2003

The Radio Broadcasting Industry

The Radio Broadcasting Industry

Alan B. Albarran
Southern Methodist University

Gregory G. Pitts
University of North Texas

Allyn and Bacon
Boston • London • Toronto • Sydney • Tokyo • Singapore

Editor in Chief: Karen Hanson
Series Editor: Karon Bowers
Editorial Assistant: Jennifer Becker
Marketing Manager: Jacqueline Aaron
Editorial Production Service: Chestnut Hill Enterprises, Inc.
Manufacturing Buyer: Julie McNeill
Cover Administrator: Jennifer Hart

Internet: www.abacon.com

Between the time Website information is gathered and published, some sites may have closed. Also, the transcription of URLs can result in typographical errors. The publisher would appreciate notification where these occur so that they may be corrected in subsequent editions.

Library of Congress Cataloging-in-Publication Data
Albarran, Alan B.
    The radio broadcasting industry / by Alan B. Albarran and Gregory G. Pitts.
       p.   cm. — (Series in mass communication)
    Includes bibliographical references and index.
    ISBN 0-205-30791-4
       1. Radio broadcasting—United States.   2. Radio broadcasting—United States—History.   I. Pitts, Gregory G. II. Title. III. Allyn & Bacon series in mass communication.
PN1991.3.U6 A43 2000
384.54'0973—dc21
                                                  00-028854
                                              CIP

Printed in the United States of Amerca
10 9 8 7 6 5 4 3 2 1   05 04 03 02 01 00

To my aunt, Judy Shaffer
ABA

To my wife, Stephanie Qualls, and my son, Garrett Pitts
GGP

Contents

Preface   **xiii**

1   Broadcast Radio: An Orientation   1
A Familiar Sound   2
Radio: It's Everywhere   2
Radio's Evolution   3
Radio—A Local Medium   4
A Look at Listeners   6
       International Listeners   6
A Thumbnail View of Radio Regulation   6
Efficient Radio Spectrum Usage   10
Radio Programming   13
The Radio Business   13
The Plan of the Book   15

2   The History and Development of Radio Broadcasting   17
Electromagnetic Spectrum   18
Marconi: Inventor, Innovator, and Entrepreneur   18
Three Inventors and Innovators: Fessenden, de Forest,
       and Armstrong   19
Growth of Public Interest in Wireless   20
The First Wireless Regulations   22
The Beginning of Programming for the Mass Audience   24
The Secretary of Commerce Attempts to Regulate Radio   25
Commercial Sponsorship Begins   27

Radio's New Regulators   *29*
The Development of Radio Networks   *30*
The Golden Age of Radio Programming   *32*
AM Radio: Standard Broadcast Service   *35*
Local Radio Service Develops   *37*
Music and More   *39*
Station Differentiation: Top 40   *39*
The Decline of AM and the Rise of FM Radio   *41*
Radio in 2000 and Beyond   *43*

3   Radio Regulation   48
Origins of Radio Regulation: The Pioneer Era   *48*
The Communications Act and Radio's Golden Age   *49*
Deregulatory Period: Round One   *51*
Deregulatory Period: Round Two   *52*
Current Regulations   *54*
    Program Content Regulations   54
Advertising   *57*
    Political Advertising   57
    Tobacco and Alcohol Advertising   57
    False or Deceptive Advertising   58
Daily Operations   *58*
    Station IDs   58
    Required Communications and Engineering Concerns   59
    Hiring Practices   60
Licensing and License Renewal   *61*
Future of Radio Regulations   *62*

4   The Radio Industry: Management and Economics   66
Radio Management: A Brief Overview   *66*
Management Responsibilities   *69*
    Levels of Management   69
    Radio Management Skills   69
    Radio Managerial Roles   70
Issues in Radio Management   *71*
    Maximizing Cash Flow   71
    Personnel Issues   72
    The Challenge of Competition   72
    The Demise of AM   73
    Embracing the Internet   73
Radio Economics   *74*
    Radio Markets: The Local Market   74

Radio Markets: The National Market   75
Supply and Demand Relationships in Radio   75
Market Structure for Radio   76
Radio Performance and Profitability   77
Summary   78

5   Radio Programming   80
Brand Name Awareness and Usage   80
Radio Becomes Brand Aware   81
Programming for a Specific Audience   81
Supplying More Than Music Utility   82
External and Internal Brand Building   83
Maintaining On-Air Consistency   86
Music Formats   89
Radio Format Segmentation   89
Radio Formats: From AC (Adult Contemporary) to UC
    (Urban Contemporary)   91
Ever-Changing Formats   98

6   The Radio Brand and Advertising   100
Radio Consolidation and the Effect on Sales   104
Radio Advertising Clients   105
Radio: Reach and Frequency   105
Research and Ratings   106
Optimum Effective Scheduling   108
Rate Cards   110
Agency Selling   111
Value-Added Selling   111
The Business of Selling   112

7   Radio Research   114
Sales Research   116
    Arbitron   116
    Sample Procedures   116
    Methodology   117
    Arbitron Report   120
    Interpreting the Arbitron Book   120
    Criticisms of Ratings Research   122
    Other Sales Research   125
Programming Research   126
    Callout Research   126
    Auditorium Testing   127

Focus Groups   128
Personal Interviews   129
Intercept Research   129
Some Considerations for Future Research   *130*
Internet Research   131

8   Noncommercial Radio Broadcasting   133
Defining Noncommercial Radio   134
The Early History of Noncommercial Radio   136
Noncommercial Radio Finds a Home on the FM Band   138
Radio Finds a Place in the Public Broadcasting Act   140
The Politics of Noncommercial Radio   141
Paying the Bills: Noncommercial Radio Economics   143
*A Refreshing Alternative: Programming on
   Noncommercial Radio   146*
Examining the Audience for Noncommercial Radio   149
The Declining Role of Education in Public Radio   150
Summary   151

9   The Contemporary Radio Industry: Movers and Shakers   156
The Moguls   157
   Thomas Hicks   157
   Lowery Mays   158
   Mel Karmazin   159
The Stars   160
   Howard Stern   161
   Laura Schlesinger   162
   Rush Limbaugh   163
   Larry King   164
   Casey Kasem   165
The Innovators   165
   Cuban and Wagner/Broadcast.com   166
Summary   167

10   Radio and the Twenty-First Century   169
The Business of Radio   169
   Consolidation   170
   Syndication Marketplace   170
   Radio Marketing   171
Technologies Impacting Radio   172
   The Internet   172
   Satellite-Delivered Radio Services   173

Globalization   173
Localism   174
Summary   175

Glossary   177

Index   187

Preface

THE RADIO BROADCASTING INDUSTRY

We *love* radio. We both had the opportunity to work professionally in the radio industry in a variety of capacities. Radio represented more than just a job in the broadcast industry, it opened our eyes to the medium's unique potential. Best of all, the radio industry we worked in placed a strong value on cross-training and multitasking before these words entered corporate America. We both "did it all" from announcing to news reporting, from sales to engineering.

Our love for radio was based not just on the fact that we both worked in the industry. We grew up listening to the radio as the medium made the transition from AM to FM broadcasting, and as the industry moved from "mom and pop owners" to radio groups of 100 or more stations. So when the opportunity came up to participate in Allyn & Bacon's *Series in Mass Communication* by writing a book on the radio broadcasting industry, we jumped at the opportunity. We're grateful to Al Greco, the series editor, and to Karon Bowers, our editor at Allyn & Bacon, for their support of this project.

In this book, we have done our best to try to provide the definitive work on the contemporary radio industry. Although the book's primary audience will be college students using this book for a course related to radio or broadcasting in general, it should also appeal to industry professionals, particularly new employees in the radio industry. The radio industry is not a stagnant entity, and there will no doubt be many changes in the coming years. In *The Radio Broadcasting Industry,* we have captured the contemporary aspects of the radio industry as it exists at the beginning of the twenty-first century.

We, the coauthors, shared in the writing of the book's first chapter. Greg is the author of Chapters 2, 5, and 6; Alan is the author of Chapters 4, 9, and 10. During the writing we shared notes, sources, and various resources to make this a labor of love. Other colleagues wrote the three remaining chapters. Chapter 1 provides an overview of the contemporary radio industry and sets the stage for the succeeding chapters. In Chapter 2, the rich history and development of radio are presented, from the earliest innovations to radio in 2000 and beyond. Contemporary readers should know that people were as excited about radio during its early years as they are about the Internet today.

Dr. David Sedman, a colleague at Southern Methodist University, is the author of Chapter 3, Radio Regulation. Professor Sedman does an outstanding job of detailing the origins of radio regulation, the deregulatory periods, and current regulations.

Chapter 4 examines radio management and economics. The topics include radio management, supply and demand relationships in radio, and radio performance and profitability. Chapter 5 covers radio programming with a thorough discussion of current programming practices and radio formats. Chapter 6 covers the subject of branding and advertising, looking in detail at the subject of radio advertising from a sales perspective.

Dr. Kathleen Fox, another colleague at SMU, has written Chapter 7, which is devoted to the subject of research in radio. Dr. Fox introduces the reader to the major topics of sales research and programming research, and explains important terminology used in research.

Chapter 8 examines noncommercial radio. Dr. Phil Thompsen of West Chester University has written this chapter. We are grateful to Phil for his fine work.

Chapter 9 focuses on key individuals in the contemporary radio industry. The chapter profiles ten individuals classified among three groups: moguls, stars, and innovators. Chapter 10 examines radio in the twenty-first century. As one might surmise, technology promises to change how the radio signal is delivered to the listener and how the listener uses the radio.

Several reviewers contributed helpful comments throughout the writing process. We thank Louise Benjamin, University of Georgia; Vin Burke, University of New Haven; Sam Sauls, University of North Texas; and Ed Shane, Shane Media Services, for providing astute and thoughtful reviews of our work.

We are fortunate to teach and to do our research in the Dallas–Fort Worth area, one of the major media markets in the United States. Here we have the opportunity to interact regularly with professional radio broadcasters. These experiences have made this book even stronger. J. T. Anderton of *Duncan's American Radio* provided insightful comments on radio format evolution.

Last, but certainly not least, we are grateful for the support of our families during the work on this project.

Alan B. Albarran
Gregory G. Pitts

1

Radio Broadcasting

An Orientation

". . . and now we know we are not the only creatures in the universe." (From the 1938 Mercury Theater Radio Broadcast of H. G. Wells's War of the Worlds.)

"This is London." (Edward R. Murrow's famous introduction during broadcasts from the Battle of Britain.)

"December 7, 1941. A day which will live in infamy. . . ." (President Roosevelt's address to Congress and the nation the day after the Pearl Harbor attack.)

"The Giants Win the Pennant! The Giants Win the Pennant!" (A screaming Russ Hodges describes the home run by Bobby Thompson that came to be known as the "shot heard round the world.")

"You're here with the Wolfman. . . ." (Wolfman Jack)

"And now, on with the countdown." (Casey Kasem, host of American Top 40.)

"And I am my kid's mom." (Dr. Laura Schlesinger)

A FAMILIAR SOUND

These clips present a brief montage of the many memorable lines drawn from the rich history of the radio industry. Perhaps no form of mass media has undergone as much change and evolution as that of radio, which continues to reinvent itself today. This chapter provides an introduction to the radio industry and previews some of the issues discussed in later chapters.

Radio remains an important entertainment and information source, not only for Americans, but also for people around the world. This book centers on the radio industry in the United States, where stations operate much like any other business— to make a profit. What you hear broadcast may sound like it's all fun. In reality, it is part of the station's strategy to attract and retain an audience that could be spending its time with other radio stations or media outlets.

RADIO: IT'S EVERYWHERE

According to the **Federal Communications Commission** (FCC), there are 4,783 **AM** stations, 5,766 commercial **FM** stations, 2,066 noncommercial FM stations, and another 3,000 FM translators or boosters.[1] With so many stations, there are few areas in the United States that do not receive multiple signals. In larger cities, a listener may be able to choose from as many as two dozen AM stations and nearly four dozen FM stations. Worldwide, there are few places on earth where the signal of a radio station intended for reception by the general public cannot be received.

These 12,000 radio stations provide local radio service to a specific geographic area, or **market.** In the radio industry, markets are not defined according to geographic borders, but rather to the range their signals can reach in a given locale. Thus, a market may contain several different communities, counties, and even carry across state lines. Because radio broadcasting is interstate, it falls under the jurisdiction of the Department of Commerce, which in turn regulates the industry via the FCC.

The FCC classifies and assigns stations to different categories based on the type of transmission (AM or FM), transmitter power, and assigned frequency. This classification system will be discussed in more detail later in the chapter. Local stations may be affiliated with a network programming service to provide news and features, and also music programming. Every station has the same goal: attract listeners, and then sell access to those listeners to advertisers.

Over the years, the U. S. radio audience has experienced a decline in terms of listenership. The typical person spent 1,205 hours per year listening to the radio in 1986.[2] That same person spent 1,082 hours with radio in 1997.[3] Listenership is expected to drop to 1,040 hours per year by 2002. Between 1992 and 1997, radio listening at home, where 40 percent of all listening takes place, had a compound annual drop of 2.3 percent, while listening in automobiles increased at a compound annual rate of 2.5 percent. Listening at places other than home or car did not change. Even as listenership drops, the number of stations on the air has continued to increase. The growth in the number of radio stations has actually given station operators new opportunities to alter the product they provide consumers.

Satellite-delivered audio programming will expand the listening options of many consumers. In the United States, two companies, Sirius Satellite Radio and XM Satellite Radio, will offer DARS (**digital audio radio service**), programming delivered nationally by geosynchronous satellites.[4] Listeners will pay a monthly subscription fee to receive the service, though each company anticipates providing fifty channels of commercial-free programming plus another fifty channels of programming that may include commercial content. WorldSpace will offer a similar product for listeners in Africa, Latin America, and the Middle East.[5]

Radio stations are also broadcasting via the Internet. College students living in a dorm hundreds of miles from their hometown can listen to a favorite station through the station's Website. The popularity of the Internet has led to the creation of several Internet-only radio stations. These facilities may sound just like any other radio site available through the Internet, but the stations do not use the electromagnetic spectrum to transmit a signal. In that regard, they are not radio broadcast stations but audio programming services, delivered over the Internet. Chapter 10 examines the impact of these services on traditional stations.

RADIO'S EVOLUTION

To better understand how today's radio industry operates, we will first review the roots of the radio industry. During the 1930s and 1940s, radio stations operated in a manner similar to the current television industry, providing the best programming during the primetime audience hours.[6] (Television stations primarily pass along their most attractive network programming during primetime.)[7] Radio stations used to rely on national radio networks to provide the bulk of their programming, and offered limited local programming.

The national radio networks' programming ranged from soap operas to classical music and opera performances. The most popular programs were comedy, variety, and drama programs that aired during primetime. With the advent of television in the 1950s, the national networks moved their most popular performers and programs to the new visual medium, forcing radio to reinvent itself as a "local" programming service. Radio stations began to adopt specific **formats,** and targeted different audience groups based on the content they offered.

Today, a multitude of radio formats offer even greater differentiation and choice to listeners. Most radio stations depend on programming they produce, combined with community identity, to attract and retain listeners. Station competition has led to the identification of niche audiences to which programming is targeted. Radio formats come with names like AAA (Triple-A) for "album adult alternative," which should not be confused with the alternative format.[8] Jammin' Oldies shouldn't be confused with oldies or golden oldies. Rhythmic Crossover shouldn't be confused with either contemporary hit radio, urban contemporary, churban, or rap. More detailed discussion on radio programming is presented in Chapter 6.

Stations have continued to face new competition for listeners, especially from recorded music. Radio was forced to compete with 8-track tapes in the 1970s, cassettes in the 1980s, and CDs in the 1990s. Minidiscs, the Internet, and MP3s will present new challenges for radio listener retention. Throughout its evolution, radio has always had great resiliency in its ability to adapt to the competitive environment.

RADIO—A LOCAL MEDIUM

For the most part, we think of radio broadcasting as being built around the concept of localism or local service.[9] Research indicates that people listen to radio the most in the morning, typically when getting ready for work or school and commuting to work or school. It's certainly true that radio is easier to mentally tune in or tune out than television. Another reason for greater morning radio listening is that radio stations provide listeners with key news, weather, traffic, and other relevant information that will help the listener prepare for the day.

Broadcasters divide the day into segments called **dayparts** that provide a means to track radio listening and schedule programming. The typical dayparts are morning drive, from 6 A.M. until 10 A.M., midday, from 10 A.M. until 3 P.M., afternoon drive, from 3 P.M. until 7 P.M., nighttime, 7 P.M. until midnight, and overnight, midnight until 6 A.M. Each of these dayparts roughly follows listener patterns. For example, the midday period from 10 A.M. until 3 P.M. corresponds with listening at work. Afternoon drive, 3 P.M. until 7 P.M. corresponds with the end of the workday and the commute home.

Each radio station serves a specific city of license. The station's programming is intended to serve that city and perhaps adjacent communities. In the cases of suburban areas, the concept of city of license has become lost. For example, the Dallas–Ft. Worth, Texas market includes stations that are licensed to a variety of communities in the DFW Metroplex. In most instances, the stations have abandoned the concept of programming to a specific community of license. Recognizing that their signals cover a much larger area, the stations target their programming to the entire metropolitan area. Table 1-1 lists some of the stations serving the Dallas–Ft. Worth market along with their actual city of license.

Stations in smaller towns have continued to retain a local identity. The smallest communities might not need traffic reports nor is there a great deal of breaking news, but these stations furnish listeners with community announcements and they are often an important source of weather and farm news. For example, WGOH-AM in Grayson, Kentucky received a Crystal Radio Award for community service in 1999 from the National Association of Broadcasters. Chapter 5 includes a profile of the local programming commitment of this station.

TABLE 1-1   Dallas Fort Worth FM Stations

These FM stations call Dallas or Fort Worth home, yet only 19 actually list Dallas or Fort Worth as their city of license.

Station Call Letters	Frequency	City of License
KNTU	88.1	Denton
KEOM	88.5	Mesquite
KTCU	88.7	Fort Worth
KETR	88.9	Commerce
KMQX	89.1	Springtown
KNON	89.3	Dallas
KERA	90.1	Dallas
K213BP	90.5	Irving
KCBI	90.9	Dallas
KDKR	91.3	Decatur
KVTT	91.7	Dallas
KTTV	92.1	Glen Rose
KXEZ	92.1	Farmersville
KZPS	92.5	Dallas
KKMR	93.3	Haltom City
KLTY	94.1	Dallas
KDGE	94.5	Gainesville
KWRD	94.9	Arlington
KHYI	95.3	Howe/Plano
KSCS	96.3	Fort Worth
KNKI	96.7	Flower Mound
KEGL	97.1	Fort Worth
KBFB	97.9	Dallas
KLUV	98.7	Dallas
KHCK	99.1	Denton
KPLX	99.5	Fort Worth
KRBV	100.3	Dallas
WRR	101.1	Dallas
KTXQ	102.1	Fort Worth
KDMX	102.9	Dallas
KVIL	103.7	Highland Park
KMRR	104.1	Sanger
KKDA	104.5	Dallas
KTCY	104.9	Pilot Point
KYNG	105.3	Dallas
KRNB	105.7	Decatur
KHKS	106.1	Denton
KDXT	106.7	Grandbury
KZDF	106.9	McKinney
KZDL	107.1	Terrell
KOAI	107.5	Fort Worth
KDXX	107.9	Corsicana

Source: Radio Digest.Com, available online at http://www.radiodigest.com/dallas/dial/fm_dial.htm and online through the FCC at http://www.fcc.gov/mmb/asd/amq.html and http://www.fcc.gov/mmb/asd/fmq.html.

A LOOK AT LISTENERS

Receiver technology also helps increase the number of different stations available to the audience. Listeners may be categorized in a number of ways. One is to talk about **preset listeners** and **scanner listeners**. The preset listener may identify six to eight "favorite" stations and set the preset buttons on the radio to these stations. While one or two of the presets may garner most of the listener's attention, when those stations are no longer airing programming the listener wants, the listener may select another preset station.

Scanners jump from one station to the next. Rather than being loyal to a group of preset stations, these listeners hit the scan or seek button on their radio whenever they hear objectionable programming. They are less concerned with who (what station) they are listening to and more concerned with what (music or other programming) they are listening to. For many of these listeners, music utility plays a prominent role in station selection.

Think of how you feel about other products you use, such as soft drinks. Are you loyal to one brand? Or is Coke equal to Pepsi and also equal to Dr. Pepper? Is it the station that matters (along with the personality of the station created by its on-air image campaign) or just the music playing at the moment that matters? Chapter 6 will discuss the efforts by stations to create brands with listener value.

International Listeners

Shortwave broadcasting continues to bring news and information to listeners in many countries in Africa, South America, and Asia. The governments of the United States and Great Britain continue to operate shortwave radio services. These program services, referred to as "external broadcasting services" because their programming is intended to be listened to by people outside of the home country, include the Voice of America (VOA) and British Broadcasting Corporation World Service (BBC World Service). VOA airs programming each week in 53 languages to an audience of 91 million people.[10] BBC World Service similarly airs programming each week in 43 languages.[11]

A THUMBNAIL VIEW OF RADIO REGULATION

Congress, in the Communications Act of 1934, created the Federal Communications Commission (FCC) to formally replace the previous Federal Radio Commission (FRC). The FCC's purpose, in part, is "regulating interstate and foreign commerce in communication by wire and radio so as to make available, so far as possible, to all the people of the United States a rapid, efficient, Nation-wide, and world-wide wire and radio communications service. . . ."[12] The five FCC commissioners are appointed by the president and confirmed by the Senate. The Mass Media Bureau has day-to-day responsibility for developing, recommending, and administering the rules governing radio and television stations.

New station allocations are based on demonstrated needs of communities for additional broadcast outlets and on engineering standards that prevent interference between stations. Though the FCC expects stations to be aware of the important problems or issues in their communities and air programming to address those issues, the FCC does not select or control the material broadcast.

The Communications Act prohibits the FCC from censoring broadcast programming. They can fine a station or revoke its license if it has, among other things, aired obscene language, broadcast indecent language when children are likely to be in the audience, broadcast some types of lottery information, or solicited money under false pretenses.[13] The FCC also licenses television stations, microwave stations, and a range of mobile radio services used by broadcasters and various industries.

Radio stations receive a renewable eight-year license. The license holder can expect nearly automatic renewal if the owners have attempted to operate the station within FCC guidelines. Each radio station produces a carrier frequency onto which the programming material is added before signal transmission. The signal will travel as far as geographic and weather conditions allow. This also means that radio signals can and do interfere with each other. Each radio station not only produces the signal on its frequency but it also creates interference for stations on nearby frequencies.

The frequencies just above and below a station's frequency are called *first adjacent frequencies*. For example, the adjacent frequencies for Z100, WHTZ-FM 100.3 MHz, in New York City are 100.1 MHz, and 100.5 MHz.[14] There are also second and third adjacent frequencies for positions two or three frequencies above or below the station's carrier.

The frequencies on which stations broadcast are part of the **electromagnetic spectrum.** The spectrum consists of invisible rays of light. The first successful commercial broadcast service for public listening in the United States used amplitude modulation (or AM) technology to transmit programming to listeners. AM listenership has been declining for the past twenty-five years but AM is still called "standard broadcasting" because it was the first system in use.

AM stations occupy a portion of the spectrum called "the medium wave band," from 535 kilohertz (kHz) to 1705 kHz. Each AM station is spaced 10 kHz apart with the first station operating at 540 kHz, the next at 550 kHz, and so on to the last station operating on 1700 kHz. The upper portion of the AM band from 1605 to 1705 kHz was authorized for broadcasting in 1991.[15] Congress, along with the FCC, sought to reduce some of the station interference on AM by adding the new spectrum space and moving some existing stations to the new band. The stations operating on the expanded AM frequencies were given higher operating power and better nighttime coverage. Millions of radios built prior to 1991 cannot receive stations on the upper portion of the band, which, along with AM's general loss of listeners, has made the move less effective than had been hoped for.

The FCC uses three classification systems to identify AM stations. Class A stations are called "Clear Channel stations" and may operate with up to 50,000 watts of power during the day and night. The Federal Radio Commission and the Federal Communications Commission created these stations to provide national radio service. The FCC has designated certain AM frequencies primarily for clear channel service. Usually no more than two stations will be authorized to operate at night on a clear channel. These stations have a coverage radius of about 750 miles. Class B stations operate day and night with power levels between 250 watts and 50,000 watts. Class C stations operate with power levels up to 1,000 watts, and broadcast on a group of local frequencies. These frequencies were designated for day and night service at a time when nearly all radio listening was to AM rather than FM. Class D stations operate with a daytime power between 250 and 50,000 watts. If nighttime broadcasting is allowed, the station's power is 250 watts or less.[16] Slightly more than half of all AM stations are limited to daytime operation.

AM signals follow the earth's surface and are called "ground wave signals." They provide primary local reception. The signal typically travels a maximum of 100 to 200 miles. The station's signal also travels into the air where it eventually attenuates or grows so weak that it fades away. At night, that same signal is reflected from the ionosphere and may be received by listeners several hundred miles away. This is why a listener, driving at night across the United States, might hear clear channel station WWL (870 kHz) from New Orleans while driving through North Carolina. The traveler might decide to change to WLW (700 kHz) in Cincinnati, or WCBS (880 kHz) in New York. These are three examples of 50,000-watt clear channel stations. Skywave signals are subject to fading and will vary with location and time of year.

While useful for the traveler, AM skywave signals can also be a form of interference among stations. To eliminate the interference, many stations are required to cease broadcasting, reduce power, or change the pattern of their station's antenna transmission at local sunset. The allocation of commercial AM service in its present medium waveband, with the static and interference that listeners sometimes think are typical of the AM band, resulted because commercial radio developed around the frequencies used by ships at sea for distress signals. Radio was first widely used for ship-to-shore communications. The limited technical knowledge about the spectrum and radio transmission led most inventors to work to improve the original ship-to-shore system rather than to try to perfect a system for home listening.

FM (or frequency modulation) stations occupy a portion of the spectrum called VHF or Very High Frequencies, from 88 megahertz (MHz) to 108 MHz. Each FM station is spaced with .2 MHz or 200 kHz separation, with the first station operating at 88.1 MHz, the next at 88.3 MHz, and so forth until the last station operating on 107.9 MHz. This produces 100 FM frequencies or channels. The lower portion of the FM band from 88.1 to 91.9 MHz is reserved for noncommercial station operation. Television channels 2–13 are also part of the VHF band.

Unlike AM stations, which produce groundwave and skywave signals, FM signals travel in a manner called "line-of-sight." The signal travels as far as it can "see" to travel. The curve of the earth and geographic features (mountains or valleys) limit the coverage area. For this reason, FM stations rely not only on the station's transmitter power to create the coverage area but also on the height of the station's antenna. FM station engineers (and the FCC) use the term *HAAT* (or height above average terrain) to determine the height of a station's antenna.

The FCC also uses three classification systems to identify FM stations. Class A stations operate with a maximum power of 6,000 watts and a HAAT of 100 meters. Class B stations operate with a maximum power of 50,000 watts and a HAAT of 150 meters. Class C stations operate with up to 100,000 watts and a HAAT of 600 meters. Additional subcategories have been created as the FCC has attempted to allow station operators to obtain the maximum coverage area possible to serve their listeners.[17] Table 1-2 lists the FM station classifications and powers. Chapter 3 provides more discussion of radio regulation.

TABLE 1-2   Station Classifications

Station Classification	Maximum Station Power and HAAT[1]	Primary Signal Radius Protection
Class A	6.0 kW / 100 meters	28.3 km
Class B1	25.0 kW / 100 meters	44.7 km
Class B	50.0 kW / 150 meters	65.1 km
Class C3	25.0 kW / 100 meters	39.1 km
Class C2	50.0 kW / 150 meters	52.2 km
Class C1	100.0 kW / 299 meters	72.3 km
Class C	100.0 kW / 600 meters	91.8 km

[1]HAAT refers to the height above average terrain of an FM station's radiating antenna. Quite literally, each FM station must determine, from its tower location, the effect the surrounding topography will have on the propagation of the station's signal. By measuring the surrounding terrain, the FM broadcaster is also able to determine the height of the station's transmission antenna above these obstacles. For FM station signals, which travel line-of-sight, HAAT is as important as transmitter power.

[2]Class B and B1 stations are authorized only in Zones I and I-A, which include the following states and areas: CA (south of 40° latitude), CT, DC, DE, IL, IN, MA, MD, coastal ME, MI (south of 43.5° latitude), NJ, NH (south of 43.5° latitude), NY (south of 43.5° latitude), OH, PA, PR, RI, northern and eastern VA, VI, VT (south of 43.5° latitude), southeastern WI, WV. Class C, C1, C2, and C3 stations are not authorized in Zones I or I-A, but may be authorized elsewhere.

This information is available online at http://www.fcc.gov/mmb/asd/fmclasses.html

EFFICIENT RADIO SPECTRUM USAGE

The licensing process and station coverage areas allow the sharing of frequencies. Dozens of stations can therefore broadcast on a single frequency. Table 1-3 lists the stations operating on 100.7 MHz, 100.9 MHz, and 101.1 MHz in Connecticut, Massachusetts, New Hampshire, and Vermont. Though stations share frequencies, each station has unique call letters that identify the station. Typically, stations east of the Mississippi River have call signs that begin with W and stations west of the Mississippi River have call signs beginning with K. There are exceptions. Usually these stations were assigned a call letter combination before the Mississippi River became the dividing line. Examples are KDKA in Pittsburgh and WHO in Des Moines, Iowa.

Many stations might use words like Power, Rock, or Kiss before their frequency (Power 97, Rock 103, and Kiss 106) or individual letters (Q-107 or Z-98). Some examples include WUSL in Philadelphia, which refers to itself as Power 99; WQLT in Florence, Alabama, calls itself Q-107; WNNX in Atlanta is 99X, and WHTZ in New York is Z-100. All stations are required by the FCC to identify themselves once each hour, near the top of the hour, by the specific call letters and the city to which the station is licensed.

TABLE 1-3   Station Frequency Sharing

Approximately 80 stations throughout the United States are licensed to operate on each of the three FM channels shown below. Even in the Northeast, where states are geographically small but have greater population density, it is possible for seven stations to share these frequencies without interfering with each other. Similar situations are present throughout the United States.

Call Letters	City of License	Power	Antenna height
100.7 MHz			
WZLX	Boston, MA	21.5 kw.	777 feet, HAAT*
WVAY	Wilmington, VT	135 watts	1,460 feet, HAAT
100.9 MHz			
WTYD	New London, CT	3 kw.	328 feet, HAAT
WRNX	Amherst, MA	1.35 kw.	692 feet, HAAT
WGTK	Middlebury, VT	3 kw.	300 feet, HAAT
101.1 MHz			
WWKJ	Mashpee, MA	3.7 kw.	253 feet, HAAT
WGIR	Manchester, NH	11.5 kw.	1,027 feet, HAAT

*Some stations may appear to exceed the FCC limits on power or HAAT. Instead, when stations increase their antenna height they must correspondingly reduce the transmitter power. Station WVAY in Wilmington, VT is a Class A station. The low power, 135 watts, is due to the extreme height of the antenna.

Worldwide, thousands of radio stations broadcast programming intended for reception by the general public. The stations include AM or medium-wave stations, FM stations, and HF or high-frequency or shortwave stations. Broadcast stations may be licensed to private owners, as is most common in the United States, the government may own the stations, or they may be operated by a government-authorized but independent agency. The best example of the latter category is the British Broadcasting Corporation (or BBC). The United Kingdom now has private station ownership but at one time the BBC held a monopoly on broadcasting in the United Kingdom.

Besides the number difference on your radio dial, there is another marked difference between AM and FM broadcasts. As mentioned earlier, all broadcast transmitters produce a **carrier wave.** The carrier wave is the frequency on which the station operates. **Modulation,** which means change, is the process by which the programming aired on the station is added to the carrier wave. How this change in the carrier wave takes place is the difference between AM and FM.

All carrier waves begin as sine waves. Figure 1-1 shows an unmodulated carrier wave, an amplitude modulated (AM) carrier wave, and a frequency modulated (FM) carrier wave. The number of sine wave cycles that are completed in one second determine a station's frequency. (We use the term *Hertz* as convenient shorthand for the longer term *cycles-per-second.*)[18] An AM station broadcasting on 870 kHz generates 870,000 sine wave cycles in one second. An FM station broadcasting on 98.7 MHz generates 98,700,000 sine wave cycles per second. What happens when the programming is added to the carrier wave is different for AM and FM stations.[19]

The modulation process for the AM station results in variation of the amplitude or height of the carrier wave. The FM modulation varies the frequency of the carrier wave. Why don't we have just one standard? Amplitude modulation was invented first. It took a number of years to perfect transmission and reception of AM signals. By the time FM was first demonstrated to the public, hundreds of radio stations were already entertaining millions of listeners. Making an abrupt change from AM to FM would have meant that all the existing AM radios would have been worthless to their owners. Just as there are two operating systems for home computers, the Windows system and the Apple system, we have two radio systems. Each broadcast service does have some distinct advantages just as each of the computer operating systems has distinct advantages. For example, AM signals have greater coverage range while FM signals can deliver higher sound fidelity.

Consumers may see another radio service added within ten years or less. Stations may begin broadcasting digital signals using a system called IBOC, or In Band-On Channel.[20] The IBOC system would allow a station to continue to broadcast programming using normal AM or FM modulation, but the station could also send through the air a digital stream of information that would also be part of the station's carrier wave. The FCC is also considering whether digital broadcasting should be moved to an entirely new portion of the spectrum. Either way, consumers

FIGURE 1-1 Carrier Waves

Unmodulated Carrier Wave

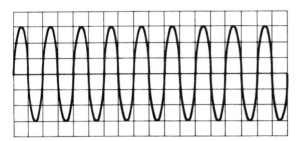

Amplitude Modulated Carrier Wave

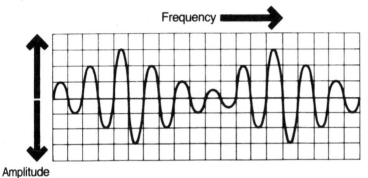

Frequency Modulated Carrier Wave

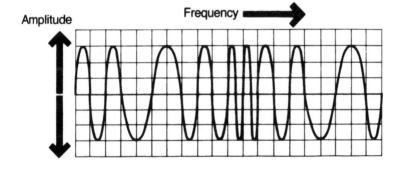

would be required to purchase new receivers to hear the digital programming. The competitive advantage provided by the IBOC system would be superior audio compared to normal AM or FM programming.

RADIO PROGRAMMING

How does a radio station determine what to air? Stations use several tactics to decide programming. The most obvious approach is to determine what the public wants. If there were no stations presently serving an area, the station might seek to discover the format that is of greatest demand by potential listeners. If stations are already serving the audience, the newest station might try to determine how good a job the existing stations are doing and whether there is a weakness in their operation that can be exploited. Market research would be helpful in both determinations.

The type of station facility and the station's power are also important when determining programming. Some formats probably no longer belong on an AM station. Would listeners want contemporary rock music on an AM station if an FM station already existed? Probably not. If no FM programmed contemporary rock and the AM station adopted this format and was successful, it is likely that an FM station might change to this format and take away the AM station's listeners. A Class A FM station (6,000 watts) might not be successful trying to program country music if the market already had one or more Class C stations (100,000 watts) airing country. Assuming that market research supported the need for an additional country station, the Class A station might adopt a niche country format. Rather than compete head-to-head, a variation on the country format might work.

Stations have a variety of sources to help them make programming decisions. Once the market research has been collected and evaluated, a number of companies can supply music to stations. The music services supply either CDs, music that can be stored on a computer hard drive, or programming that can be delivered by satellite feed. The satellite feeds can be so inclusive as to provide music and on-air talent. Using a computer system, the station can be made to sound local, even though the announcers may be hundreds of miles away. Several radio groups currently use computers and telephone data lines to feed announcer comments from a central production facility to various station affiliates. Most station owners take this approach to control costs but also to improve the quality of talent listeners in a small market might be able to hear. More about programming in Chapter 5.

THE RADIO BUSINESS

Radio isn't just a source of entertainment or information. For the publicly traded corporations that own stations and hundreds of individual station owners, radio is a business. The radio industry sold more than $15.4 billion worth of radio advertising time in 1998.[21] To answer the question of what business a radio station is in, one might respond, "it's in the business of selling opportunities for businesses to have people learn about a product." We might also say the station is in the marketing business: the station not only markets its programming but also markets the goods or services of clients who advertise with the station. The proliferation of stations means that the listener, not the manager or program director, determines the success of the station.[22] Stations must attract and retain listeners not only from song to song but from hour to hour and daypart to daypart.

The airtime the station client is buying is intangible. It has a limited lifespan and, once gone, can never be recovered. For this reason, commercial time for sale by a radio station is a perishable commodity. The job of the account executives selling the airtime is to get the highest rate possible for the station but ensure that the time gets sold. If a station hopes to air an average of twelve minutes of commercial ads per hour, it cannot increase the commercial load to eighteen minutes one hour if only six minutes were sold the previous hour. Such a practice would alienate listeners who would seek other stations and might not return to the station with the heavy commercial load.

Commercials are commonly referred to as **spots.** Most stations sell spot time in lengths of thirty or sixty seconds. Sponsorships of programs, sports events, or program time are also sold but standard commercial units produce the majority of station revenue. Commercial purchases come through three areas. Local spot sales produce the majority of station income, though the amount of income varies according to market size. A station in a small town may earn 90 percent of its revenue from local ad sales. A major market station may earn only about 50 percent of its revenue from local spot sales. The other sources of ad revenue are regional advertising and national advertising.

Even if the station sets a maximum load of twelve minutes of commercials per hour, the mix of spot lengths could cause a station to air up to twenty-four commercials in one hour if all spots are thirty seconds in length. Likewise, if the station's clients all purchased 60-second spots, only a dozen commercials would air in an hour. Not all twelve or twenty-four would run at one time of course. Spot sets, clusters of between four and eight spots, are strategically placed to run at different times in the hour depending on the station's format. Besides paid commercials, some of the station's airtime is dedicated to airing station promotional announcements (promos) or nonrevenue-producing public service announcements (PSAs).

Station programming and promotional efforts create the perceived value of the station as a tool to help market a client's products or services. The station is assigned call letters but most stations prefer to use a word or letter as part of the promotional identity the station seeks to establish. For example, an Internet search for stations on frequencies between 92.1 and 99.9 MHz located thirteen stations using the letter X and their dial position as part of their on-air identification. When a station changes formats, it is relatively easy to dump one on-air identifier for another. More discussion of the relationship with the business side of the station operation is included in

Chapter 4, which discusses the economics of the radio industry, Chapter 5, which discusses programming, and Chapter 6, which discusses radio spot sales.

Radio is an interesting business that provides numerous opportunities for people wishing to enter the business either as talent, in sales, in production, engineering, or station ownership. There are also numerous career options in ancillary fields via advertising agencies, research firms, production houses, programming services, and networks.

THE PLAN OF THE BOOK

This chapter has provided an overview of the contemporary radio industry, and many of these topics will be discussed in detail in separate chapters. Following is a description of the other chapters in the book, which can be read either in sequential order, or as stand-alone separate topics.

Chapter 2 presents a historical look at the radio industry. Here you will learn about the development of radio, from the early innovators who invented the medium to the establishment of FM service and, ultimately, digital radio.

Chapter 3 is devoted to the subject of radio regulation, while Chapter 4 examines the management and economics of the radio industry.

Chapter 5 examines programming, while Chapter 6 centers on a topic critical in today's competitive radio industry—branding.

In Chapter 7, you will learn about the importance of research, and the way the radio industry utilizes different types of research to gain a competitive edge.

Chapter 8 is devoted to noncommercial radio, an important component of the radio industry. The chapter examines "public" radio broadcasting from both a local and national perspective.

Chapter 9 looks at key individuals who have shaped the radio industry during the last decade, and who will influence the medium in the twenty-first century. The chapter considers owners, talent, and innovators.

Chapter 10 looks at the future of radio. In this capstone chapter, issues related to technology, international broadcasting, programming, and ownership serve as a guide to assess radio's future.

Radio's rich history and diversity are difficult to capture in any single text. However, when you complete this book you will have a greater appreciation, and certainly a better understanding, of the radio industry, how it functions, and the significant role radio plays in America and throughout the world.

NOTES

[1]"Broadcast Station Totals as of September 1999," available online at http://fcc.gov/mmb/asd/totals/index.html, accessed January 3, 2000.

[2]*The Veronis, Suhler and Associates Communications Industry Forecast,* 6th ed., (New York: Veronis, Suhler & Associates, 1992), p. 12.

[3]*The Veronis, Suhler and Associates Communications Industry Forecast,* 12th ed., (New York: Veronis, Suhler & Associates, 1998), p. 44.

[4]Each company offers a Website with the latest information about its service and programming options, available online at http://www.siriusradio.com and http://www.xmradio.com/have.asp.

[5]As of October 1999, WorldSpace began delivering twenty-three broadcast services with programming in sixteen languages to listeners in Africa. WorldSpace also plans to provide programming to the Middle East, Asia, Latin America, and the Caribbean. Additional information about WorldSpace is available online at http://www.worldspace.com.

[6]Chapter 2 contains a discussion of the growth and history of the radio networks and lists source references.

[7]James Walker and Douglas Ferguson, *The Broadcast Television Industry* (Boston: Allyn and Bacon, 1998).

[8]http://gavin.com lists many frequently occurring radio formats as well as current songs being played by stations with the formats.

[9]"The Public and Broadcasting, June 1999," available online at http:www.fcc.gov/mmb/prd/docs/manual.html, accessed August 19, 1999.

[10]"VOA Special English Celebrates 40 Years," available online at http://www.ibb.gov/pubaff/media.html, accessed December 29, 1999.

[11]"BBC Worldservice," available online at http://www.bbc.co.uk/worldservice/index.shtml, accessed January 3, 2000.

[12]"The Public and Broadcasting, June 1999," available online at http:www.fcc.gov/mmb/prd/docs/manual.html, accessed November 1, 1999.

[13]Ibid.

[14]Though Z-100 promotes itself as a New York station, the actual city of license is Newark, New Jersey.

[15]*Broadcasting and Cable Yearbook 1998* (New Providence, NJ: R.R. Bowker), p. xxv.

[16]"AM Station Classes: Clear, Regional and Local Channels," available online at http://www.fcc.gov/mmb/asd/amclasses.html#CLEAR, accessed July 17, 1999.

[17]"FM Station Classes and Service Contours," available online at http://www.fcc.gov/mmb/asd/fmclasses.html, accessed July 17, 1999.

[18]Heinreich Hertz was the first person to detect and measure sine waves. For this reason we use *Hertz* to refer to cycles completed per second.

[19]*Broadcast Operator Handbook,* 1st ed., Washington, DC: Government Printing Office, 1976).

[20]"Digital Audio Broadcasting Systems and Their Impact on the Terrestrial Radio Broadcast Service," *Federal Register,* November 9, 1999, 64, 216. Available online at http://frwebgate.access.gpo.gov/cgi-bin/getdoc.cgi?dbname=1999_register&docid=fr09no99-21, accessed January 3, 2000.

[21]"Radio Ad Sales Surpass $15 Billion in 1998 to Extend Industry's Record-Setting Run," available online at http://www.rad.com/pr/dec98rev.html, accessed July 6, 1999.

[22]David McFarlane, *Contemporary Radio Programming Strategies* (Hillsdale, NJ: Lawrence Erlbaum, 1990), p. 5.

2

The History and Development of Radio Broadcasting

The telephone was barely off the drawing board when the earliest radio experiments began. The purpose of this chapter is to help the reader understand and appreciate how wondrous radio (wireless) communication was as it was evolving in the early 1900s. The first practical uses for radio were to communicate with ships at sea and for military communications. But of greater significance was the realization that radio could simultaneously reach millions of listeners across a wide geographic area.

Radio has a colorful history. No single person can be credited with inventing radio. Most of radio's "inventors" should be credited with refining an idea first put forth by someone else. This chapter has space to cite only a few of the remarkable events in the fascinating history of radio. Readers are encouraged to read further about the personalities cited in this chapter. Not unlike the issue of which came first, the chicken or the egg, radio programming developed as a means of encouraging people to buy or build receiving equipment, not for the purpose of delivering news or entertainment. Until radio, it was impossible to simultaneously transmit entertainment or information to millions of people. As the acceptance of radio grew, radio networks were founded to become the first simultaneous, live, national medium of communications.

Today we enjoy the ability of the Internet to allow us to travel around the world without leaving our seat in front of the computer. For the listener in 1920 or 1930 or 1940, radio was the only way to learn about distant places.

ELECTROMAGNETIC SPECTRUM

At the turn of the twentieth century, over-the-air broadcasting was an emerging technology. Though omnipresent today, wireless communications had only been a theoretical proposition in 1864 when Scottish mathematician and physicist James Clerk Maxwell published the results of a study that suggested that a signal could be sent electromagnetically. Radio service depended on two electromagnetic spectrum characteristics: propagation of the signal at various frequencies and level of interference. Maxwell's theories predicted the existence of invisible electromagnetic frequencies that could travel through the air.

A little more than twenty years later German physicist Heinrich Hertz conducted a series of experiments in 1887 to prove that Maxwell's theories were correct. Hertz created a crude spark-gap generator that allowed an electric spark to be detected by a receiving coil. Though of limited detection range, Hertz successfully measured the presence of wireless signals. The fundamental unit of electromagnetic frequency, the Hertz (Hz) is named for him. Despite his discovery, Heinrich Hertz did not promote the use of wireless for communication.

Technological growth, inspired by the telegraph, the telephone, and other achievements, led private citizens to experiment with the new wireless communications medium. In the 1890s, three other inventors almost simultaneously worked on wireless transmission and detection. French physicist Edouard Branly invented a signal detector called a *coherer* that consisted of a glass tube filled with metal filings. The filings reacted when a signal was detected. English physicist Sir Oliver Lodge worked on the *principle of resonance tuning,* which would allow the transmitter and receiver to operate on the same wavelength. Russian Alexander Popoff developed a better coherer and a *vertical receiving antenna.*

MARCONI:
INVENTOR, INNOVATOR, AND ENTREPRENEUR

Probably the most widely known inventor–innovator in wireless is twenty-year-old Italian Guglielmo Marconi. More than one Marconi biographer has reported Marconi's pragmatic view of wireless. He was interested in getting wireless to work, and not interested in how it worked! Marconi's family affluence enabled him to perfect the wireless equipment of Hertz, Branly, and Lodge. Marconi began his wireless experiments in 1894. He improved the Hertz transmitter and determined that an elevated antenna enhanced signal travel. Marconi was able to increase the sensitivity of the Branly–Lodge coherer and he added a telegraph key to control the wireless signal transmitted. Within two years, Marconi had created a wireless system capable of sending and detecting a signal over a distance of two miles.

When the Italian government showed no interest in wireless, Marconi traveled to England. His Irish-born mother's family contacts enabled Marconi to present his wireless system to possible investors, including the head of the British Post Office. Three years after he began his first experiments, Wireless Telegraph and Signal Company was founded in 1897. Marconi marketed radio as a telegraph that did not require wires to send Morse code dots and dashes. His appreciation of wireless was limited to its use as a communications tool between ships at sea and shore stations. British Marconi and the U.S. subsidiary American Marconi dominated wireless communication of Morse code for ship-to-shore and transatlantic communications until after World War I. Noncoded broadcasts would follow.

THREE INVENTORS AND INNOVATORS: FESSENDEN, DE FOREST, AND ARMSTRONG

Unlike broadcasting today, Marconi's wireless business did not use a continuous, modulated carrier wave to transmit his dots and dashes of Morse code. His system used a spark-gap generator. Variation of the spark led to the production of dots and dashes of code. Canadian Reginald Fessenden, working in the United States, wanted to create a wireless system using a continuous carrier wave. On Christmas Eve in 1906, after a decade of work, Fessenden used an experimental alternator he had developed to broadcast programming from studios at Brant Rock, Massachusetts. Unlike Marconi's Morse code transmissions, Fessenden's transmission system allowed him to read scripture from the Bible, play "O Holy Night" on the violin, and talk to the audience. Fessenden's audience consisted primarily of radio operators on ships at sea, newspaper reporters who had been alerted to his publicity-generating broadcast, and home experimenters. The sound quality was poor but this marked the first transmission of noncoded radio signals for general reception by listeners. (Some people even claim Fessenden as the world's first disc jockey.)

What is most interesting about early wireless experimentation is that no single person or company can be credited with inventing wireless. Marconi didn't invent wireless; he recognized its commercial value and improved the operation of early wireless equipment. Fessenden, a less astute businessman than Marconi, sought to improve the transmission process. American Lee de Forest was a self-promoter and a scientist. After several failures and claims by investors that he was a fraud, de Forest created a radio company that improved existing technology and aired publicity-generating broadcasts to attract both listeners and investors. One of his most famous was a 1908 broadcast from the Eiffel Tower in Paris. In 1906, de Forest also took credit for the creation of one of the most important wireless components.

Lee de Forest invented the Audion, or triode vacuum tube, that enabled wireless signals to be amplified for improved reception. Prior to the Audion, wireless receivers lacked suitable sensitivity to detect weak signals for the operators. Radio operators had to listen for the coded signals through earphones because there was no way to amplify the reception of the weak signals. The Audion not only could be used to build an amplifier to increase the strength of the audio signals but it was also used later to build better transmitters. Author Tom Lewis, writing in *Empire of the Air,* notes that de Forest avoided giving credit to Thomas Edison, inventor of the light bulb, and John Ambrose Fleming, inventor of the vacuum tube.[1] Though de Forest held the patent for the Audion, historians note that de Forest did not fully understand what he had invented or how it worked. It would take the work of another radio innovator to develop the next use of the Audion circuit.

Edwin Howard Armstrong's fascination with wireless emerged as news of the latest developments were being reported. In 1904, at the age of thirteen, Armstrong was already studying accounts of Guglielmo Marconi's wireless system. By 1909, Armstrong had enrolled in Columbia University's engineering program to study wireless. Though the Audion was being sold for use by wireless operators, no one knew precisely how it worked. Beginning in 1912, Armstrong measured the current emitted by the Audion, made a change that refed the current back through the circuit and discovered the principle of regeneration.[2]

Regeneration enabled two things to be accomplished. First, it enhanced the quality of signal amplification. It was now possible to use an external speaker, rather than earphones, to listen to incoming signals. This principle is still used today not only in radio but also in amplifier circuits. Second, Armstrong realized that regeneration produced a constant oscillating signal, or carrier wave, that became the founding principle behind new wireless transmitters. The use of regeneration vastly shrank the size of wireless transmitters, much as transistors and integrated circuits would later decrease the size of radio transmission and reception equipment.

Armstrong delayed applying for a patent to protect his new discovery until late October 1913, more than a year after his first regeneration experiments. His failure to disclose both the reception and transmission aspects of his regeneration circuit would later provide the basis for patent infringement suits by de Forest against Armstrong. It would be a battle Armstrong would ultimately lose.

The quest for personal glory and greed—stemming from entrepreneurial opportunities that might develop from new wireless technology and perhaps simply the combination of so many individuals focusing simultaneously on the same topic—led to a number of patent disputes, lawsuits, and counterlawsuits over wireless innovations. Fessenden, Marconi, de Forest, Armstrong, and a host of lesser players threatened lawsuits, then sued and countersued each other over simultaneous developments and improvements. All the while, whether for ship-to-shore communications or other commercial applications or simply to entertain curious citizens, radio prospered.

GROWTH OF PUBLIC INTEREST IN WIRELESS

The patent disputes ended shortly after the United States entered the war against Germany in 1917. During the war, as a national security measure, the Navy took over the operation of all high-power stations, even those owned by American Marconi.[3] All amateur stations and radio experimenters were forced to cease broadcasting. The wartime demand for reliable transmitters and receivers led to an emergency pooling of patent rights; the Navy agreed to pay the damages if manufacturers were later sued for patent infringement.

After the war, the U.S. Congress considered maintaining government control over wireless operations. Changing sentiments (as well as a Republican Party victory in the elections of 1918) resulted in the government dropping its claim to operate wireless. The stations seized by the Navy were returned to the original owners. Amateurs were also able to return to the air.

American Marconi (a subsidiary of British Marconi) attempted to return to business as usual before the war but opposition to a foreign company's monopoly over wireless communications in the United States eventually led General Electric (GE) to buy a controlling interest in American Marconi. GE's interest was in manufacturing radio equipment. Along with Westinghouse and AT&T, GE established the Radio Corporation of America and transferred the tangible assets of American Marconi to RCA. GE, AT&T, and Westinghouse ended the patent disputes by pooling nearly 2,000 patents. GE and Westinghouse would make parts they would sell to RCA. RCA would then manufacture radio receiving sets. AT&T would manufacture transmitters and station equipment. The three companies, through RCA, viewed radio in much the same way as the original Marconi companies—as a means for maritime and international communications. Radio broadcasting, as we know it, was not yet being considered.

Technological growth led private citizens to experiment with the new wireless communications medium. Increasing numbers of amateur operators and commercial establishments, in the business of selling transmitting and receiving equipment, set up broadcasting stations. Not unlike computer users today, amateur wireless enthusiasts traded information among themselves, learned from magazine articles and books, and used trial and error to build a receiver or transmitter.

Readers interested in studying the early history of wireless development will note that in the sexist world of the early 1900s, most of the early books and magazine articles suggest radio projects for boys or young men. The *Boy Scout Manual* contained information about radio equipment and urged boys to make their own sets. Boy's fiction hero Tom Swift had two books built around radio adventures: *Tom Swift and His Wireless Message* and *The Castaways of Earthquake Island.* By the time of World War I, a whole generation of (primarily) American boys had grown up learning about the excitement and mystery of wireless.[4]

A wireless receiver capable of detecting Morse code could be built for as little as $2.25, with another investment of $3.00 to 4.00 for an outside antenna. Frederick Collins's 1915 text, *The Book of Wireless,* also recommends a more sophisticated receiver that could be built from parts costing less than $16.00.[5] While these amounts are paltry today, $2.00 in 1915 might have represented a day's wages for some segments of the population.

There is an important parallel between early wireless users and early adopters of virtually all technology, including computer technology. Computer users today commonly upgrade software or computer hardware and use Internet sites to share computer information. The earliest experiences of the users often involved imprecise equipment or techniques. As the skill level of the user improved, improvements in the equipment were made. The earliest radio enthusiasts were able to share information and expertise with interested citizens and they provided a ready workforce for the developing radio industries. And, as young users of wireless matured and obtained full-time jobs, the higher income could be used to purchase better receiving equipment. The wireless tinkerer of 1910 became the faithful radio listener of 1920.

Early radio listeners consisted of three groups: hams, who were as interested in transmitting signals as in receiving them, "distance fiends," interested in broadcasts from faraway places, and members of a general listening audience, fascinated by the instantaneous information available by radio.[6] All three listener groups wanted national radio services.

Probably the biggest single breakthrough in receiver design came from Edwin Armstrong. Armstrong had already patented a new application of de Forest's Audion. During service in WWI, Armstrong developed a new type of tuner that better amplified the radio signal and offered improved sound. Called the "superheterodyne receiver" and equipped with six tubes, the superiority of Armstrong's invention convinced RCA to abandon its own receiver development plans, purchase rights to Armstrong's new receiver, and begin development and then production of a moderately priced superheterodyne receiver.[7]

Equipment manufacturers and retailers interested in selling radio receiving sets not only searched for and built cheaper and better performing receiver sets, but they also operated radio stations, not as a public service, but to give the public something to listen to and, thus, a reason to buy a receiver. One of the most famous of such stations was Westinghouse station KDKA in Pittsburgh, which is still on the air.

Though KDKA can trace its roots to a prewar experimental station that began to broadcast in 1916, KDKA's first broadcast came on election night, November 2, 1920. Generally, KDKA is thought to be the oldest radio station in the United States to hold a government license, to broadcast noncoded programming intended for reception by the general public by radio waves, and to operate in a continuous and organized manner.[8] Thus, radio communications, aimed at many listeners, began to change radio into a mass medium.

THE FIRST WIRELESS REGULATIONS

As radio grew, the need to regulate wireless became more apparent. Part of the need for regulation resulted from domestic problems. Wireless had moved from ship-to-shore communications to land-based communications. Individuals interested in "tinkering" with radio could freely do so and they could expect few if any consequences resulting from the interference they created. Internationally, a protocol was needed to limit interference created by signals traveling across national boundaries.

By the early 1900s, wireless had become increasingly common aboard ships. The Marconi Company supplied the most reliable equipment, and, with the Marconi land stations, messages could be effectively sent, received, or relayed. Marconi was not the only source for equipment. The United Fruit Company used de Forest wireless equipment to schedule ships for loading fruit as soon as it was picked at the company's plantations in Latin America.

Maritime disasters were also averted through the use of wireless. In 1909, during a heavy fog, the ocean liner *Republic* collided with *Florida* off the East coast of the United States. The radio operator on *Republic* stayed at his post and was able to issue a call for help, saving nearly all the passengers on board. The *Republic* disaster made it apparent that wireless played an important role not only in the commerce of shipping but in safety as well.[9] After several legislative attempts, Congress passed the first piece of legislation to regulate broadcasting in the United States, the Wireless Ship Act of 1910. The act required that all oceangoing vessels with 50 or more passengers and crew members, traveling between ports 200 miles or more apart, carry a "radio-communication apparatus" capable of transmitting 100 miles and operated by a skilled person.[10]

Three years later, the legislation was put to the test. One of the biggest maritime disasters occurred when the *Titanic* sank on its maiden voyage. More than 1,500 passengers and crew died. While the ship *Carpathia* responded to the distress calls from *Titanic* and ultimately saved about 700 persons, that ship was 58 miles away and did not arrive until well after *Titanic* sank. A closer ship to *Titanic,* the *California,* did not respond to the distress calls because the ship's sole radio operator, after many hours on duty, was asleep when the distress messages were transmitted. Furthermore, because that ship was traveling through the same ice field as *Titanic*, the ship's captain had cut all power to the ship, ending the electrical service needed to power the wireless system.[11]

Still a third ship, the freighter *Lena,* was only thirty miles away. But because of its small crew and no regular passengers, the ship was not equipped with a wireless. News of survivors of the disaster was slow to reach the mainland because the *Carpathia's* wireless equipment had a range of only eighty-five miles. Two U.S. Navy cruisers, sent by President Taft to intercept *Carpathia* on its way to New York, couldn't effectively relay information back to New York because the wireless operators on the Navy ships weren't sufficiently skilled.[12]

The *Titanic* tragedy led newspaper and magazine editorials to call for the federal government, as an agent of the public, to establish control over wireless operation and corporate practices. The regulation of wireless was viewed as a public good, equal in importance to previous social and antitrust regulatory actions by the government to regulate the railroads, oil companies, and meatpackers. Regulation was to improve the welfare of citizens.

Within four months of the *Titanic* tragedy, transmitting in the *ether* (as the airwaves were sometimes called) would not be a personal right but a privilege assigned by the government. The Radio Act of 1912 required that all operators be licensed, that stations adhere to specific frequency allocations, that distress calls take priority over all other communications, and that the secretary of commerce had the power to issue radio licenses and make other necessary radio regulations.[13]

Amateur radio operators were relegated to a shortwave portion of the spectrum for transmission though they were free to monitor transmissions on any frequencies. *The Book of Wireless* (1915), lamented the "taming of the airwaves" through regulation by noting that the time existed "not so very long ago, when a boy could own any kind of wireless set, use any length of wave he wanted to and send messages wherever he pleased and no one could say him nay."[14] Amateur radio operators were also forbidden to reveal the contents of messages received. Divulging or publishing unauthorized information could result in a fine of $250 or imprisonment for up to three months or both!

The Navy and major corporations (primarily Marconi) strengthened their monopoly over radio technology with passage of the Radio Act of 1912, but amateurs were unwilling to abandon the airwaves. If anything, maritime tragedy, newspaper and magazine articles, and government regulation only increased public curiosity about radio. The number of licensed amateurs increased from 322 in 1913 to 13,581 in 1917.[15] As the number of operators increased, they learned how closely they had to adhere to the 1912 laws. As with laws we have against speeding on the highways, the trick for radio amateurs was to decide to what extent they would obey the laws.

THE BEGINNING OF PROGRAMMING FOR THE MASS AUDIENCE

The name of the wireless service, along with the technology, evolved. Known first as the "wireless telegraph," between 1906 and 1912 the transition from wireless telegraphy to radiotelegraphy and radiotelephony (transmission of the human voice) occurred. The term was gradually shortened to *radio* by the time of the 1912 act, and the wireless reference became obsolete. The word *broadcast* was borrowed from agriculture and referred to the practice of scattering seed across a field.[16] The earliest coded radio transmissions were from a specific sender to a specific receiver. With licensing and restrictions on who could transmit, radio broadcasts increasingly moved from messages to individual receivers to messages intended for multiple receivers.

Just as the public rushed to the Internet in the 1990s, the public, seventy-five years earlier, was rushing to the airwaves. Middle-class Americans, intrigued with the scientific applications of radio and the potential for information and entertainment, purchased radio receiving sets at an astonishing rate. Sales of radio sets and parts totaled $60 million in 1922, $136 million in 1923, and $358 million in 1924.[17] Radio listening also meant that individuals and families could enjoy the newly available information and entertainment from the comfort and privacy of their homes.

During the 1920s, the thrill of receiving signals from distant cities led many ads for manufactured receiving sets or parts (for building receivers) to emphasize the ability of the receiver or its components to bring in distant signals. By about 1925, as radio sets began to appeal to an even wider audience, manufacturers built receiver sets that looked more like furniture and did not appeal only to enthusiasts.

Radio programming evolved along with the receiving sets. During the 1920s, programming, even in major cities, often consisted of whoever was available to fill the on-air time. Local musicians, often unpaid by the station, were given time on the air to perform and promote other appearances. Informational programming consisted of federally sponsored agriculture programming from the U.S. Department of Agriculture as well as farm commodity information. Prior to radio, it wasn't unusual for local commodity buyers to cheat farmers by underreporting actual market prices. Valuable market price information became a prime motive for farmers to purchase radios. For the first time, a farmer in a rural area was able to receive accurate weather information as well as information about farm product prices. One radio magazine reported a rural listener's story related to egg prices. When a buyer told the farmer that prices were bad and getting worse, the woman told him that day's current price and advised him next time to stop by before she heard the 8 o'clock prices if he wanted to cheat her![18]

While many books talk about early radio broadcasts of classical music, country music, the music of rural America, had a major impact on radio growth and radio listening in the 1920s. Industrialization had moved many Americans from the country to the city. Radio became a way for migrants to reconnect with their roots. Saturday night barn dance programs were regular program features on many stations. When one Chicago radio station had a request for a square dance caller, a listener telephoned the station to volunteer his services!

One prominent country program began in 1925 on WSM in Nashville. The WSM program starred George D. Hay, who had previously hosted the successful "National Barn Dance" show on WLS in Chicago.[19] Within two years the "WSM Barn Dance" adopted the name "The Grand Ole Opry." Station history suggests that after an NBC network opera broadcast concluded, WSM host George Hay told the listeners they had been listening to Grand Opera but that they would now hear "The Grand Ole Opry."[20]

WSM attained clear-channel radio status in 1932 and an operating power of 50,000 watts. It continues to broadcast "The Grand Ole Opry" to much of the United States on 650 kHz every Saturday night.

THE SECRETARY OF COMMERCE ATTEMPTS TO REGULATE RADIO

While station and operator licensing instituted by the Radio Act of 1912 was intended to provide "monitored" growth of radio, the Department of Commerce failed to realize how quickly radio would grow. By the end of 1922, 690 licenses had been assigned to general broadcast stations, those airing entertainment and information.[21] All of these stations occupied one of *two frequencies*, 360 meters (833 kHz) or 400

meters (750 kHz). Interference led many stations to become inaudible. Station interference eventually led to voluntary frequency sharing (time-sharing) by some stations. In the New York area, WOR, operated by Bamberger's Department Store, found itself sharing time with WJZ, operated by Westinghouse's Newark, New Jersey manufacturing plant. It was decided that the stations would alternate days broadcasting between sunrise and sunset and sunset to sunrise.[22]

The "big four" corporations that dominated broadcasting in the 1920s, GE, Westinghouse, and AT&T, and their pooled patents, held through RCA, had an interest in developing national radio listenership but not necessarily commercial radio service. As radio interference increased, they encouraged the Secretary of Commerce to institute administrative laws, through the Department of Commerce, to regulate radio. A reluctant Herbert Hoover instituted a series of radio conferences.

Between 1922 and 1925, four annual conferences were held to discuss the problems facing corporate and amateur radio stations. The first National Radio Conference recommended complete government control and the Second National Radio Conference, in a unanimous opinion, affirmed that the Secretary of Commerce, under existing laws, had authority "to regulate hours and wave-lengths of operations of stations and to revoke or withhold licenses of stations when such action is necessary to prevent interference detrimental to public good."[23] At the meeting of the Third National Radio Conference in October 1924, Secretary of Commerce Herbert Hoover noted the need for additional frequencies for station broadcasts.

While the conferences allowed discussion of issues, there was little real resolution of conflict. They did, with the further encouragement of the RCA–GE–Westinghouse consortium, lead Hoover to begin administrative regulation of wireless. One of Hoover's first actions was to begin to establish a limited number of "superpower" radio stations around the country. Hoover authorized some stations to operate with power levels as high as 50,000 watts and he also arbitrarily began to assign frequencies based on station power; the more powerful stations received the best frequencies.[24]

At that time, both GE and Westinghouse believed not in local radio service but in the ability to cover the entire country with just a handful of high-powered stations. Their hope was to operate a sufficient number of stations to cover the United States and therefore encourage receiver sales, but at the same time to limit the operational and programming expenses by linking the stations to form a national network. (Not only had they not considered the idea of selling advertising but AT&T claimed that the patent pooling agreement had granted it exclusive rights to broadcast paid material.)

Hoover did not have the ability to deny station licenses to groups requesting them but his frequency, power assignments, and time-sharing alienated many station owners. They believed Hoover was attempting to gain favor with corporate owners. It is important for readers today to remember that computers were not available to help staff members in the Department of Commerce manage the station database. In fact, large maps were laid out on the floor at the Department of Commerce and workers used colored paper to code station operations.

It was inevitable that Hoover's powers to regulate radio would be challenged. In 1925, Eugene F. McDonald of Zenith Radio, who owned a newly licensed station in Chicago, challenged Hoover's authority. McDonald's station had been authorized to broadcast only two hours a week. McDonald moved his station to another frequency, prompting Hoover's agents to close the station. McDonald sued. Hoover viewed the suit as a means of gaining court endorsement of his authority. The judge disagreed with Hoover.

The U.S. District Court for the Northern District of Illinois, in 1926, agreed with McDonald's claim that the commerce secretary had violated the Radio Act of 1912.[25] Secretary of Commerce Hoover did not have the power to impose restrictions as to station frequency, power, hours of operation, or a station's use of a frequency not assigned to it. The next day, Hoover issued a statement abandoning all his efforts to regulate radio. He urged the stations to undertake self-regulation and his action endorsed the need for a new law to regulate broadcasting.

Beginning in mid-1926, radio became chaotic. Operators and station owners could do virtually anything they wanted with no regulatory consequence. Perhaps the only thing that kept some operators in check was the knowledge that anything they did to another station to create interference could also be done to them. New stations continued to apply for licenses to go on the air. Listeners were beginning to receive only conflicting sounds caused by interfering signals. For the first time, radio set sales dropped drastically. In his December 1926 message to Congress, President Calvin Coolidge urged passage of legislation that would save radio before it destroyed itself. A little more than two months later, in February 1927, Congress passed the Radio Act of 1927 and sent the measure to Coolidge for his signature.[26]

Rather than creating mere rules for regulating radio, the act borrowed from the language of railroad regulations. Radio was deemed to operate for the "public convenience, interest, or necessity."[27] Though the Radio Act of 1927 did not define *public convenience, interest, or necessity,* it established the idea that no one could own a radio frequency. Government's responsibility was to manage the airwaves so that the public benefited just as much as the station owner. Further, the act declared that radio would not become a monopoly enterprise controlled by a few organizations. The airwaves were a public resource, not the private property of a licensee, and the public had a right to expect something from the radio station.[28]

COMMERCIAL SPONSORSHIP BEGINS

AT&T, through the patent pooling agreement of 1919, had exclusive rights to manufacture transmitters and wireless telephony equipment. Further, AT&T claimed that the patent pooling arrangement gave it the right to sell commercials.[29] AT&T exercised its claim to air commercials by starting station WEAF in New York in 1922.

AT&T envisioned a national network of radio stations, linked by AT&T telephone lines, that could not only air programming nationally, which was distributed by the telephone lines, but also sell commercials or "toll" time, much as AT&T sold time for long-distance telephone calls.[30] Indeed, flagship station WEAF was open to anyone who wanted to buy time to speak. Just as citizens would contact the telephone company to arrange two-way phone service, so WEAF would provide one-way communications to anyone who wanted it.

AT&T viewed WEAF's telephone service comparison not only as an appropriate analogy but also as a way to answer a question that had been perplexing almost all of the early radio pioneers: how could radio be made to pay for itself?[31] The first reported radio ad was for an apartment complex in New York and aired on WEAF in 1922. It cost $100. Throughout the toll broadcasting effort, there were vigorous protests. Secretary of Commerce Hoover viewed advertising sales with "alarm."[32] In 1925, a New York representative introduced legislation to ban advertising.[33]

AT&T's vision of radio-linking the nation for important national events was attained in 1923. AT&T fed President Calvin Coolidge's first address to Congress to a network of six stations, consisting of WEAF, New York, WCAP, Washington, WJAR, Providence, KSD, St. Louis, WDAF, Kansas City, and WFAA, Dallas.[34]

Why was it that radio in the United States developed through private ownership while it was often government-run in other parts of the world? Smulyan notes that radio developed as a private enterprise in the United States due to its large geographic size, the even distribution of the population, and the linguistically homogeneous population. By contrast, England and Germany, relatively small land areas, needed but a few stations to cover each country. Australia and Canada, though large in size, had most of their populations living in close proximity to a few major cities. The (former) Soviet Union was large in size and needed to program in more than sixty languages, thus eliminating the need for national radio service.[35]

Whenever a few companies control an industry, through a monopoly or oligopoly, both government and consumer groups fear the potential harm consumers may experience. Just as the Justice Department in the 1970s began proceedings that eventually broke apart AT&T, and in the 1990s launched investigations of computer chip maker Intel and software maker Microsoft, the Justice Department of the 1920s was eyeing AT&T's wireless and telephone monopoly and the GE–Westinghouse–RCA receiver oligopoly. Concerns about control of both radio and telephone service eventually led AT&T to sell WEAF and other AT&T stations to RCA in 1926 and for RCA to use WEAF to form the National Broadcasting Corporation, NBC. The new corporation was owned by RCA (50 percent), GE (30 percent), and Westinghouse (20 percent). AT&T withdrew from radio but profited by maintaining the telephone monopoly, which now included the exclusive rights to lease telephone lines to NBC and other radio networks. AT&T ended its exclusive claim over commercial sales. Commercial radio service was created to not only pay for programming and station operational expenses but to pay the cost of the telephone lines leased from AT&T.

RADIO'S NEW REGULATORS

The Radio Act of 1927 created the **Federal Radio Commission (FRC)** with five commissioners, with limited staffing, to sort out the mess of the airwaves. The act also revoked the licenses of all radio stations, including commercial stations, trans-oceanic stations, coastal stations, experimental stations, educational, religious, and training stations, and approximately 14,885 amateur stations, more than 18,000 transmitters in all!

Despite public enthusiasm for radio, the FRC moved to reduce the number of radio stations on the air from 681 in 1927 to 606 in 1929. Also, the Commission reduced the number of stations that were allowed to broadcast at night from 565 to 397. At one point in 1928, 164 stations were notified that the Commission "was not 'satisfied that public interest, convenience or necessity' would be served by granting applications for renewal."[36]

The FRC licensing system favored high-powered stations capable of serving national audiences of listeners, especially at night. The clear channel stations operated with 50,000 watts of power both during the day and at night. Twenty-one of the twenty-four clear channel assignments went to stations that were network affiliates. The government had previously deemed citizen communication important enough to create free mail delivery for citizens in rural areas. FRC Commissioner O. H. Caldwell equated high-power radio broadcasting, capable of reaching thousands—even millions—of rural residents with rural free mail delivery.[37] Broadcast service was the first means of effectively reaching citizens in broader geographic areas. Reducing the power of existing 50,000-watt stations would be a mild inconvenience for persons in metropolitan areas but a disaster for rural listeners.

FRC licensing decisions pushed many educational stations to undesirable frequencies, low power, and, typically, no nighttime power. The FRC believed the success of radio depended not on many low-power stations but on fewer stations with higher power. By 1933, twenty-two stations were operating with the AM maximum 50,000 watts of authorized power. The clear channel-dominated standard broadcasting system was born; clear channel stations provided more than one third of the nation's voters with election returns in the 1930s. Local stations did operate but were sometimes forced to operate with powers of 250 or 500 watts. Regulators and station owners recognized that the AM station allocation scheme that was developing placed some stations in "a marked competitive advantage or disadvantage over other stations in the community."[38] Most of all, the piecemeal AM scheme, along with the future demonstration of technological advantages of FM, would eventually drive the final nails into AM radio's coffin.

The developing radio networks preferred the system of a few high-power stations across the country rather than many low-power stations. For national programmers, the greatest revenue would come from nighttime service. Though NBC and CBS embraced the network concept, the limited hours of operation by some stations still made it difficult to gain network program clearances. In Chicago the hours of station operation were so sporadic that CBS had to sign affiliation contracts with three stations to reach the residents of the city. NBC, with the Red and Blue Networks, had to sign affiliation agreements with five stations to reach the residents of the city.[39]

THE DEVELOPMENT OF RADIO NETWORKS

Broadcast historian Erik Barnouw notes that NBC, like RCA, was born with a silver spoon in its mouth. The premiere of the network broadcast era took place on November 15, 1926, when NBC aired a four-hour program from the Waldorf-Astoria Hotel in New York. The broadcast featured singers, orchestras, and comedy teams, and it included two remote broadcasts from other cities, a singer in Chicago and humorist Will Rogers in Kansas City.[40]

The event was reported to have cost $50,000, though most stars performed for free and perhaps half that amount was spent for technical arrangements, including the 3,600 miles of special AT&T telephone cable that connected the WEAF program to about two dozen stations. New NBC president, Merlin Aylesworth, estimated that as many as 12 million persons might have heard the broadcast, a sizeable audience when one remembers that the U.S. population was less than 100 million. Most of all, the broadcast created the perception that the new radio network was powerful. It could attract star performers and millions of listeners.

Less than two months later, a second NBC network was started. This network used the former RCA station WJZ in New York as the flagship for the network. The WJZ-based network became the NBC Blue Network. The WEAF-based network was the NBC Red Network. A separate West Coast NBC Pacific Coast Network operated for about a year, connecting stations between San Francisco and Seattle, until both the Red and Blue Networks began offering coast-to-coast programming.

The network radio business began slowly. Initially, both the Red and Blue Networks had difficulty attracting advertisers and affiliate stations. In 1930, government antitrust action against RCA, GE, AT&T, and Westinghouse resulted in RCA becoming the sole owner of the NBC Networks. By 1931, NBC reported a profit of more than $2.3 million and had an affiliate base of seventy-six stations.[41]

NBC was soon joined by two network competitors. The Columbia Phonograph Broadcasting System, named for its partnership with Columbia Phonograph Record Company, and later changed to Columbia Broadcasting System (CBS), was established in 1927. CPBS lost more than $100,000 in its first month of operation, prompting Columbia Phonograph to withdraw from the venture. The Congress Cigar Company then bought a controlling interest in the network to promote its cigars. William Paley, son of the firm's founder, took over the now CBS network's operation, and would head the network for more than half a century.[42]

Much of the programming carried by NBC and CBS from 1928 to 1929 was musical programming. Concerts featured classical compositions, though popular dance music and jazz received some airplay. Radio drama began to develop as the complement to the musical programming. While some programming was built around rebroadcasts of historic events, such as *Great Moments in History* on NBC, writers were recognizing the opportunity to do creative storytelling through radio. The creation of a show on WGN in Chicago, first called *Sam and Henry* and later changed to *Amos 'n Andy* when the show moved to WMAQ and NBC, is often cited as the first show to demonstrate the power of radio dramatizations.[43]

The show was about the misadventures of Amos and Andy, who were created to represent part of the migration of African Americans from the Deep South to urban cities in the North. Readers today probably cannot imagine listening to a program on which two white performers used exaggerated African American dialect to entertain listeners.[44] But minstrel jokes and burnt cork routines were decades old and continued as part of vaudeville when *Amos 'n Andy* began to air. By 1929, the radio show had created several spin-offs, including a daily comic strip, phonograph records, and a candy bar.

A telephone survey of radio listeners in 1929 found that more than half of those telephoned reported listening to *Amos 'n Andy* and the accompanying sponsor messages for Pepsodent toothpaste. At one point the audience totaled more than 40 million listeners for NBC.[45] The show was popular with white and black listeners. Though some African American leaders openly scorned the show and began unsuccessful petition drives to have the show taken off the air. *Amos 'n Andy* not only prospered on the radio; the show eventually moved to television in the 1950s, though with black actors in the starring roles.

When radio was being touted as a marvel of technology, able to open the world to isolated Americans, *Amos 'n Andy* represents a sad example of how the new medium resorted to old stereotypes. Freeman Gosden and Charles Correll, the stars of the program, were notable performers; they sometimes played up to six characters each in a single 15-minute show and they did not rehearse before a broadcast. Instead, they preferred spontaneous interaction.[46] In that regard, *Amos 'n Andy* is a notable example of radio's earliest program creativity.

What *Amos 'n Andy* did for radio was to signal a listener desire for comedy programming. Though NBC was a step ahead of CBS with *Amos 'n Andy*, William Paley began the drive to bring popular, mass appeal entertainment to CBS. The quickest way to making the biggest profits, Paley reasoned, was to appeal to the largest audience (a thought obvious to us today but novel in 1929). Paley's first coup was the signing of musician Paul Whiteman and his orchestra. Whiteman, who had created a symphonic jazz band, was paid $5,000 a week; members of the band split a $30,000 salary each week.[47]

By the early 1930s, the success and notoriety Bill Paley was achieving were akin to the fame and fortune now gained by Internet entrepreneurs. Paley had another incentive to program his network to attract the largest possible audience. In late 1929, before the stock market crash, Paley arranged a deal to sell half of CBS to Paramount Film Studies. But for the deal to be lucrative for Paley and CBS, the network needed to earn a net profit of $2 million by 1931. Paley scheduled programming designed to pander to listeners, from fortune tellers to gory thrillers. He likewise permitted commercials to become more numerous and more insistent in their pitch to listeners, even granting sponsors the right to mention product prices on the air.[48]

Advertisers began to see radio as an inexpensive and effective way to reach the national audience. Paley added hour after hour of escapist programming to the CBS Network schedule. A complainant to the Federal Radio Commission wrote that the detective stories on *Street and Smith* included "dramatic and bloody murder" scenes.[49] NBC, though the top network, would soon follow the CBS programming strategy. By 1932 CBS and NBC aired 12,546 commercial interruptions in 2,365 hours of programming![50]

The perceived commercial excesses of the radio networks in the late 1920s and early 1930s led a new group, called the National Committee on Education by Radio, to request that Congress consider legislation to regulate radio more closely than the Radio Act of 1927. The group was motivated to advocate these changes because of the perceived ill-treatment many educational stations had experienced from Secretary of Commerce Hoover. Among the regulatory changes they requested was a requirement that 15 percent of all radio channels be reserved for education use.

William Paley testified before a Senate Committee in January 1930. Paley knew that his struggling network needed more affiliates. Reserving 15 percent of the channels for education use would stifle the growth of CBS and certainly cause him to miss his $2 million profit mark by 1931. Paley told the senators that only 22 percent of CBS's programming schedule was sponsored; the other 78 percent wasn't.[51] Of course, the sponsored programming aired during the most listened-to time periods and more than two thirds of the unsponsored programming consisted of popular music or symphonic music because it was the cheapest programming the network could find to air. And, if CBS had been able to increase the amount of sponsored programming, it would have done so. Paley's testimony was enough to forestall the attempt at regulation.

The third radio network, which began operation in 1934, was the Mutual Broadcasting System (MBS). The four founding stations were WGN, Chicago, WOR, New York, WLW, Cincinnati, and WXYZ, Detroit.[52] All four stations are still on the air, though only WGN is still owned by its original owner, the *Chicago Tribune* newspaper, now Tribune Company. The Mutual Broadcasting System ceased operation in 1999.[53]

THE GOLDEN AGE OF RADIO PROGRAMMING

Whether they were local stations or clear channel stations, the public listened. Not only had radio receivers improved in quality since the late 1920s, but receiving sets capable of using household current were widely marketed. By 1935, the Department of Commerce estimated that radio broadcasts served 18.5 million families or over 50 million people. Approximately 60 percent of all homes in the United States had radios and radio sets in operation in the United States comprised 43.2 percent of the world total.[54]

Congress passed the Communications Act of 1934 to create one agency to supervise wired and wireless communication. The Federal Communications Commission (FCC) replaced the FRC. The radio portion of the Communications Act of 1934 mirrored the provisions of the 1927 Act, thus providing continuity from the FRC to the FCC.

Policymakers acknowledged radio's importance through the increased number of commentaries about radio's political and social impact. The American Academy of Political and Social Science devoted its January, 1935 and January, 1941 issues of *Annals of the Academy of Political and Social Science* to the development of United States and world radio broadcasting systems and public response to the new entertainment and information medium. In the forward of the 1941 issue, Editor Herman Hettinger writes:

> *Since 1929, radio broadcasting may be said to have emerged from youth into adolescence, and now into the beginnings of maturity. Today, broadcasting, as a medium of entertainment, cultural and political enlightenment, and more formal educational training, extends its personal and all-pervasive influence into six out of every ten American homes. It has grown into the greatest medium of mass communication to be developed since the printing press.[55]*

Critics noted that the airwaves were being choked with mass appeal, commercial-laden programming. But corporately controlled radio, via the NBC and CBS networks, was here to stay. For the public, radio offered something comforting. The stock market crash in 1929 had changed the role of radio. While unemployment was rising and wages were plummeting, radio was proving to be a Depression-proof business. Radio receiver sets were certainly not cheap but, once the receiver was purchased, the radio provided hours of programming and the only cost to the listener was the opportunity cost of listening to commercials.

CBS continued to lead the way with popular radio programming though NBC, with both the Red and Blue Networks, typically had more affiliates and stations with better signals. Some of the most popular programming of the time starred comedians, such as George Burns and Gracie Allen, Jack Benny, and Fred Allen. In the earliest days of CBS, it was not uncommon for hosts of successful shows to change to NBC once a program and its host became popular. CBS fought back by conducting talent raids against NBC to recruit better affiliate stations and to lure star talent, such as singers Al Jolsen and Nelson Eddy and variety show host Major Edward Bowes away from NBC.

Serial melodramas ran during the daytime and soon drew a large audience of housewives. These daytime serials featured the trials and tribulations of everyday people and were often sponsored by soap makers, hence the name *soap operas*.

Entertainment and informational content are so pervasive today that it is difficult to imagine what it was like in the 1920s or 1930s to finally have radio broadcasting. Comedy, drama, and music (referred to as light entertainment) were the mainstays of radio programming. Most advertisers chose not to sponsor programs that reported on contemporary problems. Perhaps most famous among radio's news-related programming was the broadcast in 1933 of four addresses to the nation by newly elected President Franklin Roosevelt. Called "fireside chats" because of Roosevelt's informal and relaxed tone as well as the perception that he was sharing his thoughts with the public, Roosevelt's speeches created goodwill among the public and enabled many of his New Deal reforms to be quickly passed by Congress.[56]

As the radio networks began to achieve profitability in the early 1930s, at both the local and network level, radio began to cover the news. Radio's news focus was not to be ignored by newspaper owners, who were already experiencing dwindling advertising revenue, partly from radio competition and partly resulting from the Depression. As NBC and CBS increased their news reporting, newspaper publishers fought back. Some local radio stations found their broadcast schedules were no longer considered "newsworthy" by the papers and therefore weren't published. Radio network advertisers experienced a newspaper publicity blackout.[57]

At a December 1933 meeting at the Biltmore Hotel in New York, between NBC, CBS, the wire services (AP, UP, and INS), and the American Newspaper Publishers Association, CBS agreed to disband its news service and NBC would refrain from building a news-gathering operation.[58] Instead, the networks agreed to pay to establish a Press-Radio Bureau, which would send broadcasters brief news items—not to exceed 30 words per item. The news bulletins would allow the networks to schedule two five-minute newscasts, one in the morning after 9:30 A.M. and another at night, after 9:00 P.M. The hours were selected to protect newspaper circulation from radio competition.

Competing news suppliers soon emerged and extended radio news coverage continued on many stations. Just as newspaper owners were pondering how they might squash the press freedom of the radio stations, advertiser interest in sponsoring several daily newscasts led UP and INS, and eventually AP, to agree to sell their news content to the radio networks. The Press-Radio Bureau soon disappeared. Newspaper owners recognized the value of owning radio stations and began to apply for licenses. As Hitler and Mussolini were gathering followers in Europe, the radio networks in the United States were building the news departments.

In a time before the Internet or television, radio was the only live, simultaneous source of mass communications. The popularity of radio and importance of radio news can easily be seen by recalling the quiet Sunday afternoon in 1941 when, at 2:31 P.M. Eastern time, a CBS newsman interrupted the regular programming to announce that the Japanese had launched a surprise air attack on Pearl Harbor in Hawaii. The next day, an estimated 62 million Americans heard President Franklin Roosevelt declare war on Japan.[59]

Radio broadcasts prior to the bombing of Pearl Harbor had told listeners of the fighting already underway in Europe. Probably the most memorable WWII broadcasts were the reports from London by CBS reporter Edward R. Murrow, who reported during actual bombings of London by the Nazis. While technology and government censorship provided some limits to news reporting, radio reporters accompanied troops into battle. For listeners at home, the battlefield reports, even though recorded, brought home sounds of war that most listeners had never before heard.

The U.S. government did not seize radio as it had during World War I, but, the government did establish the Office of War Information, headed by former CBS news commentator Elmer Davis. The OWI was charged with determining what the domestic and international audiences should be told about the war. This included both news, public affairs information about how and why the United States was fighting, and information about what the public could do to contribute to the war effort. To counter international broadcasts coming from Germany, Japan, and Italy, the OWI also established the Voice of America. VOA programming consisted of music, news, and commentary programs. By Congressional mandate, all VOA programming was transmitted for listeners outside of the United States.

AM RADIO: STANDARD BROADCAST SERVICE

Today, less than 20 percent of all radio listening is to stations operating on the AM radio band. However, from its earliest days as experimental service until the mid-1970s, radio stations using amplitude modulation were the dominant radio service. Problems with manmade interference, caused by poor receivers, natural static, and interference by other stations continued to plague AM radio even as the number of stations and listeners expanded. The FCC's 1939 *Standards of Good Engineering Practice Concerning Standard Broadcast Stations* noted that, "All classes of broadcast stations have primary service areas subject to limitation by fading and noise, and interference from other stations to the contours set out for each station."[60] The general unsuitability of the medium wave (AM) band for broadcast of information and entertainment was noted in a *New York Times* article in 1940. The article reported that the FCC, despite complaints from listeners about local interference in broadcast reception, "had no authority to investigate, or require the elimination of such prominent noise sources or other electrical apparatus, ignition systems of automobiles and electrical signs."[61]

The prospect of creating an additional radio service, using frequency modulation or FM service, was barely an issue until the late 1930s. Even then, FM service might have died for lack of support but for the dogged determination of Edwin Armstrong, who discovered the principle of regeneration and invented the superheterodyne tuner. Edwin Armstrong first began work on a radio system that would eliminate static in 1923. A decade later, in 1933, Armstrong received five patents for his new radio service.[62] Having previously sold his superheterodyne tuner to RCA, Armstrong first demonstrated his latest invention to RCA's President, David Sarnoff.

While Sarnoff recognized the quality of the FM signal, Sarnoff was unwilling to financially back the new system. Instead, RCA was already locked in battle against Philco and several smaller companies to develop television! Sarnoff saw FM as a competitor that would destabilize the growing AM radio industry, divert scientific research from television, distract the attention of the FCC from television, and compete with television for spectrum space over which to broadcast.[63]

After working for a decade on FM, Armstrong was committed to making his system a success. He demonstrated the system in 1935 before a group of radio engineers and a year later he received permission from the FCC to build an experimental station. Though he battled against the television interests for the FCC's attention, the commission recognized the potential for FM. FCC Chairman T. A. M. Craven suggested FM would allow more local stations to be licensed and that FM service would eventually replace AM.[64]

Using his own money to fund the construction, Armstrong built a 50,000-watt FM station in Alpine, New Jersey. The station finally reached full power in 1939. The other problem facing Armstrong was the absence of receivers: his new system would never gain support from the public unless the public could hear the product. Again, Armstrong supplied the financing necessary to commission General Electric to build FM receivers.[65] With available receivers and Armstrong's evangelism, FM's higher fidelity audio gained new supporters. (It's important for readers to know that Armstrong's FM system was not stereo. He was broadcasting only a monaural or single-channel transmission. The FCC would not authorize stereo transmission until 1961!)

That fall, the FCC received station applications from about 150 FM enthusiasts. The problem for the FCC became where to find the spectrum or frequencies for FM. This time Armstrong had backing from General Electric and other receiver manufacturers and a newly formed FM Broadcasters Association. To create FM spectrum, the FCC removed television Channel 1 from the TV band and assigned it to FM.

Commercial FM service was authorized in May 1940 and the FCC authorized FM sound for the newly developing television service. Military needs led Armstrong to grant the royalty-free use of FM to the government for military communications. Soon FM was used for communication in U.S. tanks, jeeps, and other military vehicles.[66] But the military needs of World War II halted civilian development of additional FM stations and FM receivers. When the United States entered the war in December 1941, FM was barely a commercial service. Fewer than 400,000 receivers were in the hands of the public.[67] By contrast, AM station programs could be heard by approximately 29 million households.

After World War II, FM should have been set to grow. Receivers for civilian use could now be manufactured, a little more than fifty FM stations were already on the air, and the quality of FM sound was attracting listeners. Then the FCC made a crucial spectrum decision to change the frequencies allocated for FM. FM was moved from 42–50 MHz to the current 88–108 MHz.[68] The new allocation created more spectrum space for future station growth and it reserved twenty channels for educational station use. But it made obsolete all 400,000 FM receivers sold before the frequency change.

With so many out-of-date receivers, a resurgence in AM station growth, and the beginning boom in television, FM growth would be slowed to a snail's crawl for the next ten years. At one point the number of FM stations actually declined from 616 in 1952 to 530 in 1957. When FM stations did go on the air, they were typically owned with an AM station and the owner was allowed by the FCC to simulcast the same programming on the FM station as the AM station.

Although RCA initially discouraged Armstrong's research into FM, it had adopted FM for use in television sets as well as FM receiver sets, and RCA had never paid Armstrong a royalty for his invention. In 1948, Armstrong sued RCA. RCA fought back by claiming it had done more than anyone to help Armstrong develop FM and was entitled to use Armstrong's technology. Armstrong was infuriated. His legal expenses soared. Finally in 1953, estranged from his family and friends, he authorized a settlement with RCA. Before the settlement was concluded, Armstrong, neatly dressed, fell to his death from his New York apartment.

LOCAL RADIO SERVICE DEVELOPS

When World War II ended, AM station applications surged. In the twenty-seven months between the close of the war and January 1, 1948, 1,054 new AM stations were authorized, more than doubling the number of licensed or authorized AM stations from 912 in 1943 to 2,034 in 1948. (At one point in 1945, engineers estimated there was only room to license about 900 AM stations.) More than *50 million* AM receivers were manufactured between 1946 and 1948. As radio set prices dropped, the multiset household developed. Radios moved from the living room to the kitchen and bedroom.

The postwar expansion of AM radio stations resulted in the first local service for many nonmetropolitan communities. As many communities were gaining their first radio service, the FCC, with the endorsement of equipment makers, was moving ahead with television. The 1952 release of the *Sixth Report and Order* created a television allocation plan for the United States, specifying minimum mileage separations, and free of any need for directional station antenna arrays. The FCC was committed to avoiding the piecemeal system that had created some of the interference problems for AM stations. NBC and CBS moved from dominant national radio networks to dominant national television networks.

Television expanded far more rapidly because it was built on the existing radio structure. Television used radio program formats with added video, television networks were operated similar to radio networks, advertisers jumped from radio to television, and radio set makers added television set manufacturing. Radio station owners were encouraged by the networks to apply for television station licenses.

Radio persevered, still bound partly to the traditional but declining radio network programming relationships, and to station owner/operator desires to provide service to more local communities. A new network quiz show introduced on radio in 1948 went from nowhere to a 20 rating by January 1949. As television grew, the rating dropped to 8.3 in 1951. Film and radio comedian Bob Hope saw radio program ratings drop from 23.8 percent in 1949 to 5.4 percent in 1953.[69] For many radio entertainers, a move to television became the only way to resurrect a career.

At the close of fiscal year 1954, licensed or authorized AM stations totaled 2,697, nearly three times the number of stations operating in 1943. A majority of new AM stations were limited to daytime operation only, when the signals would not travel as far as at night. Two factors encouraged the growth of daytime stations: first, the existing AM band crowding made it difficult to identify unlimited time frequencies, and second, the growth of television drew nightly programming and audiences from radio. Licensees thus favored stations limited to operating only during the daytime. Radio survived by adopting the all-music format and shifting to a heavier emphasis on daytime listening to withstand the evening program encroachment of television.

As radio programming changed, so did the way people used radio and how advertisers bought radio time. Television networks became the means to reach large, national audiences. Radio became a local advertising medium. The growth in the number of radio stations reflects the faith many station owners had in radio. Radio had previously been an evening entertainment medium, but in the 1950s, it shifted to "morning drive" and "afternoon drive" listening patterns. There are obvious reasons for this change.

The mid-1950s was a time of economic prosperity in the United States. Out were the Depression and the WWII food and luxury shortages. In were consumer luxuries and increased consumer confidence. Also in was the suburban housing boom, the ability of families to own a car, or perhaps two vehicles (equipped with radios), and there was a dramatic increase in births after the end of WWII.

Also in was the miniaturization of electronics through the development of the transistor. While transistors boosted the production of television sets, they also improved the quality of radios. Small, battery-power transistor radios changed how and where people could listen to the radio. AFC circuits (automatic frequency control) reduced signal drift on the receivers.

This activity on the AM band took place while television expanded and FM sought a foothold. Commercial and noncommercial television authorizations had grown from a total of 108 stations in 1952, the year the TV freeze ended, to 667 by 1959. Commercial and noncommercial FM stations, though limited by receiver availability, in 1959 numbered 769 and 165, respectively. FM receiver set sales would finally top one million in late 1958.

MUSIC AND MORE

In the 1950s, the networks shifted from controlling the programming heard on their affiliates to supplying program segments. As they had in the earliest days of radio, stations shifted more of their programming to "light entertainment" or music programming. Radio seemed to be returning to its earliest programming strategy, airing recorded music because it was cheap to program. In a major city, a station might adopt an entirely classical format. In a small town, country and western might be played. Still other stations might adopt "block programming" that might feature a two-hour country and western program, followed by two hours of popular music, followed by two hours of classical music, and perhaps then followed by a network-supplied entertainment program. Stations in many markets attempted a "one size fits all" approach by airing a middle-of-the-road (MOR) format, which probably meant playing a mix of orchestral or vocal popular music. With network affiliations virtually meaningless, something was needed to help radio stations differentiate themselves from one another.

STATION DIFFERENTIATION: TOP 40

Just as the refinement of various radio ideas and inventions by Marconi, Fessenden, de Forest, and Armstrong had led to wireless transmission to crude homemade receivers, four independent station owners began to appear in the broadcast press in the 1950s with a new approach to station programming. The four programmers were Todd Storz, Gordon McLendon, Gerald Bartell, and Harold Krelstein. Each man and the company he headed made substantial contributions to the development of the Top 40 format that would create a new identity for radio.[70]

One of the best explanations for creating a radio format built around 40 key songs came from a chance observation by Todd Storz. Storz observed customers in an Omaha bar playing the same few songs over and over on the jukebox. As customers left, the waitresses also played the same few songs over and over. Storz concluded that listeners most wanted to hear a select number of hit tunes, over and over. The music repetition was instituted by Storz at KOWH in Omaha.[71] Within two years, the station's Top 40 format was number one in all time periods!

History suggests that 40 songs were picked because that's the number of songs a jukebox could hold. Others say the 40 songs allowed the station to broadcast for several hours before having to completely start the song rotation again. The Top 40 format emphasized music, news, and local flavor supplied by the disc jockeys and the station's on-air promotions. On-air promotions that might seem obvious to us today were pioneering strategies of the Top 40 programmer. Storz first contest promised to give a homeowner $500 if the station broadcast the person's address and they called the station within a minute. *Time,* in a 1956 article, reported that Storz stations in Omaha and Minneapolis were offering to give away two bank drafts for $105,000 each to listeners who could find the checks, based on clues given on the air.[72] An insurance company underwriting the contest estimated there was only a 1 in 47 chance of someone winning the prize.

Gordon McLendon's stations used the "Oops, sorry" promotion to attract listeners. Stations in Dallas and four other markets, over a six-week period, ran ads ostensibly to apologize for language inadvertently aired. In fact, the ads were to create talk about the stations and, ultimately, cause listeners to sample the stations, perhaps in hopes of hearing other naughty words! Another promotion called "the Walking Woman contest" consisted of giving a woman/man a sizeable prize. Listeners were given clues on the air and encouraged to walk up to someone on the street and ask if they were the "Walking Woman/Man."[73]

While the number of FM stations had begun to increase, FM still constituted a small portion of total radio listening. For this reason, these programmers built Top 40 around AM stations that had typically been network stations. Each station owner tried to differentiate his station through refinement of the radio format. Station ownership was limited to only seven stations of a broadcast service (seven AM and seven FM). For the first time, programming was emphasized over sales. Owners freed themselves from the type of network programming decisions that had been influenced by advertisers and ad agencies.

Program directors at stations created "hot clocks," which presented a one-hour slice of the station's programming. The station might specify when to play an "up tempo" song, when to play a solid hit, and when to play an emerging hit. Stations also used jingles, weather forecasts, and other segments to create a unique but consistent identity for the station. A 1955 *Billboard* survey asked managers who controlled the music at their station. The survey reported that management controlled or influenced programming at more than 75 percent of the large stations and at about 60 percent of the small stations.[74]

As competition among Top 40 formats increased, stations found further need to differentiate themselves. Usually this meant expanding the playlist by adding oldies. Just as the Top 40 relied on currently popular hits, the oldies theory held that songs, once popular, would still be popular. Ultimately, Top 40 would lead stations to classify their formats in one of three ways: Roots, based on the origin of the music, such as country, reggae, or folk songs; Targets, referring to the presumed target audience for the music; Presentation, based on how each individual station chose to deliver the music to the listener.[75]

The Top 40 mix was aimed at a teenage or young adult audience. While older listeners had switched to television viewing, inexpensive and very portable radios made Top 40 a natural draw for the teen audience. Teens were also the fastest growing population segment (the segment growth was fueled by the post-WWII baby boom); they had plenty of disposable income and they had time to listen.

THE DECLINE OF AM AND THE RISE OF FM RADIO

The mix of Top 40 stations helped reposition radio in the minds of listeners but it also created a group of similar sounding stations. Many stations aired similar music and jingles, played loud and lengthy sets of commercials, and were generally of poor fidelity. The growth spurt in the number of stations had not stopped either. The number of authorized stations increased from 2,034 in 1948 to 3,456 by 1960. If it is proper to characterize the AM band in the early 1960s as being "in trouble," the FCC was aware of it.

AM radio in the early 1960s found itself in trouble similar to that of the 1920s. The number of stations in 1960 led to listener complaints about interference and poor audio quality. The low-cost receivers, which had initially encouraged listening, now discouraged listening because consumers began to want higher audio fidelity. The same transistor technology that encouraged cheap radios also led to greater audio sophistication among manufacturers. Higher fidelity phonographic systems were available. Home tape recording was beginning to gain acceptance.

In the *FCC Annual Report*, for fiscal years 1961 and 1962, the Commission notes the problems with AM service, including band congestion and programming competition. Even the National Association of Broadcasters (NAB) recognized the hazards of uncontrolled AM growth. NAB President LeRoy Collins said the FCC had licensed more stations than advertising revenue would support.[76] This gloomy AM assessment, with the endorsement of the National Association of Broadcasters, led to a partial freeze, from 1962–1964, on the acceptance of applications for new AM stations and for major changes in existing facilities.

With the freeze on AM station construction, potential station owners shifted their attention to FM. Besides the obvious FM advantage—that channels were frequently available while new AM service was frozen—operators began to recognize other benefits not available from AM stations. FM service provided day and night service, with uniform power levels and coverage areas. The 200 kHz channel width of FM produced superior audio; in 1961, FM stereo service had been authorized. The higher spectrum of FM service produced less susceptibility to atmospheric noise or radio frequency interference.

By 1963, the number of commercial FM stations had finally topped 1,000, with 1,081 authorized commercial stations and another 209 noncommercial stations. In cities with populations over 100,000, the FCC in 1964 required that half the FM station's programming not duplicate a sister AM station's programming.[77] Nonduplication, along with stereo broadcasting and wider availability of quality FM receivers would give consumers new reasons to listen to FM.

FM stations in major cities began to counter program the AM stations. If the Top 40 AM formula suggested playing no song longer than three minutes, the FM approach was to play an album cut ten minutes long.[78] Rock music, growing from the "flower children" and "make love not war" anti-Vietnam movements, featuring performers such as Jefferson Airplane, the Grateful Dead, Jimmie Hendrix, and Buffalo Springfield, provided much of the content for FM station programming. The teens and preteens of 1950s Top 40 were now the 18–34 audience and the target of FM rock stations.

The music industry also encouraged the growth of FM radio. While the playlist of the Top 40 stations had been tightly controlled, with very limited opportunity for new songs or new groups to gain on-air exposure, many of the FM stations would play virtually anything. Record companies effectively used the stations to introduce new artists and styles of music to a generation willing to listen and to buy the records.

Underground FM stations, programming long sets of rock songs, were still the minority among FM stations, but they signaled the ability for FM to attract listeners by offering counterprogramming. FM listenership was also still dwarfed by AM's listener share, but FM stations were gaining listeners and the number of stations continued to grow. By 1971, there were 4,343 AM stations and 2,196 commercial FM stations and another 472 noncommercial FM stations. Nearly half of all radios sold included FM tuners. About three-fourths of all households had FM radio. Nearly 40 percent of FM stations were broadcasting in stereo.[79] About one third of all radio listening was to an FM station.

The underground rock formats of the 1960s gave way to progressive rock formats in the 1970s. In the South and Midwest, FM stations started programming stereo country. A few FMs marketed themselves to listeners as "fine music" stations and aired instrumental or beautiful music. FM resulted in more programming choices for listeners and made AM stations respond to new competition. National FM listener share passed AM in the fall of 1978; 50.698 percent of radio listening was to FM.[80]

For both AM and FM, the number of stations has continued to rise, particularly the number of FM stations. Mass Media Docket 80–90 in 1982 created hundreds of new FM drop-in allocations (leading to a surge in the number of FM stations) and it made power increases by existing FM stations possible. While AM stations in many major markets continue to attract listeners with unique programming—particularly news, talk, sports, or "full-service" programming—for most listeners it is no longer a question of whether to listen to AM or FM. FM has become the *de facto* standard for the majority of radio listeners.

Changes in station ownership policies have also benefited FM stations more than AM stations. Station owners, since radio's infancy, had been limited to owning no more than seven stations of any one service, AM, FM, or television. (Only five of the television stations could be VHF; the other two had to be in the UHF band.) In 1985, the FCC increased station ownership to twelve stations of any one service.

This number was increased again to eighteen in 1992 and twenty in 1994. Also eliminated in 1992 was the restriction against owning more than one station of each service in a market.[81] With passage of the Telecommunications Act of 1996, broadcasters may own up to eight commercial stations, in markets with forty-five or more commercial radio stations, not more than five of the same service, and they may own as many stations nationwide as they are able to purchase.[82] The higher power levels of the FM stations, combined with stereo signals, uniform coverage areas, and static-free signals, have made the FM stations much more desirable purchases. Both of these ownership measures have led many smaller station owner groups to sell their properties to larger corporate groups. These owners have built successful stations groups that dominate not only station listening but also radio ad sales in their markets.

The AM band has been described as "saturated" for three decades. Some attempts have been made to improve AM's appeal to listeners. AM stereo, after a lengthy competition among various manufacturers, was finally approved by the FCC in 1993.[83] Though most observers say the decision was too little and too late. The FCC, in previous proposals for AM improvement, succinctly identified the difficulties inherent in AM service:

Channel congestion and interference, both radio- and environmentally-induced, have dramatically increased on the AM band. Coincident with this growth has been a decline in the fidelity of AM receivers. As a consequence, during the last twenty years there has been a well-documented shift of AM listeners to newer mass media services that offer higher technical quality and better aural fidelity. This shift in listenership has clearly dulled the competitive edge of this once vital service.[84]

RADIO IN 2000 AND BEYOND

By 2000, approximately 85 percent of all radio listening was to an FM station, even though the number of AM stations totaled 4,783 versus 5,766 commercial FM stations and 2,066 noncommercial FM stations.[85] The question now may be whether AM radio and possibly FM are simply transitional delivery technologies. Already, broadcasters are investigating (and investing in) digital terrestrial broadcasting that could eventually replace the AM and FM stations we know of. At the same time, the FCC has approved creating micro FM stations (low-power stations) to offer additional local programming.

The companies Sirius Satellite Radio and XM Satellite Radio are marketing satellite-delivered national audio service that will give subscribers national radio service.[86] Command Audio is launching a subscription audio service using FM subcarriers in the top forty markets around the country to deliver what they call "personalized content."[87] Web Radio sites provide listeners not only with the chance to listen to local radio programming but to enjoy distant stations too far away to be received over the air or to listen to "radio stations" programming solely on the Internet. These "stations" don't require a license from the FCC and can be put on the air with minimal effort and expense.

These programming options also should lead the reader to reflect on the most compelling issue facing the earliest radio station operators: How do you pay for these new services? WGN General Manager Ward Quaal, commenting in 1962 about the competition facing AM pointed out something still obvious, "we have learned the hard way that in our business additional competition does not necessarily mean a better product for the consumer."[88] More stations have not necessarily meant better programming or improved service to the public. Some critics charge, and rightfully so, that many stations are adopting formats designed only to boost profits and cut costs. In the coming chapters, we will talk about broadcast station management and sales, how stations now use research to help determine station programming, and we will look further at some of the technological issues facing the industry and the public.

NOTES

[1]Tom Lewis, *Empire of the Air: The Men Who Made Radio* (New York: Harper Collins, 1991), p. 51.

[2]Ibid., p. 70.

[3]Erik Barnouw, *A Tower of Babel: A History of Broadcasting in the United States* (New York: Oxford University Press), 1966, p. 37.

[4]George Douglas, *The Early Days of Radio Broadcasting* (Jefferson, NC: McFarland & Company, 1987), p. 39.

[5]A. Frederick Collins, *The Book of Wireless* (New York: D. Appleton and Company, 1915), p. 22.

[6]Susan Smulyan, *Selling Radio: Commercialization of American Broadcasting 1920–1934* (Washington, DC: Smithsonian Institution Press, 1994), p. 20.

[7]G. Douglas, op. cit., p. 46.

[8]Sydney W. Head, Christopher H. Sterling, Lemuel B. Schofield, Thomas Spann, & Michael A. McGregor, *Broadcasting in America: A Survey of Electronic Media* (Boston: Houghton Mifflin, 1998), p. 31.

[9]Susan J. Douglas, *Inventing American Broadcasting, 1899–1922* (Baltimore, MD: Johns Hopkins University Press, 1987), p. 200.

[10]S. J. Douglas, op. cit., p. 219

[11]S. J. Douglas, op. cit., pp. 227, 228.

[12]Ibid., p. 230.

[13]Barnouw, op. cit., p. 32.

[14]Collins, op. cit., p. 196.

[15]S. J. Douglas, op. cit., p. 293.

[16]Lewis, op. cit., p. 73.

[17]S. J. Douglas, op. cit., p. 303.

[18]Smulyan, op. cit., p. 21.

[19]Herbert H. Howard, "Country Music Radio Part I: The Tale of Two Cities," *Journal of Radio Studies 1* (1992), 107.

[20]Ibid., p. 107.

[21]G. Douglas, op. cit., p. 34.

[22]Ibid., p. 34.

[23]L. F. Schmeckebier, *The Federal Radio Commission: Its History, Activities and Organization* [Service monographs of the United States No. 65]. (New York: AMS Press, 1932), p. 5.

[24]Barnouw, op. cit., pp. 178, 179.

[25]Frank J. Kahn, (ed.), *Documents of American Broadcasting*, 3rd ed. (Englewood Cliffs, NJ: Prentice-Hall, 1978), p. 114.

[26]Barnouw, op. cit., pp. 197, 198.

[27]M. S. Mander, "The Public Debate about Broadcasting in the Twenties: An Interpretive History," *Journal of Broadcasting 28* (1984), 167–185.

[28]Frank J. Kahn, (ed.), *Documents of American Broadcasting*, 4th ed. (Englewood Cliffs, NJ: Prentice-Hall, 1984), p. 40.

[29]Smulyan, op. cit., p. 63.

[30]Smulyan, op. cit., pp. 52, 54.

[31]G. Douglas, op. cit., p. 36, also Smulyan, op. cit., p. 1.

[32]White, op. cit., p. 30.

[33]Barnouw, op. cit., p. 177.

[34]Smulyan, op. cit., p. 55.

[35]Ibid., p. 61.

[36]Schmeckebier, op. cit., p. 31.

[37]Orestes H. Caldwell, "High power is parallel to rural free delivery," *New York Times,* September 16, 1928, pp. XII, 6.

[38]W. J. Dempsey, & W. C. Koplovitz, "Radio Economics and the Public Interest," *Annals of the American Academy of Political and Social Science 213* (1941), 97–101.

[39]J. W. Spalding, "1928: Radio Becomes a Mass Advertising Medium," *Journal of Broadcasting 8* (1968): 31–44.

[40]Barnouw, op. cit., p. 190.

[41]Smulyan, op. cit., p. 63.

[42]Sally B. Smith, *In All His Glory: The Life of William S. Paley* (New York: Simon and Schuster, 1990), p. 63.

[43]Melvin P. Ely, *The Adventures of Amos 'n' Andy: A Social History of an American Phenomenon* (New York: Macmillan, 1991), pp. 54, 57.

[44]Ely, op. cit., p. 1, 2.

[45]S. Smith, op. cit., p. 73

[46]Barnouw, op. cit., p. 227.

[47]S. Smith, op. cit., p. 73.

[48]Ibid., p. 86.

[49]Ibid., p. 133.

[50]Ibid., p. 86.

[51]Ibid., p. 133.

[52]White, op. cit., p. 38.

[53]"How Sweet It Was," *Broadcasting and Cable,* April 19, 1999, pp. 74–76.

[54]Herman S. Hettinger, (ed.), Foreword. *Annals of the American Academy of Political and Social Science 177* (1935), p. vii.

[55]Herman S. Hettinger, "Organizing Radio's Discoveries for Use," *Annals of the American Academy of Political and Social Science 213* (1941), 170–189.

[56]Erik Barnouw, *The Golden Web*, (New York: Oxford University Press, 1968) p. 7.

[57]Ibid., p. 20.

[58]Ibid., p. 20.

[59]Sterling & Kittross, op. cit., p. 206.

[60]Federal Communications Commission. (1947). *Standards of Good Engineering Practice Concerning Standard Broadcast Stations* (1939). Washington, DC: GPO, p. 4.

[61]FCC urges cooperation to stop interference, *New York Times*, March 17, 1940, pp. X, 10.

[62]Lewis, op. cit., p. 248.

[63]Barnouw, 1968, op. cit., p. 42.

[64]T. A. Craven, "Radio Frontiers," *Annals of the American Academy of Political and Social Science 213* (1941), 127.

[65]Barnouw, 1968, op. cit., p. 129.

[66]Barnouw, op. cit., p. 130.

[67]Sterling & Kittross, op. cit., p. 145.

[68]Llewellyn White, *The American Radio: A Report on the Broadcasting Industry in the United States from The Commission on Freedom of the Press* (Chicago: University of Chicago Press, 1947), p. 22.

[69]Barnouw, 1968, p. 288.

[70]David T. MacFarland, *The Development of the Top 40 Radio Format* (New York: Arno Press, 1979), p. 122.

[71]David T. MacFarland, *Contemporary Radio Programming Strategies* (Hillsdale, NJ: Lawrence Erlbaum, 1990), p. 58.

[72]"King of Giveaways," *Time*, June 4, 1954, p. 100.

[73]MacFarland, 1979, op. cit., p. 397 and 401.

[74]"The *Billboard* Ninth Annual Disk Jockey Poll," *Billboard*, November 10, 1956, p. 84.

[75]MacFarland, 1990, op. cit., p. 60.

[76]Frank Kahn, "Economic regulation of broadcasting as a utility," *Journal of Broadcasting 7* (1963): 105.

[77]Federal Communications Commission, *30th Annual Report* [fiscal year 1964]. Washington, DC: GPO, 1964.

[78]Edward J. Whetmore, *The Magic Medium: An Introduction to Radio in America* (Belmont, CA: Wadsworth, 1981), p. 61.

[79]Sterling and Kittross, op. cit., pp. 381 and 633.

[80]James H. Duncan, (ed.), (1987). *American Radio: Spring 1987* (Kalamazoo, MI: Duncan's American Radio), p. A3.

[81]Kenneth C. Creech, *Electronic Media Law and Regulation* (Boston: Focal Press, 1996), p. 94.

[82]Margaret L. Tobey & Phuong N. Pham, "The Broadcast Ownership Provisions of the Telecommunication Act of 1996," *Communications Lawyer* (Summer 1996), p. 6.

[83]"AM Stereo Broadcasting," available online at http://www.fcc.gov/mmb/asd/bickel/amstereo.html, accessed January 4, 2000.

[84]Federal Communications Commission. (1991). *FCC record* [Report and order: In the matter of review of the technical assignment criteria for the AM broadcast service] (22) (pp. 6273–6472). Washington, DC: GPO, p. 6275.

[85]"Broadcast Station Totals as of September 1999," available online at http://fcc.gov/mmb/asd/totals/index.html, accessed January 3, 2000.

[86]Each company offers a Website with the latest information about their service and programming options, available online at http://www.siriusradio.com and http://www.xmradio.com/have.asp.

[87]Glen Dickson, "Delivering Audio on Command," *Broadcasting and Cable,* May 24, 1999, p. 70.

[88]Quaal Urges New Communications Act, *Broadcasting*, May 7, 1962, p. 58.

3

Radio Regulation

DR. DAVID SEDMAN
Associate Professor of Electronic Media and Film
Southern Methodist University

Twentieth-century America has been unequivocally transformed by the invention of broadcasting. The United States government, from almost the inception of the earlier of the two inventions, radio, has attempted to provide legislation that would both promote and reign in the industry for the public good. Throughout most of the century, radio has constantly had to reinvent itself to remain profitable due to increased competition from alternate media forms. The key periods of maturation within the radio industry are inexorably tied to governmental regulation and deregulation of the industry. The three stages in radio's development may be characterized as: (1) the pioneer era, (2) the "golden age," and (3) the deregulatory period.

ORIGINS OF RADIO REGULATION:
THE PIONEER ERA

The origins of radio regulation can be traced back to two laws passed by Congress during the first part of the twentieth century, the Wireless Ship Act of 1910 and the Radio Act of 1912. Both laws dealt with the requiring of emergency radio telegraphic equipment on ships at sea. During this period, the technological explosion in wireless transmission had advanced radiotelephony to enable the transmitting of voice and music. Radio science was given a tremendous boost during World War I when the United States Navy called on radio's pioneer inventors and important corporations to pool their various patents for help in winning the War. By selecting the best of the workable designs available at the time, the Navy demonstrated the great potential of radio.

In 1920, the first officially licensed radio station began operation, but soon after a myriad of technical problems threatened to stunt the new medium's growth. Herbert Hoover recognized the problems faced by radio soon after President Warren Harding appointed him Secretary of Commerce in 1921. Because broadcast transmissions crossed interstate boundaries, jurisdiction fell under Hoover's office. Hoover wasted no time in arranging a conference to bring together the key players in the emerging radio industry. Following the first Radio Conference of 1922, it was decided that more governmental control over broadcasting was going to be necessary.

Hoover decided that limitations must be placed on the number of stations that would be allowed in a given city, the number of hours a day a station could operate, and the power level and frequency on which a station could operate. Though the broadcast industry recognized the need for some form of governmental regulation, there was not unanimous support for all of Hoover's restrictions. More importantly, the courts were not ruling that the Department of Commerce had the jurisdiction to control so many aspects of the industry.[1]

While Hoover still enjoyed support from many within the industry and from the public, his court losses and the technological quagmire surrounding the radio broadcasting industry were increasingly frustrating to him. This frustration caused him to ask the Department of Justice for a definitive opinion on the scope of the broadcast business and of his power to regulate it. In 1926, the acting Attorney General under Calvin Coolidge, William Donovan, concluded, "I can only suggest that it be sought in new legislation, carefully adapted to meet the needs of both the present and the future."[2] Coolidge concurred and pushed for the passage of legislation recommended by both Hoover and Donovan.[3]

The Radio Act of 1927 established a five-member body to oversee the radio industry. The newly developed Federal Radio Commission (FRC) was given authority over basic operational guidelines including the classification of radio stations, assigning frequencies to stations, and assigning times during which a station could operate.[4] This structural regulatory approach dealing with the basic technical issues and licensing parameters rectified the transmission problems and allowed the stage to be set for entry into radio's "golden age."

THE COMMUNICATIONS ACT AND RADIO'S GOLDEN AGE

By 1934, the public's acceptance of and appetite for radio led Secretary of Commerce Daniel Roper to suggest to President Franklin Roosevelt that a more centralized approach to communications regulation would be advantageous. Roper's suggestions were quickly acted on and resulted in the Communications Act of 1934.

Prior to the Communications Act, a number of federal agencies had some measure of jurisdiction over wireless and wired communication. This control group included the Postmaster General of the United States and the Interstate Commerce Commission, as well as the FRC. The 1934 legislation concentrated these controls in a single entity and placed all forms of communication under the auspices of the Federal Communications Commission (FCC). Much like the preamble to the United States Constitution, the first paragraph of the Communications Act makes a general statement as to the FCC's responsibilities:

> *For the purpose of regulating interstate and foreign commerce in communication by wire and radio so as to make available, so far as possible, to all the people of the United States a rapid, efficient, nationwide, and worldwide wire and radio communication service with adequate facilities at reasonable charges . . . for the purpose of securing a more effective execution of this policy by centralizing authority heretofore granted by law to several agencies and by granting additional authority with respect to interstate and foreign commerce in wire and radio communication, there is hereby created a commission to be known as the "Federal Communications Commission," which shall be constituted as hereinafter provided, and which shall execute and enforce the provisions of this Act.[5]*

Provisions of the act consisted of seven major divisions. Regulatory duties in the area of broadcasting were detailed in Title III. All sections of the Communications Act were to be carried out using the overriding principle of the "public interest, convenience, or necessity." This government supervision or trusteeship of the broadcasting industry is the key component to what is commonly referred to as the "public trusteeship model" of broadcast regulation.[6]

The government's limitation on entrants into the market and the public's insatiable demand for radio programming proved to be beneficial to the industry and the listening public. Radio transmissions were generally received without interference from other stations that placated the public while profit margins were favorable for radio station owners.

With the structural issues codified, the FCC turned to the behavioral aspects of broadcast regulation. Business aspects such as prohibiting unethical practices by advertisers regarding program content, including local programming and the discussion of controversial issues of public importance, were now under the control of the FCC.

The FCC made a number of rulings that seemed to border on infringement of the First and Fourth Amendments of the Bill of Rights. Control of program content and the restricted number of stations allowed to enter the field of broadcasting would normally be considered violations of free speech. The FCC maintained this power due to the definition of broadcasting as a "unique" industry. The rationale for government control and licensing of private stations was the concept of **scarcity.** Scarcity in broadcasting exists because of the limited amount of space on the broadcast spectrum. The finite number of stations that can be placed in a given area limits the number of entrants that can be allowed into the broadcast field.

For the next two decades, during its Golden Age, radio reigned supreme, flourishing within the confines of its FCC disciplines. As alternate media sources such as broadcast television, cable television, and Internet-delivered media have proliferated, radio has had to redefine its programming and business operation to survive. Of necessity, the radio industry has transformed itself from the preeminent mass media source of news and entertainment to a niche-audience provider of narrowly defined music formats and talk shows. As a result of these changes, regulations have been pared back and this, in turn, has benefited the industry.

DEREGULATORY PERIOD: ROUND ONE

The wisdom of politicians trying to establish fairness and morality in the broadcast industry rarely goes unchallenged. During the 1960s and 1970s, the FCC imposed a number of controversial regulations on the broadcast and cable industries. These regulations affected various phases of station and cable system operations. They included programming practices (e.g., television's Prime-Time Access Rule and Financial Interest and Syndication Rule), technical considerations (e.g., cable system's requirement to have two-way communication capability by a given deadline), and content (e.g., indecency standard prompted by a radio case). These and other regulations were revisited by the FCC and Congress because a number of the rules seemed either antiquated or ineffective. A deregulatory tack first advanced by FCC Chair Charles Ferris during the Carter administration was furthered by Chairmen Mark Fowler and Dennis Patrick in the Reagan years. Throughout the 1980s, the FCC torched the "regulatory underbrush" because it felt it lacked the resources and expertise to deal with the myriad of behavioral rules on the books.[7] This attitude is best exemplified in the repeal of the Fairness Doctrine in 1987.

The **Fairness Doctrine** required broadcasters to present issues of public importance on their stations. The "fairness" portion required that stations provide the opportunity for airing opposing points of view on matters relating to the public interest. The Doctrine was used as a rationale for nonrenewal of a station's license. Many stations avoided controversial material due to the requirements of the Doctrine, the opposite of what the regulation intended. In 1987 the Fairness Doctrine was repealed from the regulatory landscape. Viewed as a hindrance to the open discussion of contemporary issues, the FCC felt that the marketplace (i.e., the listening audience, station, and advertisers) would be better arbiters of the numbers and types of issues to be discussed on the radio airwaves. The repeal of this law could not have come at a better time for the AM radio industry.

AM broadcasters, who had lost their listeners of episodic entertainment to television during the 1950s, became a poor second to FM radio in the late 1970s and 1980s. Popular music formats gravitated to FM and the loss of their audience forced some AM stations into oblivion. The repeal of the Fairness Doctrine, combined with low cost satellite transmission and reception, ushered in a new wave of long-form talk shows well suited to AM's inferior sound capability. Nationally delivered talk shows such as G. Gordon Liddy, Tom Leykis, and Rush Limbaugh would deliver solid audiences with minimal programming costs to the station.

Further deregulatory measures aimed at reducing the FCC's load also lowered the costs of station operations. It was now possible for the stations to have unattended operation with the use of automated equipment without FCC notification. The use of automated testing equipment was also allowed. Stations were able to trim personnel costs by reducing on-air personalities and contracting out and/or sharing engineering staff. A contemporary radio station could be run with a handful of employees.

An FCC ownership rule modification allowed competing stations to broker programming time and combine personnel through **local marketing agreements** (LMAs). In 1992, the FCC also eased the duopoly rule that had long prevented an owner from holding more than one AM or one FM station in a given market.[8] Obviously, these deregulatory measures aided those stations that were looking to trim operating costs and streamline operations. These incremental changes were largely welcomed by the radio industry. The second wave of deregulation, however, would forever change the concept of radio station ownership.

DEREGULATORY PERIOD: ROUND TWO

Though the daily operations of radio stations were streamlined to some degree, radio suffered unprofitable years in the late 1980s and early 1990s. With LMAs and the relaxation of the duopoly rules as appetizers, the Telecommunications Act of 1996 proved to be the main course. The 1996 measure was the first major overhaul of communications law since the Communications Act of 1934. Given the major changes that had taken place in telecommunications over a sixty-year period, the radio industry was eager to embrace any positive regulatory change that would enhance its profitability. The radio industry's benefit came directly from a provision of the Telecommunications Act that discarded the long-standing notion of scarcity.

With audio services being delivered via direct broadcast satellite (DBS), the Internet, cable audio, and more than 12,000 radio stations in the United States by 1996, the notion of scarcity within the radio industry did seem antiquated. The long-term viability of radio hinged on the regulatory changes that would see it into the twenty-first century. The Telecom Act would repeal limits on the number of radio stations a single licensee could hold. Limitations on the number of stations an entity could own in a single market were relaxed significantly (see Table 3-1).[9] This por-

TABLE 3-1   Telecommunications Act of 1996 Limits

# of Commercial Stations in the Market	Limit of Ownership
45 or more	Up to 8 with no more than 5 in FM or AM
30 to 44	Up to 7 with no more than 4 in FM or AM
15 to 29	Up to 6 with no more than 4 in FM or AM
Fewer than 14	Up to 5 with no more than 3 in FM or AM but not more than 50% of stations in market

1999 Cross-Ownership Revision

# of Media Voices in the Market	Limit of Ownership
20 or more	2 TV stations and six radio stations, or 1 TV station and seven ration stations, or 8 radio stations (see above)
10 to 19	2 TV stations and four radio stations 1 TV station and five radio stations

Source: Federal Communications Commission.

tion of the Act along with an earlier FCC provision which removed the three-year holding rule (known as the trafficking rule) which forced an owner to operate a station for three years before it could be resold, led to radio station brokering. Radio station transactions abounded.

Group owners continued to buy more stations, and consolidation within the industry continued. In the first quarter of 1997, radio station transactions (not including mergers) amounted to more than $4 billion compared with less than $800 million in the same period during 1995 and $2 billion in 1996.[10] By comparison, the total radio transactions for all of 1991 amounted to less than $1 billion.[11] Meanwhile, publicly held multiple station owners saw their stocks increase an average of 400 percent between 1993 and 1998 and 110 percent during 1997 alone.[12] After the regulation went into effect, stations traded hands so quickly that some employees would ask facetiously, "Who's my owner today?"

In 1999, the FCC again revised its ownership rules by allowing common ownership of two television stations and six radio stations by a single company in one market. For decades, licensees were restricted from adding stations within a market by cross-ownership restrictions. To qualify for the maximum number of radio and television stations, the market must contain at least twenty independent media voices. These outlets include broadcast stations, daily newspapers with circulation exceeding 5 percent of the local market, and cable service (counted as one no matter how many cable companies are represented in the market).[13] In markets with ten to nineteen media outlets, groups can own up to four radio stations and two TV stations. The revised rule also allows a company to own as many as seven radio stations in a market where it owns one TV station, or up to eight radio stations in a single market. The FCC reasoned that the rapidly evolving media marketplace necessitated the latest rule modification.

CURRENT REGULATIONS

Obviously, the radio industry is not totally deregulated and is not likely to be in the near future. The regulations that remain still affect all phases of a station's operation, including daily operations, program content, advertising, and licensing.

During the two stages of deregulation, some areas remained virtually unaffected and others were totally removed. There are some segments that would appear to be about half-gone. To some observers, these aspects of radio regulation appear to be a rather disconnected lot of odds and ends that are of great significance to the industry. During a 1999 review of ownership rules, FCC Chair Bill Kennard admitted as much when he said, "Instead of a set of rules, we just had a blur of policies."[14]

An excellent example of the controversies that have taken place as a result of regulation reform can be found in the area of program content that deals with political candidates running for office. These focus on personal attacks, editorials, and equal opportunity.

Program Content Regulations

Personal Attacks, Editorials, and Equal Opportunity
When the Commission abandoned the Fairness Doctrine, the related personal attack and political editorializing rules remained on the books. The political editorial rule requires a station that endorses a candidate for office to inform opponents of the endorsement and offer the opportunity to respond to the station's position. The personal attack rule obligates a station to contact a person whose character, integrity, or honesty is attacked on its airwaves. In addition, the station must provide the person an opportunity for response.

Opponents of the two rules, such as the Radio and Television News Directors Association (RTNDA), suggest that the rules inhibit discussion of important political issues and are an abridgement of the First Amendment. During the summer of 1999, the U.S. Court of Appeals agreed and ordered the FCC to justify the retention of both rules.[15] The rules appear to be both antiquated and disjointed in radio's contemporary regulatory framework. While the court was not favorable to the FCC's initial arguments for retention, future litigation will almost surely see a relaxation of the restrictions.

Two related provisions that have a more solid footing are found in sections 312 and 315 of the Communications Act and deal with reasonable access and equal opportunities. The reasonable access portion of the Act requires stations to make their facilities available to all candidates for federal office. Further, it states that the station must permit the purchase of commercial time for legally qualified candidates for a federal office. While the reasonable access provision applies only to federal candidates, the equal opportunities provision applies to state and local candidates.

In the event that a radio station allows any legally qualified candidate for public office to utilize its facilities, all other legally qualified candidates for the same office may request an equal opportunity to appear on that station.[16] Stations, however, are not obligated to sell local or state candidates airtime or to allow them usage of their radio facilities. Once access is given or time sold to a candidate, a recognized political opponent must be given the same access and opportunity to buy the same amount of advertisement time at the same rate and at similar airtimes. There are four exemptions from equal opportunities claims. They include appearances on bona fide news programs and spot news coverage, documentaries, interviews, and debates. The equal opportunities provision provides stations with a variety of challenges during an election season. Regulations also affect the station's profit margin at election time through the lowest unit charge. This topic is found in the advertising selection later in this chapter.

Payola and Plugola

Payola and **plugola** violations have served as black marks throughout radio's history. Payola is the unreported payment of money or a valuable gift given to a station employee in exchange for playing some form of programming. Payola is most often associated with the rock and roll era of the 1950s when payment was given to disc jockeys for playing particular songs. Today, when payment is given for playing music, stations announce the source of the payment prior to the song. Failure to report such payment is a payola violation under the Communications Act and could lead to criminal prosecution.

Plugola is a related activity in which the station employee promotes some product, service, or other item in which he or she has a direct interest or relevant, though indirect, interest. If the employee fails to note this interest, the FCC could rule the message as a violation of the sponsorship identification requirement. Such a violation carries a fine and must be placed in the station's public file. Other forms of on-air speech can lead to difficulties for the station.

Unprotected Speech

All media are subject to criminal and civil laws of the land. Broadcasters and the print media can be held liable for defamatory statements. As can be seen in the discussion of candidate endorsements, however, broadcasters have modestly restricted First Amendment rights. Whereas a newspaper can freely endorse one political candidate over another, a radio station making the same endorsement would have to offer the opportunity to respond, as noted earlier. The sliding scale of protected speech is represented in offensive speech. One such example is obscene and indecent material.

Obscenity is not protected speech. The Supreme Court in *Miller vs. California* established a three-part test to determine whether a work—be it print, audio, visual, or any other format—will be considered obscene and, therefore, a violation of the U.S. Criminal Code. The Miller test requires that: (1) the average person, applying contemporary community standards, would find that the material appeals to the prurient interest; (2) the material describes or depicts sexual conduct in a patently offensive manner; and (3) taken as a whole, the material lacks serious literary, artistic, political, or scientific value. It would be a very unusual situation for a radio station to be found guilty of obscenity.

Music lyrics, comedy routines, and air personalities' comments that would fall well shy of meeting the Miller standard of obscenity have long been the target of criticism by some in the radio listening audience. The FCC responded to the public criticism and created an indecency standard following the Pacifica case (discussed below). The contemporary definition of **indecency** is any broadcast that "depicts or describes, in terms patently offensive as measured by contemporary community standards for the broadcast medium, sexual or excretory activities or organs" will be considered indecent.

The rationale behind the FCC's creation of this standard was the fact that broadcasts can be considered as uninvited guests. Unlike books or cable television subscriptions that require a buyer or subscriber purchase, broadcasts are pervasive. In the Pacifica case, an afternoon airing of a George Carlin comedy sketch was heard by a father driving with his son. Responding to the complaint, the FCC characterized the Carlin monologue as "'patently offensive,' though not necessarily obscene," and that it be regulated much like a nuisance law whereby the "law generally speaks to channeling behavior rather than actually prohibiting it."[17]

The Commission's indecency rule was designed primarily to protect children from such indecent broadcasts. Therefore, indecent material is allowed between 10:00 P.M. and 6:00 A.M. Shock jock Howard Stern and his employer, Infinity Broadcasting, were repeatedly fined during the 1990s for indecency violations that occurred during Stern's morning show (see Chapter 9).

Another regulation designed to protect the listener is the FCC's hoax rule. The effects of radio programs on audiences date back at least to the golden age. The most famous example was Orson Welles's 1938 broadcast of H. G. Wells's *War of the Worlds.* Some listeners believed that the Martian invasion dramatized in the program was actually taking place. However, it was not until 1992 that the FCC created a rule about broadcast hoaxes.

A spate of incidents involving air personalities at various stations led to the rule. The most prominent case was a St. Louis station's airing of an emergency alert and a bulletin that the country was under nuclear attack. Because the incident took place during the Gulf War, listeners failed to grasp the intended humor of the broadcast. In another incident, a station told listeners that a vacationing air personality had been kidnapped. Listeners actually tried to aid the investigation. Because the air personality had not been kidnapped, the station received a number of complaints.

The FCC's hoax rule involves the answering of three questions: (1) Is the information known to be false? (2) Will foreseeable public harm stem from the broadcast? and (3) What was the result of the broadcast and did it directly cause public harm?[18] One place where this type of speech is protected on the broadcast airwaves is in political advertisements.

ADVERTISING

Political Advertising

The area of political advertising is well covered by the Communications Act. Radio political spots are required to disclose the identity of the organization paying for the ad. The sponsorship identification provision is found in Section 317. Stations may screen the ad to ensure that the identification provision has been met. However, this is the only action that the station may take prior to airing the spot. If the spot contains defamatory statements, the station is not allowed to edit or shelve the spot. As such, it is also protected from lawsuits or fines that could have been successfully brought against the station.

Advertising rates are generally not subject to governmental regulation and scrutiny. One anomaly is the area of political advertising. Section 315(b) ensures that stations will not favor one candidate over another by offering markedly different advertising rates. In the forty-five days preceding a primary and sixty days preceding a general or special election, ad rates are subject to the **lowest unit charge** (LUC) provision. When within the LUC window, candidates pay no more than the lowest unit charge obtained by any other advertiser for the same class of time, spot length, and during the same time period or daypart.

If the station offers volume discounts for large purchases of commercial inventory, the candidate must be offered the same rate even if he or she only purchases a single spot. Further, bonus spots and make-goods are also factored into the LUC formula. The station is obligated to disclose all rates and incentives that are made available to other advertisers. The LUC formula must be recomputed on a week-by-week schedule. Because many radio stations offer volume discounts and incentives, the LUC can affect station profit levels.

Tobacco and Alcohol Advertising

Federal law prohibits the advertising of cigarettes, mini-cigars, and smokeless tobacco products in broadcasting. The Justice Department and the Federal Trade Commission (FTC) are responsible for enforcement of the tobacco advertising prohibition. There are no federal laws or FCC regulations with respect to alcoholic beverages. The content and acceptance of advertising are ultimately in the hands of the broadcast industry, the advertising agencies, and the alcohol and tobacco companies. State laws may also affect liquor advertising. Self-regulation from broadcasters and industry trade groups has limited the appearance of hard liquor ads on radio. The alcoholic beverage industry trade group has created guidelines for the depiction of products in ads. Because this area of advertising is particularly controversial to the public and Capitol Hill, the industries are very cautious in their advertising practices. They do not want to risk governmental intervention and a possible banishment of their ads from the airwaves.

A federal law banning radio and television ads for casino advertising was struck down by a unanimous Supreme Court decision in 1999. The ruling permits the carriage of casino ads only in states that permit gambling.[19] Despite the First Amendment right to carry ads for certain types of tobacco, gambling, and alcohol, the industry does exercise varying degrees of caution when advertising these controversial products and places. Even with mundane products and services, however, the content of advertisements is always a concern due to listener criticism and advertising regulations established by the FTC.

False or Deceptive Advertising

In the 1980s, the FCC removed a number of regulations dealing with business practices. The Commission has no rules prohibiting false or deceptive advertising. However, the Federal Trade Commission does have jurisdiction over unfair and deceptive advertising.[20] The radio industry needs to practice care to ensure that commercials do not contain the elements found in previous cases of deceptive and unfair advertising practices.

The FTC is fairly clear about its standards. An ad is found to be deceptive if it contains statements or omits information that is likely to mislead consumers acting reasonably and that the information is material to the consumer's decision to take a particular course of action.[21] The FTC considers a commercial unfair if it causes or is likely to cause substantial consumer injury that the consumer could not reasonably avoid, provided that the harm is not outweighed by the benefit to the majority of consumers.[22] The screening of radio commercials is an important part of a station's regular operation.[23]

DAILY OPERATIONS

As from its outset, radio regulations continue to have a direct bearing on the daily operation of a station. These rules range from the most finite, technical aspects of the station to the hiring practices of the station to the messages heard on the station's airwaves. One of the most familiar requirements is that of the station identification.

Station IDs

All radio stations must broadcast an identification message at the beginning and ending of each operating day, as well as an hourly identification near or at the top of each hour within a natural break in programming. The message must contain the station's call letters followed by the community of license. A **legal identification ID** may also include the station's frequency, the licensee's name, and the operating wattage. Following the legal information, a station is allowed to include positioning statements or any other information it deems appropriate.

Required Communications and Engineering Concerns

The **Emergency Alert System (EAS)** was created as a means of providing emergency communications to the listening public concerning local, state, and national emergencies. The EAS superseded the **Emergency Broadcast System (EBS)** in 1997.[24] All stations must have functional EAS equipment that is certified by the FCC and must be operational, either manually or automatically, at all times of the broadcast day. (The FCC will consider waivers from translator or satellite stations that merely rebroadcast the signal of another station.) All EAS stations are considered as Participating Notification outlets (PN) and, during a national level Emergency Activation Notification (EAN), must remain on the air. Stations must monitor and may activate the EAS at the local or state level at their discretion.

EAS and the former EBS tests are familiar to both broadcasters and audience members. A weekly test is conducted at random days and times. The Emergency Communications Committee of each state coordinates an additional monthly test. All stations are required to carry these tests. On the weeks of a monthly test, carriage of the weekly EAS test becomes optional. Stations are required to log all EAS tests either by manual or automated means. A station with EAS equipment found to be defective must repair the system within sixty days or, in some circumstances, request an extension from the FCC.

Communication of another type is needed at the transmitter site. The FCC requires all radio towers to be painted and lighted per the station's authorization or as required by the Federal Aviation Administration. The lighting on tower structures should be observed at least once during twenty-four-hour intervals by observation or by automated means. The automated monitor device itself must be inspected every three months. The owner of the tower is required to contact the nearest FAA Flight Service Station to report malfunctioning lighting instruments that could pose safety threats to pilots. All information and action taken must be placed in the station's records. This became a particularly sensitive issue late in 1998 when the FCC issued two warnings to all stations following two lighting malfunctions involving emergency medical helicopter crashes.[25] Violation of tower lighting has now become one of the largest fines in terms of the base amount of forfeiture as established by the FCC.[26] Table 3-2 presents a list of selected base amounts for FCC forfeitures.

In addition to tower checks, the FCC requires stations to conduct inspections of their transmitter systems, as the operator deems appropriate. Performance measurements are also required and must be kept on file at the transmission site for a period of two years. These measurements must be signed and dated by a qualified person making the measurements.[27] With respect to station performance, the FCC's field

TABLE 3-2   Selected Base Amounts for FCC Forfeitures

Violation	Fine[1]
Failure to comply with prescribed lighting/marking	$8,000
Transmission of indecent materials	5,000
Violation of public file rules	5,000
Unauthorized discontinuance of service	2,000
Use of unauthorized equipment	2,000
Failure to file required forms or information	2,000
Failure to make required measurements	1,000
Failure to provide station identification	500
Unauthorized pro forma transfer of control	500
Failure to maintain required records	500
Miscellaneous violations	250

Source: Federal Communications Commission

[1]Fee amounts are subject to change. Refer to FCC's Internet site for current fees at http://www.fcc.gov

office inspectors arrive without notice to inspect the station. Any violation of engineering standards could result in a warning letter or the issuance of a violation notice that generally carries a fine.

Hiring Practices

Another station operation that carries a fine when not followed in accordance with FCC rules is that of hiring practices. The FCC's Equal Employment Opportunities (EEO) section was designed to ensure that stations would be forbidden in hiring to discriminate against any person because of race, religion, color, national origin, or sex.[28] Further, stations have had to adopt an affirmative action program targeted to minorities and women.[29] Stations that failed to implement an acceptable EEO program have faced sanctions including fines, short-term license renewal, and the possibility of license nonrenewal. A case involving KFUO-AM and –FM radio in Clayton, Missouri forced the FCC to alter its EEO requirements.

Both KFUO-AM, a noncommercial religious station, and KFUO-FM, a commercial classical station with a religious orientation, are situated on the Concordia Seminary campus. Its hiring practices favored campus residents because the station believed that the station positions required knowledge of the Lutheran doctrine familiar to the campus community. The FCC claimed that the station violated EEO regulations by making insufficient efforts to recruit minorities and found it unnecessary for receptionists, engineers, and business managers to have knowledge of Lutheran doctrine. The court supported the church's claim that the Commission had violated both its religious freedoms and the equal protection component of the Fifth Amendment.[30] As a result, the FCC revised the EEO provisions.

The FCC's new EEO requirements no longer compare a station's employment profile to the composition of the local workforce. The scaled-back rules require outreach efforts designed to ensure that minority and female applicants are informed of, and have an opportunity to apply for, position openings.[31] In light of the FCC's revised rules, the Commission waived at least nineteen fines against radio stations.[32] The FCC will allow radio stations to design their own outreach programs. The self-assessment may be a consideration of the license renewal process.

LICENSING AND LICENSE RENEWAL

An initial license for a broadcast station will be granted only if the licensee meets basic criteria. The licensee must be a citizen of the United States, be of good character, and have the technical and financial capabilities to institute and operate the station. In addition, the applicant must obtain, file, and pay for a construction permit. (See Table 3-3 for a list of various applications and fees.) New stations are also the only facilities that carry a minimum operating requirement period for holding a license. Unlike existing stations, which can be bought and sold at will with FCC approval, a newly constructed station must be operated by its original owner for at least one year.

The Telecommunications Act of 1996 extended the license period for a radio station from seven to eight years.[33] The station pays an annual fee to the government for operating the station. Congress required the FCC to collect fees to recover the costs of their enforcement, policy and rule-making, international and user information activities. The fees paid are based on the classification of license(s) held by the licensee (see Tables 3-3 and 3-4).

Four months before the license expires, the licensee files an application for renewal. Renewal is based on three general criteria: (1) that the broadcaster is able to serve the public interest, convenience, and necessity, (2) that the broadcaster has had no serious violation of FCC regulations, and (3) the broadcaster has had no violations that would constitute a pattern of abuse.[34]

The station maintains a public inspection file at its main studio. The file should provide the documentation needed at license renewal time. The public file contains required information such as a listing of programs aired on the station that dealt with issues of relevance to the local community. Public correspondence, time brokerage agreements involving another station in the same market, as well as the station's application, license, and construction permit must be kept in the file. Also to be included are the most current two years of the station's time allotment to political candidates, its coverage area or contour maps, and any documentation involving FCC actions or investigations. The file can be maintained in paper form, on a computer database, or a combination of both. Commercial and noncommercial public file requirements vary slightly. Although the renewal process is never guaranteed, it is extremely rare that a radio station fails to earn license renewal.

TABLE 3-3   Fee Table for Commercial AM and FM Stations

Type of Application	Fee[1]
New or Major Change Construction Permit (CP)	
AM	$2,885
FM	2,600
Minor change, AM or FM	$ 725
New License	
AM	$ 475
FM	150
Transfer of Control	
Long form, AM or FM	$ 725
Short form, AM or FM	105
License Assignment per Station	
Long form, AM or FM	$ 725
Short form, AM or FM	105
Hearing (New and major/minor change comparative CP hearing), AM or FM	$8,640
Call sign application, AM or FM	$ 75
Replacement of CP or extension of time to construction, AM or FM	$ 260
Ownership Report, AM or FM	$ 45
Main Studio Request, AM or FM	$ 725
Directional Antenna Application	
AM	$ 545
FM	$ 455

Source: Federal Communications Commission

[1]Fee amounts are subject to change. Refer to FCC's Internet site for current fees at http://www.fcc.gov

FUTURE OF RADIO REGULATIONS

There has been a consistent pattern to give more latitude to the radio industry in the areas of business practices, ownership, and free speech issues. This trend will continue as the FCC clears out the remnants of "underbrush" regulations passed over during the deregulatory stages of the 1980s and 1990s. The FCC will spend more of

TABLE 3-4   1999 FCC Fee Schedule by Market Size

Station Classification	>20,001	20,001–50K	50,001–125K	125,001–400K	400,001–1 Million	<1 Million
AM Class A	$430	$825	$1,350	$2,000	$2,750	$4,400
AM Class B	325	650	850	1,400	2,250	3,600
AM Class C	225	325	450	625	1,250	1,750
AM Class D	275	450	675	825	1,500	2,250
FM Classes A, B1, C3	325	650	875	1,400	2,250	3,600
FM Classes B, C, C1, C2	430	825	1,350	2,000	2,750	4,400

Source: Federal Communications Commission

its effort on ushering radio into the digital transmission era and will continue to study new uses for radio as prescribed by Section 303 of the Communications Act.[35] Signs of this are evident heading into the twenty-first century.

In 1999, the FCC proposed three new classes of low-power or "microradio" FM stations. The categories include: (1) a 1–10 watt station with a service radius of two miles or less, (2) a 100-watt station with a radius of under four miles, and (3) a 1,000-watt station with a service radius of nine miles or less. The Commission's goal was to encourage a new breed of licensees. To discourage group station owners, the Notice of Proposed Rulemaking (NPRM) suggested that full-power broadcasters should be prohibited from owning, creating an LMA, or brokering any of the low-power FM stations. The proposal also sought to prohibit the use of a station as a translator service that would merely rebroadcast the programming of a traditional FM station. In addition, it proposed a limit of one low-power FM station per licensee in a given community and a national limit of ten or fewer stations.

The most eagerly anticipated FCC action is radio's gravitation from the analog to the digital domain. The FCC continues to watch the progress of an in-band, on-channel (IBOC) terrestrial radio transmission system to supplant the present analog system. A separate satellite-delivered digital radio service is also under consideration and would provide even more options in the radio landscape. The public would benefit from superior digital service and alternative modes of delivery. The transition to digital service could also make the FCC inspection process more efficient through virtual inspections. The questions that remain will be the influence of group owners on the public interest and whether radio's influence will be altered as it makes use of new technology.

By freeing radio of restrictive regulations, radio is in a unique position to retain its primary audience and take further advantage of lucrative synergistic partnerships with traditional and new media companies. The FCC will balance the remaining behavioral regulations with the evolving structural nature of the medium in its supervision of the radio industry's future.

NOTES

[1]In 1923, a federal appeals court ruled that the Secretary of Commerce did not have the authority to refuse radio licenses to qualified individuals or to select the frequency on which a station would operate. Hoover v. Intercity Radio Co., Inc. 286 F. 1003 [D.C. Cir., 1923]. And in 1926, a federal district court ruled that the Radio Act of 1912 did not allow the Secretary of Commerce to require a licensee to broadcast at specific times or to broadcast on a designated channel. United States v. Zenith Radio Corporation, et al., 15 F.2d 614 [N.D. Ill., 1926].
[2]35 Ops. Att'y Gen 126 [July 1926].
[3]By February of 1927, both Houses approved of the Radio Act of 1927, and that same month Coolidge signed the Radio Act into law. See generally, Stephen Davis, *The Law of Radio Communication* (New York: McGraw-Hill, 1927).
[4]Public Law 632, "The Radio Act of 1927," 69th Congress [February 23, 1927].
[5]Communications Act of 1934.
[6]Mark S. Fowler and Daniel L. Brenner, "A Marketplace Approach to Broadcast Regulation," *Texas Law Review 60* (1982): 217.
[7]William B. Ray, *FCC: The Ups and Downs of Radio–TV Regulation* (Ames, IA: Iowa State University Press, 1990), p. 169.
[8]Federal Communications Commission, "Revision of Radio Rules and Policy," 1992.
[9]Public Law 104, "Telecommunications Act of 1996," 110 Stat. 56 [February 8, 1996].
[10]"Changing Hands," *Broadcasting,* March 30, 1998, p. 46.
[11]Vincent M. Ditingo. *The Remaking of Radio*)Boston: Focal Press, 1995).
[12]Elizabeth Rathburn, "Wall Street Tuned to Radio," *Broadcasting & Cable*, June 3, 1996, p. 58.
[13]Federal Communications Commission, "FCC Revises Local Television Ownership Rules," Report No. MM 99-8 MM Docket No. 91-221 and 87-8 [August 5, 1999].
[14]Christopher Stern. "FCC Ending Duopoly Ban: Votes Big Changes to Ownership Rules," *Daily Variety* August 6, 1999, p. 1.
[15]Radio-Television News Directors Association v. FCC, 98-1305, D.C. Cir. (August 3, 1999).
[16]Candidates have seven days from the time of their opponents' usage and/or appearance to request equal time. To be considered legally qualified, candidates must have publicly declared their candidacy. Further they must be legally qualified to hold the office for which they are running. Finally, they must qualify for a place on the ballot or publicly seek election by write-in votes.
[17]FCC v. Pacifica Foundation, 438 U.S. 726 (1978).
[18]See Broadcast Hoaxes, 47 CFR 73.127.
[19]Greater New Orleans Broadcasting Association v. U.S., No. 98-387, S. Ct. (June 14, 1999).
[20]Because the FTC is an administrative agency that regulates interstate commerce, if the product, service, or advertising medium is wholly considered intrastate (i.e., unaffected by interstate commerce), the advertisement would not be under the domain of the FTC.
[21]Federal Trade Commission, "FTC Policy Statement on Deception." Letter to the Honorable John D. Dingell, Chair of the Committee on Energy and Commerce [October 14, 1983].
[22]Federal Trade Commission. "FTC Policy Statement on Unfairness." Letter to the Honorable Wendell H. Ford Chairman, Consumer Subcommittee [December 17, 1980].

[23]For further information see, Federal Trade Commission, "Screening Advertisements: A Guide for the Media." [September 1998].

[24]In the Matter of Amendment of Part 73, Subpart G, of the Commission's Rules Regarding the Emergency Broadcast System, FO Docket 91-171 [June 4, 1997].

[25]FCC and FAA members also reminded tower owners that registration of towers that are 200 feet tall and higher or that are within 20,000 feet (approximately 3.8 miles) of a public use airport is required. See Federal Communications Commission. "FCC Hosts Forum on Tower Lighting and Year 2000 Issues, Urges Compliance with Tower Registration Rules" (Press release, December 14, 1998).

[26]Other infractions can result in markedly higher fines, generally many multiples higher than the FCC's base amount. These large fines, such as for the transmission of indecent material, are usually the result of repeated violations, the nature of the violation, and/or the degree of recklessness on the part of the licensee.

[27]The FCC used to require "licensed operators" to observe and adjust the transmission instruments of an attended station. The Commission now allows stations to determine the qualification of their operators. See Harold Hallikainen, "Chronicles of Transmitter Control," *Radio World*, June 23, 1999.

[28]47 C.F.R. 73.2080(a) (1997).

[29]47 C.F.R. s 73.2080(b) & (c) (1997).

[30]Lutheran Church–Missouri Synod v. FCC, No. 97-1116, D.C. Cir. (April 14, 1998).

[31]Federal Communications Commission, "Revision of Broadcast and Cable EEO Rules and Policies," MM Docket No. 98-204 (December 1, 1998).

[32]Jeremy Shweder, "FCC Waives Fines against 19 EEO Violators," *Radio and Records,* July 30, 1999, p. 4.

[33]110 Stat. 56 at 112 [February 8, 1996].

[34]110 Stat. 56 at 112-113 [February 8, 1996].

[35]Under the Powers and Duties of Commission, the FCC shall "regulate the kind of apparatus to be used with respect to its external effects and the purity and sharpness of the emissions from each station and from the apparatus therein" and "study new uses for radio, provide for experimental uses of frequencies, and generally encourage the larger and more effective use of radio in the public interest. . . ." Sections 303 E and G, Communications Act of 1934.

4

The Radio Industry
Management and Economics

This chapter centers on the role management and economics play in the radio industry. Radio management and economics are interdependently linked in radio; both areas influence and impact one another. The value of a radio station is directly related to management's ability to manage the operation's **cash flow** (the inflow and outflow of revenues and expenses for a specific time period). In turn, cash flow is but one variable used to monitor a station's economic performance.

To increase performance and efficiency, management must understand the economics of radio in terms of a single station operation, a cluster of owned and operated stations, and the broader industry level. At the same time, managers must understand how to motivate and lead employees toward completion of organizational goals and objectives.

The first part of this chapter examines the role of management in the contemporary radio industry. The remainder examines radio industry/station economics. Throughout the chapter, key concepts are introduced in order to understand the complexities associated with the changing world of radio management and economics.

RADIO MANAGEMENT: A BRIEF OVERVIEW

Radio has a rich and colorful history, as discussed in Chapter 2. As a result, radio station management has been in a continual state of evolution. Historically, each radio station had its own unique management team, which at a minimum usually consisted of a general manager (often the owner in a small market), a sales manager, and a program director. As radio stations grew in size and complexity, departments were expanded and the range of managerial responsibilities increased and was shared with other management-related positions.

Radio ownership and management underwent massive changes with the passage of the 1996 Telecommunications Act. As detailed in Chapter 3, the 1996 Act eliminated previous national caps on ownership limits. Prior to the new legislation, individuals and corporations had been limited to the number of radio stations they could own nationally.[1] Originally, ownership limits followed the "rule of sevens," meaning an owner was limited to a total of seven AM and seven FM stations. Further, the old rules limited ownership in an individual market. Previously, owners could own only one type of station in each class (AM/FM).[2]

Over the years, as the industry evolved, the ownership rules were modified several times to reflect changes in the marketplace. Owners were given the opportunity to acquire more stations, but always capped by a national limit.

But the limitations on station ownership still negatively affected the radio industry for its owners. By the early 1990s, many radio stations were losing money due to a national recession that dramatically impacted local economies, the primary source of radio station revenues. Part of the problem lay in the FCC's controversial 80–90 docket, which allowed a number of new additional radio stations to begin operation in the 1980s. The 80–90 decision created a glut of radio stations, further increasing competition in many markets. When local markets suffer a downturn in the business cycle, many small businesses cut back on local advertising. Radio stations began losing money in all types of markets: large, medium, and small. In 1991, three out of every four stations suffered a loss for the year.

Responding to radio's financial crisis, in 1992 the FCC eased the restrictions on the original **duopoly** rule that limited ownership to one type of station in each class in a given market. In large markets (defined as markets with forty-five or more stations) owners could own up to four radio stations. In markets with less than fifteen stations, an owner was limited to a total of three stations.

The revision of the duopoly rules enabled radio groups to begin clustering their operations on a very small scale. By adding additional stations in a market, owners could now consolidate management responsibilities and other areas where duties overlapped. For example, one general manager could be responsible for the station cluster, as would a single engineer and a central office staff. The ability to combine operations led to some job losses, but also allowed stations to reduce overhead expenses and improve their revenue picture, enabling the industry to engage in what economists call **economies of scale.**[3] Basically, radio operators realized they could minimize the fixed costs of operating a series of stations, while at the same time increasing profit margins.

Radio owners continued to be frustrated with the ownership limitations, despite the modifications in the original duopoly rule. Radio's related industries, television and cable, were also clamoring for major reforms and relaxation of many governmental policies. It was this environment, coupled with a strong national economy and increasing technological convergence among the computer, broadcast, and tele-communications industries that led to the passage of the 1996 Act.[4]

While Congress removed national ownership limits, local market limits were enacted using a tiered system. In the largest radio markets, if there were at least forty-five stations, an owner was now limited to a total of eight stations, with no more than five in a single class. In a market with thirty to forty-four stations, owner-ship was capped at seven with a maximum of four in each class. Markets with fifteen to twenty-nine stations limited ownership to six stations (four in a single class); while markets with less than fifteen stations limited ownership to five stations with three in a single class.[5]

With national ownership caps removed, a number of owners began rapid acqui-sition of stations and smaller groups. In a span of two years following the passage of the 1996 Act, the top seventy-five radio companies were consolidated into four giant radio companies: Chancellor, Infinity, Clear Channel, and Jacor.[6] By mid-1999, the number was reduced to three major players. Chancellor (renamed AMFM, Inc. in 1999), the largest, acquired several groups including Evergreen and Capstar. Infin-ity was acquired by CBS. Clear Channel acquired Jacor. In October 1999, Clear Channel announced it was acquiring AMFM, creating a massive radio conglomer-ate. The top ten radio groups are listed in Table 4-1.

The impact of this consolidation affected management more than any other level in a radio station's operation. Instead of being responsible for a maximum of four stations, many managers found themselves managing clusters of stations, espe-cially in large- and medium-size markets where merger and acquisition activity were particularly high.

TABLE 4-1   Top 10 Radio Group Owners (as of September 1, 1999)[1]

Owner by Rank	Stations Owned
Clear Channel Communications	830[2]
Infinity (CBS)	163
ABC Radio	43
Entercom Communications	85
Cox Radio	58
Hispanic Broadcasting	42
Cumulus Media	248
Citadel Communications	118
Susquehanna Radio	29
Emmis Communications	18

Source: Adapted from Special Report: Radio, *Broadcasting & Cable*, August 30, 1999, pp. 26–32, and other trade publications.

[1]Station acquisitions affect the data in this Table on a monthly basis. Consult trade publications such as *Broadcasting & Cable* to locate ownership updates.

[2]The number of stations Clear Channel is expected to own following its approved merger of AMFM Inc.

Taking on the management of additional stations (often with different formats) meant spending more time and effort on effectively managing the resources and personnel within each station operation. The term **multitasking** became commonplace in management vocabulary. The term presented an entirely new dimension for many radio managers, who found the increasing workload and stress levels to be higher than anticipated.[7]

MANAGEMENT RESPONSIBILITIES

Managers of radio stations engage in similar responsibilities, whether they manage a cluster of up to eight stations in a given market or a stand-alone station. These responsibilities are best described by breaking down responsibilities into the different levels of management, the skills required of radio managers, and the roles radio managers play.[8]

Levels of Management

One common misconception regarding management is that there is one person who leads an organization. This is rarely true, especially in the radio industry. Management is often described as operating across three distinct levels. The **General Manager** (GM) represents the executive level of management. This person is vested with the control of the station, and is accountable to the ownership for its successes and failures. Middle managers are delegated responsibility for a specific unit, and usually have decision-making authority for the personnel and budget with the approval of the GM. In a typical station, the **Station Manager,** the **General Sales Manager,** and **Office Manager** would be considered middle management representatives. Supervisors oversee other employees and monitor their performance. Supervisory or lower level managers might include the Local Sales Manager, Program Director, and Promotions Director. It is important to recognize that management is not accomplished through one person, but with a group of people working together to achieve organizational goals and objectives.

Radio Management Skills

Management theorists often identify three areas where different skill sets are utilized: technical skills, interpersonal or people skills, and conceptual/problem-solving skills. In reality, these skill sets are interrelated and sometimes overlap. Technical skills are needed in radio management to understand basic differences between AM and FM broadcasting, analog and digital transmission, engineering standards, and computer applications. Interpersonal skills are critical in radio management. Managers must be able to understand, relate, and communicate with employees, provide motivation, and build a sense of working toward achieving organizational goals. Conceptual skills are used in a number of different ways.

Radio is heavily dependent on its external environment, or relationship to the community in which it operates. Management must understand the complexity of both the internal (station) and external environments, and be able to respond quickly to changes and adapt as necessary.

Two other skill sets are also needed in today's competitive radio industry, financial skills and marketing skills. Financial skills require an understanding of the financial statements used to evaluate economic performance. Typically, these statements include the income or profit/loss statement, the balance sheet, and the statement of cash flows. But, in addition to knowing how to read and interpret financial data, managers need to have strong budgeting skills, meet revenue projections, and manage a station's cash flow.

Marketing skills involve utilizing any and all available methods to effectively market and sell the radio station to target advertisers and audiences. In today's strategic radio environment, marketing involves using other media (e.g., television, newspapers, Internet) to broaden and expand the station's promotional reach. In managing clusters of stations, marketing becomes even more challenging. One key issue is being able to effectively market each individual station, usually toward a different demographic group with a different format, while at the same time marketing the entire group of stations to prospective advertisers. Generating new business in terms of retail and local sales is a critical part of local marketing efforts.

As seen in this limited discussion, a number of skill sets are needed to be an effective radio manager. These skill sets do not function in isolation; they overlap and intertwine with one another. There is debate within the industry as to the best way to acquire these skills, whether by sheer experience or a combination of education and experience. Further, few individuals will have an equal balance of these skills, meaning some managers may be more oriented toward conceptual and marketing skills as opposed to technical and financial skills. Finding competent, experienced managers who have command of these skill sets remains a long-term challenge for the radio industry.

Radio Managerial Roles

Radio managers, like many people in management, find themselves in a variety of different roles depending on whom they interact with in various situations. Much of the management literature presents mixed findings on the different types of roles needed in management. In terms of radio management, managers tend to exhibit three types of roles: leadership, representative, and liaison. Leadership is a given for any manager, and better managers are often perceived by their employees as being strong leaders. Leadership involves a number of traits, including adapting to change, ability to make decisions, good communication skills, and character.

Radio managers serve in representative roles, involving the local, state, and national level. The General Manager or Station Manager typically represents the station to the community in which it is licensed. This may involve speaking engagements and other civic responsibilities. The GM also represents the station to various trade organizations at the state and national levels, and, where appropriate, labor unions. Middle managers, like Sales Managers (and their respective staffs), interact on a daily basis with their client base of advertisers. Being a public licensee, radio stations recognize their community responsibilities, and many employees aside from management assist in this representative role.

Finally, the liaison role refers to the relationship between the station and its parent owner. As more and more stations have become part of larger group operations, managers of single stations or station clusters must represent their respective station(s) to the parent company. In this sense, management serves as a conduit between the parent company and the individual station. Managers in the liaison role facilitate the flow of information between the owner and the local station, and communicate company-wide objectives and strategies.

ISSUES IN RADIO MANAGEMENT

Having discussed radio management in general terms in regard to managerial levels, skills, and functions, we now turn to a review of some of the key management issues facing today's radio manager. While management takes place at different levels, the focus in this section centers on the issues requiring the decision making of the General Manager. Further, these issues are applicable to managers in all types of markets, from small markets to urban top ten markets.

Maximizing Cash Flow

Radio is first and foremost a business, and while all stations are expected to operate to serve the public interest, ownership expects profitability. Meeting revenue goals and projections has always been critical in evaluating management success, but in today's competitive environment the ability to effectively manage and maximize cash flow is critical.

Historically, the radio industry has produced stable profits for its owners except in times of recession. Following the last major recession in the early 1990s, the radio industry bounced back to generate double-digit profit margins, with some station groups earning as much as 50 percent on the dollar.

This is not meant to suggest that owning a radio station automatically results in heavy profits. There is considerable competition for advertising dollars at the local level, from newspapers and television to Internet and alternative forms of advertising. The ability of the GM to effectively manage cash flow, meet revenue projections, and handle contingencies in a quickly changing world is extremely demanding.

Personnel Issues

Radio is a people business, and ultimately the success of any organization depends primarily on the people it employs. Managers need to be involved in all aspects of employee selection, training, and evaluation. Further, management must keep abreast of labor laws, union requirements (where applicable), and the needs of the employees.

Today's radio staffs tend to be more multicultural, better educated, and have a higher degree of mobility (less likely to remain in a position for an extended length of time). Consolidation has forced many personnel changes, with some job areas actually declining over the years (e.g., engineering, office staff), and other areas expanding (e.g., sales and marketing, Webmasters). Maintaining a productive and contributing workforce continues to be a key issue for radio managers.

Management must also control personnel costs. In any organization, personnel usually represent the greatest expense of doing business. Radio salaries vary across positions in a radio station, and across market size. Examples of average salaries in the radio industry are presented in Table 4-2.[9]

The Challenge of Competition

Radio faces more competition today for audiences than at any time in its history. There are now over 12,000 radio stations in operation in the United States. There are hundreds of Internet-only radio stations available on the Web, with thousands of on-

TABLE 4-2   Examples of Radio Station Salaries (1999)

Job Title	Average Total Compensation*
General Manager	$189,726
General Sales Manager	132,708
Local Sales Manager	108,761
Morning Drive Talent	114,277
Program Director	89,494
Music Director	46,695
News Director	43,838
Promotion Director	42,615
Account Executive	50,884
Receptionist	19,765

Source: Adapted from *1999 Radio Station Salaries*. Washington, DC: National Association of Broadcasters.

*Salary figures are based on total compensation (including bonuses and incentives) for all stations, nationwide. It should be noted that salaries vary considerably based on size of market, station revenues, region, and format. The authors are grateful to Mark Fratrick, Vice President/Economist with the National Association of Broadcasters, for providing the data.

air stations from around the world accessible to listeners via shortwave and the Internet. **Digital Audio Radio Services (DARS)** and other types of digital subscription services have announced various stages of deployment.

In 1999, the FCC shocked the radio industry with an announcement that the Commission would consider establishing hundreds of lower-powered **microradio** stations (e.g., limited to 10, 100, or 1000 watts). The industry, led by the National Association of Broadcasters, reacted very negatively toward the proposal. If microradio stations become reality, competition would take on an entirely new dimension. These new stations would compete for the same audiences now served by the radio industry. It is unclear if the Commission will allow this new class of stations to be noncommercial or have the option of carrying advertising. If allowed to sell advertising, the decision could negatively affect existing radio broadcasters.[10]

Radio stations draw and build audiences from the same base that watches television, movies, and videos, reads newspapers, magazines, and books, and engages in other media-related activities. Dealing with competitors by garnering effective and consistent marketing and promotion strategies is an ongoing daily activity for today's radio managers. Further, the microradio issue illustrates the need for the radio industry to maintain strong lobbying efforts in Washington to stave off policy decisions that could prove economically harmful.

The Demise of AM

Despite the growth of popular national radio hosts like Dr. Laura, Rush Limbaugh, Don Imus, and Howard Stern, the AM side of the radio bandwidth continues to suffer from lower audience levels. In addition to talk formats, AM has become the home for news and news talk, sports and sports talk, and niche/ethnic programming. Most importantly, the age of the AM audience continues to be dominated by people over forty.

While AM audiences will never again surpass FM audiences, the long-term erosion and aging of the AM audience raises questions about the future of the medium. AM is not likely to wither and go away, but as audiences continue to decline, the ability to maintain profitability remains a key issue. Further, AM has failed to attract new, younger listeners to the medium. To date, news talk and sports talk stations have been the most successful in terms of generating revenues for AM, primarily in major markets.

Embracing the Internet

The majority of the radio stations in the United States have linked home pages to the Internet for listener access and Internet broadcasting. The challenge for radio management lies in how to effectively transition the station's Web presence from an informational/broadcasting mode to a medium that can complement the existing radio industry.

Ultimately, radio owners would like to use the Internet for many different purposes, especially in generating additional revenue streams. Ideally, the radio industry needs to be part of the electronic commerce revolution. For that to happen, successful business models on how to best embrace the Internet need to be developed.

Clearly, the Internet can help in terms of providing additional marketing support and research information about the station's audience. Questions remain as to the best way to fully utilize the Internet to supplement the radio industry's primary mission of linking audiences with advertisers while serving the public interest.

These issues are not exhaustive but illustrate the diversity of challenges faced by contemporary radio management. Radio is not a static industry, and the issues the industry faces will continue to change and evolve. Interestingly, many of these issues have economic implications for the radio industry. Understanding the economics of the radio industry, the next topic of this chapter, is paramount to achieving success in this dynamic media industry.

RADIO ECONOMICS

Radio economics is best understood when considered as a part of the larger field of media economics.[11] Media economics is defined as "the study of how media industries use scarce resources to produce content that is distributed among consumers to satisfy various wants and needs."[12] Media economics considers the role of both macroeconomics and microeconomics in media industry analysis.

Briefly, *macroeconomics* refers to the entire economic system and is typically studied at a national level. *Microeconomics* considers individual markets, firms, and consumers. The radio industry can be studied from both macro- and microeconomic perspectives. Considering the aggregate impact of the radio industry at the national level would require macroeconomic analysis. Here the focus of topics studied might include the economic performance of the radio industry in comparison to other media industries, the profitability of national radio networks, impact of policy decisions on industry performance, or trends in labor (employment) for the entire radio industry.

Examining individual markets or firms operating in the radio industry would require a microeconomic examination. Such analysis might involve case studies of a selected radio company, the analysis of individual radio markets, the structure of individual radio markets, or ratings analysis of individual stations/markets. In this chapter, the primary focus will be on microeconomic aspects of the radio industry. Where applicable, macroeconomic concepts will be discussed.

Radio Markets: The Local Market

The radio industry operates in two distinct markets: local and national. In terms of local markets, radio stations are individually licensed to serve specific geographical markets and the FCC assigns the classification and maximum power the station can transmit. Markets with larger populations have more radio signals than smaller, more rural communities. The stations assigned to a specific geographic area constitute a local radio market. Within the local market smaller submarkets exist, such as the market for female listeners between the ages of 18–49, or the market for a particular type of format, such as country music.

Radio stations draw the majority of their revenues from the sale of local advertising, so the local economy directly influences the station's economic performance. When the local economy is strong, local advertising also tends to be strong, or, to use the appropriate term, in high demand. Conversely, if the economy is in a downward cycle, local advertising tends to decline, resulting in a greater supply of available advertising time. Supply–demand relationships in the radio industry will be discussed in more detail later in the chapter.

Radio Markets: The National Market

At the national level, radio networks and programming services attract audiences through their distribution on local stations. Radio networks consist of traditional services offering packages of news, features, and sports programming, as well as twenty-four-hour satellite-delivered formats (such as ABC Radio Networks) that can supply the entire programming for a local station. Ultimately, these aggregate local audiences are used to attract national advertisers seeking to use radio to complement their advertising mix.

Data on the national radio industry is compiled by several different sources. The **Radio Advertising Bureau (RAB)** gathers information on radio advertising in terms of local, network, and national spot advertising. National radio listening to networks is provided by **RADAR (Radio's All-Dimensional Audience Research),** which provides ratings estimates for nationally distributed radio programming. Several publications detail the economic state of the radio industry, such as **Duncan's American Radio,** and the Veronis, Suhler and Associates annual *Communications Industry Report.* The Federal Communications Commission maintains data on station transactions.

SUPPLY AND DEMAND RELATIONSHIPS IN RADIO

Supply and demand make up two of the key concepts in the field of economics. In terms of application to the radio industry, supply can be thought of primarily as the entire radio industry or individual radio stations. Supply takes on different meanings in regard to listeners, advertisers, and owners. The number of stations in the local market makes up the available listening outlets; the types of programming they provide to listeners constitute the supply of entertainment and information available to the audience via radio.

From the advertiser's point of view, radio stations represent an outlet for their messages, and a chance to target messages toward specific demographic groups that are desired. Advertisers then think of radio stations as suppliers of advertising time that can be acquired to reach audiences. Most national advertisers utilize radio to cross-market products and services in conjunction with television and print advertising. Radio's cost efficiency and audience reach make the medium a strong complement to other forms of advertising.

From an ownership perspective, individual stations represent commodities that can be acquired or sold to other owners. Cash flow is the most critical variable used in assessing the valuation of a radio station. Stations in larger markets are more valuable to an owner's portfolio than stations in smaller markets. Frequency location and class of station also affect station values.

In turn, audiences, advertisers, and owners represent the three primary categories of demand for radio stations. Listeners love radio. According to estimates provided by the Radio Advertising Bureau, 95.8 percent of all people age twelve and up listen to radio during a given week.[13] Weekday listening averages around three hours and eighteen minutes a day, with higher averages (over five hours) found on weekends.

Advertisers have found radio to be a cost-effective and efficient means of reaching key demographic groups. Radio advertising is segmented into three categories: local, spot (national advertising found on local stations), and network. With both the national and local economies experiencing strong growth during the mid-1990s, radio advertising increased dramatically from 1994 to 1998. In 1998, local advertising totaled $11.9 billion, spot $2.77 billion, and network $720 million for total advertising revenue of $15.4 billion.[14]

Demand for stations increased dramatically after the passage of the 1996 Telecommunications Act that eliminated national ownership restrictions. Radio acquisitions soared in 1996 and 1997 as the industry pursued consolidation. Prior to the 1996 Act, there were an estimated 5,222 owners that controlled approximately 10,250 stations. By 1999 the number of owners declined to 4,500, a loss of over 720 owners.[15] Acquisitions have slowed in 1998 and 1999, leading one analyst to remark that "for all practical purposes [radio] is consolidated . . . there are less stations to sell."[16]

In summary, supply and demand relationships differ in regard to the market structure of an industry. Radio continues to experience an evolving market structure.

MARKET STRUCTURE FOR RADIO

Media economists use different labels to characterize the market structure of an industry.[17] Historically, the radio industry has resembled a monopolistic competitive structure, which features a number of suppliers that offer a product that is similar in nature, but qualitatively different from one another. Such a definition aptly describes radio formats, which may appeal to similar age groups but differ in the presentation of the format.

For years the radio industry operated in a monopolistic competitive structure at both the national and local levels. But given the consolidation of ownership in the industry, there is growing evidence that the industry is moving toward an oligopoly at both the local and national levels. In an oligopoly, a smaller number of players tend to dominate an industry by controlling the majority of the market share.

There is no question this is happening with the huge radio companies like CBS and Clear Channel, which not only dominate local radio, but also network radio as well. According to estimates from Duncan Radio, in 1997 the top fifty radio groups reported revenue totaling $6.99 billion, representing 56 percent of the total radio revenue for the year.[18] In 1996, the top fifty groups accounted for 51 percent of the total radio revenue, and in 1995 approximately 41 percent of the total radio revenue. Duncan estimates that by the year 2000 the top fifty groups may control as much as 65 percent of the total radio revenue unless additional regulation is enacted.

Radio's evolving market structure means higher revenue potential for larger station groups, as the medium becomes more appealing to advertisers who can acquire access to larger audiences with greater efficiency. The radio industry continues to exhibit good growth potential. From 1992 to 1997, the radio industry grew at an average compound rate of 9.3 percent with the same growth rate projected through 2002.[19] Stable audience levels, consolidation of ownership, and cross-media marketing potential lead to high economic expectations for the radio industry.

RADIO PERFORMANCE AND PROFITABILITY

Overall, the radio industry has been attractive to investors because industry performance remains strong. Radio stations have the ability to generate strong cash flows while holding expenses relatively constant. Profit margins and performance measures for the industry have averaged double-digit growth since 1994. With projections for growth averaging near 10 percent through 2002, analysts remain bullish on radio's potential.

Long-term industry performance has been threatened by the large amount of debt some companies have acquired in order to become larger group owners. In particular, the former AMFM and Entercom are representative of this trend. The stock of both companies suffered strong declines during 1999 as Wall Street analysts downgraded the stock when it failed to meet revenue projections.[20] Much of the pessimism has centered on management's ability to effectively manage the huge debt load, resulting in depreciation of stock.

The performance of the radio industry will be enhanced by the industry's ability to generate additional revenue streams. Radio remains too dependent on local advertising, drawing over 70 percent of its revenues from the local market.[21] In this regard, the Internet and electronic commerce hold great potential for the radio industry, but no clear-cut business models exist as to the best way to generate revenues.

SUMMARY

This chapter has presented a general discussion of current trends and issues in radio management and economics. Management and economics function in an interdependent relationship in the radio industry; the actions of one area influence the other.

Management has undergone significant change and modification due to the rapid consolidation of the radio industry, and escalated with the passage of the 1996 Telecommunications Act, which removed national ownership limits and ushered in an area of unparalleled merger and acquisition. Many radio managers found themselves managing clusters of stations as opposed to single-station entities or AM/FM combos.

Industry consolidation gave the radio industry the opportunity to engage in economies of scale by reducing overlapping employment areas and lowering operational costs. The industry has experienced strong economic growth since the passage of the 1996 Act, and future projections reflect a healthy economic future.

At the same time, consolidation has also affected the debt load carried by some of the larger radio companies. Uncertainty over debt may continue to affect the performance of these companies. Still, radio remains a lucrative investment for its owners and stockholders. Management's challenge is to maintain the positive performance and continue to increase the cash flow and ultimate value of the stations under their direction.

NOTES

[1]Ownership limits were placed on radio and later television due to the principle of *scarcity*, the notion that more individuals desired a license to broadcast than there were available frequencies to operate. Today, the concept of scarcity is still widely debated. On one side, proponents argue that scarcity remains, otherwise there would not be such high valuations placed on individual stations. Skeptics claim the marketplace no longer suffers from scarcity, given the range of outlets for expression and dissemination of information.
[2]Limitations on owning only one type of station in each class became commonly known as the "duopoly rule."
[3]Economies of scale, or "scale economies," allow a company to spread costs across several different operations. In the case of radio, a group of stations located in a single market could theoretically share the same physical location, transmitter tower, and employees, allowing for considerable cost savings. Economies of scope, a related concept, allow the company to share similar expenses (e.g., programming, research) across geographical operations.
[4]The 1996 Telecommunications Act was signed into law by President Bill Clinton on February 8, 1996.

[5]Alan B. Albarran, *Media Economics: Understanding Markets, Industries, and Concepts* (Ames, IA: Iowa State University Press, 1996), p. 68.

[6]Chancellor changed its name to AMFM during the summer of 1999. AMFM, CBS/Infinity, and Clear Channel also own television stations.

[7]See Alan B. Albarran, *Management of Electronic Media* (Belmont, CA: Wadsworth, 1997) for a discussion on multitasking in the new managerial environment.

[8]Material in this section was culled from a number of sources including *Management of Electronic Media* (Albarran, 1997, Wadsworth); *Electronic Media Management,* 3rd ed. (Pringle, et al., 1995, Focal Press), and *Telecommunications Management* (Sherman, 1995, McGraw-Hill).

[9]See *1999 Radio Station Salaries.* Washington, DC: National Association of Broadcasters.

[10]Bill McConnell, "Big Flap over Small Stations," *Broadcasting & Cable,* April 18, 1999, pp. 26–36.

[11]For more information on media economics, see Albarran, *Media Economics* (1996); Robert Picard, *Media Economics: Concepts and Issues* (Sage, 1989); and Alexander, et al., *Media Economics: A Reader,* 2nd ed. (Hillsdale, NJ: Lawrence Erlbaum, 1998).

[12]Albarran, *Media Economics,* p. 5.

[13]See http://www.rab.com/station/mgfb98/fact1.html

[14]"Radio Revenue Is Growing," available http://www.rab.com/station/mgfb99/fac28.html

[15]"The State of the Industry Radio Report," available http://www.bia.com/state_radio.htm

[16]Elizabeth A. Rathburn, "Going, going, gone . . ." *Broadcasting & Cable,* February 15, 1999, pp. 33–34.

[17]These labels are *monopoly, duopoly, oligopoly, monopolistic competition,* and *perfect competition.* For more information, see Albarran, *Media Economics* (1996) and Picard, *Media Economics: Concepts and Issues* (1989).

[18]Available http://www.duncanradio.com/rankings13.html

[19]See "Radio Broadcasting," Veronis, Suhler, and Associates, *Communications Industry Forecast,* October, 1998, p. 150.

[20]Steve McClellan and Joe Schlosser, "Street Spanks Station Groups," *Broadcasting & Cable,* February 15, 1999, pp. 8–9.

[21]The NAB published the most recent study on industry revenues and expenses in 1992 and reported that local advertising made up over 70 percent of a station's revenue base.

5

Radio Programming

*Programming that attracts listeners is the dynamo
that propels radio. But today, the proliferation of
media choices has put the listener in the driver's seat.*
DAVID MACFARLAND, CONTEMPORARY
RADIO PROGRAMMING STRATEGIES[1]

BRAND NAME AWARENESS AND USAGE

The last time you purchased a beverage from a vending machine or at a convenience store, you probably examined various beverage options that were available. They ranged from colas and other carbonated drinks to juices and bottled water. The beverages were packaged in aluminum cans, glass, or plastic bottles of several sizes. Brightly colored packaging presented the product logo and name. You selected your beverage, paid for it and consumed the product. It would seem to be an unremarkable experience except when you consider the variety of factors that ultimately led to your product selection. These factors included price and packaging, product taste, and the product image. These and other factors contribute to the brand awareness consumers associate with the product.

A brand is more than the name a company uses for a product or line of products. The brand is a perceived image residing in the mind of the consumer. Brands help consumers differentiate between similar products manufactured by different companies. Brands also help the sellers of goods or services establish a presentation of their products. If the product is readily available to the consumer, at a reasonable price, and a product of consistent quality is offered, consumers become brand loyal.[2] To the extent that a brand has a positive image, it can be thought of as an asset of a company.

The brand and the brand image are the result of extensive consumer research by manufacturers. Consumer products manufacturer Proctor and Gamble (P&G) uses consumer brand research to make certain their products appeal to the proper consumer segment. P&G also looks for ways to extend the appeal of a brand. Brand extensions might be as simple as Proctor and Gamble marketing Tide laundry detergent in a variety of fragrances (or perhaps with no fragrance), or a brand extension might include adding bleach to Tide. Another way to extend the sales appeal of the familiar Tide name is to create a new product category with the familiar name, such as Liquid Tide. Of course, the product has to satisfy the need of the user in a similar manner. If the product does not satisfy the consumer need, the brand name is damaged. One of the best examples of a branding disaster was the decision by the Coca-Cola Company to change the formula for Coke. "New Coke" was rejected by consumers, resulting in the Coca-Cola Company's having to reintroduce the old Coke formula, this time called "Classic Coke."

RADIO BECOMES BRAND AWARE

As discussed in Chapter 2, the limited number of radio stations during radio's infancy enabled station owners and the radio networks to offer almost any type of programming they wanted. Most consumers were so taken with the technology of radio—the fact that they could sit at home and receive *anything* through the radio receiver was a small miracle—that they would listen to whatever programs were offered. As the number of radio stations increased, competition fostered greater choice.

Beginning in the 1950s, the growth in television service killed radio as the national source of entertainment and information. Individual radio station owners began to apply **demand marketing** to their operations. Demand marketing simply means that the station owners analyzed the listener market to determine the product listeners wanted. Perhaps the best example of early demand marketing was Todd Storz's observance of the waitress playing the same favorite songs. Gordon McLendon used a variety of stunts and promotions to create word-of-mouth interest in his stations.

PROGRAMMING FOR A SPECIFIC AUDIENCE

Radio has changed from being a program-specific medium to a format medium.[3] More radio stations choose to air a music format than any other programming option. These stations know that they must do more than serve as jukeboxes for their listeners. The station's on-air sound includes the music and announcer presentation but also of great importance is the listener perception of additional "value" the station provides. Radio analyst J. T. Anderton of Duncan's American Radio says, "It is essential that you mean something to the listener. Otherwise there's no point in turning on the transmitter."[4] Anderton adds that radio should be a showcase for entertainment and information that listeners can't get through the Internet or from listening to CDs. Contests, concert information, and listener "lifestyle" information are used to create the perception of added value. News and talk stations cultivate an image of dependability as a source for breaking news and as a source for talk programming that agrees with the listeners' political or social values. All radio stations use a combination of jingles and other promotional announcements to reinforce the station's call letters and logo. Station jingles are discussed later in this chapter.

The radio station and its format seek to satisfy consumer needs. Radio listeners are most interested in how a radio station's format will provide the gratification they desire. The station must, in the execution of its format, enhance the presentation of the programming with on-air and off-air marketing efforts that create a brand name in the minds of the listeners. This brand must not only be thought of as one that satisfies consumer wants and needs, but it also must be a brand that is easy to recognize, remember, and return to for additional consumption. While the listener expects the station to play different songs from one hour to the next or from one day to the next, the listener also expects a certain sameness in the sound or style of the music or the artists played. This is referred to as *format continuity;* maintaining a consistent on-the-air sound that satisfies listeners is essential. The radio listener seeks a product that is familiar. This doesn't mean that individual announcers at a station must sound the same. But it does mean that the announcer working a particular shift should do things in a similar way from day to day.

Radio listeners consume the on-air product "sold" by a radio station. While the programming does not have the sort of literal cost as a beverage, the sheer number of stations competing for listener attention does create a cost for listening. The primary listener cost is time. The station attempts to maximize the total time spent listening. The magic of radio has always been its accessibility and unique ability to deliver a product with a low cost to use, a modest expenditure for a receiver and the time cost of listening to commercials. But listeners can't effectively listen to more than one station at a time. When the station plays a song a listener does not like, the commercial breaks are too long, or the announcer says something that isn't interesting, the listener may conclude he or she has the wrong product and may make another selection.

SUPPLYING MORE THAN MUSIC UTILITY

Increasingly, consumers will encounter two kinds of entertainment and information programming: direct programming by the listener and programming done by the station. Through cable television, CDs or other recorded music sources, and the Internet, consumers have come to see themselves as the producers or programmers of the content they want to consume. The number of available cable television channels gives consumers more control over how they will spend their viewing time. CDs, minidisks, and MP-3 files provide consumers with the opportunity to determine what they hear. The number of Websites and the variety of customizable content on the Internet give the consumer the chance to tailor the media experience. Radio stations don't provide the kind of custom experience of these other media. But, at the same time, the radio station must do more than attract listeners through **music utility.**[5] CDs or other recorded forms can replace radio stations that are only in the business of supplying music. The radio station that works to create a brand identity that demonstrates value to the listener will create product sampling and encourage loyal product users.

In the crowded and competitive radio marketplace, most stations no longer try to program for a single mass audience. They customize their programming to reach a particular group of listeners. This customization means paying considerable attention to the perceived product needs of their anticipated listeners. Just as the soft drink company uses a logo, package design, and advertising to promote the beverage, the radio station also has a logo or on-air persona. Its programming is designed around the image the station wishes to portray. The station uses a combination of on-air promotion and advertising through other media—such as television or billboards—to reach potential listeners. Part of the radio station's persona may be created with a combination of letters or words. These range from "B" (B-97.9), "Q" (Q-107), or "Z" (Z-100) to "Lite" (Lite Rock and Less Talk) to "Magic" (Magic 102). Three common animal names currently used as part of station brand building include *wolf, duck,* and *frog* (99.5, The Wolf, K-Duck 100, or Froggy 94). These letter or word combinations afford the station the opportunity to create an identify or brand that customers will remember, particularly through the use of jingles or other on- and off-air promotions. This brand image should be easier to remember than the usual set of call letters that the station must use to meet FCC requirements.

EXTERNAL AND INTERNAL BRAND BUILDING

Radio ratings company Arbitron identifies what it calls External and Internal factors that affect programming and decision making within a radio station.[6] The external factors include market competition, both from other stations and other media. Stations compete directly for listeners with stations playing similar music, but they also complete with other media and all other activities. Consumers increasingly have the ability to sample radio signals from other parts of the country through using their computer; CD players or MP-3 files can allow listeners to create custom music blends. Even though radio programmers are fond of talking about the portable nature of radio, other demands for time—whether at work or during leisure activities—can limit radio listening.

Music availability and the quality of the music determine the sound of a radio station. If the station plays mostly current hit songs, the number of new releases and corresponding quality of the music will influence the station's sound. Record companies have an incentive to supply new music but the cost of producing, distributing, and promoting new music also means that record companies don't produce an unlimited supply of new product for consumers or radio programmers to select from. As electronic distribution of recorded music has increased, record companies have a distribution system that can bypass the traditional music sellers. This will allow record companies to increase the number of music products they offer. While the increased product range may give radio stations more music to select from, it will also give consumers a similar choice. This may make it even harder for radio stations to select the "right" songs that will attract and retain a sizeable listening audience.

Changes in lifestyles, most notably the aging of the baby boomers, have resulted in an increase in the number of stations playing Classic Rock and playing 1970s disco and R&B music. Stations in the latter group are airing the Jammin' Oldies format. Lifestyle changes also cause stations to reposition themselves in the audience marketplace. *Duncan's American Radio* reported 374 stations airing beautiful music or easy listening formats in 1977. That number dropped to 179 in 1986.[7] Beautiful music/easy listening did not make the list of national format shares in the **Radio and Records Directory** in 1999.[8] What lifestyle change contributed to the format change? As the baby boom generation aged, they were not interested in listening to the traditional easy listening or beautiful music format that their parents or grandparents listened to. And the pool of previous listeners kept shrinking as a result of natural mortality (advancing age and death). Some of the stations repositioned themselves as light rock or soft adult contemporary stations. Still others changed their formats entirely. We will talk further about the differences in formats (such as light rock and soft adult contemporary) later in the chapter.

The growth in the number of radio stations (from about 3,000 FM stations in 1980 to 5,700 in 2000) has meant that stations must work harder to be noticed in the marketplace. Additionally, stations must give consumers a reason to listen to the radio rather than prerecorded music. Except for a few heritage stations with long traditions in the community, most stations can't expect listeners to just happen to know about the station. Off-air or **external promotions** allow the station to introduce its logo and brand identity to consumers. Typical external promotions include bumper stickers and billboards. Station promotions also include remote broadcasts from concerts and sporting events and Friday afternoon "bring-in-the-weekend" type remotes from a restaurant or bar. Selling T-shirts, caps, or sweatshirts with the station logo or brand will not only enhance listeners' awareness of the station but may contribute additional revenue to the station. For stations with particularly mass appeal formats, television advertising may be used to promote cash or automobile giveaways. Most of these external promotional efforts reinforce the brand value of the station to existing listeners or encourage nonlisteners or infrequent listeners to sample the product at other times.

Internal factors affecting station programming include the number of songs a station plays and the quality of the songs, on-air promotions, quality of production, commercial load, and announcer performance. Listeners often think that radio stations play any song that matches the station's general format. In fact, nothing could be further from the truth. Radio stations typically have a tightly controlled library of song titles. Becoming part of the **music library** often depends on station testing of the song to determine what listeners think of it (see Chapter 7, Radio Research, for more information), the addition of the song to the playlist by other stations in a station's peer format group, or perhaps the recommendation of a programming consultant. Monitoring services such as *Radio and Records, Billboard,* and *The Gavin Report* also track current hit songs and may be another source of information for determining which songs are added to a station's playlist. This is especially true for stations airing any sort of "hit music" format that relies on the latest hits to "drive" the sound of the station.

Think of all the songs that are written and released in a single year. Multiply that number by the number of years of music represented in a station's format. Ultimately, only a small number of the total number of songs released will make it into the station's active music library. A station playing Classic Rock might have between 700 and 1000 titles in its music library. A Contemporary Hit Radio (CHR) station might have between 400 and 600 titles in its music library. A country station might have 700 to 900 titles in its music library.

Listeners sampling the music or "sound" of the station for the first time hear not only the music but also a variety of **on-air promotion** segments that help shape their opinion of the station. On-air promotions may be as simple as announcer-delivered commentary about the station or as complex as a multitrack audio production complete with a variety of sound effects, music segments, and radio production techniques. Effective on-air promotion depends not only on the quality or quantity of the audio production but also on the nature of the promotion. Most on-air promotions accomplish one of two things. The promotions encourage longer listening—this might be as simple as an announcer previewing or teasing the upcoming songs. If the listener hears a song title or artist she likes, listening may continue. Or on-air promotion may try to recycle listeners by getting them to listen at another time of the day.

Production quality refers not only to the production of commercials and station promotional announcements but also to the overall execution of the station's format. The effectiveness of the production staff determines whether the station has a consistent sound. Just as you might be unlikely to return to a restaurant where you received poor service or a bad-tasting meal, listeners are less willing to return to a station that is inconsistent, though, at least in the case of the radio station, the listener is not required to make a monetary expenditure to sample the station's product. Even the time spent listening to the station can be as short as the time it takes to push a button to go to the next station.

Commercials are probably the single biggest irritant to radio listeners but for the station management the commercials are the most important part of the station's programming. Station owners or managers establish the number of commercial minutes aired each hour. At one time, the National Association of Broadcasters enacted codes for radio and television advertising.[9] The NAB's voluntary codes suggested that radio stations limit advertising to no more than eighteen minutes per hour and that television limit advertising to no more than fourteen minutes per hour. In 1979, the U.S. Justice Department brought suit against the imposition of commercial limits, charging that the NAB Code artificially limited the supply of advertising time and thus unfairly increased the price of television and radio advertising. In response, the NAB, in 1982, voluntarily dissolved the radio and television codes.[10]

Station competition, after the limit was ended, was expected to keep the amount of commercials aired in check. A strong economy and radio consolidation have made it difficult for some stations to say no to potential advertisers. The radio ad market has been robust. Debt burden from various station purchases has pushed managers to take the ad revenue as it has become available. Advertisers have fewer ad options because of consolidation. They may be able to purchase advertising on a variety of different stations but ultimately only two or three owners may control the top stations in the market. Consumers find themselves sitting through long commercial breaks with no legitimate radio option because all the stations in the market are under similar pressure to air more radio ads. The variety of radio formats and the audiences targeted by those formats make it easier for radio to reach large but narrowly defined audiences. Consumer products manufacturer Proctor and Gamble has increased its use of radio to advertise twenty of its national brands.[11] Internet or "Dot-com" companies have found radio to be an effective way to reach consumers with brand information.[12]

Announcer performance refers to the quality of the on-air staff as demonstrated by its ability to relate to the listeners. Depending on the station's format, the announcers may need to be funny, conversational, or opinionated, or all of these, simultaneously. Announcers must demonstrate consistency within a day or several days. For most listeners, the announcer is the radio station. Internal or external promotion influences the sound of the station but execution of the on-air sound of the station depends on the announcer. If the announcer is perceived to have done something wrong, the listener may push the button and listen to another station.

MAINTAINING ON-AIR CONSISTENCY

How do radio stations maintain a consistent on-air sound? Historically, the station would have maintained a **continuity book.** The continuity book listed the introductory and closing comments for any program or broadcast aired on the station as well as provided background material to the announcers. Stations are now less likely to have a continuity book, but they will have a list of liner phrases or positioning statements that the announcers will use—a **hot clock,** a **program log,** and a **music log.**

The liners or positioning statements reinforce the brand image the station wants to create. Every time the announcer speaks, the first thing out of the announcer's mouth will be either the station's call letters (WBAP, Newstalk 820), a station brand identifier (The Wolf, 99.5), or a positioning statement (Your Dance and Party Station, Hot 100.) These identifiers reinforce the station brand and are intended to help listeners who may be participating in station ratings reporting. Stations register with Arbitron or other ratings services the various liners, slogans, or statements their announcer staff will use on-air to refer to the station. Additionally, stations may air a jingle identification package that will reinforce the call letters or station logo, type of programming, or other programming element. Figure 5-1 discusses several of the successful jingle production companies.

A hot clock is a visual representation of one-hour of the station's programming. Shown on the hot clock will be the approximate times when commercial breaks are taken, when particular types of songs are to be played (a current hit, new song, or oldie), and, perhaps, when the announcer should talk on-air (and with the help of liner phrases or positioning statements, what the announcer should say). Radio may sound like one big jukebox for the person sitting at home or in the car but what and when the listener hears something does not occur by chance. The hot clock ensures format consistence by providing the announcer with a visual representation of the elements the listener is to hear.

Announcers also typically follow a program log, which lists not only program names or time periods, but also the commercials the station will be airing. Most music-oriented stations air few actual programs but newscasts, traffic reports, or weather updates are common programming elements that are listed on the program log. Commercials include sponsor names and are usually allotted to clusters or spot sets. The music-oriented station is also likely to have a music log for the announcer. The music log, produced with the help of scheduling software, will list every song the announcer will play. Most stations preselect the songs to provide tighter control over the music played not just on-the-air, but to control songs played within even a selected time of the day. Both the hot clock and the music log will list songs according to various categories including top hits or currents, oldies and golden oldies, or perhaps by tempo (slow, medium, or fast) or artist (group, male soloist or female soloist). The number and type of songs played on a station will depend on the station's format and target audience.

David MacFarland suggests that perhaps stations don't want to be too consistent in what they do. Too much consistency makes the radio station too much like a jukebox, supplying only music. It also means the station may not have anything that makes its brand unique. Even McDonald's, which prides itself on providing consistent products from its thousands of franchised restaurants around the world, offers more than a single menu item and the food company develops advertising campaigns to increase consumer awareness of new product offerings. Consistency is one thing but consumer boredom with the product is another. Listeners should receive a "good" product every day but it should be a "fresh" product that offers a slightly new experience. Whether stations are effective in delivering consistent, yet fresh, on-air content each day depends on how well the station knows its audience and what the audience wants.[13] Among other things, MacFarland argues that radio

FIGURE 5-1   The Radio Jingle Capital of the World: Dallas, Texas

A favorite on-air promotional tool for many radio stations has been the station jingle package. Jingles, whether a cappella or with musical accompaniment, can be used by almost any format as one of the elements contributing to a station's unique sound. Jingles contribute to the image or identity the station wants to create and help listeners remember the call letters or station logo. Jingles are also a programming transition device. The jingle signals the end of a commercial break and the return to music, introduces a contest, or serves as a transition between two songs.

Dallas, Texas isn't the exclusive location for jingle production but the jingle industry's presence dates back to the 1950s and the use of jingles by Gordon McClendon. Probably the grandfather of all jingle companies was PAMS, "Production Advertising Merchandising Service," founded in 1951 by William (Bill) Meeks in Dallas, Texas. Meeks, after working for Gordon McLendon's legendary Top 40 radio station KLIF, including creating jingles for the station, formed PAMS to begin marketing jingles to other stations. PAMS's clients during the 1960s and 1970s, included some of the most widely listened to radio stations in the country, including: WABC and WNBC in New York, WLS in Chicago, WXYZ in Detroit, KFWB in Los Angeles, WKYC in Cleveland, KJR in Seattle, WAYS in Charlotte, WWWE in Cleveland, WCBS-FM in New York, WLW in Cincinatti, and KDKA in Pittsburgh.

JAM Creative Productions
Dallas is also home to JAM Creative Productions, founded by Jon and Marylyn Wolfert in 1973. Jon Wolfert became interested in the radio jingle through listening to WABC, 770 kHz. Located in New York, it is a station some regard as one of the greatest Top 40 stations in the history of the format. Wolfert worked for PAMS, which for more than a decade created most of the WABC jingles. JAM Creative Productions produces jingles for radio and television stations around the world, creates custom commercials for advertisers, supplies postscoring for film or video production, and owns the rights to the jingles created by Bill Meeks PAMS that launched many Top 40 formats. Production facilities at JAM include two twenty-four-track studios. JAM productions are sold to a worldwide customer list, including the BBC as well as other stations in Europe, South America, and Africa.

Thompson Creative Services
Founded in 1986 by broadcasters Larry and Susan Thompson, Thompson Creative Services produces jingles and station ID packages as well as customized ads for radio & TV promo, voiceovers, and turnkey radio commercials. Production facilities include a twenty-four-track recording studio.

TM Century Productions
TM Century Productions began as two separate companies: Century 21 Productions and TM Productions. The companies merged to become TM Century, a publicly traded company listed under the symbol TMCI. TM Century, Inc. creates, produces, and distributes music-based products for broadcast media use. Product lines include music libraries and music services, production music, commercial jingles, and radio and TV station jingle packages. TM Century's clients include radio and television stations; satellites and Internet networks; Websites and portals; the American Forces Radio Network; advertising agencies and commercial businesses.

TM Century can furnish clients with complete music libraries for formats ranging from adult contemporary to traditional country. Clients can download music files from the TM Century Website.

Jingle packages are prepared on a market-exclusive basis; only one station in a market will have jingles of a particular sound. However, the goal of most jingle companies is to create a jingle concept that can be sold to a number of different stations around the country. While 50 or even 100 stations might buy the full package of jingles, each station will have exclusive use of the jingles within a market area.

Sources: Al Brumley, "Jingles: All the way," *Dallas Morning News,* January 3, 1999, p. C1 and C6, and Jam Creative Productions, http://www.jingles.com/, PAMS, http://www.pams.com/, Thompson Creative Services, http://www.thompsoncreative.com/index.htm, TM Century Productions, http://www.tmcentury.com/. Visit the Websites to listen to audio files containing jingle demos.

stations should apply a higher standard of research to determine precisely what they play on the air.

MUSIC FORMATS

The magazine *Television/Radio Age* quoted author Tom Ratner as noting that "music programming on radio is swinging into an era of fickle formats and shifting audiences."[14] What is most remarkable about this observation is when it was made. The quote, while not identified by specific date, was used in the book *The Radio Format Conundrum*, published in 1978. The book's authors devote nine chapters to specific radio formats and their subformats. They note that a radio station may select a format to fill an immediate void in the radio market, but once the format is selected the format will likely "be subjected to a dozen subtle or obvious shifts and adjustments" as the station determines its sound.[15] This observation is still true today. It illustrates how a station must be both proactive and reactive as it determines not only the music to be played but also the other elements that contribute to the station sound or brand.

We have discussed a number of elements that contribute to the station brand though, for most listeners, ultimately it is the music played by the station that is the primary factor in determining whether they will listen even once to the station or not. Once the listener has sampled the product, the station hopes that other elements it contributes will encourage the listener to remain with the station or to return to listen again at another time.

At one point, most mainstream radio formats could fit in one of five categories: contemporary, country, black, middle-of-the-road (MOR), and other. Today, radio formats have splintered into multiple formats; one radio industry-tracking group identifies at least thirty-seven formats and that number will likely continue to grow. Figure 5-2 provides a glimpse of radio format growth over a twenty-year period. New formats often represent a further segmentation of existing formats or the creation of subformats or niche formats. Top 40 of the 1950s led to the creation of rock and adult contemporary. Rock spawned mainstream rock, hard rock, classic rock, and alternative. Adult contemporary led to oldies, soft rock, classic hits, hot AC, and modern adult contemporary. Each format variant represents an effort by a radio station or group of stations to establish a programming identity for themselves that will set their station apart from others in the market. The stations no longer are trying to be "all things for all people." They recognize that it is better to have a strong listener base among a particular audience segment.

RADIO FORMAT SEGMENTATION

Three factors have been the driving force behind the growth in radio format segmentation: the sharp rise in the number of radio stations on the air, a greater awareness of audience segmentation, and radio consolidation. As more radio stations (primarily

FIGURE 5-2   Just how many radio formats are there, anyway? Format categories used in *Duncan's American Radio* to track stations beginning in 1977.

1977	1986	1998
CHR/AOR/ Contemporary	CHR/Top 40/Contemporary	Adult Contemporary
MOR/AC	AOR	Modern AC
Country	MOR/Variety	AOR
Black/Urban	AC/Soft Oldies	New Rock
News/Talk	Country	Progressive Rock
Beautiful Music/Easy Listening	Black/Urban	Black
Spanish	News/Talk	Black Adult Contemporary
Religion/Gospel	Beautiful Music/Easy Listening	Black Oldies
Classical	Spanish	Business News/Talk
Other	Religion/Gospel	Country
	Classical	Classic Country
	Other	Contemporary Hit Radio/Top 40/Contemporary
		Classical
		Classic Hits/70's Oldies
		Ethnic (usually Foreign Language)
		Easy Listening/Beautiful Music
		Full Service
		Gospel
		Jazz & New Adult Contemporary
		News
		Oldies
		Religion/Christian
		Contemporary Christian
		Soft Adult Contemporary
		Hispanic/Spanish
		Hispanic Contemporary
		Hispanic News/Talk/ Information
		Hispanic-Regional
		Hispanic-Tropical
		Hispanic-Variety
		Tejano
		Sports
		Standards, Big Band, Nostalgia
		Talk
		Urban
		Variety/Other

Source: *Duncan's American Radio Tenth Anniversary Issue, 1976–1986* and *Duncan's American Radio Fall 1998 Ratings Report.* Used with permission, Duncan's American Radio.

FM) have gone on the air, new stations have realized they need to offer a product slightly different from the competition if the new station is to succeed. These new stations have also displaced many AM stations. As the new FM stations began airing programming similar to the AM stations' offerings, listeners abandoned AM service. The AM station owners needed something new.

Awareness of changing audience demographics has given stations the impetus to redirect their programming. The music we listen to no longer has the same meaning to various segments of our population; there is no one format or musical sound that is a common part of the U.S. culture. Just as music has broadened to appeal to a variety of age and ethnic groups, advertisers no longer covet only the 25–54 or 25–49-year-old listener groups. The U.S. population includes segments of affluent consumers in other age ranges and ethnic backgrounds who can be reached effectively through radio programming.

Radio consolidation refers to the growth in the number of large radio groups that began after the Telecommunications Act of 1996 increased the number of radio stations a single owner could control in a market. Consolidation has put stations that were once fierce competitors in a market under common corporate ownership. The new owners, unwilling to have their stations compete with themselves, have mandated both subtle and extreme format changes at the stations they purchased. The format changes sometimes allow two stations to develop even greater strength among their listening audience. For example, two stations previously targeting a listener group of women, ages 25–54, might now split the demo into two categories. One station might try to reach women ages 18–34 and the other station might reach women ages 35–54. Some of the music aired on the two stations might be the very same; at the very least, the programming on the stations would complement each other.

RADIO FORMATS:
FROM AC (ADULT CONTEMPORARY)
TO UC (URBAN CONTEMPORARY)

Adult Contemporary (AC) has traditionally been one of the top radio formats both in terms of the number of stations airing the format and the number of listeners. Adult Contemporary developed from the Top 40/Pop sound of the 1960s as that format began to split. The AC station targets an audience between the ages of twenty-five and fifty-four; while both male and female listeners are sought, women often constitute about two-thirds of the format's audience. The broad age range for Adult Contemporary listeners also suggests that not all AC stations will program the same mix of music. The AC format has gradually fragmented to include Mainstream AC (current hits and older AC hits), Hot AC (a cross between mainstream AC and Contemporary Hit Radio), Full Service AC (older skewing with a softer music appeal), Urban AC (a hybrid between traditional AC and Urban Contemporary), Modern AC (a blend of AC and pop/alternative) and Light AC (also sometimes called Soft Rock).

Contemporary Hit Radio or CHR is the grandchild (or great grandchild) of Top 40 radio. The format mostly closely resembles the traditional Top 40 sound; stations air a limited music playlist of current hit songs, the format is high energy, and often includes contests, promotions, and strong on-air personality identification. Most CHR stations target listeners 18–34, though the station may also have especially strong listenership among teens. The station's format depends heavily on current music trends. The CHR format also includes the variation CHR/Rhythmic (a mix of contemporary hits and dance and Urban hits). The format appeals to the same general age audience, though this format variation likely includes a greater percentage of Hispanic and African-American listeners.

Country music moved from a regional format of the South and Southwest (Country & Western) to a national format during the 1970s as a result of U.S. population changes, television and movie exposure to the country genre (from *Donnie and Marie* to *The Urban Cowboy*), and crossover artists who also appeared on AC stations. The country format attracts a broad audience; the 25–54 age group is the traditional audience. Women compose slightly more than half of all country listeners. As with other music, some format segmentation has occurred.

The Country format has fragmented to include Classic Country (past hits and the traditional country sounds of the 1960s, 1970s, or early 1980s), which appeals to listeners 35+, Young Country/Modern Country (current hits with a strong emphasis on the young country stars who are also popularized through music videos), and Americana (a blend of Traditional Country and Young Country). Still, compared with some music formats, country has failed to reach the fractionalization of some formats.

The News/Talk format includes stations airing all news, all talk, all sports, all business, or a mixture of the four. The format usually targets both male and female listeners, though its strongest following is among men, who comprise about 60 percent of the listener base. The listener age range is 25+; the news/talk format is especially strong among 35–54-year-old listeners, though audiences 55–64 and 65+ can also be regular listeners.

Traditionally, All News stations operated with each programming hour split into two or three segments of thirty minutes or twenty minutes each. The typical listener could expect to hear local, national, and international news, weather, sports, business news, and traffic within a segment. The cycle would then repeat itself, with fresh copy or updated information being added when possible. Gradually, some news stations recognized the desire for listener discussion of news topics and the talk component was added to the news format. The talk radio phenomenon fragmented to include sports talk. The typical all-sports or sports talk station will likely anchor its on-air brand around one or more major professional teams, then establish talk programming to provide a platform for fan discussion of the teams' performance.

Growing public interest in the stock market and investing, along with the stock market's strong performance in the 1990s, led to the creation of the all business format. All business radio usually relies on a network provider to supply the latest breaking national and international business trends. The affiliate station will focus on local business stories as well as traffic information. The latest twist on business news has been technology news and information company CNET's deal with

AMFM Inc. (Chancellor Media) to create a business technology radio format to extend CNET's reach beyond the Internet. While many readers may view the Internet as more powerful than "mere radio," CNET views the radio format as an effective method to build its brand recognition as "the center for tech information."[16]

Urban Contemporary (UC) is a mixture of dance, rap, R&B, and Contemporary Hits. The format itself is actually a fragmentation of what was once called Black or Ethnic radio. The UC format is now more widely used to cover a category of stations that appeal to women, men, and teens, with slightly more women than men. While the format is strongest among African Americans, more than one fourth of the listeners are Caucasian. The Urban Contemporary format includes: Churban (dance tempo hit format consisting of Urban and contemporary hits targeted especially at African American and Caucasian women, 18–34), Urban AC (a slower version of the UC format targeted to reach an older audience than the usual UC station), Black Oldies (R&B and soul hits targeted to reach an audience age 35+), Rap (rap music without the CHR or dance crossover music and targeted to an under 25 audience), and Urban (similar to UC but the programming is designed to attract an audience consisting almost exclusively of African Americans).

The term *Ethnic radio* has come to include foreign-language programming aimed at a local audience segment. Examples of such stations might include a station airing programming intended to attract Korean listeners. Some AM station owners have found market success by selling blocks of programming time to entrepreneurs who produce programming in a variety of languages ranging from Indian to Korean to Chinese to Arabic. Most communities could not sustain a single station airing programming in one or two of these languages, but by airing programming in multiple languages the local communities are served and the station's ethnic format is economically sustainable.

Oldies/Classic Rock, while often lumped into one broad category, actually consists of formats appealing to different listener groups. The oldies format has greater listener appeal among women while classic rock is stronger among men. Oldies may include hits from the 1950s—the earliest years of the Top 40 format—to an oldies AC or Classic Hits format consisting of music from the 1980s and 1990s. The Classic Rock format may include music from the early 1970s through the early 1980s; most of the artists are male performers.

Rock/Active rock is a mixture of current rock music and older rock music and is another of the lifestyle formats that gears the listening experience not only to include music but also contests, promotions, and personalities. Two-thirds of Rock/Active Rock listeners are likely to be men; most of the format's listeners are Caucasian. The target audience consists of listeners ages 25–44, with additional appeal to 18–24-year-olds.

Rock has become one of the most fragmented formats. The earliest pure rock format was Album Oriented Rock (AOR), which emerged on FM stations in the early 1970s as a response to Top 40 radio. Today, rock includes Alternative (also called Modern Rock), New Rock, Mainstream Rock, and Album Adult Alternative

(Triple-A) or Progressive Rock. Stations establish their niche through music selection and presentation and both on-air and off-air promotional appeals. The Modern Rock format may target the 25–34-year-old audience segment of recent college graduates or high school grads early in their careers. The Triple-A station may focus on the 35–44-year-old adults who have been out of college for more than a decade, are likely to own a home, and may be concerned with family and individual issues. The number of radio signals available in most markets, plus the wide use of CDs or other playback sources, suggests that the rock station would face a daunting task if it tried to be all things for all rock listeners. Figure 5-3 discusses the unique efforts of one station owner to establish a variation of the rock format on two newly purchased stations.

Spanish is a broad label given to a category of radio formats that range in age appeal from attracting teen listeners to adults 45+. Population and economics experts recognize that the U.S. Hispanic market has one of the highest percentage growth rates both in population and economic clout. This segment growth has led to format delineation. Spanish formats now include Hispanic/Spanish, Hispanic Contemporary (an Hispanic version of AC), Hispanic News/Talk/Information, Hispanic Regional, Hispanic Tropical, Hispanic Variety, Tejano, and religious Spanish. Language is often the one aspect that separates these formats from other radio formats. Many of the stations include on-air delivery in English and Spanish by the announcing staff and in commercials; other stations focus exclusively on Spanish delivery.

Spanish formats have provided opportunities for station owners to better use an existing AM radio signal. Small AM stations that might not be able to sustain a music format if forced to compete against FM stations, have established a viable listenership with a Spanish format. Cities such as Nashville, Tennessee (sometimes called the Cradle of Country Music) or Springfield, Missouri, which might not be thought of as having a sizeable Hispanic population now have sufficiently large Hispanic populations to justify the operation of Spanish-formatted radio stations in such cities. If the format succeeds on AM and the market's Hispanic population continues to grow, the format will migrate to FM.

Standards, Big Band, and Nostalgia refer to stations airing music from the 1940s up to the 1960s, including some of the songs that might be thought of as early rock and roll or pop. The term Middle-of-the-Road (MOR) is another name used for Standards. While not exclusively an AM format, Standards/Nostalgia is one of the remaining music formats present in regular numbers on the AM band. The format appeals to listeners thirty-five to sixty-four years of age, many of whom grew up listening primarily to AM radio. Many of the older recordings were not originally produced in stereo.

Easy Listening/Beautiful music is a close relative of Standards. The EZ format sounds very different—consisting of instrumentals and slower remakes of hit songs—but the audience appeal is to listeners in the 35–64 age range. Easy Listening was once a standard FM radio format; today it can be found on a limited number of AM or FM stations. Many Easy Listening stations repositioned themselves as

FIGURE 5-3   What's in a Name?

Susquehanna Radio Corporation, headquartered in York, Pennsylvania, is one of the largest privately owned radio broadcast group owners in the United States. In 1997, Susquehanna purchased a two FM stations in the Dallas–Ft. Worth, Texas, radio market to join other properties they already owned. One station was licensed to Haltom City, Texas, a community situated between Dallas and Ft. Worth; the other station was located in Sanger, Texas, a community situated northwest of Dallas. The Haltom City station's power was upgraded to 50,000 watts, making it a class C2 FM. The Sanger station is a class C3 FM, with 1 kw and 150 m HAAT.

Once you buy a new radio station (or two stations) how do you program them? The stations initially simulcast a Triple-A, album adult alternative format using the on-air promotion The Zone. After failing to break into the Top 20 stations in the Dallas–Ft. Worth market, Susquehanna unveiled a new format and positioning campaign during the fall of 1999.

Calling the station Merge Radio, the stations began airing what they called "Cool Rock Smart Pop." Not only does the programming air on the FM band but listeners can also receive the music via the Internet at Merge933.net. Unlike other stations that operate a Website and stream audio, the station maintains a staff of fulltime "Webjammers" who can interact with online listeners, and the Merge Radio site is updated regularly during the day. The site even informs listeners about MP-3 audio files, what they are, and where they can be found on the Internet.

The station's Website describes the format and station brand this way: "Where the Burning Passion of music meets the cool steely gleam of the digital future! At Merge Radio 93.3 FM and Merge 933.net, we offer an innovative, new brand of adult alternative music for Dallas/Fort Worth, Cool Rock Smart Pop. R.E.M., Pearl Jam, Lenny Kravitz, Collective Soul, Foo Fighters. Along with established bands that we love, count on Merge 933.net to embrace emerging music from bands that will define the future."

The Merge Radio signal is completely digital from the time the music is played back via CD or hard-drive audio file to the time the station's programming reaches the transmitter. Unfortunately, the over-the-air is still an analog FM broadcast signal.

How is the station doing with listeners? Ratings were not available at the time this book was being published. Readers can check one of the online radio Websites to find the most recent ratings. *Radio and Records* (http://www.rronline.com/) provides a free quarterly listing of radio ratings data supplied by Arbitron. Merge Radio (http://www.merge933.net) uses the call letters KKMR-FM, Haltom City/Dallas and KMRR-FM, Sanger, Texas.

Merge Radio, Cool-Rock-Smart-Pop, and Webjammer are copyrighted service marks of Susquehanna Radio. Used with permission, Susquehanna Radio Corporation.

Light Adult Contemporary stations in an effort to improve their listenership and ability to sell advertising time.

Religious radio refers to a broad category of formats ranging from radio preachers to music programming of several different styles and appeals. Many of the first radio stations to begin operation in the 1920s or 1930s were run by evangelists who wanted to use the airwaves to save souls. Religious radio grew from this tradition to include Gospel formatted stations: both black gospel and white gospel, Contemporary Christian programming, and religious talk/information programming. Contemporary Christian has become a strong FM format in many large cities. While the market may only support one such station, it is a viable format that appeals to a 25–54-year-old audience. Gospel programming in large cities is more likely to be found on the AM band than the FM, but in small towns gospel may occupy a sizeable portion of the airtime on small market AM or FM stations. Religious news/information formats may consist of individual stations selling airtime in program length segments varying from fifteen minutes in length to two or three hours. The stations furnish the airtime and the program producers provide the program content. Another religious format present in many markets occupies the noncommercial portion of the FM band (discussed in Chapter 8). Low-power translator stations rebroadcast religious programming that is beamed in by satellite.

Full Service is the format description for a handful of mostly clear channel AM stations. Most of these stations began broadcasting in the 1930s and have survived the public shift from AM to FM by continuing to build on their traditional success in the market as news and information leaders. Unlike a News/Talk station, Full Service stations emphasize their heritage in the market and commitment to community service, including news coverage. One of the best examples of the Full Service format is number one-rated WGN radio in Chicago. *Duncan's American Radio* lists WGN's format as Full Service/Talk; the station is the flagship radio station for Chicago Cubs baseball. WGN was estimated to have billed $32.5 million in 1997 for its owners, making the station not only the top billing station in Chicago but one of the highest billing stations in the country.[17]

The Full Service approach isn't limited only to Clear Channel AM stations. In small to medium markets, many AM stations have also built their identity through community heritage and service. These stations place a heavy emphasis on **localism** and typically air local events such as high school football and basketball broadcasts. Some stations may choose to identify their format as Variety or Block Programming to reflect a mixture of various types of music, local news and talk, local sports, and community announcements. While they may not be as successful as WGN, the stations have created a visible community brand name. A great example of localism comes from stations WGOH-AM and WUGO-FM, owned by Carter County Broadcasting, in Grayson, Kentucky. Though each station does air a specific music format, the stations pride themselves on serving the local community. WGOH-AM received the NAB's Crystal Award for Community Service in 1999, and the stations have been named one of the Top Five Small-town stations in the United States. Figure 5-4 provides a profile of the stations' programming.

New Adult Contemporary/Smooth Jazz is one of the most recent radio formats to develop. The format is a blend of soft adult contemporary ballads and instrumental jazz sounds that emerged beginning in the late 1980s. In some respects, NAC has tried, unsuccessfully, to become the millennium version of easy listening. The format lacks a sufficiently large library of familiar music capable of helping the station reach the critical audience mass. NAC/Smooth Jazz targets the 35–54-year-old audience and attracts slightly more female listeners than male listeners. Additionally,

FIGURE 5-4   Community Radio Service the Old Fashioned Way

Radio station licensing in the United States historically sought to establish stations capable of addressing the needs of a local community. Changes in ownership and changing perceptions of radio's role as a mass medium have altered the level of community service provided by many radio stations. The National Association of Broadcasters recognizes radio public service through its annual Crystal Award. Crystal Award winner WGOH-AM and sister station WUGO-FM in Grayson, Kentucky demonstrate outstanding community service. WGOH/WUGO, known by the radio brand "Go Radio," serves Carter County (population 26,848) and residents in surrounding counties, a blend of information, entertainment, and public service more reminiscent of radio from an earlier time than what people usually hear today.

WGOH-AM went on the air in 1959 and WUGO-FM was established in 1967; both stations are owned by Carter County Broadcasting, an independent group of local owners. The stations describe themselves as home-owned and operated by a staff that has been with the station an average of thirty years. General Manager Francis Nash joined the station as an announcer in 1966. Go Radio operates with computer-controlled studios, operates a Website, and programs and sells ad time on a community cable channel.

The stations feature more than 210 minutes of news each day, including a morning news block from 6:00–8:15 A.M. called *Mornings on the Go*. As part of its Crystal Award, WGOH documented airing more than 5,000 public service announcements for the community. The stations' other accomplishments include airing a radio auction to raise funds to keep open an Adult Education Center, a Kids Safety Fair each fall, staging a Christmas Parade for foster children, helping restock the community pantry to feed the needy, sponsoring a record-breaking blood drive, and helping clean up forty tons of trash.

WGOH-AM, 1370 khz, with 5,000 watts of daytime power and up to 500 watts of presunrise and postsunset power, airs a country gold format but includes midday segments of bluegrass and gospel programming. WUGO-FM, 102.3 MHz, with a power of 4.8 kw and an antenna height of 111 meters, airs an adult lite rock format and provides complete coverage of local high school sports from East and West Carter High Schools, plus University of Kentucky sports and Cincinnati Reds baseball. Station programming also includes the *Trading Post* program (listeners call in items to sell, buy, or trade), the *Great Person of the Day* program (a community citizenship feature), community bulletin board, church news and obituaries, a weekly call-in public affairs program with county leaders, and color Doppler weather radar. The stations are also affiliated with the CBS Radio Network and with the Kentucky News Network.

Advertising rates on the stations range from a low of $2.80 for a :15 commercial purchased through a yearly contract to a high of $6.00 for a :60 commercial purchased through a weekly contract. All members of the staff serve as account executives and thus share in sales commissions. These ad rates might seem low compared to major market rates but they reflect the size of the market and the pledge of the station owners to serve the community and have fun with local radio. Go Radio has twice been nominated for the NAB's Marconi Award as Best Small-Market Radio Station in the United States.

Folksy community programming is one of the things that adds a personal dimension to radio. Radio is a mass medium, but it can retain the ability to speak to individual listeners.

Sources: GO Radio Rate Card, 1999; Francis M. Nash, *Towers over Kentucky*, (Lexington, KY: Host Communications, 1995); Francis Nash personal correspondence; and "WGOH–WUGO Website." Available at http:www.wgohwugo.com, accessed November 2, 1999. Used with permission, Francis Nash.

NAC/Smooth Jazz crosses ethnic lines to attract Caucasian, African-American, and Hispanic listeners. The greatest listener strength for this format is on the U.S. West coast although stations may be found throughout the United States.

Classical music, with a few exceptions, was once limited to airplay only on noncommercial radio stations. Increasingly, commercial station programmers have recognized that Classical, while not a ratings winner, can be a revenue winner for the station owner and the station can virtually *own* a desirable segment of the radio listening audience. Slightly more than half of the Classical listeners are female. While a sizeable number of listeners are over the age of 65, the format has a significant following among listeners ages 35–64. Classical listeners are also more likely to belong to households with higher incomes than listeners of other formats. The audience characteristics of the classical radio listener can help the station sell advertising time to advertisers who otherwise might not buy radio advertising time.

EVER-CHANGING FORMATS

All radio formats remain in a state of flux; the station desires consistency but it doesn't want its sound to become stale so new approaches are tested. Likewise, stations monitor the on-air sound of their competitors. When one station is successful with a new song, a new contest idea, a new promotion, a new identifier, other stations are quick to copy the successful strategy. Quincy McCoy, Senior Editor with Gavin.Com, notes that, "Content drives the radio industry . . . compelling content is what radio needs."[18] Content includes music, news, and talk but it also refers to air talent who remember that they provide a product that must be consistently important to the listener.

Who is actually in charge of the programming has changed as the radio industry has changed. Historically, an individual with the title of program director (PD) would program the station. Today, if the station has a program director, he or she likely will be responsible for the daily execution of the format by the staff of the station. This will include seeing that announcers follow the hot clock, use the correct positioning statements on-air, and generally maintain format continuity. Sometimes the PD may carry the title Operations Manager. The actual programming of the station is more likely to come through involvement of various research companies or programming consultants along with input from the program director, general manager, and probably the sales manager. These changes reflect both the competitive nature of the radio market and the increased pressure from profit-driven owners for the stations to perform well.

Radio stations have been facing increased competition from home audio sources, the Internet, and now from satellite-delivered audio services. Satellite-delivered radio programming, since the 1980s, has been available to station owners who wanted to cut costs while maintaining a consistent on-air sound. The latest satellite technology bypasses the terrestrial radio broadcaster much as Direct TV and The Dish Network have bypassed local television stations. Consumers seem to be less concerned with where the content comes from as long as it is content that satisfies their needs. Consumers, in droves, demonstrated this as they abandoned AM monaural signals for FM stereo.

It would be wrong to suggest that new technology is beginning to write the obituary of the radio industry; radio's obit has been incorrectly written in the past. Building a radio brand does become all the more important. A familiar product, one that consistently brings listeners back to a station on a daily basis, will determine the success of not just that individual station but it will also contribute to continuing consumer preference for over-the-air broadcasting. Success as a radio programmer is no longer a matter of selecting the right music or being an effective announcer. Yes, both are part of the equation. Figuring out who the audience is and what they want from a radio station, then consistently satisfying their wants, is the radio station's objective.

NOTES

[1] David MacFarland, *Contemporary Radio Programming Strategies* (Hillsdale, NJ: Lawrence Erlbaum, 1990), p. 1.

[2] Brian Mullen and Craig Johnson, *The Psychology of Consumer Behavior* (Hillsdale, NJ: Lawrence Erlbaum, 1990), p. 120.

[3] David MacFarland, loc. cit.

[4] J. T. Anderson, Duncan's American Radio, personal conversation, October 18, 1999.

[5] MacFarland, p. 21.

[6] Peter K. Pringle, Michael F. Starr and William McCavitt, *Electronic Media Management* (Woburn, MA: Butterworth-Heinemann, 1999), p. 123.

[7] Jim Duncan, *Duncan's American Radio: Tenth Anniversary Issue* (Kalamazoo, MI: Duncan's American Radio), p. A-29.

[8] National Format Shares, *R&R Ratings Report & Directory*, Vol. 1, 1999, p. 6.

[9] Kenneth C. Creech, *Electronic Media Law and Regulation,* 2nd ed. (Boston, MA: Focal Press, 1996), p. 186.

[10] Ibid.

[11] Katherine Young, "Radio Wins Ad Dollars as It Grows More Efficient," *Dallas Morning News,* November 8, 1998, p. 3H.

[12] Martin Peers, "Radio's Results: Genuine Gains, or a Dirge for the Urge to Merge?" *Wall Street Journal*, December 27, 1999, p. B8.

[13] MacFarland, p. 22.

[14] Edd Routt, Dr. James B. McGrath and Frederic A. Weiss, *The Radio Format Conundrum* (New York: Hastings House, 1978), p. 10.

[15] Ibid, p. 1.

[16] Kara Swisher, "Latest Twist for CNET: A Radio Deal," *Wall Street Journal*, January 4, 2000, pp. B1, B4.

[17] *Duncan's American Radio Fall 1998 Ratings Report* (Cincinnati, OH: Duncan's American Radio, L.L.C.), no page given. See listing for Chicago.

[18] Quincy McCoy, Gavin.Com, available at http://www.gavin.com/industry/9909/content.shtml

6

The Radio Brand
and Advertising

What do your favorite radio station and your favorite fast-food restaurant have in common? The instinctive answer a reader of a chapter on radio sales might give is to say that the radio station helps promote the fast-food restaurant by airing commercials. A better answer might be to suggest that the consumer has found the radio station and the fast-food restaurant to be acceptable **brands.** The products supplied by each business satisfy a user need.

Once the radio station has found a programming approach that satisfies listener needs, the station must begin to satisfy the needs of another group. The second group consists of advertising clients who purchase the radio station's ad time. For the potential advertiser, the radio station is not in the entertainment business but the **ear leasing** business. Just as the radio station must build listener awareness of its programming, advertising clients need listener awareness of the goods or services they sell and, most importantly, the clients need customer traffic. Selling any product involves satisfying needs. The job of the radio station is to provide the ears of listeners who will hear the ad buyer's message, then visit the store or otherwise obtain the product.

It is easy for listeners to criticize radio advertising. Commercials interrupt the music or talk programming we want to listen to. Commercials are played in blocks or sets sometimes consisting of six or more commercial units. Depending on spot lengths, a commercial break might consume five minutes of airtime. As distracting as commercials may sometimes seem to the listeners, radio stations from the earliest days recognized that there had to be a way for the station to pay for the operating expenses. For radio stations in the United States, this meant the adoption of commercial advertising.[1] Some countries, most notably the United Kingdom, funded their broadcast services by charging receiver license fees to pay for the operation of the broadcast services. Eventually, British listeners demanded more programming choices than the BBC provided and the British government authorized private, ad-supported broadcasters to begin operation.

At the least, listeners should think of advertising as the fuel that keeps the station running. And, when the advertising is sold effectively—based on the station's target audience and programming niche—the listener actually benefits by receiving worthwhile consumer information.

Radio stations and radio networks have increased the amount of money their clients spend on radio advertising. More than $15.4 billion was spent on radio advertising in 1998; about $11.9 billion was spent on local spot advertising.[2] Radio commercials are usually sold in lengths of :30 or :60 seconds. A Sales Manager or General Sales Manager supervises the day-to-day sales operation and helps make revenue projections for the station. The members of the sales staff are usually called "account executives" though some stations may refer to their AEs as Marketing Executives or Marketing Consultants.

It is the job of the **account executives** to prospect for potential clients, develop client presentations, secure advertising buys, and then service the account. Servicing includes ensuring that the ads run when they should, updating the ad copy as needed, and, in some smaller markets, even collecting payment from the client. This last issue can be especially awkward for the AE and client if the client fails to pay on time. Clients who don't pay their bills may cause the AE to receive a "charge back" (money previously paid to the AE is taken back out of a future paycheck) if the client never pays the bill. Some stations avoid this by only paying their staff based on revenue collected from clients.

As with any electronic medium, the biggest problem stations face is inventory management. For any broadcast station (radio or television), **inventory** refers to the number of commercials the station has available for sale. A newspaper has the ability to increase or decrease the number of pages printed or to increase or decrease the amount of news (versus advertising) that is published. For electronic media, advertising time is a product inventory that is an absolutely perishable commodity. Any commercial inventory not sold by the station is lost forever. There is no effective way for the station to store, save, or warehouse the unsold commercial inventory for use at a future time when demand is higher. Stations that add extra commercials to their schedule may experience short-term revenue increases but they are likely to experience declining ratings at a later time when listeners tune out the station because of the heavier commercial loads.

Radio, when compared with television, cable, newspaper, or magazine advertising, offers the advertiser some unique advantages. Nearly everyone listens to the radio. Radio reaches more than three fourths of all consumers every day and about 95 percent of all consumers each week.[3] That number exceeds the number of newspaper readers and television viewers. The typical person spends about three hours and eighteen minutes listening to radio on the average weekday.

Just as radio offers advantages, competitors can cite disadvantages of radio advertising. It is virtually impossible to buy advertising on just one or two radio stations and find that this meets the advertiser's marketing needs. The number of stations and their niche formats often mean that the advertiser must make a multiple-station buy. Radio is sometimes considered a "background" medium. Listeners often tune out commercials or, even worse, go to another station when the commercials air. Where people listen to the radio makes it difficult for consumers to benefit from certain types of product information, such as telephone numbers, addresses, or other product attributes. When a station's audience is perceived as being small, the client may think the ad buy will not be effective. When the station's listening audience is too large, the client may think an ad campaign involves overspending.

A strong economy in the 1990s, along with regulatory changes, has provided a robust advertising market. This market has encouraged the radio mergers and shielded station groups from potential problems associated with advertising sales. These problems include declining listenership and increasing ad costs. Thom Moon, director of research for Duncan's American Radio, estimates that radio listening is at its lowest level in twenty years.[4] *The Wall Street Journal* cites two studies that identify reasons for decreased listening.[5] A survey of 1,071 respondents by Edison Media Research found listener perceptions of increased ad clutter on many stations. The Wall Street firm BancBoston Robertson Stephens found commuters who owned a cell phone reported listening to the radio less than a year earlier.

Most radio sales managers will tell you the first job of the sales staff is to help clients understand how effective the radio medium is when compared with competing advertising media. The second job is to sell advertising time on the account executive's station. This is the toughest job. As with the increasing number of fast-food restaurants, the proliferation of radio stations and continued fragmentation of audiences have made it even more important for stations to market a station brand not only to listeners but to advertisers as well.

Advertisers are no longer buying just a mass audience from the station. An advertising executive once suggested that advertisers wanted the sizzle as well as the steak. For radio advertisers, this includes the station's **listener demographics** and the on-air presence of the station, which includes the announcers, music, and promotional events. As discussed in Chapter 5, listener demographics refers to the listener age range, gender, ethnicity, socioeconomic background, consumer spending patterns, plus a host of other qualitative variables.

The advertiser is interested in both the literal and hidden costs of advertising. The obvious cost is the cost of an advertisement, represented either through an actual dollar cost for the spot or the **cost per thousand (CPM).** The hidden cost refers to the quality or nature of the audience the advertiser is buying. How closely does this audience match the advertiser's customer profile? Significant deviation from the audience the advertiser needs to reach probably means the advertiser is making an inefficient advertising purchase.

Radio station owners and the industry trade organization, **The Radio Advertising Bureau,** work to maintain radio's position as a valuable ad source. (See RAB Profile, Figure 6-1.) Most radio station managers acknowledge that their biggest competitor is *not* another radio station in the market playing the same music and

FIGURE 6-1   Radio Advertising Bureau

The Radio Advertising Bureau (RAB) describes itself as the sales and marketing arm of the radio industry. Nearly 5,000 member stations, networks, and sales organizations in the United States and abroad are members of RAB. The RAB promotes the effectiveness of radio advertising, helps its members effectively market radio advertising to station clients, provides sales training for station employees, and serves as an information resource for station members.

A continuing theme for the RAB has been to promote the effectiveness of the radio industry as an advertising medium against other competing media. RAB's current campaign, titled Radio Gets Results, includes a focus on local stations providing specific examples of how the stations have solved marketing problems for clients. Gary Fries, President and CEO of the RAB, described the Radio Gets Results campaign as a way to provide the radio industry with documented proof of radio's unique ability to deliver outstanding results for its advertisers.

RAB has been aggressive in its use of the World Wide Web to supply station members with information (www.rab.com). *RadioLink* is RAB's twenty-four-hour Internet access service. Available through the World Wide Web is information to help radio account executives find clients, prepare client proposals, make client presentations, and become a marketing resource for advertising clients. RAB members will find RAB *Instant Backgrounds* on 150 businesses, promotional and sales ideas, consumer information from Simmons Study of Media and Markets and media information, including not only facts on radio usage but information to help account executives sell against other media such as newspapers, television, Yellow Pages, and the Internet.

Professional development is another role of RAB. Station members receive an RAB Sales and Marketing kit each month to help sales managers conduct successful sales meetings and to highlight new sales opportunities for account executives. RAB sales training includes four levels of sales certification: RMP (Radio Marketing Professional), CRMC (Certified Radio Marketing Consultant), CRMS (Certified Radio Marketing Specialist), and CRME (Certified Radio Marketing Expert). RAB calls certification, "the Radio equivalent to a CPA and the mark of a Radio Marketing Professional."* The first RAB training program was established in 1973. Persons wishing to receive the CRMA designation must combine knowledge gained from studying CRMC materials with what they know from day-to-day experience as a radio account executive. The three-hour written examination requires the demonstration of knowledge of the media industry to solve marketing problems for clients. RAB holds an annual three-day conference to bring together sales and marketing trainers and radio station staff members.

Unfortunately, much of the RAB's information is available only to members. The RAB's Website (http://www.rab.com) includes the *Radio Gets Results* station testimonials, media statistics, links to other sites, and the latest press releases from RAB, which often highlight industry trends.

Source: Used with permission, Radio Advertising Bureau.

*http://www.rab.com/pr/crmc.html

attempting to attract the same listener group. The biggest competitor for most radio stations are other media forms, such as television stations, newspapers, the Yellow Pages, billboards, and direct mail. Radio advertising, in 1998, received about 10 cents of every dollar spent on advertising. Television and newspapers each received about 33 cents of each advertising dollar. Yellow Pages advertising received about 8 cents of every dollar spent on advertising. On-line advertising is one of the fastest advertising growth segments, but only received about 1 cent of every dollar spent on advertising.[6] Convincing advertisers to divert money from other media buys to radio would increase the size of the advertising pie slice for the radio industry.

RADIO CONSOLIDATION AND THE EFFECT ON SALES

The radio industry has been influenced in several ways by passage of the Telecommunications Act of 1996. As we've talked about in Chapter 3, the Telecommunications Act enabled station owners to increase the number of station properties they owned in a single market. Radio consolidation has not yet helped the radio industry to sell more advertising, but consolidation has provided cost savings to the owners.[7] It has also allowed the radio industry to move away from its mom-and-pop status. In most of the major media markets, two-four owners have been able to purchase as many as eight stations each. This has affirmed the need for station account executives to sell the virtues of the radio medium and then to sell the specific audience of a radio station or stations they represent. Account executives who tried selling "against" other stations might find themselves selling against stations also owned by the same parent company. Besides buying multiple stations in the same market, some station groups have built regional station clusters.

Prior to its purchase by Clear Channel Communications, Jacor Communications was one of the first group owners to build station clusters. Jacor's strongest cluster was in its home market of Cincinnati, where the company controlled nearly half of the radio advertising revenue in the market. Cumulus Broadcasting has devised a station clustering technique that consists of small market stations. Chancellor Broadcasting, a successful large market station group, was itself purchased by Clear Channel Communications. Consolidation has led to a slowdown in sale approval for some radio properties as the Department of Justice has investigated the potential for monopoly control of the radio ad market by one or two owners. In some instances, stations groups have been forced to divest ownership of some stations before a consolidation purchase would be approved. Probably the best example of consolidation causing station divestiture was Chancellor Media's merger with Clear Channel Communications. Approximately 125 stations needed to be spun off to gain FCC and DOJ antitrust approval of the purchase of Chancellor by Clear Channel.

RADIO ADVERTISING CLIENTS

Radio stations generally sell advertising to three distinct groups of clients: local clients, regional clients, and national clients. The percentage of clients in each category usually depends on the size of the market the station operates in and the station's ratings. Successful stations in large markets command more national and regional advertising. Small market stations air primarily local ads. About 75 percent of all radio ad dollars are spent on local spot radio purchases.[8]

Even though most radio ad purchases are local, national manufacturers or distributors are often involved in local ad sales through **cooperative advertising programs.** Cooperative advertising, or co-op advertising, is a shared-cost ad program involving local retailers and national manufacturers or distributors. The national company provides an advertising allowance to the local retailer, usually determined by the dollar value of the inventory purchased from the national company. This advertising allowance can then be used to buy ads to promote the national brand and the local retailer.

A typical co-op plan might provide the local retailer with an ad allowance equal to 2 to 3 percent of the inventory brand purchased from the national company. The local retailer can use this money to pay advertising expenses to promote the national brand, though some national companies also require the local retailer to contribute to the ad costs. Depending on the size of the local retailer purchases, the money provided by a co-op program could range from several hundred to several thousand dollars. Cooperative ads also may include nationally produced radio commercials that only need the retailer's name added as a "local tag" at the end of the ad.

RADIO: REACH AND FREQUENCY

Radio advertising effectiveness is gauged by measuring the **reach** and **frequency** of ad exposure. *Reach* refers to the number of different people who are exposed to the ad while *frequency* refers to the number of times different people hear the ad. Most radio and television ads probably won't produce the degree of effectiveness the advertiser wants if consumers are exposed to the ad only one time. The nature of radio and television use suggests that consumers are often engaged in other activities while they listen to the radio or watch television. To create an impression in the consumer's mind, repeated exposure to the message (frequency) is typically needed.

Generally, if an advertiser began an advertising campaign by planning to run one commercial per hour between 6 A.M. and 6 P.M., the advertiser might reach the majority of the radio station's listeners. But, because people don't listen to the radio continuously, each listener might hear the ad only once or twice. To increase the likelihood that the ads would actually cause the consumer to take action, frequent exposures to the message are desired. Instead of scheduling only one day of commercials, the advertiser might schedule multiple days of advertising with one or more ads per hour during a selected time period.

RESEARCH AND RATINGS

How does the radio station account executive know how many listeners the station has? Just as research is important in programming a radio station, research is essential to the sales staff. The most widely used supplier of radio ratings information is the Arbitron Company, headquartered in Columbia, Maryland. Arbitron has been measuring radio listening since 1964. The company uses a personal, seven-day diary to measure radio listening in 260 markets, with 94 markets being measured year-round.[9]

Arbitron research data is an important part of station sales though Arbitron data and other forms of research are also used to help the station program effectively. Radio research plays three important roles for the radio station. First, research helps the station determine its programming approach. Second, once the programming is on the air, research enables the station's program director to determine the effectiveness of the format and to make appropriate adjustments in the on-air sound. These first two steps are brand building for the station, creating the ear product (listeners) the advertiser will want to buy. Third, research helps the station quantify and qualify the listening audience—advertisers want to know how many people are listening and just who the listeners are, with respect to age, income or gender. Most station account executives try not to sell a station solely on the ratings. Ratings will vary somewhat and most stations feel they can offer other marketing services to a business than just a quantitative number of listeners. But ratings are important.

Advertising agencies, representing national or international clients, need a way to compare the cost of advertising on various stations. Ratings data provides the comparison. Radio listening is tracked using fifteen-minute increments called *Average Quarter Hour* measures. Audience estimates can be expressed as rating percentages or as actual listener estimates in hundreds or thousands.

Gross Impressions and Cost Per Thousand are probably the two most common ad calculation comparisons. Gross Impressions provide a quantitative way to compare the ad exposures delivered by a proposed ad schedule or station with another ad schedule or station. Cost Per Thousand provides a way to compare the cost of reaching the targeted audience either on a single station or among multiple stations. Evaluations can be made based on all station listeners, usually referred to as listeners 12+, or evaluations can be made for particular audience segments, such as women 25–49 years of age.

Gross impressions (GI) are the actual number of impressions an ad schedule will deliver. GIs are calculated by multiplying the AQH persons estimate for the particular daypart by the number of spots to be run in the daypart.[10] The number of listeners or AQH persons is the number of persons listening to the station in a fifteen-minute period. Consider an ad schedule during morning drive to be purchased on stations A and B. One spot will air each hour between 6 and 10 A.M. Station A's AQH persons estimate is 100,000. Thus 4 spots × 100,000 AQH persons = 400,000 GIs. Station B's AQH persons estimate is 20,000 AQH. Thus 4 spots × 20,000 AQH persons = 80,000 GIs. If more than one daypart is involved in the ad purchase, the GIs for the various dayparts are summed to determine the total number of GIs for the ad schedule. GI calculations allow ad buyers to compare different stations in a market or different ad schedule proposals on a single station. They can also give the client a comprehensive look at what is being purchased when ads are placed on multiple stations within a radio market.

Cost per thousand, abbreviated as CPM, (the Roman numeral M equals 1,000) allows the advertiser to know how much money it costs to reach one thousand of the station's listeners. (This is sometimes referred to as *Listeners Per Dollar.*) The simplest way to calculate cost per thousand is to divide the cost of the ad by the number of listeners (in thousands) who are expected to hear the ad. Thus, if the commercial costs $50 and the station reaches 20,000, the cost per thousand is calculated by dividing $50 by 20. The resulting CPM is $2.50 to reach each one thousand listeners. The biggest problem many people face when doing CPM calculations is to remember that they are figuring a cost per thousand listeners. The listener figure needs to be thought of as twenty one-thousand listener groups rather than dividing the cost by 20,000 individual listeners.

Consider the example of morning drive advertising purchased on two radio stations. Station A charges $100.00 for a :30 spot that reaches 100,000 listeners. Station B charges $25.00 for a :30 spot that reaches 20,000 listeners. Which ad purchase is a better value for the advertiser? Station A's CPM is $1.00 ($100.00 ÷ 100 = $1). Station B's CPM is $1.25 ($25.00 ÷ 20 = $1.25). Station A, based solely on CPM, has a lower cost for each 1,000 persons reached and is a better ad buy. Other issues to consider might be station listener demographics. It is certainly possible that a more suitable listener profile might make the station with the higher CPM a more appropriate ad buy.

Another method for calculating CPM is to divide the total cost of the ad schedule by the total number of Gross Impressions:

A one-day ad schedule consisting of five spots costing $100.00 each and reaching an AQH of 100,000 persons, plus another seven spots costing $80.00 each and reaching an AQH of 70,000 persons, would produce the following calculations:

Total Gross Impressions for the schedule equal:

5 spots × 100,000 AQH = 500,000 GIs plus 7 spots × 70,000 AQH = 490,000 GIs, for a total of 990,000 GIs.

Total cost of the schedule equals:

5 spots × $100.00 = $500.00 plus 7 spots × $80.00 = $560.00 or a total schedule cost per day of $1,060.00.

To calculate CPM we take total schedule cost and divide this by GIs. $1,060.00 ÷ 990,000 GIs = .00107 × 1,000 = $1.07 CPM. *(This number has been rounded.)*

In this case, after we have divided the cost of the schedule by the GIs, we must multiply that product by 1,000 to arrive at a cost that represents the cost for reaching 1,000 listeners. (We might also choose to drop the extra zeros in our calculation: $1,060 ÷ 990 GIs = $1.07 CPM.)

Cost Per Thousand can be used to compare ad rates for different dayparts on the same station or to compare ad rates among several stations in the market. Cost Per Thousand is an effective way to evaluate station ad costs but usually isn't the only thing for an ad buyer or seller to consider. The listener profile of the station is important, as is the station's image in the community. There are stations and products that might not want to be associated with each other. A station with a religious format would probably never want to sell advertising time to an establishment that made most of its money from the sale of alcoholic beverages. An urban contemporary station would not likely sell ad time to a client who sold western boots and clothing. A traditional country station would probably never sell advertising to a teen-oriented clothing store.

It is also helpful for account executives and advertisers to know a station's **cume listeners.** *Cume listeners* refers to the exclusive listeners a station has. Rather than count listeners multiple times during the day, this calculation allows the advertiser to see how many different people listen to the station during a day. A CHR format will usually have greater listener turnover and a higher cume because there are usually several stations in a market with this format or a complementary format. A classical format, usually present on one station in the market, will have a smaller exclusive audience or cume.

Figure 6-2 illustrates additional calculations that can be used to evaluate ad purchases.

OPTIMUM EFFECTIVE SCHEDULING

Another ratings-related strategy used by radio stations to increase the effectiveness of a client's ad schedule is a technique called **Optimum Effective Scheduling (OES).** OES is based on the concept of audience turnover. Think about people who patronize a library and a convenience store. You will likely find the library has customers who stay for a longer period of time but it may have fewer total customers than the convenience store. If you were trying to reach customers in the convenience store with radio ads, you would need to repeat the ad broadcast in the convenience

FIGURE 6-2   Additional Advertising Buying and Selling Formulas

A variation on **Gross Impressions** is **Gross Ratings Points (GRPs)**. GRPs are the number of ratings points a schedule will deliver. GRPs may be calculated by dividing the Gross Impressions of an ad schedule by the market population. Another variation is to multiply the number of ratings delivered in a time period by the total number of spots to be aired in that time period. Five spots that air during a time period with an **Average Quarter Hour Rating (AQHR)** of 9 deliver 45 GRPs. Gross Ratings Points are, however, only a summary of the number of ratings points in an ad schedule. One hundred GRPs does not mean that 100 percent of the audience has been reached by the ad schedule.

Reverse Gross Impressions is a term used when calculating the number of spots needed on a competing station to match your station's Gross Impressions. To calculate, divide your station's Gross Impressions by the AQH Persons on a Competing Station.

Gross Impressions on Your Station ÷ AQH Persons on Competing Station = # of spots needed.

Cost Per Gross Rating Point is the average cost for one GRP in an ad schedule. Calculate by dividing the total cost of the schedule by the total number of GRPs.

Cost of Schedule ÷ GRPs = Cost Per Point

Reverse Cost Per Thousand is the maximum rate per spot that a competing station can charge to remain as cost-effective as your station.

(Your Station CPM × Competing Station AQH Persons) ÷ 1,000 = Reverse CPM

Account Executives sometimes perform CPM or other calculations with the help of a pocket calculator, but most stations also have a software program available to simplify the calculations. Arbitron provides Maximi$er 99[SM] for radio stations and Media Professional[SM] for advertising agencies and advertisers. TAPSCAN WORLDWIDE® is a division of Arbitron and offers additional software services to simplify ratings data analysis. Their services include software to analyze radio, TV, cable, print, and outdoor media through TAPSCAN®, TVSCAN®, QUALITAP[SM], TAPSCAN CUSTOM COVERAGE[SM], PRINTSCAN[SM], and MEDIAMASTER[SM]. These are proprietary software systems available to subscribing stations or station groups.

store more often because the customer group is constantly changing. That's the principle behind OES.[11]

Steve Marx and Pierre Bouvard wanted to balance the desire for ad frequency and reach while producing an effective commercial schedule. To accomplish their goal they developed Optimum Effective Scheduling.[12] Marx and Bouvard use station turnover or *T/O* (cume audience ÷ AQH) times a constant, 3.29, to determine the number of spots an advertiser should schedule each week. Thus a station with a turnover ratio of five would need 16 spots per week while a station with a turnover ratio of twenty would need to air about 66 spots each week to produce an effective ad schedule for the client.

From the standpoint of generating ad revenue for the radio station, stations with low turnover may be at a disadvantage when using OES. Because their listeners spend more time with the station, fewer spots are needed to produce an effective schedule of reach and frequency. Assuming ad rates per thousand listeners are reasonably comparable, these stations must attract more clients to generate the same amount of ad revenue as would a station with high listener turnover. Of course, as we discussed in Chapter 5, stations with high listener turnover have higher programming costs. They must spend more to promote the station's format and to attract new listeners.

RATE CARDS

Radio station advertising rates are typically shown on the station's **rate card.** Historically, the station produced one rate card that was typically valid for six months to a year. The card might list rates for program sponsorships, such as sponsoring a newscast or remote broadcast. The card also might specify a price discount provided to the advertiser for increasing the quantity of spots purchased. This rate card is sometimes referred to as a "quantity card" or "quantity-discount rate card." In some situations, especially in smaller markets, the quantity card may be an effective way of rewarding a client who spends more money with the station. The obvious drawback to this card is that the radio station, which has a limited inventory of commercial time, must discount the price of its product. The discount applies, no matter what the available advertising situation is like.

A better option used by most radio stations is the grid rate card system. The grid system is based on computerized inventory tracking that helps the radio station determine how much of its inventory is still available for sale. Depending on how the station chooses to track its inventory, the station can tabulate total commercial minutes sold or total number of commercial units available (:30 or :60 spots). The computer inventory tracking also allows the radio station to change the price of advertising on a daily basis.

Basic economic principles suggest that when the supply of a good decreases but demand remains high, the price of the good should increase. When the station has sold nearly all of the advertising it can effectively run, this indicates not only that the station has an effective sales force but that the station is perceived to be an effective marketing tool by its advertisers. Therefore, a successful station, as determined by high advertiser demand, should be able to charge more money for the remaining commercial units. A grid-rate card enables the station to adjust its ad rates according to the amount of inventory remaining.

Stations sometimes encounter clients who are hesitant to commit early to an ad schedule on the station. The grid-rate card can help the account executives pre-sell the station's inventory prior to peak demand periods. A retailer wanting to get the lowest ad rates available for pre-Christmas advertising would want to place an order with the station as soon as possible for Christmastime, perhaps as early as January 2. The longer an individual waits to place an order for a flight of commercials, the more likely the available supply of ad time will decrease and, correspondingly, the price of the remaining time will increase.

AGENCY SELLING

Account executives often do not deal directly with retailers or manufacturers. Instead, **advertising agencies** are the contact source the account executive must deal with if the AE wants to sell advertising time to retailers or manufacturers. The advertising agency may serve as a creative development center for the client by devising the marketing approach and advertising campaign for the client as well as coordinating advertising placement among various media including radio, television, and newspapers. Typically, the ad agency is paid a fee or commission based on the cost of a station's advertising. Not only does the radio station account executive receive a sales commission but the ad agency also receives a commission. The standard agency commission is 15 percent. If the ad agency buys $1,000.00 of advertising on a radio station, the purchase price is **grossed up** to include the agency commission. To add a 15 percent commission you would actually multiply $1,000.00 by the constant 1.1765. When you do the reverse math on $1,176.50 and subtract 15 percent, you will arrive at the $1,000.00 purchase price.

What did the advertising agency do to earn the 15 percent commission? Very little, some station account executives say. In fact, the ad agency serves as a gatekeeper to evaluate the effectiveness of a variety of advertising options and coordinate ad placement. Agencies evaluate station strength and ad costs by examining station ratings and computing CPMs and GIs. This is a vital role for large retailers or national brands. The client holds the ad agency accountable for the success of the marketing campaign.

VALUE-ADDED SELLING

Unlike television advertising or newspaper advertising, one of the strengths of radio advertising has always been **value-added selling.** Rather than sell a client only a schedule of commercials, many radio stations market the client's products through on-air giveaways, remote broadcasts, or other creative approaches that join the client brand with the station brand/image. These value-added approaches create value for the advertiser and offer another reason why the client should purchase advertising on the radio station.

Examples of value-added selling can include station giveaways. When a station gives away a vehicle or vacation package, the station probably wants to accomplish two things: to promote the station's format with current and potential listeners and create additional advertising opportunities. The giveaway allows the account executive to offer something special to a select group of sponsors. These sponsors may have remote broadcasts scheduled from their business or perhaps receive registration forms for customers to fill out to enter to win the vehicle. On-air announcer mentions identify registration locations and generate store traffic.

Radio production techniques offer additional value for the client. Radio copy and production techniques appeal to the "theater of the mind." While television ads may involve costly location shooting and tedious editing, radio copywriters and production staff can create multiple ad appeals for the client and typically not charge a production fee to the client. Production techniques allow minor changes to be made in the voice track of an ad while the same music and sound effects appear in the background.

THE BUSINESS OF SELLING

Radio account executives are usually paid according to their sales performance. This may mean they are paid a straight commission or a percentage of the sales dollars they generate. This compensation plan carries a strong incentive for the salesperson to produce results, but it also means the account executive has little job security. Another approach is to pay the account executive a draw against commission. The draw enables the account executive to establish a minimum compensation amount based on anticipated sales. Once this minimum is reached, additional compensation is paid through sales commissions. If an account executive accepts a draw and commission but later has a client who defaults on a bill, the account executive may have a **charge back** to the draw and commission. In other words, the account executive must return any income earned on ads that aired but were not paid for by the client.

Radio advertising sales, then, is a relationship business built on trust between the account executive and the client. It is in the best interest of both parties that each succeeds. The account executive (AE) is there to solve a problem for the client—generating store traffic and increasing sales. The relationship between the two is not a one-time event. Successful account executives may spend years working with successful business clients. As the client's business increases, the client may spend more money on the AE's station. Successful clients also provide sales referrals to other prospective clients of the account executive. The account executive also recognizes that the relationship with the client involves consultant selling or consultant marketing. Effective account executives may recommend other radio stations or advertising approaches for the business owner. This may initially reduce the ad money spent on the AE's station but it reflects the obvious: One radio station or even a station group in a major market can't accomplish everything a business owner may need to market his or her products or services.

As a matter of business ethics and professionalism, the radio account executive wants the business owner to succeed. A successful business is part of a healthy economy and means continued prosperity for the business owner and the radio station. It eventually means repeat advertising business for the radio station and thus strengthens the consultative relationship between the account executive and the business owner. Establishing this relationship is essential for the millions of people who make their living through some form of consultative sales.

Money magazine once asked its readers to determine what "Steve" did for a living. Among other things, a former neighbor described Steve as shy and withdrawn and meek and tidy. *Money* asked whether Steve was likely to make his living as a librarian or a salesman. The natural assumption is that Steve's personality type is that of a librarian. In fact, *Money* notes that Steve is about 75 times more likely to be a salesman.[13] The point of this example is to not ignore the obvious: Millions of people make their living in sales. They do sell a product or service but a sale occurs only if the client is convinced that the product satisfies a need. Successful account executives solve problems for their clients.

Radio consolidation has pushed radio stations into the most competitive environment the industry has encountered. While consolidation will result in greater pressure on general managers and sales managers to establish revenue forecasts and resulting pressure on account executives to achieve the revenue goals, the changes in the industry will likely produce a better trained sales force. To achieve the revenue objectives the owners need, they will need not only highly motivated employees but they will also need to train them to succeed, thus creating outstanding career opportunities.

NOTES

[1]Thomas Streeter, *Selling the Air: A Critique of the Policy of Commercial Broadcasting in the United States.* (Chicago: University of Chicago Press, 1996). This book provides an informative history of how commercial broadcasting developed in the United States.

[2]"Radio Revenue Is Growing," available online at http://www.rab.com/station/mgfb99/fac28.html, accessed January 4, 2000.

[3]Radio Reaches 75% of All Consumers Every Day," available at http://www.rab.com/station/mgfb99/fac1.html, accessed January 4, 2000 and "Radio Reaches 95% of All Consumers Every Week," available online at http://www.rab.com/station/mgfb99/fac2.html, accessed January 4, 2000. Calculated using data collected by RADAR ® 59, Fall 1998, © Statistical Research, Inc.

[4]Martin Peers, "Radio's Results: Genuine Gains or a Dirge for the Urge to Merge?" *Wall Street Journal*, December 27, 1999, p. B8.

[5]Ibid.

[6]Calculated from advertising spending estimates provided in *The Veronis, Suhler & Associates Communication Industry Forecast*, 12th ed. (New York: Veronis, Suhler & Associates, 1998), p. 84.

[7]See Martin Peers, op. cit.

[8]"Radio Revenue Is Growing," available online at http://www.rab.com/station/mgfb99/fac28.html, accessed January 4, 2000. Calculated using revenue totals supplied by RAB.

[9]*A Guide to Understanding and Using Radio Audience Estimates*, Arbitron, 1996, p. i.

[10]Ibid., p. 36.

[11]Ed Shane, *Selling Electronic Media* (Woburn, MA: Focal Press, 1999), p. 384.

[12]Steve Marx and Pierre Bouvard, *Radio Advertising's Missing Ingredient: The Optimum Effective Scheduling System*, 2nd ed. (Washington, DC: NAB Publications, 1993).

[13]Clint Willis, "The Ten Mistakes to Avoid with Your Money," *Money*, June 1990, p. 87.

7

Radio Research

DR. KATHLEEN A. FOX
Assistant Professor of Electronic Media and Film
Southern Methodist University

Radio consists of many intangible variables that affect its success as a business. Due to the nature of radio's product as one that people cannot touch or see, radio professionals have difficulty explaining the importance of their product to outsiders. Radio's profitability depends on selling advertising time to many companies unaware of radio's impact on its listeners. Historically, potential advertisers have been skeptical of radio's potential to attract loyal and attentive audiences. Advertiser skepticism is due to their doubt that an intangible medium like radio could persuade large numbers of consumers to purchase a product. This skepticism led to the rise of radio research initiated by advertisers, not broadcasters, to investigate how many people heard their messages and how effective the messages were.[1] Radio research still exists today to persuade advertisers that radio is a viable medium for advertiser money, and researchers continuously strive to improve the research process.

Research is the tool all radio stations use to measure their success. Radio research is important because it allows individual stations to compare themselves with other stations in the market, evaluate promotional activities, and examine trends in programming. Without research, stations would have little evidence of the size of their audience and the tastes of their audience. Not only does research serve as a vehicle to estimate audiences, but research also helps radio stations improve their ability to serve the needs of their audiences and advertisers.

One method of categorizing radio research is to divide the process into the divisions of sales research and programming research. Sales research is primarily concerned with ratings research, in other words, the *hard* numbers estimating the size of a station's audience. Account executives use these numbers to explain to potential advertisers the number of possible consumers, including the anticipated demographic makeup of the audience available through buying time at that radio station.

Programming research, on the other hand, is concerned with investigating the quality of the station's music, radio personalities, and promotions. Programming researchers examine listener attitudes to understand listening trends and motivations. Programming and sales research are essential to the success of a radio station. Programming research focuses on delivering a quality product to the station's listeners so they tune in to that particular station. Furthermore, programming research is important to the sales process because, without quality programming, audience numbers will decrease. If audience numbers decrease, sales research will reflect poor numbers and harm the sales process.

So, who conducts all this essential research? Research is usually generated by one of three groups of people: rating firms, individual consultants, or an in-house department. Rating firms collect data from listeners regarding listening patterns for an entire radio market without special attention to any one station. The most widely known and used rating firm in radio is **Arbitron Research,** discussed in some detail later in this chapter. Examples of other radio ratings services include AccuRatings from Strategic Media Research and Statistical Research.

Another group of researchers is individual consultants. Many radio stations hire individual consultants (i.e., Ed Shane, Mike McVay) to conduct programming research for them. These consultants analyze data concerning listener perceptions of the station exclusively for that station. Often consultants help a station to gain a competitive edge over other stations in the market.

Finally, some stations have an in-house department that conducts research for the station. This research is usually programming research because no one would believe ratings collected by the station itself. An in-house research department can be very beneficial because researchers gathering the information are in tune with the programming needs of the station. However, due to their high cost, in-house research departments are usually only found in larger market radio stations, which draw more advertising revenue and can afford the cost.

It is essential to understand the importance of research to the success of a radio station before attempting to understand how to interpret radio research. Advertisers need proof that their money is being spent wisely and that the message is actually reaching potential consumers. Not only does research help estimate the total number of listeners being reached, but research helps paint a picture of who those listeners are. Advertisers are concerned with reaching only their specific target audience, in other words, those people who are most likely to purchase their particular product. This is where the beauty of radio lies. Radio, due to formatting, is an ideal medium for targeting a specific *demographic* group.

For example, a local beauty salon may wish to advertise on the radio, but may only want to reach women because they are the most frequent users of a salon. A locally owned beauty salon, which probably does not have a great deal of money to spend on advertising, would only want to buy time on a radio station geared toward women. An adult contemporary station would be ideal for the salon to consider because it targets women between the ages of 25–49. Furthermore, radio is relatively inexpensive for the local advertiser compared to mediums such as television or magazines. Buying time in a medium that has a mass audience of both men and women would waste the advertising money on a great number of people who have no intention of using the product.

Radio is an ideal advertising medium for both local and national companies. However, radio needs to continually improve its own product, which is entertainment, and prove that people are listening. This is where radio research enters the picture. The remainder of this chapter will demonstrate in detail the importance of sales research and programming research, and conclude with some thoughts on future advances in radio research.

SALES RESEARCH

Radio sales research consists of two different types of research: quantitative and qualitative research. Quantitative research explains the data in numbers. Quantitative research asks questions such as "How many people listen to radio?" and "How many hours a day does the average person listen to the radio?" Qualitative research gathers more in-depth data that explains the reasons why something occurs. Qualitative research asks questions such as "Why do you listen to radio?" and "What qualities do you look for in a radio station?" Quantitative research uses methods such as survey research, while qualitative research employs methods such as personal interviews and focus groups.

Arbitron

An important tool for account executives in the radio sales business is "the book." The *Arbitron Market Report,* commonly referred to as "the book," is the industry standard for quantitative radio data. Arbitron, a company that surveys radio listeners in local markets nationwide, sells its book of listener behavior data to radio stations to use in their sales and programming decisions. While other companies have attempted to compete with Arbitron to be the national leader in quantitative data for radio, Arbitron remains the industry leader in ratings research. Because Arbitron is the leader in ratings research, the next several pages will concentrate solely on how Arbitron gathers radio data and how to interpret Arbitron data.

Sample Procedures

One of the most important questions to ask when interpreting research data is "How was the sample constructed?" A **sample** is simply the group of people who participated in the study. It is important that one group of people (i.e., men) is not given more opportunity to participate in a study than another group of people because it will skew the results. In a quantitative study, every member of the population should have an equal chance of being selected.

In creating a sample, Arbitron defines radio markets as one of the following: the Metro, TSA, or DMA (see Figure 7-1). The **Metro** is a geographic area used by Arbitron and is defined by Arbitron subscribers.[2] The Metro is the smallest of the three geographic distinctions. **TSA,** the next geographic distinction, stands for Total Survey Area. The TSA is a geographic area that expands the Metro by a few additional counties. **DMA** stands for Designated Market Area, defined using A. C. Nielsen's television rating report. The DMA is composed of sampling units and every county or split county within the sampling unit is assigned exclusively to only one DMA. Arbitron uses the DMA distinction in only the top fifty radio market reports.[3]

In evaluating research, it is not only important to know who was included in a sample, it is just as important to understand how a sample is derived. Arbitron generates a sample through a random selection process of both listed and unlisted telephone numbers. The addresses for these households are then located and initial contact is made by mail, informing them of their selection and that they will be telephoned soon about their participation in the study. Households are telephoned to gain consent, to determine the number of persons over the age of twelve, and to determine the race/ethnicity and demographics of the household. Arbitron includes all persons over the age of twelve who have consented to the study in the sample. Arbitron includes monetary incentives of varying amounts, depending on race/ethnicity, to encourage greater participation.[4]

Methodology

Arbitron conducts its survey on a quarterly basis. Large markets are surveyed four times a year for a twelve-week period in the winter, spring, summer, and fall. Every Arbitron market is surveyed at least once a year in the spring; some markets are surveyed twice a year every spring and fall.[5] While all radio stations are included in the survey, it is important to note that it is the decision of each individual station as to whether it decides to purchase the results of the study.

Arbitron distributes a **diary** to the sample to measure radio audience listening behaviors (see Figure 7-2). All members of the sample receive a personal diary. Each person is asked to record all radio usage both in and outside of the home. The Arbitron diary week begins on Thursday and ends on Wednesday. Respondents are expected to record the time they began listening, station call-letters, station name, program name, whether the station is AM or FM, and where they were listening to the radio. In some of the smaller markets, Arbitron also asks a few qualitative questions in the back of the radio diary. The qualitative questions include information concerning employment, retail purchases, fast-food consumed, television networks viewed, and other categories.[6]

Dallas-Ft. Worth

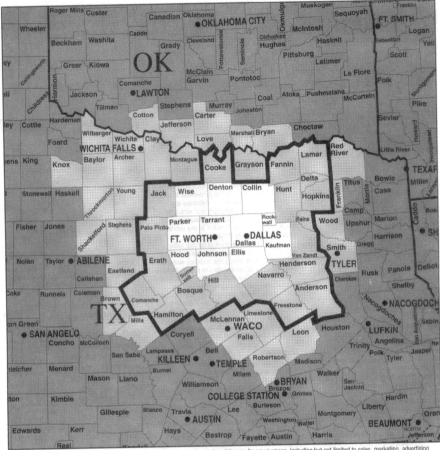

© 1999 The Arbitron Company   Nonsubscribers to this report may not reproduce this map for any purpose, including but not limited to sales, marketing, advertising or promotional purposes, without the express written permission of The Arbitron Company.

☐ **Metro**   ▨ **TSA**   ▩ **DMA**®

TSA and DMA sampled in Spring and Fall only.
For definitions of the terms Metro, TSA and DMA, see Page M3, Paragraph 1, and Page M7, "Selected Arbitron Terms."

Metro Rank: 7
Market Surveyed: Winter, Spring, Summer, Fall

Station Subscribers to This Report*					
KBFB-FM	KDGE-FM	KDMX-FM	KDXX-AM	KDXX-FM	KEGL-FM
KESS-AM	KHCK-FM	KHKS-FM	KHVN-AM	KKDA-AM	KKDA-FM
KKZN-FM	KLIF-AM	KLUV-AM	KLUV-FM	KMEO-FM	KOAI-FM
KPLX-FM	KRBV-FM	KRLD-AM	KRNB-FM	KSCS-FM	KTCK-FM
KTXQ-FM	KVIL-FM	KYNG-FM	KZPS-FM	WBAP-AM	

Station subscribers as of release to print.

ARBITRON

FIGURE 7-1   Dallas–Ft. Worth Radio Market (Metro, TSA, DMA)
© 1999 The Arbitron Company

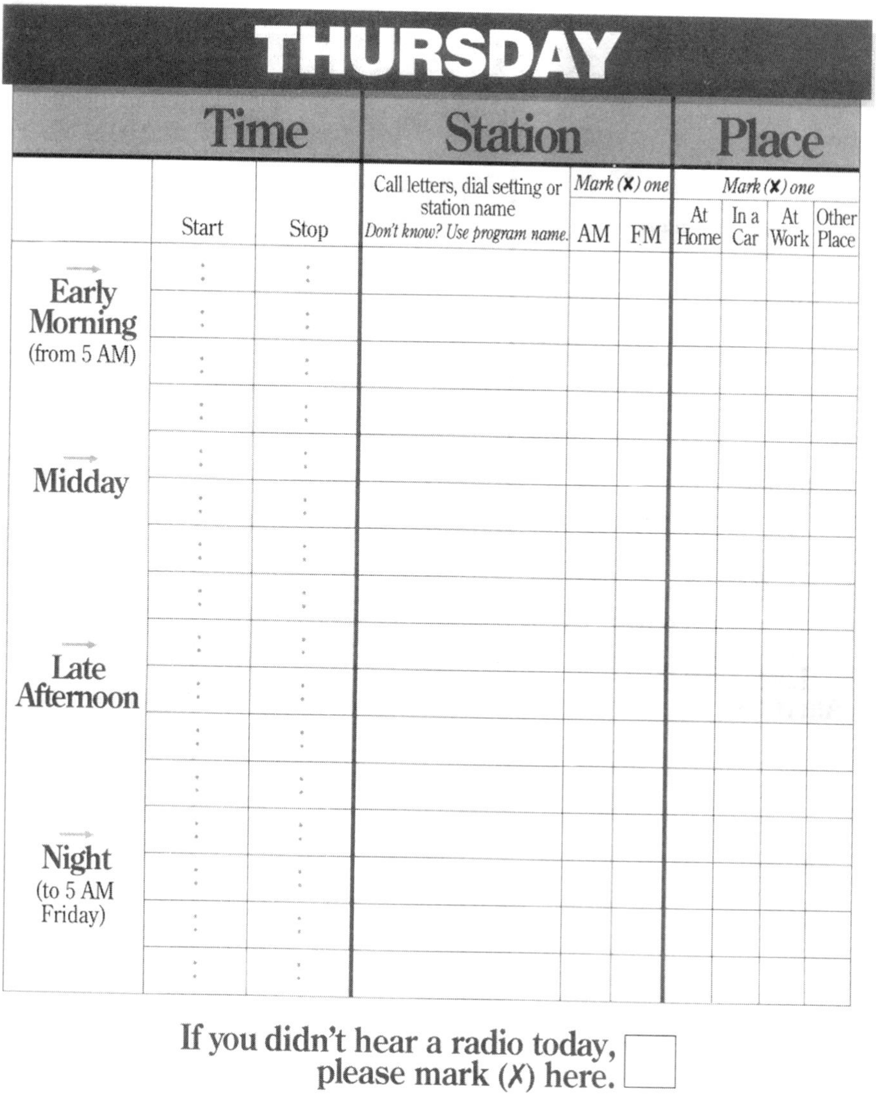

THURSDAY

Time		Station			Place			
Start	Stop	Call letters, dial setting or station name *Don't know? Use program name.*	*Mark (✗) one* AM	FM	*Mark (✗) one* At Home	In a Car	At Work	Other Place
Early Morning (from 5 AM)								
Midday								
Late Afternoon								
Night (to 5 AM Friday)								

If you didn't hear a radio today, please mark (✗) here. ☐

FIGURE 7-2   Arbitron Company Sample Diary Page
© 1999 The Arbitron Company

After placing the diaries with sample members, Arbitron makes further contact reminding individuals to return the diary to achieve a high return rate. The more diaries returned the more accurate the results of the study; however, the company is lucky if a 50 percent response rate is achieved in a local market.[7]

After Arbitron collects the diaries, the data is analyzed. Diaries that are not legible or accurate are eliminated from the sample. The usable diaries are tabulated and quantified into numbers. Arbitron has a complex process of creating numbers that reflect a demographic breakdown of listener behavior during the particular survey period. Arbitron breaks listener responses into demographic groups, separating overall audience, men, and women in the following age designations: 12+, 12–24, 18–34, 18–49, persons 25–49, 25–54, and 35–64. Teen listening is also included in the market report.

Arbitron Report

The *Arbitron Market Report,* once completed, is distributed to corporations, stations, advertising agencies, and other clients that have paid Arbitron for its services. Radio stations purchase the Arbitron book primarily for one reason: to sell radio time. While the book does help programming understand how it fares compared to other stations, radio managers buy the book to help their sales staff sell advertising time. Having high numbers in the Arbitron book can mean great profits for a radio station and high commissions for account executives. Every station eagerly awaits the distribution of the Arbitron Report each quarter with the hope of high ratings.

Once the Arbitron book reaches individual stations, managers and account executives analyze the numbers and demographic data to determine the best way to approach current and potential advertising clients. Advertising clients want some proof that if they buy advertising time they will get a return on their investment. Radio account executives use the *Arbitron Market Report* to convince clients that buying time on their station will allow the client to reach the number of people reflected in the book. It is important to remember, however, that the numbers reflect how the station has performed in the past, not how the station will perform in the future. The account executive's job is to convince the client that, of course, the station will reach at least as many people in the future.

Of all sales professions, radio account executives have one of the most difficult products to sell. Many clients are skeptical of radio's ability to reach consumers because they have difficulty visualizing the results. The Arbitron book provides account executives with tangible numbers to help convince clients that the people the client wants to reach are listening to their radio station. In order to sell radio, account executives need to be able to understand and explain the Arbitron book to clients. The following section provides a brief explanation of selected Arbitron terms.

Interpreting the Arbitron Book

At first glance, the Arbitron book appears to be an endless number of pages with strange numbers and charts. However, Arbitron has separated the material into relatively easy-to-understand sections so advertising clients, who have less training in the book's content, can understand the importance of the numbers. Before understanding how to read individual Arbitron pages, one must understand a few essential terms.

Average Quarter Hour
Radio listening is measured using the average quarter hour. Listeners must report listening to a particular radio station for at least five minutes within a period of fifteen minutes in order to be counted. In radio research, each hour is separated into quarter hours instead of half hours or hours because radio listeners often switch stations.

PUR
PUR stands for **persons using radio.** Reflected as a number, this term represents the total number of people who have a radio turned on. This term is important in calculating share (discussed later).

Daypart
Radio listening is separated into different time periods throughout the day. Arbitron separates these time periods, called *dayparts,* into the following categories: 6 A.M.–10 A.M., 10 A.M.–3 P.M., 3 P.M.–7 P.M., 7 P.M.–midnight, and overnights.

TSL
TSL stands for **time spent listening**. TSL estimates the amount of time an average person spends listening to a particular station or radio in general, during a specific daypart. This estimate is provided for the Metro only. Time spent listening numbers are important because advertisers want to be convinced that listeners do not switch radio stations every time a commercial break begins. This figure helps account executives persuade advertisers that listeners tune to their station even through the commercials.

Cume
The term *cume* stands for *cumulative audience.* Cume is the estimated number of *different* people who have listened to a particular station for a minimum of five minutes during the quarter hour. A cumulative audience may be important to an advertiser who wants to reach a large number of different people instead of reaching the same people repeatedly. For example, a store with a grand opening may be more concerned with advertising its location to every person in the area once rather than only a few people several times.

Rating
Possibly, the most important and well-known term of the Arbitron book is **rating.** To calculate a rating, use the following formula:

$$\text{Rating} = \frac{\text{People tuned to a particular station}}{\text{Population}}$$

Ratings estimate the number of people within the target population that are tuned to a particular station and the market in general. This number is important in the sales process because it estimates a percentage of the total population that tunes to a particular station.

Share

A share is an estimate of the number of people who have their radios turned on and tuned to a particular station. Share is calculated through the following formula:

Share = People tuned to a particular station
         PUR (Persons Using Radio)

While share can be important to radio sales, it is more critical in radio programming decision making. Share differs from rating because it estimates the number of people who cared to turn on their radio that are listening to your station; rating estimates people who have their radio on or off that are listening to your station. In other words, share penetration gives programmers an idea of how many people who want to listen to the radio have tuned to their station instead of the competition.

Now that you understand some of the key terms of an *Arbitron Radio Market Report,* let's examine a page from the Report (Figures 7-3 and 7-4). Figure 7-3 represents Target Listener Estimates for Persons 12+ in the Dallas–Fort Worth radio market. The page is separated into five dayparts across the top of the page to illustrate listening patterns at different times of the day. Underneath the dayparts are estimates for the AQH, Cume, AQH rating, and AQH share. The left side of the page lists individual station call letters listed along with their numbers for that particular book and the totals for all four quarterly reports in that year.

Let us examine one station, KSCS-FM in the Dallas–Fort Worth market in both Figure 7-3, persons 12+, and Figure 7-4, women 18–49. For persons 12+ during the Monday–Friday 6 A.M.–7 P.M. time slot, KSCS has an AQH rating of 1.1 and an AQH share of 5.2 for the winter of 1999. For women 18–49 in the same time slot, KSCS has an AQH rating of 1.6 and an AQH share of 6.8. As you can see, KSCS's rating and share rise when broken down into the demographic of women 18-49. Actually, no other station in the market has a higher rating or share for this demographic group during the summer of 1999. This is where the Arbitron rating book will help KSCS sell airtime. KSCS will showcase the book's numbers to advertisers desiring to reach women within this age group and point out that no other station in the market reached as many women in the 18–49 category.

Criticisms of Ratings Research

Arbitron is the leader of ratings research in the radio industry. However, its research process is not without fault. Most people within the radio industry would agree that ratings research is flawed but accept the system because it is the industry standard in

Listener Estimates/Metro

Target Listener Estimates

Persons 12+

	Monday-Friday 6AM-7PM				Weekend 6AM-MID				Saturday 6AM-10AM				Saturday 10AM-3PM				Saturday 3PM-7PM			
	AQH (00)	Cume (00)	AQH Rtg	AQH Shr	AQH (00)	Cume (00)	AQH Rtg	AQH Shr	AQH (00)	Cume (00)	AQH Rtg	AQH Shr	AQH (00)	Cume (00)	AQH Rtg	AQH Shr	AQH (00)	Cume (00)	AQH Rtg	AQH Shr
+KXZN-FM																				
WI '99	**	38	**	**	2	11	**	**	**	**	**	**	**	**	**	**	**	**	**	**
4-Book	**	**	**	**	**	**	**	**	**	**	**	**	**	**	**	**	**	**	**	**
KLTY-FM																				
WI '99	306	2665	.8	3.7	181	2159	.5	4.3	168	606	.4	3.5	312	1013	.8	4.4	231	807	.6	4.3
4-Book	257	2482	.7	3.2	149	1951	.4	3.6	142	539	.4	3.1	251	837	.7	3.6	175	620	.5	3.4
+KLUV-AM																				
WI '99	41	520	.1	.5	19	318		.4	24	106	.1	.5	48	158	.1	.7	37	109	.1	.7
4-Book	39	543	.1	.5	18	283		.4	21	71	.1	.5	36	114	.1	.5	22	64	.1	.5
KLUV-FM																				
WI '99	265	2794	.7	3.2	133	2019	.3	3.1	166	574	.4	3.5	225	832	.6	3.2	177	665	.5	3.3
4-Book	277	3436	.7	3.4	163	2328	.4	3.9	179	604	.5	3.9	299	1019	.8	4.2	225	786	.6	4.3
+KMEO-FM KNKI-FM																				
WI '99	70	1029	.2	.8	53	751	.1	1.2	41	162	.1	.9	99	322	.3	1.4	96	282	.3	1.8
4-Book	**	**	**	**	**	**	**	**	**	**	**	**	**	**	**	**	**	**	**	**
KOAI-FM																				
WI '99	244	2347	.6	3.0	123	1412	.3	2.9	116	394	.3	2.4	198	561	.5	2.8	165	560	.4	3.0
4-Book	248	2328	.7	3.1	140	1641	.4	3.3	123	440	.3	2.7	243	670	.7	3.5	180	531	.5	3.5
KPLX-FM																				
WI '99	306	3084	.8	3.7	167	1906	.4	3.9	214	642	.6	4.5	279	812	.7	3.9	192	607	.5	3.5
4-Book	296	3193	.8	3.7	154	1983	.4	3.7	161	569	.5	3.5	296	891	.8	4.2	194	636	.5	3.8
KRBV-FM																				
WI '99	137	1948	.4	1.7	108	1532	.3	2.5	93	325	.2	2.0	147	580	.4	2.1	134	427	.4	2.5
4-Book	172	1984	.5	2.1	119	1499	.3	2.8	110	358	.3	2.4	174	548	.5	2.5	128	385	.4	2.5
KRLD-AM																				
WI '99	331	3896	.9	4.0	111	1799	.3	2.6	254	856	.7	5.3	180	681	.5	2.5	98	417	.3	1.8
4-Book	320	3898	.9	4.0	122	1929	.3	2.9	245	832	.7	5.3	181	676	.5	2.5	83	345	.2	1.6
KRNB-FM																				
WI '99	52	938	.1	.6	35	491	.1	.8	23	69	.1	.5	34	119	.1	.5	51	120	.1	.9
4-Book	56	918	.2	.7	38	572	.1	.9	34	111	.1	.8	47	181	.1	.7	52	173	.1	1.0
KSCS-FM																				
WI '99	430	3690	1.1	5.2	215	2507	.6	5.1	239	744	.6	5.0	382	1177	1.0	5.4	301	904	.8	5.5
4-Book	420	3964	1.1	5.2	208	2602	.6	5.0	244	776	.7	5.3	346	1145	.9	4.9	287	930	.8	5.5
KTCK-AM																				
WI '99	215	1490	.6	2.6	51	1018	.1	1.2	75	295	.2	1.6	95	358	.2	1.3	64	242	.2	1.2
4-Book	256	1739	.7	3.2	58	917	.1	1.4	98	326	.3	2.1	109	362	.3	1.6	58	239	.2	1.1
KTXQ-FM																				
WI '99	271	2989	.7	3.3	158	1955	.4	3.7	151	519	.4	3.2	310	956	.8	4.4	264	724	.7	4.9
4-Book	233	2947	.6	2.9	123	1780	.3	2.9	119	420	.3	2.6	246	817	.7	3.5	183	629	.5	3.5
KVIL-FM																				
WI '99	406	3815	1.1	4.9	187	2087	.5	4.4	224	795	.6	4.7	307	932	.8	4.3	217	679	.6	4.0
4-Book	429	4005	1.2	5.3	186	2664	.5	4.5	203	731	.6	4.4	274	942	.7	3.9	215	696	.6	4.2
KWRD-FM																				
WI '99	53	807	.1	.6	9	210		.2	22	50	.1	.5	15	53		.2	7	36		.1
4-Book	56	718	.1	.7	10	191		.3	17	52	.1	.4	15	45		.2	11	33		.2
KXEB-AM																				
WI '99	57	571	.1	.7	48	503	.1	1.1	45	173	.1	.9	113	358	.3	1.6	90	235	.2	1.7
4-Book	**	**	**	**	**	**	**	**	**	**	**	**	**	**	**	**	**	**	**	**
KYNG-FM																				
WI '99	210	2433	.5	2.5	132	1554	.3	3.1	156	515	.4	3.3	197	642	.5	2.8	160	579	.4	2.9
4-Book	219	2786	.6	2.7	127	1664	.3	3.0	131	422	.4	2.8	210	722	.6	3.0	159	556	.4	3.0

** Station(s) not reported this survey. * Listener estimates adjusted for reported broadcast schedule. + Station(s) changed call letters – see Page 13. 4-Book: Avg. of current and previous 3 surveys. 2-Book: Avg. of most recent 2 surveys.

DALLAS-FT. WORTH

ARBITRON

20

WINTER 1999

FIGURE 7-3   Dallas–Ft. Worth Market, Persons 12+ Target Listener Estimates

© 1999 The Arbitron Company

Target Listener Estimates

Women 18-49

Station	MF 6AM-7PM AQH (00)	Cume (00)	AQH Rtg	AQH Shr	WE 6AM-MID AQH (00)	Cume (00)	AQH Rtg	AQH Shr	Sat 6AM-10AM AQH (00)	Cume (00)	AQH Rtg	AQH Shr	Sat 10AM-3PM AQH (00)	Cume (00)	AQH Rtg	AQH Shr	Sat 3PM-7PM AQH (00)	Cume (00)	AQH Rtg	AQH Shr
+KXZN-FM WI '99	**	9	**	**	**	**	**	**	**	**	**	**	**	**	**	**	**	**	**	**
4-Book																				
KLTY-FM WI '99	165	1382	1.4	5.9	98	1055	.8	7.4	83	298	.7	6.4	186	530	1.5	8.2	126	407	1.0	7.4
4-Book	133	1224	1.1	4.9	75	944	.6	5.8	68	275	.6	5.3	130	435	1.1	5.7	91	321	.8	5.6
+KLUV-AM WI '99	3	63		.1	1	44		.1	2	9		.2	2	8		.1	8	26	.1	.5
4-Book	6	96	.1	.2	2	43		.2	3	4		.2	6	17		.3	7	15	.1	.5
KLUV-FM WI '99	105	903	.9	3.8	38	635	.3	2.9	45	165	.4	3.5	79	250	.7	3.5	52	198	.4	3.1
4-Book	94	1158	.8	3.4	49	752	.4	3.8	54	194	.5	4.2	91	309	.8	4.0	67	263	.6	4.1
+KMEO-FM KNKI-FM WI '99	26	346	.2	.9	18	254	.1	1.4	11	43	.1	.8	26	94	.2	1.1	20	66	.2	1.2
4-Book	**	**	**	**	**	**	**	**	**	**	**	**	**	**	**	**	**	**	**	**
KOAI-FM WI '99	103	878	.9	3.7	36	498	.3	2.7	30	119	.2	2.3	54	160	.4	2.4	48	175	.4	2.8
4-Book	92	794	.8	3.4	42	517	.4	3.2	31	124	.2	2.4	74	199	.6	3.2	58	175	.5	3.5
KPLX-FM WI '99	116	1173	1.0	4.2	49	719	.4	3.7	54	221	.4	4.2	79	301	.7	3.5	81	263	.7	4.8
4-Book	110	1272	1.0	4.1	48	732	.4	3.7	45	190	.4	3.6	99	338	.8	4.4	66	241	.6	4.0
KRBV-FM WI '99	73	848	.6	2.6	52	715	.4	3.9	40	146	.3	3.1	56	244	.5	2.5	55	182	.5	3.2
4-Book	82	853	.7	3.0	55	666	.5	4.2	45	153	.4	3.5	77	245	.7	3.4	57	168	.5	3.5
KRLD-AM WI '99	62	854	.5	2.2	11	251	.1	.8	19	79	.2	1.5	15	91	.1	.7	14	66	.1	.8
4-Book	69	886	.6	2.6	18	310	.2	1.3	36	136	.3	2.8	29	114	.2	1.3	12	56	.1	.7
KRNB-FM WI '99	25	460	.2	.9	22	283	.2	1.7	19	40	.2	1.5	28	86	.2	1.2	33	90	.3	1.9
4-Book	27	439	.2	1.0	20	304	.2	1.5	13	41	.1	1.0	24	98	.2	1.1	26	99	.2	1.6
KSCS-FM WI '99	190	1469	1.6	6.8	80	1033	.7	6.1	59	195	.5	4.5	159	521	1.3	7.0	110	336	.9	6.5
4-Book	154	1458	1.3	5.6	71	954	.6	5.5	73	238	.6	5.7	123	438	1.0	5.4	98	334	.8	6.0
KTCK-AM WI '99	4	109		.1	2	112		.2		6			2	16		.1	3	11		.2
4-Book	12	188	.1	.4	5	107	.1	.4	2	13		.2	9	37	.1	.4	6	25		.3
KTXQ-FM WI '99	124	1440	1.0	4.4	77	997	.6	5.8	63	288	.5	4.9	157	480	1.3	6.9	125	384	1.0	7.3
4-Book	87	1118	.7	3.1	47	720	.4	3.6	42	169	.3	3.3	99	333	.8	4.4	64	236	.5	3.9
KVIL-FM WI '99	155	1480	1.3	5.6	44	699	.4	3.3	55	215	.5	4.2	72	273	.6	3.2	66	186	.5	3.9
4-Book	192	1665	1.6	7.0	57	950	.5	4.4	67	248	.6	5.2	91	354	.8	4.0	75	247	.6	4.6
KWRD-FM WI '99	20	332	.2	.7	1	35		.1		4			1	6			1	16		.1
4-Book	20	282	.2	.7	1	44		.1	1	4		.1	2	9		.1	1	6		.1
KXEB-AM WI '99	1	22			2	27		.2	2	8		.2	1	18			7	18	.1	.4
4-Book	**	**	**	**	**	**	**	**	**	**	**	**	**	**	**	**	**	**	**	**
KYNG-FM WI '99	80	1131	.7	2.9	55	680	.5	4.2	56	185	.5	4.3	75	283	.6	3.3	78	265	.6	4.6
4-Book	92	1262	.8	3.4	48	698	.4	3.7	44	152	.4	3.4	86	323	.7	3.7	63	227	.5	3.8

** Station(s) not reported this survey.   * Listener estimates adjusted for reported broadcast schedule.   + Station(s) changed call letters - see Page 13.   4-Book: Avg. of current and previous 3 surveys.   2-Book: Avg. of most recent 2 surveys.

FIGURE 7-4   Dallas–Ft. Worth Market, Women 18–49 Target Listener Estimates

© 1999 The Arbitron Company

audience measurement. Many radio stations are able to compete effectively by using the Arbitron book to sell airtime and therefore feel no need to change the system. Ratings research is often criticized for its sampling process and methodology. Some people believe that not enough people or the wrong people are included in ratings research. Others say using a diary to collect data is a poor way to estimate radio audience size. In the book *Audience Ratings,* Hugh "Mal" Beville summarized the national criticisms of ratings research as the following:

1. Ratings are not accurate.
2. Ratings are biased.
3. Ratings are misleading.
4. Ratings are misused.[8]

First, some people believe ratings data is not accurate because samples are too small, listeners may not accurately complete the diary, and ethnic groups tend to be underrepresented. Second, ratings are biased in the sense that stations have more promotion and publicity during rating periods. Third, ratings can be misleading because they only determine if a listener had a particular radio station tuned in, not whether the commercials were effective in gaining listener attention. Fourth, ratings can be misused because programmers may retain poor quality programs because they create high ratings, or ratings can cause stations to overemphasize ratings and profits over quality.[9]

Ratings research is regulated by the **Electronic Media Rating Council (EMRC).** The EMRC serves as a watchdog within the broadcast industry to assure that research is conducted honestly and that stations do not unfairly use their programming to boost ratings. Arbitron, as well as many other firms, receives accreditation by the EMRC to demonstrate its integrity to clients.

Other Sales Research

Arbitron, while the leader in providing ratings research, is not the only company involved in providing research data for local radio sales. AccuRatings also collects data for local radio stations to assist them in their sales efforts. Network radio audiences are collected and measured by Statistical Research in the **Radio All-Dimensional Audience Report (RADAR).**

Another research firm used widely in the sales process is Scarborough research. While not a research firm that measures radio alone, Scarborough is a leading local market research tool providing qualitative research. Scarborough surveys consumer behavior for 64 DMAs and provides comprehensive market measurements of media usage, retail shopping, demographics, lifestyle, and other consumer behaviors.[10] Scarborough research does help local radio sell airtime because it serves as a tool for account executives to explain the needs and wants of local consumers to potential advertising clients.

While not considered a research method, another sales technique should be mentioned in this chapter. Arbitron has created several software tools to help local stations analyze Arbitron research data and incorporate it in their local marketing plans. Some of the key applications Arbitron offers its radio clients are Maximi$er 99SM and TAPSCAN. The computer applications help stations customize survey areas, demographics, dayparts, and target audience to help account executives sell the airtime for a station.[11]

PROGRAMMING RESEARCH

While sales research is concerned with selling radio airtime, programming research is concerned with improving the quality of programming at the radio station. Programming departments at radio stations are constantly evaluating their performance. Good programmers understand the tremendous impact quality programming has on the success of a radio station. Quality programming brings listeners to a station, which brings high ratings, which in turn brings advertising dollars.

Every year radio stations invest thousands of dollars, either in-house or through consultants, to improve their programming. Stations spend this money so they can understand listener tastes in music, news, personalities, and promotions. In order to understand listener tastes, stations usually turn to researchers specializing in qualitative research. Qualitative research is important to programming because it centers on producing in-depth information from listeners regarding opinions, attitudes, and behaviors. Furthermore, qualitative data is often important to the research process because it complements quantitative research. For example, a station with low ratings can conduct focus groups or interviews with listeners to gather data on listener perceptions in order to improve programming. This section discusses some of the various qualitative and quantitative methods employed by researchers in their quest for information on listener preferences.

Callout Research

Callout research uses both quantitative and qualitative research. A method where telephone operators interview people regarding their listening preferences, callout research is widely used in the radio industry for programming research.

Callout research can be quite beneficial to individual radio stations. The advantage of callout research is that a large number of people can be accessed in a relatively short time frame regarding listening tastes. Furthermore, according to Ed Shane, in his book *Cutting Through,* "some programmers claim they can increase their station's share by as much as 20 percent with regular music callout."[12]

During callout research, trained interviewers telephone people and ask several hundred people the same question. Callout research is often conducted to understand listeners' musical preferences. Interviewers play a **music hook** (a short sample of music usually about 10 seconds long) and ask the listener to rate the piece on a scale. Music hooks are a common radio research term. Music callouts generally answer the following questions for researchers: "How familiar has the record become? How popular is it? Has the record become burned out?"[13] Programmers use this information to plan music programming based on the research data.

Another use for callout research is to gain quantitative information regarding radio listening behavior. In this case interviewers telephone listeners and ask questions such as: What is your favorite radio station? How often do you listen to the radio? Where do you listen to the radio? The interviewer also asks questions regarding the respondent's age, sex, race, and so forth. Information from this type of callout research can be used to gain quick insight into which stations people are tuning into and why, without waiting several months for the *Arbitron Radio Market Report* to be published.

There are many advantages to using callout research in programming decisions. One great advantage is that several hundred people can be surveyed in a relatively short period. Also, callout research is inexpensive. The primary cost involved is interviewer salaries. Furthermore, callout research can be conducted on a continual basis.

Callout research also has disadvantages. One main disadvantage is the growing distaste of telemarketing among consumers. Consumers for years have been bombarded with telephone calls from companies trying to sell them one product or another. The backlash of telemarketing causes great frustration to researchers because it lowers response rates. This provides a great challenge to interviewers trying to persuade potential respondents to answer a few questions.

Auditorium Testing

Auditorium testing is another popular method employed by radio programming researchers. Usually conducted for an individual radio station's programming, auditorium research tests music preferences by that station's target audience. Similar to callout research, this method of testing is very popular with radio industry researchers.

The first step in auditorium testing is telephoning potential subjects and determining if they qualify for the research. In order to qualify, a person must fit the station's target audience, respond to a few questions regarding radio listening, and be willing to spend some time listening to music in an auditorium. Researchers provide a monetary stipend to respondents in order to persuade the subject to attend the testing.

Once all respondents are selected (usually 75–200 people) everyone is gathered in an auditorium to begin testing.[14] Respondents are asked to evaluate music hooks and score each hook by marking his or her opinion on a score sheet or by using an electronic device. The electronic device is a handheld meter; each respondent turns the knob to the point on the scale that most accurately represents his or her feelings toward the music hook. If a score sheet is used, all score sheets are collected after completion and scanned by a machine that tabulates the scores.

Music testing is the most common form of auditorium testing. However, auditorium testing is used for other programming concerns. For example, respondents could be asked to score their feelings toward a disc jockey, a news topic, or station promotion.

Auditorium testing has several advantages. One advantage is that auditorium testing offers a higher sound quality for playing music hooks than callout research. Another advantage is that several hundred respondents can be tested in only a couple of nights.

The main disadvantage of auditorium testing is its high cost. Auditorium research can cost $20,000–$40,000 to test 800 songs.[15] Paying respondents, researchers, and renting the facilities are only a few of the costs involved in auditorium research. Another disadvantage is respondent burnout during the testing period. Often auditorium research attempts to test several hundred hooks in a session. During this testing period respondents may tire of the process and score the hooks with little effort or thought, leading to inaccurate results.

Focus Groups

Focus groups are a very popular research tool in many industries. Companies use focus groups during the marketing of their products. In particular, radio often uses focus groups in order to better understand listener tastes.

Focus groups, the grouping of six to twelve similar people to discuss a particular issue, are used to gather qualitative data.[16] Focus groups should be used to explore topics and gather rich information. In radio, focus groups can be used for various topics such as musical tastes, promotions, commercials, and specific programs. The key to focus groups is group dynamics. When gathered in a group, people discuss topics in a different manner. One person's comment may spur another person to think of the topic in a different way.

Subjects are recruited by telephone and later given a monetary reward for agreeing to participate in the focus group. They must meet certain criteria. The main criterion is for subjects to create a homogeneous group with one special characteristic in common. Sometimes focus groups are all men, sometimes all women, and sometimes represent a single ethnic group. In focus groups for radio, researchers are usually concerned with ensuring that all group members listen to a particular station or type of music. People agreeing to participate in the focus group are arranged into groups of six to twelve people and gathered around a large table. A facilitator guides the group through the topic at hand while trying to have as little impact on the group dynamics as possible. The facilitator is present to guide the group, not to offer her or his own opinion. After the focus group is completed, the facilitator should be able to summarize the group's discussion. A good focus group discussion will provide information not previously thought of and raise more questions.

A major aspect of focus groups is that they are qualitative, and, like all qualitative research, results cannot be generalized. The study's results provide information on listener attitudes but do not necessarily represent *all* listener attitudes. Recall that focus groups have only six to twelve people; this sample is too small to generalize to an entire population. Many researchers conduct several focus groups to gather information on one topic. However, this type of research will seldom reach a sufficient sample size to be generalized. Focus groups should be used to explore information, not draw conclusions.

The major advantage of focus groups is the rich in-depth information that can be collected. However, focus groups are extremely costly. The cost of paying subjects, paying a good facilitator, renting a room, buying food, and so on is extremely high. Therefore, while focus groups are one of the best ways to gather qualitative information, be prepared to spend a great deal of money.

Personal Interviews

Personal interviews are a less widely used research method in radio than auditorium testing, callout research, and focus groups. This is mainly due to the long period of time it takes to conduct a quality one-on-one interview. However, personal interviews often provide considerable quality information. In radio, personal interviews might be conducted to gain insight into topics such as a listener's attitude toward a disc jockey or a talk radio program.

One-on-one interviews last anywhere from a few minutes to more than an hour. The interviewer asks the respondent specific questions to gain insight into his or her opinions. The interviewer is usually free to probe into a respondent's answer and is trained to gather as much quality information as possible. Personal interviews are qualitative in nature and thus gather in-depth information that cannot be quantified.

An advantage of personal interviews is that they can gather large amounts of data regarding listener attitudes and beliefs. Another advantage is that the interviewer can read nonverbal responses to questions as well as verbal responses. The major drawbacks of personal interviews are that they are time-consuming and cannot be generalized. Hundreds of personal interviews would need to be conducted in order for the sample to be large enough to be generalized.

Intercept Research

Intercept research is another form of a personal interview, conducted spontaneously in a public area such as a shopping mall.[17] During intercept research the researcher looks for shoppers with certain characteristics. If the researcher, through visual observation, feels the person meets the criteria, he or she stops the person and asks her or him to participate in the study. People who agree to participate are asked a few questions and given a monetary reward.

The advantage of intercept research is that it can be conducted quickly. Depending on the size of the interview, anywhere between five and fifty people can be interviewed in a day by one researcher. Intercept research is ideal for a station needing quick responses. For example, a station may wish to test listener opinions to a disc jockey who had recently used inappropriate language without consulting the station. The station may choose intercept research to determine whether damage control needs to be taken or whether listeners liked the disc jockey's show. Furthermore, intercept research can be conducted to gather quantitative or qualitative data.

The main drawback of intercept research is getting the desired respondents to participate in the study. Depending on the desired subjects, getting people to take even five minutes out of their day can be a difficult task.

Callout research, auditorium testing, focus groups, personal interviews, and intercept research are all legitimate research methods that can provide great data about the radio industry. However, each method has a specific purpose, and should be used only if the method fits the study's research question or reason for being conducted.

SOME CONSIDERATIONS FOR FUTURE RESEARCH

As mentioned earlier in this chapter, researchers are continuously striving for new and improved methods to study radio research. This section will discuss a few possibilities for future research.

One new method for collecting ratings is currently being researched by Arbitron: the possibility of using electronic meters. In 1998, Arbitron announced its first field test of the personal portable meter (PPM) to be tested in the United Kingdom. The meter was created to read inaudible codes embedded in audio signals. Through the reading of audio signals, the PPM would be able to read codes from radio stations, TV stations, and cable systems. If successful, the meter would replace Arbitron diaries as the method of collecting radio measurements. Consumers would carry the meter with them everywhere and each night the meter would transmit the data to processing stations.[18] The meter would allow broadcasters to more accurately measure radio listenership without relying on the consumer to complete a diary accurately. However, even if the testing of the PPM is successful, the technology may prove too expensive for broadcasters to adopt for ratings research. Only time will tell.

Ed Shane of Shane Media has some interesting forecasts for radio research. One of his forecasts is that music testing will be conducted with computers instead of auditorium testing. Shane predicts people will be asked to participate in music testing and allowed to show up for the testing according to their own schedule. Instead of being asked to attend a music test at a set time, a person would be allowed to drive to the radio station or music consultant's office at his or her own preferred time. At the office respondents would listen to music hooks and score them by touching a computer screen. Not only would this be more convenient for the respondent and increase response rates, but it would also increase the accuracy of responses. A person would be able to listen to hooks, repeat a hook if necessary, and take as much time as he or she feels is necessary to complete the study. Also, music testing would be relatively inexpensive and it would be possible to conduct it on a continuous basis.[19]

One interesting new development in radio research already in existence is called the Living Room Music Test. In 1998, Kelly Music Research received a patent for the Living Room Music Test; many stations have already seen positive results. The Living Room Music Test survey takes place in the comfort of the respondents' own homes. Respondents are mailed a music cassette along with a survey, instructions, and cash honorarium. The respondents complete the survey by listening to the cassette and return the survey for tabulation.

The difference between the Living Room Music Test and other music tests lies in the sampling process. Kelly Music Research knows that mainly avid radio listeners will complete their at-home test and they know that these are the people most likely to complete an Arbitron diary. In reality, radio stations care mainly about people who complete Arbitron diaries because those people determine the ratings of the station. Therefore, radio stations are making their music programming decisions to please Arbitron diary holders. According to Kelly Music Research, "The Living Room Music Test is designed to create a research sample of listeners similar to that created by Arbitron to determine ratings. The objective is to increase audience share by projecting the opinions of the types of listeners who are likely to participate in the diary and ratings process." Kelly Music Research's new test shows stations how to play the radio ratings game and win.[20]

Internet Research

The rise of the Internet in our society has widespread implications for the broadcast industry (see Chapter 10 for more on the impact of the Internet on the radio industry). In particular, radio has been using the Internet to promote and air radio programs. Radio stations use the Internet to sell T-shirts, hats, promote radio personalities, and promote programs. Even more importantly, radio is using streaming technology to air radio programs via the Internet. Internet radio will be a growing trend because of the quality and clarity of sound. With the growth of radio's prominence on the Internet comes the problem of measuring radio's impact on Internet users.

Research professionals are currently examining methods to measure Internet audiences. The Internet is one of the most difficult mediums to measure audiences. Internet researchers currently know how many people hit a Website and can even measure how long they stay connected. The problem lies in determining who are the people using each individual Website. Advertisers are interested in specific demographics when using radio to advertise their products. Researchers currently know how many people are listening to the radio via the Internet, but are not able to adequately measure the Internet listener's age, sex, race, education, and so on. Radio researchers understand the importance of the Internet to radio's future and the importance of measuring Internet audiences. Researchers are currently scrambling to develop new research methods that include measuring the Internet.

There are many other researchers currently planning new research methods for the radio industry. Time will determine which new strategies will be successful. Those researchers that will find success in the future will undoubtedly have superb research knowledge in sampling techniques, quantitative and qualitative methods, and a great understanding of the radio industry.

NOTES

[1]Roger D. Wimmer and Joseph R. Dominick, *Mass Media Research* (Belmont, CA: Wadsworth), p. 289.

[2]Ed Shane, *Selling Electronic Media* (Boston: Focal Press, 1999), p. 157.

[3]Arbitron Company, *Radio Market Report: Dallas–Ft. Worth,* Summer, 1996, p. 2.

[4]Ibid., p. 3.

[5]Shane, p. 157.

[6]Shane, p. 158.

[7]Wimmer and Dominick, p. 292.

[8]Hugh Malcom Beville, Jr., *Audience Ratings* (Hillsdale, NJ: Lawrence Erlbaum, 1988), pp. 223–224.

[9]Ibid., p. 224.

[10]Scarborough Sales Packet.

[11]Arbitron, *Radio Survey Information.* Available online at http://www.arbitron.com/radiosurvey.htm, (accessed 7/15/99).

[12]Ed Shane, *Cutting Through: Strategies and Tactics for Radio* (Houston: Shane Media Services, 1991), pp. 54–55.

[13]Shane, 1991, p. 55.

[14]Wimmer and Dominick, p. 307.

[15]Wimmer and Dominick, p. 307.

[16]Richard Krueger, *Focus Groups* (Thousand Oaks, CA: Sage, 1994), p. 78.

[17]Shane, 1991, pp. 62–63.

[18]Bachman, Katy, "Arbitron Goes Portable," *MediaWeek,* October 19, 1998, p. 10.

[19]Shane, 1991, p. 58.

[20]Kelly Music Research, Inc., *Test Design & Procedure* (Kelly Music Research, June 1999).

8

Noncommercial Radio Broadcasting

Dr. Philip A. Thompsen
Assistant Professor of Communication Studies
West Chester University

This is a chapter about a different kind of radio broadcasting than has been the subject of previous chapters in this book. Noncommercial broadcasting is the oldest form of radio broadcasting in the United States, for the commercialization of radio came after the invention of the technology. **Noncommercial radio** arose from the radio broadcasting pursuits of college students, community groups, political parties, and nonprofit organizations. The use of radio waves to train and educate both students at a high school or university and students who composed the listening audience led noncommercial broadcasting to sometimes be referred to as "educational broadcasting." Despite the many challenges and struggles faced by noncommercial stations, it is a story that has only just begun.

We begin the chapter with an extended look at the early development of noncommercial radio in the United States. Two important events in this history merit special attention: the reservation of FM frequencies for noncommercial radio in 1945, and the last-minute inclusion of radio in the Public Broadcasting Act in 1967. We then turn our attention to the last quarter of the twentieth century. While a time for growth in the number of stations and listenership, it was also a politically turbulent time for the Corporation for Public Broadcasting. We examine the peculiar economics of noncommercial radio, the diversity of noncommercial radio programming, and the noncommercial radio audience. Though much of this chapter will focus on federally funded noncommercial radio stations, we will also include the story of the sometimes-overlooked majority of noncommercial radio licensees who don't receive any federal funding.

DEFINING NONCOMMERCIAL RADIO

It may be an understatement to say that it is difficult to define *noncommercial radio*. A logical starting point for such a definition is the special status given noncommercial radio by the Federal Communications Commission. With few exceptions, these stations hold a special class of broadcast license for a "noncommercial educational FM." As of July 1999, the FCC reported that there were 2,055 noncommercial educational FM broadcast stations operating in the United States.[1] The vast majority of these stations operate in a portion of the FM band that the FCC has reserved for educational use. In 1945, when the FCC allocated the frequencies 88 to 108 MHz for FM broadcasting, they designated the first one-fifth of that band—from 88.1 to 91.9 MHz—for the exclusive use of noncommercial educational radio.[2]

Yet the "noncommercial educational" designation is now an inadequate label for stations operating in this portion of the band for two reasons. First, noncommercial radio stations have adopted many of the strategies of their commercial counterparts, including the deliberate targeting of audiences that appeal to corporate sponsors. It is common to reward the generosity of such "program underwriters" with on-air announcements that have become nearly indistinguishable from the spot ads heard on commercial radio stations. Second, most noncommercial radio stations have distanced themselves from their educational roots, often minimizing the role of faculty and replacing student volunteers with professional staffs. It would similarly be a stretch to call the programming on many noncommercial stations "educational," as the majority of stations typically fill their broadcast day with programs designed as much to entertain as to enlighten.

The term **public radio** is sometimes used by listeners and holders of noncommercial educational FM licenses to refer to FM stations operating between 88.1 and 91.9 MHz. In fact, all AM and FM radio service in the United States is public. Any listener with a receiver can pick up the broadcasts of stations serving the listener's community. The listener is not required to pay a receiver license fee, nor is the over-the-air signal scrambled or otherwise encoded to limit access to the broadcast. In this regard, all AM and FM radio broadcasting is "public." Yet, noncommercial radio stations, particularly stations affiliated with National Public Radio (NPR), have appropriated the term *public broadcasting*. In this chapter, when the term *public broadcasting* is used, it will generally refer to these affiliated stations.

One can identify at least four types of noncommercial radio stations: CPB-qualified noncommercial stations, student stations, community stations, and religious stations. CPB-qualified refers to those stations that have met the requirements set by the Corporation for Public Broadcasting (CPB) to receive federal money, and are members of National Public Radio (NPR), a private organization created by the CPB in 1970. As of July 1999, about 560 stations or about a fourth of the noncommercial radio stations in the United States were CPB-qualified stations.[3] Most are full-power stations, and many have additional "translator" stations, low-power stations that serve specific communities outside the range of the station's main signal. Many NPR affiliates trace their origins to stations started at colleges and universities, and about half still maintain ties to a sponsoring educational institution.

The majority of noncommercial educational licenses are used to operate *student* or *campus radio stations*. According to the Intercollegiate Broadcasting System, there are over 1,300 student radio stations in the United States.[4] Student stations can be found at colleges, universities, high schools, and other educational institutions. These stations are student-operated and usually student-managed stations, although typically a faculty advisor provides some oversight. They are generally not eligible to receive money from the CPB, because they rarely meet the minimum requirements to receive federal funds. (In particular, CPB requires that there be five full-time noninstructional paid employees on the station's staff.) Although there are exceptions, most student stations operate with relatively low power (sometimes less than 1,000 watts), projecting a limited reception range that extends only a few miles. Many student stations serve as training laboratories for broadcast education programs, but more than a few have earned reputations as "electronic sandboxes" where students "play radio."[5] A great variety of programming can be found on student radio stations, but generally such stations feature music from new artists who have yet to achieve popularity on commercial radio. In this role, the student radio station can be an effective venue for introducing new music to student listeners who may be receptive to new performers or music styles. Groups such as R.E.M., Nirvana, and Pearl Jam were introduced to listeners through college radio stations.[6]

Providing programming that is an alternative to the programming found on most commercial radio stations, both musically and politically, is also a task of *community radio stations*. These noncommercial stations are typically run by volunteers, although there often is a core staff of paid professionals. Some of the larger community stations receive grants from the CPB, but most community stations rely extensively on listener donations and support from nonprofit organizations. Most are members of the National Federation of Community Broadcasters, which represents the interests of about 140 community radio stations in the United States.[7] Many community stations are affiliated with Pacifica, an alternative programming network that was started in 1949 at KPFA in Berkeley, California, which held "the first noncommercial license that did not go to an educational or religious institution."[8] Perhaps the most distinctive feature of community radio stations is what Ralph Engelman has called their "commitment to sustain an independent, critical, and oppositional public sphere on the broadcast spectrum."[9]

A significant number of noncommercial radio licensees are *religious radio stations*. While only a minority of the 1,600 religious stations in the United States hold noncommercial licenses, a rapidly growing number of noncommercial educational FM licenses are being granted to religious organizations.[10] Many of these stations are affiliated with a religious radio network, such as Family Life Radio, the Bible Broadcasting Network, or the Christian Broadcasting Network. Most feature evangelical Christian programming, often with a fundamentalist and charismatic flavor. Although these stations often solicit listener support, they also take advantage of the fact that the FCC allows noncommercial licensees to sell airtime to nonprofit organizations, such as churches, charities, and evangelistic organizations. Religious broadcasters have aggressively pursued noncommercial FM translators, which rebroadcast satellite-delivered programming over low-power transmitters. The rapid growth of noncommercial religious radio translators has other noncommercial stations concerned over the increasing congestion of the noncommercial FM band.[11]

In general, however, these four types of noncommercial radio broadcasting coexist today in relative harmony. There are even a few stations that straddle the boundaries, such as student-operated stations with religious formats and community stations that broadcast NPR programming. But for the most part, each type focuses on its own unique strengths and largely ignores its siblings. This is particularly true of CPB-qualified radio stations; they represent a minority of noncommercial licensees yet command the lion's share of both transmission power and funding support. Noncommercial radio stations, despite some clear compromises with regard to noncommercial status, can rightfully claim a legacy that started long before the CPB and NPR. It is a legacy that is as old as radio itself.

THE EARLY HISTORY OF NONCOMMERCIAL RADIO

As we said in Chapter 2, the early history of radio is very much like the early history of a more recent communication medium, the Internet. Both radio and the Internet grew out of pioneering experiments in electronic communication. Both were noncommercial in nature for many years, with early ties to the military and education. Once business interests were introduced, however, both communication media became commercial very quickly. And with the blessing of the federal government, both radio and the Internet dramatically mushroomed to become dominant economic forces of their time.

The Internet today is driven by advertising and e-commerce, but the Internet has its roots in the computer communication networks jointly developed over the past thirty years by the military, various government agencies, electronic hobbyists, and educational institutions.[12] In much the same way, radio began not as a business, but as a noncommercial experiment in wireless communication. The government's first attempt to regulate radio, the Wireless Ship Act of 1910, made no mention of the commercial use of radio, but rather addressed the use of radio to promote maritime safety.[13] Colleges and universities started many of the earliest radio broadcast stations, typically by electrical engineering departments.[14]

Although KDKA received the first official broadcast license in 1920, a number of stations operated with experimental licenses before KDKA, and many of these early broadcasters had roots in educational broadcasting. One of the first radio stations in the country was established by Charles David "Doc" Herrold of San José, California in 1909. "San José Calling," as the station was originally known, was operated as part of Herrold's School of Radio. Lee de Forest said that Herrold's station, which eventually would become KCBS, "can rightfully claim to be the oldest broadcasting station of the entire world."[15]

Another early radio broadcaster was WHA at the University of Wisconsin. Faculty in the university's physics department began radio experiments in 1902, and within a few years had built the radio transmission facility that would eventually become WHA. Professors Earle Terry and Edward Bennett received an experimental license from the federal government to operate the station, which was initially granted the call sign 9XM. During much of the 1910s it broadcast weather forecasts in Morse code. Unlike most experimental radio stations at the time, 9XM was allowed to stay on the air during World War I, and the station began broadcasting voice transmissions shortly after the war.[16] Because other early stations (including Herrold's) were forced off the air by the military during World War I, many radio historians feel WHA has a justified claim of being "the Oldest Station in the Nation . . . in existence longer than any other."[17]

Regardless of which radio station has the most substantiated claim of being the first on the air, it is clear that colleges and universities, as well as other noncommercial organizations, were a significant presence in early radio. A 1923 tabulation by the Department of Commerce reported that educational institutions owned 13 percent of the radio stations then in existence, second only to radio manufacturers in station ownership.[18] The same report showed that a number of other stations in operation at the time were also owned by noncommercial organizations, such as churches, YMCAs, police and fire departments, and cities. Broadcast historians Christopher Sterling and John Kittross argue that even among commercial broadcasters, "a radio station was seldom the primary concern" but was "nearly always an arm of some other business or activity, often promotional but mostly noncommercial."[19]

As radio broadcasting developed in the 1920s, however, the noncommercial flavor of early radio would fade. The stage was being set for what Robert McChesney has called "the battle for the control of U.S. broadcasting."[20] On one side of this battle were those who favored advertiser-supported radio. On the other side, a loose coalition of educational institutions, churches, labor unions, civic groups, and charitable foundations fought to preserve a significant place on the airwaves for noncommercial, public-service radio. The federal government played a decisive role in this battle when Congress created the Federal Radio Commission (FRC) in 1927. The

FRC decision to mandate a frequency reallocation plan that favored high-powered stations on "clear channels" required the vast majority of stations to switch frequencies. Noncommercial stations could not easily afford the expense of changing to a new frequency, and many simply went off the air. The FRC also established a competitive hearing procedure for determining who could use the limited number of available frequencies, a process that clearly favored wealthy corporations over nonprofit organizations.

Supporters of noncommercial radio fought valiantly during the early 1930s to keep the airwaves from becoming completely commercialized. In 1930, the Association of College and University Broadcast Stations called on Congress to reserve some frequencies for the exclusive use of noncommercial broadcasters. The Payne Fund's National Committee on Education by Radio also pressured Congress to pass legislation requiring that at least 15 percent of all frequencies be reserved for noncommercial use. There were sympathetic ears in Congress, including legislators sensitive to complaints from the listening public of the increasingly blatant commercial nature of radio broadcasting. At the 1932 convention of the National Association of Broadcasters, FRC Commissioner Harold Lafount warned commercial broadcasters that "an irate public is besieging Congress to stop overcommercialism of radio in America."[21] From 1931 to 1933, Ohio Senator Simeon Fess repeatedly introduced legislation that would allocate frequencies for noncommercial radio, but the Senate never brought his bill to a vote.[22]

During congressional debate over the bill that would eventually create the Communications Act of 1934, New York Senator Robert Wagner and West Virginia Senator Henry Hatfield proposed an amendment that would require that one fourth of all frequencies be designated for noncommercial use. This amendment garnered considerable support in the Senate, though the Wagner–Hatfield amendment fell to a counterproposal from Washington Senator Clarence Dill that the FCC study the proposal to reserve frequencies for noncommercial use and report its findings to Congress within a year. Not surprisingly, the newly formed FCC turned out to be as procommercial as the FRC. Its 1935 report to Congress recommended against any allocation of frequencies for noncommercial use.[23] It would seem that the "battle for the control of U.S. broadcasting" was over, and the commercialization of radio was complete.

NONCOMMERCIAL RADIO FINDS A HOME ON THE FM BAND

A decade after the FCC's report to Congress on noncommercial radio, the number of noncommercial stations in the United States had fallen to its lowest point. Only about twenty-five of the nearly one thousand radio stations on the air in 1945 were noncommercial.[24] Despite this spiraling decline, supporters of noncommercial radio, and in particular educational broadcasters, continued to call for frequency reservation. The Association of College and University Broadcast Stations, which had changed its name in 1934 to the National Association for Educational Broadcasters (NAEB), was particularly persistent. In 1945, the NAEB successfully persuaded the FCC to reserve for noncommercial use 20 percent of the band allocated for Frequency Modulation (FM), a newly approved technology for radio broadcasting.[25] The role of the educational community in this action is evident in the name the FCC gave to this new kind of radio license, noncommercial educational FM. Finally, noncommercial radio had found a home.

It was a quiet home at first. Few commercial broadcasters saw any value in starting an FM station; they were more interested in starting ventures in television broadcasting. By the end of 1945, only fifty-four FM stations were on the air in the United States, and eight of these held noncommercial educational licenses.[26] With so few FM stations to choose from, and with most commercial FM stations **simulcasting** the programming of a sister AM station, most Americans had little motivation to purchase an FM radio receiver. Many colleges and universities wanted to venture back into radio, but starting and operating an FM station was an expensive proposition, with little assurance there would be an audience.

Sensing the need for a nudge, the NAEB petitioned the FCC to consider lowering the minimum operating power requirements for noncommercial educational FM radio stations. In 1948, the FCC created the Class D educational FM license, which permitted schools to go on the air with as little as 10 watts of output power. (FM station classes A, B, and C are discussed in Chapter 1.) This was the spark that reignited the flame of noncommercial radio. The number of noncommercial educational FM stations shot up dramatically, from 10 stations in 1947 to 125 stations in 1957.[27] Many of these stations participated in the NAEB "bicycle network," the first national cooperative program distribution service for noncommercial radio, which enabled college stations to share programs with each other through a tape exchange system.

Class D gave a needed boost to both student radio and FM radio. It's interesting to note that in the decade after the FCC started granting Class D licenses, the number of commercial FM licensees actually declined, while the number of educational FM licensees increased tenfold. By 1966, over half of the nearly 300 noncommercial FM stations on the air were Class D stations. These low-power stations were inexpensive to start and maintain. Many college and university programs in broadcasting were eager to take advantage of a great opportunity to provide a "real world" laboratory for students. Class D stations were particularly appealing to land-grant universities and liberal arts colleges. And for the predominantly youthful FM radio audience of the 1960s, Class D stations greatly added to the diversity of programming available, often featuring alternative or progressive music, providing an outlet for local talent, and covering news and public affairs with a very local flavor. It was the heyday of the hippie, and Class D stations were one of the few media outlets for the countercultural "underground" of the era.

RADIO FINDS A PLACE IN THE PUBLIC BROADCASTING ACT

It was from the 1960s that modern **public radio** would arise. It was a time of revolutionary idealism, of protests against the "establishment" of white middle-class values, and bitter division over the war in Vietnam. It was a time of tragic assassinations—of a President, a younger brother who wanted to be one, and a civil rights leader whose dream still lives today. It was a time of technological change, of television and computers and astronauts landing on the moon. And in this climate of social and cultural introspection, it was the perfect time for a new vision of noncommercial broadcasting, one that could finally provide a viable alternative to the overtly commercial fare that dominated the airwaves.

The distinguished Carnegie Commission on Educational Television powerfully articulated this new vision. Their report, "Public Television: A Program for Action," outlined a bold vision of what noncommercial educational television should strive to become.[28] The Carnegie Commission saw an opportunity to harness the miracle of television—at that time still a technological marvel to the general public—for enhancing the quality of the American way of life, for fostering the cultivation of the mind, and for advancing television programming of diversity and excellence. It called on Congress to form a Corporation for Public Television, which would provide federal funds to make the vision a reality.

Strangely missing from the Carnegie Commission report was noncommercial educational radio. Once again, the NAEB lobbied on behalf of noncommercial radio. While Congress was considering the formation of a Corporation for Public Television, it was the NAEB and, in particular, its radio division head Jerry Sandler, who pressed for the inclusion of noncommercial radio in the Public Broadcasting Act. With support from the Ford Foundation, Sandler commissioned a study of noncommercial radio, which resulted in a report appropriately entitled *The Hidden Medium*.[29] The report was released in early April 1967, just days before the Senate Commerce Committee began hearings on the Public Television Act.[30] These hearings were broadcast live on many noncommercial radio stations, a fact that helped underscore the potential of including radio in the proposed legislation.[31] Testimony from educational radio stations, which substantially outnumbered educational television stations, as well as the extensive lobbying efforts of NAEB, convinced Congress to include radio in the bill, which was renamed the Public Broadcasting Act.

There was little resistance to the Public Broadcasting Act from the commercial broadcast industry. At the time, few believed that a stronger system of noncommercial broadcasting would substantially threaten the audience for commercial stations. Most noncommercial radio stations were safely segregated from their commercial counterparts at the lower end of the still struggling FM band. Only the most optimistic observers in the mid-1960s could foresee that the audience for FM would someday surpass that of AM radio. Of all the radios sold in 1965, only 15 percent could receive FM signals, and only 6 percent of new car radios included the FM band.[32] Commercial broadcasters may have also seen an opportunity for some relief from their own FCC-mandated public service obligations. A federally funded radio service would greatly increase the public interest programming available on the airwaves, which in turn could lead the FCC to relax some of the programming requirements for commercial stations. This scenario, in fact, was realized to a great extent during the FCC's deregulation of radio broadcasting, which began during the 1980s and has continued to this day. Without significant opposition from the powerful commercial broadcasting lobby, the Public Broadcasting Act was quickly passed, and was signed into law by President Lyndon Johnson on November 7, 1967.

THE POLITICS OF NONCOMMERCIAL RADIO

The inclusion of radio wasn't the only change Congress made to the Carnegie Commission's vision. A more significant modification was the rejection of the Carnegie Commission's call for a dedicated tax on radio and television receiving sets to finance noncommercial broadcasting. Instead, the Public Broadcasting Act called on Congress to make regular appropriations for the newly formed Corporation for Public Broadcasting (CPB), which would in turn distribute funds to noncommercial broadcast stations. Since the passage of the Public Broadcasting Act, the CPB has had to argue its case to every newly elected Congress, requiring it to respond to the ever-changing political landscape. Rather than creating the politically neutral "heat shield" between the federal government and noncommercial broadcasters originally envisioned by the Carnegie Commission, the Public Broadcasting Act created a CPB that was a political animal from the very beginning.

It wouldn't take long before politics would take center stage in the unfolding saga of noncommercial broadcasting. Although the Public Broadcasting Act of 1967 was signed by President Johnson, the CPB and NPR came into being a few years later during President Nixon's Administration. A conservative Republican, Richard Nixon made a concerted effort to steer noncommercial broadcasting away from its liberal roots. Nixon applied pressure through a 1972 veto of CPB's funding authorization bill, and by directing his chief of telecommunication policy, Clay Whitehead, to take an active role in shaping the nascent public broadcasting system. Nixon's actions antagonized many in the noncommercial broadcasting community, and prompted the resignations of CPB chairman Frank Pace and CPB president John Macy, whom Nixon replaced with individuals more open to his influence.[33] With the broad support of local stations, NPR was able to stand up to the Nixon-compromised CPB, but the resulting wounds have been slow to heal.

When Democrat Jimmy Carter became president, the battle-scarred CPB community tried to regain its original sense of mission. In 1976, the CPB and NPR approached the Carnegie Corporation about funding a study that would focus on the future of public broadcasting. This second Carnegie Commission finished its inquiry in 1979, producing a much more comprehensive and critical document than the original Carnegie Commission report.[34] It was particularly critical of the CPB, which it said had "failed to function as the catalyst for creative programming envisioned by the first Carnegie Commission and the Public Broadcasting Act."[35] The Commission recommended that the CPB be abolished and replaced by a new "Public Telecommunications Trust" that would "provide financial protection both for broadcast licensees and for a highly insulated, self-directed division of the Trust, the Program Services Endowment."[36] Most CPB-qualified broadcasters applauded what has become known as Carnegie II; policymakers largely ignored the report. As public broadcasting scholar Willard Rowland put it, "Carnegie II was too aloof from both the general U.S. telecommunications policy environment and the realities of the structural changes and power relationships within public broadcasting that had emerged since Carnegie I to be effective in the applied political realm where its recommendations would have to be enacted."[37] To put it bluntly, public broadcasting was no longer "a public trust," as the second Carnegie Commission described it. Public broadcasting, as it has evolved from the Public Broadcasting Act, has become a federally subsidized industry preoccupied with survival.

The will to survive would continue to be tested in the 1980s and 1990s. Republican President Ronald Reagan twice vetoed public broadcast funding bills, and Congress upheld both vetoes. As one observer noted, "[f]rom 1981 to 1986 public broadcasters had to live with the very real fear that federal funding might be totally eliminated."[38] Although this fear was never realized, appropriations for CPB dropped significantly in the early 1980s, and NPR member radio stations were hurt by these cuts to a more dramatic degree than were their PBS television siblings. Many stations were forced to scale back personnel and programming budgets, and most became increasingly focused on generating financial support from local businesses and loyal listeners.

Some members of the noncommercial radio community may have breathed a sigh of relief when Democrat Bill Clinton was elected President in 1992. As it has turned out, however, the Clinton years haven't been particularly kind to the Corporation for Public Broadcasting. When the Republicans gained control of both houses of Congress in 1994, public radio was once again up against the ropes. Speaker of the House Newt Gingrich and South Dakota Senator Larry Pressler led the congressional effort to end federal funding of broadcasting, charging that its programming had a liberal bias and didn't reflect the values of most Americans. Among the complaints was the fact that it was NPR that broke the story about sexual harassment charges against Judge Clarence Thomas after his nomination to the Supreme Court.[39] These experiences have entrenched NPR member stations' fear of losing government dollars, dramatically changing how the stations view the role of federal funding.

PAYING THE BILLS:
NONCOMMERCIAL RADIO ECONOMICS

Money is a problem that has always plagued noncommercial radio. Before 1967, most stations scraped by on meager budgets, typically provided by a university or college. Although the Public Broadcasting Act introduced federal funding for noncommercial radio, the shifting political terrain has prevented secure, long-range financing. The first Carnegie Commission report called for a tax on television sets; it never happened. The second Carnegie Commission suggested a spectrum use fee to fund public broadcasting; the proposal was ignored. Other ideas that have been suggested include a tax on commercial broadcasters, a tax on long-distance carriers, an advertising tax, and a per-household license fee on radio and television receivers. Even the radical idea of noncommercial broadcasters selling commercials was considered by Congress in the early 1980s, and a few stations were permitted to do so on a trial basis. Ultimately, however, none of these potential solutions survived the force of competing political interests.

As a result, most noncommercial radio stations operate largely at the mercy of short-term funding sources, assiduously courting favor with a broad base of constituents. Of particular significance are five funding sources that provide most of the financial backing for noncommercial radio. These major sources of support are: (1) grants from federal, state, and local governments, (2) budgets from the institutions that hold the broadcast licenses, (3) corporate underwriting, (4) gifts from the listening audience, and (5) the sale of airtime to nonprofit organizations. This mix of funding sources varies for each of the four types of noncommercial radio stations mentioned earlier in this chapter. CPB-qualified stations receive a significant, but dwindling, level of support from government sources. Student-operated stations rely primarily on institutional budgets. Community stations rely heavily on donations from the audience, although nearly all noncommercial stations now ask listeners for money. This includes religious stations that hold noncommercial licenses, which are also more likely to sell airtime to nonprofit organizations.

One may be surprised to learn that government support typically provides less than a third of a CPB-qualified radio station's budget. What may be even more surprising is that it is money from state governments, not the federal government, that provides the largest share of government funding. It should be pointed out, however, that state funds for radio may in turn rely on federal grants, so it is sometimes difficult to distinguish state support from federal. Further, most state money comes from state-supported universities or colleges, which in turn rely on a variety of funding sources, including the federal government. Nevertheless, state governments are a crucial source of funding for public radio. According to recent figures from the CPB, states provide about 18 percent of the total revenue of the public radio system, with 5.2 percent coming directly from state governments, and 12.8 percent funneled through state universities and colleges.[40] Much of the direct state support goes to the

10 percent of noncommercial radio stations that are licensed to state authorities or commissions.[41]

This is not to say that money from the federal government isn't significant, but on a percentage basis, federal dollars represent a declining share of total income. Federal support was much more important in the early years of noncommercial television and radio broadcasting. Many stations would not be on the air today if it weren't for construction grants from the National Telecommunications and Information Administration's Public Telecommunications Facilities Program (PTFP). This program, created by Congress in 1962 as the Educational Broadcasting Facilities Program, was the first significant infusion of federal money into noncommercial broadcasting. While PTFP grants continue to provide an important source of funding for construction and expansion of broadcast facilities, most of the ongoing federal support for noncommercial radio today is funneled through the Corporation for Public Broadcasting. Federal money accounts for 14.7 percent of public radio's total income, with the bulk of that (13.4%) coming directly from the CPB. Stations receive this CPB money primarily in the form of two types of grants. Annual community service grants are unrestricted funds that the CPB provides to all qualified stations. For stations in small towns or remote areas, the community service grant often represents the single most significant source of revenue. Most noncommercial radio stations also receive federal support in the form of restricted grants for programming development, production, and acquisition. Independent program producers, as well as NPR, also compete for programming grants from the CPB.

In addition to state and federal money, some noncommercial radio stations receive funding from local government authorities, such as cities, community colleges, and school districts. Local government support, however, represents only 2.6 percent of the total income of the public radio system, and many noncommercial radio stations receive no local government money at all. In a few cases, however, city governments hold the license of a noncommercial radio station and pay for much of the operational cost from the city treasury. The nation's most listened-to public radio station, WNYC, was licensed for many years to the City of New York, and until it recently gained independence from the city, it had relied almost exclusively on city support.[42] Still, local government agencies operate less than 5 percent of the nation's noncommercial radio stations, and these stations account for most of the local government funding.

The entities that hold noncommercial radio station licenses are ultimately responsible for financing the operations of their stations, and such institutional support is an important source of income. In the case of CPB-qualified public radio stations, slightly more than half (54%) are licensed to universities and colleges.[43] Most of these institutions of higher learning are supported in part by states or local municipalities, which makes it difficult to distinguish between government and institutional support. However, private colleges and universities account for 27 percent of noncommercial radio's funding from educational institutions. Student-operated radio stations tend to rely extensively on institutional support, usually in the form of school budgets. Student stations that exist primarily as a "student voice on the airwaves" typically rely on budgets drawn from student fees and administered by student governments. Stations that primarily provide facilities for student training are usually funded by academic departments. Many student stations rely on a combination of student fees, department support, and donations from local businesses.[44] Sometimes institutional support for a station takes the form of free studio space and utilities that the station is not required by a college or university to pay.

Corporate underwriting represents a significant and growing piece of the noncommercial radio financing pie. Donations from the business community in support of programming represent approximately 15 percent of public radio's income. The role of corporations and local businesses in supporting noncommercial radio has increased dramatically since the early 1980s. In response to the Reagan Administration's attacks on federal support for CPB, Congress created the Temporary Commission on Alternative Financing, which explored a variety of funding options, including the sale of commercials. Indeed, a handful of noncommercial broadcasters were granted permission to sell commercial time on a trial basis. Although the Commission ultimately recommended against commercials, it urged the FCC to relax its rules regarding the identification of program underwriters. The FCC obliged in 1984 with what has become known as the "enhanced underwriting" rules. Prior to this, noncommercial stations could mention only the name of the underwriter. With enhanced underwriting, noncommercial radio stations could broadcast more detailed acknowledgment announcements, including nonpromotional information about the business or corporation, such as a description of goods and services, a business's location, and even a "value-neutral" company slogan. In general, most noncommercial stations are careful not to promote a business in such announcements, but a few (including student stations) have crossed the fuzzy line separating enhanced underwriting from commercials and have been fined by the FCC.[45]

Another important source of revenue is listener support. This is the primary source of income for community stations, and is becoming increasingly important to all noncommercial stations. The idea of "listener-supported" radio is generally attributed to Lewis Hill, the founder of KPFA in Berkeley, California, the flagship station of the Pacifica network.[46] In 1949, Hill's Pacifica Foundation launched KPFA as an alternative to commercial radio, accountable only to listeners, who were asked to become "subscribers" by donating $10.00 a year.[47] KPFA struggled at first but eventually became self-sufficient, and during the 1960s it was a driving force in the San Francisco counterculture movement. The Pacifica Foundation established additional radio stations in Los Angeles, New York, Houston, and Washington, D.C., created a low-cost programming service for other noncommercial stations, and inspired a community radio movement that continues to this day. Many noncommercial radio stations were slow to adopt the listener-supported model, perhaps in part to politically distance themselves from leftist-leaning community stations. By 1977, only 7.5 percent of the stations' income came from private donations.[48]

But twenty years later, listener support would account for nearly 30 percent of non-commercial radio's revenue. Today, most noncommercial stations, including NPR member stations, religious, community, and even some student stations, regularly ask their audiences for money.

Finally, some noncommercial stations rely on the sale of airtime to nonprofit organizations. Although noncommercial stations are prohibited from selling airtime to for-profit entities, they may legally sell airtime to nonprofit organizations, as long as the time is not used to promote a commercial enterprise. This is the primary source of income for noncommercial religious radio stations, many of which publish rates for "preaching programs," just as their commercial counterparts do. Some student stations, especially at church-related colleges, also take advantage of this source of revenue. Noncommercial radio stations have generally not derived a significant portion of their budget from the sale of airtime to nonprofits, although this may change in the coming years if government funding continues to decline.

In addition to these five major sources of revenue, noncommercial stations have found a number of other creative ways of paying the bills. One of the most popular is the fund-raising auction, which has become a quarterly event at some stations. These auctions often include frequent mentions of donated items from local businesses, providing much more detail about a product or service than would be permissible in underwriting announcements. Other sources of income include philanthropic foundations and charitable organizations, and many radio programs are underwritten in part by foundation grants. Some noncommercial radio stations earn extra cash by leasing their subcarriers to specialized broadcast ventures, such as background music companies, wireless stock quotes, and radio reading services for the blind. Stations also earn revenue from the sale of program-related merchandise. Minnesota Public Radio, for example, has been particularly aggressive in the direct marketing of products related to the very popular radio program *A Prairie Home Companion*. And noncommercial stations were among the first to embrace the potential of the World Wide Web, not only for promoting programming, but also as an opportunity to more explicitly acknowledge the generosity of their program underwriters. National Public Radio has even ventured into e-commerce, selling books, tapes, and promotional paraphernalia on the Web.[49]

A REFRESHING ALTERNATIVE: PROGRAMMING ON NONCOMMERCIAL RADIO

Noncommercial stations are sometimes referred to as "alternative" radio, suggesting that they offer a programming alternative to the content found on most commercial AM and FM stations. Despite their financial challenges, noncommercial radio stations provide the U.S. public with a wide variety of innovative, interesting, and illuminating programs. In terms of technical quality, artistic creativity, social relevancy, and journalistic integrity, NPR member radio stations arguably provide some of the best news and cultural programming available. Community stations add a more clearly alternative flavor to the mix, and serve as an important outlet for minority voices. Student stations typically feature new music from struggling artists, and occasionally provide cutting-edge social commentary of a genuinely unique nature. Even noncommercial religious radio stations, while having much in common with their commercial counterparts, have nevertheless expanded the variety of religious programming in this country, and have been a major force in the surging popularity of alternative forms of religious music. When taken as a whole, the noncommercial radio stations of America provide a refreshing alternative to the programming of commercial radio.

The programming of CPB-qualified public radio stations serves the largest segment of the audience for noncommercial radio. These stations receive much of their programming from two national services: National Public Radio (NPR) and Public Radio International (PRI). NPR is the older of the two organizations. CPB created NPR in 1970 to provide programming and interconnection for a national public radio system. The first NPR network relied on telephone lines for programming distribution, but by 1980 NPR had established a state-of-the-art satellite delivery system. The semiautonomous Public Radio Satellite System provides NPR stations with multiple simultaneous program feeds, allowing stations great flexibility in the selection of network programming. This system not only distributes NPR network programming but also a wide variety of programs from independent producers, including those represented by PRI. Originally known as American Public Radio, Minnesota-based PRI does not produce programs itself, but rather serves as a distributor of radio programming. Its first and still predominant client is Minnesota Public Radio, but PRI has expanded rapidly in recent years to become a major producer and distributor of radio programs.

NPR is particularly known for its two "drive-time" news programs. NPR's longest-running program, and one of the most highly respected programs in public radio, is the afternoon news program *All Things Considered*. Launched in 1971, this "news magazine of the air" features news summaries, in-depth investigative reports, insightful analysis and commentary, unique public interest stories, and brief musical interludes that tie it all together. The musical breaks also provide "cutaway" points where stations can insert local news and weather. A faster paced morning version of the program, *Morning Edition*, debuted in 1979. Although both programs have weekly audiences approaching eight million, *Morning Edition* has a slight lead, making it the most listened-to program on noncommercial radio. Other popular programs from NPR includes *Car Talk*, which features the playful banter of two automobile mechanics dispensing advice; *Fresh Air with Terry Gross*, a daily interview program with a focus on literature and the arts; *Talk of the Nation*, an issue-oriented discussion program; and *Performance Today*, a classical music program with live performances, artist interviews, and extensive commentary.

Public Radio International is perhaps best known for the long-running *A Prairie Home Companion*. Since its debut in 1974, fans of this weekly aural journey to Lake

Wobegon have been among the most loyal in the public radio audience. But PRI's most popular program, heard by nearly 3 million people a week, is the daily business-oriented program *Marketplace*. PRI is also the U.S. distributor of the *BBC World Service*, which provides many CPB-qualified radio stations (as well as some community and student stations) with hourly news updates. Until the *Christian Science Monitor* suspended the program in 1997, PRI distributed *Monitor Radio*, a widely respected news service. Other notable programs distributed by PRI include *Michael Feldman's Whad'ya Know?*, a humorous call-in quiz show; *St. Paul Sunday*, a weekly program of chamber music; *Pipedreams*, a program featuring pipe organ music; and *Schickele Mix*, an engaging and entertaining program for music lovers. PRI also distributes a twenty-four-hour classical music service as well as a variety of jazz programs, including *Jazz After Hours*.

Although programming from these two national radio networks represents an important part of a typical CPB-qualified radio station's schedule, about half of its programming is locally produced. Most stations have a news department that provides local news and weather updates during breaks in *Morning Edition* and *All Things Considered*. But the most common local programs feature announcers introducing recorded music. Classical music programs are the most popular choice, with some stations featuring classical music exclusively. Jazz is also a staple at many stations. In markets where there is more than one CPB-qualified station, often one will focus on classical music while the other will concentrate on jazz. Another common programming strategy is to "daypart" by airing classical music during the day (between the two NPR drive-time programs) and airing jazz in the evening hours. On the weekends, most stations add some specialty music programs to their schedule, such as folk, "world," latino, and "new age" music programs.

In most cases, however, the diversity of music programming on CPB-qualified radio does not match that of community and student radio. Community stations tend to provide the most diverse program mix on the air. Most community stations rely on a staff of volunteer announcers, each of whom brings his or her own unique tastes in music and public interest programming. Pursuing the spirit of the Pacifica model, community stations focus on serving the interests of the audience that are not satisfied by the commercial market, even if that audience is very small. Ironically, this approach of serving small audience segments is currently at the center of an ongoing controversy at KPFA. Attempts by management to increase audience share and make programming tamer have led to violent confrontations at Pacifica's flagship station.[50] Similar shifts toward the mainstream at student stations have also led to conflict.[51] But for the most part, community and student stations take pride in their efforts to provide genuine alternatives to commercial radio, and they tend to take more programming risks than CPB-qualified radio stations. Community stations provide an outlet for radical thought and minority interests, challenging the status quo and expanding the diversity of voices on the airwaves. Student stations provide an outlet for new forms of alternative music and have been a significant force in the rise of independent record labels.[52]

EXAMINING THE AUDIENCE
FOR NONCOMMERCIAL RADIO

The audience for noncommercial radio has been gradually but steadily growing. From 1986 to 1996, the weekly national audience for public radio increased more than 80 percent, from 11 million to 20 million.[53] Today, noncommercial radio signals are available to 91 percent of Americans, and 9 percent of the population tunes in to a noncommercial radio station at least once a week. The average listener spends more than eight hours per week listening to public radio, with most of that time spent listening to NPR's daily news magazine programs. The audiences for community stations tend to be smaller, but they also tend to be more diverse in racial composition and educational attainment. Student stations, because they typically have weaker signals, serve a more geographically bounded audience, and one that tends to be skewed toward young men of high school and college age.

The radio audience of the CPB-qualified public station is skewed toward older, well-educated, white middle-class men.[54] Although men represent 48 percent of the adult population in America, the public radio audience is over 59 percent male. Well over two-thirds of the audience is 35+ years of age, and almost a third is 50+. The audience is also overwhelmingly white. Only about one in seven public radio listeners is a member of a racial or ethnic minority.[55] Less than 9 percent of the audience is black, and only 3.5 percent is Hispanic. Recently, NPR was hit with a lawsuit charging the network with making racist business decisions, further fueling the attacks on what critics have called National Public Racism.[56] But NPR contends that the main reason for the low representation of minorities in its listening audience is that public radio programming tends to attract highly educated listeners, and there are unfortunate but real long-standing racial inequities in educational attainment in the United States. Most listeners in public radio's minority audience have at least a bachelor's degree. Black public radio listeners are three times as likely to have a college degree than blacks who don't listen to public radio, and Hispanic public radio listeners are five times as likely to have a college degree.[57] Public radio stations that feature classical music, the most common local programming format, attract the most highly educated—and white—audience. Jazz public radio stations, on the other hand, tend to attract a more diverse audience, both in racial composition and educational attainment.[58]

CPB-qualified radio stations are facing mounting pressures to expand their audience, and much of that pressure comes from NPR. Starting in late 1999, NPR dropped its long-standing practice of charging stations for programs based on their operating budgets, an arrangement that helped stations of all sizes focus more on the quality of programming than on the quantity of listeners. Now NPR charges stations for programming based on audience size.[59] The larger the audience, the more a station must pay for NPR programs. This policy is forcing stations to increase their reliance on corporate underwriting and listener support to pay NPR fees. Perhaps more significantly, it is causing stations to take an increasingly hard look at the "cost per listener hour" versus the "return per listener hour."

These phrases are used repeatedly in the CPB-funded Audience 98 study.[60] In essence, "cost per listener hour" refers to the cost a station must pay (expressed in cents) to get one person to listen one hour to public radio, while "return per listener hour" refers to the listener-sensitive income generated by an hour of public radio programming, in the form of audience support and corporate underwriting. By comparing these two figures for individual programs, a radio programmer can more precisely identify which programs are the most successful in generating income for the station. For example, the Audience 98 study found that PRI's business-oriented program *Marketplace* had the highest gross return of any NPR program, largely because underwriters are willing to pay a high premium for the listeners of this program. *Car Talk* was another program identified by the study as a "high yield" program, because on a per-listener basis it generated the most listener donations. While programming strategies based on financial return are essential in commercial radio, many question the appropriateness of such strategies in noncommercial radio.

THE DECLINING ROLE OF EDUCATION IN PUBLIC RADIO

Many also question how far noncommercial radio has strayed from its educational heritage. The early years were a time of division among noncommercial educational radio stations. When the first federal funds were distributed in 1970, only 17 percent of the noncommercial educational stations on the air were eligible to receive those funds.[61] The strict CPB guidelines for federal funding were ostensibly established to encourage stations to expand and become more professional. But the effect of those guidelines was quite different. Noncommercial radio was being divided into two camps: the respectable, professionally staffed CPB-qualified public stations, and the scrappy, student-operated stations at colleges and universities. The divisiveness would escalate in 1976, when the CPB and NPR petitioned the FCC to reconsider the allocation of low-power Class D stations. NPR wanted to expand into a network of full-power stations, and all those pesky 10-watters were cramping the airwaves. In 1978, the FCC ruled that it would no longer issue Class D licenses, and it put pressure on 10-watters to increase their power to at least 100 watts by 1981 or face being reduced to secondary status. Although many of these stations were able to increase their power to the new minimum, some were forced off the air to make room for full-power NPR stations. Whatever their eventual fate, all Class D stations received the unmistakable message that the Corporation for Public Broadcasting was determined to distance itself from its educational roots.

Public radio even turned its back on the NAEB, the very organization that championed the cause of noncommercial radio for over half a century. NPR essentially took over the program distribution system that NAEB had created. In 1981, during its final year of operation, the NAEB launched a newsletter called *Current*, which today continues on its own as the major trade publication for the public broadcasting industry. For a few old-timers, this newsletter is a perpetual reminder of the long-severed ties between academia and public radio. With the end of the NAEB came the end of the last scholarly home for public broadcasting research in America. As public broadcasting scholar Robert Avery has noted, "The single most important factor in explaining the failure of communication researchers to focus their attention on U.S. public broadcasting in recent years is the demise of the National Association of Educational Broadcasters."[62]

To put it bluntly, the demise of the NAEB, and the death of Class D, gave a one-two knockout punch to educational involvement in public broadcasting in the early 1980s. The passing of the NAEB was largely a blow to faculty, as academics lost a credible voice in the public broadcasting industry, and scholars lost a vital forum to publish research. The successful attack on Class D extended the damage to students, as college radio was shoved to the backwaters of obscure closed-circuit broadcast technologies like carrier current and "leaky FM." Changing institutional priorities, waning faculty involvement, and growing student apathy only accelerated student radio's descent into the "electronic sandbox."[63] Even though most CPB-qualified radio stations today are still affiliated with a college or university, the relationship is often a strained one, with little real interaction between public broadcasters and the campus community.[64] Today's public radio, for all of the wonderful programming it has brought to the American people, has largely abandoned the educational mission that once was at its core.

SUMMARY

As noncommercial radio enters a new century, its mission is increasingly being shaped by the demands of the marketplace. Public radio broadcasters find themselves pulled in opposite directions, compelled by ideological tradition to serve a broadly defined public interest, but pushed by the instinct for survival into focusing on a narrow agenda of maximizing support from their diverse pool of funding sources. While the ideals of noncommercial radio support an educational mission of public service to the community, the practice of public radio reveals a business plan of selling the attention of an elite audience to commercial underwriters. The rationale for doing so has less to do with the public interest than it has to do with the desire to maintain marketplace viability by capturing audiences that remain underserved by the commercial system. Public radio is desperately seeking to claim the gaps in the audience that commercial radio fails to fill.

Unfortunately, those gaps are closing in on public radio. As the number of channels in the radio marketplace increases, the niche audiences targeted by public radio stations are shrinking precariously. This trend is likely to be even more pronounced in the near future, as alternative audio delivery systems, such as direct satellite radio, further dissect the radio audience.[65] By yielding to the seductive logic of the market-place view of the public interest, some noncommercial radio stations may have sealed their own fate, giving up long-term ideological vitality for short-term economic viability. And as one critique put it, "Once sold, the soul of public service broadcasting may never be recovered."[66]

Both critics and supporters wonder how long public radio can last in the new century. Some believe public radio is an anachronism of a bygone era, a bureaucratically burdened solution to the problem of an overwhelmingly commercial marketplace limiting diversity of programming, a problem technology presumably has solved with today's abundance of program options. Others support the mission of noncommercial radio, but argue that it has lost that mission, that it has trapped itself into a desperate Faustian bargain with big business and big government to survive at any cost, even at the cost of the public interest principles it is supposed to serve.

The public broadcasting community even has a name for those who bemoan the drift away from public interest principles: "mission-firsters." Robert Duffey complains that this shrinking group of holdouts "think of themselves and their stations more as social institutions than media outlets, their charters being to stand fast and not yield in the onslaught of new media influences and market forces."[67] Yet to many long-term observers of noncommercial broadcasting, it is remarkable that so many broadcasters do not see their stations as "social institutions" distinctive from the realm of commercial broadcasting. For this is precisely what the Carnegie Commission had in mind, "a system that in its totality will become a new and fundamental institution in American culture."[68]

This institution has endured political trials, economic uncertainties, and ideological angst. Noncommercial radio stations, including public, community, student, and religious stations, have together created a unique national treasure. For many in the listening audience, noncommercial radio is a treasure waiting to be discovered, a "hidden medium" on the left end of the radio dial. But for a growing number of Americans, noncommercial radio is a vital alternative source of information, dialogue, and music. As we move into the twenty-first century, there undoubtedly will be many challenges ahead for the noncommercial radio community. It has already successfully met numerous significant challenges in its history, and, if the past is any predictor of the future, there is ample reason to believe that the story of public broadcasting is far from over. It may be just beginning.

NOTES

[1]"Broadcast Station Totals," available online at http://www.fcc.gov/mmb/asd/totals/bt990731.html, accessed August 30, 1999.
[2]Robert Blakely, *To Serve the Public Interest: Educational Broadcasting in the United States* (Syracuse, NY: Syracuse University Press, 1979), p. 75.

[3]"Who are the Stations and Organizations?," available online at http://www.cpb.org/research/faq/faqp3.html, accessed July 1999.

[4]Fritz Katz, Intercollegiate Broadcasting System. Personal Correspondence, November 1998.

[5]Philip A. Thompsen, "Enhancing the Electronic Sandbox: A Plan for Improving the Educational Value of Student-Operated Radio Stations," *Feedback*, Winter 1992, pp. 1, 12–15.

[6]Lynne Schafer Gross, *Telecommunications: An Introduction to Electronic Media* (Dubuque, IA: Broan and Benchmark, 1997), p. 111.

[7]National Federation of Community Broadcasters, "NFCB Members," available online at http://www.nfcb.org/members.html, accessed September 30, 1999.

[8]Peter M. Lewis and Jerry Booth, *The Invisible Medium: Public, Commercial, and Community Radio* (Washington, DC: Howard University Press, 1990), p. 116.

[9]Ralph Engelman, *Public Radio and Television in America: A Political History* (Thousand Oaks, CA: Sage, 1996), p. 82.

[10]National Religious Broadcasters, *1999 Directory of Religious Media* (Manassas, VA: National Religious Broadcasters, 1998).

[11]Bruce F. Elving, *FM Atlas and Station Directory*, 12th ed. (Esko, MN: FM Atlas Publishing, 1989), p. 2.

[12]Barbara K. Kaye and Norman J. Medoff, *The World Wide Web: A Mass Communication Perspective* (Mountain View, CA: Mayfield, 1999), pp. 14–16.

[13]Ibid., pp. 37–39.

[14]Donald N. Wood and Donald G. Wylie, *Educational Telecommunications* (Belmont, CA: Wadsworth, 1977), p. 18.

[15]Christopher Sterling and John Kitross, *Stay Tuned: A Concise History of American Broadcasting*, 2nd ed. (Belmont, CA: Wadsworth, 1990), p. 40.

[16]Sydney Head, Christopher Sterling and Lemuel Schofield, *Broadcasting in America: A Survey of Electronic Media*, 7th ed. (Boston, MA: Houghton Mifflin, 1994), p. 265.

[17]"Who's on First?," available online at http://www.oldradio.com/archives/general/first.html, accessed September 1999. WHA continues to operate as a noncommercial public radio station, one of the few on the AM band.

[18]Sterling and Kittross, p. 62.

[19]Ibid.

[20]Robert W. McChesney, *Telecommunications, Mass Media and Democracy: The Battle for the Control of U.S. Broadcasting, 1928–1935* (New York: Oxford University Press, 1994).

[21]Ibid., p. 123.

[22]Blakely, p. 59.

[23]Ibid., p. 68.

[24]Head, et al., pp. 266–267.

[25]Ibid., p. 266.

[26]Sterling & Kittross, p. 632.

[27]Ibid., pp. 632–633.

[28]Carnegie Commission on Educational Television, *Public Television: A Program for Action* (New York: Bantam Books, 1967).

[29]Herman W. Land Associates, *The Hidden Medium: A Status Report on Educational Radio in the United States* (New York: National Association of Educational Broadcasters, 1967).

[30]Blakely, p. 149.

[31]Ibid., p. 185.

[32]Sterling and Kittross, p. 657.
[33]Robert K. Avery and Robert Pepper, "Interconnection Redirection: Public Broadcasting Conflicts and the Emerging Alternatives," *Public Telecommunications Review* 6 (1978): 7–25.
[34]Carnegie Commission on the Future of Public Broadcasting, *A Public Trust* (New York: Bantam Books, 1979).
[35]Ibid., p. 57.
[36]Ibid., p. 66.
[37]Willard D. Rowland, Jr., "Public Service Broadcasting in the United States: Its Mandate, Institutions, and Conflicts," in Robert K. Avery, Ed., *Public Service Broadcasting in a Multichannel Environment: The History and Survival of an Ideal* (New York: Longman, 1993), pp. 157–194.
[38]Richard Somerset-Ward, "The Story So Far" in *Quality Time?: The Report of the Twentieth Century Fund Task Force on Public Television* (New York: Twentieth Century Fund Press, 1993), p. 95.
[39]Bruce Drushel, "If You Take the King's Shilling, You Do the King's Bidding." Paper presented to the Speech Communication Association, November 1995.
[40]Corporation for Public Broadcasting, *Public Broadcasting Revenue, Fiscal Year 1997 Final Report* (Washington, DC: Corporation for Public Broadcasting, 1999). Unless otherwise noted, funding figures in this section are from this report.
[41]Corporation for Public Broadcasting, "Financial Profiles of Public Radio Grantees by Licensee Type and Budget Size, Fiscal Year 1997 (Research Note No. 112)" (Washington, DC: Corporation for Public Broadcasting, 1999).
[42]Engelman, pp. 119–120.
[43]Corporation for Public Broadcasting, "Who are the Stations and Organizations?" Available at http://www.cpb.org/research/faq/general/faqp4.html, accessed March 17, 2000.
[44]Robert McKenzie, "We Can Do More to Enhance the Electronic Sandbox," *Feedback*, Summer 1992, pp. 27–30.
[45]See, for example, the list of recent cases of underwriting abuse available from the Audio Services Division of the FCC, available online at http://www.fcc.gov/mmb/asd/nature.html, accessed October 1999.
[46]Lewis Hill, "The Theory of Listener-Sponsored Radio," in Eleanor McKinney, ed., *The Exacting Ear* (New York: Pantheon, 1966), pp. 19–26.
[47]Engelman, p. 49.
[48]Carnegie Commission on the Future of Public Broadcasting, 1979, p. 111.
[49]"National Public Radio and Minnesota Public Radio and Teaming Up to Offer Access to Information about their Shows over the Internet," *Broadcasting & Cable*, March 15, 1999, p. 89.
[50]Alexander Cockburn, "Rebellion at Pacifica," *The Nation*, April 26, 1999, p. 8.
[51]Kenneth Nagelberg, "'What is the Frequency, Kenneth?': A Case Study of the Mainstreaming of College Radio." Paper presented to the Speech Communication Association, San Antonio, TX, 1995.
[52]Jeffrey Wilkinson, "Managing Anarchy, A Prescription for Public Radio," *Feedback*, Winter 1998, pp. 14–20.
[53]"What's on Public Radio and TV?," available online at http://www.cpb.org/research/faq/faqp11.html, accessed July 1999.

[54]"Looking Back at the Audiences of Public Broadcasting (Current Online Briefing)," available online at http://www.current.org/pb/pbaud1.html, accessed September 1, 1999.

[55]Leslie Peters, ed., "Audience 98: Public Service, Public Support" (Washington, DC: Corporation for Public Broadcasting, 1999), p. 43.

[56]"National Public Racism?," *U.S. News & World Report*, January 25, 1999, p. 11.

[57]Ibid., p. 46.

[58]Ibid., pp. 30–31.

[59]Andrea Adelson, "The Business of National Public Radio," *New York Times*, April 5, 1999, p. 9.

[60]Peters, p. 43.

[61]Engelman, p. 92.

[62]Robert K Avery, "Contemporary Public Telecommunications Research: Navigating the Sparsely Settled Terrain," *Journal of Broadcasting and Electronic Media 40* (1996): 132–139.

[63]Thompsen, p. 12.

[64]Jacqueline Conciatore, "Rifts Open between Radio Stations and the Universities," *Current*, August 24, 1998, p. 1.

[65]Jacqueline Conciatore, "NPR, PRI Make Satellite Deals with CD Radio," *Current*, June 21, 1999, p. 1.

[66]Willard D. Rowland, Jr. and Michael Tracey, "Worldwide Challenges to Public Service Broadcasting," *Journal of Communication 40* (1990): pp. 8–27.

[67]Robert Duffey, *Boosting the Signal* (Washington, DC: Corporation for Public Broadcasting, 1996), p. 13.

[68]Carnegie Commission on Educational Television, 1967, p. 4.

9

The Contemporary Radio Industry
Movers and Shakers

The radio broadcast industry has been influenced by a number of key individuals throughout its history. In radio's infancy, inventors and scientists such as Hertz, de Forest, and Armstrong paved the way for the creation of a new medium. Innovators like Sarnoff and Paley recognized the ability of radio to bring audiences together and then sell access to these audiences to potential advertisers. Performers realized that being on the radio was critical for name recognition and the hope of eventual stardom. Politicians found a way to reach their constituency in a timely and cost-efficient manner. Audiences found in radio a medium that could deliver instant news, information, and entertainment programming.

Today, the contemporary radio industry continues to be influenced by a number of key individuals. Who are the movers and the shakers in the contemporary radio industry that will continue to shape and influence the medium in the twenty-first century? This chapter looks at a number of key individuals who have shaped the radio industry during the past ten years and will likely continue to influence the medium for years to come.

Our discussion of these individuals is, by nature, arbitrary in its selection. However, we feel we have identified key individuals who, by their contributions at the time of publication, are major figures in the radio industry. Rather than offer a biographical entry for each person, the chapter highlights the individual's place in the industry, and how this person influences the medium.

THE MOGULS

As discussed in earlier chapters, consolidation became the norm for the radio industry during the 1990s due to passage of the 1996 Telecommunications Act, which eliminated national ownership limits on radio stations. The result has been a rapidly consolidating industry, with the number of companies owning radio stations shrinking rapidly.

Two companies dominate the radio landscape. Clear Channel Communications, through its merger with AMFM Inc. (formerly Chancellor Media), and CBS/Infinity (to be merged with Viacom) have emerged as the key players in radio ownership, with each company controlling hundreds of stations. The leaders who built these powerful radio companies—Thomas Hicks, Lowery Mays, and Mel Karmazin— make up the radio moguls of the twenty-first century. Each of them is profiled below.

Thomas Hicks

Thomas O. "Tom" Hicks is best known in the financial world as the CEO of Dallas-based Hicks, Muse, Tate & Furst, a leverage buyout financier. Interestingly, Hicks, Muse has only existed since 1989, when he and his partners formed the private investment firm after leading several key soft-drink industry buyouts. Today, the portfolio of companies controlled by the LBO firm consists of real estate, consumer products, movie theaters, sports franchises, and broadcast stations.

Hicks became a common name in the radio industry during his tenure as CEO for AMFM Inc., the umbrella name for the media company built during the 1990s. Hicks grew up with an understanding of the radio business. His father owned a few stations in small markets in Texas, and during his teenage years he worked for a time as a radio disc jockey. Hicks began acquiring stations in earnest in 1993 via Hicks, Muse, with Chancellor Broadcasting and CapStar forming the cornerstones of the radio group as part of the Hicks, Muse overall investment strategy.

Acquisitions continued in 1996 and 1997 as Chancellor became Chancellor Media and acquired several key radio holdings, including Evergreen, SFX, and Viacom. Hicks, Muse ventured into television with the purchase of stations owned by LIN Television, as well as several outdoor advertising companies. Hicks attempted to merge the television holdings into Chancellor, but was rebuked by shareholders.[1] In July 1999, shareholders approved the former merger of Chancellor Media and Capstar into a new company known as AMFM Inc. to reflect the emphasis on radio as well as matching the name of the company's national radio network. In 1999, AMFM owned 460 radio stations.[2] In October 1999, Hicks shocked the radio industry with the announcement that Clear Channel Communications would merge with AMFM.[3] Hicks was set to become the Vice Chairman of Clear Channel Communications following the merger.

Aside from building one of the largest radio companies in the country, Hicks brought a new type of entrepreneurial spirit to the radio industry. By clustering stations in geographical areas and appealing to different target audiences, Hicks understood the changing economics of radio and the resultant cash flow that would come with streamlined operations. In an interview published in 1997, Hicks called radio "one of the all-time great businesses for pre-cash flows . . . with no capital expenditures than keeping your physical plant in order."[4]

Hicks's attitudes toward radio spurred other groups to consolidation in order to maintain a national presence in the radio industry. Ultimately, the wave of consolidation proved to be more profitable for Hicks, Muse to become a seller rather than a buyer. Hicks showed other investors that radio was still a profitable investment. While consolidation has not been without controversy, there is no doubt the radio industry has achieved renewed interest among the investment community and higher valuation as an industry group with Hicks as one of radio's leading advocates.

Lowery Mays

Lowery Mays is the Chairman and CEO of Clear Channel Communications, a San Antonio-based company that has been building a radio empire since 1972. The company became a publicly traded entity in 1984. At the time of publication, Clear Channel was the largest owner of radio stations in the world.[5] A former investment banker, Mays runs Clear Channel with the help of his two sons, Mark, who is President and Chief Operating Officer, and Randall, who is Executive Vice President and Chief Financial Officer.

For years Clear Channel was considered a steady, conservative radio company. Beginning with a singe station purchase in 1972, the company was built very slowly during the 1970s and 1980s. By 1993, the company owned thirty-one radio stations (the maximum number any group could own at the time was forty) and seven television stations. In mid-1999, Clear Channel's holdings included 492 radio stations, 19 television stations, and over 425,000 outdoor billboards in twenty-seven different countries. But Clear Channel made the biggest acquisition in radio history with its announcement of a merger with AMFM Inc. in October 1999, a $23.5 billion deal. Once approved by the FCC, Clear Channel would own 830 radio stations in America.[6]

Clear Channel's business philosophy is rather simple: Cut costs while at the same time increasing revenue. But Clear Channel, with Mays as its guiding force, has been able to do it with greater success than most other companies. Mays comments that "We're trying to create shareholder value because we're (family members) the largest shareholders in this company."[7]

Interestingly, Mays believes his company is not so much in the broadcasting business as it is in selling products to consumers. This entrepreneurial philosophy is certainly appreciated by advertisers in the cities where Clear Channel stations conduct business because of its customer-oriented focus.

In addition to being one of the most aggressive buyers of radio stations and outdoor advertising displays, Clear Channel has also invested in new media technologies. In 1999, the company invested $15 million in Tunes.com, an Internet music network. The company also signed a contract with StarGuide Digital Networks to provide satellite-based distribution equipment for radio programming. Clear Channel will use StarGuide equipment to deliver programming originated by its regional and sports networks as well as content created at Premiere Radio Networks, Clear Channel's wholly owned programming subsidiary.

The company has invested heavily in outdoor display advertising in foreign markets, as well as partial ownership in broadcasting operations in several countries. For example, Clear Channel has interest in Australian Radio Networks, Grupo Acir Communcaciones in Mexico, and Radio Bonton in the Czech Republic.[8]

Many challenges await the company, including managing such a large conglomerate, and using the Internet to extend the reach and marketing potential of Clear Channel's radio holdings. As the largest radio station operator in the United States, Clear Channel has positioned itself as one of the largest media companies in the world. Its potential cumulative audience reaches an estimated 100 million people with annual revenues expected to reach around $3 billion.

Mel Karmazin

Mel Karmazin became President and CEO of CBS in 1998 following the retirement of Michael Jordan, who had guided the merger of Westinghouse and CBS several years earlier. Karmazin's rise to the top of the well-known "tiffany" network happened just three years after the company acquired Infinity Broadcasting, at the time one of the largest and most profitable radio companies in the United States.

Karmazin's business skills of increasing stock values and profits were honed in the radio industry. Infinity Broadcasting focused on acquiring the best stations in the largest radio markets. Infinity was also well known as the company with the most controversial talent in the radio industry—Howard Stern. Infinity fought the FCC over the issue of indecency for years with the Stern program, and Karmazin was often called on to defend Stern and the First Amendment, a role that he found uncomfortable.[9] Regulators continued to fine Infinity millions of dollars for numerous Stern violations.

With radio consolidation moving at a record pace after the passage of the 1996 Act, Infinity faced a decision many other radio companies pondered, whether to sell the company to another entity or try to become one of the major players in a revamped industry. The latter would mean investing billions of dollars in more stations. CBS not only made the most competitive offer for Inifinity, but the stations owned by CBS fit nicely with the Infinity holdings.

By folding Infinity into CBS, Karmazin became the President of CBS Radio, and because of his huge personal investment in Infinity, he became the single largest shareholder in the new CBS. The years following the merger were tough for the parent company. The television network had lost part of the lucrative NFL contract to the Fox network. Ratings for primetime television were falling as audiences shifted to cable television channels. An effort to establish a presence in cable television (CBS "Eye on People") failed to attract audiences.

While CBS suffered financially with several of its business segments, the radio division under Karmazin was generating most of the positive cash flow for the company. Karmazin became upset as he learned the economics of television, particularly with the way account executives were compensated. In an interim move to the top of the CBS board, Karmazin was assigned responsibility for the CBS television network. He quickly moved to cut costs at CBS-owned stations, virtually eliminating salaries for account executives and placing the staff on compensation-only income, a move that shocked long-time sales employees of CBS. Internal cost reductions, plus better television ratings for the TV network, led to a rebound in CBS's financial picture.

It was this environment that led Jordan to retire earlier than anticipated, paving the way for Karmazin to become the head of CBS, the first person with a background in radio to lead a major network since David Sarnoff. Interestingly, Karmazin is indifferent about television programming, and even radio programming. In an interview after becoming CEO of CBS, Karmazin claimed he spent little time as a consumer of TV or radio.[10]

But Karmazin's tenure as CEO of CBS would evolve in a manner of a few months. In November 1999, the largest media merger in history was announced: Viacom was buying CBS, creating a media company rich in radio and television stations, programming, cable services, publishing, film production, and other assets. Karmazin was set to become the President and Chief Operating Officer of the new company, second in command to Viacom CEO Sumner Redstone. On Redstone's retirement, Karmazin would become CEO.

While Karmazin's career has shifted toward oversight of a large media conglomerate, he will always be remembered as the man who built Infinity Broadcasting into one of the premiere radio groups in the country. Further, with his support of Howard Stern, Mel Karmazin will likely also be remembered as the man who financially backed the development of the shock radio format.

THE STARS

The power of radio to attract and maintain audiences has always been vested in human talent. During radio's golden age, the medium's talent rivaled that of the film industry. Today, talent is no less important, with several individuals emerging as not only radio stars, but multimedia stars as well. This section focuses on five of the most famous contemporary radio stars: Howard Stern, Laura Schlesinger, Rush Limbaugh, Larry King, and Casey Kasem.

Howard Stern

Howard Stern is the self-proclaimed "king of all media," and perhaps rightly so. Stern remains one of the most listened to voices in America, and he has successfully parlayed his unique style to other media, including television, film, and books. Stern's nationally syndicated radio program is a blend of talk involving sexuality, society, and politics. The program has become a showcase for freedom of expression because Stern talks—and will talk with his studio family and guests—on just about any topic.

Stern was introduced to the radio industry through his father, who worked as a sound engineer.[11] A 1976 communications graduate from Boston College, Stern's early career was far removed from his later success. As typical with many young radio announcers, Stern moved from job to job and format to format. Eventually, Stern was teamed with his sidekick Robin Quivers, and his program evolved into more talk and less music.

Stern and Quivers were fired from WNBC-AM, New York, in 1982 following a dispute with management. By 1985, "The Howard Stern Show" found its home on WXRK-FM, a station owned at the time by Infinity Broadcasting. The program began national syndication the following year.

While Stern's outrageous humor was attractive to his predominantly male audience with references to sex, celebrities, naked women, and an overemphasis on bodily functions, it was not so popular with members of a conservative Federal Communications Commission. The Stern program was levied with over $2 million in fines, the majority of which were related to indecency.[12] Invoking his First Amendment rights, Stern refused to change his program and Infinity, his employer, continued to support his program and paid the fines.

During the 1990s Howard Stern became a multimedia star. Portions of his daily radio show were taped for later broadcast on the E! cable channel, eventually moving to daily status. Stern's autobiography *Private Parts* was published in 1993, and became the fastest selling book in the history of Simon and Schuster.[13] The film adaptation of the book was also a box office success, bringing Stern even greater notoriety. A pay-per-view New Year's Eve special became the most watched PPV event in history.

A second book, *Miss America*, was published in 1995, and reached the top position on many best-seller lists. In 1998, Stern was given the opportunity to have his own national television program when the CBS network gave him the late-night time slot opposite NBC's *Saturday Night Live*. But the Stern program suffered in the television ratings, and several CBS affiliates dropped the controversial program.[14]

Howard Stern is often described as a "shock radio" jock, a title he openly resents in *Private Parts* because he never intended to shock anybody with his radio show.[15] Stern writes "what I . . . set out to do was to talk just as I talk off the air, to talk the way guys talk sitting around a bar."[16] Surprisingly, this bar talk has made Stern a millionaire, and forever changed the way talk radio is perceived by American listeners.

Laura Schlesinger

Dr. Laura Schlesinger is the most listened to woman in America, and, like Howard Stern, has taken her unique brand into other forms of mass media. Like Stern, Schlesinger deals primarily in talk radio, but her expertise is in helping callers who are faced with moral dilemmas. Schlesinger eschews an old-fashioned sense of mores and personal responsibility, and she has been known to yell at and even hang up on whiners.[17]

Schlesinger began her radio career in the 1970s, serving first as an expert on human sexuality on another talk show hosted by Bill Balance before landing her own daily program. Her show went into national syndication in 1994, and became immensely popular with listeners for her frank and candid style.

Schlesinger does not have formal training in counseling or sex therapy; in fact her Ph.D. is in physiology from Columbia University.[18] She prefers to be known as "her kid's mom," reflecting her devotion to her son. With each telephone call, Dr. Laura encourages her listeners to do what is morally right, and she is quick to condemn premarital sex, adultery, infidelity, and mistreatment of children.

In addition to hosting her daily radio program, Schlesinger also has a weekly syndicated newspaper column. She has authored several books, including *How Could You Do That?*, *The Abdication of Character, Courage, Conscience; Ten Stupid Things Men Do to Mess Up Their Lives*, *Ten Stupid Things Women Do to Mess Up Their Lives*, and *The Ten Commandments: The Significance of God's Laws in Everyday Life.*

Schlesinger experienced embarrassment in 1998 when a series of nude photographs of the radio star taken when she was in her twenties appeared on the Internet.[19] Bill Balance, the man who gave Schlesinger her start in radio in 1976, took the photos while the couple was allegedly having an affair. Balance sold the pictures to Internet Entertainment Group for several thousand dollars, which loaded the pictures on their Website. Schlesinger took legal action to stop the postings, but the courts ruled in favor of IEG.

An unauthorized biography was published in 1999, which also turned out to be very unflattering to Dr. Schlesinger.[20] Despite these personal setbacks, Schlesinger's popularity continued to grow. She will host a television talk show that will be distributed by Paramount Domestic Television, expected to begin airing during the fall of 2000. Like her radio show, the program is expected to deal with a combination of ethical and moral issues.[21]

Laura Schlesinger stands alone as the most recognizable female talent in the radio industry. She has successfully found a niche among listeners, and has been able to redirect her content into other media forms. Hopefully, her success will generate even more opportunities for women in radio.

Rush Limbaugh

Rush Limbaugh burst onto the national radio scene in 1988, proclaiming himself as "a man, a legend, a way of life." Rush Limbaugh is the ultimate political conservative, and he spent most of the 1990s bashing liberalism, the Clinton administration, the Democratic Party, feminism, and government bureaucracy on his daily three-hour radio talk show.

Limbaugh is credited with revitalizing AM radio, and he certainly has contributed to a resurgent interest in AM as a talk medium. Heard on over 600 AM stations across the country, Limbaugh broadcasts over his "Excellence in Broadcasting" (EIB) network from its Manhattan base.[22] His program attracts millions of listeners, ranking him with Stern and Schlesinger as the most listened to voices in America.

Limbaugh's rise to the top of conservative talk radio didn't happen overnight. A native of Cape Girardeau, Missouri, Limbaugh grew up in a Republican household with both of his parents active in the GOP.[23] He began working in radio as a teenager, and like Howard Stern, rotated through a number of stations in different markets. At one point in his career, Limbaugh left radio to work for the Kansas City Royals baseball team in their marketing department.

Eventually moving back into radio, Limbaugh had the chance to replace the fired Morton Downey, Jr., on a talk show in Sacramento in 1984. His program became very popular, leading to an opportunity to audition for a national talk show with WABC in New York in 1988. From that point forward, the rest is history. Limbaugh's program soared in popularity, with hundreds of stations acquiring the syndicated talk program that airs for three hours every weekday afternoon.

Who listens to Limbaugh? Audience data indicates his audience is almost entirely male, white, with more than half ages 22–54.[24] These "dittoheads" as Limbaugh refers to his minions, are conservative citizens who share his concern on topics such as illegal immigrants, the media, environmentalists, feminists, liberals, Democrats, Affirmative Action, and, yes, the Clinton Administration.

Limbaugh is not just a radio celebrity, he is an active public speaker. He developed a half-hour syndicated television program and authored two books: *The Way Things Ought to Be*, and *See, I Told You So*. Both books were bestsellers.

Many of Limbaugh's critics expected his popularity to wane by the end of the decade, but it clearly has not happened. Rush Limbaugh will likely be a part of radio well into the millennium. Limbaugh is a product of the medium, and he is extremely skillful at harnessing the power of radio and its ability to impact audiences.

Larry King

Larry King is no longer a fixture on national radio, but deserves mention for his development of the talk radio phenomenon. Born in Brooklyn, New York, King wanted a career in radio as early as age five. King's father died when he was only nine years old, causing the family to become dependent on welfare for its survival.

King first ventured into radio in 1957 as a disc jockey, working long shifts and covering every type of programming, music, news, and sports.[25] Early in his career he had the opportunity to conduct interviews, and it was here where King began to build a niche. In 1960, King was working in radio in South Florida, and had the opportunity to do a local television show that also consisted of interviews and debates. King credits Arthur Godfrey on radio and Jackie Gleason on television as two mentors who strongly influenced his young career.[26]

King lost his jobs in the media during the early 1970s after his involvement with a shady financier was made public. He toiled with various jobs until he was eventually able to return to the air in Miami, where he regained his popularity. In 1978, Larry King began hosting a national talk show on the Mutual Broadcasting System, and it was this forum that gave King his greatest recognition as a masterful interviewer.

In 1985, the fledging Cable News Network offered King the opportunity to host an hour-long live talk program, featuring audience call-ins. It was the first show of its kind in television history, and immediately became CNN's highest rated television program, a position the program still maintains.[27] In 1994, *Larry King Live* became the first talk show to be simulcast on both television and radio.

King has conducted more than 30,000 interviews during his broadcasting career. His guest list features the biggest names in world politics, entertainment, sports, and the media. The popularity of his television show led to King's retirement from radio in 1996.

King is the author of eleven books, and also writes a weekly column entitled *Larry King's News & Views* every Monday in *USA Today*. He has also made cameo appearances in a number of feature films. In 1987, King suffered from serious heart problems, leading to quintuple bypass heart surgery. That experience led King to establish the Larry King Cardiac Foundation, which helps heart patients with financial need have the necessary surgery and medical care they need to live. A nonprofit entity, the Foundation is supported by proceeds from the sale of King's books, public speaking engagements, and an annual fundraiser.[28]

Larry King's contributions to the development of talk radio and the radio interview program is enormous. Through his years on the old Mutual network and his live television show, King demonstrated that talk could not only be interesting, but profitable as well. His ability to simultaneously engage studio guests, call-ins, and audience members set the standard for talk radio personalities.

Casey Kasem

Aside from James Earl Jones, Casey Kasem probably has the most recognized voice in America. A longtime radio and television performer, Kasem is best known as the man who for years has provided a weekly rundown of the country's hottest music on the syndicated program "American Top 40."

Kasem began his radio career in 1950 in his native Detroit at WXYZ performing dramatic roles on *The Lone Ranger* and *Sergeant Preston of the Yukon.*[29] He worked various jobs in radio at several different stations, and also worked for Armed Forces Radio after he was drafted for service during the Korean War.

In 1970, Kasem and his friend Don Bustany co-created *American Top 40,* and later *American Country Countdown.* The program was extremely timely in that many FM stations were starting to adopt music formats that were being abandoned by AM stations. *AT40* was the vehicle that made Kasem a star, and the program became one of the most popular weekly syndicated radio shows in the history of the industry. *AT40* was syndicated nationally by ABC/Watermark until 1988 when Kasem left over a contract dispute.[30] From there the program moved to Westwood One, where it would remain until 1998.

In addition to his work on *AT40,* Kasem has hosted a number of other countdown programs over the years including *Casey's Top 40, Casey's Hot 20, Casey's Biggest Hits,* and *Casey's Countdown.* Kasem's voice can be heard in a number of other forums. Among his credits are a number of cartoon programs, including "Shaggy" on *Scooby-Doo,* the voice of Robin on *The Adventures of Batman and Robin* and *The All New Super Friends Hour,* and Cliffjumper on *Transformers.* Kasem has also made cameo appearances in several movies and television programs as himself.

In 1998, Kasem angered his former employer, Westwood One, by signing with AMFM Radio Networks to move *AT40* to a new forum. A lawsuit followed, with the parties eventually reaching a settlement that allowed Kasem to move to AMFM.[31]

During his long career, Kasem has received numerous honors and awards over the years, including his 1998 induction into the Broadcasting and Cable Hall of Fame. On receiving this honor, Kasem thanked several industry executives, including a mentor in Detroit that was "kind enough . . . to wait six months to tell me what I was doing wrong so it wouldn't crush my enthusiasm." Kasem called himself "The person trying to live up to the positive image which I hope I've projected over the air all these years."[32]

THE INNOVATORS

What does the future hold for the radio industry? While no one is entirely certain, there are clear indications that radio continues to adapt and evolve to its changing environment. Revisions of regulatory policy results in implications for market structure and competition. New technologies push and extend the medium to new levels of presentation and packaging.

The emergence of the Internet has had an enormous impact on traditional broadcasting, especially with the development of streaming media. One company that became an early leader in streaming digital media is Dallas-based Broadcast.com, a company formed in 1995 by Mark Cuban and Todd Wagner.

Cuban and Wagner/Broadcast.com

Mark Cuban and Todd Wagner are the cofounders and innovators behind Broadcast.com, the pioneering company that invented Internet broadcasting. Friends since their days at Indiana University, Cuban combined an entrepreneurial spirit with a zest for technology. Wagner, on the other hand, spent his early career as a corporate attorney working his way through major law firms.

In 1995, Wagner and Cuban were both living in Dallas. Wagner asked Cuban if there was some way to listen to Indiana University basketball games over the Internet. That conversation was the genesis for a company that would eventually be valued at over $5 billion by 1999.

Cuban used about $5,000 worth of equipment to create the company, and convinced Dallas radio station KVIL to give them permission to broadcast their signal over the Internet. In a short amount of time, the popularity of the site grew, and the pair realized they had a viable business model. The pair formed a company called AudioNet and began selling Internet distribution to radio stations and sports teams across the country.[33]

The young company was off to a fast start, with a number of content providers jumping on board. From a strategic standpoint, Cuban and Wagner recognized that if they could control access to the content, it would be much more difficult for competitors to encroach on their market. Thus, AudioNet emerged as an exclusive provider of Internet content for many providers.[34]

In 1998, AudioNet changed its name to Broadcast.com, to reflect the fact that the company now offered video distribution as well as audio broadcasting. An initial public offering of company stock on July 17, 1998, was one of the most successful in Wall Street history. On that day, the stock of Broadcast.com grew some 249 percent, raising more than $40 million in operating capital and making Cuban and Wagner and their other investors instant millionaires.[35]

The company continued to achieve great notoriety, especially with its Internet broadcast of a live Victoria's Secrets fashion show on February 3, 1999.[36] The show attracted 1.5 million viewers, but thousands more Internet users were denied access due to network capacity, demonstrating the power of the Internet to attract audiences. More and more businesses began to utilize Broadcast.com for audio and video streaming as interest in the company continued to grow.

The tremendous success of the young company, coupled with Internet euphoria, led to another major financial windfall for Broadcast.com. Yahoo!, the original Internet portal/search engine, announced plans to acquire Broadcast.com for $5.6 million on April 1, 1999.[37] Merging the leading Internet portal with the leading provider of audio/video content on the Web was a natural fit, allowing the merged companies to share synergies and develop new revenue streams. Renamed Yahoo Broadcast Services after the merger, Cuban and Wagner continue to hold important leadership roles with the company.

SUMMARY

This chapter introduced some of the key individuals who have had a significant impact on the radio industry in recent years. We looked at ten individuals divided into three categories: moguls, stars, and innovators. Their contributions have been felt in markets large and small, and across geographic boundaries. No doubt, their presence in the industry will be felt for many years to come.

Radio is a business, but it has always been a business about people. Radio brings people together, whether in the form of audiences, advertisers, talent, or musicians. And it will continue to do so.

Historians have written that the "golden age" of radio occurred in the 1930s and 1940s. Looking back fifty years from now, many may surmise that the last decade of the twentieth century was truly radio's golden age, when innovation and vision collided with technology and forever changed the industry.

NOTES

[1]"An Ambition as Big as Texas," *Business Week*, July 26, 1999, pp. 66–67.

[2]"Special Report on Radio Ownership," *Broadcasting & Cable*, August 30, 1990, p. 26.

[3]Elizabeth A. Rathburn, "Count 'em: 830," *Broadcasting & Cable*, October 11, 1999, p. 12.

[4]"Thomas Hicks Follows the TV-Radio Muse," *Broadcasting & Cable*, June 23, 1997, p. 40.

[5]See http://www.clearchannel.com, company overview.

[6]Rathburn, p. 12.

[7]Elizabeth A. Rathburn, "Clear Channel Builds a Broadcast Dynasty," *Broadcasting & Cable*, October 7, 1996, p. 56.

[8]1998 10-K Annual Report, Clear Channel Communications, p. 3.

[9]Peter Viles, "Mel Karmazin and the Infinite Possibilities of Radio," *Broadcasting & Cable*, September 6, 1993, p. 32.

[10]Martin Peers and Josef Adalian, "The King and Eye," *Variety*, November 16, 1998, p. 1.

[11]"Year in Review 1997: Biography," *Encyclopedia Britannica Online*, http://www.eb.com: 180/bol/topic?eu=124834&sctn=1 [Accessed 23 August 1999].

[12]"Stern's Comments Cost Company $1.7 Million," *News Media & the Law, 19,* Fall 1995: pp. 45–46.

[13]Year in Review 1997.

[14]Michael Freeman, "Howard Gets a Tweaking," *Mediaweek,* September 7, 1998, p. 9.

[15]Ruth Bayard Smith, "Absolute Talk on the Radio," *Media Studies Journal* (Spring/Summer 1998): p. 77.

[16]Howard Stern, *Private Parts* (New York: Simon & Schuster, 1993).

[17]Smith, p. 78.

[18]Smith, p. 78.

[19]Elizabeth A. Rathburn, "Dr. Laura—Naked?" *Broadcasting & Cable,* November 2, 1998, p. 34.

[20]Vicki Bane, *Dr. Laura: The Unauthorized Biography* (St. Martin's/Thomas Dunne, 1999).

[21]Joe Schlosser, "The Doctor Is In," *Broadcasting & Cable,* May 17, 1999, p. 34.

[22]Smith, p. 75.

[23]Philip Seib, *Rush Hour* (Fort Worth: The Summit Group): p. 23.

[24]Tom Lewis, "Triumph of the Idol—Rush Limbaugh and a Hot Medium," *Media Studies Journal 7* (Summer 1993): p. 53.

[25]Rich Cohen, "The King and I," *Rolling Stone,* November 14, 1996, Pp. 74–75.

[26]See Larry King—Biography, available at www.achievement.org/people/lking

[27]See http://www.cnn.com/anchors/larry_king.htm

[28]See http://www.lkcf.org

[29]See *Broadcating & Cable,* Hall of Fame program insert, November 9, 1998.

[30]Carrie Borzillo, "Casey Kasem Counts Down 25 Years on the Radio," *Billboard,* July 8, 1995, p. 79.

[31]See "Year in Review 1998" *Encyclopedia Britannica Online,* http://www.eb.com:180/bol/ topic?eu=136370&sctn=4&pm=1 [Accessed 23 August 1999].

[32]"The Winner's Circle," *Broadcasting & Cable,* November 16, 1998, p. 46.

[33]Richard Murphy, "Mark Cuban and Todd Wagner," *Success,* May, 1999, p. 54.

[34]Murphy, op cit.

[35]Ibid.

[36]Adam Penenberg, "Informercial.com," *Forbes,* March 8, 1999, p. 116.

[37]"Yahoo!'s Broadcast Bonanza," *Business Week,* April 12, 1999, p. 44.

10

Radio and the Twenty-First Century

Trying to assess the future of the radio broadcasting industry is a daunting task, given the numerous twists, turns, and reinventions during the medium's first century. During radio's first hundred years of existence, the medium grew from an experimental system of sending Morse code to a multibillion-dollar entertainment and informational companion. Modes of transmission, programming, and audience uses of the medium have undergone massive shifts over the years.

There are however, trends in the past twenty years that provide at least some direction as to how the radio industry will continue to evolve during the twenty-first century. Our focus in this final chapter will be on four broad categories that, in our view, provide a road map for radio's future. These four categories are: (1) the Business of Radio, (2) Technologies Impacting Radio, (3) Globalization, and (4) Localism.

THE BUSINESS OF RADIO

Radio's resurgence as an intensive cash-flow medium attracted investor attention following the elimination of national ownership caps in the 1996 Telecommunications Act. More than at any time in its history, the radio industry truly was looked on as a business. Here are a few areas that illustrate radio's business environment.

Consolidation

Industry consolidation escalated during the 1990s, with a number of companies gobbled up in the acquisition frenzy. While the industry is dominated by a shrinking number of large companies like Clear Channel and Viacom/CBS, there is still room for further consolidation, especially involving medium and small market stations. Look for further efforts among industry players to consolidate operations, especially with the development of regional station clusters.

As mentioned in Chapter 3, the relaxation on television duopoly ownership rules will produce ripple effects for the radio industry. The new rules allow TV broadcasters to own two television stations in the same market, provided there are eight stations operated by different owners. However, the maximum number of radio stations owned varies. If an owner acquires a second TV station, he or she is limited to owning six radio stations in the market. If he or she only owns one television station, the owner is limited to owning seven radio stations in the market. As TV consolidation continues, there will be spin-off sales to allow companies to meet the new rule requirements.[1]

Further ownership regulatory decisions, whether involving the FCC, Congress, or the Courts, may affect radio consolidation in the years ahead. At the time of publication, the Commission was considering further ownership modifications, especially in regards to cross-media ownership involving newspapers and broadcast stations. It is unclear how changes in cross-media ownership might affect further radio consolidation.

Syndication Marketplace

Another likely business trend is the continuing growth of the syndication market for national radio programming. This market revolves around two separate directions: individual syndicated programs and features and 24-hour format services.

In terms of individual programs, popular national talents like Stern, Limbaugh, and Schlesinger have already led to a number of other syndicated talk efforts, involving a number of hosts: Art Bell, Oliver North, G. Gordon Liddy, and others. Talk will remain an AM fixture, built around news, sports, and politics. In addition to the talk format, several morning shows from around the country emerged during the 1990s. In the Southeast, John Boy and Billy found regional success with their blend of Southern-fried humor and interest in auto racing. In the Midwest, Madcow Muller began to syndicate his shock-style morning show. And on the West Coast, KFI-AM (Los Angeles) morning team John and Ken began syndicating their morning show, which emphasizes news and politics.[2]

Countdown programs, such as *American Top 40, American Country Countdown* and other radio programming features, have become mainstays of radio programming. New features will continue to be introduced in the years ahead to complement existing formats.

Satellite-delivered formats are extremely popular among radio managers for their ability to deliver strong talent and quality programming, while reducing overhead and local personnel costs. ABC Radio Networks, based in Dallas, Texas, is the leading provider of 24-hour radio formats in the country, offering ten different formats targeted to specific demographic groups. The rise of newer radio services, such as ESPN Radio and Radio Disney, both extensions of existing national brands, have also been very successful innovations. The StarSystem, another programming service located in the South and Southeast, has targeted smaller and medium-size cities to deliver programming.[3]

In summary, the syndication marketplace for radio is stronger than ever, with more content available for station programmers than can be utilized by any one station. The growth in programming material in turn has made radio even more marketable, especially as an advertising medium.

Radio Marketing

Growing clusters of powerful stations offering quality programming generate sizeable audiences that can be effectively marketed to national, regional, and local advertisers. The consolidation of radio ownership will give the industry greater leverage in negotiating with national advertisers.[4] Still, with the price of all advertising mediums rising, radio remains an affordable and targeted advertising vehicle.

Building on its strength as an advertising medium, the radio industry is well positioned to maximize and expand its advertising base. During the 1990s, annual radio advertising exhibited strong double-digit growth from 1993–1998.[5] Although data for 1999 was not available prior to publication, it was anticipated that the industry would continue to experience increases averaging around 10 to 13 percent on an annual basis. During the 1990s, radio advertising increased at a higher annual rate than advertising in newspapers and television.

But the radio industry will need to continue to emphasize its marketing strengths to advertisers at all levels. Television, newspapers, magazines, and other mediums compete for the same ad dollars as radio, along with the Internet. Not surprisingly, the Internet has quietly skipped past radio in terms of national advertising.[6] Paradoxically, radio has become a preferred advertising medium for many Web startups as a fast and reliable way to build audiences.[7] For the radio industry, the local market will remain the most efficient and lucrative category for advertising revenues.

Marketing will need to involve strong promotion efforts as well. Aside from traditional AM and FM stations, listeners now have hundreds of Internet radio stations promoting niche formats and trying to lure audiences and advertisers.[8] New satellite-delivered radio services (e.g., DARS) are also trying to capture the same listeners. At a time when the potential of the radio medium is so great, the competitive marketing challenges have never been greater.

TECHNOLOGIES IMPACTING RADIO

Radio's technological capabilities in the twenty-first century are numerous, and will no doubt impact the direction of the medium. Today, radio programming can reach audiences via a number of distribution options. Traditional AM and FM broadcasting continue to be the primary avenues, but new distribution technologies have emerged. In this section of the chapter, we will focus on two areas: the Internet and the deployment of satellite-delivered digital radio services.

The Internet

Like many forms of existing media, radio stations embraced the Internet early in its diffusion. Radio stations recognized that a complementary Web page would enable the stations to extend their brand, and help in the marketing and promotion of the stations. Soon, station personnel recognized that the Web page could aid in providing another form of audience research, as well as continuous interaction with the audience through electronic mail.

The advent of streaming media provided another revolution in Internet capability. As discussed in Chapter 9, broadcast.com (now a part of Yahoo!), located in Dallas, Texas, began live Internet broadcasting with radio station KLIF. The trend caught on quickly with other radio stations, domestically and around the world. Now it was possible for anyone with an Internet connection to listen to a station anywhere in the world. And because the transmission involved only an audio channel, most household computer modems could easily reproduce the originating station's signal with little difficulty. Live Internet broadcasting became a way to extend a station's listener base, and allow for out-of-home listening for travelers as well as people living in another country wanting to listen to their "home" stations.

But Internet broadcasting would not be confined to delivering programming from existing radio stations. The Internet offered an outlet for anyone who wanted to broadcast, leading to the creation of thousands of Internet-only radio stations.[9] Cyber-radio stations utilize a server with a high-speed connection and software capable of streaming audio files. The user simply needs speakers or headphones and a media player that can be downloaded for free for any home computer.

Internet-only radio stations recognize that in order to be unique, they must differentiate themselves from stations on the Web. One service, GoGaGa, epitomizes this trend. The service displays a list of all the music they play, with each song linked to an online retailer like Amazon.com, enabling the listener to purchase a song seamlessly while listening.[10] Listeners also are fed advertisements on login, something broadcast stations can't offer.

The latest innovation in Internet-related broadcasting is the development of **personal radio**.[11] The personal radio service utilizes thousands of digital music cuts stored on a server. In a personal radio system, the user first sets up a listener profile through an existing service. The user enters his or her music preferences, either using a genre or selecting individual artists. By adding a zip code to the profile, the listener can also access local weather. Eventually, the services plan to offer traffic and local news information.

Internet-only radio stations and the continuing development of personal radio may attract some listeners from traditional radio stations, especially those who are male, younger, and more technologically oriented. It is unlikely these new startups will impact radio advertising in any measurable way in the immediate future. At the least, the Internet has given radio broadcasting a whole new perspective—and more possible competitors than one could imagine.

Satellite-Delivered Radio Services

Satellite-delivered radio services, labeled as DARS (Digital Audio Radio Services), have been in development for several years. Two services, Sirius Satellite Radio and XM Satellite Radio, are set to debut in 2000. Originally licensed in 1995 by the FCC, DARS has the ability to deliver CD-quality audio to either the home or the automobile via a special receiver.[12] Offered as a subscription-based service, companies licensed to provide the DARS service will offer a number of music formats for a monthly fee.

Terrestrial broadcasters fought unsuccessfully against the establishment of DARS, fearing the new services would erode local audiences. Plagued by regulatory hurdles and financing, the services are expected to debut over the next few years.

Will DARS be successful? That will ultimately be up to consumers to decide. Some argue that DARS will provide the same content available on radio for free, while others claim the superior sound quality will make the service preferable to standard radio receivers. DARS will finally enter the radio marketplace, but its long-term ability to survive remains in question.

The development of new communication technologies will continue to affect the radio industry. Eventually, radio will move to distribution in a totally digital environment, meaning broadcasters will be known as datacasters, with content being repurposed in a number of unenvisioned means. Radio has shown its ability to adapt and survive during its first century of existence. If the past is prologue to the future, we can expect radio to continue to adapt and evolve as technology requires.

GLOBALIZATION

The globalization of the media industries continues at an unprecedented pace. Exactly how globalization may affect the United States domestic radio industry remains to be seen. What is much more concrete is the influence of U.S. radio companies abroad.

During the 1990s, several radio companies began limited investment in foreign companies. In most cases, ownership interests were of a minority interest (less than

50% ownership). Clear Channel Communications has been particularly aggressive, with ownership interests in twenty-eight different countries, primarily in Western and Eastern Europe and countries in the Pacific Rim. In the case of Clear Channel, holdings include a number of outdoor (billboard) advertising companies, as well as radio operations.[13]

While it is unlikely that a U.S. "Westernization" of radio will take place around the globe, there is little doubt that the United States has influenced other countries with its development of commercial radio. Even the stoic British Broadcasting Corporation (BBC) is restructuring itself along the lines of U.S. broadcast companies.[14] And, in the United Kingdom, commercial radio stations have doubled since the country passed a 1990 Act that provided more permissive licensing.[15]

Domestic radio companies will continue to look for good investment potential in other regions of the world. While business opportunities will drive such actions, one concern is that U.S. radio's influence will result in a lack of diversity of program offerings. Ownership concentration, whether at domestic or international levels, tends to lead to homogeneous products, especially where media oligopolies exist.[16] Policymakers in other countries will no doubt monitor U.S. investment and ownership in their native countries in order to limit undue concentration.

Given the relaxation in radio ownership rules in the United States, is increased foreign ownership of U.S. radio stations likely in the twenty-first century? Currently, foreign ownership of domestic stations is limited to a minority interest. Other media industries have significant foreign ownership including newspapers, film studios, recording companies, and book and magazine publishers. If U.S. companies can invest in radio in other countries, shouldn't foreign companies be allowed to invest in radio stations operating within the United States?

Ultimately, the Congress, courts, and the FCC may tackle the emotional issue of foreign ownership of U.S. broadcast interests. Given the increasing globalization of the media industries, revamped foreign investment and ownership may become a reality in the years ahead.

LOCALISM

As discussed in Chapter 2, the advent of television in the 1950s forced radio to reposition itself as a local rather than national medium. Today, the radio broadcasting industry offers localism as its greatest asset. In the future, localism will continue to be one of the primary ingredients driving the success of the medium.

In order to exhibit a strong sense of localism, radio stations will have to establish a clear identity in their respective markets. Strong branding and promotion will be the cornerstones of building a local identity, along with good programming and sophisticated and varied research efforts. An editorial in *Broadcasting & Cable* offered sage advice on the topic of localism: "Broadcaster's edge is localism and tailoring programming to individual markets and listeners."[17] Programming will remain music-centered on FM. AM will continue to market talk, sports, and ethnic/ niche formats.

Regardless of the type of transmission, radio must deliver enough information needed by the respective audience to maintain listeners. Over the years, many stations abandoned news in order to reach the growing baby boomer audience. As baby boomers mature, look for more news and information to flow back into radio formats during drive times, especially those geared toward an audience age forty and higher.

During the 1980s and 1990s, many music-formatted radio stations adopted a **formula radio** approach. Such a format consisted of several sets of music interspersed with blocks of radio commercials, along with traffic, weather, and minimal news and information. Regardless of the type of music (e.g., country, rock, Top 40) the presentation remained the same. Formula radio meant that stations in San Francisco sounded like stations in Houston, which sounded like stations in Chicago. Missing from the medium was much in the way of creativity. Even contests sounded the same from market to market.

While imitation is the ultimate form of flattery, the most successful radio stations in the future will be those that once again find creative ways to reach and retain listeners in their local markets. This will mean constant interaction with the community, using any and all available means, such as the station's Web page, research, and even personal appearances by talent. It will mean being responsive to listener wants and needs. And it will require consistent analysis and innovation.

Even in a world of instantaneous communication and personal radio, no medium has the power to reach millions of daily commuters and office personnel like the radio. When a change in the weather is approaching people most often turn to radio. Traffic information is also easily found on the radio. And for the first bit of important news or information on a breaking story, radio is, for many people, the first stop. Why? Radio is ubiquitous, reliable, and local.

SUMMARY

The competitive challenges facing the radio industry are numerous. Today there are more entertainment and information options available to consumers than at any point in media history. How will radio respond as an industry? Will the radio industry continue to hold an important role in society? Or will new technologies and the Internet push radio into the dreaded category referred to as "old media"?

At this particular stage in history, the radio industry finds itself financially strong and rather secure. A strong national economy coupled with low unemployment and inflation rates has also stimulated local economies, resulting in a high demand for advertising and positive cash flows. But we know the business cycle doesn't continue indefinitely on a high note. The financial good times for radio may pass. Still, the industry is in a good position to reinvest in itself, to again draw on the innovation and creative spirit that led to the founding of radio as we know it nearly a century ago.

As the first electronic medium, radio holds a special place in the lives of its listeners. If the medium continues to develop and appreciate its relationship to its audience and the community it serves, there is no reason to think the radio industry won't be around for many more decades. The first century of radio has been colorful and remarkable. Many in the industry think the best is yet to come.

NOTES

[1] See "FCC Revises Local Television Ownership Rules," available online at http://www.fcc. gov/Bureaus/Mass_Media/News_Releases/1999/nrmm9019.html

[2] Donna Petrozello, "Expanding Horizons," *Broadcasting & Cable*, June 9, 1997, p. 26.

[3] Katherine Yung, "New Wave," *Dallas Morning News*, January 10, 1999, pp. 1H, 6H.

[4] Katheryn Kranhold, "Clear Channel Deal to Further Reduce Radio Options," *Wall Street Journal*, October 5, 1999, p. B8.

[5] See Media Facts, available online at http://www.rab.com/station/mediafact/medfcts99/mfradio.html

[6] "Online Ad Spending . . ." *Wall Street Journal*, August 12, 1999, p. B5.

[7] Suen L. Hwang, "Old Media Get a Web Windfall," *Wall Street Journal*, September 17, 1999, p. B1, B4.

[8] See William M. Bulkeley, "Radio Stations Make Waves on the Web," *Wall Street Journal*, July 23, 1998, p. B1.

[9] Thomas E. Weber, "Web Radio: No Antenna Required," *Wall Street Journal*, July 28, 1999, pp. B1, B4.

[10] Weber, p. B4.

[11] William M. Bulkeley, "Start-Up Wants Web Surfers to Play Tunes," *Wall Street Journal*, September 9, 1999, p. B8.

[12] Lynne Gross, *Telecommunications: An Introduction to Electronic Media* (New York: McGraw-Hill, 2000), p. 32.

[13] See the Clear Channel Website for current ownership information, available online at http://www.clearchannel.com

[14] "The New-look BBC," *Economist*, August 29, 1998, p. 53.

[15] "Commercial Radio. Switched on," available online at http://www.economist.com/archive, accessed August 11, 1999.

[16] See Alan B. Albarran, *Media Economics: Understanding Markets, Industries and Concepts* (Ames, IA: Iowa State University Press, 1996), p. 36.

[17] "Size Matters," *Broadcasting & Cable*, October 11, 1999, p. 110.

Glossary

account executives (AES)   The sales staff of a radio station. They are responsible for identifying potential clients, qualifying the clients, developing sales presentations, closing the sale, and servicing the account. AEs are also known as marketing executives or marketing consultants.

advertising agencies   The contact source for account executives who want to sell advertising time to larger retailers or manufacturers. The advertising agency may serve as a creative development center for the client by devising the marketing approach and advertising campaign for the client as well as coordinating advertising placement among various media including radio, television, and newspapers.

amplitude modulation (AM)   The modulation process for AM stations that results in variation of the amplitude or height of the carrier wave; also, the first system of broadcasting technology to develop.

Arbitron Research   The most widely used supplier of radio ratings information. The company uses a personal, seven-day diary to measure radio listening in 260 markets, with 94 markets being measured year-round.

auditorium testing   A type of programming research done by radio stations to test audience reactions and preferences for different types of music. Auditorium testing is done with a large group of subjects in a single location.

average quarter hour (AQH)   Radio listening is tracked using 15-minute increments called Average Quarter Hour (AQH); it measures an estimate of the number of people listening to a particular station during any five-minute interval in a particular daypart. Audience estimates can be expressed as AQH rating percentages or as AQH actual listener estimates in hundreds or thousands.

Billboard A trade industry publication that tracks music sales and radio station song airplay. Available online at http://www.billboard.com/. Billboard Online & Yahoo! Broadcast.com provide a weekly audio show featuring The Billboard Hot 100 on Billboard Radio. The site allows listeners to hear the week's most popular singles and tracks as compiled from a national sample of Broadcast Data Systems radio playlists, retail store, mass merchant, and Internet sales reports.

brand An umbrella term used to refer to radio station formats and their accompanying promotional images. Brand has also been used to equate station listening (usage) with preferences consumers have for other goods or services.

call out research A type of programming research used to collect listener preferences for different types of music; it uses professional interviews to collect data from eligible respondents.

carrier wave The frequency on which the station operates. The station's programming is placed on the carrier wave through modulation and then broadcast through the air for listener reception.

cash flow The amount of cash that "flows" through a radio station. Cash flow is the revenues of a radio station minus expenses, taxes, depreciation, and interest. Cash flow is often used to estimate the value of a station.

charge back Requiring an account executive to repay any previously paid commission in the event a client fails to pay for ad time already run and for which the account executive has already been paid.

continuity book A list of the introductory and closing comments for any program or broadcast aired on the station; it provides background material to the announcers as well. It is not as likely to be seen today in a radio station, but stations may make programming reference material available via computer files.

cooperative advertising or **co-op advertising** A shared-cost ad program involving local retailers and national manufacturers or distributors. The national company provides an advertising allowance to the local retailer, usually determined by the dollar value of the inventory purchased from the national company. This advertising allowance can then be used to buy ads to promote the national brand and the local retailer.

cost per gross rating point The average cost for one GRP in an ad schedule; it is calculated by dividing the total cost of the schedule by the total number of GRPs.

cost per thousand (CPM) A figure that compares the cost of reaching the targeted audience either on a single station or across different media. The simplest way to calculate cost per thousand is to divide the cost of the ad by the number of listeners (in thousands) who are expected to hear the ad.

cume listeners A shortening that stands for *cumulative audience,* an estimate of the total number of listeners reached by a radio station during a typical week. Cume estimates indicate the level of reach or penetration in a market. Rather than count listeners multiple times during the day, this calculation allows the station to know how many different people listen to the station during a day.

daypart Divisions of the broadcast day created to track radio listening and aid in program scheduling. Dayparts include morning drive, midday, afternoon drive, nighttime, and overnight. Dayparting can also refer to slight variations in the music played on the station at various times of the day.

demand marketing As applied to radio, an audience analysis that enables station owners to determine the product listeners wanted. As television replaced radio in the 1950s as the nation's dominant entertainment medium, radio operators were forced to pay attention to what a potential listening audience segment might want to hear on the radio.

demographics A term used to describe the characteristics of radio audience in terms of gender and age. Adults 18–49, W 18–35, M 25–54 are examples of demographic categories.

designated market area (DMA) A term used by Nielsen and Arbitron to indicate concentration of listeners in a geographical market.

diary A long-standing method of collecting audience listening data; each respondent fills out a diary (log) of daily listening for a one-week period. Diaries are collected and tabulated and used to produce a ratings report.

digital audio radio services (DARS) A new technology enabling the distribution of satellite-delivered audio services to consumers for a monthly fee. The FCC authorized DARS service in 1995.

Duncan's American Radio A radio industry research group that tracks station trading and radio listenership, and provides individual radio market reports of station ratings and revenue performance throughout the United States.

duopoly Prior to 1996, regulations prevented one owner from owning another station of the same type or class within the same market. This provision was known as the "duopoly rule."

ear leasing Radio stations' use of their programming to attract listeners and then sell access to these listeners to advertising clients. Effectively, the ad client is paying the radio station rent in order to have station listeners hear a commercial about the client's products or services.

economies of scale A term used by economists to describe efficiencies in production and ownership. In radio, economies of scale have been realized due to consolidation, where fixed costs can be reduced by combining operations.

electromagnetic spectrum Invisible rays of light. The various frequencies used by radio, television, and other means of wireless communications are part of the electromagnetic spectrum.

Electronic Media Ratings Council (EMRC) An independent council that monitors and verifies standards for audience research methods used in the broadcasting industry.

Emergency Broadcast System (EBS)/Emergency Alert System (EAS) A system designed to utilize the country's airwaves to deliver warnings related to weather, threats of war, and other catastrophes. The EAS replaced the old EBS in 1997. All radio stations are required to have working EAS equipment.

external promotions Promotional efforts that make use of media or promotional channels other than direct on-the-air promotion. Two common forms of external radio promotion include billboard advertising and bumper stickers.

Fairness Doctrine Repealed by the FCC in 1987, the doctrine required broadcasters to cover controversial matters of public importance and to present both sides of an issue. Failure to do so could result in a challenge to the license. Broadcasters argued that the doctrine stifled the presentation of such material rather than encouraging its presentation.

Federal Communications Commission (FCC) The Communications Act of 1934 established the FCC to replace the Federal Radio Commission as the primary regulatory body for radio and television. The Mass Media Bureau (MMB) within the FCC regulates the television and radio stations. The Bureau issues broadcast licenses specifying the community of license, the channel, and operating power of the station. FCC rules generally do not govern the selection of programming; exceptions are: restrictions on indecent programming, limits on the number of commercials aired during children's programming, and rules involving candidates for public office.

Federal Radio Commission (FRC) The Radio Act of 1927 established the Federal Radio Commission, the forerunner of the FCC. The FRC was given responsibility to regulate the radio industry.

focus groups A type of qualitative research method; focus groups involve six to twelve subjects led by a group facilitator. Focus groups offer richer, more detailed information in contrast to survey research.

format The general term used to refer to the programming aired by a radio station. Usually, the term *format* refers to music programming though all news, all talk, or all sports are common nonmusic formats.

formula radio A term used to describe radio formats that cluster music together in blocks separated by commercial or promotional announcements.

frequency The number of times different people hear the sales advertising message.

frequency modulation (FM) The modulation process for FM stations that varies the frequency of the carrier wave.

general manager (GM) A person responsible for total station operation and performance; the GM normally reports to the station's owners.

general sales manager (GSM) A person responsible for advertising sales at a station; the GSM's staff consists of local account executives and, in some markets, national sales executives.

gross impressions (GI) A quantitative way to compare the ad exposures delivered by a proposed ad schedule or station with another schedule or station; the actual number of impressions an ad schedule will deliver. GIs are calculated by multiplying the AQH persons estimate for the particular daypart by the number of spots to be run in the daypart.

gross ratings points (GRPs)   The number of ratings points a schedule will deliver. GRPs may be calculated by dividing the Gross Impressions of an ad schedule by the market population. Another variation is to multiply the number of ratings delivered in a time period by the total number of spots to be aired in that time period.

grossed up   Adding an advertising agency commission to the cost of media advertising. To add the typical 15 percent agency commission, the constant 1.1765 is multiplied by the dollar value of the advertising purchased. The net revenue to the station is arrived at by deducting the 15 percent commission from the product.

hot clock   A pie chart showing a visual representation of one hour of the station's programming. Shown on the hot clock are approximate times when commercial breaks are taken, when particular types of songs are to be played (a current hit, new song, or oldie), and perhaps when the announcer should talk on-air (and with the help of liner phrases or positioning statements, what the announcer should say). The hot clock ensures format consistency by providing the announcer with a visual representation of the elements the listener is to hear.

indecency   A category of speech that is protected by the First Amendment. The Pacifica case defined *indecent speech* as that which "depicts or describes, in terms patently offensive as measured by contemporary community standards for the broadcast medium, sexual or excretory activities or organs." Over the years the FCC has issued numerous fines to stations broadcasting indecent material.

intercept research   A type of research conducted at a shopping mall or other public venue; eligible respondents are "intercepted" by researchers and asked to answer a short series of questions.

inventory   The commercial ad time for sale by a broadcast station. Advertising time is an absolutely perishable commodity. Unsold commercial time cannot be put into storage for sale at a later time. Failing to sell ad time means the station has forever given up the potential revenue available from its sale.

legal identification (ID)   This is required for every radio station; a legal station identification consists of call letters followed by the city of license. A station must identify itself as close to the top of the hour as possible.

listener demographics   A station's listener age range, gender, ethnicity, socioeconomic background, consumer spending patterns, plus a host of other qualitative variables.

local marketing agreements (LMAs)   In an LMA, one station in the market takes over the operation of another station, especially in regard to advertising sales and programming. LMAs do not involve a transfer of station ownership.

localism   The idea that stations best serve their listening audience by providing unique locally based programming that reflects the specific community of licensing. Ideally, *localism* means that the station is actively involved in local news coverage and in covering various issues of important public concern.

lowest unit charge (LUC)   The amount a radio station must charge a legally qualified candidate for public office for radio advertising.

market   Geographic coverage area that may contain several different communities or counties and even carry across state lines. This area, as covered by the signals of several radio stations and identified by a ratings service, such as Arbitron, is referred to as a "market."

metro   A ratings term used by Arbitron to reflect the concentration of radio listeners in a given market.

microradio   A new class of radio stations approved by the FCC. Microradio stations would operate at reduced power of 10 or 100 watts. Commercial stations aggressively oppose microradio.

modulation   The process by which a broadcast station's programming is added to the carrier wave. AM stations use *amplitude modulation* and FM stations use *frequency modulation*.

multitasking   A term used to describe multiple managerial duties that are often done in a simultaneous fashion.

music hook   A term used in radio programming research; subjects listen to different segments or hooks of music and are asked to indicate their preferences regarding likes and dislikes.

music library   Recordings available for on-air playback by a radio station. Generally, stations attempt to limit the number of songs that may appear on-air by conducting listener tests to determine which selections appeal most favorably to their listeners.

music log   A computer-generated listing of the material to be played on the radio station during a 24-hour period. The music log is prepared from the available recordings in the station's music library. Music-scheduling software can be used to categorize selections by tempo, sex of performer, age of recording, or other factors.

music utility   The idea that a radio station only serves as a jukebox or source for music to listeners. Music utility cannot produce a viable radio station.

noncommercial radio   Stations, primarily FM, operating between 88.1 and 91.9 MHz. These stations are prohibited by the FCC from airing commercial ads though many noncommercial stations do air underwriting announcements.

obscenity   Speech that is not protected by the First Amendment. In *Miller vs. California,* the Supreme Court defined obscene material using three criteria: (1) The average person, applying contemporary community standards, would find that the material appeals to the prurient interest; (2) the material describes or depicts sexual conduct in a patently offensive manner; and (3) taken as a whole, the material lacks serious literary, artistic, political, or scientific value.

office manager   An umbrella title for the person who handles a variety of administrative responsibilities for a radio station. The office manager usually oversees the reception and secretarial positions and assists with accounting functions.

on-air promotions   These can be as simple as announcer-delivered commentary about the station or as complex as a multitrack audio production complete with a variety of sound effects, music segments, and radio production techniques. Stations commonly use on-air promotion to encourage listeners to keep listening for longer periods of time.

optimum effective scheduling (OES)   An ad scheduling strategy based on audience turnover. A calculation that uses station turnover *(T/O)* (cume audience ÷ AQH) times a constant, 3.29, to determine the number of spots an advertiser should schedule each week.

payola   Illegal compensation, usually offered to program directors or radio announcers, to make sure certain recordings are played over the air. Payola was a widespread practice in radio during the 1950s.

personal interviews   A type of radio research that involves individual, in-person interviewing. It provides rich data, but is tedious to gather and analyze.

personal radio   A term used to describe Internet capability of creating a listener's ideal radio station by selecting type of music, artists, and other information.

persons using radio (PUR)   An estimate of the number of people in a given market who have their radio sets turned on.

plugola   An employee's promotion over the air of a particular product or service in which the employee has a direct or indirect interest. Plugola is a violation of the sponsorship identification requirement.

preset listeners   Radio listeners who identify six to eight "favorite" stations and set the preset buttons on the radio to these stations. While one or two of the presets may garner most of the listener's attention, when those stations are no longer airing programming the listener wants, the listener may select another preset station.

program log   A computer-generated listing of all the programs and commercials to be aired each day on the radio station. The program log is normally produced by the radio station's traffic department, which handles commercial billing and related business transactions. Announcers are responsible for airing the scheduled commercials and programs during their shift. The program log may take the form of a printed document or it may appear only as an electronic file on a computer screen.

public radio   The identifier used primarily by noncommercial affiliates of National Public Radio to position their programming with listeners and the general public. All AM and FM radio broadcasts in the United States are noncoded signals and can be received by listeners without paying a listener or receiver license fee. In this respect, all U.S. radio stations are public.

Radio Advertising Bureau (RAB)   An industry organization that provides research and other resources to member radio stations to help in the marketing and selling of radio advertising.

Radio All-Dimensional Audience Ratings (RADAR)   The service that provides ratings estimates for national radio networks and syndicated national radio programming.

Radio and Records   A trade publication specializing in business, regulatory, and programming news of the radio industry. Available online at http://www. rronline.com/

rate card   The list or schedule of ad charges for a radio station, television station, or other media outlet. Rate cards can be quantity-based cards, offering a price discount for increasing the number of ads purchased, or grid cards, which base ad price according to client demand for a diminishing inventory of ad time.

rating   An estimate of the number of people listening to a radio station at a given time, based on the total population of people with radio sets.

reach   The number of different people who are exposed to an advertisement or who have an opportunity to hear the spot.

reverse cost per thousand   The maximum rate per spot that a competing station can charge to remain as cost-effective as a competitor.

reverse gross impressions   A term used when calculating the number of spots needed on a competing station to match another's Gross Impressions. To calculate, divide the station's Gross Impressions by the AQH Persons on a competing station.

sample   Subjects selected for a research study; in a ratings period the sample consists of those listeners provided with a diary to record radio listening.

scanner listeners   Radio listeners who jump from one station to the next. Rather than being loyal to a group of preset stations, these listeners hit the scan or seek button on their radio whenever they hear objectionable programming. They are less concerned with who (what station) they are listening to and more concerned with what (music or other programming) they are listening to. The *music utility* of radio plays a more prominent part in their listening habits.

scarcity   The concept on which early broadcast regulation was based. Because there were initially few frequencies available for broadcasting, coupled with many who sought a license, regulation was needed to ensure that broadcasters would operate to serve the public interest, convenience, or necessity.

share   An estimate of the number of people listening to a radio station at a given time, based on the total population of people using radio (PUR).

shortwave broadcasting   Broadcast services that use the high-frequency portion of the electromagnetic spectrum. Shortwave signals can cover vast geographic areas during both daytime and nighttime broadcasts. Often, shortwave signals provide government radio programming through external broadcasting services, and such programming is intended to be listened to by people outside of the home country. Voice of America (VOA) and British Broadcasting Corporation World Service (BBC World Service) are examples of external broadcasters.

simulcasting   Simultaneously airing the same programming on more than one station owned by an individual or station group. Historically, simulcasting meant airing the same programming on an FM station and an AM station. Once FM gained listener dominance, the situation often was reversed.

spot   Any announcement, commercial, station promo, or public service announcement that is scheduled for airplay.

station manager   Person responsible for the overall operation of the organization; reports directly to the general manager. In smaller markets, the duties of the station manager and general manager are often combined into a single position.

time spent listening (TSL)   An estimate of the amount of time a listener spends with a given station; the higher the TSL the more loyal the listener is to a station.

total survey area (TSA)   The term used by Arbitron to represent the total market area surveyed for a ratings report. The TSA is the largest geographical area, followed by the DMA and the Metro.

value-added selling   The practice of marketing a client's products through on-air giveaways, remote broadcasts, or other creative approaches that join the client brand with the station brand/image, in addition to airing a traditional flight of spot ads.

War of the Worlds   The 1938 CBS *Mercury Theater of the Air* broadcast on Halloween night that many listeners believed was an attack by the planet Mars. Directed and performed in part by Orson Welles, the broadcast demonstrated the power of radio drama and led to a public apology by CBS.

Index

ABC, 75, 171
Account executive (AE), 101, 112
AccuRatings, 115
Adult Contemporary (AC) format, 91
Advertising, 13–14, 100–113
  advantages and disadvantages of radio, 101–102
  agency selling, 111
  business of selling, 112–113
  clients for, 105
  consistency and, 87
  consolidation of radio stations and, 104
  cooperative, 105
  effectiveness of, 76
  false or deceptive, 58
  frequency, 105–106
  in future of radio, 171
  growth of, 32
  local, 38
  Optimum Effective Scheduling (OES), 108–110
  origins of, 27–28
  political, 57
  rate cards, 110
  ratings research, 106–108, 114–115, 116–126. *See also* Research
  reach, 105–106
  regulation of, 57–58
  revenues from, 75
  segments, 14, 76
  spending on radio, 101
  supply and demand relationships and, 75–76
  tobacco and alcohol, 57–58
  value-added selling, 111–112
Advertising agencies, 111
Agency selling, 111
Alcohol advertising, 57–58
All business format, 92–93
Allen, Fred, 33
Allen, Gracie, 33
All News format, 92
Amateur radio operators, 24
American Marconi, 20–21
American Public Radio, 147
AMFM, Inc., 68, 77, 92–93, 157–158
Amos 'n Andy, 31
AM stations, 2
  authorized power, 29
  carrier waves, 11, 12
  classification of, 8, 9
  decline of, 41–43, 52, 73
  growth in number, 37, 38
  history of, 35–37, 38, 41–43
  in medium wave band, 7–8
  standard broadcast service, 35–37
Anderton, J. T., 81–82
Announcer performance, 86

Arbitron Research, 83, 87, 106, 115,
  116–125
  criticisms of, 122–125
  future, 130–131
  interpreting, 120–122
  methodology, 117–120
  report distribution, 120
  sample procedures, 116–117
  software tools, 126
Armstrong, Edwin Howard, 20, 22, 35–
  36, 37
Association of College and University
  Broadcast Stations, 138–139
AT&T, 21, 26–28, 30
Audience. *See* Listeners
Audion, 19–20, 22
Auditorium testing, 127–128, 130–131
Average quarter hour rating (AQHR), 106–
  107, 109, 121, 122
Avery, Robert, 151
Aylesworth, Merlin, 30

Balance, Bill, 162
Barnouw, Erik, 30
Bartell, Gerald, 39
Bell, Art, 170
Bennett, Edward, 137
Benny, Jack, 33
Beville, Hugh "Mal," 125
Billboard, 40, 85
Block programming, 39
Bouvard, Pierre, 109
Bowes, Major Edward, 33
Brands, 100
  brand awareness, 80–81
  brand building, 83–86
Branly, Edouard, 18
British Broadcasting Corporation (BBC), 6,
  11, 100–101, 174
Broadcast, as term, 24
Broadcast.com, 166–167, 172
Brumley, Al, 88
Burns, George, 33
Business of radio, 13–15
  commercials. *See* Advertising
  consolidations in, 68, 91, 104, 113, 157–
    160, 170, 171
  daily operations, 10, 14, 58–61, 86–87
  economics in, 74–78
  future of, 169–171
  management in, 60–61, 66–74
  programming. *See* Programming
  promos, 14, 81–84

public service announcements, 14, 59
  syndication and, 170–171

Cable audio, 52
Cable News Network (CNN), 164
Caldwell, O. H., 29
Call letters, 10, 14, 58–59, 86–87
Callout research, 126–127
Carlin, George, 56
Carnegie Commission on Educational
  Television, 140–142, 143
Carrier frequency, 7–9
Carrier waves, 11, 12
Carter, Jimmy, 51, 141–142
Cash flow, 66, 71, 76
CBS, 29–32, 33, 34–35, 68, 77, 157, 159–
  160, 170
CDs, 83
Censorship, 7
Chancellor Media, 68, 92–93, 104, 157
Charge back, 112
Classical music format, 98
Clear Channel Communications, 68, 77, 96,
  104, 157, 158–159, 170, 174
Clear-channel stations, 29
Clinton, Bill, 142, 163
CNET, 92–93
Coca-Cola Company, 81
Coherer, 18
Collins, Frederick, 21
Collins, LeRoy, 41
Commerce Department, U.S., 25–27, 49
Communications Act of 1934, 6–9, 33, 49–
  51, 52, 54–55, 63
Community radio stations, 135
Competition, 4, 72–73, 98–99, 101–
  102, 171
Consistency, 85, 86–89
Consolidation of radio stations, 68, 91, 104,
  113, 157–160, 170, 171
Contemporary Hit Radio (CHR) format,
  91–92
Continuity book, 86–87
Coolidge, Calvin, 27, 28, 49
Cooperative advertising programs, 105
Corporation for Public Broadcasting (CPB),
  134–135, 136, 140–145, 147,
  149–150
Correll, Charles, 31
Cost per gross rating point, 109
Cost per thousand (CPM), 102, 106–108
Country format, 92
Craven, T. A. M., 36

Cross-ownership restrictions, 52, 53–54
Cuban, Mark, 166–167
Cume, 121, 122
Cume listeners, 108
Cumulus Broadcasting, 104
Customization, of programming, 82–83,
172–173

Daily operations, 58–61
engineering concerns, 59–60
hiring practices, 60–61, 72
required communications, 59
station identification, 10, 14, 58–59,
86–87
Dallas-Fort Worth Metroplex, 4, 5
DARS (Digital Audio Radio Services), 3,
43–44, 52, 73, 98, 159, 171, 173
Davis, Elmer, 35
Dayparts, 4, 121
Deceptive advertising, 58
de Forest, Lee, 19–20, 22, 23, 137
Demand marketing, 81
Demographics, 102, 115–116
Diary, 117–120, 131
Digital Audio Radio Services (DARS), 3,
43–44, 52, 73, 98, 159, 171, 173
Digital radio, 11–13, 63
Dill, Clarence, 138
Direct broadcast satellite (DBS), 52
Distance fiends, 22
DMA (Designated Market Area), 117
Dr. Laura, 73, 162–163, 170
Donovan, William, 49
Downey, Morton, Jr., 163
Duncan's American Radio, 75, 77, 81–82,
84, 90, 96, 102
Duopoly rule, 52, 53–54, 67–68

EAN, 59
Ear leasing, 100
EAS, 59
Easy Listening/Beautiful music format,
94–95
Economics. *See* Radio economics
Economies of scale, 67
Eddy, Nelson, 33
Edison, Thomas, 20
Edison Media Research, 102
Electromagnetic spectrum
early technology and, 18–20
efficient usage of, 10–13
radio frequencies on, 7–9

Electronic Media Rating Council
(EMRC), 125
Electronic sandboxes, 135
Emergency Activation Notification, 59
Emergency Alert System, 59
Emergency Broadcast System (EBS), 59
Engelman, Ralph, 135
Enhanced underwriting, 145
Entercom, 77
Equal Employment Opportunities (EEO),
60–61
ESPN Radio, 171
Ether, 23–24
Ethics, 112
Ethnic radio, 93, 94
External promotions, 84

Fairness Doctrine, 51–52, 54
False advertising, 58
Federal Aviation Administration (FAA), 59
Federal Communications Commission
(FCC), 6–9
AM standards, 35–37
Bill of Rights violations and, 50–51
classification of radio stations, 2, 8, 9,
13, 134, 139, 151
daily operations regulation, 10, 14,
58–61
deregulatory periods, 51–54
FM quality, 36–37
licensing and renewal regulations, 7, 51,
61–62
origins of, 33, 50
program content regulations, 54–57
Federal Radio Commission (FRC), 29–30,
32, 49–50, 137–138
Federal Trade Commission (FTC), 57–58
Ferris, Charles, 51
Fess, Simeon, 138
Fessenden, Reginald, 19
First adjacent frequencies, 7
Fleming, John Ambrose, 20
FM stations, 2
carrier waves, 11, 12
classification of, 9, 13, 134, 139, 151
decline in number, 37
growth in number, 38–39, 41–43, 52, 84
history of, 36–37, 38–39, 41–43
micro, 43, 63, 73
noncommercial, 138–141. *See also*
Noncommercial radio
quality of signal, 36–37
in very high frequency wave band, 8–9

Focus groups, 128–129
Ford Foundation, 140
Formats, 3–4, 82. *See also* Music formats
Formula radio, 175
Fowler, Mark, 51
Frequency, 105–106
Frequency sharing, 10, 25–26
Full Service format, 96
Future of radio, 43–44, 169–176
    advertising and, 171
    business of radio and, 169–171
    globalization and, 173–174
    innovators in, 165–167
    localism, 174–175
    regulation in, 62–63
    research in, 130–132
    technology and, 172–173

Gavin Report, The, 85
General Electric (GE), 21, 26–27, 28,
    30, 36
General Manager (GM), 69, 70–71
General Sales Manager, 69, 101
Gingrich, Newt, 142
Gleason, Jackie, 164
Globalization, 173–174
Godfrey, Arthur, 164
GoGaGa, 172
Gosden, Freeman, 31
Gospel format, 95–96
Government regulation. *See* Regulation
    of radio
Great Moments in History, 31
Grossed up, 111
Gross impressions (GI), 106–107, 109
Gross ratings points (GRPs), 109
Ground wave signals, 8

Harding, Warren, 49
Hatfield, Henry, 138
Hay, George D., 25
Herrold, Charles David "Doc," 137
Hertz (Hz), 11, 18
Hertz, Heinrich, 18
Hettinger, Herman, 33
Hicks, Thomas, 157–158
Hill, Lewis, 145
Hiring practices, 60–61, 72
History of radio, 17–47
    AM stations, 35–37, 38, 41–43
    commercials, 27–28, 38
    early technology, 18–20

FM stations, 36–37, 38–39, 41–43
    future and, 43–44
    growth of public interest, 20–22
    local service, 37–39
    networks, 29–32
    noncommercial, 133–134, 136–138
    programming, 24–25, 32–35, 39–41
    regulation, 22–24, 25–27, 29–30
Hoax rule, 56–57
Hoover, Herbert, 26–27, 28, 32, 49
Hope, Bob, 38
Hot clocks, 40, 86, 87

IBOC (In Band-On Channel), 11–13, 63
Imus, Don, 73
Indecency, 56, 159, 161–162
Infinity Broadcasting, 56, 68, 157, 159, 161
Intercept research, 129–130
Intercollegiate Broadcasting System, 135
International listeners, 6
Internet, 3, 4, 21–22, 24, 43–44, 52, 72–74,
    86, 98
    future of, 172–173
    research, 131–132
Internet Entertainment Group, 162
Inventory, advertising, 101

Jacor, 68, 104
Jingles, 88
Johnson, Lyndon, 141
Jolsen, Al, 33
Jukebox, 39, 87
Justice Department, U.S., 28, 49, 57–58, 86

Karmazin, Mel, 159–160
Kasem, Casey, 165
KDKA (Pittsburgh), 22, 137
Kelly Music Research, 131
Kennard, Bill, 54
KFI-AM (Los Angeles), 170
KFUO (Clayton, Missouri), 60
King, Larry, 164
Kittross, John, 137
KOWH (Omaha), 39–40
KPFA (Berkeley), 135, 145, 148
Krelstein, Harold, 39
KSCS-FM (Dallas-Fort Worth), 122

Lafount, Harold, 138
Leaky FM, 151
Legal ID, 59
Levels of management, 69

Lewis, Tom, 20
Leykis, Tom, 52
Licensing
  current regulation of, 61–62
  Federal Radio Commission (FRC),
    29–30
  renewals, 7, 51, 61–62
Liddy, G. Gordon, 52, 170
Light entertainment, 39
Limbaugh, Rush, 52, 73, 163, 170
Line-of-sight signals, 9
Listeners, 2–3
  cume, 108
  demographics of, 102, 115–116
  early types, 22
  international, 6
  noncommercial radio, 149–150
  preset, 6
  programming for specific, 81–83
  scanner, 6
Listener-supported radio, 145
Living Room Music Test, 131
Localism, 96, 174–175
Localization, 4–5, 37–39, 74–75
Local marketing agreements (LMAs),
  52, 68
Lodge, Oliver, 18
Lowest unit charge, 57

MacFarland, David, 87–89
Macroeconomics, 74, 75
Macy, John, 141
Management. See Radio management
Marconi, Guglielmo, 18–19, 20
Marconi Company, 20–21, 23, 24
Market, 2–3
Market structure, 76–77
Marx, Steve, 109
Mass Media Bureau, 7
Mass Media Docket, 42
Maxwell, James Clerk, 18
Mays, Lowery, 158–159
McChesney, Robert, 137
McCoy, Quincy, 98
McDonald, Eugene F., 27
McLendon, Gordon, 39, 40, 81
McVay, Mike, 115
Metro, 117
Microeconomics, 74–75
Micro FM stations, 43, 63, 73
Middle-of-the-road (MOR) format, 39,
  89, 94

Miller vs. California test, 56
Minidiscs, 4, 83
Minnesota Public Radio, 146, 147
Modulation, 11. See also AM stations;
  FM stations
Money magazine, 113
Moon, Thom, 102
Morse code, 18–19, 21, 137
MP3, 4, 83
Multitasking, 69
Murrow, Edward R., 35
Music formats, 89–99
  in brand building, 83–86
  ever-changing, 98–99
  range of, 91–98
  segmentation of, 89–91
  Top 40, 39–41, 42, 89, 165
Music hooks, 126–128
Music library, 85
Music log, 86, 87
Music utility, 83
Mutual Broadcasting System (MBS),
  32, 164

Nash, Francis M., 97
National Association of Broadcasters
  (NAB), 41, 73, 85–86, 138
National Association of Educational
  Broadcasters (NAEB), 139, 140,
  150–151
National Federation of Community
  Broadcasters, 135
National Public Radio (NPR), 134–135,
  142, 144, 146–148, 149, 150
NBC, 28, 29–31, 34
  Red and Blue Networks, 30, 33
Networks
  development of, 29–32
  origins of, 27–28
New Adult Contemporary/Smooth Jazz
  format, 96–98
Newspapers, 34, 55, 101
News/Talk format, 92–93, 96, 161–164
Noncommercial radio, 133–155
  audience for, 149–150
  defining, 134–136
  economics of, 143–146
  education and, 134–135, 138–139,
    150–151
  on the FM band, 138–139
  history of, 133–134, 136–138
  politics of, 141–142

Noncommercial radio *(continued)*
programming, 140–141, 146–148
Public Broadcasting Act of 1967, 133–134, 140–142, 143
Nonduplication, 41
North, Oliver, 170

Obscenity, 56
Office Manager, 69
Office of War Information (OWI), 35
Oldies/Classic Rock format, 93
On-air promotion, 85
Optimum Effective Scheduling (OES), 108–110
Ownership rules, 52, 53–54, 67–68

Pace, Frank, 141
Paley, William, 30, 31–32
Patrick, Dennis, 51
Payola, 55
Performance measurements, 59–60
Personal attack, 54
Personal interviews, 129
Personal portable meter (PPM), 130–131
Personal radio, 172–173
Personnel issues, 72
hiring practices, 60–61, 72
levels of management, 69
managerial roles, 70–71
radio management skills, 69–70
Playlist, 85
Plugola, 55
Political advertising, 57
Political editorializing, 54
Popoff, Alexander, 18
Positioning statement, 86–87
Prairie Home Companion, A, 146, 147–148
Present listeners, 6
Pressler, Larry, 142
Press-Radio Bureau, 34
Proctor and Gamble (P&G), 81, 86
Profitability, 77–78
Program log, 86, 87
Programming, 13, 14–15, 80–99
brand awareness and, 80–81
brand building and, 83–86
comedy, 31, 33, 34
consistency of, 85, 86–89
customization of, 82–83, 172–173
drama, 31, 33, 34
educational, 32, 134–135, 138–139, 150–151
formats, 3–4

golden age of, 32–35
history of, 24–25, 32–35, 39–41
music, 30–32, 34, 38, 39–41, 42.
See also Music formats
network, 30–31
news, 34–35, 82
noncommercial radio, 140–141, 146–148
origins of, 24–25
quiz show, 38
regulation of, 54–62
responsibility for, 98–99
for specific audience, 81–83, 172–173
Programming research, 126–130
auditorium testing, 127–128, 130–131
callout research, 126–127
focus groups, 128–129
future, 130–131
intercept research, 129–130
nature of, 107
personal interviews, 129
Promos, 14, 81–84
Public Broadcasting Act of 1967, 133–134, 140–142, 143
Public radio. *See also* Noncommercial radio
defined, 134
modern, 140–141
Public Radio International (PRI), 147–148
Public service announcements, 14, 59
Public Telecommunications Facilities Program (PTFP), 144
PUR (persons using radio), 121

Quaal, Ward, 44
Qualitative research, 116
Quantitative research, 116
Quivers, Robin, 161

RADAR (Radio All-Dimensional Audience Research), 75, 125
Radio
advertising. *See* Advertising
business of. *See* Business of radio
competition and, 4, 72–73
evolution of, 3–4
future of. *See* Future of radio
history of. *See* History of radio
as local medium, 4–5, 37–39, 74–75
popularity of, 2–3
programming. *See* Programming
regulation of. *See* Regulation of radio
research. *See* Research
Radio Act of 1912, 23–24, 25, 27, 48

Radio Act of 1927, 27, 29, 32, 33, 49
Radio Advertising Bureau (RAB), 75, 76, 103–104
Radio and Records Directory, 84, 85
Radio and Television New Directors Association (RTNDA), 54
Radio Corporation of America (RCA), 21, 26–27, 28, 30, 36–37
Radio Disney, 171
Radio economics, 74–78
  local market, 74–75
  market structure, 76–77
  national market, 74, 75
  noncommercial radio, 143–146
  performance and profitability, 77–78
  supply and demand relationships, 75–76
Radio management, 66–74
  cash flow in, 66, 71, 76
  issues in, 60–61, 71–74
  levels of, 69
  local market limits, 52, 68
  overview, 66–69
  ownership rules, 52, 53–54, 67–68
  roles in, 70–71
  skills in, 69–70
Rate cards, advertising, 110
Ratings. *See* Research
Ratner, Tom, 89
Reach, 105–106
Reagan, Ronald, 51, 142, 145
Redstone, Sumner, 160
Regeneration, 20, 35–36
Regulation of radio, 6–9, 48–65
  advertising, 57–58
  Communications Act of 1934, 6–9, 33, 49–51, 52, 54–55, 63. *See also* Federal Communications Commission (FCC)
  current regulations, 54–62
  daily operations, 58–61
  deregulatory periods, 51–54
  Federal Radio Commission (FRC), 29–30, 32, 49–50, 137–138
  future of, 62–63
  licensing and license renewal, 7, 51, 61–62
  origins of, 22–24, 48–49
  program content, 54–57
  Secretary of Commerce and, 25–27, 49
Religious format, 95–96, 135–136
Repetition, 39–40
Research, 114–132
  considerations for future, 130–132

programming, 115, 126–131
  sales, 106–108, 114–115, 116–126
Resonance tuning, 18
Reverse cost per thousand, 109
Reverse gross impressions, 109
Rock/Active Rock format, 93–94
Rogers, Will, 30
Roosevelt, Franklin D., 34, 49–50
Roper, Daniel, 49–50
Rowland, Willard, 142

Sales research, 106–108, 114–115, 116–126
  Arbitron Research, 83, 87, 106, 115, 116–125
  future, 130, 131–132
  nature of, 106–107
Sample, 116–117
Sandler, Jerry, 140
Sarnoff, David, 36, 160
Satellite-delivered radio, 3, 43–44, 52, 73, 98, 159, 171, 173
Scanner listeners, 6
Scarborough research, 125
Scarcity, 51
Schlesinger, Laura, 73, 162–163, 170
Shane, Ed, 115, 126, 130–131
Share, 122
Shortwave radio, 6, 24
Signal amplification, 20
Simulcasting, 139
Sirius Satellite Radio, 3, 173
Skywave signals, 8
Soap operas, 33
Spanish format, 94
Spots, 14, 76
StarGuide Digital Networks, 159
Station Manager, 69, 70–71
Statistical Research, 115
Stereo transmission, 36
Sterling, Christopher, 137
Stern, Howard, 56, 73, 159, 161–162, 170
Storz, Todd, 39–40, 81
Strategic Media Research, 115
Streaming media, 172
Superheterodyne receiver, 22
Supply and demand relationships, 75–76
Syndication, 170–171

Talk radio. *See* News/Talk format
Technology
  early, 18–20
  future and, 172–173

Telecommunications Act of 1996, 43, 52–
    54, 61, 67, 76, 91, 104, 157, 169–170
Television, 37–39, 51, 53, 81, 164
Television/Radio Age, 89
Terry, Earle, 137
Thomas, Clarence, 142
Titanic tragedy, 23–24
Tobacco advertising, 57–58
Top 40 format, 39–41, 42, 89, 165
Total radio listening, 40
Trafficking rule, 52–53
Transistors, 38
TSA (Total Survey Area), 117
TSL (time spent listening), 121

United Fruit Company, 23
Unprotected speech, 55–57
Urban Contemporary (UC) format, 93

Value-added selling, 111–112
Value-neutral company, 145
Viacom, 157, 160, 170
Voice of America (VOA), 6, 35

Wagner, Todd, 166–167
War of the Worlds hoax, 56
WCBS (New York), 8

WEAF (New York), 27–28, 30
Web Radio, 43–44
Welles, Orson, 56
Wells, H. G., 56
Westinghouse, 21, 22, 26–27, 30
WGN (Chicago), 31, 32, 44, 96
WGOH-WUGO (Grayson, Kentucky),
    96, 97
Whiteman, Paul, 31
Wireless Ship Act of 1910, 23, 48, 136–137
Wire services, 34
WJZ (New York), 30
WJZ (Newark), 26
WLW (Cincinnati), 32
WNBC-AM (New York), 161
WNYC (New York), 144
WOR (New York), 26, 32
WorldSpace Radio, 3, 16
WSM (Nashville), 25
WWL (New Orleans), 8
WXRK-FM (New York), 161
WXYZ (Detroit), 32, 165

XM Satellite Radio, 3, 173

Zenith Radio, 27

U^{the}nofficial Guide® to

New Orleans

4th Edition

the Unofficial Guide® to New Orleans

4th Edition

Eve Zibart
with
Bob Sehlinger

WILEY

Please note that prices fluctuate in the course of time, and travel information changes under the impact of many factors that influence the travel industry. We therefore suggest that you write or call ahead for confirmation when making your travel plans. Every effort has been made to ensure the accuracy of information throughout this book, and the contents of this publication are believed correct at the time of printing. Nevertheless, the publishers cannot accept responsibility for errors or omissions or for changes in details given in this guide or for the consequences of any reliance on the information provided by the same. Assessments of attractions and so forth are based upon the author's own experience, and therefore, descriptions given in this guide necessarily contain an element of subjective opinion, which may not reflect the publisher's opinion or dictate a reader's own experience on another occasion. Readers are invited to write the publisher with ideas, comments, and suggestions for future editions.

Published by:

John Wiley & Sons, Inc.

111 River Street

Hoboken, NJ 07030

Produced by Menasha Ridge Press

Cover design by Michael J. Freeland

Interior design by Michele Laseau

For information on our other products and services or to obtain technical support please contact our Customer Care Department within the U.S. at 800-762-2974, outside the U.S. at 317-572-3993 or fax 317-572-4002

Wiley also publishes its books in a variety of electronic formats. Some content that appears in print may not be available in electronic formats.

ISBN 0-7645-2632-4

ISSN 1096-5211

Manufactured in the United States of America

5 4 3 2 1

Contents

List of Maps   x
About the Author and Contributors   xi
Acknowledgments   xii

Introduction   1

Let the Good Times Roll   1
About This Guide   3
   How Come "Unofficial"?   3
   Creating a Guidebook   3
   How *Unofficial Guides* are Different   4
   How This Guide Was Researched and Written   5
   Letters, Comments, and Questions from Readers   6
"Inside" New Orleans for Outsiders   6
   How Information is Organized: By Subject and by Geographic
      Zones   8

Part One   Understanding the City   26

A Too-Short History of a Fascinating Place   26
   The French Flag   27
   The Spanish Flag   28
   Three Flags in Forty Years   29
   "The Whites of Their Eyes"   31
   Free Blacks, Slaves, and Mulattos   31
   The War Between the States and Reconstruction   33
   The 20th Century and the New Millennium   34
Parishes, Neighborhoods, and Districts   35
   The French Quarter (Zone 1)   36
   Central Business District (Zone 2)   37
   Uptown below Napoleon (Zone 3)   38
   Uptown above Napoleon (Zone 4)   38
   Downtown/St. Bernard (Zone 5)   39
   Mid-City/Gentilly (Zone 6)   40
   Lakeview/West End/Bucktown (Zone 7)   40

New Orleans East (Zone 8)   40
Metairie below Causeway (Zone 9)   41
Metairie above Causeway/Kenner/Jefferson Highway (Zone 10)   41
West Bank (Zone 11)   41
North Shore (Zone 12)   42
The Fictional City   42

Part Two   **Planning Your Visit to New Orleans   44**

When to Go   44
Pick Your Party   44
Weather or Not . . .   45
Gathering Information   46
Using the Internet   47
New Orleans on the Internet   48
Major Travel and Information Sites   48
Some Reservation Sites to Check Out   50
Travel and Local Information Resources   50
Search Engines and Directories   51
A Calendar of Festivals and Events   52–57
Special Considerations   56
What to Pack   56
Playing Host   58
Exchanging Vows   59
New Orleans for Families   59
Tips for International Travelers   61
Tips for the Disabled   62
For the Nose that Knows   62

Part Three   **New Orleans's Major Festivals   63**

Mardi Gras Mania   63
Jazz and Heritage Fest   74
Halloween   75
Creole Christmas   76
Cajun Country Festivals   78

Part Four   **New Orleans Lodging   79**

Deciding Where to Stay   79
Some Considerations   80
Getting a Good Deal on a Room   82
Value Season   82
Special Weekday Rates   82
Getting Corporate Rates   82
Half-Price Programs   82
Preferred Rates   83
Wholesalers, Consolidators, and Reservation Services   84
How to Evaluate a Travel Package   85

Helping Your Travel Agent Help You   86
If You Make Your Own Reservation   87
Hotels and Motels: Rated and Ranked   88
What's in a Room?   88
Hotel Ratings   91
How the Hotels Compare   92
The Top 30 Best Deals in New Orleans   101
Hotel Information Chart   104–131

Part Five   **Visiting New Orleans on Business   132**

New Orleans Lodging for Business Travelers   132
Convention Rates: How They Work and How to Do Better   133
The Ernest N. Morial Convention Center   134
Getting Food   137

Part Six   **Arriving and Getting Oriented   138**

Coming into the City   138
By Plane   138
By Car   140
By Bus or Train   141
Where to Find Tourist Information in New Orleans   141
Getting Oriented   141
Finding Your Way around the French Quarter   143
Things the Natives Already Know   144
New Orleans Customs and Protocol   144
Talking the Talk   145
Dress   146
Eating in Restaurants   146
Tipping (and Stripping)   147
New Orleans on the Air   148
How to Avoid Crime and Keep Safe in Public Places   148
Crime in New Orleans   148
Crime Prevention Planning   150
Personal Attitude   152
Self-Defense   152
More Things to Avoid   153
Carjackings   153

Part Seven   **Getting around New Orleans   154**

Public Transportation   154
Walking the Walk   156
Public Accommodations   157

Part Eight   **Sight-Seeing, Tours, and Attractions   158**

Guided Sight-Seeing   159
Walking Tours   159

Bus Tours and Trolleys   160
Carriage Tours   160
Special-Interest Tours   161
Swamp Tours   163
River Cruises   165
Self-Guided Tours   166
Exploring New Orleans's Diversity   166
Neighborhood Walking Tours   170
Plantation Tours and Excursions   186
New Orleans Attractions   189
Zone 2: The Central Business District   190
Zone 3: Uptown below Napoleon (Garden District)   190
Zone 4: Uptown above Napoleon/University (191)   191
Zone 5: Downtown/St. Bernard   192
Zone 7: Lakeview/West End/Bucktown   192
Zone 10: Metairie above Causeway/Kenner/Jefferson Highway   193
Attraction Profiles   196

Part Nine   **Dining in New Orleans   228**

Chowing Down in the Big Easy   228
A New Orleans Culinary Calendar   230
Hype and Glory   231
New Restaurants   232
The Restaurants   232
Our Favorite New Orleans Restaurants: Explaining the Ratings   232
Our Pick of the Best New Orleans Restaurants   234
More Recommendations   241
Best Sunday Brunch   241
Best Breakfast   242
Best Hamburgers   242
Most Striking Architecture   242
Best Cafés for Desserts and Coffee   243
Best for Children   243
Best Local Color   243
Best Muffulettas   244
Best Outdoor Dining   244
Best Pizza   245
Best Casual Seafood Houses   245
Restaurant Profiles   246

Part Ten   **Shopping in New Orleans   307**

The French Quarter   308
Other French Quarter Collectibles   311
Magazine Street   313
The Warehouse District   315
Malls of Americas   317

Part Eleven **Exercise and Recreation   320**

   Working Out and Playing Hard   320
      Walking   320
      Running and Jogging   321
      Biking   321
      Tennis   322
      Golf   322
      Gyms and Health Clubs   322
      Other Recreational Activities   323
   Spectator Sports   324

Part Twelve **Entertainment and Nightlife   325**

   Performing Arts   325
   New Orleans Nightlife   326
      The Quarter   326
      The Jazz Scene   330
      What Else Is There?   331
      A Note on Safety   333
   Nightclub Profiles   335

Index   364

List of Maps

New Orleans Touring Zones   10–11
Zone 1: French Quarter   12–13
Zone 2: Central Business District   14–15
Zone 3: Uptown below Napoleon   16
Zone 4: Uptown above Napoleon   17
Zone 5: Downtown/St. Bernard   18
Zone 6: Mid-City/Gentilly   19
Zone 7: Lakeview/West End/Bucktown   20
Zone 8: New Orleans East   21
Zone 9: Metairie below Causeway   22
Zone 10: Metairie above Causeway/Kenner/Jefferson Highway   23
Zone 11: West Bank   24
Zone 12: North Shore   25
Ernest N. Morial Convention Center   135
Walking Distance from the Convention Center   136
St. Charles Streetcar Route   155

About the Author and Contributors

Eve Zibart is a native of Nashville who began her career as a reporter at age 17 at *The Tennessean* (Nashville). She moved to Washington and *The Washington Post* in 1977 and has served as critic, editor and columnist at various times for "Style," "Weekend," "TV," "Metro," and "Magazine" sections. For the past decade, she has roamed Washington's restaurants, carryouts, bars, and nightclubs, with the occasional foray into museums and legitimate theater. In addition to her *Post* columns, Eve has written or co-written eight books and regularly appears in a variety of lifestyle magazines. Despite God's repeated physical admonishments, Eve continues to play a variety of sports, split her own firewood and haul rocks into what she hopes will become a Japanese garden within her lifetime.

Bob Sehlinger is the creator of the *Unofficial Guide* series and author of more than two dozen travel guides.

Chris Rose is an entertainment columnist for the *New Orleans Times-Picayune* newspaper, covering nightlife, personalities, and the generally offbeat. He lives by the Audubon Zoo with his wife and three children. He boils crawfish better than anyone he knows—and that includes Emeril.

Tom Fitzmorris has written a weekly restaurant review column in New Orleans for over 30 years. He is also the host of the daily three-hour "Food Show" on WSMB radio, and he publishes the New Orleans Menu Daily at **www.nomenu.com.** He has written 20 dining guides and cookbooks about the New Orleans food scene. Tom was born on Mardi Gras.

Acknowledgments

Scores of New Orleanians were gracious enough to talk about their city, both on and off the record, and I thank them all, especially Lea Sinclair and Diane Genre.

Everybody needs a place to hang out: Thanks to Jeanine, Julie and Kim (we won't forget the *real* Old Absinthe), Tiffany, Michael, Mark, Karen, Amy and Sean of the International House and Loft 523, St. James, and Char Thian from the Ritz-Carlton.

Very special thanks to tour guide and amateur historian Noah Robert for more good stories than I could fit in; to Grace Rogers for taking on the chauffeuring duty; and to Tom Fitzmorris, Chris "Jr. Nightlife" Rose and F. Lynne Bachleda for their contributions.

As always, thanks to Bob, Molly, Gabbie, Chris, and Annie for pushing forward and reading behind.

And—always and everywhere—Margi Smith and Joe Hemingway, the best dinner companions any traveler could have. A dozen cities and counting . . .

—Eve Zibart

Introduction

Let the Good Times Roll

A fine spring evening in Jackson Square. As the sun gradually lowers, the shadows of St. Louis Cathedral and the Cabildo stretch across the flagstones, brushing the tables of the tarot readers; young couples with souvenir hurricane cups stand around a man playing saxophone, its case open in front of him.

And there it is, the mystique of New Orleans in a single vignette: empire, religion, music, voodoo, and alcohol. *Laissez les bons temps rouler* —let the good times roll.

And yet there are some who say that what passes for "good times" is rolling too long and too strong these days. There is a battle raging for the soul of New Orleans, most visibly in and around the French Quarter; and while it is not a contest between good and evil, at least not in the classical sense, it will, in the next few years, determine whether the character of this unique city is lost, restored, or permanently altered.

That the character of the Vieux Carré has already changed is clear from a few hours' acquaintance. An odd confluence of factors—renovation of some older houses into upscale condominiums and the gradual decline of others; a much-publicized increase in street crime and heavy investment by outside commercial interests into redevelopment, frequently uprooting smaller local firms—has reduced the number of the French Quarter's permanent residents from about 15,000 a generation ago to fewer than 3,300 today. And of those, a dispiriting percentage are derelicts, street kids, and drunks, all looking for handouts and all with their vanished ambitions etched in their faces.

A high tide of cheap-souvenir and T-shirt shops has swamped Bourbon Street, and glossy, private club–style strip joints, several bankrolled from out of town, are squeezing out the older, more authentic burlesque houses. At the same time, the number of bars offering heavily amplified rock and blues music, their doors open and competing for volume dominance, makes the retreat of jazz and Dixieland more obvious. Sit-down bars that specialized in classic New Orleans cocktails such as hurricanes and Sazeracs, touristy though they may have seemed before, now appear almost quaintly sophisticated in the face of the carryout frozen margarita and daiquiri counters with crayon-colored mixes spinning in laundromat-like rows.

Yes, souvenir shops are brighter than bars, but they certainly have less character. Sure, live blues is great, but it's more Texan than Louisianan. Mardi Gras, once the most elegant and elaborate of festivities, has become the world's largest frat party, its traditions degraded, its legends distorted, and its principal actors, the Grand Krewes, overshadowed by the mobs of drinking and disrobing "spectators." Several of the oldest and most prestigious krewes have withdrawn from the celebration, and travel agents say as many residents flee New Orleans during Carnival as tourists come in.

Altogether, New Orleans is in danger of becoming a parody of itself, a mini-Epcot or Busch Gardens' Old Country simulacrum. The posters and prints feature wrought-iron fences, but the real courtyards are gated and locked tight. Steamboats play recorded music intentionally out of tune— "old-fashioned" in the hokiest sense. Self-appointed tour guides mix all their legends together: The statue in St. Anthony's Garden behind St. Louis Cathedral, memorializing French sailors who volunteered as nurses during a yellow fever epidemic, has even been explained as "the Mardi Gras Jesus" because the statue's outstretched hands are supposedly reaching for throws! And now life imitates, well, imitation: a 100-acre theme park called Jazzland is under construction only a few miles out of town.

And yet for all the tawdriness and commercialization, one cannot help falling under the city's spell. It is a foreign country within American borders, not merely a multilingual hodgepodge like Miami or New York, but a true Creole society blended through centuries. It is Old South in style, New South in ambition. It has a natural beauty that refutes even the most frivolous of franchised structures, a tradition of craftsmanship and even luxury that demands aesthetic scrutiny and surrender, and a flair for almost exquisite silliness—like those Jackson Square psychics with their Pier 1 Imports turbans—that keeps all New Orleanians young. Fine arts, fashionable cuisine, voodoo, vampires, and Mardi Gras. It's all muddled up, sometimes enchanting, sometimes infuriating.

We hope to help you find the real New Orleans, the old and gracious one, that is just now in the shadow of the Big Too-Easy. We want to open your heart, not your wallet. We think you should leave Bourbon Street behind and visit City Park, one of the finest and most wide-ranging public facilities in the United States. We want you to see Longue Vue House as well as St. Louis Cemetery. We'd like you to admire not only the townhouses of Royal Street and the mansions of St. Charles but the warehouses and row houses of the Arts District— the combined Greenwich Village and TriBeCa of New Orleans. We hope you'll walk Chartres Street in the evening shade, watch the mighty Mississippi churn contemptuously past the man-made barriers, and smell the chicory, whiskey, and pungent swamp water all mixed together the way Andy Jackson and Jean Lafitte might have the night before the great battle.

So get ready, get set, go. *Laissez les bons temps rouler!*

About This Guide

How Come "Unofficial"?

Most guides to New Orleans tout the well-known sights, promote the local restaurants and hotels indiscriminately, and leave out a lot of good stuff. This one is different.

Instead of pandering to the tourist industry, we'll tell you if the food is bad at a well-known restaurant, we'll complain loudly about high prices, and we'll guide you away from the crowds and traffic for a break now and then.

Visiting New Orleans requires wily strategies not unlike those used in the sacking of Troy. We've sent in a team of evaluators who toured each site, ate in the city's best restaurants, performed critical evaluations of its hotels, and visited New Orleans's wide variety of nightclubs. If a museum is boring, or standing in line for two hours to view a famous attraction is a waste of time, we say so—and, in the process, make your visit more fun, efficient, and economical.

Creating a Guidebook

We got into the guidebook business because we were unhappy with the way travel guides make the reader work to get any usable information. Wouldn't it be nice, we thought, if we were to make guides that are easy to use?

Most guidebooks are compilations of lists. This is true regardless of whether the information is presented in list form or artfully distributed through pages of prose. There is insufficient detail in a list, and prose can present tedious helpings of nonessential or marginally useful information. Not enough wheat, so to speak, for nourishment in one instance, and too much chaff in the other. Either way, these types of guides provide little more than departure points from which readers initiate their own quests.

Many guides are readable and well researched, but they tend to be difficult to use. To select a hotel, for example, a reader must study several pages of descriptions with only the boldface hotel names breaking up large blocks of text. Because each description essentially deals with the same variables, it is difficult to recall what was said concerning a particular hotel. Readers generally must work through all the write-ups before beginning to narrow their choices. The presentation of restaurants, nightclubs, and attractions is similar except that even more reading is usually required. To use such a guide is to undertake an exhaustive research process that requires examining nearly as many options and possibilities as starting from scratch. Recommendations, if any, lack depth and conviction. These guides compound rather than solve problems by failing to narrow travelers' choices down to a thoughtfully considered, well-distilled, and manageable few.

How *Unofficial Guides* Are Different

Readers care about the authors' opinions. The authors, after all, are supposed to know what they are talking about. This, coupled with the fact that the traveler wants quick answers (as opposed to endless alternatives), dictates that authors should be explicit, prescriptive, and above all, direct. The authors of the *Unofficial Guide* try to do just that. They spell out alternatives and recommend specific courses of action. They simplify complicated destinations and attractions and allow the traveler to feel in control in the most unfamiliar environments. The objective of the *Unofficial Guide* authors is not to give the most information or all of the information, but to offer the most useful information.

An *Unofficial Guide* is a critical reference work; it focuses on a travel destination that appears to be especially complex. Our authors and research team are completely independent from the attractions, restaurants, and hotels we describe. *The Unofficial Guide to New Orleans* is designed for individuals and families traveling for the fun of it, as well as for business travelers and conventioneers, especially those visiting the Crescent City for the first time. The guide is directed at value-conscious, consumer-oriented adults who seek a cost-effective, though not Spartan, travel style.

Special Features

The *Unofficial Guide* offers the following special features:

- Friendly introductions to New Orleans's most fascinating neighborhoods and districts.

- "Best of" listings giving our well-qualified opinions on things ranging from raw oysters to blackened snapper, 4-star hotels to 12-story views.

- Listings that are keyed to your interests, so you can pick and choose.

- Advice to sight-seers on how to avoid the worst of the crowds, and advice to business travelers on how to avoid traffic and excessive costs.

- Recommendations for lesser-known sights that are away from the French Quarter but no less worthwhile.

- A zone system and maps that make it easy to find places you want to go to and avoid places you don't.

- Expert advice on avoiding New Orleans's notorious street crime.

- A hotel chart that helps you narrow down your choices fast, according to your needs.

- Shorter listings that include only those restaurants, clubs, and hotels we think are worth considering.

- A table of contents and detailed index to help you find things fast.

- Insider advice on the French Quarter, Mardi Gras, Jazz Fest, best times of day (or night) to go places, and our secret weapon—New Orleans's streetcar system.

What you won't get:

- Long, useless lists where everything looks the same.

- Information that gets you to your destination at the worst possible time.

- Information without advice on how to use it.

How This Guide Was Researched and Written

Although many guidebooks have been written about New Orleans, very few have been evaluative. Some guides come close to regurgitating the hotels' and tourist office's own promotional material. In preparing this work, nothing was taken for granted. Each hotel, restaurant, shop, and attraction was visited by a team of trained observers who conducted detailed evaluations and rated each according to formal criteria. Team members conducted interviews with tourists of all ages to determine what they enjoyed most and least during their New Orleans visit.

While our observers are independent and impartial, they do not claim to have special expertise. Like you, they visited New Orleans as tourists or business travelers, noting their satisfaction or dissatisfaction.

The primary difference between the average tourist and the trained evaluator is the evaluator's skills in organization, preparation, and observation. The trained evaluator is responsible for much more than simply observing and cataloging. Observer teams use detailed checklists to analyze hotel rooms, restaurants, nightclubs, and attractions. Finally, evaluator ratings and observations are integrated with tourist reactions and the opinions of patrons for a comprehensive quality profile of each feature and service.

In compiling this guide, we recognize that a tourist's age, background, and interests will strongly influence his or her taste in New Orleans's wide array of attractions and will account for a preference for one sight or museum over another. Our sole objective is to provide the reader with sufficient description, critical evaluation, and pertinent data to make knowledgeable decisions according to individual tastes.

Letters, Comments, and Questions from Readers

We expect to learn from our mistakes, as well as from the input of our readers, and to improve with each new book and edition. Many of those who use the *Unofficial Guides* write to us asking questions, making comments, or sharing their own discoveries or lessons learned in New Orleans. We appreciate all such input, both positive and critical, and encourage our readers to continue writing. Readers' comments and observations will be frequently incorporated in revised editions of the Unofficial Guide, and will contribute immeasurably to its improvement.

How to Write the Authors:

Eve and Bob
The Unofficial Guide to New Orleans, 4th edition
P.O. Box 43673
Birmingham, AL 35243

When you write, be sure to put your return address on your letter as well as on the envelope—sometimes envelopes and letters get separated. And remember, our work takes us out of the office for long periods of time, so forgive us if our response is delayed.

Reader Survey

At the back of the guide you will find a short questionnaire that you can use to express opinions about your New Orleans visit. Clip the questionnaire out along the dotted line and mail it to the above address.

"Inside" New Orleans for Outsiders

It's a funny thing about New Orleans travel guides: most of them tell you too much, and a few tell you too little. That's because New Orleans is such a complex city, so ornate and enveloping and layered with history and happenstance, that it's hard to stop acquiring good stories and passing them on.

But statistics show that the majority of visitors to New Orleans stay only three or four days—and frequently that even includes spending part of the time in seminars or conventions. How much can you squeeze into a long weekend? How much do you want to see? Walking tours of the French Quarter and Garden District often point to buildings with obscure claims to fame and with only partial facades to their name (and no admission offered in any case). Walking tours of the farther reaches are often redundant; even the keenest architecture critic will probably lose heart trying to cover the third or fourth neighborhood in 48 hours. Some tour books either stint on shopping or endorse every dealer in town; some forget any fine arts or theater productions at all, as if Bourbon Street bars were the sole form of nightlife available in the city. Some are too uncritical, some too "insider." Some have all the right stuff, but are poorly organized; some are easy to read, but boring.

So, hard as it is to limit this book, we have—sort of. We have tried to make the do-it-yourself walking tours short enough that they won't exhaust you, but full enough of sights and stories to give you the city's true flavor. (And if you want to do more, we'll tell you how.) We've tried to take things easy, but we don't forgive exploitation or boost unworthy distractions. If it isn't fun, informative, or accurate, we don't want you to go. If there's a better alternative, we want you to know. We don't make purely philosophical judgments—some people believe in the supernatural, some don't—but we do try to evaluate in a dispassionate fashion what you get for your money. We hope to keep the quality of your visit high, and the irritation quotient low.

We've also divided the attractions up in various ways, often overlapping, so you can pick out the ones you'd most enjoy: In Part Two, Planning Your Visit to New Orleans, we suggest attractions by type—family style, musical, festive, spooky, and so on. The neighborhood profiles in Part One, Understanding the City, are more strictly geographical descriptions to help you get your bearings and focus your interests, while the zone maps are designed to help you with the logistics of arranging accommodations and sight-seeing. More elaborate walking tours are laid out for you in Part Eight, Sight-Seeing, Tours, and Attractions, and particular museums and exhibits in each zone are explored in more detail and rated for interest by age group. And for those who don't wish to do-it-themselves at all, we have listed a number of commercial and customized tours tailored to almost any interest.

In addition, even granting that your time will be tight, we have included a list of opportunities to exercise or play. That's partly because we at the *Unofficial Guides* try to keep up with our workouts when we're on the road, and also because you may be visiting old friends, old teammates, and tennis players. Beyond that, although you may not think you'll want to make time for a run or ride, experience has taught us that sight-seeing and shopping can be exhausting, make you stiff, and make you long for the outdoors—and New Orleans has some of the prettiest outdoors you'll ever see.

Finally, for visitors lucky enough to have more than a couple of days to spend, or who are returning for a second or third go-round, we have sketched out a few excursions outside the city.

Please do remember that prices and hours change constantly. We have listed the most up-to-date information we can get, but it never hurts to double-check times in particular (if prices of attractions change, it is generally not by much). And although usually a day or so is all the advance notice you need to get into any attraction in New Orleans, if your party is large, you might try calling ahead.

How Information Is Organized:
By Subject and by Geographic Zones

To give you fast access to information about the best of New Orleans, we've organized the material in several formats.

Hotels   Since most people visiting New Orleans stay in one hotel for the duration of their trip, we have summarized our coverage of hotels in charts, maps, ratings, and rankings that allow you to focus quickly your decision-making process. We do not go on page after page, describing lobbies and rooms which, in the final analysis, sound much the same. Instead, we concentrate on the specific variables that differentiate one hotel from another: location, size, room quality, services, amenities, and cost.

Restaurants   We provide plenty of detail when it comes to restaurants. Since you will probably eat a dozen or more restaurant meals during your stay, and since not even you can predict what you might be in the mood for on Saturday night, we provide detailed profiles of the city's best restaurants in Part Nine, Dining in New Orleans.

Entertainment and Nightlife   Visitors frequently try several different clubs or nightspots during their stay. Because clubs and nightspots, like restaurants, are usually selected spontaneously after arriving in New Orleans, we believe detailed descriptions are warranted. The best night-spots, clubs, and lounges in New Orleans are profiled in Part Twelve, Entertainment and Nightlife.

Geographic Zones   Once you've decided where you're going, getting there becomes the issue. To help you do that, we have divided the city into geographic zones:

Zone 1	French Quarter
Zone 2	Central Business District
Zone 3	Uptown below Napoleon
Zone 4	Uptown above Napoleon
Zone 5	Downtown/St. Bernard
Zone 6	Mid-City/Gentilly
Zone 7	Lakeview/West End/Bucktown
Zone 8	New Orleans East
Zone 9	Metairie below Causeway
Zone 10	Metairie above Causeway/Kenner/Jefferson Highway
Zone 11	West Bank
Zone 12	North Shore

All profiles of hotels, restaurants, and nightspots include zone numbers. If you are staying at the Royal Orleans, for example, and are interested in Creole restaurants within walking distance, scanning the restaurant profiles for restaurants in Zone 1 (the French Quarter) will provide you with the best choices.

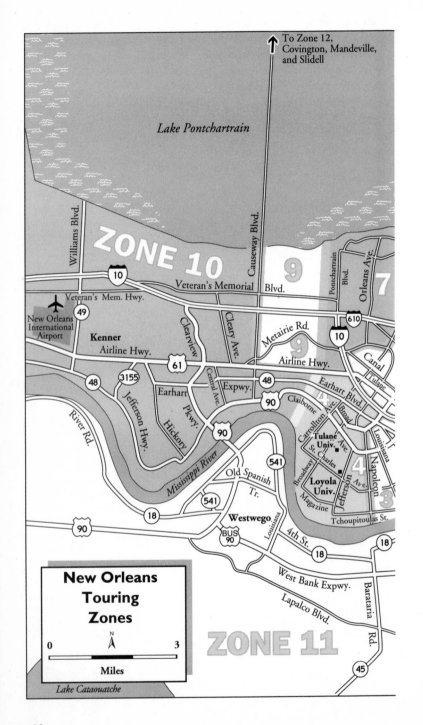

To Zone 12, Covington, Mandeville, and Slidell

Lake Pontchartrain

Williams Blvd.

ZONE 10

Causeway Blvd.

9

Pontchartrain Blvd.

Orleans Ave.

7

10

Veteran's Memorial Blvd.

Veteran's Mem. Hwy.

49

New Orleans International Airport

Kenner

Airline Hwy.

61

Clearview

Cleary Ave.

Metairie Rd.

9

Airline Hwy.

610

10

Canal

Tulane

48

3155

Earhart

Central Ave. Expwy.

48

90

Earhart Blvd

Claiborne

4

Jefferson Hwy.

Pkwy.

Hickory

90

Mississippi River

River Rd.

Carrollton Ave.

Broad

Louisiana

Tulane Univ.

St. Charles

90

Broadway

541

Loyola Univ.

Magazine

Jefferson Ave.

Napoleon

4

3

Old Spanish Tr.

541

Tchoupitoulas St.

18

Westwego

Louisiana

BUS 90

90

4th St.

18

18

West Bank Expwy.

Barataria Rd.

Lapalco Blvd.

New Orleans Touring Zones

N

0   3

Miles

ZONE 11

45

Lake Cataouatche

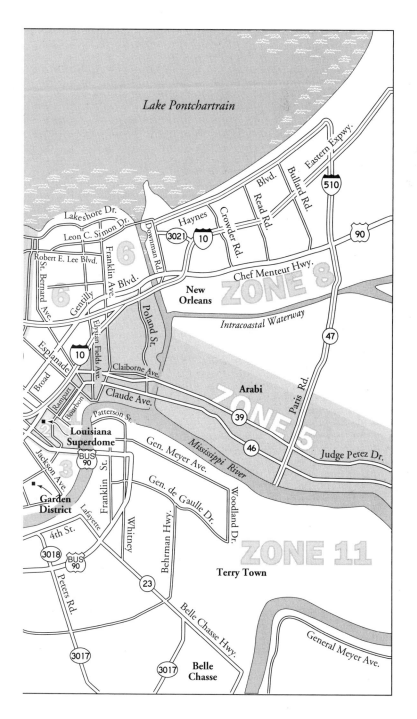

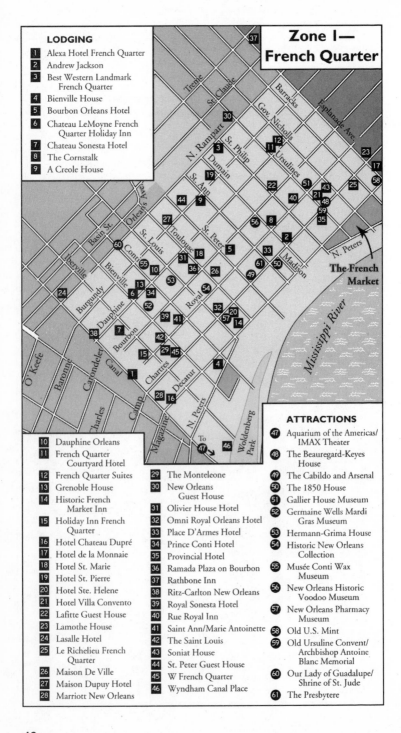

Zone 1—
French Quarter

LODGING

1	Alexa Hotel French Quarter
2	Andrew Jackson
3	Best Western Landmark French Quarter
4	Bienville House
5	Bourbon Orleans Hotel
6	Chateau LeMoyne French Quarter Holiday Inn
7	Chateau Sonesta Hotel
8	The Cornstalk
9	A Creole House
10	Dauphine Orleans
11	French Quarter Courtyard Hotel
12	French Quarter Suites
13	Grenoble House
14	Historic French Market Inn
15	Holiday Inn French Quarter
16	Hotel Chateau Dupré
17	Hotel de la Monnaie
18	Hotel St. Marie
19	Hotel St. Pierre
20	Hotel Ste. Helene
21	Hotel Villa Convento
22	Lafitte Guest House
23	Lamothe House
24	Lasalle Hotel
25	Le Richelieu French Quarter
26	Maison De Ville
27	Maison Dupuy Hotel
28	Marriott New Orleans
29	The Monteleone
30	New Orleans Guest House
31	Olivier House Hotel
32	Omni Royal Orleans Hotel
33	Place D'Armes Hotel
34	Prince Conti Hotel
35	Provincial Hotel
36	Ramada Plaza on Bourbon
37	Rathbone Inn
38	Ritz-Carlton New Orleans
39	Royal Sonesta Hotel
40	Rue Royal Inn
41	Saint Ann/Marie Antoinette
42	The Saint Louis
43	Soniat House
44	St. Peter Guest House
45	W French Quarter
46	Wyndham Canal Place

ATTRACTIONS

47	Aquarium of the Americas/ IMAX Theater
48	The Beauregard-Keyes House
49	The Cabildo and Arsenal
50	The 1850 House
51	Gallier House Museum
52	Germaine Wells Mardi Gras Museum
53	Hermann-Grima House
54	Historic New Orleans Collection
55	Musée Conti Wax Museum
56	New Orleans Historic Voodoo Museum
57	New Orleans Pharmacy Museum
58	Old U.S. Mint
59	Old Ursuline Convent/ Archbishop Antoine Blanc Memorial
60	Our Lady of Guadalupe/ Shrine of St. Jude
61	The Presbytere

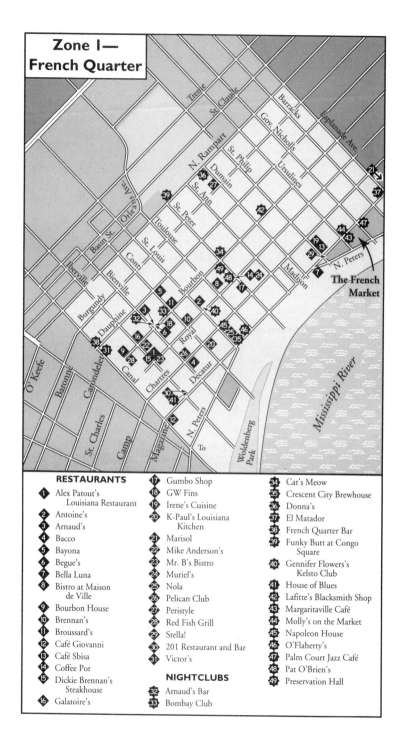

Zone 1— French Quarter

RESTAURANTS

1. Alex Patout's Louisiana Restaurant
2. Antoine's
3. Arnaud's
4. Bacco
5. Bayona
6. Begue's
7. Bella Luna
8. Bistro at Maison de Ville
9. Bourbon House
10. Brennan's
11. Broussard's
12. Café Giovanni
13. Café Sbisa
14. Coffee Pot
15. Dickie Brennan's Steakhouse
16. Galatoire's
17. Gumbo Shop
18. GW Fins
19. Irene's Cuisine
20. K-Paul's Louisiana Kitchen
21. Marisol
22. Mike Anderson's
23. Mr. B's Bistro
24. Muriel's
25. Nola
26. Pelican Club
27. Peristyle
28. Red Fish Grill
29. Stella!
30. 201 Restaurant and Bar
31. Victor's

NIGHTCLUBS

32. Arnaud's Bar
33. Bombay Club
34. Cat's Meow
35. Crescent City Brewhouse
36. Donna's
37. El Matador
38. French Quarter Bar
39. Funky Butt at Congo Square
40. Gennifer Flowers's Kelsto Club
41. House of Blues
42. Lafitte's Blacksmith Shop
43. Margaritaville Café
44. Molly's on the Market
45. Napoleon House
46. O'Flaherty's
47. Palm Court Jazz Café
48. Pat O'Brien's
49. Preservation Hall

13

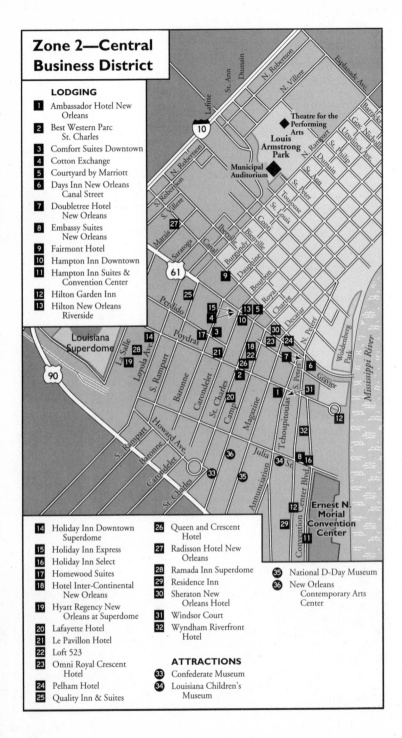

Zone 2—Central Business District

LODGING

1. Ambassador Hotel New Orleans
2. Best Western Parc St. Charles
3. Comfort Suites Downtown
4. Cotton Exchange
5. Courtyard by Marriott
6. Days Inn New Orleans Canal Street
7. Doubletree Hotel New Orleans
8. Embassy Suites New Orleans
9. Fairmont Hotel
10. Hampton Inn Downtown
11. Hampton Inn Suites & Convention Center
12. Hilton Garden Inn
13. Hilton New Orleans Riverside

14. Holiday Inn Downtown Superdome
15. Holiday Inn Express
16. Holiday Inn Select
17. Homewood Suites
18. Hotel Inter-Continental New Orleans
19. Hyatt Regency New Orleans at Superdome
20. Lafayette Hotel
21. Le Pavillon Hotel
22. Loft 523
23. Omni Royal Crescent Hotel
24. Pelham Hotel
25. Quality Inn & Suites
26. Queen and Crescent Hotel
27. Radisson Hotel New Orleans
28. Ramada Inn Superdome
29. Residence Inn
30. Sheraton New Orleans Hotel
31. Windsor Court
32. Wyndham Riverfront Hotel

ATTRACTIONS

33. Confederate Museum
34. Louisiana Children's Museum
35. National D-Day Museum
36. New Orleans Contemporary Arts Center

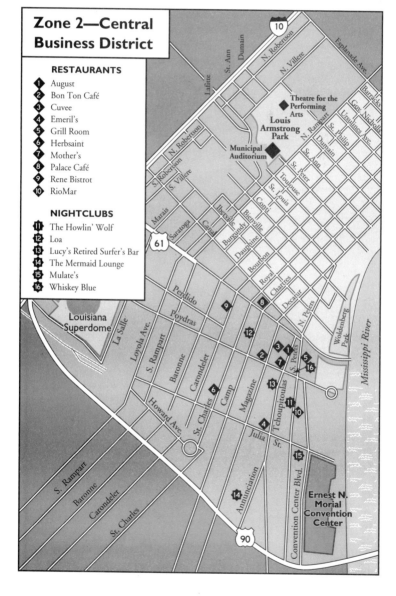

Zone 2—Central Business District

RESTAURANTS
1. August
2. Bon Ton Café
3. Cuvee
4. Emeril's
5. Grill Room
6. Herbsaint
7. Mother's
8. Palace Café
9. Rene Bistrot
10. RioMar

NIGHTCLUBS
11. The Howlin' Wolf
12. Loa
13. Lucy's Retired Surfer's Bar
14. The Mermaid Lounge
15. Mulate's
16. Whiskey Blue

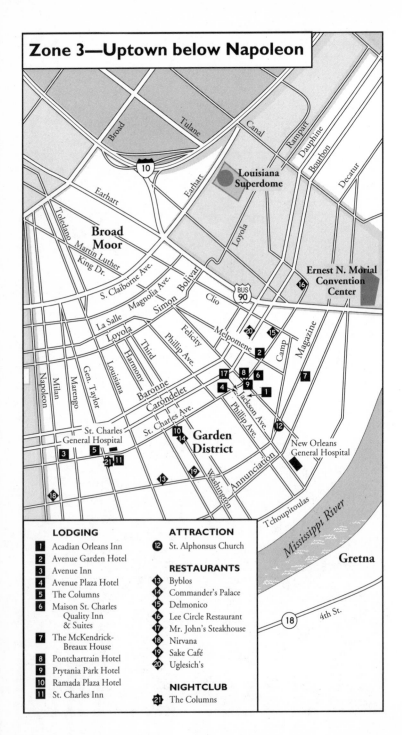

Zone 3—Uptown below Napoleon

Louisiana Superdome

Broad Moor

Ernest N. Morial Convention Center

Garden District

St. Charles General Hospital

New Orleans General Hospital

Mississippi River

Gretna

LODGING

1. Acadian Orleans Inn
2. Avenue Garden Hotel
3. Avenue Inn
4. Avenue Plaza Hotel
5. The Columns
6. Maison St. Charles Quality Inn & Suites
7. The McKendrick-Breaux House
8. Pontchartrain Hotel
9. Prytania Park Hotel
10. Ramada Plaza Hotel
11. St. Charles Inn

ATTRACTION

12. St. Alphonsus Church

RESTAURANTS

13. Byblos
14. Commander's Palace
15. Delmonico
16. Lee Circle Restaurant
17. Mr. John's Steakhouse
18. Nirvana
19. Sake Café
20. Uglesich's

NIGHTCLUB

21. The Columns

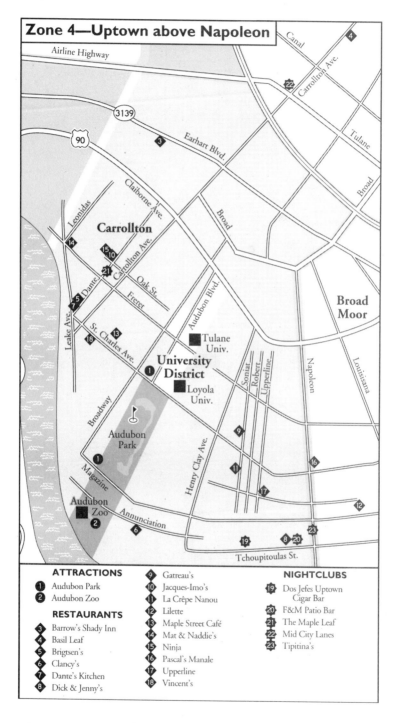

Zone 4—Uptown above Napoleon

Airline Highway

Canal

Carrollton Ave.

Tulane

3139

US 90

Earhart Blvd.

Broad

Claiborne Ave.

Leonidas

Carrollton

Carrollton Ave.

Dante

Oak St.

Freret

Leake Ave.

St. Charles Ave.

Audubon Blvd.

■ Tulane Univ.

University District

■ Loyola Univ.

Soniat

Robert

Upperline

Broad Moor

Napoleon

Louisiana

Broadway

Audubon Park

Henry Clay Ave.

Magnolia

Magazine

■ Audubon Zoo

Annunciation

Tchoupitoulas St.

ATTRACTIONS
1. Audubon Park
2. Audubon Zoo

RESTAURANTS
3. Barrow's Shady Inn
4. Basil Leaf
5. Brigtsen's
6. Clancy's
7. Dante's Kitchen
8. Dick & Jenny's
9. Gatreau's
10. Jacques-Imo's
11. La Crêpe Nanou
12. Lilette
13. Maple Street Café
14. Mat & Naddie's
15. Ninja
16. Pascal's Manale
17. Upperline
18. Vincent's

NIGHTCLUBS
19. Dos Jefes Uptown Cigar Bar
20. F&M Patio Bar
21. The Maple Leaf
22. Mid City Lanes
23. Tipitina's

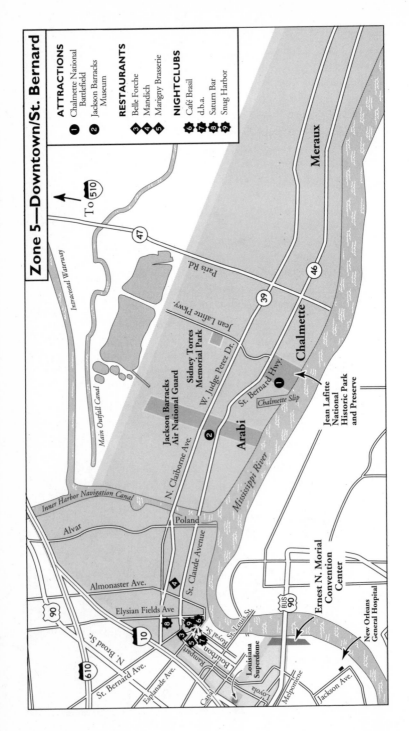

Zone 5—Downtown/St. Bernard

ATTRACTIONS
1. Chalmette National Battlefield
2. Jackson Barracks Museum

RESTAURANTS
3. Belle Forche
4. Mandich
5. Marigny Brasserie

NIGHTCLUBS
6. Café Brasil
7. d.b.a.
8. Saturn Bar
9. Snug Harbor

To 510

Intracoastal Waterway

Meraux

47

Paris Rd.

Main Outfall Canal

Jean Lafitte Pkwy.

39

46

Chalmette

Sidney Torres Memorial Park

W. Judge Perez Dr.

Jackson Barracks Air National Guard

N. Claiborne Ave.

St. Bernard Hwy.

Chalmette Slip

1

Arabi

2

Jean Lafitte National Historic Park and Preserve

Inner Harbor Navigation Canal

Alvar

Poland

Mississippi River

St. Claude Avenue

Almonaster Ave.

4

90

Elysian Fields Ave.

N. Broad St.

10

8

3

9

6

5

1

7

St. Louis St.

Royal St.

Bourbon

Rampart

Ernest N. Morial Convention Center

New Orleans General Hospital

BUS 90

St. Bernard Ave.

Esplanade Ave.

Loyola

Canal

Louisiana Superdome

610

Melpomene

Jackson Ave.

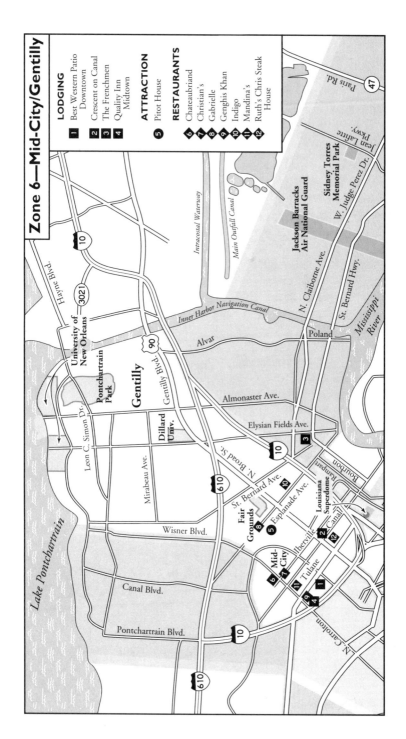

Zone 6—Mid-City/Gentilly

LODGING

1. Best Western Patio Downtown
2. Crescent on Canal
3. The Frenchmen
4. Quality Inn Midtown

ATTRACTION

5. Pirot House

RESTAURANTS

6. Chateaubriand
7. Christian's
8. Gabrielle
9. Genghis Khan
10. Indigo
11. Mandina's
12. Ruth's Chris Steak House

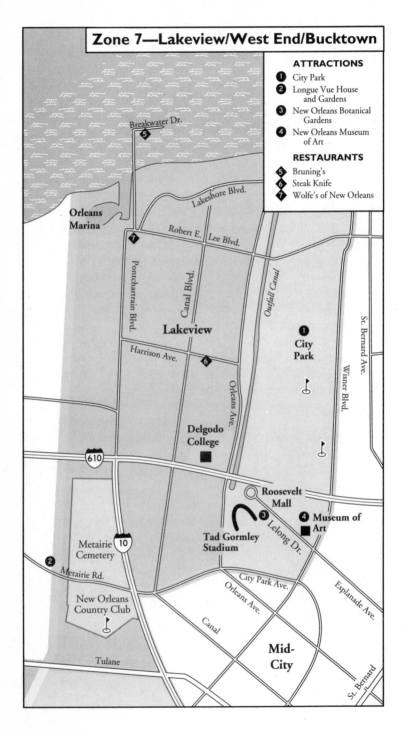

Zone 7—Lakeview/West End/Bucktown

ATTRACTIONS
1. City Park
2. Longue Vue House and Gardens
3. New Orleans Botanical Gardens
4. New Orleans Museum of Art

RESTAURANTS
5. Bruning's
6. Steak Knife
7. Wolfe's of New Orleans

Breakwater Dr.

Orleans Marina

Lakeshore Blvd.

Robert E. Lee Blvd.

Pontchartrain Blvd.

Canal Blvd.

Outfall Canal

St. Bernard Ave.

Lakeview

City Park

Harrison Ave.

Wisner Blvd.

Orleans Ave.

Delgodo College

610

Roosevelt Mall

Museum of Art

Tad Gormley Stadium

Lelong Dr.

Metairie Cemetery

10

Metairie Rd.

City Park Ave.

Esplanade Ave.

New Orleans Country Club

Orleans Ave.

Canal

Mid-City

Tulane

St. Bernard

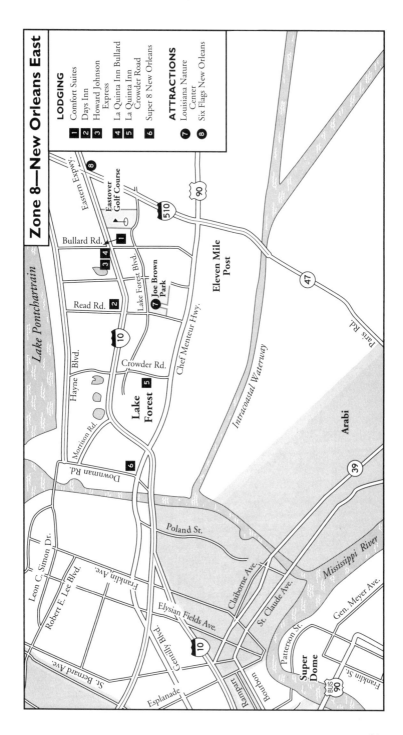

Zone 8—New Orleans East

LODGING

1. Comfort Suites
2. Days Inn
3. Howard Johnson Express
4. La Quinta Inn Bullard
5. La Quinta Inn Crowder Road
6. Super 8 New Orleans

ATTRACTIONS

7. Louisiana Nature Center
8. Six Flags New Orleans

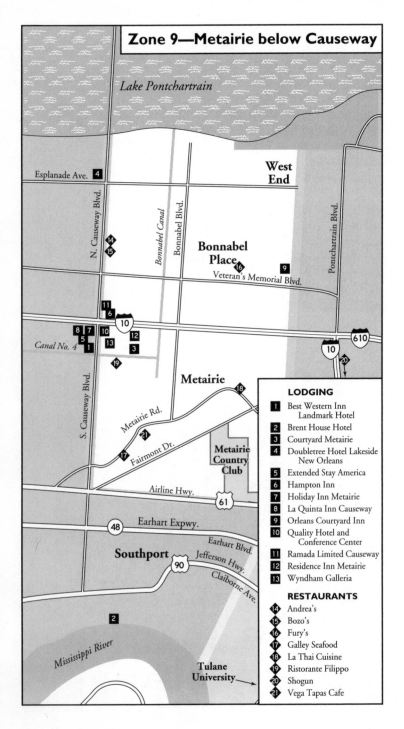

Zone 9—Metairie below Causeway

Lake Pontchartrain

Esplanade Ave. **4**

West End

N. Causeway Blvd.

Bonnabel Canal

Bonnabel Blvd.

Pontchartrain Blvd.

14
15

Bonnabel Place

16
9

Veteran's Memorial Blvd.

11
6
10

8 **7** **10** **12**

5
1 **13** **3**

Canal No. 4

19

S. Causeway Blvd.

Metairie

18

Metairie Rd.

21

17 Fairmont Dr.

Metairie Country Club

Airline Hwy.

61

Earhart Expwy. **48**

Earhart Blvd.

Southport Jefferson Hwy.

90

Claiborne Ave.

2

Mississippi River

Tulane University →

LODGING

1 Best Western Inn Landmark Hotel
2 Brent House Hotel
3 Courtyard Metairie
4 Doubletree Hotel Lakeside New Orleans
5 Extended Stay America
6 Hampton Inn
7 Holiday Inn Metairie
8 La Quinta Inn Causeway
9 Orleans Courtyard Inn
10 Quality Hotel and Conference Center
11 Ramada Limited Causeway
12 Residence Inn Metairie
13 Wyndham Galleria

RESTAURANTS

14 Andrea's
15 Bozo's
16 Fury's
17 Galley Seafood
18 La Thai Cuisine
19 Ristorante Filippo
20 Shogun
21 Vega Tapas Cafe

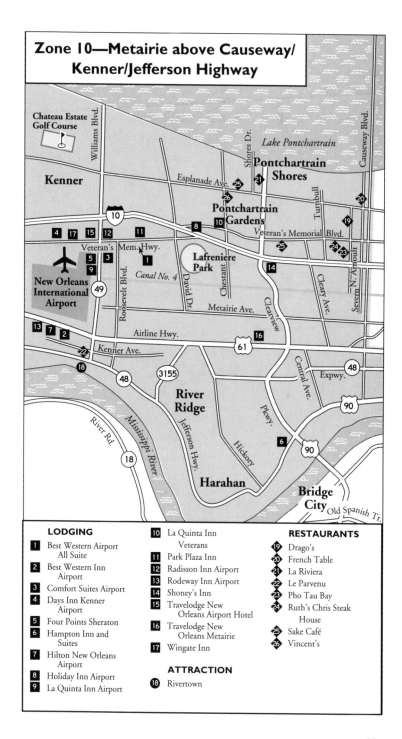

Zone 10—Metairie above Causeway/ Kenner/Jefferson Highway

Chateau Estate Golf Course

Williams Blvd.

Kenner

Esplanade Ave.

Shores Dr.

Lake Pontchartrain

Causeway Blvd.

Pontchartrain Shores

Turnbull

Pontchartrain Gardens

Veteran's Memorial Blvd.

Veteran's Mem. Hwy.

Lafreniere Park

Roosevelt Blvd.

Canal No. 4

David Dr.

Chestant

Clearview

Cleary Ave.

Severn

N. Arnoult

New Orleans International Airport

Metairie Ave.

Airline Hwy.

Kenner Ave.

Mississippi River

River Rd.

River Ridge

Jefferson Hwy.

Hickory

Harahan

Pkwy.

Central Ave.

Expwy.

Old Spanish Tr.

Bridge City

LODGING

1 Best Western Airport All Suite
2 Best Western Inn Airport
3 Comfort Suites Airport
4 Days Inn Kenner Airport
5 Four Points Sheraton
6 Hampton Inn and Suites
7 Hilton New Orleans Airport
8 Holiday Inn Airport
9 La Quinta Inn Airport

10 La Quinta Inn Veterans
11 Park Plaza Inn
12 Radisson Inn Airport
13 Rodeway Inn Airport
14 Shoney's Inn
15 Travelodge New Orleans Airport Hotel
16 Travelodge New Orleans Metairie
17 Wingate Inn

ATTRACTION

18 Rivertown

RESTAURANTS

19 Drago's
20 French Table
21 La Riviera
22 Le Parvenu
23 Pho Tau Bay
24 Ruth's Chris Steak House
25 Sake Café
26 Vincent's

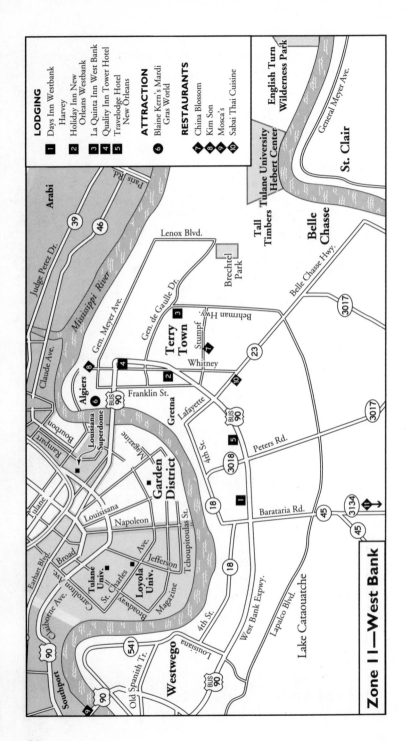

LODGING

1. Days Inn Westbank Harvey
2. Holiday Inn New Orleans Westbank
3. La Quinta Inn West Bank
4. Quality Inn Tower Hotel
5. Travelodge Hotel New Orleans

ATTRACTION

6. Blaine Kern's Mardi Gras World

RESTAURANTS

7. China Blossom
8. Kim Son
9. Mosca's
10. Sabai Thai Cuisine

Zone 11—West Bank

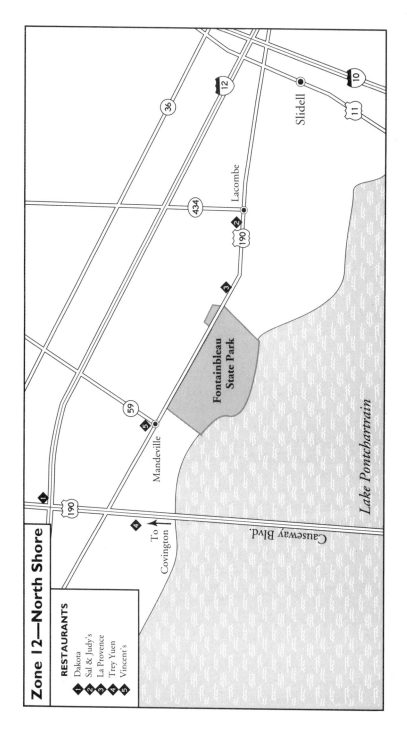

Zone 12—North Shore

RESTAURANTS

1. Dakota
2. Sal & Judy's
3. La Provence
4. Trey Yuen
5. Vincent's

Slidell

Lacombe

Mandeville

To Covington

Causeway Blvd.

Fontainbleau State Park

Lake Pontchartrain

Part One

Understanding the City

A Too-Short History of a Fascinating Place

New Orleans exercises a strange fascination over the rest of the country, and for good reasons. It's foreign territory at heart. It has flown three national flags—four if you count the Confederate States of America—and changed hands a couple more times than that. Like several other southern cities, it was "occupied" by then-hostile Union forces, had to repulse periodic Indian raids, and might briefly have flown a British flag as well if the Battle of Chalmette had turned out differently. (And legend aside, it might easily have done so.) Andy Jackson notwithstanding, New Orleans's legal system is still based upon the Napoleonic code.

New Orleans lives an unnatural, enchanted life, an island dug out of the swamp some yards lower than the river that embraces it, tethered to the world by bridges, ferries, and causeways. Its proximity to the swamps exposed it to almost yearly epidemics; in the course of just over 100 years, between 1795 and 1905, an estimated 100,000 lives were lost to yellow fever, malaria, or cholera. The city has been flattened by hurricanes and nearly erased by floods. And despite all that water around it, it has been destroyed twice by fire too—catastrophes that wiped out almost the entire first century of construction.

New Orleans has been identified with both the most sophisticated Creole culture and good ol' boy corruption; it has produced a rich ethnic melting pot and the most virulent racism. Oil drillers rescued it in the first half of the 20th century, and international petroleum prices nearly strangled it in the second half. Mardi Gras is the world's most famous frat party, yet when New Orleans threw a World's Fair to celebrate itself, it nearly went bankrupt.

Somehow, as low as New Orleans gets—as much as ten feet below sea level in some places—it never quite goes under. Like that Ol' Man River that surrounds it, like those famous good times, it just keeps rollin' along.

The French Flag

Louisiana stood at the center of imperial rivalries right from the beginning. Columbus had claimed the New World for Spain, but the other seagoing nations also pursued colonial territory and (as they believed) Asian trade. In 1519, the Spanish explorer Alonzo de Pindea sailed at least past, if not up, the mouth of the river. In 1534, Cartier sailed down the St. Lawrence waterways from Canada into the northeast. Only a few years later, Hernando de Soto established settlements along the southeastern coast and actually reached the Mississippi River, but the Spanish attention was distracted by the conquest of Mexico and the expansion into the American Southwest and northern South America.

In the 1670s, while the British were planting Union Jacks up and down the Atlantic Coast from Maine to the Carolinas, Rene Cavelier, Sieur de la Salle, set out from Canada with the intention of following the Illinois River all the way to the mouth of the Mississippi River in the Gulf of Mexico and, in 1682, claimed for France all the land drained by the Mississippi. He named the land Louisiana in honor of his sovereign lord King Louis XIV, the Sun King. Spain launched a huge manhunt in an attempt to intercept Rene Cavelier (when they finally reached his settlement, mutineers had already murdered him), but by the turn of the 17th century, other Frenchmen had established settlements all over Louisiana and what is now the state of Mississippi.

In 1699, the Sieur de Bienville planted a huge cross at the bend of the Mississippi River, and 20 years later his brother, the Sieur d'Iberville, stood looking out over the Mississippi where it connected to Lake Pontchartrain through Bayou St. John and ordered the construction of his "city." He named it La Nouvelle Orleans in honor of Phillipe, Duc d'Orleans, who was then the Regent of France.

It was probably fortunate that the name of the river eventually settled into Mississippi, a corruption of the name of the Mamese-Sipou tribe that lived along its banks. At various times, it was referred to as the Sassagoula, the Saint Louis, the Escondido, and most curiously for such a muddy stream, the Immaculate Conception.

Marshy, mosquito-infested, and oppressively hot, New Orleans became the subject of a real-estate scam that might have inspired the Florida land boom of the 1920s. Posters and supposed "eyewitness" tales of the gold-rich territories—most promulgated by an unscrupulous Scottish crony of the regent's with the ironic name of John Law, though even he thought Baton Rouge a liklier site. These stories lured thousands of French optimists and opportunists to the crude settlement, where they had little choice but to build the city they had been told already existed. Life in the settlement was so meager that in 1727, 88 women convicts were released from prison on the condition they accompany the Ursuline nuns to New Orleans as mail-order brides.

These were not the only unaristocratic imports: In fact, there were probably far more exiles, common soldiers, petty thieves, intractable slaves, and indentured servants than blue-bloods, and fewer "casket girls"—the respectable but impoverished girls who also came out as wards of the Ursuline Sisters with their few belongings packed in small trunks—than street women. (It should be remembered, however, that life in Paris was very hard, and that many young girls fell or were sold into prostitution as a last resort, so that their records should perhaps not be held against them. They worked pitifully hard for their "freedom" in New Orleans, in any case.)

The city was laid out with the streets in a grid around a central square that faced the river—the Place d'Armes, now Jackson Square. "Vieux Carré" means Old Square, and it almost was square: it extended from the Mississippi River to Rampart Street, which was once literally a rampart or wall, and from Esplanade Avenue to Iberville. (It's generally said to extend to Canal Street, but Canal Street was originally intended to be just that, a canal dividing the French Quarter from the American sector in what is now the Central Business District.) Gradually the settlement grew, and merchants, traders, and practical farmers, as well as more restless aristocrats, came to Louisiana to stay. With them came the beginning of a caste system—aristocrats, merchants, farmers, and servants—that became a hallmark of Creole society.

The Spanish Flag

In the 1760s, two other groups arrived, one in extremity and one in force. The first were the Acadians—the Cajuns—whom the British forced to leave their homes in Nova Scotia, and who settled in the bayou country west of New Orleans. Though most New Orleanians looked down on the Acadians whom they considered countrified (to say the least) and speaking an "uncultured" dialect, the Cajuns were French nationals driven into exile by France's enemy, Britain, and so they were accepted.

The other new arrivals were anything but welcome: the Spanish. To their dismay, the ethnically proud New Orleanians discovered that King Louis XV had secretly surrendered the Louisiana Territory to his Spanish cousin Charles III (some writers say it was used to pay off huge gambling debts). The residents violently resisted the Spanish takeover and succeeded in routing the first commissioner sent from Madrid. But in 1769, a more determined mercenary with the intriguing name of Don Alexander O'Reilly, or "Bloody Reilly," arrived with an armada of 24 warships and 2,000 soldiers. He executed several of the most prominent rebels and made swift work of the insurrection. The Arsenal and Cabildo were erected on the square (*cabildo* is actually the term for governing body), and French and Spanish aristocrats began inviting each other to dinner.

By the time the American colonies declared independence from Britain, New Orleans was an important Spanish outpost, which made the entrance of the Spanish on either side potentially decisive. Finally, Oliver Pollack, a New Orleans native who had become a member of the Continental Congress, persuaded the then-governor of New Orleans, Bernardo de Galvez, to send a convoy of 20 supply ships to New York to aid the American revolutionaries. Great Britain then declared war on Spain, and de Galvez proceeded to roll over the British colonies along the Gulf of Mexico. Consequently, although Lafayette and the French are usually remembered as the key European allies of the American forces, the Spanish also played an essential role.

Three Flags in Forty Years

Unsettled as New Orleans's first 60 years had been, the next 40 or so were just as dramatic.

The city was devastated by two great fires, the first in 1788 and the second, which came before the community had rebuilt, in 1794. Only a couple of buildings remain from before that time: the Old Ursuline Convent, whose age is undisputed; and Madame John's Legacy, which is the subject of some debate. Determined to prevent a third disaster, the Spanish promulgated new building codes: All roofs had to be tiled, houses were to be made of brick or plaster rather than wood, high walls had to separate gardens so one fire wouldn't spread from house to house, and alleys were eliminated to prevent a bellows effect that might feed a blaze. So what is considered classical French Quarter architecture, including arches, rear courtyards, and the famous ornamental wrought iron of the balconies and fences, is actually Spanish.

Meanwhile, the city's merchants and shippers continued to prosper. The city was not only a major exchange point between the eastern and midwest markets, but it also controlled much of the European-American import and export trade. New Orleans's strategic position, both for trade and defense, made the city highly attractive to the new government of the United States, and a source of great regret to the French government. The city remained solidly French at heart, with a royalist cast of mind— another wave of French aristocrats had fled the Revolution in 1789—and so when Napoleon set out to establish his own French Empire, New Orleans became a spoil of war. In 1800, by yet another secret treaty, Spain ceded the Louisiana Territory back to France.

Napoleon became a romantic idol to the colonists, who proudly named a battalion of streets after his battle victories—Marengo, Milan, Perrier, Constantinople, Austerlitz, Prytania, Cadiz, Valence, Jena, and even Forcher (after his great general)—not to mention Napoleon and Josephine themselves.

But when things began to turn sour for him, Napoleon decided to cash in the American colonies to finance his European campaigns and the effort to reclaim Santo Domingo (Haiti) after the great slave rebellion of Toussaint L'Ouverture. When President Thomas Jefferson offered to buy the port of New Orleans, Napoleon surprised him by offering to sell the entire Louisiana Territory—more than 500 million acres—for the sum of $15 million ($11 million in cash and $4 million in forgiven debt). The sale was officially transacted in the Cabildo on December 20, 1803. Louisiana became a U.S. territory, and in 1812 it was granted statehood, a fact commemorated in the arrival of the first steamboat, the *New Orleans.* It is one of those curiosities of political history that this exchange, facilitated by British and Dutch banks, provided Napoleon with funds to continue his war against those same nations.

Despite Napoleon's apparent betrayal, in 1820 loyal New Orleans Creoles plotted to rescue the deposed emperor from his prison on St. Helena, but he died before it could be attempted. His death mask, however, was delivered to his followers and is still on display at the Cabildo.

The purchase of Louisiana by the United States inspired thousands of Americans—and not-yet-Americans, recent immigrants still looking to make their home there—to ride, raft, barge, stage, and even walk to the thriving port. In the first seven years, the population of New Orleans more than tripled, from 8,000 to 25,000. A huge non-Creole community sprang up just upriver of the Vieux Carré, near the older sugar plantations and sometimes on top of them, and out into what is now the Garden District. The new arrivals were not exactly welcomed by the more-civilized-than-thou New Orleanians. The Scotch-Irish, who had already settled along the Carolina and Virginia mountains, were a new and particularly rough presence among the old Creole families; they took the word "riffing," Gaelic for "rowing," and contemptuously referred to all the laboring men and hardscrabble farmers who poled their way down the Mississippi as "riff raff."

A huge drainage canal emptying into the river was marked out along the upriver edge of the French Quarter, ostensibly as part of the construction of the booming city, but also to serve as an emotional if not actual barrier between the French Quarter, now also known as the First Municipality, and the American quadrant, officially the Second Municipality. In response to this subtle but elegant slight, the Americans laid out their sector, called Faubourg Ste. Marie, as a sort of mirror image of the Vieux Carré, with Lafayette Square (a seemingly polite tribute, but subtly claiming the marquis for the Americans) as a Place d'Armes; St. Patrick's as a rival to St. Louis Cathedral; and Gallier Hall, which was the official City Hall until the 1950s, in place of the old Cabildo. Each had its own mayor and council, each its own regulations. The city was not officially united until 1852.

As it happened, the canal was never built; and for a time, although it was referred to as the "neutral ground," the swath was the site of repeated brawls between Creole residents and brash, aggrandizing newcomers. Eventually a grand boulevard, divided by a great median, was paved through the strip instead and was dubbed Canal Street. Even so, it remained the acknowledged border between the two communities, and ever since, the New Orleans term for a median strip is the neutral ground.

"The Whites of Their Eyes"

The winning of the Battle of New Orleans has become such a touchstone of American pride that it has inspired hit songs (Johnny Horton's "Battle of New Orleans") and Hollywood epics (*The Buccaneer*, with Charlton Heston as Andrew Jackson and Yul Brynner as Jean Lafitte). The legend is glorious and shining—overnight excavations, secret meetings, Redcoats coming ghostlike through the fog to the banshee wailing of bagpipes, and Jackson shouting, "Don't shoot until you see the whites of their eyes!"

As is frequently the case with warfare, the truth is a little muddier. It is true, however, that the ruthless and lucky Jackson lost only 13 men while killing 2,000 British Army soldiers. It's probably true that without the combined efforts of 5,000 American, Creole, black, and Indian volunteers—not to mention the heavy arms and ammunition donated by Lafitte from his store of plunder—Jackson's Tennessee soldiers would have had a much harder time. And considering how intensely most Native Americans hated Jackson, who had commanded many brutal campaigns against the Creek and Choctaw tribes, their participation was even more remarkable.

The great irony is that the war was already over. The Treaty of Ghent had been signed a fortnight earlier. However, the campaign and victory served to unite the previously rancorous Creole and American communities, along with the smaller Scots-Irish, German, mestizo, and native-Creole outposts, and to establish New Orleans, distinctive as it might be, as an all-American city.

Free Blacks, Slaves, and Mulattos

The presence of African and Caribbean blacks, both free and slave, in New Orleans can be documented as far back as the early clearing of the French Quarter neighborhood. In 1721, only a couple of years after the city's founding, there were 300 slaves for only 470 Europeans, and a "code noir" was enacted in 1724 as a way of regulating the slave trade.

Free blacks, people "of color" (meaning of mixed blood in almost any proportion), and slaves made up a substantial portion of the population; the free blacks of New Orleans outnumbered those of any other Southern city. In fact, by 1803 there were exactly as many blacks and mixed-blood residents as whites: 4,000 of each, with 1,300 (40%) of the blacks being free. By the beginning of the Civil War, there were an estimated 30,000 free blacks in New Orleans.

An elaborate caste system emerged, in which the mulattos assumed social rank according to the amount of white (Creole) blood in their veins. Mulattos were half black, half white; quadroons were one-quarter white (meaning one white grandparent); and octaroons were one-eighth white. Women of mixed blood were considered exceedingly handsome, and though the Creole aristocrats would never have dreamed of marrying a black woman, it was considered a mark of wealth and good taste—another bit of conspicuous consumption—to have a well-spoken, elegantly dressed black or mixed-blood mistress. Many of these women became heads of the Creoles' city homes, running second establishments, in effect, and if they were really lucky, might be freed at their master's death. If not, at least their children might be recognized as illegitimate offspring and left some money.

This was such a widely recognized custom that the Creoles might even formally court these women, making semi-official offers to their mothers or owners that included property settlements, allowances, etc. So the annual Quadroon Balls became notorious tableaux of young "available" beauties, something between an auction and a debutante ball. Many of these balls were held in the Orleans Ballroom, a grandiose hall built in 1817 and now a special-events site within the Bourbon Orleans Hotel.

As time went on, the *gens de couleur libre*—literally "free men of color"—developed their own quite sophisticated culture; the sons of Creole aristocrats were often given first-class education befitting their (fathers') status, and some were even sent to Europe, where such colonial cross-breeding was commonplace. Alexandre Dumas, the author and playwright, was mulatto, and by some accounts Napoleon's Josephine, from the island of Martinique, had some mixed-blood ancestors as well. Both free and slave blacks were allowed to congregate in Congo Square, near North Rampart and Orleans streets in what is now Louis Armstrong Park; as many as 2,000 gathered in this onetime Choctaw meeting place on Sundays to sing, dance, trade, eat, fight, and perhaps practice a little voodoo until the "curfew," a cannon in the Place d'Armes, sounded. (In tribute, the first New Orleans Jazz and Heritage Festival in 1969 was held in Congo Square.)

In the years just before the Civil War, New Orleans was the largest slave market in the nation. Blacks, even well-to-do mulattos and freemen, remained mere residents rather than citizens; blacks were not granted the vote until 1868, during Reconstruction and despite a campaign of terror by the Ku Klux Klan. They were effectively disenfranchised again in 1898 through a legislative maneuver requiring stringent proof of literacy. The vote was returned only in 1965, and although African Americans make up more than half of the city's population, the first black mayor, Ernest Morial, was not elected until 1978. (His son Marc became mayor in 1994 and was re-elected in 1998.) Carnival krewes were not integrated until 1991, and some krewes boycotted or even withdrew from Mardi Gras when that happened.

The War Between the States and Reconstruction

The port of New Orleans practically floated on money in the decades after the Treaty of Ghent. Steamboats were in their prime; at the peak, there were some 11,000 plying the waters of the Mississippi; some of the luxury paddle wheelers, the "show boats," had capacities of 600 and served 500 for dinner. It was, so to speak, the beginning of New Orleans's tourism industry. Cotton, tobacco, and the slave trade fueled the economy. By 1840 New Orleans was the second-busiest port in the nation, after New York, and had a population of more than 100,000. The Irish Famine of 1841 sparked another flood of immigrants, who settled northwest of the American sector in what gradually became known as the Irish Channel; a large number of Germans also moved in. Unfortunately, their arrivals were offset by the yellow-fever epidemic of 1853, which killed 11,000 people and incapacitated another 40,000, thus becoming the most deadly epidemic in the nation's history.

But in 1861, with the secession of the Confederate States, Louisiana changed flags for the fourth time—and with the taking of New Orleans by Union forces under Admiral David Farragut in 1862, flew its sixth.

The Union occupation (as New Orleanians saw it, although officially it ceased to be an "occupation" after 1865) lasted 15 years. New Orleans fell so early that its three-year occupation by "enemy troops" is the longest unfriendly occupation of any city in the United States, and amnesty was not granted Confederate officers until 1872. Reconstruction was a period of tremendous unrest in the entire region.

It was the rapid evolution of steamboat travel that helped resurrect interest in the city. As trips became faster and shorter, a craze for unofficial river races took hold, and steamboats vied to set speed records between St. Louis and New Orleans, often with great sums wagered on the outcomes. In the summer of 1870, the then-recordholder, the *Natchez,* belonging to Thomas P. Leathers, took up the challenge of Capt. John W. Cannon, owner of the *Robert E. Lee.* The two steamed out of New Orleans on June 30 with a reported $1 million, much of it from European gamblers, riding on the race. By stripping his boat to a near shell, and arranging for mid-river refueling—a very modern concept— Cannon managed to beat Capt. Leathers by six-and-a-half hours, arriving in St. Louis on Independence Day after a trip of 3 days, 18 hours, and 14 minutes. After that contest, the steamboat race craze subsided.

In the final two decades of the 19th century, as the reviving port began to bring new industry and pleasure seekers into the city, what might be called the Bourbon Street culture made its first bow. By 1880 there were almost 800 saloons operating in New Orleans, along with about 80 gambling parlors and even more bordellos, which, though officially banned, had never been prosecuted or even regulated. New Orleans was starting to develop a reputation as a party town, a reputation that many people resisted and resented.

In 1897, an alderman named Sidney Story proposed that all these activities be restricted to a red-light district along Basin Street adjoining the French Quarter. The business of vice prospered almost virtuously in what was quickly dubbed "Storyville." The fanciest bordellos boasted not only elegant décor, sophisticated refreshments, and fine entertainment (these "sporting palaces" were where many of the great jazz improvisors got their start), but also well-dressed and willing ladies whose names, addresses, and race mix were listed in "blue books" that parodied social registers. One of the few surviving blue books is in the Old U.S. Mint Museum, along with several beautiful stained-glass windows from a bordello.

The 20th Century and the New Millennium

The century began promisingly: oil was discovered in Louisiana, and the new dredging and refining industry pumped new money into the regional economy (and pollutants into the water). But a second potential moneymaker, jazz, which had struck its first ragtime notes just before the turn of the 19th century, was turned out: the Storyville neighborhood, the bordello area and center of the burgeoning "jass" movement, was closed and virtually bulldozed off the face of the earth. "King" Oliver, Jelly Roll Morton, and other prominent musicians moved north to New York and Chicago, launching successful careers and a nationwide craze.

Some New Orleanians might have felt that the Great War was being fought at home. A massive hurricane struck the city in 1915, devastating the economy and widening the division between the well-to-do and the subsistence farmers; and although a cure for the dreaded yellow fever had been discovered in the early years of the century, the great influenza epidemic of 1918 killed at least 35,000 residents. In 1927 one of the worst floods in history flattened the city, ushering the Depression into the state even before it struck the rest of the nation. (Such natural disasters continue to harass Louisiana: hurricanes Betsy in 1965 and Camille in 1969 caused billions of dollars' worth of damage, and periodic floods have caused even more damage.)

Louisiana would have remained a virtual feudal society had it not been for the anti-establishment revolution of Huey Long, the "Kingfish"—a populist, demagogue, and drunk, who became governor in 1928 and bullied, bludgeoned, and blackmailed the state legislature into expanding public education, roads, and hospitals. Within a year he had been indicted on bribery charges, but was not convicted and instead was elected U.S. Senator. He began as a vocal New Deal supporter, but soon developed a populism that bordered on socialism and alarmed even the most liberal of Washingtonians. In 1935, on a trip home, he was assassinated, but the Long arm of their family law stretched on: his brother Earl was a two-time governor, and his son Russell served in the U.S. Senate from 1948 until 1986.

The growth of industry, particularly oil and natural gas, has been a boon to the state economy, if not the ecology. By 1980 there were more than 40 countries maintaining consular offices in New Orleans, an indication of the power of a trade port that accommodated more than 5,000 international vessels every year. But in 1984 the massive World's Fair Exposition, set up along three wharves with an eye toward the rejuvenation of the Warehouse District, ran heavily into debt and, combined with the collapse in world oil prices, came perilously close to bankrupting the city. What resulted was symbolic: the harder industries turned to the softer tourism industry for partnership. The wharf areas that were renovated for the World's Fair are now the site of the Riverwalk Marketplace and the vast and expanding Convention Center, which brings in more than a million people a year by itself. The luxury hotels along Canal Street and in the burgeoning Warehouse/Arts District owe their existence primarily to the face-lift connected to the fair. And the legalization of gambling has brought in some money to the state (although the on-again, off-again construction of the massive Harrah's casino near the foot of Canal Street bankrupted many smaller subcontractors along the way).

Nowadays the Mississippi riverfront is a microcosm of the city's spirit (for good or ill), combining franchised entertainment, name-brand boutiques and music clubs, huge international tankers and simulated steamboats, "real" Civil War coffee with chicory, reinvented Cajun cuisine, 18th-century voodoo, and 21st-century vampires. They *laissez les bons temps rouler,* all right; they just make sure it's your money roll that's good-timing.

Parishes, Neighborhoods, and Districts

It might surprise those who think that "old" New Orleans is limited to the Vieux Carré and the Garden District, but metropolitan New Orleans has 16 National Historic Districts, including Tremé and Faubourg Marigny as well as the Warehouse/Arts District and the often-denigrated Ninth Ward.

These are all within Orleans Parish (the central portion of greater New Orleans), which is roughly defined by the U-shaped bowl of the Mississippi River—the eponymous "crescent"—and lines running more or less north to Lake Pontchartrain. Many of these neighborhoods were originally laid out along fairly regular street grids, easily negotiated by newcomers, but because of the snaking of the Mississippi, the overall pattern of the center city now resembles a spider's web: sets of parallel streets occasionally are "pieced out" or head off at wider angles, and a few great, long, curving avenues, such as St. Charles, Claiborne, and Magazine, follow the curve of the river. It takes a little getting used to.

New Orleans also incorporates Jefferson Parish to the west beyond Audubon Park, and St. Bernard Parish downriver to the east. ("Parish" is no longer a religious jurisdiction, but the equivalent of a county.)

Only a few of New Orleans's neighborhoods are of real interest to tourists, but a quick overview of them, and how we have arranged them into zones, may help you plan your trip. These are the same zones we have used to cluster special attractions, restaurants, nightlife, entertainment, and hotels.

The French Quarter (Zone 1)

Although Vieux Carré literally means "Old Square," the French Quarter is, of course, not perfectly square, as it rides a hump of Mississippi sidesaddle. And because it's tilted, it's actually closer to the shape of a diamond. (Ironically, considering the Creoles' long rivalry with their American governors, the Quarter is a fair mirror image of Washington, D.C., only in miniature.) Nevertheless, it's the easiest neighborhood to grasp logistically, because the streets do proceed in a perpendicular grid, most of them one way in alternating directions.

The boundaries are Canal Street to the southwest, North Rampart Street to the northwest, Esplanade Avenue on the northeast, and the concave line of the Mississippi to the southeast. (The legal border on the southwest is Iberville Street, but we have used Canal Street as the border throughout this book.) If you look at the neighborhood square-on, with Rampart running across the top of the grid, Jackson Square and Artillery Park are in the center at the bottom, like a stem.

This is tourist central, the neighborhood of Bourbon Street and all-night beignets, St. Louis Cathedral, Preservation Hall, and Pat O'Brien's hurricanes. It includes the oldest architectural examples in the city, the most inexhaustible souvenir vendors, and the finest antique shops, plus a handful of franchised star-power hangouts à la Planet Hollywood. The French Quarter is something of a year-round party, justly famous for strip joints and street drinking. It has also developed a second kind of "street life" in recent years, with some of the longtime street musicians giving way to groups of punk-styled teenagers and young adults, panhandlers, and vagrants; so you may want to be less freestyle with your partying. There are still full-time residents here, but in general they have withdrawn to the quieter edges of the neighborhood.

For a full description, see the walking tour of the French Quarter in Part Eight, Sight-Seeing, Tours, and Attractions.

Central Business District (Zone 2)

The Central Business District, generally shortened to the CBD, is a cleaver-shaped area adjoining the French Quarter on the southwest side of Canal Street and also bordering it on the northwest side of North Rampart. Zone 2 also includes two historic neighborhoods: the Warehouse/Arts District and the historic Tremé neighborhood, which itself is incorporated in the Warehouse/Arts District. On our map, the zone is defined by South Claiborne Avenue/Interstate 10 on the northwest side, Business 90/Pontchartrain Expressway on the southwest, and the Mississippi on the east, with a jag from Canal Street across Rampart to Esplanade. This is also the beginning of "uptown" New Orleans, that is, upriver from Canal Street, as opposed to "downtown."

The CBD includes the Ernest N. Morial Convention Center, the Louisiana Superdome and Arena, Riverwalk Marketplace, Harrah's Casino, the World Trade Center, and City Hall. In the beginning this neighborhood was known as Faubourg Ste. Marie, and was the site of some early sugar plantations. However, when the Americans flooded in after the Louisiana Purchase, they chopped up the old plantations and began settling on the "other" side of Canal Street. Though it was begun long after unification, the U.S. Customs House on Canal Street sits as a sort of hinge between the two neighborhoods. The heart of the CBD is Lafayette Square, the Americans' answer to Jackson Square just as St. Patrick's Cathedral was their version of St. Louis.

Tremé is one of the old Creole neighborhoods, part of the plantation of Claude Tremé that was bought by the city for residential development in the early 19th century. (The reputation of the same Claude Tremé was somewhat elevated when St. Claude Avenue was named after him.) Tremé is where the famous Storyville red-light district was established, now the site of a disgracefully decrepit housing project. Tremé is also the area where you'll find Louis Armstrong Park, the Theatre for the Performing Arts, and the famous Congo Square, home of jazz; St. Louis Cemetery (Nos. 1 and 2); and Our Lady of Guadalupe Chapel.

The Warehouse/Arts District, on the other hand, is a fairly recent concept. The huge old storehouses, light industrial hangars, and factories on the streets south of Lafayette Square and west of the Convention Center originally had easy access to the docks. Many had been abandoned or allowed to fall into disrepair in the 1960s and 1970s, and the neighborhood was ripe for redevelopment. But when plans were made to transform the dock area for the World's Fair, artists and performers began moving in, turning them into lofts, studios, and display galleries. Now it's a trendy area, with several hot restaurants, hotels, many of the city's best galleries, most of the museums, and more coming in around Lee

Circle. A strong campaign is being mounted to preserve and restore the buildings rather than raze them.

And in a peculiar turnabout, the trendiness of the Warehouse/Arts District is one of the factors that has encouraged the revitalization of Canal Street not merely as a shopping strip but as a haven for high-profile hotels, including the Orient Express-owned Windsor Court, the Ritz-Carlton, constructed behind the facade of the old Maison Blanche department store, and one of two W hotels in the neighborhood. Even the old streetcar rails are being restored down the middle of Canal Street. (Unfortunately, much of the development near the foot of Canal was slowed by the ongoing financial travails of the huge Harrah's Casino.) For more information, see the walking tours of both the CBD and Warehouse/Arts District in Part Eight, Sight-Seeing, Tours, and Attractions.

Uptown below Napoleon (Zone 3)

This is the area of the Garden District, New Orleans's second most famous neighborhood, the upper-class residential portion of the old "American sector," and visually as well as historically a world away from the French Quarter. Originally there were some Creole plantation homes here, but after the turn of the 19th century, as Americans moved in above Canal Street, this became incorporated as the City of Lafayette (hence Lafayette Cemetery at its heart). It was annexed into New Orleans in 1852. Although real-estate promoters and area residents constantly stretch the description, the true Garden District is generally considered to fall between St. Charles Avenue and Magazine Street, Jackson Avenue on the northeast and Louisiana Avenue on the west.

However, for our purposes, Zone 3 is a somewhat larger, skirt-shaped wedge stretching from the Pontchartrain Expressway on the northeast, South Claiborne/Route 90 on the northwest, Napoleon Avenue to the west, and the river curving along the east and south.

Although the area's streets occasionally shift a little as the Mississippi curves back up, like the skirt's pleats, the Garden District is fairly gridlike within its borders and a fine residential neighborhood for exploring (see the walking tour of this area as well). Magazine Street had become somewhat run down, but its ongoing revitalization has made it a popular shopping area (see Part Ten, Shopping in New Orleans).

Uptown above Napoleon (Zone 4)

This area, along with the Garden District, is most often what is meant by the general phrase "uptown." Its northwest border, Monticello Avenue, which strikes off from the rim of the river's "cup," marks the line between Orleans and Jefferson parishes, so in one sense the area is at the far end of the Crescent City. (Some residents of the Metairie and Kenner suburbs would say that New Orleans's older families seem to think so, too.)

The area is also called University, sort of shorthand for the "university neighborhood," because of the adjoining campuses of Loyola and Tulane universities. It is split virtually down the middle by the St. Charles Avenue streetcar, which makes it, like the Garden District, easily accessible from the French Quarter or hotel district. Its most famous landmark is Audubon Park, which stretches from the universities right to the spot where the Mississippi River turns back north, with a fine view of both banks.

At the northwest edge of the area is the neighborhood called Riverbend, which is sort of Uptown's own counter–French Quarter, with boutiques and art galleries, bookstores, and a booming restaurant scene. See Part Ten, Shopping in New Orleans, for more information.

For the purposes of this book, Zone 4 is defined by Napoleon Avenue on the east, the Mississippi River on the south and west, Monticello up to Highway 61 (Old Airline Highway) on the north, and I-10 to the north and northeast.

Downtown/St. Bernard (Zone 5)

This area, which adjoins the French Quarter's east side, has suffered a great deal more than the French Quarter from the vicissitudes of time and industrial development, but it contains many fine old houses, the eccentric St. Roch Cemetery, Chalmette Battlefield and Jackson Barracks, and the Old U.S. Mint Museum. Zone 5 is defined by Esplanade Avenue on the west, I-10 to the Industrial Canal on the north, the Back Levee and Florida Avenue on the east, and the river on the south.

It actually includes parts of two parishes, since the neighborhood of Faubourg Marigny, which faces the French Quarter across Esplanade Avenue, is part of Orleans Parish; the rest is St. Bernard Parish. In fact, St. Claude Avenue becomes St. Bernard Highway at the parish line, and leads down along the Mississippi to the city of St. Bernard, where you can visit the Isleño Center and the Ducros Museum. This is also, you should note, the Ninth Ward, which is the way locals refer to it in terms of crime (see "How to Avoid Crime and Keep Safe in Public Spaces" in Part Six, Arriving and Getting Oriented).

But it has great beauty, still: Blanche DuBois's famous directions, "They told me to take a streetcar named Desire, transfer to one called Cemeteries, ride six blocks and get off at Elysian Fields," owes most of its charm to streets in Faubourg Marigny, although to be truthful, the routes wouldn't intersect. Faubourg Marigny is named for one of the greatest charmers and also greatest wastrels in New Orleans lore, Bernard Xavier Phillipe de Marigny de Mandeville, who gambled away an immense fortune and gradually sold off his vast holdings to developers. In 1807 he subdivided his own plantation ("faubourg" means something like suburb or cluster development), and it became the second-oldest neighborhood in the city; and it was he who named Elysian Fields Avenue. (He also gave the name

Rue d'Amour, the Street of Love, to what is now the far more truculent Rampart Street.) These days, the western part of Faubourg Marigny, from the edge of the French Quarter past Washington Square to Elysian Fields, is a mixed but lively neighborhood of artists, gays, hip straights, musicians, and young couples working to renovate the rambling old homes, something like the downtown Riverbend, but funkier and dicier.

Mid-City/Gentilly (Zone 6)

This is a fat-topped Santa's boot of a zone. Its cuff is the lakefront, which runs from the inner harbor canal on the east to I-10, follows the interstate southeast along the calf, until it makes a sharp right at the heel of the boot and runs back up the sole toward the northwest; the toe is at City Park Avenue, and the shin goes up Wisner Boulevard to Lake Pontchartrain. Within this zone are the Fairgrounds, where the Jazz and Heritage Fest is held; the University of New Orleans and Kiefer Lakefront Arena; and Bayou St. John, the original passage the French took moving in from Lake Pontchartrain toward the Mississippi (and a Native American route long before that). And the stretch of Esplanade Avenue near the Fairgrounds and bayou, known as Esplanade Ridge, makes for a nice mini-walking tour.

Lakeview/West End/Bucktown (Zone 7)

This zone is a sort of bridge between Mid-City and Metairie, borrowing a little from each. From Lake Pontchartrain, it follows Wisner Boulevard down to City Park on the east; takes City Park Avenue west to I-10 and zigs down to Highway 61; and turns back up along the Jefferson Parish line, the 17th Street Canal, and Chickasaw Street to the lake.

Within this zone are lovely City Park (which includes the New Orleans Museum of Art, Botanical Gardens, etc.), Longue Vue House and Gardens, and Lake Lawn Metairie Cemetery. At the edge of Pontchartrain, along Lakeshore Drive, what is now developed was mostly fishing camps and speakeasies, gambling dens and partyhouses. Now it's a much fancier version, with fine yacht clubs, the West End Park, and Lakeshore Drive Park, a five-mile-long promenade (stretching into Zone 8) that includes the New Canal Lighthouse (a Coast Guard rescue center not open to the public) and the Mardi Gras Fountain.

New Orleans East (Zone 8)

This zone runs west from the Inner Harbor Canal to the St. Bernard Parish line, above the Back Levee and Florida Avenue on the south. It's dominated by bayous, lakes, and marshland and includes New Orleans Lakefront Airport and the Louisiana Nature Center.

Metairie below Causeway (Zone 9)

If this sounds like a strange location, remember that in New Orleans, "below" and "above" are derived from the flow of the Mississippi, and that Causeway is local shorthand for Causeway Boulevard, not the Pontchartrain Causeway it runs off; so to be below Causeway in this case means on the east side of the highway, not beneath a bridge. Zone 9 is a rectangular section bordered by Causeway on the west, Highway 61/Old Airport Highway on the south, the Jefferson/Orleans parish line, the Metairie Outfall Canal and Chicasaw on the east, and the lake on the north.

Both Zone 9 and Zone 10 are suburbs with multi-ethnic populations, so there are lots of up-and-coming or locals-only restaurants here, though it's best to go with friends from town if possible.

Metairie above Causeway/Kenner/Jefferson Highway (Zone 10)

This booming suburban area lies just beyond the university neighborhood, bounded by Causeway Boulevard and a zigzag of Highway 61 and the Jefferson Parish line on the east, the Mississippi on the south, the Jefferson/Orleans parish line on the west, and Lake Pontchartrain on the north. Within Zone 10 are New Orleans International Airport (and so quite a number of less expensive hotels), the newly expanded Six Flags New Orleans amusement park, and the Rivertown museum complex.

West Bank (Zone 11)

The apparently contradictory name—from most of New Orleans, this appears to be the *East* Bank, not to mention south!—comes from the fact that the Mississippi makes another of its huge loops east of the city, and these towns all lie west of that portion of the river. Among these are Algiers, Gretna, Harvey, Terrytown, and Marerro. Although Algiers is slowly being regentrified, and there are walking tours of the area designed to raise its profile, it is still not an area that offers much to the tourist, with the exception of the Canal Street Ferry landing and Blaine Kern's Mardi Gras World (see Part Eight, Sight-Seeing, Tours, and Attractions). Like its namesake, Algiers is regarded as foreign territory—there wasn't even a bridge from the city to Algiers until 1958—but the major ethnic presence there is now Vietnamese, not North African.

Golf fans may also find themselves on the west bank, since several of the golf courses are across the river (see Part Eleven, Exercise and Recreation). If you go down to English Turn Wilderness Park or to English Turn country club, where the PGA tournament is held, you can see two other huge curves of the Mississippi River.

North Shore (Zone 12)

This is literally the north shore of Lake Pontchartrain, a zone that includes Slidell, Mandeville, Covington, Folsom, and other areas. Few tourists will get to this side of the lake unless they are looking for the Joyce Wildlife Management Area and Global Wildlife Center (see "Swamp Tours" in Part Eight, Sight-Seeing, Tours, and Attractions), or perhaps are lured by some of the restaurants there. The Joyce area is actually crossed by Interstate 55 and Highway 51, if you happen to be able to drive into New Orleans using that route. However, if you are part of a packaged tour, you may wind up at the factory outlet stores in Slidell. This is Tammany Parish, a pretty and mostly quiet area.

The Fictional City

There are many wonderful histories and cultural studies of New Orleans, but for some reason, fiction always seems to convey more of the atmosphere and is more fun to take along on a vacation. Some of my personal favorites (not all currently in print, but widely available in secondhand stores and libraries) include the following.

Anne Rice's books about the Vampire Lestat, the Mayfair Witches, and Lasher, etc., all have New Orleans settings, of course; but far more gripping is her historical novel, *The Feast of All Saints,* about the free people of color and their culture in the years leading up to the Civil War. And if you enjoy the old-fashioned style of murder mysteries, John Dickson Carr's *Papa La-Bas,* set amid the era of Marie Laveau and the Quadroon Balls, is as good as a voodoo tour of the French Quarter.

The posthumously published black-humor masterpiece *A Confederacy of Dunces,* by John Kennedy Toole, contains some of the best dialect and Bourbon Street camp of all time. Ellen Gilchrist's interrelated short stories of Garden District life in "Victory over Japan" and "In the Land of Dreamy Dreams," and the contemporary crime novels of James Lee Burke and his Cajun hero Dave Robichaux, are quite different, but all first rate.

If you can find the books of George Washington Cable, you will love his late-19th-century stories of Creole romance and adventure. (One of his stories inspired the name of Madame John's Legacy, a historic house in the French Quarter.) The same is true of the novels of Frances Parkinson Keyes, notably *Dinner at Antoine's, Steamboat Gothic* (set at San Francisco Plantation), and *Madame Castel's Lodger,* about the house she and Beauregard both lived in. (See a description of this house, now a museum, in Part Eight, Sight-Seeing, Tours, and Attractions.)

Walker Percy might be the city's foremost "serious" novelist, edging out William Faulkner by dint of long residence (Faulkner only stayed a few years). Percy had an almost unequaled sense of the minute degrees of social distinction, coming as he did from one of the area's most prominent clans. Most of his novels, among them *The Moviegoer* and *Love among the Ruins,* are set in the New Orleans area. Faulkner's novel *Pylon* and several of his short stories have New Orleans backgrounds. So do Tennessee Williams' *A Streetcar Named Desire, The Rose Tattoo,* and *Suddenly Last Summer,* among others. The residences of Williams, Faulkner, and several others are pointed out in the walking tour of the French Quarter described in Part Eight, Sight-Seeing, Tours, and Attractions.

In recent years, Kate Chopin's works, particularly *The Awakening,* one of the first great feminist novels of the late 19th century (and set in New Orleans), have been rediscovered, and deservedly so. William Sidney Porter, better known as O. Henry, lived in New Orleans for a little while before the turn of the 19th century, and some of his stories, including "Cherchez la Femme," are set in the city. In fact, local legend has it that he borrowed his famous pseudonym from a popular bartender, whose services were routinely summoned by a call of "Oh, Henry!" The city also makes several cameo appearances in Mark Twain's *Life on the Mississippi,* the sketches he wrote about piloting a steamboat.

Finally, if you'd like to raise a toast to your favorite writer, O. Henry fans should head to Tujague's (823 Decatur Street). For almost everyone else—Hearn, Twain, Walt Whitman, William Makepeace Thackeray, and even Oscar Wilde—go to the Old Absinthe House at 240 Bourbon Street. Ask for a Sazerac.

Part Two

Planning Your Visit to New Orleans

When to Go

Pick Your Party

Meteorologically speaking, most residents consider that New Orleans really has only two seasons: summer—a sticky, sweltering Southern classic prone to afternoon showers and dramatic sunsets that lasts roughly from May 1 to October 1; and a long, cool, and almost identically damp fall-into-spring that rarely dips to the freezing point.

But in terms of tourism, New Orleans has gradually developed four major holiday "seasons": Carnival (or, as most people think of it, Mardi Gras), which leads up to that Fat Tuesday blowout somewhere between February 3 and March 9; the New Orleans Jazz and Heritage Festival, from the last weekend of April through the first weekend of May; Halloween, which boomed in the Anne Rice era; and Creole Christmas, a lower-key but increasingly popular group of events spread throughout December and lasting through New Year's Eve and the Sugar Bowl. And that doesn't even count the occasional Super Bowl, NCAA Final Four, or the dozens of other less famous festivals and celebrations around the city.

If you plan to come during the four big holidays, there are a few things you ought to consider. First, the fun is only nominally free. Don't be surprised if you have to pay premium rates for hotel rooms and airline seats, especially around Mardi Gras and Jazz Fest, *if* you can get them. That's another thing to know: you'd better get a hotel reservation immediately, because most of the events are sold out well in advance, and some people make reservations for Mardi Gras more than a year ahead. Mardi Gras can fall on any Tuesday between February 3 and March 9. It falls on February 24 in 2004, February 8 in 2005, February 28 in 2006, February 20 in 2007, and February 5 in 2008. (The festival moves because it is fixed 46 days before Easter, which is itself fixed by the lunar schedule, falling on the first Sunday after the first full moon after the equinox.) You might seriously consider staying in the suburbs to avoid the almost 24-hour noise; or at least try to get something in the Garden District or Warehouse/Arts District, where you can enjoy the traditional decorations without the full French Quarter hedonism.

A third factor is that the sheer size of the crowd may begin to sour on you after a while. Many restaurants and bars simply pack up the tables during Mardi Gras and settle for making money on the itinerant drinkers; restaurants that maintain their poise may refuse to make reservations or require you to leave a deposit or credit card number in case you fail to show up. (And realize again that with such a crowd, getting around town is really tricky.) Rest rooms quickly overload, and overloaded drinkers may settle for the street. An increasing number of nicer restaurants, especally along parade routes, are opting to close entirely during the last week of Carnival.

If you're coming in a Super Bowl or Final Four year, you'll have the same problem with overcrowding: even football fans without game tickets flock to the city, either in hopes of scalping seats or just to enjoy the televised hoopla. But if you can't resist these famous events, read the special information on each in Part Three, New Orleans's Major Festivals.

If you have more general interests or want to take the family, pick a less frenetic time to go: Between Easter and the Jazz Fest, usually in early May, is very quiet, and you can enjoy the French Quarter Festival, a smaller and more local (and more agreeable) jazz and heritage festival not yet too crowded; September and early October are warm and usually fine; in March you can enjoy another underestimated attraction—the astonishing, high-spirited, and eccentric Tennessee Williams Festival. Even winter can be nice if you like a brisk walk, and there are certainly no crowds in the museums. If you're traveling on business, of course, you may not have much of a choice.

The good news is that except during the big festivals, you will rarely have to stand in line, except for a table. There are so many distractions in New Orleans that only a couple of attractions (the ticket booth at the Aquarium of the Americas and IMAX theater, perhaps) collect much of a queue. And you can usually avoid that by going early or buying tickets a day in advance.

Weather or Not ...

If you aren't used to Southern summers, you may find your visit to New Orleans a sticky experience. (You'll see T-shirts all over the French Quarter that read, "It's not the heat, it's the stupidity," which gives you some idea how tired the natives are of hearing tourists complain.) Thunderstorms are almost a daily occurrence in June, July, and August, but they provide only temporary relief. The epidemics of yellow fever, malaria, and cholera that used to strike from the swamp are a thing of the past, but the social and performance calendars still tend to duck the extremes of summer, and so should you, when the sun is highest. If you skim the calendar of special events, you'll see they drop off in summertime, because even in early May, during the Jazz and Heritage Festival, temperatures can hit 100°.

On the other hand, compared to most places the climate is pretty mild. Snow is a rare and festive occurrence, and the average low temperature, even in January, is 43. (The average high is 69, which should also give you an idea of how much the mercury can swing from midnight to mid-afternoon.) So you can easily consider an off-peak vacation.

There is one more fact to remember about late summer and early fall: hurricanes. These are extremely rare, and generally there is plenty of warning from local authorities. However, just in case you have to deal with some temporary disaccommodation because of bad weather, it's a good idea to have any essential medication on hand and perhaps to pack a small flashlight. If you're going to sign up for one of those haunting expeditions, you'll want it anyway.

New Orleans's Average Temperatures and Precipitation

	Average High	Average Low	Average Rainfall
January	69	43	4.97"
February	65	45	5.23"
March	71	52	4.73"
April	79	59	4.50"
May	85	65	5.07"
June	90	71	4.63"
July	91	74	6.73"
August	90	73	6.02"
September	87	70	5.87"
October	79	59	2.66"
November	70	50	4.06"
December	64	45	5.27"

Gathering Information

Brochures, historical background, and up-to-date schedules are available from the **New Orleans Metropolitan Convention and Visitors Bureau** (1520 Sugar Bowl Drive, New Orleans, LA 70112-1259, (800) 672-6124 or (504) 566-5011; **www.neworleanscub.com**). For information targeted to African-American visitors, contact the **Greater New Orleans Multicultural Tourism Network** at (800) 725-5652, or check out their website at **www.soulofneworleans.com.** Gay and lesbian visitors may want to contact the **New Orleans Gay and Lesbian Community Center** at (504) 945-1103; **www.lgccno.org.** Jewish visitors can call the **Jewish**

Community Center at (504) 897-0143; **www.nojcc.com.** The area code for the entire New Orleans metro area is 504; that should be assumed for all phone numbers in this guide unless otherwise noted.

Using the Internet

The advent of the Internet and its immense popularity have brought about many changes in the way we seek out everyday information. Travel information is one of the most popular and useful areas of publishing and access on the Internet. In just a few short years we have gone from getting most of our travel information from printed books or magazines and our favorite travel agent to a time where we can book entire vacations online. But as wonderful as this sounds, there are pitfalls. It's no small task figuring out how to find the information you need and understanding the tricks that make navigating the Internet easy. Finally, even as an accomplished Internet user, you may be surprised to find that your most valuable travel resource is still your tried-and-true travel agent.

You may have heard that travel providers like to sell directly to consumers on the Internet in order to avoid paying commissions to travel agents, and that the commission savings are passed along to the buyer. While there is some truth in this, discounts (online or anywhere else) have much more to do with time perishability of travel products than with commissions. An empty seat on an airliner, for example, cannot be sold once the plane has left the gate. As the point of perishability approaches, the travel provider (hotel, airline, cruise line, etc.) begins cutting deals to fill its rooms, cabins, and seats. Websites provide a cheap, quick, and efficient way for travel sellers to make these deals known to the public. You should understand, however, that the same deals are usually also communicated to travel agents.

We like the Internet as a method of window-shopping for travel, for scouting deals, and for obtaining information. We do not believe that the Internet is necessarily the best or cheapest way of purchasing travel or that it can be substituted for the services of a good travel agent. The people who get the most out of the Internet are those who work in cooperation with their travel agent, using it as a tool to help their agent help them. First, almost any deal you locate online can be purchased through a travel agent, and second, the more business you give your travel agent, the harder your agent will work for you. It's all about relationships.

It is a bit convoluted to write about the interactive travel experience on paper without the benefit of the very medium we are discussing. We urge you to use your computer or to find a friend with a computer and Internet connection in order to get the most out of these guidelines. We guarantee that you will discover some wonderful things along the way, many things in all likelihood that even we haven't seen. Each person's experience on the Internet is unique, and you'll find many compelling distractions along the way. But bring your patience, because it can take some time getting used to the Internet, and it is not perfect. Once you know your way around even slightly, you will save a lot of time, and occasionally, some money. When you find resources that you like, bookmark them in your browser. The more you use them the more efficient you will become.

New Orleans on the Internet

Searching the Internet for New Orleans information is like navigating an immense maze in search of a very small piece of cheese. There are quite a few New Orleans web pages that offer information, advertisements, and services. To be sure, there is a lot of information available on the Internet, but if you do not use specific addresses, you may have to wade through list after list until you find the addresses you need. Once you have them, finding information can also be time consuming.

Here are some addresses we found helpful:

- **www.neworleans.com** is maintained by the New Orleans Publishing Group and contains advertisements, travel coupons, a hotel booking service, and articles on various subjects. Business people researching New Orleans will find useful articles on banking, industry, and trade.

- **www.neworleansonline.com** is a fun web page that is maintained by a group called the New Orleans Marketing Corporation. Subjects found on this page include music, history, people, and dining. On the practical side, you can search by amenity for a hotel room or check out the calendar of events.

- **www.nawlins.com** is an extensive web page maintained by the New Orleans Convention and Visitors Bureau. Although this page contains helpful information for leisure travelers, meeting and convention planners will find it particularly useful.

- **www.nola.com** is maintained by the New Orleans *Times-Picayune* and offers information on news, events, entertainment, and festivals. It also offers a five-day weather forecast and a chat forum.

Major Travel and Reservation Sites

The travel and booking sites are some of the most useful sites on the Internet today. They allow you to designate your destinations and preferences and then immediately check on a variety of available flights, cruises, tours, hotels, and rental cars. If you see something you like, you can purchase the ticket online. Each service has its own unique interface and design, and you may find one easier to use than another, depending on the kind of travel you do.

You should fill out a travel profile in each site you try; it is what allows you to indicate your preferences, such as favorite airline, aisle seat, or cheapest fare. Most of these sites allow you to register to receive an e-mail notification when a great fare or special deal comes up for your favorite destinations. Websites always have the latest information on any fare wars that might be happening. Just like any bargain, if you see a good price you should try to make a decision about it as soon as possible, because if you take too much time it could easily be gone when you come back.

Although there are great deals to be found on the Internet, remember that each travel provider's site is nothing more than an electronic media billboard. Be prepared for all of the hype, purple prose, and exaggeration you would find in any other kind of advertisement. Also be aware that filling out a profile will potentially make you a target for all of the provider's promotional messages. If you like to receive a lot of e-mail, fine. Otherwise, be selective.

When a deal comes along that you like, do not assume that it is the best you can do. Check the websites of direct competitors as well as deals in newspapers that target the travel provider's primary geographic market. Los Angeles, for example, is a primary market for most Las Vegas casinos, and you can often find deals in the Sunday travel section of the *Los Angeles Times* that equal or beat what you find on the Internet. When you have narrowed your possibilities, bring your travel agent into the loop and give him or her an opportunity to improve on any deals you have found.

There's a fair amount of cross-pollination in websites, with some companies sharing information and features. Some have travel content along with booking features (Travelocity and ITN), and others offer a variety of vacation packages along with the comprehensive booking information (**www.previewvacations.com**). But even if you just need a flight from San Francisco to Los Angeles, with the cheapest fare, at the most convenient time, and don't need the other travel information, you can bookmark the page of the site that allows you to set up an itinerary or go directly to it.

If you make a reservation online, remember that it's just like making reservations on the phone or through your travel agent. Make sure that you are aware of any restrictions or refund policies that the sites or the related companies have in place. If you make a reservation with an airline through a website, you can generally assume that this airline's policies apply. If you are purchasing a vacation package or something else from one of the vacation sites, be sure to visit the policies or disclaimer sections of the site so you understand what will happen if you need to change or cancel your plans. Always check this before you submit your order.

You may have read some of the news stories about the security of doing transactions over the Internet and presenting your credit card online. Much progress has been made in this area in the past year, and you'll find that most, if not all, of these sites allow you to enter through a secure server, which simply means that they are taking extra steps to protect your personal information. As the online transaction businesses grow, the technology will only get better. In reality, there have been very few problems with completing transactions online, but if you prefer, most sites will give you the option to call a toll-free number to make your purchase.

Some Reservation Sites to Check Out

Listed below are some sites we find particularly useful. We are not listing all the reservation sites with booking capabilities—just the main ones as of this writing. New sites are launched every month.

www.travelocity.com   www.sabre.com   www.itn.com

www.expedia.com   www.outtahere.com   www.trip.com

www.previewvacations.com

The Airlines

Most of the airlines have sites these days, and they can be quite useful if you like to stick to one carrier. These sites will include flight schedules, information about frequent-flier clubs, policies, and specials. One of the best things about airline-specific sites is the information on fare specials and last-minute discounts. There are often excellent deals available. Sometimes the deals are so good you want to look for a reason to go.

If you just want the best fare or the most convenient itinerary, then looking only at one airline's schedule will not give the full picture. You should also be aware that there are certain airlines, generally those that offer extra-discounted fares most of the time, that are not part of the major reservation systems. So if you want to fly on these airlines you either have to call them directly, use your travel agent, or go to their web-sites. At the time of this writing, Southwest Airlines is one of the airlines not participating in the main reservations systems.

Hotels and Rental Cars

Most of the travel sites listed above also have connections to hotel and rental-car booking services, and they work in much the same way as making airline reservations. On the airlines' sites you will find that air-lines generally have a relationship with one or two car-rental companies and will put you in touch with them for reservations. And like the air-lines, the rental-car companies have their own sites, but that means if you want to comparison-shop you have to go to multiple sites.

Travel and Local Information Resources

The most dynamic places to find all kinds of travel information are the unique travel websites that present information in a totally new way. There are also many sites presented by some of the big players in the Internet business that are designed to provide detailed information about particular cities—not only travel information, but also information on the government, schools, movies, shopping, services, and transportation. These sites can be very useful as you prepare to leave for your destination or, if you are lucky enough to have a computer with you, after you arrive. One of the best all-around resources for finding information on just about any place in the world is Excite's City.Net (**www.city.net** or through **www.excite.com**). While it presents some information directly on its site, City.Net is primarily a resource of other travel providers on the Internet. Almost all of these sites have direct links or partnerships with the reservations sites listed above.

At this point most major cities' newspapers have websites, and they are often excellent sources of local information. You may also want to check with your regional AAA office to see if they have a website. For example, AAA of Northern California, Nevada, and Utah has an excellent website that contains information about the auto club's road services and their extensive travel planning services. It is a great resource.

Listed below are some of our favorite travel and local-information resource sites:

www.city.net	www.citysearch.com	www.gorp.com
www.digitalcity.com	www.csaa.com	www.sfgate.com
www.nytimes.com	www.latimes.com	www.tribune.com
www.washingtonpost.com		

Search Engines and Directories

One of the best ways to make your time on the Internet the most useful and fun is to learn how to use one or more search engines. Some of the most popular—and arguably best—include Yahoo! (**www.yahoo.com**), Excite (**www.excite.com**), Lycos (**www.lycos.com**), Infoseek (**www.infoseek.com**), and Alta Vista (**www.altavista.com**), which is also the search engine that is used in Yahoo! along with their directories. The "directories" in Yahoo! and the "channels" in Excite, for example, are lists of sites that are already organized into categories and can be very useful. But if you don't see what you want in these directories, read on.

If you can, we suggest that you take an hour or two and just experiment. Input the same search topic in each and compare the results. For example: *Alaskan Cruises*. You will get different results from each site (sometimes slightly different, sometimes totally different), but each should give you some useful sites. These are essential tools if you can describe what you are looking for but have no idea where to find it, or if you have looked in the better-known travel sites and have not seen the information you want. There is usually a tutorial or "help" area on the search-engine site that will show you how to get the most out of that particular service. All of these services figure importantly in having a good Internet experience. You will probably find a favorite service and use it frequently.

Before you take your trip you should take a few minutes and visit a few other sites. One is Amazon.com (**www.amazon.com**). Its bookstore contains millions of titles you can order, so if you want to know more about the history, culture, or sights in the region you will be visiting, Amazon is a terrific resource. When it comes time to pack, you can go to the Weather Channel online (**www.weather.com**) and see a forecast, precipitation

A CALENDAR OF FESTIVALS AND EVENTS

These are New Orleans's major celebrations and their approximate dates (specific ones where possible). Remember, if the event requires tickets, it's best to try to arrange them before leaving home; otherwise you may find yourself paying extra or being locked out entirely. Please note that many festivals, especially in the summer, move around from year to year, and that some close down or are replaced by others; so if you are interested, contact organizers as soon as possible.

In addition to the contacts listed below, **TicketMaster** (522-5555) may be able to supply tickets to particular events, although there will be an additional handling charge.

January

Sugar Bowl   One of the three major collegiate alliance bowls, held New Year's Day. For information on tickets and festivities, contact organizers at 1500 Sugar Bowl Drive, New Orleans, LA 70112, or call 525-8573. Sugar Bowl tickets can be purchased through TicketMaster, or by calling (877) 99-SUGAR. Associated with the football classic are other sporting events, including flag football, tennis, races, and basketball.

Super Bowl   Apart from the football showdown itself, events include a celebrity golf tournament, a huge public meet-the-players party, and a "theme park" of football games at the convention center. Contact the Convention and Visitors Bureau, 1520 Sugar Bowl Drive, New Orleans, LA 70112, or visit **www.superbowl.com.**

Twelfth Night   January 6, or the Feast of Epiphany, when the Three Wise Men reportedly reached Bethlehem, also marks the beginning of Carnival season in New Orleans; contact the Convention and Visitors Bureau.

The Anniversary of the Battle of New Orleans   Early January. The actual date is January 8, and the special mass is held on that day (see the profile of St. Ursuline's Convent in Part Eight, Sight-Seeing, Tours, and Attractions). However, the reenactment of the battle, with Redcoats, cannons, and encampment demonstrations, varies slightly around that. Call Chalmette National Park at 281-0510.

February

NCAA Baseball   For tickets and times contact the Superdome Ticket Office, P.O. Box 50488, New Orleans, LA 70150, or call 587-3663.

Mardi Gras   February 24 in 2004, February 8 in 2005, February 28 in 2006, February 20 in 2007, and February 5 in 2008. (Although it can run into March, Mardi Gras most often falls in February.) Contact the Convention and Visitors Bureau and ask for the latest schedules. The day before, now called Lundi Gras or "Fat Monday," is also an organized and highly recommended event; contact Riverwalk, 1 Poydras Street, New Orleans, LA 70130, or call 522-1555.

March

Louisiana Black Heritage Festival   Early March. A two-day celebration, with exhibits and concerts set up along Riverwalk, Audubon Park, and the Louisiana State Museum buildings. Contact the festival at 6500 Magazine Street, New Orleans, LA 70118, or 861-2537.

St. Patrick's Day   Mid-March. The actual date is March 17, but the parade dates vary (and you may catch the Mardi Gras Indians in an annual encore). For information on the French Quarter celebration, contact Molly's Pub at the Market, 1107 Decatur Street, New Orleans, LA 70116, or call 525-5169.

St. Joseph's Day   Mid-March. The Italian equivalent of St. Patrick's Day salutes Jesus's adoptive father and officially falls on March 19. But like St. Paddy's, the celebrations spread out a little. The gift of the feast is fava beans, which the saint is believed to have showered upon the starving of Sicily. Contact the American Italian Renaissance Foundation at 522-7294.

Spring Fiesta   Mid-March. A five-day celebration, dating back to the 1930s, featuring tours of historic homes, courtyard receptions, and plantation tours, culminating in a grand parade down River Road with costumed figures from history riding in horse-drawn carriages. Arias pour out over the French Quarter in honor of such past stars as Adelina Patti and Jenny Lind. Tickets are $20 for city tours, $50 for the plantation tours. Contact organizers at 826 St. Ann Street, New Orleans, LA 70112, or call 581-1367.

Tennessee Williams New Orleans Literary Festival   Third week of March to early April. This five-day event features seminars, dramatic readings (often featuring Hollywood and Broadway celebrities), theatrical productions, walking tours of the French Quarter, and the popular Stella & Stanley Shouting Competition in Jackson Square. Contact the Tennessee Williams/New Orleans Literary Festival, 5500 Prytania Street, Suite 217, New Orleans, LA 70115, call 581-1144, or go to their website at **www.tennesseewilliams.net.**

April

French Quarter Festival   Mid-April. This began as something of an apology to area residents (and performers) for the fact that the Jazz and

A CALENDAR OF FESTIVALS AND EVENTS *(continued)*

Heritage Festival had gotten so large and so national. However, it's now more popular with locals than the more crowded events. Throughout the Quarter, free concerts are performed on 11 separate stages, and there are patio tours, fireworks, and second-lining brass parades. The whole of Jackson Square and the riverfront down to the aquarium become a huge jazz buffet, thanks to the efforts of several dozen Cajun and Creole restaurants. Contact the French Quarter Festival office at 100 Conti Street, New Orleans, LA 70130, or call 522-5730.

Crescent City Classic   Mid-April. An international field runs this scenic 10K race from Jackson Square to Audubon Park. Write the CCC at 8200 Hampson Street, Suite 217, New Orleans, LA 70118, or call 861-8686.

New Orleans Jazz and Heritage Festival   Last weekend in April and the first weekend in May. See details in Part Three, New Orleans's Major Festivals, or contact Jazz Fest, P.O. Box 53407, New Orleans, LA 70153, or call 522-4786; **www.nojazzfest.com.**

May

Zoo-To-Do   Early May. The fundraiser for Audubon Zoo is one of the most profitable events in the country and includes food, decorations, and special performances. Call 565-3020, ext. 602.

Compaq Classic of New Orleans   Early May. This PGA tournament sports a million-dollar purse and is held at the English Turn Golf & Country Club in Metairie. Contact Beth Bares, 110 Veteran's Blvd. #170, New Orleans, LA 70148, or call 831-4653; **www.pgatour.com.**

Greek Festival   Late May. All those streets around Lee Circle didn't get to be named for the Muses for no reason. Enjoy folk dancing, Greek food, music, and crafts. The $3 fee enters you in a drawing for a trip to Greece. Contact festival organizers at Holy Trinity Cathedral, 1200 Robert E. Lee Boulevard, New Orleans, LA 70122, or call 282-0259; **www.greekfestnola.com.**

New Orleans Food & Wine Experience   Late May. The premier taste-of-the-town event distributes goodies from more than 40 restaurants and 150 wineries. Contact organizers at P.O. Box 70514, New Orleans, LA 70172, or call 529-WINE.

June

The Great French Market Tomato Festival   Around the first of June. Cooking demonstrations, tastings, and music along the French Market promenade. Contact organizers at P.O. Box 51749, New Orleans, LA 70151, or call 522-2621.

Reggae Riddums Festival   Mid-June. City Park hosts a weekend of international performers of reggae, calypso, and soca, surrounded by booths selling food and African-American crafts. Contact Ernest Kelly, P.O. Box 6156, New Orleans, LA 70174, or call (504) 367-1313.

July

Go Fourth on the River   July 4. Independence Day celebrations include street performances, shopping specials, discounts to riverfront attractions, concerts, parades, and fireworks. Contact the French Quarter Festival office.

Essence Music Festival   Early July. A half million people hear four days of soul, jazzy R&B, and blues in the Superdome, along with seminars, crafts, and a book fair. Contact the Visitors Bureau for more information.

August

White Linen Night   Early August. Warehouse/Arts District galleries mount simultaneous openings with performing arts along Julia Street. Contact the Contemporary Arts Center, 900 Camp Street, New Orleans, LA 70130, or call 523-1216.

October

Jazz Awareness Month   Throughout October. Concerts, many of them free, lectures, and family events. Contact the Louisiana Jazz Federation at 522-3154; **www.gnofn.org.**

Octoberfest   Weekends throughout the month. Venues and restaurants around town set out German food and drink; watch for polka lessons. Call 522-8014.

Swamp Festival   Early to mid-October. Sponsored by the Audubon Institute and held at the zoo over two weekends, this offers close encounters with indigenous animals, a taste of Cajun food, and music and crafts. Contact the Audubon Institute, 6500 Magazine Street, New Orleans, LA 70118, or call 861-2537.

New Orleans Film & Video Festival   Mid-October. Regional and world premieres of films and screenings of award-winners; the main screenings are at Canal Street Cinemas. For more information, call 523-3818; or visit **www.neworleansfilmfest.com.**

A CALENDAR OF FESTIVALS AND EVENTS *(continued)*

Jeff Fest   Mid-October. This onetime family picnic is now an annual community event with 30 bands and plenty of food in Metairie's Lafreniere Park. Contact organizers at 3816 Haring Road, Metairie, LA 70006, or call 888-2900.

Fresh Art Festival   Third weekend of the month. The new season kicks off with a juried festival of sculpture, painting, metalworks, jewelry, ceramics, fiber pieces, baskets, glass, and photography along the 700 block of St. Joseph Street between Carondelet and St. Charles, near the Louisiana ArtWorks site. For information, call the Arts Council of New Orleans at 425-1465 or 529-2430.

Boo at the Zoo   End of October. Annual Halloween extravaganza at Audubon Zoo with special children's entertainment, a "ghost train," and a haunted house. Contact the Audubon Institute, 6500 Magazine Street, New Orleans, LA 70118, or call 861-2537.

November

Racing Season at the Fairgrounds   Late November to early January. The country's third-oldest racetrack still hosts thoroughbred races Thursday

map, the business travelers' forecast with airport delays, and much more. It is even better than their cable channel because you don't have to wait until your area comes on the air—you can just go directly to it.

All of these services will only get better with time and improved technology. While the amount spent on online booking of travel is only a tiny fraction of what is spent today, the predicted growth rate of these businesses is nothing short of phenomenal. So go online and try booking a trip today.

Special Considerations

What to Pack

Perhaps a little sadly, this once most elegant of societies has become extremely informal. You probably won't see a black tie or tuxedo outside of a wedding party unless you are fortunate enough to be invited to a serious social event. Even an old, established restaurant such as Galatoire's requires only a jacket (after 5 p.m. and all day Sunday) but not a tie, and most others only "recommend" a jacket.

Shorts and polo shirts are everywhere, night or day, and a sundress or reasonably neat pair of khakis will make you look downright respectable.

through Monday during the holiday season—opening day is Thanksgiving. For reservations call (800) 262-7893 within Louisiana, or 944-5515.

Celebration in the Oaks   Late November to early January. City Park kicks off the holiday season with a display of 750,000 lights, music, seasonal foods, and special events. Contact City Park, #1 Palm Drive, New Orleans, LA 70124, or call 482-4888.

Bayou Classic   Late November. One of collegiate football's long-standing rivalries. Grambling and Southern University wind up the season at the Superdome; P.O. Box 50488, New Orleans, LA 70150, or call 587-3663.

December

New Orleans Christmas   Throughout the month. See Part Three, New Orleans's Major Festivals, for details.

New Year's Eve   December 31. Jackson Square may not be as big as Times Square, but it holds a heck of a street party, complete with countdown and, yes, a lighted ball that drops from the top of Jax Brewery. Contact the Convention and Visitors Bureau, 1520 Sugar Bowl Drive, New Orleans, LA 70112, or call 566-5005.

A rainproof top of some sort, a lightweight jacket, and a sweater, even a sweatshirt, may be all you'll need in the summer, and remember that you will probably be going in and out of air conditioning as well as rain. Something along the lines of a trenchcoat with zip-in lining or a wool walking coat with a sweater will usually do in winter. (Fur coats are not a moral issue in New Orleans, but are rarely necessary, and the constant bustle of people carrying glasses and food around on the streets might make it a risk unless you plan to spend most of the time in nicer hotels and restaurants.)

Frankly, the two most important things to consider when packing are comfortable shoes (this is a culture of asphalt, concrete, and flagstone streets) and skirts or pants with expandable waistlines. Even if you don't think you're going to eat much, the scent of food constantly fills the air, and the Café du Monde by Jackson Square is still making those beignets—fried doughnuts dusted with powdered sugar, three for a buck—24 hours a day. Second, there is no other city in which the food is so rich and full of fat, cholesterol, salt, and calories as this, and even if you don't eat more than usual, you may temporarily feel the effects. (Add a third item to your packing list—Alka Seltzer.) If you don't want to pack "fat day" clothes, you'd better pack your running shoes, too.

And finally, this city has developed a crime problem (see "How to Avoid Crime and Keep Safe in Public Spaces" in Part Six, Arriving and Getting Oriented), so there is no good reason to walk around flashing expensive jewelry. Leave it at home and stick to the Mardi Gras beads.

Playing Host

If you are coming in with a family or business group and are in charge of arranging some sort of party or reception, there are plenty of restaurants, music clubs (check out the Voodoo Garden at House of Blues or the private room at Lucky Cheng's), steamboats, and hotels with private rooms. But there are also a few less ordinary places to throw a party, if you really want to make an impression. Within City Park, for example, the New Orleans Botanical Garden has the 9,000-square-foot **Pavilion of the Two Sisters** (488-2896), and **Storyland and Carousel Gardens** (483-9356) can be reserved after hours. The carousel provides on-site catering as well. The **Contemporary Arts Center** (528-3400) and the **Louisiana Children's Museum** (523-1357), both within easy walking distance of the Convention Center, have spaces for rent. Blaine Kern's **Mardi Gras World** in Algiers lets guests try on the parade masks (361-7821). The restored third-floor "Appartement de l'Empereur" at the **Napoleon House** (524-9752) can be reserved as well, and even though Bonaparte himself never came here, the atmosphere is quite imperial.

But here's another idea that might enliven either a purely social event, such as a family reunion or wedding, or provide an unusual "spouses' function" during a business convention: playing chef for a day.

The only thing more famous than Mardi Gras is probably New Orleans's food, and devotees of Cajun and Creole cuisine can not only indulge in it, but also apprentice to it, at least temporarily. There are several cooking schools in New Orleans, most associated with local celebrity chefs, that offer classes during which visitors can either actively participate or simply watch and taste, depending on their ambitions.

The shortest and least expensive of the schools is the **New Orleans School of Cooking** at 524 St. Louis Street (525-2665). Monday through Saturday, it offers three-hour Cajun/Creole cooking classes for $25; this covers the class-cooked lunch (something like jambalaya and bananas Foster) and a Dixie beer. Groups of 25 or more can arrange a private demonstration.

The **Cookin' Cajun Cooking School** (586-8832) in the Riverwalk development offers two-hour sessions that cover either an actual meal or a private midafternoon lesson. Students learn to make the likes of shrimp rémoulade or chicken-andouille gumbo. Cost is $20 per person.

The **Culinary Institute of New Orleans** (2100 St. Charles Avenue; 525-CHEF; (888) 525-CHEF; **www.ciachef.edu**) is in the Garden District, where former G&E Courtyard chef Mark Uddo is one of the instructors. Classes are actually run out of the Chef's Table restaurant, and visitors can choose from a three-hour guest lecture with meals ($25), a three-class series ($75), or four-hour hands-on classes for which day chefs get to wear chef's jackets and toques ($125). Classes, which can be either classic New Orleans–style or not, as you desire (but which go beyond gumbo to oysters Rockefeller and veal with grits, even if you do go native), are made by appointment; larger groups of up to 300 can be accommodated with advance notice—another convention blockbuster.

Chef Horst Pfeifer of **Bella Luna** restaurant in the French Market (914 N. Peters Street; 529-1583), which despite its name is as much Creole-Southwestern fusion as Italian, has expanded what were only small, rare classes to regular demonstration lunches. Pfeifer's classes include a trip to his herb garden on the grounds of the historic Ursuline convent and are held in his own home across the street from the convent. He also does large convention classes for groups of up to 100 at the restaurant.

Another longtime local chef, Richard Bond, leads all-day classes for 2 to 12 at the Mardi Gras World complex across the river in Algiers. The **Mardi Gras School of Cooking** (362-5225) is $90 for the day, including beer, wine, and soft drinks (plus, the ferry ride is free). Bond also caters private dinner parties and leads demonstration classes for groups of up to 2,000 for $38.50 per person.

Exchanging Vows

Carried away by the romance of it all? Want to make it permanent? There is a three-day waiting period between getting a license and being married, but the judge has the option of waiving it, so your weekend could turn pretty spectacular. And he may even waive the requirement for your birth certificate if you seem sober enough. Contact the Marriage Clerk at 568-5182, 8 a.m.–4 p.m. weekdays.

For designer gowns for the bride, her mother, and any available friends, try **Harold Clarke** (568-0440) at the corner of Iberville and Dauphine in the French Quarter.

New Orleans for Families

Of course, New Orleans is most famous as a sort of adults' playground, but if you're considering a family vacation here, don't worry. Despite all the round-the-clock bars and burlesque houses, New Orleans is full of family-style attractions, both in and out of the French Quarter. And since these are year-round, you can avoid the special-event crowds altogether. Just remember that warnings about dehydration in the city's heat go double for children.

Within the Vieux Carré is the entire **French Market, Jackson Square** with all its balloon twisters, clowns, and mule-drawn carriages that, while somewhat undependable as far as historic detail is concerned, are very entertaining. The **Musée Conti Wax Museum** is a perennial favorite, as is the free **Canal Street ferry** ride across the Mississippi. There are several doll and toy museum-stores that may attract some children, as well as Le Petit Soldier store and, for some, the **Pharmacy Museum.** Kids who play dress-up will love the Carnival exhibit at the **Old U.S. Mint,** with its Aladdin's cave of crowns and pins. (And you should check the schedule of **Le Petit Théâtre du Vieux Carré,** which sometimes has children's productions.)

The state-of-the-art **Louisiana Children's Museum** is in the Ware-house/Arts District. At the edge of the riverwalk area is the Aquarium of the Americas, from which you can take a boat directly to **Audubon Zoo** in the Garden District. (The Zoo is also accessible from the St. Charles streetcar, which is another family possibility.)

City Park in Mid-City has an antique carousel, miniature rideable trains, a toy museum, the Storyland playground designed around Mother Goose characters, plus botanical gardens and a riding stable. Beyond that, in eastern New Orleans, is the **Louisiana Nature Center,** which has a planetarium, hands-on exhibits, and 86 acres of forest trails.

East of the city on the way to Chalmette National Battlefield, site of the Battle of New Orleans, is a remarkable military museum at the **Jackson Barracks** that will almost certainly transfix any normally bloody-minded kid. **The Confederate Museum,** while more specific and semi-hagiographic, is close to the new D-Day Museum and the Louisiana Children's Museum.

Near the airport is a treasure trove for families, a complex of attractions called **Rivertown** that includes an observatory and planetarium, Mardi Gras and toy-train museums, the New Orleans Saints Hall of Fame, a Native American–living museum within the Louisiana Wildlife Museum, and the Children's Castle, where puppet and magic shows are staged. There is also a repertory theater there.

And if you're interested in swamp and bayou life, you can either sign up for one of the several swamp tours or cruises or take a short drive to the **Barataria Preserve**—Jean Lafitte's old stronghold and now a 20,000-acre park with a Park Service visitors center, trails, and boardwalks that wind among the cypress swamps and freshwater branches. Or spend the night at the **Global Wildlife Center** near Folsom and go nose-to-nose with a giraffe (see Part Eight, Sight-Seeing, Tours, and Attractions).

If you bring the kids along for the convention but have to get a little work time in, contact **Accents on Arrangements** (524-1227) to hook up with children's tours; or the day care/field trip–oriented **Conference Child Care Service** (248-9457), which is a member of the Greater New Orleans Multicultural Tourism Network.

Tips for International Travelers

Visitors from Western Europe, the United Kingdom, Japan, or New Zealand who stay in the United States fewer than 90 days need only a valid passport, not a visa, and a round-trip or return ticket. Canadian citizens can get by only with proof of residence. Citizens of other countries must have a passport (good for at least six months beyond the projected end of the visit) and a tourist visa as well, available from any U.S. consulate. Contact consular officials for application forms; some airlines and travel agents may also have forms available.

If you are taking prescription drugs containing narcotics or requiring injection by syringe, be sure to get a doctor's signed prescription and instructions (good advice for all travelers). Pacemakers, metal implants, and surgical pins may set off security machines, so a letter from your doctor describing your condition is a wise precaution (again, this applies to domestic travelers as well). Also check with the local consulate to see whether travelers from your country are currently required to have any inoculations; there are no set requirements to enter the United States, but if there has been any sort of epidemic in your homeland, there may be temporary restrictions.

If you arrive by air, be prepared to spend as much as two hours entering the country and getting through Customs. Canadians and Mexicans crossing the borders either by car or by train will find a much quicker and easier system. Every adult traveler may bring in, duty-free, up to 1 liter of wine or hard liquor; 200 cigarettes, 100 non-Cuban cigars, or 3 pounds of loose tobacco; and $100 worth of gifts, as well as up to $10,000 in U.S. currency or its equivalent in foreign currency. No food or plants may be brought in. For information on sales tax refunds, see Part Ten, Shopping in New Orleans.

Credit cards are by far the most common form of payment in New Orleans, especially American Express, Visa (also known as BarclayCard in Britain), and MasterCard (Access in Britain, Eurocard in Western Europe, or Chargex in Canada). Other popular cards include Diners Club, Discover, and Carte Blanche. Travelers checks will be accepted at most hotels and restaurants if they are in American dollars; other currencies should be taken to a bank or foreign exchange and turned into dollar figures (the Mutual of Omaha office offers this service and wires funds in or out).

The dollar is the basic unit of monetary exchange, and the entire system is decimal. The smaller sums are represented by coins. One hundred cents (or pennies, as the 1-cent coin is known) equal one dollar; 5 cents is a nickel (20 nickels to a dollar); 10 cents is called a dime (10 dimes to a dollar); and the 25-cent coin is called a quarter (4 to a dollar). The dollar coin is the only one that is not perfectly round, but octagonal, so it's easily identified. Beginning with one dollar, money is in currency bills (there are both one-dollar coins and bills). Bills come in $1, $5, $10, $20, $50, $100, $500, and so on, although you are unlikely to want to carry $1,000 or more. Stick to $20s for taxicabs and such; drivers rarely can make change for anything larger.

International visitors who shop at stores participating in the Louisiana Tax-Free Shopping (LTFS) program can get a refund on the taxes on retail purchases; see Part Ten, Shopping in New Orleans, for details.

If you need any additional assistance, there is an Immigration Service desk at the airport (467-1713). For language assistance, try the AT&T language line at (800) 874-9426.

And throughout the United States, if you have a medical, police, or fire emergency, dial 911, even on a pay telephone, and an ambulance or police cruiser will be dispatched to help you.

Tips for the Disabled

Visitors who use walking aids should be warned: only the larger museums and the newer shopping areas can be counted on to be wheelchair accessible. Many individual stores and smaller collections are housed in what were once private homes with stairs, and even those at sidewalk level are unlikely to have wider aisles or specially equipped bathrooms. The restaurants that we profile later in the book all have a disabled access rating, but you need to call any other eatery or store in advance. Similarly, you need to call any stores you're interested in. Antique stores in particular tend to be tightly packed and with shelving at all levels.

For the Nose that Knows

If you are allergy sensitive, watch out for spring. As for smoking, it is prohibited in any public building, on the streetcars, and in taxis. Restaurants with more than 50 seats have to have a nonsmoking section, but that's not practical in a smaller restaurant; bars welcome smokers.

Part Three

New Orleans's Major Festivals

Mardi Gras Mania

You could write a book about Mardi Gras, and many people have. The big picture, you already know: it's a loud, public, and highly indulgent series of parades, "second-line" dancing (that refers to the parasol-wielding high-steppers who traditionally formed a second line behind the brass band, and who gradually acquire a civilian train like a comet attracting cosmic detritus), and formal masques and balls. There's partying in the streets, in the bars, in the restaurants, in the courtyards, in the parks, in the alleys—no wonder most French Quarter residents rent their homes out for the week and flee uptown, or even out of town. There's little sleep to be had, with more than a million visitors—an estimated two million in 2003—packed elbow to armpit and mug to go-cup. Tourism officials estimate that Mardi Gras spending has reached a billion dollars a year.

But in recent years, the ever-increasing incidents of public inebriation, fighting, nudity, petty (and occasionally greater) crime, and general vagrancy have for many people irretrievably tarnished the event; some of the oldest and most respected societies have pulled out entirely. Some, it must be pointed out, have pulled out with less plausible excuses: After the City Council ruled in 1991 that the all-white krewes had to integrate their parades, two of the three oldest parading krewes, the venerable Comus and Momus, chose to stop parading rather than integrate. They were followed the next year by Proteus, the fourth-oldest parading krewe, though it returned to active duty in 2000. They now maintain their balls strictly as private parties. A recent Rex float, florid with flames and demons, was titled "Momus in Hades," a tribute to one of the most famous parades in Mardi Gras history, the 1877 "Hades, a Dream of Momus," which managed to insult nearly every politician at the state or national level; however, some city residents took it as a poke from Rex to its less amenable rival. (It would have been more appropriate than they knew: Although it's not often mentioned, white supremacists and antifederalist groups often used Mardi Gras parades, and costume masks, as a cover for rallies and sometimes riots during Reconstruction. Some, including the Mystick Krewe of Comus, were at times virtual fronts for such groups.)

The pleading for beads and other *lagniappes* (pronounced lan-yap) and the traditional cries of "Throw me somethin', mister," have degenerated to the point where members of even the highest-profile krewes knowingly twirl their fanciest prizes and demand that women bare their breasts to earn the treasure. Grown-ups (we use the phrase ironically) now far outperform the most spoiled and insatiable small children by stealing beads tossed to others, concealing the size of their trove, and even snatching stuffed animals and toys. Wearing the biggest and showiest beads is now a sort of measure of either testosterone or nubility, depending on the wearer. It's no wonder that the locals tend to avoid Bourbon Street and enjoy smaller parties in the suburbs; or they pick and choose their events.

But tarnished or not, no city, except perhaps for Rio de Janeiro, is so closely associated with Carnival as New Orleans. In fact, it almost seems as if the city's destiny was to be the biggest Mardi Gras party town in the world: On March 3, 1699, when the Sieur d'Iberville (brother of the Sieur de Bienville) camped on the Mississippi River, the day *was* Mardi Gras, and that was what he named the site—Mardi Gras Point. Hedging a little bit, perhaps, the city declared the 1999 Carnival season the 300th anniversary celebration. Nevertheless, it is clear that there were some rudimentary carryings-on in the area—Mobile had a Boeuf Gras, a "fatted calf" club, even before the city of New Orleans formally existed—almost from the very beginning, so observing Mardi Gras in the Crescent City is one of those things a lot of people feel they ought to do at least once. If you want to immerse yourself in the spirit, we can try at least to make it a little easier on you.

Mardi Gras, for those who think it means "bottoms up," actually translates as "Fat Tuesday"; it's so called because it's the last day before Lent, when observant Catholics were supposed to give up meat-eating (and, ideally, various other fleshly pleasures). The weeks between Twelfth Night and Lent are called "Carnival," from the Latin for "farewell to meat," although the festival season certainly involves plenty of feasting—stocking up, so to speak. Although many people refer to the entire Carnival season as Mardi Gras, that title rightfully applies to only the one day, and using the term wrongly is one way to brand yourself a really green outsider. The day after Fat Tuesday is Ash Wednesday, the beginning of the sober Lenten season, which continues until Easter. In other words, Tuesday is supposed to be the last day to enjoy oneself for nearly seven weeks. Hence it became an occasion for overindulgence, followed by extreme penitence, beginning smack on the mark with midnight mass. Nowadays most people settle for the indulgences and watch the tape replay of Ash Wednesday services on television later. In fact, St. Louis Cathedral doesn't even hold midnight mass at the end of Mardi Gras any more because of the unruly crowds.

Mardi Gras is also a legal holiday in Louisiana, so get your banking done on Monday. (But be sure to check the calendar there, too; in 1999, for example, the Monday before Mardi Gras coincided with the federal holiday Presidents' Day, so there was no banking from Friday to Wednesday, and no postal service from Saturday to Wednesday. It was also Valentine's Day on Sunday, and the end of spring break for a lot of college students; so now you know how they wound up with two million people in the streets.)

Mardi Gras has a long and suitably flamboyant history in New Orleans. The French colonists celebrated Mardi Gras, or more generally, Twelfth Night, in some form for nearly 50 years, but when the city was turned over to the Spanish empire, which adhered to a much more rigorous and ascetic form of Catholicism, the governor banned the festivities—and the anti-Catholic Americans who took over after the Louisiana Purchase weren't favorably inclined toward such Papist displays, either. In fact, there was nearly a serious dust-up over whether the music played at Carnival season was to be in English or in French. However, there was always at least some private partying to keep the spirit alive. By 1823 the balls were legal again, and within a few years the street parties took hold; the first walking parades were organized in 1837. As in modern times, the crowds kept swelling; a parade of mounted "Bedouins" was a huge public success in 1852, but by 1855, newspaper reports, focusing on the violence of the rabble and the drunkenness of some participants (ahem), called for an end to the celebrations.

Instead, a group of aristocratic Creoles formed the first secret krewe, the Mystick Krewe of Comus, to give the mayhem some form. It was Comus that designed the first great classical tableaux and theme parade floats and debuted them in early 1857. The Twelfth Night club first selected a queen and threw trinkets soon after the Civil War (during which, due to the occupation, all celebrations were cancelled); the Krewe of Rex designed the first "doubloon" in 1884. That same year, incidentally, Comus picked its first queen, Mildred Lee, daughter of the "sainted" Robert E. Lee—payback for those four years, perhaps. The theme song, the rather sappy "If Ever I Cease to Love," was a signature song of New York vaudeville star Lydia Thompson, who was performing in New Orleans in 1872. The lovesick Grand Duke Alexis of Russia followed her south, and in his honor every krewe played the number in its parade (except Momus, which fortunately had thrown its inaugural parade on New Year's Eve). Now it's not so common, but Rex and his court still begin their ball with it.

The first "electric parade" was in 1889, when the appropriately named Krewe of Electra wired the headdresses of more than 125 paraders. The first black organization, the Original Illinois Club, was founded in 1895; the first all-woman krewe, Les Mysterieuses, followed suit the next year and held a formal ball, though the first all-woman parade, by the Krewe of Venus, wasn't launched until 1941. (It has since disbanded.) The gay Krewe of Petronius threw its first ball in 1962; there are now four gay krewes. Mardi Gras has survived wars (though the only times it has been cancelled were during the Civil War and World Wars I and II), Prohibition (only Rex paraded in 1920), fires, blizzards, monsoons, epidemics (most of it was lost to yellow fever in 1879), racial tensions (with losses, as mentioned), and hurricanes (1965's Betsy chewed up a chunk of several krewes).

The major parades include dozens of floats, punctuated by marching bands and mounted police, and may require the talents of 2,000 or 3,000 people. Mardi Gras expert Arthur Hardy, who has been publishing the semi-official guide to Mardi Gras for more than 20 years, has calculated that the parades of Endymion, Bacchus, and Orpheus, which are held the three nights leading up to Mardi Gras, among themselves account for 3,750 members, 110 floats, 90 marching bands, and 375 units.

Most of the krewes (the only correct spelling for Mardi Gras "crews") have names and themes taken from classical mythology: Aphrodite, Pegasus, Mercury, Ulysses, Saturn, Rhea, Argus, Atlas, Atreus, Helios, Orion, Poseidon, Pan, Hermes, Zeus, Juno, Diana, Hercules, Venus, Midas, Mithras, Isis, Iris, Thor, and Thoth ("tote," as it's pronounced locally) have all had their own krewes, although not all survive or parade. Most members are masked, and many never even reveal their membership, especially those who belong to charitable clubs.

Although the strict secrecy has eased a little, some krewes still keep parade themes and rulers quiet until the last minute. The captain of the krewe, who is actually the executive officer, is a permanent position, but the king, queen, and court change from year to year. Rex, considered the real King of Carnival, is never publicly identified until the night before. The "dictator" or the Krewe d'Etat, which was formed only in 1996 and is trying to return the parades to their original political and satirical tone, is never publicly identified. Depending on the krewe, the royals may either be mature members of the business/social communities, or up-and-comers, with queens and ladies drawn from the debutante circle. In the older social families, there may be more than one generation of kings and queens, and several lesser lights.

Bacchus, on the other hand, is most celebrity-conscious and regularly crowns actors of, let us say, obvious appetites, such as John Goodman and James Belushi, and the verbally voracious Larry King. The Krewe of Orpheus, named after the musician so eloquent he persuaded Pluto to release his dead wife (although she slipped away again), was founded in

1994 by Harry Connick Jr. as the first "super krewe" with male and female members, and its parade on Saturday night is considered one of the modern highlights. Over the years, celebrities as wide-ranging as the Beach Boys, Dolly Parton, Stevie Wonder, Whoopi Goldberg, Bob Hope, Britney Spears, and Jackie Gleason have been lured to the throne of Parade floats.

In its heyday, and even up until fairly recently, Creole Carnival season was a much more elegant affair, with fancy dress and masquerade balls, elaborate trinkets, and lagniappes, a word meaning something like "a little extra" and applied to any small gift or token, even a nibble or free drink. Nowadays, yelling "Throw me somethin', mister" may get you beads, candy, bikini pants, or almost anything—if you can wrest it away from the next guy, or the girl on his shoulders. (The familiar purple, green, and gold colors represent justice, faith, and power, and you may need all three to survive.) Even now, being a krewe member is fairly expensive; it costs more than $3,000 to ride with Krewe of America.

Obviously, you need not be a New Orleans resident to participate— the Southern Trial Lawyers Association annually schedules its convention in New Orleans to coincide with Mardi Gras so that members may parade with the Bards of Bohemia—but the most traditional dances are still sponsored by old-line krewes, and their parties are still by closely guarded invitation only, many of them doubling as the debutante balls of their members' daughters. They often get to sit in special boxes along the parade routes and be saluted by their loyal following on the floats, and some actually ride and toss themselves.

Even if somehow you do get invited to a traditional krewe ball, remember that you are not a member and can only sit in the spectator seats and enjoy the show. (The only exception is a woman guest issued a "call-out card"; she will sit with the other called women until the dancing begins and her escort calls her out.) And it is quite a show: the last year's court will be presented, and the costumes displayed in tableaux. The ball of the Krewe of Rex, for example, which is probably the most intently traditional, follows so rigid a line that the stories in the *Times-Picayune* are reprinted almost word for word every year—sort of an inside joke:

It begins about 6 p.m. the day before Mardi Gras (Lundi Gras or "Fat Monday") with Rex's being ferried downriver (in the 19th century it was a paddleboat; these days, he's transported by Coast Guard cutter) to land at Spanish Plaza at the foot of Canal Street. There he is greeted by the King of Zulu. Rex reads a proclamation declaring the advent of festivities—a little late, but then he is the official King of Carnival—fireworks ensue, and he and his retainers head for their ball, usually held at a downtown hotel or the convention center. The captain announces the arrival of the court, in order of precedence; the court dances the first dance and then everybody gets to join in. Around 9 p.m., however, a messenger from the Krewe of Comus is announced; he invites Rex and his Queen to visit the Comus court (usually in the neighboring ball-room), and Rex and company head over for another presentation to the King of Comus, who, unlike Rex, is never unmasked.

Some outsiders may find all this pompous circumstance a little strange, especially in contrast to the other parties in the street. (Among the better-natured spoof parades is the annual Mystic Krewe of Barkus parade, a fundraiser for the LSPCA that has chosen such themes as "Lifestyles of the Bitch and Famous" and "Jurassic Bark.") However, there are many newer and more liberal krewes that throw more public and less tradition-bound "supper dances," and you may be able to get tickets to some of those. Orpheus and Tucks, for example, sell party tick-ets through TicketMaster. You can even join a krewe and ride for a few hundred bucks. Get a copy of Arthur Hardy's annual *Mardi Gras Guide* magazine for more information. It will probably be all over town when you get there, but you would be smart to have one in advance, because it includes maps, schedules, tips, gossip, features, and even the occasional coupon. Write to P.O. Box 19500, New Orleans, LA 70005, call (504) 838-6111, or write to him via his e-mail address: mardihardy@aol.com.

Carnival season in New Orleans traditionally begins with the Krewe of Twelfth Night ball held on Twelfth Night or Epiphany (January 6), but the pace gradually picks up: The last 10 or 12 days of Carnival is high parade season, when at almost any moment police sirens announce the imminent arrival of a marching band, motorcycle drill team, or horseback troupe, stilt-walking clowns, acrobats, balloon-twisters, and professional and amateur dancing girls. Although these are rarely as elab-orate or as lengthy as those in the final few days, they are often just as entertaining and not nearly so crowded. The French Quarter in particu-lar erupts into walking parades of ordinary celebrants that form behind the bands and second-liners. One of the sweetest is a parade of elemen-tary-school children, with a tiny king who sometimes loses his crown as his mule-drawn carriage turns a corner. (For renting or buying costumes, see "Mardi Gras and Music" in Part Eight, Sight-Seeing, Tours, and Attractions; or look in Part Ten, Shopping in New Orleans.)

And since any real business pretty much comes to a halt after lunch on Friday, the city has instituted a more recent celebration on Lundi Gras. It's actually one of the best things about Carnival these days, involving a whole day of music (two stages' worth) on the riverfront and in front of the Aquarium of the Americas. That's followed by the landing of Rex and the fireworks on the Spanish Plaza, a free public masquerade ball, and the lavish one-two parades of the Bards of Bohemia (all professional enter-tainers, including the fire-swallower who was married to his assistant on the float as they passed City Hall), and the celebrity-laden Orpheus.

Though the most famous parades use St. Charles Avenue and Canal Street, not all the parades do: Various routes go uptown, downtown, or into the suburbs, and some guidebooks have maps and information. (The French Quarter is no longer used for the big parades except in a few cases, and only for a couple of blocks.) The *Times-Picayune* publishes a daily list of routes and times of parades—along with anecdotes, full-color photographs, ball-queen presentations, and literally pages of trivia—throughout the Carnival season.

Mardi Gras day more or less officially kicks off with one of the real highlights, the Zulu Social Aid and Pleasure Club parade. The role of Zulu is a key one, because it brings up some racial issues still not very smoothly settled in New Orleans, as we've mentioned elsewhere. The Zulu parade dates from early in the 20th century, when a black resident named William Storey parodied the elaborately crowned Rex by strutting behind his float wearing an old lard can on his head and calling himself "King Zulu."

Gradually, however, the Zulus' plucky sense of humor, their no-holds-barred self- *and* social parody, and their very serious accomplishments (like the best of the old krewes, Zulu is made up of respected professionals and community activists) have given it a rare prestige in that often narrow-minded city. Nowadays the Zulu's gilded coconut shells are among the most coveted throws, and it is an even greater honor, especially for a white resident, to be invited to participate. Of course, they have to wear blackface and a grass skirt; but then even the black members and the king himself do the minstrel-show makeup thing.

And finally, in 1999, at "the last Mardi Gras of the millennium" as they said inaccurately but grandly, Rex not only accepted King Zulu's greeting at the river, but also exchanged greetings, king to king. It was a subtle shift, but one obvious to everyone in the crowd, and it may have been the most important event of the entire festival. It was also the 50th anniversary of the year that Louis Armstrong rode as King Zulu, and that was frequently alluded to as one of Fat Tuesday's greatest moments. (Armstrong's wife returned as queen in 1973.)

So the parade of Zulu, which leads straight into Rex, is a touchstone event of the day—the inaugural event, in fact. It begins at 8:30 a.m. (theoretically), and heads off toward downtown as the various "walking clubs" are promenading about town to set the tone. These range from the Half-Fast Walking Club, founded by legendary jazz clarinetist Pete Fountain, that walks the traditional Canal and St. Charles route; to more daringly clad entertainers of Bourbon Street's bars and strip joints; to the fantastically beaded and befeathered black "Indians" of Kenner and Metairie, such as the revered Wild Tchoupitoulas tribe, whose chiefs are required to sew their costumes themselves and indulge in great competitions of face, style, and song. The highly competitive Bourbon Street Awards, the gay costume competition around the intersection of St. Ann and Burgundy streets outside the Rawhide Bar, warms up around midday, as less formal processions are forming all over town.

The most elaborately "classical" float, the crown-shaped vessel of Rex, King of Carnival, takes off at 10 a.m. and arrives at Gallier Hall around midday, preceded by a cohort of gold-helmeted lieutenants and white horses. Atop one of Rex's floats is a papier-mâché fatted ox, or "boeuf gras," reminding you of that meatless future. The parade route goes across St. Charles Avenue starting as far back as Napoleon Street, so if you can find a place along St. Charles, you can see everything without being swamped by the Bourbon Street brawlers. There are limited bleachers put up, but the public tickets generally go on sale right after Christmas; contact the Metropolitan Convention and Visitors Bureau. (The Hotel Inter-Continental at 444 St. Charles is among those setting up grandstand seats and selling them in a package with buffet meals; call 525-5566.)

Don't worry about running dry; to accommodate early parade-goers, many bars open at 8 a.m., and, of course, the convenience stores along the parade routes do a continual carry-out business as well. But remember, Fat Tuesday ends on Ash Wednesday, and like Cinderella's coach, it turns into a pumpkin exactly at midnight. This is the one and only time that "time" is definitely called in New Orleans, so be prepared. The police, led by the many mounted officers who warm up for duty by parading during the day, "sweep" the French Quarter in a maneuver that is as invariably part of the next day's newspaper photo spread as Miss America jumping in the surf off Atlantic City the morning after the pageant.

In the meantime, try to pace yourself. Consider the paucity of rest rooms; most hotels issue colored wristbands to make sure only paying guests get in, and no bar or restaurant is going to welcome you if you don't plan to purchase anything. The city does place some portable toilets around the parade routes, near the music stages along the riverfront, but they quickly become overloaded, and many people, especially the younger guys, are reluctant to go so far from their parade-side stations to use them. Unfortunately, since a lot of people will lose either patience or control, you'll have to be careful where you walk, much less sit, especially in the Quarter.

However, if you do some careful scouting early in the day, you may see a fairly new Mardi Gras phenomenon: pay-per-visit portapotty parks. A few clever entrepreneurs have taken to renting toilets, setting them up in strategic locations, and charging for their use. A couple of years ago, a guy put up 28 of them near Bourbon Street and Iberville, and clients paid $1 per visit during the day and $2 after 6 p.m., or bought an all-day pass for $10. In return, a host stayed on duty to maintain order, keep the johns as clean as possible, and spray them with air freshener. The next year, several more porto-parks appeared, including one right on Canal Street. Some restaurants and shops also put signs up advertising toilet privileges for $2 or $3 a trip, but the quality control leaves a lot more to be desired.

To be quite frank, the best way to enjoy Mardi Gras is to pick a couple of days, immerse yourself in the party spirit, and be gone by the time Fat Tuesday gets into high gear. You could come for Friday and Saturday, see the Endymion and Bacchus parades, among others, and get your fill of beads and friendly strangers while the bloom is still on the rose. (Traditionally, many local residents pull out on Sunday morning.) Or even come in as the first wave of hotel guests goes, spend Sunday and Monday, getting the most out of Lundi Gras, and take the early Tuesday flights out. The detritus starts to build up pretty heavily by Monday—in 1999 streetcleaners, sweeping up right behind the police, gathered up an estimated 932 tons of garbage and that's just in New Orleans alone, not counting the neighboring parishes.

But if you want to see the real thing, here are some tips on how to have fun and look like a native. If you're going to be within tossing distance at a night parade—that is, either in a stand with fairly good access or staked out right behind the barricades—you should also have a handful of quarters in your pocket to throw to the torch bearers, called *flambeaux*. They are reminders of the men who carried real flaming-pitch torches (these are naphtha) for the Krewe of Comus, which was the first to figure out how to turn parading into a nighttime spectacle. Really experienced flambeaux carriers not only twirl these heavy torches; they can spot the glint of coin from yards away. They have to—although this traditional tribute goes back a long way, few non-natives know about it, and so despite the huge popularity of Mardi Gras, the cut of flambeaux carriers has been getting pretty short in recent years. So if you feel like looking for dollar coins to toss, they'd be grateful.

In terms of food supplies, it's smart to bring your own. Aside from a couple of vendor trucks offering steam-table Thai or Chinese, you'll probably have to settle for a hot dog or pizza. (This is along the parade route; there will be more of those turkey leg and jambalaya concessionaires along the river.) Plastic containers are a lot safer than glass or metal, but since so many people will be buying alcohol as the day goes on, you'll be surrounded by both eventually, so real shoes are a good idea, too. And you should bring a lot of water or soda, because you will be dehydrated, and the mark-ups at quick-stops are steep.

Veteran parade-goers also take along duffle bags or shopping totes to put their goodies in. You can only put so many beads over your shoulders—you will find that the cumulative weight is pretty surprising—and come the next parade, or the next morning, it starts all over again. According to "Mardi Gras Man" Hardy again, just those same three parades, Endymion, Bacchus, and Orpheus, toss more than 1.5 million plastic cups, 2.5 million doubloons, and around 25 million beads. And they aren't even the only krewes parading at a time. So you might as well be picky; hold on to the good ones, and let the cheapies go to the kids.

(One of the perennial mysteries of Ash Wednesday is not a spiritual but a material one: What do you do with all those trinkets? Do you ship them home? Throw them out? Try to sell them to a bead merchant for the next year? Good luck. Personally, I suggest donating them to a shelter, a hospital children's ward, or the like. You could decorate your Christmas tree with them, but you'll still have to store them for eight months. Trust me, a few strands will do you.)

Another thing that comes in handy if you're serious about being really close to the action is goggles of the sort used in racquetball, especially for children whose reflexes may not be as quick. A slung rope of beads is like an Argentine bolo, and pretty dangerous. There are likely to be incoming missiles from several angles at once; and as the parades get more elaborate and the crowds get rowdier, you are almost certain to get a few bruises. It may come as a rude surprise, but the 50-year-old tourist trying to revive his career as a Lothario can be just as much of a toss hog as any teenager. Worse, in fact. And now that beads are bigger and heavier, and the float riders start showing off by slinging out huge handfuls of them at a time, you can occasionally take quite a shot. Even large cheap sunglasses might help, if you can keep them on.

Don't carry a lot of cash, and put it someplace other than your pocket. Leave your car well out of the neighborhood if possible; many streets are closed off, and parking regulations are vigorously enforced. If you inadvertently drive into a parade route, it can cost you a cool $100.

First-time Mardi Gras celebrants, many of whom have never been to New Orleans at all, frequently come anticipating dinner at the famous restaurants of the French Quarter. Be sure to make your reservations well in advance, because a fair number of the trendiest ones will be closed Tuesday or even for several days beforehand because the closing-off of parade routes makes it so hard for their patrons to get in and out that it's not worth staying open. Some give up the sit-down dishes in favor of sandwiches and salads. Others that are located in hotels, such as the Windsor Grill in the Windsor Court, are open only to hotel guests who can show their identification bands. So do some advance work. And if you get the little doll in your slice of the tricolor King Cake, you have to throw the next party.

Here's another piece of logic that often fails to dawn on outsiders: Since so many of the parade routes include St. Charles Avenue and Canal Street, the streetcar doesn't run on Fat Tuesday, and not for huge parts of the days and nights beforehand. (The parade routes are not only marked off by portable fences, they are actively patrolled by police officers, who are reluctant to let civilians cross the road and are sometimes downright truculent about the available options.) Similarly, since many of the parades wind up down at the convention center or major hotels where the krewe balls are held, the Riverfront Line is blocked off. So quaint as they are, and handy as it may seem, this is one time you're not going to be able to use public transportation. Cabs are going to have a hard time negotiating the area as well, so the best thing is to have a coherent plan and be ready to walk it.

And you should also realize that these parades are long, long affairs, several hours' worth—sometimes all day. For one thing, you have to beat the band. Unless you have a grandstand ticket (and to some extent, even if you do, because they are only for sections, not specific seats), you need to stake out a position along the parade route a couple of hours early. Many people who want prime territory spend all night or show up at the literal crack of dawn toting sofas, stepladders, and lawn chairs. So if, for example, you decide to view Zulu and Rex from further uptown, and Zulu is scheduled to start off at 8:30 a.m., you need to be down on the street by 6:30 or 7 a.m., if not sooner.

Then, even if Zulu does get off on time, it will be 10:30 or 11 a.m. before it turns the corner of St. Charles onto Canal (so you need to be in position by 8:30 or 9 a.m., and then expect to have to hold your ground against invaders). Each parade takes a couple of hours to pass, followed immediately by Rex, followed by the dozen of Elks club trucks, followed by the Crescent City Trucks, which are huge semis honking and wheezing, all still bearing dozens of bead-tossers, followed by the Krewe of America . . . and sometimes the police barricades never open in between. So if you stake out your position at 8 a.m., it may be 6 p.m. before you can cross the parade without going a very, very long way out of your way. Especially if you're downtown, you need to be sure which side of Canal—in the Quarter or out—you want to spend most the day. If you want to see the costume parades and balcony parties on Bourbon Street, plan to cross Canal before 9:30 a.m., catch a bit of Zulu, and cut away.

The same goes at night; if you enjoy the Lundi Gras festival at Spanish Plaza, which generally lasts until around 7:30 p.m., then get into position for Bards of Bohemia, you may be there until after midnight waiting for Orpheus to finish up. So make sure you consider the map in advance. (It's midnight: do you know where your hotel is?)

If you want to come to Mardi Gras and bring your kids, but don't necessarily want to take them to the parades with you (or don't think they need to get their first lessons in anatomy along Bourbon Street), there are a fair number of activities for them in addition to those mentioned earlier in "New Orleans for Families"; check the *Times-Picayune*. Several of the hotels provide kids' carnivals or parties, and the Louisiana Children's Museum offers special in-house parades, mask-making classes, and so on.

You could opt for seeing the parades in Metairie or Kenner: these are much more family-style events, and the "Indian" walking parades are famously rousing, with good music and flamboyant costumes of a huge and feathered sort particularly attractive to kids. You could go out to the fairgrounds racetrack and see an afternoon of races; in 1999, jockey Julie Kron won her 350th race on Mardi Gras and turned back flips for the crowd.

Or you could skirt the entire issue: there is a rather different but fascinating Cajun Mardi Gras celebration in Lafayette, Louisiana, about three hours from the city; see "Cajun Country Festivals" at the end of this chapter.

Jazz and Heritage Fest

The New Orleans Jazz and Heritage Festival spans a ten-day period in late April and early May. It's usually called Jazz Fest for short, and in fact the first festival, organized over a quarter century ago by the same folks who brought you the Newport Jazz Festival, featured such stars as Duke Ellington, Mahalia Jackson, and Al Hirt. Now, however, the folk, gumbo, zydeco, Latin, R&B, swamp rock, brass, bounce (brass crossed with rap), ragtime-revival, bluegrass, gospel, and even klezmer performers far outnumber the jazz traditionalists; it's estimated that close to 5,000 musicians show up.

Long a favorite of lower-key visitors, in recent years it has come to rival Carnival in its crowds and extravagance (although not yet in its sheer overindulgence). The main stages, a dozen of them, are erected at the Fair Grounds near City Park, with the biggest performance stage right in the racetrack infield and tents all around the 25-acre site. The music is big-time but wide-ranging: veterans include the Neville Brothers, the Marsalis brothers (and sometimes patriarch Ellis as well), Irma Thomas, Gladys Knight, Wilson Pickett, the Indigo Girls, the Dave Matthews Band, Walter "Wolfman" Washington, Raful Neal, Kenny Neal, the Radiators, Buckwheat Zydeco, Joan Baez, and Van Morrison. You just wander around until something grabs your fancy. There are related concerts at clubs and venues all around the city, some even on the water, and the streets are full.

Meanwhile, parts of the Fair Grounds are spread out with scores of food concessions—not the usual fast-food junk, but gumbo, fried alligator, red beans and rice, jambalaya, crabs, oysters, po-boys, and even roast pig. Jewelry, hand-crafted furniture, finer hand-crafted instruments, decoys, beadwork, and baskets make for some of the most worthwhile souvenirs the city has to offer.

The Fair Grounds are in a constant state of ferment from 11 a.m. to 11 p.m.; tickets are $20 in advance or $25 at the gate (kids tickets are $1.50 in advance, $2 at the gate). Nighttime concerts, with tickets ranging up to $30, are held at various locations, although if you cock an ear toward the nicer hotel lounges and jazz clubs, you may pick up a free jam or two.

The fest is actually two long weekends (Thursday through Sunday), but the city is trying out on interim party to keep interest (and tourist money) flowing midweek. The MoFest (as in, mo' music) is held on the Monday and Tuesday between the two weekend lineups, and, much like the French Quarter Fest, features local musicians and restaurant booths set up along the riverfront.

If you have to choose, go for the second part of the festival—on Sunday morning, New Orleans's most famous falsetto, Aaron Neville, usually steps up with the famous Zion Harmonizers at the gospel show. And since it generally dovetails with the Cinco de Mayo festivities—an appropriate party for New Orleans, as it commemmorates one of the many Spanish-French battles fought over the southern North American continent—it's even more high-spirited.

Note that this festival frequently falls during one of the first real heat waves, so be sure to pack sunglasses, sunblock, water, and a hat or at least a bandanna. And forget driving there; either take public transportation or a cab. Or hoof it.

For more information, contact the **Jazz and Heritage Festival** office at P.O. Box 53407, New Orleans, LA 70153; call 522-4786; or check out **www.nojazzfest.com.** *Off Beat* magazine puts out a comprehensive guide to the festival every year, although after the fact, but check their website for hints: www.offBEAT.com. You can also buy advance tickets through **TicketMaster:** (800) 488-5252 or (504) 522-5555.

Incidentally, if you're more interested in Cajun, Indian, and island music, consider the **Festival Internationale de Louisiane** in Lafayette at the end of April, which takes over a five-block piece of downtown and draws about 100,000 fans. For more information, call (337) 232-8086 or go to **www.festivalinternational.com.**

Halloween

If you want to dress for the occasion in ultra-Lestat mode, there are plenty of stores that will frill you and thrill you to the utmost. One of the most luxuriantly decadent is **Armed and Dangerous** (529 Dumaine Street; 568-1100). It stocks wonderful velvet coats in which you can pass either as Louis the vampire or Louis XIV, with ruffled shirts to match, swords to swash, and wide belts to buckle, plus all the gauntlets, ornaments, and daggers to match—even the fanciest neoromantic crosses, if you dare.

But you don't have to be invited to the coven ball to enjoy Halloween in New Orleans. In fact, if you have any love for dressing up and acting out, this is one of the most wonderful times to be in the city. It's as flamboyant as Mardi Gras, but with far more wit, sheer theatricality (as opposed to theatrical classicism), and fun—and not nearly so much puking and public urination. The weather is apt to be warmer, and the restaurants stay open. And, since the event has become a great draw for gay costumers and drag queens, any display of breasts is at least scientifically interesting. Drag bars have a long illustrious history in New Orleans, going back at least a century and probably longer. And in addition to the fine professional drags in the Quarter and over in Faubourg-Marigny, you are apt to be serenaded, fondled, and generally scooped up by a raft of, as they used to say of Emma Peel, herself an obvious favorite of the gay crowd here, "talented amateurs." Informal parades and smartly turned-out paraders are showered with beads and coins from the galleries just as they are during Mardi Gras. Altogether, it's a great affair, unless you're uptight about who's tight in those tights.

There are costume parties all over the French Quarter, a huge one at the Convention Center (an annual fundraiser for New Orleans regional AIDS groups; call 945-4000 or 821-2601 for more information), a midnight **"Witches' Run"** (not so much to offset all that trick-or-treating as an excuse to run in costume), and for kids, the **Boo at the Zoo** festival (see "A Calendar of Special Events" in Part Two, Planning Your Visit to New Orleans). Contact the **Metropolitan Convention and Visitors Bureau,** 1520 Sugar Bowl Drive, New Orleans, LA 70112; 566-5011.

Of course, between Lestat and Marie Laveau, you can make a Halloween holiday of your own any time; see the sections on "Walking on the Dark Side" and "The Great Hereafter" in Part Eight, Sight-Seeing, Tours, and Attractions.

Creole Christmas

This is the sort of tourism-industry creation that still seems a little packaged—in fact, some brochures refer to it as "New Orleans Christmas" or "Christmas, New Orleans style" because, although old Creole society supplied the inspiration for many of the events, visitors tend to lump Cajun and Creole culture together. (If you're confused yourself, see "A Too-Short History of a Fascinating Place" in Part One, Understanding the City.)

Gradually, however, New Orleans Christmas has developed some fine moments—and in fact, the week before Christmas is described by locals as one of the best times to be in the city. Starting at Thanksgiving, City Park's old live oaks are hung with thousands of lights in the shapes of fleur-de-lis, harps, and stars, and you can ride the miniature trains or even hire a carriage. Many fine older homes are decorated in the old style and lit up at night. Plenty of holiday events are free—special walking tours and concerts, parades (with Papa Noel himself heading up the second line), brass bands, museum exhibits, house tours, tree lightings, cooking and ornament-making workshops for kids, cooking exhibitions, and candlelight caroling in Jackson Square—and perfect for a family vacation. The whole French quarter is lit up, and street performers, jugglers, and dancers fill the parks. Midnight mass in St. Louis Cathedral is lovely, even if you aren't Catholic, with carols, candles, wonderful stained glass, and so on. There are almost nightly gospel concerts as well, either in St. Louis Cathedral or historic St. Mary's on Chartres. (There are also menorah lights and Kwanzaa activities and other cultural celebrations.)

Many hotels, both chain and independent, offer special low "Papa Noel" or "Creole Christmas" rates, while restaurants of the quality of Arnaud's, Brennan's, Galatoire's, Boussard's, Upperline Café, and Commander's Palace set out "Reveillon" menus adapted from old Creole celebrations which usually include champagne or eggnog and perhaps a little *lagniappe*. ("Reveillon" means "awakening," because the great Creole houses used to celebrate the holiday with a huge dinner after attending midnight mass on Christmas Eve.) Costumed impersonators from New Orleans history (Baroness Pontalba, Lola Montez, Andrew Jackson, Edgar Degas, Buffalo Bill Cody, and so on) walk the street to talk with passers-by.

Probably the most famous Christmas display in town outside City Park, and one that's nearly as elaborate although not as restrained, is at the Metairie home of entrepreneur Al Copeland, founder of the Popeye's and Copeland's restaurant chains. Just follow the line of cars taking Veterans Highway to Transcontinental Avenue, turn right, then left onto Folse, and go two blocks. You can't miss it.

At 7 p.m. on Christmas Eve, scores of huge bonfires are set up and down the Mississippi around the plantations (by some estimates 100 of them in 50 miles) and across the river from the city on the West Bank of Algiers. Homes in the country are all decked out, which makes this a really good time to plan your plantation tour. For more about New Orleans Christmas, plus a second booklet of caroling schedules, lightings, fireworks, and so on, as well as discount coupons on shopping, dining, and attractions, call (800) 474-7621.

Of course, major party town that it is, New Orleans doesn't really surrender the Christmas season until New Year's Eve, which is another wild, woolly, loud, and lively night on the town, culminating with a giant crowd singing "Auld Lange Syne" in Jackson Square. New Year's Eve also coincides with the collegiate football championship Sugar Bowl, held in the Superdome. Just as for Mardi Gras, you need to make your hotel reservations early; however, you may be able to sneak in a good airfare by waiting to come until, say, December 27 or 28 and staying over until after New Year's Day. Or you could stay through until Twelfth Night on January 6, when the first Carnival krewe kicks off the pre–Mardi Gras season . . . or even January 8, for the annual celebration of Jackson's victory at the Battle of New Orleans . . .

Cajun Country Festivals

There is more and more interest in Cajun culture—just notice what sort of music all those souvenir shops are blaring out onto Bourbon Street these days. What's called "Cajun Mardi Gras" in Lafayette, Louisiana, about three hours west of New Orleans, is a much more family-style festival than the Bourbon Street blowout. There the festival's sovereigns are King Gabriel and Queen Evangeline, from Longfellow's epic story of the Cajun diaspora, and several of the events are geared specifically to children. And unlike the Rex ball, the final party is open to the public (though you should still tie that black tie). You can also participate in some even older, country-style events, such as house-to-house partying. For information, contact the **Lafayette Parish Convention and Visitors Commission,** P.O. Box 52066, Lafayette, LA 70505; call (800) 346-1958 or visit **www.cajunhot.com.**

In Euince, Louisiana, about two hours west of Baton Rouge, the tradition of *courir de Mardi Gras* ("running of Mardi Gras") means that hundreds of costumed revelers parade in trucks and trailers from house to house, singing, dancing, busking, or begging for the ingredients of a huge, city-sized gumbo made at day's end. Fore more information, visit **www.eunice-la.com.**

Around the third week of September, Lafayette is the site of a multi-theme celebration, the **Festivals Acadiens,** spotlighting Cajun traditions and history. The best-known part is the **Festival de Musique Acadienne,** now more than 20 years old and drawing 50,000 fans of two-step, zydeco, and traditional Cajun-French music. Set up alongside the music stages is the **Bayou Food Festival,** a mouthwatering abundance of smothered quail, oysters en brochette, boudin sausages, and other Cajun specialties, prepared by area restaurants. The **Louisiana Native Crafts Festival** spotlights traditional methods and native materials: duck decoy carving, caning, basket weaving, quilting, pottery-making, jewelry, and even alligator skinning. Artists over 60 have their own seniors circuit, so to speak, the **RSVP** (Retired Senior Volunteer Program) **Fair,** where you get the tall tales along with the traditional crafts.

There are also Mardi Gras celebrations along the Mississippi Gulf Coast, notably in Biloxi and Gulfport. Contact the Mississippi Gulf Coast Convention and Visitors Bureau at P.O. Box 6128, Gulfport, MS 39506-6128; call (888) 467-4853; or go to **www.gulfcoast.org.**

And although it's not truly Cajun, the various celebrations of Isleño culture—Louisianans descended from Canary Island fishermen—held just outside New Orleans are of unusual interest. Contact the **Canary Islands Descendants Association** (682-1010) or the **Los Isleños Heritage and Culture Society** (682-0862) about festivals and events.

Part Four

New Orleans Lodging

Deciding Where to Stay

New Orleans, you must understand, has an almost palpable feel. History here is cumulative, and from the French to the Spanish to the Confederacy to the present, every sailor, gambler, barmaid, and merchant has left something for you to savor. When you are in New Orleans, you know without being told that you are someplace very different. In fact, it's not so much a place to be as a place to know. Even as a first-time tourist, your heart aches to know this city intimately, to be part of its exotic rhythms and steaminess. The city never, never leaves your consciousness. You wear it and breathe it at the same time, all of it, and hundreds of years of blues in the night, chicory coffee, and sweat on the docks become part of your reality.

This reality is sustained by the river, the humidity, the narrow streets, and even by the city's grittiness and poverty. And it is reflected by its small, quirky hotels and inns. Some of the most delightful, interesting, and intimate hotels in America can be found in New Orleans. Ditto for guest houses and bed-and-breakfasts. Zoning and historic preservation ordinances, particularly in the French Quarter, have limited the construction of modern high-rise hotels and stimulated the evolution of an eclectic mix of medium- and small-sized properties, many of which are proprietorships. In an age of standardization and cookie-cutter chain hotels, these smaller hotels, distinguished by cozy courtyards, shuttered windows, balconies, and wrought-iron trim, offer guests a truly unique lodging experience.

Hotels in New Orleans are concentrated in the French Quarter and along Canal Street between Claiborne Avenue and the river. Most of the larger, modern chain hotels are situated near the convention center at the river end of Canal Street. Smaller hotels, inns, and guest houses are sprinkled liberally around the French Quarter and along St. Charles Avenue west of Lee Circle. Historically, there have been relatively few hotels located in other parts of town. Although today there are some hotels near the airport and along

I-10 east of the city, hotels outside of the downtown/French Quarter area are relatively scarce.

Because New Orleans thrives on tourism, weekday hotel rates are often lower than weekend rates (the opposite of most cities where business travel rules). If you would like to visit during any holidays other than Mardi Gras or Jazz Fest, make your reservations six months or more in advance. For Mardi Gras (late February to early March) you need to plan nine months to one year ahead, and for the New Orleans Jazz and Heritage Festival (late April to early May), give yourself at least ten months.

While we would not dissuade you from experiencing Mardi Gras, be advised that the city is pretty much turned upside down. Hotels are jammed, prices are jacked up, parking is impossible, and the streets are full of staggering drunks. In the French Quarter many bars and restaurants dispatch their furniture and fixtures to warehouses to make room for the throng of wall-to-wall people. While Mardi Gras is a hell of a good party, it essentially deprives visitors of experiencing "the real" New Orleans.

If you happen to be attending one of the big conventions, book early and use some of the tips listed below to get a discounted room rate. To assist you in timing your visit, we have included a convention and trade-show calendar in Part Five, Visiting New Orleans on Business.

Some Considerations

1. When choosing your New Orleans lodging, make sure your hotel is situated in a location convenient to your recreation or business needs, and that it is in a safe and comfortable area.

2. New Orleans hotels generally offer lower-quality rooms than those in most cities profiled by the *Unofficial Guides.* A meager 21% of the hotels in New Orleans merit a quality rating of four stars or higher. Compare this with Chicago, where 36% of the hotels are rated four stars and higher, Washington, D.C., where 37% of the hotels are four stars or higher, and San Francisco, which boasts 40% of its hotels as four- and five-star properties. Need we mention New York City's impressive 84%? As a consequence of the generally lower-quality standard, newer chain hotels have not had to invest in superior rooms in order to be competitive.

   Surprisingly, New Orleans is not home to a single five-star hotel. Two of the nicest hotels in New Orleans, the **Windsor Court** and the **Omni Royal Crescent,** are older properties that have found ways to cram insane amounts of luxurious amenities into shoebox-sized rooms. These hotels rely as much on their dignified reputations as on their guest-room quality to attract guests. Although extremely nice, their rooms lack the square footage to be called "luxurious" by any standard. One hotel that satisfies all requirements of space and opulence has finally made its way into the French Quarter. The **Ritz-Carlton** on the French-Quarter side of Canal Street, which opened its doors in October 2000, has set a new standard for New Orleans expectations.

New Orleans is full of old hotels, some well maintained, some not. Many are situated in ancient buildings, with guest rooms in varying states of renovation and dilapidation. Lobbies of the nicer hotels are characteristically decorated in gaudy antique gilt, with Old World sculptures and crystal chandeliers. Along similar lines, you are likely to find more antique and antique-replica furniture in New Orleans hotel rooms than in most any other U.S. tourist destination. Four-poster rice beds are a particular favorite.

And it's gonna cost you. In general, New Orleans hotels are pricey. But good deals can be found, and upon inspection, a pattern emerges. With a handful of exceptions, the hotels that offer the best values are found outside the French Quarter. And within the French Quarter, those hotels found on or within one block of Bourbon Street are often outrageously expensive. So, as is often the case with urban hotels, the address of the hotel is the deciding factor in the room price.

For example, the most expensive hotel in New Orleans, the **Best Western Inn** on Bourbon, is located right in the middle of the Bourbon Street action. Although the Best Western Inn on Bourbon offers only a three-star room, it is continually booked due to location.

Before making any reservations, find out when the guest rooms in your prospective hotel were last renovated. Request that the hotel send you its promotional brochure. Ask if brochure photos of guest rooms are accurate and current.

3. If you plan to take a car, inquire about the parking situation. Some hotels offer no parking at all, some charge dearly for parking, and some offer free parking. Check the Hotel Information Chart at the end of this chapter for availability and prices.

4. If you are not a city dweller, or perhaps are a light sleeper, try to book a hotel on a quieter side street. In the French Quarter, avoid hotels on Bourbon Street. If you book a Central Business District or Canal Street hotel, ask for a room off the street and high up.

5. When you plan your budget, remember that New Orleans's hotel tax is 11%.

6. The ratings and rankings in this chapter are based solely on room quality and value. To determine if a particular hotel has room service, a pool, or other services and amenities, see the alphabetical Hotel Information Chart at the end of this chapter.

Getting a Good Deal on a Room

Value Season

New Orleans's value season generally starts the first weekend in July (it seems New Orleans is not a popular Fourth destination) and ends on the first weekend in September.

Special Weekday Rates

Although well-located New Orleans hotels are tough for the budget-conscious, it's not impossible to get a good deal, at least relatively speaking. For starters, many French Quarter hotels that cater to tourists offer special weekday discount rates that range from 5 to 25% below weekend rates. You can find out about weekday specials by calling individual hotels or by consulting your travel agent.

Getting Corporate Rates

Many hotels offer discounted corporate rates (5–12% off rack). Usually you do not need to work for a large company or have a special relationship with the hotel to obtain these rates. Simply call the hotel of your choice and ask for their corporate rates. Many hotels will guarantee you the discounted rate on the phone when you make your reservation. Others may make the rate conditional on your providing some sort of bona fides, for instance a fax on your company's letterhead requesting the rate, or a company credit card or business card on check-in. Generally, the screening is not rigorous.

Half-Price Programs

The larger discounts on rooms (35–60%), in New Orleans or anywhere else, are available through half-price hotel programs, often called travel clubs. Program operators contract with an individual hotel to provide rooms at deep discounts, usually 50% off rack rate, on a "space available" basis. Space available generally means that you can reserve a room at the discounted rate whenever the hotel expects to be at less than 80% occupancy. A little calendar sleuthing to help you avoid Mardi Gras, Jazz Fest, special events, and city-wide conventions will increase your chances of choosing a time when the discounts are available.

Most half-price programs charge an annual membership fee or directory subscription charge of $25 to $125. Once enrolled, you are mailed a membership card and a directory that lists participating hotels. Examining the directory, you will notice immediately that there are many restrictions and exceptions. Some hotels, for instance, "black out" certain dates or times of year. Others may offer the discount only on certain days of the week, or require you to stay a certain number of nights. Still others may offer a much smaller discount than 50% off the rack rate.

Programs specialize in domestic travel, international travel, or both. More established operators offer members between 1,000 and 4,000 hotels to choose from in the United States. All of the programs have a heavy concentration of hotels in California and Florida, and most have a very limited selection of participating properties in New York City or Boston. Offerings in other cities and regions of the United States vary considerably. The programs with the largest selections of New Orleans hotels are Encore, ITC-50, Great American Traveler, and Entertainment Publications. Each of these programs lists between 9 and 30 hotels in the greater New Orleans area.

Encore	(800) 444-9800
ITC-50	(800) 987-6216; www.itc50online.com
Great American Traveler	(800) 833-0123
Entertainment Publications	(800) 445-4137; www.entertainment.com

One problem with half-price programs is that not all hotels offer a full 50% discount. Another slippery problem is the base rate against which the discount is applied. Some hotels figure the discount on an exaggerated rack rate that nobody would ever have to pay. A few participating hotels may deduct the discount from a supposed "superior" or "upgraded" room rate, even though the room you get is the hotel's standard accommodation. Though hard to pin down, the majority of participating properties base discounts on the rate published in the *Hotel & Travel Index* (a quarterly reference work used by travel agents) and work within the spirit of their agreement with the program operator. As a rule, if you travel several times a year, your room-rate savings will easily compensate you for program-membership fees.

A noteworthy addendum: deeply discounted rooms through half-price programs are not commissionable to travel agents. In practical terms this means that you must make your own inquiry calls and reservations. If you travel frequently, however, and run a lot of business through your travel agent, he or she will probably do your legwork, lack of commission notwithstanding.

Preferred Rates

If you cannot book the hotel of your choice through a half-price program, you and your travel agent may have to search for a lesser discount, often called a preferred rate. A preferred rate could be a discount made available to travel agents to stimulate their booking activity, or a discount initiated to attract a certain class of traveler. Most preferred rates are promoted through travel industry publications and are often accessible only through an agent.

We recommend sounding out your travel agent about possible deals. Be aware, however, that the rates shown on travel agents' computerized reservations systems are not always the lowest rates obtainable. Zero in on a couple of hotels that fill your needs in terms of location and quality of accommodations, and then have your travel agent call the hotel for the latest rates and specials. Hotel reps are almost always more responsive to travel agents because travel agents represent a source of additional business. There are certain specials that hotel reps will disclose only to travel agents. Travel agents also come in handy when the hotel you want is supposedly booked. A personal appeal from your agent to the hotel's director of sales and marketing will get you a room more than 50% of the time.

Wholesalers, Consolidators, and Reservation Services

If you do not want to join a program or buy a discount directory, you can take advantage of the services of a wholesaler or consolidator. Wholesalers and consolidators buy rooms, or options on rooms (room blocks), from hotels at a low, negotiated rate. They then resell the rooms at a profit through travel agents or tour operators, or directly to the public. Most wholesalers and consolidators have a provision for returning unsold rooms to participating hotels, but are not inclined to do so. The wholesaler's or consolidator's relationship with any hotel is predicated on volume. If they return rooms unsold, the hotel may not make as many rooms available to them the next time around. Thus wholesalers and consolidators often offer rooms at bargain rates, anywhere from 15–50% off rack, occasionally sacrificing their profit margins in the process, to avoid returning the rooms to the hotel unsold.

When wholesalers and consolidators deal directly with the public, they frequently represent themselves as "reservation services." When you call, you can ask for a rate quote for a particular hotel or, alternatively, ask for their best available deal in the area you prefer to stay. If there is a maximum amount you are willing to pay, say so. Chances are the service will find something that will work for you, even if they have to shave a dollar or two off their own profit. Following is a list of several services that sell rooms in New Orleans:

Hotel Reservations Network	(800) 715-7666; www.hoteldiscount.com
Room Finders USA	(800) 473-7829; www.roomfinders.com
	(headquartered in New Orleans)
RMC Travel	(800) 245-5738; www.rmcwebtravel.com
Accommodations Express	(800) 444-7666; www.accommodationsexpress.com

The discount available (if any) from a reservation service depends on whether the service functions as a consolidator or a wholesaler. Consolidators are strictly sales agents who do not own or control the room inventory they are trying to sell. Discounts offered by consolidators are determined by the hotels with rooms to fill. Consolidator discounts vary enormously depending on how desperate the hotel is to unload the rooms. When you deal with a room reservation service that operates as a consolidator, you pay for your room as usual when you check out of the hotel.

Wholesalers have longstanding contracts with hotels that allow the wholesaler to purchase rooms at an established deep discount. Some wholesalers hold purchase options on blocks of rooms, while others actually pay for rooms and own the inventory. Because a wholesaler controls the room inventory, it can offer whatever discount it pleases, consistent with current demand. In practice, most wholesaler reservation-service discounts fall in the 10–40% range. When you reserve a room with a reservation service that operates as a wholesaler, you must usually pay in advance with your credit card for your entire stay. The service then sends you a written confirmation and usually a voucher (indicating prepayment) for you to present at the hotel.

Our experience has been that the reservation services are more useful in finding rooms when availability is scarce than in obtaining deep discounts. Calling the hotels ourselves, we were often able to beat the reservation services' rates when rooms were generally available. When the city was booked, however, and we could not find a room by calling the hotels ourselves, the reservation services could almost always get us a room at a fair price.

How to Evaluate a Travel Package

Hundreds of New Orleans package vacations are offered to the public each year. Packages should be a win/win proposition for both the buyer and the seller. The buyer has to make only one phone call and deal with a single salesperson to set up the whole vacation: transportation, rental car, lodging, meals, attraction admissions, and even golf and tennis. The seller, likewise, has to deal with the buyer only once, eliminating the need for separate sales, confirmations, and billing. In addition to streamlining sales, processing, and administration, some packagers also buy airfares in bulk on contract like a broker playing the commodities market. Buying a large number of airfares in advance allows the packager to buy them at a significant savings from posted fares. The same practice is also applied to hotel rooms. Because selling vacation packages is an efficient way of doing business, and because the packager can often buy individual package components (airfare, lodging, etc.) in bulk at discount, savings in operating expenses realized by the seller are sometimes passed on to the buyer so that, in addition to convenience, the package is also an exceptional value. In any event, that is the way it is supposed to work.

All too often, in practice, the seller cashes in on discounts and passes none on to the buyer. In some instances, packages are loaded with extras that cost the packager next to nothing, but inflate the retail price sky-high. Predictably, the savings to be passed along to customers do not materialize.

When considering a package, choose one that includes features you are sure to use; whether you use all the features or not, you will most certainly pay for them. Second, if cost is of greater concern than convenience, make a few phone calls and see what the package would cost if you booked its individual components (airfare, rental car, lodging, etc.) on your own. If the package price is less than the à la carte cost, the package is a good deal. If the costs are about the same, the package is probably worth buying just for the convenience.

If your package includes a choice of rental car or airport transfers (transportation to and from the airport), take the transfers if you plan to spend most of your time in the French Quarter or the Central Business District. If you want to run around town or go on excursions outside the city, take the car. If you take the car, be sure to ask if the package includes free parking at your hotel.

The following tour operators specialize in vacation packages to New Orleans. Book directly or through your travel agent.

Atlas Tours	(504) 483-0607
Destination Management	(800) 366-8882
Travel New Orleans	(800) 535-8747

Tour operators, of course, prefer to sell you a whole vacation package. When business is slow, however, they will often agree to sell you just the lodging component of the package, usually at a nicely discounted rate.

Hotel-Sponsored Packages

In addition to tour operators, packages are frequently offered by hotels. Usually "land only" (i.e., no airfare included), the hotel packages are sometimes exceptional deals. New Orleans hotels (especially those that are larger and closest to the Convention Center) seem to have good package deals that include room upgrades, special services (e.g. concierge, dry cleaning, etc.) and some meals for those in town for multiple nights over large convention weekends. Many packages are specialized, offering plantation tours, jazz tours, or the like, while others are offered only at certain times of the year, such as "Papa Noel" deals during the December holiday season. Promotion of hotel specials tends to be limited to the hotel's primary markets, which for most properties are Louisiana, Texas, Alabama, Florida, Mississippi, Georgia, Arkansas, and Tennessee. If you live in other parts of the country, you can take advantage of the packages but probably will not see them advertised in your local newspaper. An important point regarding hotel specials is that the hotel reservationists do not usually inform you of existing specials or offer them to you. In other words, *you have to ask.*

Helping Your Travel Agent Help You

When you call your travel agent, ask if he or she has been to New Orleans. If the answer is no, be prepared to give your travel agent some direction. Do not accept any recommendations at face value. Check out the location and rates of any suggested hotel and make certain that the hotel is suited to your itinerary.

Because some travel agents are unfamiliar with New Orleans, they may try to plug you into a tour operator's preset package. This essentially allows the travel agent to set up your whole trip with a single phone call and still collect an 8–10% commission. The problem with this scenario is that most agents will place 90% of their New Orleans business with only one or two wholesalers or tour operators. In other words, it's the line of least resistance for them, and not much choice for you.

Travel agents will often use wholesalers who run packages in conjunction with airlines, like Delta's Dream Vacations or American's Fly-Away Vacations. Because of the wholesaler's exclusive relationship with the carrier, these trips are very easy for travel agents to book. However, they will probably be more expensive than a package offered by a high-volume wholesaler who works with a number of airlines in a primary New Orleans market.

To help your travel agent get you the best possible deal, do the following:

1. Determine where you want to stay in New Orleans, and if possible, choose a specific hotel that meets your needs. This can be accomplished by reviewing the hotel information provided in this guide, and by writing or calling hotels that interest you.

2. Check out the hotel deals and package vacations advertised in the Sunday travel sections of the *Atlanta Journal-Constitution, New Orleans Times-Picayune,* or *Dallas Morning News* newspapers. Often you will be able to find deals that beat the socks off anything offered in your local paper. See if you can find specials that fit your plans and include a hotel you like.

3. Call the hotels or tour operators whose ads you have collected. Ask any questions you have concerning their packages, but do not book your trip with them directly.

4. Tell your travel agent about the deals you find and ask if he or she can get you something better. The deals in the paper will serve as a benchmark against which to compare alternatives proposed by your travel agent.

5. Choose from the options that you and your travel agent uncover. No matter which option you select, have your travel agent book it. Even if you go with one of the packages in the newspaper, it will probably be commissionable (at no additional cost to you) and will provide the agent some return on the time invested on your behalf. Also, as a travel professional, your agent should be able to verify the quality and integrity of the deal.

If You Make Your Own Reservation

As you poke around trying to find a good deal, there are several things you should know. First, always call the specific hotel rather than the hotel chain's national 800 number. Quite often, the reservationists at the national 800 number are unaware of local specials. Always ask about specials before you inquire about corporate rates. Do not be reluctant to bargain. If you are buying a hotel's weekday package, for example, and want to extend your stay into the following weekend, you can often obtain at least the corporate rate for the extra days. Do your bargaining, however, before you check in, preferably when you make your reservations.

Hotels and Motels: Rated and Ranked

What's in a Room?

Except for cleanliness, state of repair, and décor, most travelers do not pay much attention to hotel rooms. There is, of course, a discernible standard of quality and luxury that differentiates Motel 6 from Holiday Inn, Holiday Inn from Marriott, and so on. In general, however, hotel guests fail to appreciate the fact that some rooms are better engineered than others.

Contrary to what you might suppose, designing a hotel room is (or should be) much more complex than picking a bedspread to match the carpet and drapes. Making the room usable to its occupants is an art, a planning discipline that combines both form and function.

Décor and taste are important, certainly. No one wants to spend several days in a room whose décor is dated, garish, or even ugly. But beyond the décor, several variables determine how livable a hotel room is. In New Orleans, for example, we have seen some beautifully appointed rooms that are simply not well designed for human habitation. The next time you stay in a hotel, pay attention to the details and design elements of your room. Even more than décor, these will make you feel comfortable and at home.

It takes the *Unofficial Guide* researchers quite a while to inspect a hotel room. Here are a few of the things we check that you may want to start paying attention to:

Room Size   While some smaller rooms are cozy and well designed, a large and uncluttered room is generally preferable, especially for a stay of more than three days.

Temperature Control, Ventilation, and Odor   The guest should be able to control the temperature of the room. The best system, because it's so quiet, is central heating and air conditioning, controlled by the room's own thermostat. The next best system is a room module heater and air conditioner, preferably controlled by an automatic thermostat, but usually by manually operated button controls. The worst system is central heating and air without any sort of room thermostat or guest control.

The vast majority of hotel rooms have windows or balcony doors that have been permanently sealed. Though there are some legitimate safety and liability issues involved, we prefer windows and balcony doors that can be opened to admit fresh air. Hotel rooms should be odor and smoke free, and not feel stuffy or damp.

Room Security   Better rooms have locks that require a plastic card instead of the traditional lock and key. Card-and-slot systems allow the hotel, essentially, to change the combination or entry code of the lock with each new guest. A burglar who has somehow acquired a conventional room key can afford to wait until the situation is right before using the key to gain access. Not so with a card-and-slot system. Though larger hotels and hotel chains with lock-and-key systems usually rotate their locks once each year, they remain vulnerable to hotel thieves much of the time. Many smaller or independent properties rarely rotate their locks.

In addition to the entry lock system, the door should have a deadbolt, and preferably a chain that can be locked from the inside. A chain by itself is not sufficient. Doors should also have a peephole. Windows and balcony doors, if any, should have secure locks.

Safety   Every room should have a fire or smoke alarm, clear fire instructions, and preferably a sprinkler system. Bathtubs should have a nonskid surface, and shower stalls should have doors that either open outward or slide side-to-side. Bathroom electrical outlets should be high on the wall and not too close to the sink. Balconies should have sturdy, high rails.

Noise   Most travelers have been kept awake by the television, partying, or amorous activities of people in the next room, or by traffic on the street outside. Better hotels are designed with noise control in mind. Wall and ceiling construction are substantial, effectively screening routine noise. Carpets and drapes, in addition to being decorative, also absorb and muffle sounds. Mattresses mounted on stable platforms or sturdy bed frames do not squeak, even when challenged by the most acrobatic lovers. Televisions enclosed in cabinets, and with volume governors, rarely disturb guests in adjacent rooms.

In better hotels, the air conditioning and heating system is well maintained and operates without noise or vibration. Likewise, plumbing is quiet and positioned away from the sleeping area. Doors to the hall, and to adjoining rooms, are thick and well fitted to better block out noise.

If you are easily disturbed by noise, ask for a room on a higher floor, off main thoroughfares, and away from elevators and ice and vending machines.

Darkness Control   Ever been in a hotel room where the curtains would not quite meet in the middle? Thick, lined curtains that close completely in the center and extend beyond the edges of the window or door frame are required. In a well-planned room, the curtains, shades, or blinds should almost totally block light at any time of day.

Lighting Poor lighting is an extremely common problem in American hotel rooms. The lighting is usually adequate for dressing, relaxing, or watching television, but not for reading or working. Lighting needs to be bright over tables and desks, and beside couches or easy chairs. Since so many people read in bed, there should be a separate light for each person. A room with two queen beds should have individual lights for four people. Better bedside reading lights illuminate a small area, so if one person wants to sleep and another to read, the sleeper will not be bothered by the light. The worst situation by far is a single lamp on a table between beds. In each bed, only the person next to the lamp will have sufficient light to read. This deficiency is often compounded by weak light bulbs.

In addition, closet areas should be well lit, and there should be a switch near the door that turns on room lights when you enter. A seldom seen but desirable feature is a bedside console that allows a guest to control all or most lights in the room from bed.

Furnishings At bare minimum, the bed(s) must be firm. Pillows should be made with nonallergic fillers and, in addition to the sheets and spread, a blanket should be provided. Bedclothes should be laundered with fabric softener and changed daily. Better hotels usually provide extra blankets and pillows in the room or on request, and sometimes use a second topsheet between the blanket and spread.

There should be a dresser large enough to hold clothes for two people during a five-day stay. A small table with two chairs, or a desk with a chair, should be provided. The room should be equipped with a luggage rack and a three-quarter- to full-length mirror.

The television should be color and cable-connected; ideally, it should have a volume governor and remote control. It should be mounted on a swivel base, and preferably enclosed in a cabinet. Local channels should be posted on the set and a local TV program guide should be supplied. The telephone should be touchtone, conveniently situated for bedside use, and should have, on or near it, easy-to-understand dialing instructions and a rate card. Local telephone directories should be provided. Better hotels install phones in the bathroom and equip room phones with long cords.

Well-designed hotel rooms usually have a plush armchair or a sleeper sofa for lounging and reading. Better headboards are padded for comfortable reading in bed, and there should be a nightstand or table on each side of the bed(s). Nice extras in any hotel room include a small refrigerator, a digital alarm clock, and a coffeemaker.

Bathroom Two sinks are better than one, and you cannot have too much counter space. A sink outside the bath is a great convenience when one person bathes as another dresses. Sinks should have drains with stoppers.

Better bathrooms have both a tub and shower with a nonslip bottom. Tub and shower controls should be easy to operate. Adjustable shower heads are preferred. The bath needs to be well lit and should have an exhaust fan and a guest-controlled bathroom heater. Towels and wash-cloths should be large, soft, and fluffy, and generously supplied. There should be an electrical outlet for each sink, conveniently and safely placed.

Complimentary shampoo, conditioner, and lotion are a plus, as are robes and bathmats. Better hotels supply bathrooms with tissues and extra toilet paper. Luxurious baths feature a phone, a hair dryer, some-times a small television, or even a jacuzzi.

Vending   Complimentary ice and a drink machine should be located on each floor. Welcome additions include a snack machine and a sun-dries (combs, toothpaste) machine. The latter are seldom found in large hotels that have restaurants and shops.

Hotel Ratings

Zone   The Zone column identifies the New Orleans zone where you will find a particular property.

Overall Quality   To distinguish properties according to relative quality, tastefulness, state of repair, cleanliness, and size of standard rooms, we have grouped the hotels and motels into classifications denoted by stars. Star ratings in this guide apply to New Orleans–area properties only and do not necessarily correspond to stars awarded by Mobil, AAA, or other travel critics. Because stars carry little weight in the absence of common standards of comparison, we have linked our ratings to expected levels of quality established by specific American hotel corporations.

★★★★★	Superior	Tasteful and luxurious by any standard
★★★★	Extremely Nice	What you would expect at a Hyatt Regency or Marriott
★★★	Nice	Holiday Inn or comparable quality
★★	Adequate	Clean, comfortable, and functional without frills (like a Motel 6)
★	Budget	Spartan, not aesthetically pleasing, but clean

Star ratings describe the property's standard accommodations. For most hotels, a "standard accommodation" is a room with either one king bed or two queen beds. In an all-suite property, the standard accommo-dation is either a one- or two-room suite. In addition to standard accom-modations, many hotels offer luxury rooms and special suites not rated here. Star ratings are assigned without regard to whether a property has restaurant(s), recreational facilities, entertainment, or other extras.

Room Quality   In addition to stars (which delineate broad categories), we also employ a numerical rating system. Our rating scale is 0 to 100, with 100 as the best possible rating, and zero (0) as the worst. Numerical ratings are presented to show the difference we perceive between one property and another. Rooms at the Grenoble House, Hotel de la Monnaie, and Dauphine Orleans are all rated as three and a half stars (★★★½). In the supplemental numerical ratings, the Grenoble House is rated an 82, the Hotel de la Monnaie an 80, and the Dauphine Orleans a 79. This means that within the three-and-a-half-star category, the Hotel del la Monnaie is a bit nicer than the Dauphine Orleans, and the Grenoble House has an edge over both.

Cost Cost estimates are based on the hotel's published rack rates for standard rooms. Each "$" represents $50. Thus, a cost symbol of "$$$" means a room (or suite) at that hotel will cost about $150 a night.

How the Hotels Compare

Below is a hit parade of the nicest rooms in town. We've focused strictly on room quality, and excluded any consideration of location, services, recreation, or amenities. In some instances, a one- or two-room suite can be had for the same price or less than that of a hotel room.

If you use subsequent editions of this guide, you will notice that many of the ratings and rankings change. In addition to the inclusion of new properties, these changes also consider guest-room renovations or improved maintenance and housekeeping. A failure to maintain guest rooms properly or a lapse in housekeeping standards can affect negatively the ratings.

Finally, before you begin to shop for a hotel, take a look at this letter we received from a couple in Hot Springs, Arkansas:

> *We cancelled our room reservations to follow the advice in your book [and reserved a hotel room highly ranked by the Unofficial Guide]. We wanted inexpensive, but clean and cheerful. We got inexpensive, but [also] dirty, grim, and depressing. I really felt disappointed in your advice and the room. It was the pits. That was the one real piece of information I needed from your book! The room spoiled the holiday for me aside from our touring.*

Needless to say, this letter was as unsettling to us as the bad room was to our reader. Our integrity as travel journalists, after all, is based on the quality of the information we provide our readers. Even with the best of intentions and the most conscientious research, however, we cannot inspect every room in every hotel. What we do, in statistical terms, is take a sample: We check out several rooms selected at random in each hotel and base our ratings and rankings on those rooms. The inspections are conducted anonymously and without the knowledge of the management. Although unusual, it is certainly possible that the rooms we randomly inspect are not representative of the majority of rooms at a particular hotel. Another possibility is that the rooms we inspect in a given hotel are representative, but that by bad luck a reader is assigned a room that is inferior. When we rechecked the hotel our reader disliked, we discovered our rating was correctly representative, but that he and his wife had unfortunately been assigned to one of a small number of threadbare rooms scheduled for renovation.

The key to avoiding disappointment is to snoop around in advance. We recommend that you ask for a photo of a hotel's standard guest room before you book, or at least get a copy of the hotel's promotional brochure. Be forewarned, however, that some hotel chains use the same guestroom photo in their promotional literature for all hotels in the chain; a specific guest room may not resemble the brochure photo. When you or your travel agent call, ask how old the property is and when your guest room was last renovated. If you arrive and are assigned a room inferior to that which you had been led to expect, demand to be moved to another room.

HOW THE HOTELS COMPARE

Hotel	Zone	Overall Quality	Room Quality	Cost ($=$50)
Ritz-Carlton New Orleans	1	★★★★½	94	$$$$−
Windsor Court	2	★★★★½	94	$$$$$$$
Wyndham Canal Place	1	★★★★½	90	$$$$$$+
Omni Royal Crescent Hotel	2	★★★★½	88	$$$$$
Residence Inn Metairie	9	★★★★	89	$$−
Pelham Hotel	2	★★★★	89	$$$+
Royal Sonesta Hotel	1	★★★★	89	$$$$$$−
Le Pavillon Hotel	2	★★★★	89	$$$$$$$$$$−
Ambassador Hotel New Orleans	2	★★★★	88	$$
The McKendrick-Breaux House	3	★★★★	88	$$$+
Loft 523	2	★★★★	88	$$$$
Fairmont Hotel	2	★★★★	88	$$$$+
Hilton New Orleans Riverside	2	★★★★	88	$$$$$+
The Monteleone	1	★★★★	88	$$$$$−
Residence Inn	2	★★★★	87	$$$+
Omni Royal Orleans Hotel	1	★★★★	87	$$$$$$−
Sheraton New Orleans Hotel	2	★★★★	87	$$$$$$$$$+
Hilton Garden Inn	2	★★★★	86	$$
Hampton Inn Suites & Convention Center	2	★★★★	86	$$$$$−
Wyndham Riverfront Hotel	2	★★★★	85	$$$$$$
Hotel Inter-Continental New Orleans	2	★★★★	85	$$$$$$$
Wyndham Galleria	9	★★★★	84	$$+

HOW THE HOTELS COMPARE *(continued)*

Hotel	Zone	Overall Quality	Room Quality	Cost ($=$50)
Hyatt Regency New Orleans Superdome	2	★★★★	84	$$$$$–
Embassy Suites New Orleans	2	★★★★	84	$$$$$
Doubletree Hotel Lakeside New Orleans	9	★★★★	83	$$$–
Queen and Crescent Hotel	2	★★★★	83	$$$–
Chateau Sonesta Hotel	1	★★★★	83	$$$$+
Holiday Inn Select	2	★★★½	83	$$+
Avenue Inn	3	★★★½	82	$$
Courtyard by Marriott	2	★★★½	82	$$$$–
Grenoble House	1	★★★½	82	$$$$$–
Hotel de la Monnaie	1	★★★½	80	$$$–
Prince Conti Hotel	1	★★★½	80	$$$–
Provincial Hotel	1	★★★½	80	$$$–
Maison Dupuy Hotel	1	★★★½	81	$$$+
Soniat House	1	★★★½	80	$$$$
W French Quarter	1	★★★½	80	$$$$$$$$$
Dauphine Orleans	1	★★★½	79	$$+
Hotel St. Marie	1	★★★½	79	$$+
The Cornstalk	1	★★★½	79	$$$
Rathbone Inn	1	★★★½	78	$$–
Hilton New Orleans Airport	10	★★★½	78	$$
Holiday Inn Downtown Superdome	2	★★★½	78	$$+
Pontchartrain Hotel	3	★★★½	78	$$$
Bourbon Orleans Hotel	1	★★★½	77	$$$$$–
Avenue Garden Hotel	3	★★★½	76	$
Comfort Suites Airport	10	★★★½	76	$$–
Avenue Plaza Hotel	3	★★★½	76	$$
Bienville House	1	★★★½	76	$$
Best Western Airport All-Suite	10	★★★½	76	$$+
Hampton Inn and Suites (Suites)	10	★★★½	76	$$$–
Holiday Inn French Quarter	1	★★★½	76	$$$+
Lafayette Hotel	2	★★★½	76	$$$+
The Saint Louis	1	★★★½	76	$$$$–
Maison De Ville	1	★★★½	76	$$$$$
Brent House Hotel	9	★★★½	75	$$–
Place D'Armes Hotel	1	★★★½	75	$$$–
Hotel Ste. Helene	1	★★★½	75	$$$
Hampton Inn Downtown	2	★★★½	74	$$$+

HOW THE HOTELS COMPARE (continued)

Hotel	Zone	Overall Quality	Room Quality	Cost ($=$50)
Acadian Orleans Inn	3	★★★	75	$$–
Cotton Exchange	2	★★★	75	$$
Hotel Chateu Dupré	1	★★★	75	$$+
Doubletree Hotel New Orleans	2	★★★	75	$$$$+
Homewood Suites	2	★★★	74	$$–
Alexa Hotel French Quarter	1	★★★	74	$$$–
Radisson Hotel New Orleans	2	★★★	74	$$$
Marriott New Orleans	1	★★★	74	$$$$$+
Comfort Suites	8	★★★	73	$$–
Ramada Inn Superdome	2	★★★	73	$$–
Hampton Inn and Suites (Rooms)	10	★★★	73	$$
Holiday Inn Airport	10	★★★	73	$$$–
Ramada Plaza Hotel	3	★★★	73	$$$–
Courtyard Metairie	9	★★★	72	$$–
Wingate Inn	10	★★★	72	$$$–
Four Points Sheraton	10	★★★	72	$$$+
Lafitte Guest House	1	★★★	72	$$$$–
Ramada Plaza on Bourbon	1	★★★	72	$$$$+
Ramada Limited Causeway	9	★★★	71	$+
Holiday Inn Express	2	★★★	70	$+
Radisson Inn Airport	10	★★★	70	$$$–
Chateau LeMoyne French Quarter Holiday Inn	1	★★★	70	$$$$–
Prytania Park Hotel	3	★★★	69	$+
Extended Stay America	9	★★★	69	$$–
Le Richelieu French Quarter	1	★★★	69	$$$–
Best Western Patio Downtown	6	★★★	69	$$$+
Holiday Inn Metairie	9	★★★	68	$$–
Quality Inn & Suites	2	★★★	68	$$–
Best Western Inn Landmark Hotel	9	★★★	68	$$+
French Quarter Suites	1	★★★	68	$$+
Crescent on Canal	6	★★★	68	$$$+
Historic French Market Inn	1	★★★	68	$$$+
Maison St. Charles Quality Inn & Suites	3	★★★	67	$$–
Hampton Inn	9	★★★	67	$$+
Best Western Parc St. Charles	2	★★★	66	$$
Hotel Villa Convento	1	★★★	66	$$+
Olivier House Hotel	1	★★★	66	$$$–

HOW THE HOTELS COMPARE *(continued)*

Hotel	Zone	Overall Quality	Room Quality	Cost ($=$50
Holiday Inn New Orleans Westbank	11	★★★	65	$$−
La Quinta Inn Crowder Road	8	★★½	64	$+
New Orleans Guest House	1	★★½	64	$$
Quality Inn Tower Hotel	11	★★½	64	$$
French Quarter Courtyard Hotel	1	★★½	64	$$+
Comfort Suites Downtown	2	★★½	64	$$$−
La Quinta Inn Airport	10	★★½	63	$$−
Saint Ann/Marie Anntoinette	1	★★½	63	$$$$−
Best Western Inn Airport	10	★★½	62	$$
Rue Royal Inn	1	★★½	62	$$
La Quinta Inn Bullard	8	★★½	61	$+
La Quinta Inn Veterans	10	★★½	61	$$−
La Quinta Inn West Bank	11	★★½	61	$$−
The Columns	3	★★½	61	$$$
The Frenchmen	6	★★½	60	$$+
Best Western Landmark French Quarter	1	★★½	60	$$$+
Quality Inn Midtown	6	★★½	60	$$$$$$$$
St. Charles Inn	3	★★½	59	$+
Orleans Courtyard Inn	9	★★½	59	$$−
Super 8 New Orleans	8	★★½	58	$
Shoney's Inn	10	★★½	58	$+
Travelodge New Orleans Airport Hotel	10	★★½	58	$+
La Quinta Inn Causeway	9	★★½	58	$$−
Andrew Jackson	1	★★½	58	$$$−
Rodeway Inn Airport	10	★★½	56	$+
Days Inn Westbank Harvey	11	★★	56	$+
Park Plaza Inn	10	★★	55	$−
Lamothe House	1	★★	55	$$$−
Days Inn New Orleans Canal Street	2	★★	54	$$−
St. Peter Guest House	1	★★	54	$$+
Days Inn	8	★★	52	$+
Days Inn Kenner Airport	10	★★	50	$
Travelodge Hotel New Orleans	11	★★	48	$+
Hotel St. Pierre	1	★★	48	$$+
Travelodge New Orleans Metairie	10	★★	47	$+
A Creole House	1	★★	47	$$−

HOW THE HOTELS COMPARE (continued)

Hotel	Zone	Overall Quality	Room Quality	Cost ($=$50
Quality Hotel and Conference Center	9	★½	45	$+
Lasalle Hotel	1	★½	44	$$−
Howard Johnson Express	8	★½	41	$

NEW ORLEANS HOTELS BY ZONE

Hotel	Overall Quality	Room Quality	Cost ($=$50
Zone 1: French Quarter			
Ritz-Carlton New Orleans	★★★★½	94	$$$$−
Wyndham Canal Place	★★★★½	90	$$$$$$+
Royal Sonesta Hotel	★★★★	89	$$$$$$−
The Monteleone	★★★★	88	$$$$$−
Omni Royal Orleans Hotel	★★★★	87	$$$$$$−
Chateau Sonesta Hotel	★★★★	83	$$$$+
Grenoble House	★★★½	82	$$$$$−
Maison Dupuy Hotel	★★★½	81	$$$+
Hotel de la Monnaie	★★★½	80	$$$−
Prince Conti Hotel	★★★½	80	$$$−
Provincial Hotel	★★★½	80	$$$−
Soniat House	★★★½	80	$$$$
W French Quarter	★★★½	80	$$$$$$$$$
Dauphine Orleans	★★★½	79	$$+
Hotel St. Marie	★★★½	79	$$+
The Cornstalk	★★★½	79	$$$
Rathbone Inn	★★★½	78	$$−
Bourbon Orleans Hotel	★★★½	77	$$$$$−
Bienville House	★★★½	76	$$
Holiday Inn French Quarter	★★★½	76	$$$+
The Saint Louis	★★★½	76	$$$$−
Maison De Ville	★★★½	76	$$$$$
Place D'Armes Hotel	★★★½	75	$$$−
Hotel Ste. Helene	★★★½	75	$$$
Hotel Chateu Dupré	★★★	75	$$+
Alexa Hotel French Quarter	★★★	74	$$$−
Marriott New Orleans	★★★	74	$$$$$+

NEW ORLEANS HOTELS BY ZONE *(continued)*			
Hotel	Overall Quality	Room Quality	Cost ($=$50
Zone 1: French Quarter (continued)			
Lafitte Guest House	★★★	72	$$$$–
Ramada Plaza on Bourbon	★★★	72	$$$$+
Chateau LeMoyne French Quarter Holiday Inn	★★★	70	$$$$–
Le Richelieu French Quarter	★★★	69	$$$–
French Quarter Suites	★★★	68	$$+
Historic French Market Inn	★★★	68	$$$+
Hotel Villa Convento	★★★	66	$$+
Olivier House Hotel	★★★	66	$$$–
New Orleans Guest House	★★½	64	$$
French Quarter Courtyard Hotel	★★½	64	$$+
Saint Ann/Marie Anntoinette	★★½	63	$$$$–
Rue Royal Inn	★★½	62	$$
Best Western Landmark French Quarter	★★½	60	$$$+
Andrew Jackson	★★½	58	$$$–
Lamothe House	★★	55	$$$–
St. Peter Guest House	★★	54	$$+
Hotel St. Pierre	★★	48	$$+
A Creole House	★★	47	$$–
Lasalle Hotel	★½	44	$$–
Zone 2: Central Business District			
Windsor Court	★★★★½	94	$$$$$$$
Omni Royal Crescent Hotel	★★★★½	88	$$$$$
Pelham Hotel	★★★★	89	$$$+
Le Pavillon Hotel	★★★★	89	$$$$$$$$$$–
Ambassador Hotel New Orleans	★★★★	88	$$
Loft 523	★★★★	88	$$$$
Fairmont Hotel	★★★★	88	$$$$+
Hilton New Orleans Riverside	★★★★	88	$$$$$+
Residence Inn	★★★★	87	$$$+
Sheraton New Orleans Hotel	★★★★	87	$$$$$$$$$+
Hilton Garden Inn	★★★★	86	$$
Hampton Inn Suites & Convention Center	★★★★	86	$$$$$–
Wyndham Riverfront Hotel	★★★★	85	$$$$$$
Hotel Inter-Continental New Orleans	★★★★	85	$$$$$$$
Hyatt Regency New Orleans Superdome	★★★★	84	$$$$$–
Embassy Suites New Orleans	★★★★	84	$$$$$

Hotel	Overall Quality	Room Quality	Cost ($=$50
NEW ORLEANS HOTELS BY ZONE *(continued)*			
Zone 2: Central Business District *(continued)*			
Queen and Crescent Hotel	★★★★	83	$$$−
Holiday Inn Select	★★★½	83	$$+
Courtyard by Marriott	★★★½	82	$$$$−
Holiday Inn Downtown-Superdome	★★★½	78	$$+
Lafayette Hotel	★★★½	76	$$$+
Hampton Inn Downtown	★★★½	74	$$$+
Cotton Exchange	★★★	75	$$
Doubletree Hotel New Orleans	★★★	75	$$$$+
Homewood Suites	★★★	74	$$−
Radisson Hotel New Orleans	★★★	74	$$$
Ramada Inn Superdome	★★★	73	$$−
Holiday Inn Express	★★★	70	$+
Quality Inn & Suites	★★★	68	$$−
Best Western Parc St. Charles	★★★	66	$$
Comfort Suites Downtown	★★½	64	$$$−
Days Inn New Orleans Canal Street	★★	54	$$−
Zone 3: Uptown below Napoleon			
The McKendrick-Breaux House	★★★★	88	$$$+
Avenue Inn	★★★½	82	$$
Pontchartrain Hotel	★★★½	78	$$$
Avenue Garden Hotel	★★★½	76	$
Avenue Plaza Hotel	★★★½	76	$$
Acadian Orleans Inn	★★★	75	$$−
Ramada Plaza Hotel	★★★	73	$$$−
Prytania Park Hotel	★★★	69	$+
Maison St. Charles Quality Inn & Suites	★★★	67	$$−
The Columns	★★½	61	$$$
St. Charles Inn	★★½	59	$+
Zone 6: Mid-City/Gentilly			
Best Western Patio Downtown	★★★	69	$$$+
Crescent on Canal	★★★	68	$$$+
The Frenchmen	★★½	60	$$+
Quality Inn Midtown	★★½	60	$$$$$$$$
Zone 8: New Orleans East			
Comfort Suites	★★★	73	$$−
La Quinta Inn Crowder Road	★★½	64	$+
La Quinta Inn Bullard	★★½	61	$+

NEW ORLEANS HOTELS BY ZONE *(continued)*

Hotel	Overall Quality	Room Quality	Cost ($=$50
Zone 8: New Orleans East *(continued)*			
Super 8 New Orleans	★★½	58	$
Days Inn	★★	52	$+
Howard Johnson Express	★½	41	$
Zone 9: Metairie below Causeway			
Residence Inn Metairie	★★★★	89	$$−
Wyndham Galleria	★★★★	84	$$+
Doubletree Hotel Lakeside New Orleans	★★★★	83	$$$−
Brent House Hotel	★★★½	75	$$−
Courtyard Metairie	★★★	72	$$−
Ramada Limited Causeway	★★★	71	$+
Extended Stay America	★★★	69	$$−
Holiday Inn Metairie	★★★	68	$$−
Best Western Inn Landmark Hotel	★★★	68	$$+
Hampton Inn	★★★	67	$$+
Orleans Courtyard Inn	★★½	59	$$−
La Quinta Inn Causeway	★★½	58	$$−
Quality Hotel and Conference Center	★½	45	$+
Zone 10: Metairie above Causeway/Kenner/Jefferson Highway			
Hilton New Orleans Airport	★★★½	78	$$
Comfort Suites Airport	★★★½	76	$$−
Best Western Airport All-Suite	★★★½	76	$$+
Hampton Inn and Suites (Suites)	★★★½	76	$$$−
Hampton Inn and Suites (Rooms)	★★★	73	$$
Holiday Inn Airport	★★★	73	$$$−
Wingate Inn	★★★	72	$$$−
Four Points Sheraton	★★★	72	$$$+
Radisson Inn Airport	★★★	70	$$$−
La Quinta Inn Airport	★★½	63	$$−
Best Western Inn Airport	★★½	62	$$
La Quinta Inn Veterans	★★½	61	$$−
Shoney's Inn	★★½	58	$+
Travelodge New Orleans Airport Hotel	★★½	58	$+
Rodeway Inn Airport	★★½	56	$+
Park Plaza Inn	★★	55	$−
Days Inn Kenner Airport	★★	50	$
Travelodge New Orleans Metairie	★★	47	$+

NEW ORLEANS HOTELS BY ZONE (continued)			
Hotel	Overall Quality	Room Quality	Cost ($=$50
Zone 11: West Bank			
Holiday Inn New Orleans Westbank	★★★	65	$$–
Quality Inn Tower Hotel	★★½	64	$$
La Quinta Inn West Bank	★★½	61	$$–
Days Inn Westbank Harvey	★★	56	$+
Travelodge Hotel New Orleans	★★	48	$+

The Top 30 Best Deals in New Orleans

Having listed the nicest rooms in town, let's reorder the list to rank the best combinations of quality and value in a room. As before, the rankings are made without consideration of location or the availability of restaurant(s), recreational facilities, entertainment, and/or amenities.

A reader recently complained to us that he had booked one of our top-ranked rooms in terms of value and had been very disappointed in the room. We noticed that the room the reader occupied had a quality rating of ★★½. We would remind you that the value ratings are intended to give you some sense of value received for dollars spent. A ★★½ room at $30 may have the same value rating as a ★★★★ room at $85, but that does not mean the rooms will be of comparable quality. Regardless of whether it's a good deal or not, a ★★½ room is still a ★★½ room.

Listed below are the best room buys for the money, regardless of location or star classification, based on averaged rack rates. Note that sometimes a suite can cost less than a hotel room.

THE TOP 30 BEST DEALS IN NEW ORLEANS			
Hotel	Overall Quality	Room Quality	Cost ($=$40)
1. Avenue Garden Hotel	★★★½	76	$
2. Residence Inn Metairie	★★★★	89	$$–
3. Rathbone Inn	★★★½	78	$$–
4. Ambassador Hotel New Orleans	★★★★	88	$$
5. Hilton Garden Inn	★★★★	86	$$
6. Ramada Limited Causeway	★★★	71	$+
7. Wyndham Galleria	★★★★	84	$$+
8. Brent House Hotel	★★★½	75	$$–
9. Holiday Inn Express	★★★	70	$+

	Overall Quality	Room Quality	Cost ($=$40)
THE TOP 30 BEST DEALS IN NEW ORLEANS *(continued)*			
Hotel			
10. Comfort Suites Airport	★★★½	76	$$–
11. Prytania Park Hotel	★★★	69	$+
12. Avenue Inn	★★★½	82	$$
13. Ramada Inn Superdome	★★★	73	$$–
14. Extended Stay America	★★★	69	$$–
15. Avenue Plaza Hotel	★★★½	76	$$
16. Bienville House	★★★½	76	$$
17. Acadian Orleans Inn	★★★	75	$$–
18. La Quinta Inn Crowder Road	★★½	64	$+
19. Super 8 New Orleans	★★½	58	$
20. Hilton New Orleans Airport	★★★½	78	$$
21. Doubletree Hotel Lakeside New Orleans	★★★★	83	$$$–
22. Queen and Crescent Hotel	★★★★	83	$$$–
23. Quality Inn & Suites	★★★	68	$$–
24. Park Plaza Inn	★★	55	$–
25. Holiday Inn Downtown Superdome	★★★½	78	$$+
26. Homewood Suites	★★★	74	$$–
27. Ritz-Carlton New Orleans	★★★★½	94	$$$$–
28. Holiday Inn Select	★★★½	83	$$+
29. Best Western Airport All-Suite	★★★½	76	$$+
30. Comfort Suites	★★★	73	$$–

Hotel	Overall Quality	Room Quality	Zone	Address
Acadian Orleans Inn	★★★	75	3	2041 Prytania Street New Orleans, 70130
Alexa Hotel French Quarter	★★★	74	1	119 Royal Street New Orleans, 70130
Ambassador Hotel New Orleans	★★★★	88	2	535 Tchoupitoulas Street New Orleans, 70130
Andrew Jackson	★★½	58	1	919 Royal Street New Orleans, 70116
Avenue Garden Hotel	★★★½	76	3	1509 St. Charles Avenue New Orleans, 70130
Avenue Inn	★★★½	82	3	4125 St. Charles Avenue New Orleans, 70130
Avenue Plaza Hotel	★★★½	76	3	2111 St. Charles Avenue New Orleans, 70130
Best Western Airport All-Suite	★★★½	76	10	2438 Veterans Memorial Boulevard Kenner, 70062
Best Western Inn Airport	★★½	62	10	1021 Airline Drive Kenner, 70062
Best Western Inn Landmark Hotel	★★★	68	9	2601 Severn Ave Metairie, 70002
Best Western Landmark French Quarter	★★½	60	1	920 N. Rampart Street New Orleans, 70116
Best Western Patio Downtown	★★★	69	6	2820 Tulane Ave New Orleans, 70119
Best Western Parc St. Charles	★★★	66	2	500 St. Charles Avenue New Orleans, 70130
Bienville House	★★★½	76	1	320 Decatur Street New Orleans, 70130
Bourbon Orleans Hotel	★★★½	77	1	717 Orleans Street New Orleans, 70116
Brent House Hotel	★★★½	75	9	1512 Jefferson Hwy Jefferson, 70121
Chateau LeMoyne French Quarter Holiday Inn	★★★	70	1	301 Rue Dauphine New Orleans, 70112
Chateau Sonesta Hotel	★★★★	83	1	800 Iberville Street New Orleans, 70112
The Columns	★★½	61	3	3811 St. Charles Avenue New Orleans, 70115
Comfort Suites	★★★	73	8	7051 Bullard Avenue New Orleans, 70128

Phone	Fax	Reservations	Cost	# of Rooms
(504) 566-1411	(504) 561-8510	(877) 566-1411	$$–	22
(504) 962-0600	(504) 962-0501	(888) 487-9643	$$$–	515
(504) 527-5271	(504) 527-5270	(888) 527-5271	$$	165
(504) 561-5881	(504) 596-6769	(800) 654-0224	$$$–	22
(504) 521-8000	(504) 528-3180	(800) 379-5322	$	23
(504) 269-2640	(504) 269-2641	(800) 490-8542	$$	19
(504) 566-1212	(504) 525-6899	(800) 535-9575	$$	258
(504) 469-2800	(504) 469-4177	(800) WESTERN	$$+	78
(504) 464-1644	(504) 469-1193	(800) WESTERN	$$	166
(504) 888-9500	(504) 889-5792	(800) WESTERN	$$+	342
(504) 524-3333	(504) 523-5431	(800) WESTERN	$$$+	102
(504) 822-0200	(504) 822-2328	(800) WESTERN	$$$+	75
(504) 522-9000	(504) 522-9060	(800) WESTERN	$$	120
(504) 529-2345	(504) 525-6079	(800) 535-7836	$$	83
(504) 523-2222	(504) 571+4666	(800) 996-3426	$$$$$–	216
(504) 835-5411	(504) 842-4164	(800) 535-3986	$$–	168
(504) 581-1303	(504) 523-5709	(800) 447-2830	$$$$–	171
(504) 586-0800	(504) 586-1987	(800) SONESTA	$$$$+	251
(504) 899-9308	(504) 899-8170	(800) 445-9308	$$$	20
(504) 244-1414	(504) 240-1414	(800) 228-5150	$$–	65

Hotel	Pool	Sauna	Room Service
Acadian Orleans Inn	N	N	Y
Alexa Hotel French Quarter	Y	N	Y
Ambassador Hotel New Orleans	N	N	Y
Andrew Jackson	N	N	N
Avenue Garden Hotel	N	N	N
Avenue Inn	N	N	N
Avenue Plaza Hotel	Y	Y	N
Best Western Airport All-Suite	Y	Y	N
Best Western Inn Airport	N	Y	N
Best Western Inn Landmark Hotel	Y	Y	Y
Best Western Landmark French Quarter	Y	N	Y
Best Western Patio Downtown	Y	y	N
Best Western Parc St. Charles	Y	N	N
Bienville House	Y	N	N
Bourbon Orleans Hotel	Y	N	Y
Brent House Hote	Y	N	Y
Chateau LeMoyne French Quarter Holiday Inn	Y	N	Y
Chateau Sonesta Hotel	Y	N	Y
The Columns	N	N	N
Comfort Suites	Y	N	N

Parking	Breakfast	Exercise Room
Street	N	N
Valet, $10; lot	N	Y
Valet, $12	Buffet	N
Street	Contintental	N
Garage, $10	Contintental	Adjacent
Lot	Contintental	N
Valet, $18	N	Spa
Free lot	Contintental	N
Street	N	Y
Free lot	N	Y
Lot, $12	N	N
Free garage	Continental	Adjacent
Lot, $18	N	Y
Lot, $19	Continental	Off site
Valet, $25	N	Off site
Garage, $3	N	Y
Valet, $20	N	Off site
Valet, $20	N	Y
Street	Full	N
Free lot	Continental	Y

Hotel	Overall Quality	Room Quality	Zone	Address
Comfort Suites Airport	★★★½	76	10	2710 Idaho Avenue Kenner, 70065
Comfort Suites Downtown	★★½	64	2	346 Baronne Street New Orleans, 70112
The Cornstalk	★★★½	79	1	915 Royal Street New Orleans, 70113
Cotton Exchange	★★★	75	2	231 Carondelet Street New Orleans, 70130
Courtyard by Marriott	★★★½	82	2	124 St. Charles Avenue New Orleans, 70130
Courtyard Metairie	★★★	72	9	2 Galleria Boulevard Metairie, 70001
A Creole House	★★	47	1	1013 St. Ann Street New Orleans, 70116
Crescent on Canal	★★★	68	6	1732 Canal Street New Orleans, 70112
Dauphine Orleans	★★★½	79	1	415 Dauphine Street New Orleans, 70112
Days Inn	★★	52	8	5801 Read Road New Orleans, 70127
Days Inn Kenner Airport	★★	50	10	1300 Veterans Memorial Boulevard Kenner, 70065
Days Inn New Orleans Canal Street	★★	54	2	1630 Canal Street New Orleans, 70112
Days Inn Westbank Harvey	★★	56	11	3750 Westbank Expressway Harvey, 70058
Doubletree Hotel Lakeside New Orleans	★★★★	83	9	3838 N. Causeway Boulevard Metairie, 70002
Doubletree Hotel New Orleans	★★★	75	2	300 Canal Street New Orleans, 70130
Embassy Suites New Orleans	★★★★	84	2	315 Julia Street New Orleans, 70130
Extended Stay America	★★★	69	9	3300 I-10 & Causeway Boulevard Metairie, 70001
Fairmont Hotel	★★★★	88	2	123 Baronne Street, University Pl New Orleans, 70112
Four Points Sheraton	★★★	72	10	6401 Veterans Memorial Boulevard Metairie, 70003
French Quarter Courtyard Hotel	★★½	64	1	1101 N. Rampart New Orleans, 70116

Phone	Fax	Reservations	Cost	# of Rooms
(504) 466-6066	(504) 466-8282	(877) 424-6423	$$–	95
(504) 524-1140	(504) 523-4444	(800) 524-1140	$$$–	102
(504) 523-1515	(504) 522-5558	N/A	$$$	14
(504) 962-0700	(504) 962-0701	(888) 884-6126	$$	102
(504) 581-9005	(504) 581-6264	(800) 654-3990	$$$$–	141
(504) 838-3800	(504) 838-7050	(800) 654-3990	$$–	153
(504) 524-8076	(504) 581-3277	(800) 535-7858	$$–	19
(504) 558-0201	(504) 529-1609	(800) 236-6119	$$$+	1036
(504) 586-1800	(504) 586-1409	(800) 521-7111	$$+	111
(504) 241-2500	(504) 245-8340	(866) 233-9300	$+	143
(504) 469-2531	(504) 468-1269	(800) 325-2525	$	324
(504) 586-0110	(504) 581-2253	(800) 325-2525	$$–	216
(504) 348-1262	(504) 348-0624	(800) 325-2525	$+	106
(504) 836-5253	(504) 846-4562	(800) 222-TREE	$$$–	210
(504) 581-1300	(504) 522-4100	(800) 222-TREE	$$$$+	363
(504) 525-1993	(504) 525-3437	(800) 362-2779	$$$$$	372
(504) 837-5599	(504) 837-5009	(800) 326-5651	$$–	102
(504) 529-7111	(504) 529-4764	(800) 441-1414	$$$$+	700
(504) 885-5700	(504) 888-5815	(800) 325-3535	$$$+	220
(504) 522-7333	(504) 522-3908	(800) 290-4233	$$+	54

Hotel	Pool	Sauna	Room Service
Comfort Suites Airport	Y	N	N
Comfort Suites Downtown	N	Y	N
The Cornstalk	N	N	N
Cotton Exchange	Y	N	N
Courtyard by Marriott	N	N	N
Courtyard Metairie	Y	N	N
A Creole House	N	N	N
Crescent on Canal	N	N	N
Dauphine Orleans	Y	N	N
Days Inn	Y	N	N
Days Inn Kenner Airport	Y	N	N
Days Inn New Orleans Canal Street	Y	N	N
Days Inn Westbank Harvey	Y	N	N
Doubletree Hotel Lakeside New Orleans	Y	Y	Y
Doubletree Hotel New Orleans	Y	N	Y
Embassy Suites New Orleans	Y	Y	Y
Extended Stay America	N	N	N
Fairmont Hotel	Y	N	Y
Four Points Sheraton	Y	N	Y
French Quarter Courtyard Hotel	Y	N	N

Parking	Breakfast	Exercise Room
Free lot	Continental	Y
Valet, $20	Continental	Y
Lot, $15	Continental	N
Valet, $20	N	N
Lot, $19	N	Y
Free lot	N	Y
Lot, $16	Continental	N
Lot, $17	Continental	N
Valet, $18	Continental	Y
Free lot	N	Y
Free lot	N	N
Free lot	N	Y
Free lot	Continental	N
Free lot	N	Y
Valet, $25	N	Y
Valet, $15	Full	N
Free lot	N	N
Lot, $19	N	Y
Free lot	N	Y
Lot, $20	N	N

Hotel	Overall Quality	Room Quality	Zone	Address
French Quarter Suites	★★★	68	1	1119 N. Rampart New Orleans, 70116
The Frenchmen	★★½	60	6	417 Frenchmen Street New Orleans, 70116
Grenoble House	★★★½	82	1	329 Dauphine Street New Orleans, 70112
Hampton Inn	★★★	67	9	2730 N. Causeway Boulevard Metairie, 70002
Hampton Inn and Suites	★★★ ★★★½	73 76	10	5150 Mounes Street Harahan, 70123
Hampton Inn Downtown	★★★½	74	2	226 Carondelet Street New Orleans, 70130
Hampton Inn Suites & Convention Center	★★★★	86	2	1201 Convention Center Boulevar New Orleans, 70130
Hilton Garden Inn	★★★★	86	2	1001 S. Peters Street New Orleans, 70130
Hilton New Orleans Riverside	★★★★	88	2	Poydras at Mississippi River New Orleans, 70140
Hilton New Orleans Airport	★★★½	78	10	901 Airline Highway Kenner, 70062
Historic French Market Inn	★★★	68	1	501 Decatur Street New Orleans, 70130
Holiday Inn Airport	★★★	73	10	2929 Williams Boulevard Kenner, 70062
Holiday Inn Downtown Superdome	★★★½	78	2	330 Loyola Avenue New Orleans, 70112
Holiday Inn Express	★★★	70	2	221 Carondelet Street New Orleans, 70130
Holiday Inn French Quarter	★★★½	76	1	124 Royal Street New Orleans, 70130
Holiday Inn Metairie	★★★	68	9	3400 S. I-10 Service Road Metairie, 70001
Holiday Inn New Orleans Westbank	★★★	65	11	100 Westbank Expressway Gretna, 70053
Holiday Inn Select	★★★½	83	2	881 Convention Center Boulevar New Orleans, 70130
Homewood Suites	★★★	74	2	409 Baronne Street New Orleans, 70122
Hotel Chateau Dupré	★★★	75	1	131 Rue Decatur New Orleans, 70130

Phone	Fax	Reservations	Cost	# of Rooms
(504) 524-7725	(504) 522-9716	(800) 457-2253	$$+	18
(504) 948-2166	(504) 948-2258	(800) 831-1781	$$+	25
(504) 522-1331	(504) 524-4968	(800) 722-1834	$$$$$–	17
(504) 831-7676	(504) 831-7478	(800) HAMPTON	$$+	112
(504) 733-5646	(504) 733-5609	(800) HAMPTON	$$	128
(504) 529-9990	(504) 529-2466	(800) 292-0653	$$$+	187
(504) 566-9990	(504) 566-9997	(800) 292-0653	$$$$$–	288
(504) 525-0044	(504) 525-0035	(800) HILTONS	$$	284
(504) 561-0500	(504) 584-1721	(800) HILTONS	$$$$$+	1616
(504) 469-5000	(504) 466-5473	(800) 872-5914	$$	317
(504) 561-5621	(888) 211-3448	(888) 277-3447	$$$+	68
(504) 467-5611	(504) 469-4915	(800) HOLIDAY	$$$–	303
(504) 581-1600	(504) 586-0833	(800) 535-7830	$$+	297
(504) 962-0800	(504) 962-0801	(800) HOLIDAY	$+	120
(504) 529-7211	(504) 522-7930	(800) 447-2830	$$$+	374
(504) 833-8201	(504) 838-6829	(800) HOLIDAY	$$–	195
(504) 366-2361	(504) 362-5814	(800) HOLIDAY	$$–	307
(504) 524-1881	(504) 528-1005	(800) 535-7830	$$+	170
(504) 581-5599	(504) 581-9133	(800) CALL-HOME	$$–	166
(504) 569-0600	(504) 569-0606	(888) 211-3447	$$+	54

Hotel	Pool	Sauna	Room Service
French Quarter Suites	Y	Y	N
The Frenchmen	Y	Y	N
Grenoble House	Y	Y	N
Hampton Inn	Y	N	N
Hampton Inn and Suites	Y	N	N
Hampton Inn Downtown	N	N	N
Hampton Inn Suites & Convention Center	Y	N	N
Hilton Garden Inn	Y	Y	Y
Hilton New Orleans Riverside	Y	Y	Y
Hilton New Orleans Airport	Y	Y	Y
Historic French Market Inn	Y	N	Y
Holiday Inn Airport	Y	Y	Y
Holiday Inn Downtown Superdome	Y	N	Y
Holiday Inn Express	Y	N	N
Holiday Inn French Quarter	Y	N	Y
Holiday Inn Metairie	Y	Y	Y
Holiday Inn New Orleans Westbank	Y	N	Y
Holiday Inn Select	N	N	Y
Homewood Suites	Y	Y	N
Hotel Chateau Dupré	N	N	N

Parking	Breakfast	Exercise Room
Lot, $18	Continental	N
Street	Continental	N
Street	N	N
Free lot	Continental	Y
Free lot	Continental	Off site
Valet, $19	Continental	Y
Lot, $19	Continental	Y
Valet, $19	N	Y
Valet, $25; lot, $20	N	Y
Free lot	N	Y
Lot, $15	N	N
Free lot	N	Y
Lot, $13	N	Y
Valet, $20	Continental	Y
Lot, $20	N	Y
Street	N	Y
Street	N	Y
Lot, $18	N	Y
Valet, $20	Continental	Y
Valet, $19	Continental	N

Hotel	Overall Quality	Room Quality	Zone	Address
Hotel de la Monnaie	★★★½	80	1	405 Esplanade Avenue New Orleans, 70116
Hotel Inter-Continental New Orleans	★★★★	85	2	444 St. Charles Avenue New Orleans, 70130
Hotel St. Marie	★★★½	79	1	827 Toulouse Street New Orleans, 70112
Hotel St. Pierre	★★	48	1	911 Burgundy Street New Orleans, 70116
Hotel Ste. Helene	★★★½	75	1	508 Rue Chartres New Orleans, 70130
Hotel Villa Convento	★★★	66	1	616 Ursulines Street New Orleans, 70116
Howard Johnson Express	★½	41	8	4200 Old Gentilly Road New Orleans, 70126
Hyatt Regency New Orleans Superdome	★★★★	84	2	500 Poydras Plaza New Orleans, 70113
La Quinta Inn Airport	★★½	63	10	2610 Williams Boulevard Kenner, 70062
La Quinta Inn Bullard	★★½	61	8	12001 I-10 Service Road New Orleans, 70128
La Quinta Inn Causeway	★★½	58	9	3100 I-10 Service Road Metairie, 70001
La Quinta Inn Crowder Road	★★½	64	8	8400 I-10 Service Road New Orleans, 70127
La Quinta Inn Veterans	★★½	61	10	5900 Veterans Memorial Boulevar Metairie, 70003
La Quinta Inn West Bank	★★½	61	11	50 Terry Parkway Gretna, 70056
Lafayette Hotel	★★★½	76	2	600 St. Charles Avenue New Orleans, 70130
Lafitte Guest House	★★★	72	1	1003 Bourbon Street New Orleans, 70116
Lamothe House	★★	55	1	621 Esplanade Avenue New Orleans, 70116
Lasalle Hotel	★½	44	1	1113 Canal Street New Orleans, 70112
Le Pavillon Hotel	★★★★	89	2	833 Poydras Street New Orleans, 70112
Le Richelieu French Quarter	★★★	69	1	1234 Chartres Street New Orleans, 70116

Phone	Fax	Reservations	Cost	# of Rooms
(504) 947-0009	(504) 945-6841	N/A	$$$–	53
(504) 525-5566	(504) 523-7310	(800) 327-0200	$$$$$$$$	479
(504) 561-8951	(504) 581-3802	(800) 366-2743	$$+	100
(504) 524-4401	(504) 593-9425	(800) 225-4040	$$+	74
(504) 522-5014	(504) 523-7140	(800) 348-3888	$$$	29
(504) 522-1793	(504) 524-1902	(800) 887-2817	$$+	25
(504) 944-0151	(504) 945-3053	(800) 446-4656	$	100
(504) 561-1234	(504) 587-4141	(800) 233-1234	$$$$$–	1184
(504) 466-1401	(504) 466-0319	(800) 531-5900	$$–	196
(504) 246-3003	(504) 242-5539	(800) 531-5900	$+	130
(504) 835-8511	(504) 837-3383	(800) 531-5900	$$–	101
(504) 246-5800	(504) 242-5091	(800) 531-5900	$+	106
(504) 456-0003	(504) 885-0863	(800) 531-5900	$$–	153
(504) 368-5600	(504) 362-7430	(800) 531-5900	$$–	154
(504) 524-4441	(504) 523-7327	(800) 733-4754	$$$+	44
(504) 581-2678	(504) 581-2677	(800) 331-7971	$$$$–	14
(504) 947-1161	(504) 943-6536	(800) 367-5858	$$$–	30
(504) 523-5831	(504) 525-2531	(800) 521-9450	$$–	64
(504) 581-3111	(504) 529-4415	(800) 535-9095	$$$$$$ $$$$–	226
(504) 529-2492	(504) 524-8179	(800) 535-9653	$$$–	86

Hotel	Pool	Sauna	Room Service
Hotel de la Monnaie	N	N	N
Hotel Inter-Continental New Orleans	Y	N	Y
Hotel St. Marie	Y	N	Y
Hotel St. Pierre	Y	N	N
Hotel Ste. Helene	Y	N	N
Hotel Villa Convento	N	N	N
Howard Johnson Express	Y	N	N
Hyatt Regency New Orleans Superdome	Y	N	Y
La Quinta Inn Airport	Y	N	N
La Quinta Inn Bullard	Y	N	N
La Quinta Inn Causeway	Y	N	N
La Quinta Inn Crowder Road	Y	N	N
La Quinta Inn Veterans	Y	N	N
La Quinta Inn West Bank	Y	N	N
Lafayette Hotel	N	N	Y
Lafitte Guest House	N	N	N
Lamothe House	Y	Y	N
Lasalle Hotel	N	N	N
Le Pavillon Hotel	Y	N	Y
Le Richelieu French Quarter	Y	N	Y

Parking	Breakfast	Exercise Room	
Street	N	Y	
Valet, $25; lot, $12	N	Y	
Valet, $20	N	N	
Free lot	Continental	N	
Lot, $20	Continental	N	
Lot, $6	Continental	N	
Street	Continental	N	
Valet, $21	N	Y	
Free lot	Continental	Y	
Free lot	Continental	N	
Free lot	Continental	N	
Free lot	Continental	Off site	
Free lot	Continental	N	
Free lot	Continental	N	
Valet, $20	N	N	
Lot, $15	Continental	N	
Free lot	Continental	N	
Valet, $10	Continental	N	
Lot, $25	N	Y	
Free lot	N	N	

Hotel	Overall Quality	Room Quality	Zone	Address
Loft 523	★★★★	88	2	523 Gravier Street New Orleans, 70130
Maison De Ville	★★★½	76	1	727 Rue Toulouse Avenue New Orleans, 70130
Maison Dupuy Hotel	★★★½	81	1	1001 Rue Toulouse New Orleans, 70112
Maison St. Charles Quality Inn & Suites	★★★	67	3	1319 St. Charles Avenue New Orleans, 70130
Marriott New Orleans	★★★	74	1	555 Canal Street New Orleans, 70140
The McKendrick-Breaux House	★★★★	88	3	1474 Magazine Street New Orleans, 70130
The Monteleone	★★★★	88	1	214 Rue Royal New Orleans, 70130
New Orleans Guest House	★★½	64	1	1118 Ursulines Street New Orleans, 70116
Olivier House Hotel	★★★	66	1	828 Toulouse Street New Orleans, 70112
Omni Royal Crescent Hotel	★★★★½	88	2	535 Gravier Street New Orleans, 70130
Omni Royal Orleans Hotel	★★★★	87	1	621 St. Louis Street New Orleans, 70140
Orleans Courtyard Inn	★★½	59	9	3800 Hessmer Avenue Metairie, 70002
Park Plaza Inn	★★	55	10	2125 Veterans Memorial Boulevar Kenner, 70062
Pelham Hotel	★★★★	89	2	444 Common Street New Orleans, 70130
Place D'Armes Hotel	★★★½	75	1	625 St. Ann Street New Orleans, 70116
Pontchartrain Hotel	★★★½	78	3	2031 St. Charles Avenue New Orleans, 70140
Prince Conti Hotel	★★★½	80	1	830 Conti Street New Orleans, 70112
Provincial Hotel	★★★½	80	1	1024 Rue Chartres New Orleans, 70116
Prytania Park Hotel	★★★	69	3	1525 Prytania Street New Orleans, 70130
Quality Hotel and Conference Center	★½	45	9	2261 N. Causeway Boulevard Metairie, 70001

Phone	Fax	Reservations	Cost	# of Rooms
(504) 200-6523	N/A	N/A	$$$$	18
(504) 561-5858	(504) 528-9939	(800) 634-1600	$$$$$	23
(504) 586-8000	(504) 525-5334	(800) 535-9177	$$$+	200
(504) 522-0187	(504) 529-4379	(800) 831-1783	$$−	130
(504) 581-1000	(504) 523-6755	(800) 654-3990	$$$$$+	1310
(504) 586-1700	(504) 522-7138	(888) 570-1700	$$$+	9
(504) 523-3341	(504) 528-1019	(800) 535-9595	$$$$$−	600
(504) 566-1179	(504) 566-1179	(800) 562-1177	$$	14
(504) 525-8456	(504) 529-2006	866-525-9748	$$$−	42
(504) 527-0006	(504) 523-0806	(800) 843-6664	$$$$$	98
(504) 529-5333	(504) 529-7089	(800) 843-6664	$$$$$$−	346
(504) 455-6110	(504) 455-0940	N/A	$$−	52
(504) 464-6464	(504) 464-7532	N/A	$−	129
(504) 522-4444	(504) 539-9010	(888) 211-3447	$$$+	64
(504) 524-4531	(504) 571-2803	(800) 366-2743	$$$−	80
(504) 524-0581	(504) 529-1165	(800) 777-6193	$$$	118
(504) 529-4172	(504) 581-3802	(800) 366-2743	$$$−	73
(504) 581-4995	(504) 581-1018	(888) 594-5271	$$$−	94
(504) 524-0427	(504) 522-2977	(888) 209-9002	$+	62
(504) 833-8211	(504) 833-8213	(800) 228-5151	$+	205

Hotel	Pool	Sauna	Room Service
Loft 523	N	N	Y
Maison De Ville	Y	N	Y
Maison Dupuy Hotel	Y	Y	Y
Maison St. Charles Quality Inn & Suites	Y	Y	N
Marriott New Orleans	Y	Y	Y
The McKendrick-Breaux House	N	N	N
The Monteleone	Y	N	Y
New Orleans Guest House	N	N	N
Olivier House Hotel	Y	N	N
Omni Royal Crescent Hotel	Y	N	Y
Omni Royal Orleans Hotel	Y	N	Y
Orleans Courtyard Inn	Y	N	N
Park Plaza Inn	Y	N	Y
Pelham Hotel	N	N	Y
Place D'Armes Hotel	Y	N	N
Pontchartrain Hotel	N	N	Y
Prince Conti Hotel	N	N	Y
Provincial Hotel	Y	N	Y
Prytania Park Hotel	N	N	N
Quality Hotel and Conference Center	Y	Y	Y

Parking	Breakfast	Exercise Room
Valet, $22	N	Y
Lot, $23	Continental	Off site
Valet, $18	N	Y
Lot, $12	N	N
Valet, $21	N	Y
Free lot	Continental	N
Lot, $19	N	Y
Free lot	Continental	N
Free lot	N	N
Valet, lot, $22	N	Y
Valet, $21	N	Y
Free lot	Continental	Y
Free lot	Continental	Y
Valet, $20	N	N
Valet, $20	Continental	N
Valet, $18	N	Off site
Valet, $20	N	N
Lot, $15	N	N
Lot, $10	Continental	Off site
Free lot	N	Y

Hotel	Overall Quality	Room Quality	Zone	Address
Quality Inn & Suites	★★★	68	2	210 O'Keefe Avenue New Orleans, 70112
Quality Inn Midtown	★★½	60	6	3900 Tulane Avenue New Orleans, 70113
Quality Inn Tower Hotel	★★½	64	11	100 Westbank Expressway Gretna, 70053
Queen and Crescent Hotel	★★★★	83	2	344 Camp Street New Orleans, 70130
Radisson Hotel New Orleans	★★★	74	2	1500 Canal Street New Orleans, 70112
Radisson Inn Airport	★★★	70	10	2150 Veterans Memorial Boulevard Kenner, 70062
Ramada Inn Superdome	★★★	73	2	1315 Gravier Street New Orleans, 70112
Ramada Limited Causeway	★★★	71	9	2713 N. Causeway Boulevard Metairie, 70002
Ramada Plaza Hotel	★★★	73	3	2203 St. Charles Avenue New Orleans, 70140
Ramada Plaza on Bourbon	★★★	72	1	541 Bourbon Street New Orleans, 70130
Rathbone Inn	★★★½	78	1	1227 Esplanade Avenue New Orleans, 70116
Residence Inn	★★★★	87	2	345 St. Joseph Street New Orleans, 70130
Residence Inn Metairie	★★★★	89	9	3 Galleria Boulevard Metairie, 70001
Ritz-Carlton New Orleans	★★★★½	94	1	921 Canal Street New Orleans, 70112
Rodeway Inn Airport	★★½	56	10	851 Airline Highway Kenner, 70062
Royal Sonesta Hotel	★★★★	89	1	300 Bourbon Street New Orleans, 70140
Rue Royal Inn	★★½	62	1	1006 Royal Street New Orleans, 70116
Saint Ann/ Marie Anntoinette	★★½	63	1	717 Rue Conti New Orleans, 70130
The Saint Louis	★★★½	76	1	730 Bienville Street New Orleans, 70130
Sheraton New Orleans Hotel	★★★★	87	2	500 Canal Street New Orleans, 70130

Phone	Fax	Reservations	Cost	# of Rooms
(504) 525-6800	(504) 525-6808	(877) 424-6423	$$–	100
(504) 486-5541	(504) 488-7440	(800) 228-5151	$$$$$$$$	102
(504) 366-8531	(504) 362-9502	(800) 228-5151	$$	175
(504) 587-9700	(504) 587-9701	(800) 975-6652	$$$–	129
(504) 522-4500	(504) 525-2644	(800) 333-3333	$$$	759
(504) 467-3111	(504) 469-4634	(866) 292-6118	$$$–	244
(504) 586-0100	(504) 527-5263	(800) 535-9141	$$–	176
(504) 835-4141	(504) 833-6942	(800) 228-3838	$+	138
(504) 566-1200	(504) 566-0761	(800) 2-RAMADA	$$$–	132
(504) 524-7611	(504) 568-9427	(800) 272-6232	$$$$+	186
(504) 947-2100	(504) 947-7454	(800) 947-2101	$$–	14
(504) 522-1300	(504) 522-6060	(800) 654-3990	$$$+	231
(504) 832-0888	(504) 832-4916	(800) 654-3990	$$–	120
(504) 524-1331	(504) 524-7675	(800) 241-3333	$$$$–	452
(504) 467-1391	(504) 466-9148	(800) 228-2000	$+	98
(504) 586-0300	(504) 586-0335	(800) SONESTA	$$$$$$–	500
(504) 524-3900	(504) 558-0566	(800) 776-3901	$$	39
(504) 581-1881	(504) 524-8925	(800) 535-9111	$$$$–	66
(504) 581-7300	(504) 524-8925	(800) 535-9111	$$$$–	83
(504) 525-2500	(504) 595-5552	(888) 396-6364	$$$$$ $$$$+	1110

Hotel	Pool	Sauna	Room Service
Quality Inn & Suites	N	N	N
Quality Inn Midtown	Y	Y	Y
Quality Inn Tower Hotel	Y	N	N
Queen and Crescent Hotel	N	N	N
Radisson Hotel New Orleans	Y	N	Y
Radisson Inn Airport	Y	N	Y
Ramada Inn Superdome	Y	N	N
Ramada Limited Causeway	Y	N	N
Ramada Plaza Hotel	N	N	Y
Ramada Plaza on Bourbon	Y	N	Y
Rathbone Inn	Y	Y	N
Residence Inn	Y	N	N
Residence Inn Metairie	Y	Y	N
Ritz-Carlton New Orleans	Y	Y	Y
Rodeway Inn Airport	Y	N	N
Royal Sonesta Hotel	Y	N	Y
Rue Royal Inn	N	N	N
Saint Ann/Marie Anntoinette	Y	N	Y
The Saint Louis	N	N	Y
Sheraton New Orleans Hotel	Y	Y	Y

Parking	Breakfast	Exercise Room	
Valet, $25	Continental	N	
Free lot	N	Y	
Free lot	N	N	
Valet, $23	Continental	Y	
Valet, $18	N	Y	
Free lot	N	Y	
Lot, $12	N	N	
Free lot	Continental	Y	
Valet, $18	N	Off site	
Lot, $18	N	Y	
Free lot	Continental	N	
Valet, $20; lot, $17	Y	Y	
Free lot	Continental	Y	
Valet, $25	N	Y	
Street	Continental	N	
Lot, $20	N	Y	
Lot, $19	Continental	N	
Valet, $19	N	N	
Lot, $19	N	N	
Valet, $28	N	Y	

Hotel	Overall Quality	Room Quality	Zone	Address
Shoney's Inn	★★½	58	10	2421 Clearview Parkway Metairie, 70001
Soniat House	★★★½	80	1	1133 Chartres Street New Orleans, 70116
St. Charles Inn	★★½	59	3	3636 St. Charles Avenue New Orleans, 70115
St. Peter Guest House	★★	54	1	1005 St. Peter Street New Orleans, 70116
Super 8 New Orleans	★★½	58	8	6322 Chef Menteur Highway New Orleans, 70126
Travelodge Hotel New Orleans	★★	48	11	2200 Westbank Expressway Harvey, 70058
Travelodge New Orleans Airport Hotel	★★½	58	10	2240 Veterans Memorial Boulevard Kenner, 70062
Travelodge New Orleans Metairie	★★	47	10	5733 Airline Highway Metairie, 70003
W French Quarter	★★★½	80	1	316 Chartres Street New Orleans, 70130
Windsor Court	★★★★½	95	2	300 Gravier Street New Orleans, 70130
Wingate Inn	★★★	72	10	1501 Veterans Memorial Boulevard Kenner, 70062
Wyndham Canal Place	★★★★½	90	1	100 Rue Iberville New Orleans, 70130
Wyndham Galleria	★★★★	84	9	Galleria Boulevard Metairie, 70005
Wyndham Riverfront Hotel	★★★★	85	2	701 Convention Center Boulevard New Orleans, 70130

Phone	Fax	Reservations	Cost	# of Rooms
(504) 456-9081	(504) 455-6287	(800) 552-4667	$+	146
(504) 522-0570	(504) 522-7208	(800) 544-8808	$$$$	33
(504) 899-8888	(504) 899-8892	(800) 489-9908	$+	40
(504) 524-9232	(504) 523-5198	(800) 535-7815	$$+	28
(504) 241-5650	(504) 241-2178	(800) 800-8000	$	96
(504) 366-5311	(504) 368-2774	(800) 578-7878	$+	210
(504) 469-7341	(504) 469-7922	(800) 578-7878	$+	197
(504) 733-1550	(504) 733-1554	(800) 578-7878	$+	80
(504) 581-1200	(504) 523-2910	(800) 448-4927	$$$$$$ $$$$	98
(504) 523-6000	(504) 596-4749	(800) 262-2662	$$$$$$$	324
(504) 305-1501	(504) 305-1500	(800) 228-1000	$$$−	102
(504) 566-7006	(504) 553-5120	(800) WYNDHAM	$$$$$$+	438
(504) 837-6707	(504) 837-6906	(800) WYNDHAM	$$+	182
(504) 524-8200	(504) 524-0600	(800) WYNDHAM	$$$$$$	202

Hotel	Pool	Sauna	Room Service
Shoney's Inn	Y	N	N
Soniat House	N	N	N
St. Charles Inn	N	N	N
St. Peter Guest House	N	N	N
Super 8 New Orleans	Y	N	N
Travelodge Hotel New Orleans	Y	N	Y
Travelodge New Orleans Airport Hotel	Y	Y	Y
Travelodge New Orleans Metairie	Y	N	N
W French Quarter	Y	N	Y
Windsor Court	Y	Y	Y
Wingate Inn	N	Y	N
Wyndham Canal Place	Y	N	Y
Wyndham Galleria	Y	N	Y
Wyndham Riverfront Hotel	N	N	Y

Parking	Breakfast	Exercise Room
Street	Continental	N
Valet, $19	N	N
Street	Continental	N
Valet, $18	Continental	N
Free lot	Continental	N
Free lot	Continental	N
Free lot	N	N
Free lot	N	N
Valet, $32	N	N
Lot, $22	N	Y
Free lot	Continental	Y
Valet, $25; lot, $12	N	Y
Free lot	N	Y
Valet, $25	N	Y

Part Five

Visiting New Orleans on Business

New Orleans Lodging for Business Travelers

The primary hotel considerations for business travelers are affordability and proximity to the site or area where you will transact your business. Identify the zone(s) where your business will take you, and then use the hotel chart to cross-reference the hotels located in that area. Once you have developed a short list of possible hotels that are conveniently located, fit your budget, and offer the standard of accommodations you require, you (or your travel agent) can make use of the cost-saving suggestions discussed in the previous part to obtain the lowest rate.

Lodging Convenient to Morial Convention Center

If you are attending a meeting or trade show at **Morial Convention Center,** the most convenient lodging is in the Central Business District or in the French Quarter. Closest to the convention center are the **Hampton Inn and Suites** and the **Hilton Garden Inn** directly across the street, and the **Residence Inn** on St. Joseph. Next are the **Embassy Suites,** the **Holiday Inn Select** and the **Wyndham Riverfront Hotel.** The hotels on Canal Street and those in the western side of the French Quarter are also within decent proximity. Two Vieux Carré shuttle bus routes combine with the Riverfront Streetcar to make commuting from the French Quarter to the convention center easy. It takes about 10–12 minutes to walk from the exhibit halls to the river end of Canal Street and about 5–12 minutes more to reach hotels in the upper Quarter (between St. Peter and Canal streets). Parking is available at the convention center, but it is expensive and not all that convenient. We recommend that you leave your car at home and use shuttles, streetcars, or cabs.

Commuting to Morial Convention Center from the suburbs or the airports during rush hour should be avoided, if possible. If you want a room near the convention center, book early—very early. If you need a room at the last minute, try a wholesaler or reservation service, or one of the strategies listed below.

Convention Rates:
How They Work and How to Do Better

If you are attending a major convention or trade show, the meeting's sponsoring organization probably has negotiated convention rates with a number of hotels. Under this arrangement, hotels agree to block a certain number of rooms at an agreed-upon price for conventioneers. Sometimes, as in the case of a small meeting, only one hotel is involved. In the event of a large convention at Morial Convention Center, however, a high percentage of Central Business District and larger French Quarter hotels will participate in the room block.

Because the convention sponsor brings a lot of business to the city and reserves a large number of rooms, it usually can negotiate a volume discount on the room rate, a rate that should be substantially below rack rate. The bottom line, however, is that some conventions and trade shows have more bargaining clout and negotiating skill than others. Hence, your convention sponsor may or may not be able to obtain the lowest possible rate.

Once a convention or trade-show sponsor has completed negotiations with participating hotels, it will send its attendees a housing list that includes all the hotels serving the convention, along with the special convention rate for each. When you receive the housing list, you can compare the convention rates with the rates obtainable using the strategies listed below. If the negotiated convention rate doesn't sound like a good deal, you can try to reserve a room using a half-price club, a consolidator, a reservations service, or a tour operator. Remember, however, that many of the deep discounts are available only when the hotel expects to be at less than 80% occupancy, a condition that rarely prevails when a big convention comes to town.

Strategies for Beating Convention Rates

There are several tactics for getting around convention rates:

1. Reserve early. Most big conventions and trade shows announce meeting sites one to three years in advance. Get your reservation booked as far in advance as possible using a half-price club. If you book well ahead of the time the convention sponsor sends out the housing list, chances are good that the hotel will accept your reservation.

2. Compare your convention's housing list with the list of hotels presented in this guide. You may be able to find a suitable hotel that is not on the housing list.

3. Use a local reservations service, a wholesaler, or a room consolidator. This is also a good strategy to employ if you need to make reservations at the last minute. Local reservations services, wholesalers, and consolidators almost always control some rooms, even in the midst of a huge convention or trade show.

The Ernest N. Morial Convention Center

The Ernest N. Morial Convention Center is located at 900 Convention Center Boulevard, New Orleans, LA 70130. The phone number is 582-3023, the fax is 582-3088; the website is **www.mccno.com.**

The Morial Convention Center includes 1.1 million square feet of contiguous exhibit space under one roof since its Phase III expansion was completed in early 1999. All this muscle backs up to and stretches out along the bank of the Mississippi. The front of the Center runs along South Front Street, also called Convention Center Boulevard, reached easily from Interstate 10 by the Tchoupitoulas/St. Peter exit. For pedestrians attending an event at the Convention Center, the battle is won after you've found the front door. For many attendees coming from the Canal Street major hotels and the French Quarter lodgings, the way in is simply not clear from a distance, nor is it distinctly marked once you come to it. The primary entrance is on Convention Center Boulevard, but the doors are actually perpendicular to the street, not parallel to the facade. The entrance is not marked by a plaza, flags, sculpture, or a fountain—nothing really shouts, "Enter Here!"

This only poses a problem on that first critical day of registration when many people still feel disoriented. The best advice is to head for the Riverwalk Marketplace shopping center, which is highly visible on the Mississippi at Canal, Poydras, and Julia streets. As you face it (and the River), go to your right and have faith that the door will appear. It is a low-key ramp leading to a series of glass doors. Once you're inside, the facility is very well marked. The exhibit halls are alphabetically labeled, with "A" nearest the main entrance.

If the original architect missed the downbeat, the Convention Center administration does its best to set the right tempo. Clear, handsome promotional literature is readily available by calling the marketing and sales-department office. The publication details the floor plans of the facility, including the capacities of the various spaces. There are 55 spaces for highway vans and 13 freight drive-in entrances. The same brochure specifies the dimensions of these entrances, the floor load capacity (350 pounds per square foot), and a host of other details needed by exhibitors. The facility is non-union.

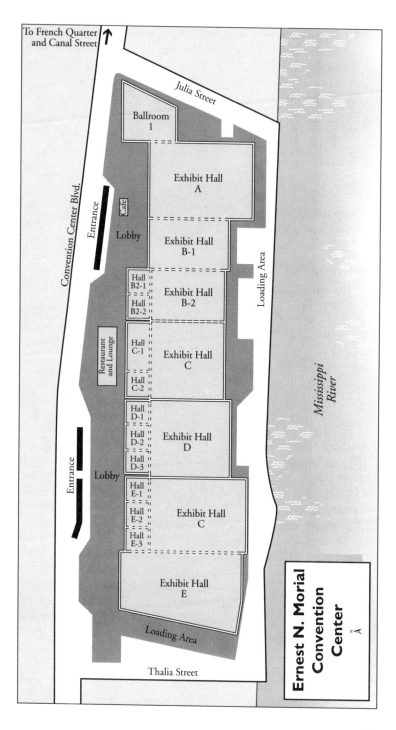

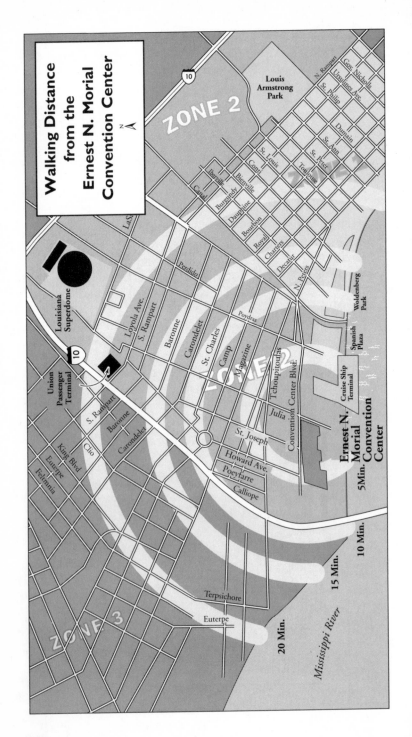

Walking Distance from the Ernest N. Morial Convention Center

ZONE 2

Louis Armstrong Park

ZONE 2

ZONE 3

Louisiana Superdome

Union Passenger Terminal

Ernest N. Morial Convention Center

Cruise Ship Terminal

Spanish Plaza

Woldenberg Park

Mississippi River

5 Min.

10 Min.

15 Min.

20 Min.

Another handy piece to help you get around is "Walking Tours of the Warehouse District & Lafayette Square: Art, History & Architecture," produced by the Downtown Development District in cooperation with the Warehouse District Arts Association. (Ask the Convention Center or the Chamber of Commerce for it. You can also find it in hotel lobby racks.) The Convention Center borders this district, and this brochure lists museums and institutions, galleries, landmarks, hotels, cafes and restaurants, and the St. Charles streetcar route, all within walking distance of the Center.

Getting Food

The food in the Center is definitely above average, and the promo literature makes much of their prize-winning chef, Leon West, who supervises the production of two kitchens, each of which can produce 20,000 meals in a 24-hour period. In the 400-seat Atrium/Restaurant Lounge you can order Cajun and Creole favorites. There are conventional concession/refreshment areas located off each exhibit hall floor. Prices are not as high as they could be, but no bargains can be found either.

If you can break free, there are several good restaurants within a 10–15-minute walk. A terrific, delicious value is at **Taqueria Corona** (857 Fulton; 524-9805), where an outstanding Mexican lunch can be yours for about $8. They also serve dinner later in the day (they're closed in the midafternoon). **True Brew Coffee** (200 Julia Street; 520-8441) can make the vegetarians happy; they also have a pastrami and pepper-cheese sandwich. Some sidewalk seating is available, and they have a bar. The **Red Bike Café** (746 Tchoupitoulas; 529-2453) specializes in bakery goods and vegetarian delights. **Ernst Café** (600 South Peters; 525-8544) offers plate lunches and sandwiches. Business people needing a quieter atmosphere can dine at the **Sugar House Restaurant** (inside the Embassy Suite Hotel at 315 Julia Street; 525-993). The muffuletta joints across the street from the Convention Center are another quick option. There are also many choices, some featuring local cuisine on short order, at the **Bon Fête Food Court** inside the Riverwalk Marketplace next door to the Convention Center.

Part Six

Arriving and Getting Oriented

Coming into the City

Nothing spoils a vacation quicker than a traffic jam, a missed connection, or a too-long walk with luggage—the sorts of misadventures that often are overlooked in the excitement of planning a trip. New Orleans happily abandons its claim to mystery when it comes to making tourists comfortable: It's well supplied with public transportation; the airport is new and efficient but not impersonal or intimidating; and once you sling a little lingo, you can get directions from anyone. Just take a few minutes to get organized before you cut loose.

By Plane

New Orleans Moisant International Airport (phone (504) 464-0831; **www.flymsy.com**) is located about ten miles west of New Orleans, in Kenner. At four feet above sea level, it's a frequent source of jokes about "high-flying" airstrips and so on, but it is relatively high and dry, at least compared to the surrounding area—and if you fly in, watching the complex gradually take shape from the swampland around it, you'll see why that's important.

The airport is fully wheelchair accessible, and the telephone banks in each concourse have TDD phones. Ticket counters are in the center on the upper level, with the four concourses at the ends, and information counters, concessions, and gift stands scattered about. A full-service Whitney National Bank, 24-hour automated-teller machines, and a post office are in the main central hall. There is a **Traveler's Aid Booth** (464-3522) in the east end of the lobby, as well as general information desks on both ends. The **Mutual of Omaha Business Service Center** (465-9647) office and an American Express traveler's check machine are in the west lobby. Transportation and baggage claim are downstairs, with additional ATMs; there are elevators at each end. The airport-shuttle desk downstairs (465-9780) is staffed around the clock.

New Orleans is served by more than a dozen airlines. American, Northwest/KLM, USAirways, and USAir Express all use Concourse A. Some American Airlines flights also go into the larger Concourse B, along with Continental, Continental Express, Southwest, and TWA. Aeromexico, Aviateca, LACSA, TACA, and United Air Lines all use Concourse C, and Delta uses Concourse D.

Incidentally, the rest rooms in the airport are very nice. The toilets are automatically sanitized with each flush, and motorized seat covers slip over the seats at the push of a button. All faucets are touch-free as well, operated by electric eyes.

Getting to the City from the Airport

To get from the airport to the city, you may take the **Airport Shuttle** (592-0555) for $10 per person; the van, which operates around the clock, will take you directly to the hotel. If you want to have the shuttle pick you up and take you back to the airport, call 24 hours in advance with your flight-departure information, and they will schedule a pickup.

Taxi fare from the airport is currently $28 for one or two passengers, and $12 per person for three or more. You can either pick one up off the line or contact **United Cabs** in advance (call (800) 323-3303 or 522-9711) and arrange to have a driver waiting for no additional charge. (Never accept an offer for a cab or limo made by a stranger in the terminal or baggage claim. At best, you will be significantly overcharged for the ride. At worst, you may be abducted.) A limo can be ordered from the airport shuttle service, or a luxury-class stretch limo can be hired from **London Livery** (831-0700): $103 for the six-passenger model and uniformed chauffeur—great for honeymooners. Other limousine services include **Carey Bonomolo** (523-5466), and **A Touch of Class** (522-7565). Rates from the airport to Downtown/French Quarter range from about $85–$120 (plus 15–20% for driver) for a six-passenger limo. *Hint:* If you want a showy chauffeur during any of the special events in town (i.e., Super Bowl or Mardi Gras), better call in early.

A **Jefferson Transit** (818-1077; **www.jeffersontransit.org**) express bus to the Central Business District puts you within a few blocks' walking distance of many of the newer hotels along Canal Street; it costs only $1.50, which may be the best choice if you are not lugging tons of baggage. The bus leaves the airport every 20 minutes or so, but it is available only between 6 a.m. and 6:30 p.m. The terminus is on Tulane Avenue between Elks Place and South Saratoga Street.

There are also regular **Regional Transit Authority** buses that may serve your route; call RTA at 827-7802 for exact times; or visit the website at **wwwregionaltransit.org.** (For more on RTA passes, see "Public Transportation" in Part Seven, Getting around New Orleans.)

The rent-a-car counters are in the lower level of the airport: **Hertz,** (800) 654-3131; **Avis,** (800) 331-1212; **Budget,** (800) 527-0700; **National,** (800) 227-7368; and **Thrifty,** (800) 847-4389, are all on site and also have second offices downtown, if for some reason you don't want to return the car to the airport. **Alamo,** (800) 327-9633, has an airport lot only. From the rental-car lots, signs will direct you onto Interstate 10 to the city (be sure to read "By Car" below).

For Private Planes

There is a small private airstrip for those who fly or charter their own aircraft. **New Orleans Lakefront Airport,** on the south side of Lake Pontchartrain, also has some rentals; call 243-4010 or 241-9400, or visit **www.lakefrontairport.com** for more information.

By Car

New Orleans is connected to the interstate highway system by Interstate 10, which goes pretty much right through the city east and west, with a few tricky spots. One thing to remember is that I-10 makes an unusual V-dip toward the French Quarter and Central Business District (CBD), while I-610 sails straight across the midcity region and dumps you back out on I-10 at the east end of town; it won't get you where you want to go, and it is a rush-hour trap of the first order. The other thing to know is that there is no marked French Quarter exit off I-10; it's marked Vieux Carré, Exit 235A. (If your hotel is along Canal Street in the CBD, take the Poydras Street exit.) Signage is not particularly good here in any case, and turn signal indicators seem to be a lost art, so be careful.

If you are driving in from the east along I-10, there is a Visitors Information Center at the Paris Road exit where you can pick up brochures, maps, discount coupons, and coffee, and make last-minute hotel reservations, if necessary.

East-west US 61 is Airline Highway, the older route from Kenner into the city, and becomes Tulane Avenue heading to the CBD near the French Quarter. US 90, also called the Old Spanish Trail, makes a squiggly circle around the river, curving around uptown and the West Bank before scooting back south and west toward New Iberia and Lafayette. (US 90 is the scenic route to Cajun country, but you can take I-10 nearly to Lafayette and on to Baton Rouge.)

Interstate 12 runs east-west as well, but along the north shore of Lake Pontchartrain, as if putting a lid on the bowl of I-10. From I-12 you can take either I-59 or I-56 south. The 24-mile-long Lake Pontchartrain Causeway (toll road) is the world's longest over-water bridge, and it's a beautiful drive; sometimes you can see nothing but sky and water, and sometimes even glimpses of the skyline or sailboat fleets. The causeway comes straight south and joins I-10, US 61/Airline Highway, US 90/Claiborne Avenue, and so on. Interstate 59 (north-south) intersects I-10 east of the city; I-56 from Jackson, Mississippi, joins I-10 west of the city.

By Bus or Train

Greyhound Bus Lines coaches (call (800) 231-2222) roll into Union Terminal at Loyola and Howard Avenues at the edge of the Central Business District not far from the Superdome. Ticket counters are open 24 hours.

Union Terminal is also the **Amtrak** station (call (800) 872-7245 or 524-7571) with connections to New York/Washington, Miami, Los Angeles, and Chicago. Ticket counters are open 24 hours (check for senior-citizen discounts and special fares). There is a taxi stop outside the terminal, of course.

Where to Find Tourist Information in New Orleans

You can get an amazing amount of material and background from the **New Orleans Metropolitan Convention and Visitors Bureau** (1520 Sugar Bowl Drive, New Orleans, LA 70112-1259; 566-5011), which also operates information centers within each terminal of the New Orleans Moisant International Airport. For specialized information, contact the **Greater New Orleans Multicultural Tourism Network** (523-5652). In the French Quarter itself, there is a combined **Louisiana state welcome office** and **NOMCVB info center** right on Jackson Square in the Pontalba Apartments (529 St. Ann Street; 566-5011) that has hundreds of brochures on attractions and tours and street maps. And the visitors bureau also distributes these brochures on a motorized cart that stops during the day at such gathering spots as Union Terminal, Aquarium of the Americas, Spanish Plaza, the Louisiana Children's Museum, and the 600 block of Canal Street.

If you have trouble, contact the **Traveler's Aid Society** (464-3522) or stop by the booth in the east lobby of the airport.

Once you are in town, the main source of information on special events, sports, arts, and tours is the *Times-Picayune,* which has an entertainment calendar every day and a special pull-out section on Fridays, called "Lagniappe," devoted to recreation and family fun. Among the free magazines you'll see around town and in hotel and restaurant lobbies are *OffBeat,* which covers the local music and nightlife scene (you can peruse it in advance at **www.nola.com**), *Gambit, Arrive,* and *Where. Ambush* magazine (**www.ambushmag.com**) and *Impact Gulf South News* are gay-and-lesbian publications. Or check in bookstores for *New Orleans Magazine* and the black-oriented monthly *New Orleans Tribune.*

Getting Oriented

New Orleans geography is confusing (even for locals), because it conflicts with our notion of U.S. geography and our basic sense of north/south orientation. Louisiana is shaped like an L. New Orleans is at the bottom of the L on the east end and is sandwiched between Lake Pontchartrain to the north and the Mississippi River to the south. Most folks picture the Mississippi River as flowing due south and emptying into the Gulf of Mexico. While this is correct, generally speaking, the river happens to snake along in west-to-east fashion as it passes New Orleans, not veering south again until after Chalmette, where the battle of New Orleans was fought in the War of 1812. To the surprise of many, the mouth of the Mississippi River is actually more than five hours south of New Orleans by boat.

If you spend time in New Orleans, the presence of the lake and the river are inescapable. As you begin to explore, you will discover that much of the city is tucked into one long bend of the river and that many of the streets and highways follow the curve of that bend. The curve in question, when viewed in the customary north/south orientation, is shaped like the smile of a happy face. Although suburbs and industrial areas parallel the river both east and west of the smile (and also across the river—south of the smile), the areas of the city most interesting to visitors are located within the curve. This curve, or smile as we put it, is why New Orleans is called The Crescent City.

The oldest part of the city, the French Quarter or Vieux Carré, is situated at the right (east) corner of the smile, while the University District, with Tulane and Loyola Universities, is located at the left (west) corner. Moving from the right corner toward the bottom of the smile, you will leave the French Quarter, cross Canal Street, and enter the Warehouse/Arts and Central Business Districts. The Central Business District is New Orleans's *real* downtown. The warehouses line the river and serve the city's bustling port.

If you look at a map of downtown, you will notice that all the streets emanating from the French Quarter change names after they cross Canal Street. Royal Street in the French Quarter becomes St. Charles Avenue in the business district (easy to remember if you think of King Charles) and parallels the river like a mustache above the smile. On St. Charles, you can drive or take the St. Charles streetcar around the curve of the smile to visit some of New Orleans's most interesting neighborhoods. As you work down the smile to the bicuspids and incisors, you will encounter the Arts District, the Irish Channel, the Garden District, and finally, the University District, including Audubon Park (described in Part Eight, Sight-Seeing, Tours, and Attractions).

If you are driving in New Orleans, picture holding a fan upside-down over the happy face. Position the fan so that the handle points north toward the lake and the curved spread of the fan aligns with the bend in the river (the smile). Tchoupitoulas Street runs at the edge of the fan along the river. A few blocks inland is St. Charles, paralleling both Tchoupitoulas and the river. Farther away from the river toward the handle is Claiborne

Avenue, following the same crescent-shaped route. The sides of the fan angling up to the handle are Esplanade on the right (east) and Carrollton on the left (west). The handle of the fan extends to the lake and includes City Park. Tourists, convention-goers, and most business visitors spend the vast majority of their time within the area of the fan.

Just outside the fan to the west is Metairie, where you can access the Lake Pontchartrain Causeway. Farther west is Kenner and the airport. To the northeast is Elysian Fields and Gentilly, where you will find Dillard and Southern Universities, the University of New Orleans, and Pontchartrain Park. To the southeast along the river is the Chalmette Battlefield, Jean Lafitte National Historic Park, and Pakenham Oaks.

Finding Your Way around the French Quarter

While orientation in the greater New Orleans area tends to be confusing, finding your way around the French Quarter is a cinch. The French Quarter is rectangular and arranged in a grid, like Midtown Manhattan. The river forms one long side of the rectangle, and Rampart Street forms the other. The short sides of the rectangle are Canal Street, New Orleans's main downtown thoroughfare, and Esplanade Avenue.

The longer streets paralleling the river are the French Quarter's primary commercial, traffic, and pedestrian arteries. Moving from the river inland, these streets are Decatur, Chartres, Royal, Bourbon, Dauphine, Burgundy, and Rampart. The more commercially developed blocks toward Canal Street are traditionally known as the Upper Quarter, while the quieter, more residential blocks toward Esplanade are called the Lower Quarter.

As recently as 30 years ago, upper Decatur, next to the river, was the domain of visiting sailors and home of the fabled Jax Brewery. Lower Decatur then, as now, was home to the French Market. With the closing of the brewery and the advent of the Riverwalk promenade, Decatur was effectively sanitized and turned into a souvenir shopping mall and restaurant venue. St. Louis Cathedral and Jackson Square face Decatur, and most of the modern tourist development is between Jackson Square and Canal Street. Moving down Decatur toward Esplanade is a rejuvenated French Market, the timeless Café du Monde, and the Central Grocery, with its signature muffuletta Italian sandwich.

Heading away from the river, you'll come to Chartres, with its galleries, restaurants, cozy taverns, and small hotels. Chartres, perhaps more than any other French Quarter street, has maintained its historic identity. Commerce rules here, as elsewhere, but it's softer, less crass, and much more respectful of its heritage.

Royal, the next street over, has always been the patrician of the Quarter's main thoroughfares. Lined with antique and art galleries, as well as some of the city's most famous restaurants, hotels, and architecture, Royal Street is the prestige address of the Vieux Carré.

One block walking takes you from the grand and sophisticated to the carnal and crass: you have arrived on Bourbon Street. While Bourbon Street has always appealed to more primitive instincts, it did so within the worn, steamy context of its colorful past. But today, Bourbon Street is a parody of itself, a plastic corporate version of the honky-tonks, burlesque shows, and diners that molded its image. Between the T-shirt shops, trendy bars, and modern, upscale strip clubs, you can still find a few survivors from Bourbon Street's halcyon days, but they are an endangered species.

Burgundy and Dauphine, the two streets between Bourbon and the boundary of the French Quarter at Rampart Street, were once primarily residential. During the past two decades, however, homes have made way for small hotels, shops, and restaurants. Burgundy and Dauphine, while less architecturally compelling than Royal or Chartres, are nonetheless quite lovely. Quieter and less commercial than the streets between Bourbon and the river, Burgundy and Dauphine provide a glimpse of what the Quarter was like when it was still a thriving neighborhood.

Rampart Street, like Canal and Esplanade, is essentially a border street: broad, heavily trafficked, and very different from the streets within the French Quarter. Twelve streets run from Rampart to Decatur, intersecting the main commercial thoroughfares discussed above and completing the grid.

St. Peter and St. Ann Streets bisect the Vieux Carré halfway between Canal and Esplanade. St. Peter, especially the block between Bourbon and Royal, is regarded by many as the "heart of the Quarter." Most of the tourist and commercial activity in the French Quarter occurs toward Canal Street, and from Bourbon Street down to the river. Except for lower Decatur and the French Market, the Esplanade half of the Vieux Carré remains residential, albeit with an increasing number of proprietary hotels and guest houses.

Things the Natives Already Know

New Orleans Customs and Protocol

New Orleans is a city that prides itself on Southern hospitality, and most residents and business owners have learned to be very patient with tourists. They need to be. And so may you.

To be blunt about it, for all the mutterings about crime you will hear from locals (see "How to Avoid Crime and Keep Safe in Public Places," below), it's almost certain that the biggest problem you'll run into in New Orleans is other tourists, particularly on Bourbon Street. Women will have to be prepared for a few juvenile remarks from the inebriated and the eternally self-deluded (amazing how attractive some people seem to consider themselves). There is a vital gay community here, and gay and lesbian visitors are welcome, but as always, there may be a few ill-mannered heteros to ignore. And a few visitors may be taken aback by the number of extravagantly dressed punksters on the streets, with their Technicolor spiked hair and heavy leathers. Longtime locals seem to find them a little scary, but they don't seem particularly interested in bothering anyone so far as we can tell. And there are more panhandlers than there used to be, though most of them will spin you a tale rather than just accost you.

Otherwise, just go by what you might call the flip side of the Golden Rule: Do nothing unto others that would be embarrassing if done unto you.

Incidentally, sections of the French Quarter—specifically parts of Bourbon Street, Royal, and some areas around Jackson Square—are often closed to cars, encouraging pedestrian traffic. And many intersections have stop signs in both directions (these are one-way streets, remember). But don't let that lead you into dropping your guard on other streets. Just be aware of where you are, or you may find yourself stepping in front of a moving vehicle.

Talking the Talk

Ironically, for a city with so many obvious European influences, New Orleans talks with a very American accent. (So American, in fact, that a lot of "dese guys," especially the ones with roots in the Irish Channel and Metairie, sound as if they just disembarked from Brooklyn or New Jersey, because they come from the same river roustabout stock.)

What that means for outsiders is that local names can be wildly confusing—not to mention the name of the city itself. Much has been written about how to say it (and to be fair, there isn't an easy answer), but what it is *not,* is Nawlins, in two syllables, or Noo OrLEENS in three or New Or-Lee-Uns in four. It's something in between: Noo-AW-lins, or, in what's left of the Creole dialect, New-YAW-yuns, with the first two syllables blending together, sort of two-and-a-half beats. Unfortunately, Orleans Street *is* pronounced Or-LEENS, and so is Orleans Parish.

Then comes the Vieux Carré (View Kah-RAY), the original name for the French Quarter; it's one of the few things around that are still spoken with a French accent aside from beignets (ben-YAYS), Arnaud's (Ar-KNOWS), and Treme and Faubourg Marigny (TRUH-may and FOH-burg MARE-in-yee), the neighborhoods adjoining the Vieux Carré. Metairie is pronounced MET-uh-ree; Pontchartrain is PAWN-cha-tren. And Marie Laveau is mar-EE lah-VOH, Jean Lafitte is ZHAWN lah-FEET, and Mardi Gras is MAR-dee GRAH, of course.

Most confusing of all are the street names, which have in many cases been translated first from Spanish to French (memorialized on blue-and-white tile signs on the sides of buildings at intersections throughout the French

Quarter), and then from French to fractured French, or to Italianese, or occasionally to English (for example, most people say Royal Street now, though you will still see Rue Royale on some business cards).

Burgundy is pronounced bur-GUN-dee; Conti is con-TIE; Chartres is CHAR-ters; Esplanade is es-pluh-NADE; Carondelet is kuh-ron-duh-LET (not LAY); Milan is MY-lun; and Iberville is EYE-ber-ville.

Even worse is what happened to the classic Greek names of the Muses east of the Garden District: Terpsichore is TERP-si-core; Calliope is KAL-ee-ope; Clio is KLIE-oh; Melpomene is MEL-poe-mean; and so on.

The Indian Tchoupitoulas is easier than it looks, like an old tomahawk joke on "Laugh-In": chop-it-TOOL-us.

As for the city's various nicknames—"The Big Easy," "Crescent City," or the older "Paris of America" and "The City That Care Forgot"—none is particularly popular, and you probably will never hear a resident use one.

Incidentally, although it works wonderfully in literary sense to speak of Desire, as in *A Streetcar Named Desire,* the line's destination was originally pronounced Desiré (dez-ih-RAY), a popular woman's name, and like many other ladies' names was applied to a wharf—just in case you wondered.

Dress

In a town as hot and humid as New Orleans, only bankers, lawyers, and maitres d' regularly wear suits. That's something of an exaggeration, but not much: what it really boils down to is that self-respecting New Orleanians dress, tourists don't. Decades of Southern culture still persuade many women to wear dresses and hose, and you'll notice the docents and information ladies usually do. The minimum "dress" for women is nice earrings and long pants rather than shorts, shoes rather than athletic wear or sandals for men. But again, this is a tourist town, and you're on vacation, so you can decide how much you care about sticking out or fitting in. Except for social occasions, you're not likely to be penalized for wearing shorts or sports clothes anywhere around town. It's just that those who do dress neatly may get better treatment or tables than those who don't.

Even at night, only a few restaurants ask men to wear a jacket, mostly the older standbys such as Antoine's and Arnaud's. But "dressy casual" is the style at most of the new celebrity spots such as Nola, Emeril's, and Mr. B's, and you may feel more comfortable in a jacket, even wearing it over a golf shirt or nice T-shirt—that is, unmarked and monotone, à la Don Johnson. The most famous exception is Galatoire's, which continues to demand jacket and tie at dinner and all day Sunday.

Eating in Restaurants

New Orleans fare may be famous, but it's not all that varied. Continental, Creole (which is very similar, but has kept more traditional, rich cream sauces than modern Continental), and Cajun styles dominate, particularly in the areas tourists are most likely to visit. And to be honest, you may find several days of such food not only filling but a trifle too rich; go slow. Most other restaurants are either new-American or Italian (or franchised).

Compared to many cities, the number of restaurants in New Orleans that do not accept reservations is fairly high. (During Mardi Gras, you may not find anybody willing to take a reservation.) Standing in line at Galatoire's, where the host is amazingly deft at juggling parties in his head, and at K-Paul's Louisiana Kitchen, where you may share your table with another party, is the stuff of legend. (K-Paul's now takes reservations for its upstairs dining room.)

As a rule, the restaurants that require reservations tend to be the same ones that require a jacket. In the same way, however, many of those would be willing to seat you, perhaps at the bar, if you are dressed at least neatly.

(A tip for dining at Antoine's: If you can make a reservation with a particular waiter, you can enter through the unmarked door just to the left of the main entrance, go down the hallway, ask for said waiter, and be seated with a little more respect and speed than if you just arrive at the "tourist" entrance. This probably means, however, that you have a friend who is a regular there—in which case you should get him to take you, anyway—or you should become a repeat customer.)

It shouldn't require saying, but having seen too many slightly overexuberant tourists trying to slip into restaurants past the queue, we will say it: Please be considerate and stay in place. Besides, these hosts are pros; they'll catch you.

Tipping (and Stripping)

New Orleans is a service-oriented economy, and you should expect to recognize that. The going tip rate for bartenders or waiters and taxi drivers is 15–20%, although if you use them as sources of local information—which is always a good bet—add a dollar for luck. In your hotel, you should leave the maids at least $1 per day of your stay, and it really should be $2. If there is a bellman, give him $1 per suitcase, and while it isn't quite rude not to slip the doorman a buck for getting you a taxi, it never hurts. After all, it might be a longer wait next time.

As for tipping strippers, it's usually $1 in one of the older, cheaper joints, or $5 for something special (you will probably be offered a "table dance," which offers a sort of up-close-and-personal view). In the really upscale places, such as Maiden Voyage or Rick's, the going rate may be a little higher, but it's up to you. Total nudity is prohibited, so there will be some sort of G-string, skimpy bathing suit, or garter to tuck it into.

However, there are a few strip-joint no-nos you should be aware of (all common sense, but as we've said, the behavior of some tourists will astound you): Absolutely no fondling of the dancers is allowed, and you may find the dancers ready to retaliate if you try. If you visit a burlesque house (this reminder more often applies to women who are escorted by men), behave yourself; don't make faces, denigrate the dancers, or pull on your escort to get away. If you are offended by the spectacle, don't go.

New Orleans on the Air

Aside from the usual babble of format rock, talk, easy-listening, and country-music stations, New Orleans is home to a few stations that really stand out for high-quality broadcasting. Tune in to what hip locals are listening to.

NEW ORLEANS'S RADIO STATIONS

Station	Frequency	Format
WWNO	89.9 FM	National Public Radio
WWOZ	90.7 FM	Lots of music with local history
WQUE	93.3 FM	Hip-hop, soul, R&B
WEZB	97.1 FM	Conventional and mainstream Top-40 radio
WNOE	101.1 FM	New Orleans's country-music flagship
KKND	106.7 FM	Hottest alternative and modern rock
WODT	1280 AM	All-blues radio

How to Avoid Crime and Keep Safe in Public Places

Crime in New Orleans

From the news clips of Mardi Gras, New Orleans may seem like an X-rated Disney World, but this is real life—and it's real life in a city with big gaps in income levels and housing. That, combined with a history of police corruption, translated into a dire and long-standing crime problem from which the city has only recently begun to recover.

New Orleans was in an unfortunate contest with Washington, D.C., for that infamous title, Murder Capital of the Nation; its murder rate was five times that of New York City, and only about a third of New Orleans murders were being solved. In 1994, homicides hit a record high of 421. New Orleans's poverty level is the third worst in the country. It is legal in New Orleans to carry a concealed weapon. And since the 1980s, crack cocaine has been big bad business here, fueling tensions and gang machismo.

While the overwhelming majority of violent crimes still occur in the poorest parts of town, around the housing projects, you cannot take for granted that you are safe even in the French Quarter. After all, that's where the rich—or at least those who appear rich by housing-project standards—are to be found.

Tourists are particularly easy marks; so are the dancers and waitstaff at bars, who earn much of their money in cash tips. During the 1996 Thanksgiving holidays, an advertising executive was raped and killed by a parking-lot attendant near the Ursuline Convent, and three of four employees of the Louisiana Pizza Kitchen in the French Market died of gunshot wounds they received during a hold up. And in May 1997, a Kentucky postal worker and father of three visiting New Orleans for a convention was shot and killed in a botched robbery as he and a companion walked through the Quarter to their hotel.

To make matters worse, the New Orleans Police Department has a long history of notorious corruption. In the last decade NOPD officers were convicted of having witnesses beaten and even executed, of robbery and murder, and of institutional extortion.

Admittedly, such reports make things sound pretty bad, and local authorities finally began to take them—and their effect on the city's reputation—seriously. The latest attempt to reform the police department began with the hiring of former D.C. deputy police chief Richard Pennington in 1994. Pennington launched a number of highly publicized police initiatives, as well as numerous anticorruption efforts, firing or disciplining hundreds of officers, hiring hundreds more, and raising salaries and standards. A private coalition of New Orleans businesses and residents kicked in the money to hire consultants Jack Maple, former deputy commissioner of the New York Police Department, and John Linder to set up a computerized "map" of the city's highest crime spots; the same method is credited with having cut the New York murder rate in half since 1993.

In general, the perception of Pennington's success is directly proportionate to the distance people live from the French Quarter. Suburban commuters think things are much better, while French Quarter residents say they never see any police except those sitting in their cars around the Royal Street precinct station. Nevertheless, crime statistics have dropped while property values have risen. In June of 2000, New Orleans was given the City Livability Award by the United States Conference of Mayors, placing the city first among 14 other major cities. The award came as a result of police reform and crime reduction.

Still, you should be careful, as you would in any major city. The whole French Quarter is pretty safe during the day, but after dark you should stick to the more populated streets—Bourbon, Royal, Chartres, Decatur, Canal, and Dauphine; and Burgundy between Dumaine and Canal—and even then you should be wary of the outer blocks. Avoid walking alone outside the commercial areas, and be sure not to flash your personal belongings if you do. Jackson Square is a good bet at all hours, thanks to the round-the-clock crowd at the Café du Monde. Still, travel in a group or take a cab; if you aren't sure how safe an area is, ask one of the locals.

The cemeteries may seem pretty quiet, but they have become particularly dangerous to visitors wandering about; even in daylight, you should go only with a tour or at least several friends. Audubon Park and City Park are both fine and busy during the day, but again, you shouldn't be strolling through them after sunset, and you should probably avoid Armstrong Park altogether, at least until the city's elaborate plans to fix it up as a community music center and to secure it are complete. Although the St. Charles Streetcar runs 24 hours a day, it's best to use it in the wee hours only if your destination is within sight of the stop, or perhaps if you just want to take a round trip to view the great houses of the Garden District lit up.

Don't leave a lot of money or traveler's checks in your hotel room; even though the employees are probably dependable, the older, smaller buildings are not exactly inaccessible. And if you buy any valuable antiques of the sort that can be easily pawned, such as silver or gems, ask the hotel to lock them in the safe.

Unless you actually drove into the city, you will find that you don't really want a car. Wait until you're headed into the country to rent one, or just take a cab. Parking can be tough and several days' parking is quite expensive; traffic customs carry more weight than laws in some cases. Tickets are stiff, and unless you're familiar with all the one-way roads and eccentric highway signage, you can make life harder on yourself. Besides, a parked car is another target for criminals and drunks.

The worst time, not surprisingly, is around Mardi Gras, when the throngs and lubrication invite pickpockets. In any case, if you are accosted by a thief, don't argue; try to stay calm, and hope he or she does, too.

Crime Prevention Planning

Random violence and street crime are facts of life in any large city. You've got to be cautious and alert and plan ahead. Police are rarely able to actually foil a crime in progress. When you are out and about you must assume that you must use caution because you are on your own; if you run into trouble, it's unlikely that police or anyone else will be able to come to your rescue. You must give some advance thought to the ugly scenarios that might occur, and consider both preventive measures that will keep you out of harm's way and an escape plan just in case.

Not being a victim of street crime sort of parallels the survival of the fittest theory. Just as a lion stalks the weakest member of the antelope herd, muggers and thieves target the easiest victims. Simply put, no matter where you are or what you are doing, you want potential felons to think of you as a bad risk.

On the Street   You seldom represent an appealing target if you are with other people and act alert. Felons gravitate toward the preoccupied, the kind found plodding along staring at the sidewalk, with both arms encumbered by briefcases or packages. Visible jewelry (on either men or women) attracts the wrong kind of attention. Men, keep your billfolds in your front trouser or coat pocket. Women, keep your purses tucked tightly under your arm; if you're wearing a jacket, put it on over your shoulder bag strap.

Carry Two Wallets   If you're really concerned about mugging, this can give you a little peace of mind. Carry one inexpensive wallet, kept in your hip pocket, containing about $20 in cash and some expired credit cards. This is the one you hand over if you're accosted. Your real credit cards and the bulk of whatever cash you have should be in either a money clip or a second wallet hidden elsewhere on your person. Women can carry a fake wallet in their purses, and keep the real one in a pocket or money belt.

If You're Approached   Police will tell you that a felon has the least amount of control over his intended victim during the first few moments of his approach. A good strategy, therefore, is to short-circuit the crime as quickly as possible. If a felon starts by demanding your money, for instance, quickly take out your billfold (preferably your fake one), and hurl it in one direction while you run shouting for help in the opposite direction. Most likely, the felon would rather collect your billfold than pursue you. If you hand over your wallet and just stand there, the felon will likely ask for your watch and jewelry next. If you're a woman, the longer you hang around, the greater your vulnerability to personal injury or rape.

Secondary Crime Scenes   Under no circumstances, police warn, should you ever allow yourself to be taken to another location—a "secondary crime scene" in police jargon. This move, they explain, provides the felon more privacy and consequently more control. A felon can rob you on the street very quickly and efficiently. If he tries to remove you to another location, whether by car or on foot, it certainly indicates that he has more in mind than robbery. Even if the felon has a gun or knife, your chances are infinitely better running away. If the felon grabs your purse, let him have it. If he grabs your jacket, slip out of it. Hanging onto your money or jacket is not worth getting mugged, raped, or murdered.

Don't Believe Anything a Criminal Says   This holds true even if he's telling you something you desperately want to believe, for example, "I won't hurt you if you come with me." No matter how logical or benign he may sound, assume the worst. Always, *always,* break off contact as quickly as possible, even if that means running.

In Public Transportation   When riding a bus, try to take a seat as close to the driver as you can; avoid riding in the back if possible. Likewise, on the streetcars, sit near the driver's or attendant's compartment. These people have a phone and can summon help in the event of trouble.

In Cabs While it is possible to hail a cab on the street in New Orleans at night, it's best to go to one of the hotel cabstands or to call a reliable cab company, remaining inside while they dispatch a cab to your door. When your cab arrives, check the driver's certificate, which must, by law, be posted on the dashboard. Address the cabbie by his last name (for example, Mr. Jones) or mention his cab number. This alerts the cab driver that you are going to remember him and/or his cab. Not only will this contribute to your safety, it will keep your cabbie from trying to run up the fare. If you are comfortable reading maps, familiarize yourself with the most direct route to your destination ahead of time; this makes the driver less likely to take a longer route so he can charge for extra mileage.

If you need to catch a cab at the train station or at one of the airports, always use the taxi queue. Taxis in the official queue are properly licensed and regulated. Never accept an offer for a cab or limo made by a stranger in the terminal or baggage claim area. At best, you will be significantly overcharged for the ride. At worst, you may be abducted.

Personal Attitude

Although some areas of every city are more dangerous than others, never assume that any area is completely safe. You can be the victim of a crime pretty much anywhere. If you go to a restaurant or night spot, use valet parking or park in a well-lighted lot. Women leaving a restaurant or club alone should never be reluctant to ask to be escorted to their car.

Never let your pride or sense of righteousness and indignation imperil your survival. This is especially difficult for many men, particularly for men in the presence of women. It makes no difference whether you are approached by an aggressive drunk, an imbalanced street person, or an actual felon, the rule is the same: forget your pride and break off contact as quickly as possible. Who cares whether the drunk insulted you, if everyone ends up safely back at the hotel? When you wake up in the hospital with a concussion and your jaw wired shut, it's too late to decide that the drunk's filthy remark wasn't really all that important.

Self-Defense

In a situation where it is impossible to run, you'll need to be prepared to defend yourself. Most police officers insist that a gun or knife is not much use to the average person. More often than not, they say, the weapon will be turned against the victim. Additionally, concealed firearms and knives are illegal in most jurisdictions. The best self-defense device for the average person is Mace. Not only is it legal in most states, it is nonlethal and easy to use.

When you shop for Mace, look for two things: it should be able to fire about eight feet, and it should have a protector cap so it won't go off by mistake in your purse or pocket. Carefully read the directions that come with your device, paying particular attention to how it should be carried and stored, and how long the active ingredients will remain potent. Wearing a rubber glove, test-fire your Mace, making sure that you fire downwind.

When you are out about town, make sure your Mace is someplace easily accessible, say, attached to your keychain. If you are a woman and you keep your Mace on a keychain, avoid the habit of dropping your keys (and your Mace) into the bowels of your purse when you leave your hotel room or your car. *Mace will not do you any good if you have to dig around in your purse for it.* Keep your keys and your Mace in your hand until you have safely reached your destination.

More Things to Avoid

When you do go out, walk with a minimum of two people whenever possible. If you have to walk alone, stay in well-lighted areas that have plenty of people around. And don't walk down alleys. Be careful about whom you ask for directions. (When in doubt, shopkeepers are a good bet.) Don't count your money in public, and carry as little cash as possible. At public phones, if you must say your calling card number to make a long-distance call, don't say it loud enough for strangers around you to hear. Avoid public parks and beaches after dark.

Carjackings

With the surge in carjackings, drivers also need to take special precautions. Keep alert when driving in traffic, and keep your doors locked, with the windows rolled up and the air conditioning on. Leave enough space in front of your car so that you're not blocked in and can make a U-turn if someone approaches your car and starts beating on your windshield. Store your purse or briefcase under your knees or seat when you are driving, rather than on the seat beside you.

Part Seven

Getting around New Orleans

New Orleans is a very hands-on, hospitable city. And the main neighborhood attractions, especially for tourists, are accessible by public transportation, give or take a taxi or two. But you will probably be asking for directions and addresses, and those are two of the most peculiar things about this idiosyncratic city. Names can be unrecognizable, and maps can seem upside down. In fact, in at least one case, west really is east, as you'll see below.

Public Transportation

As we pointed out earlier, you probably don't need or want a car in the city. Most of the time, whether you're in the French Quarter or any other neighborhood, you'll be walking. If you think you'll want a car, you should figure out exactly what excursions you want to take outside the city and only rent one for those days. Otherwise you'll have to worry about parking lots, parking tickets, and perhaps vandalism—not to mention being impounded. (If you are, call the **Claiborne Auto Pound** at 565-7450.) If you are staying at one of the larger hotels around Canal Street or in the suburbs, it may have parking (which may or may not be free). But most visitors will find the buses, streetcars, and taxis handy to any place they want to go.

By far the nicest way to get from one neighborhood to the other, or to rest your feet after a good promenade, is the streetcar. (Locals always used to call them "trolleys," but perhaps because of the heavy promotion the lines are getting these days, the word "streetcar" is gradually winning out. Still, you will sound less like a tourist if you refer to them as trolleys.)

There is one streetcar that runs the length of the Quarter, the **Riverfront Streetcar** (red trolleys), which originates near Esplanade Avenue and makes stops all the way to the Warehouse/Arts District near the Convention Center. Each trip costs $1.50. The Riverfront Streetcar operates from 6 a.m. to midnight weekdays and 8 a.m. to midnight on weekends.

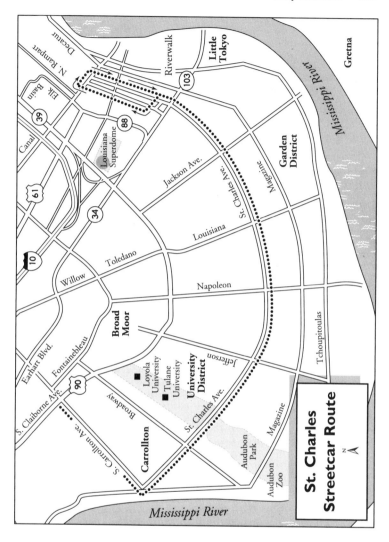

The more famous **St. Charles Avenue Streetcar** (green trolleys) originates at Canal Street and runs 24 hours a day through the Garden District past Audubon Park and Riverbend. Each one-way trip is $1.25.
But, although the St. Charles line has cars running about every 18 minutes most of the day, it runs only once an hour after midnight, so keep
that in mind if you have a late dinner planned.

A second red-line streetcar runs down the center of Canal Street to the
top of the French Quarter, and a transfer between this trolley and the
Riverfront streetcat is $0.25. Unfortunately, since the city, in a previous

face-lift, had decided the streetcar was dispensable, it had long since paved over the old Canal Street tracks, and the median had to be dug up for the tracks to be re-laid. In a few years, the resurrected streetcar will run some six miles to City Park.

The **Vieux Carré Jitney** bus route circles the French Quarter and hotel district across Dauphine and Baronne to Poydras, down Magazine to the Convention Center, and back across Chartres and Decatur—from 5 a.m. to 7:15 p.m. daily; it costs $1.25 per trip and $0.25 per transfer.

City bus trips are also $1.25 and transfers are also $0.25. Both the streetcars and the buses are operated by the Regional Transit Authority, and you can get one- or three-day VisiTour passes good for unlimited rides on any of them. A one-day pass is $5, and a three-day pass is $12. Most hotels and information centers, and many shops, sell the RTA passes, or you can buy them at the Grayline Tours kiosks around town. For bus routes and times, call the 24-hour RTA RideLine at 248-3900.

Taxicabs are pretty easy to find in the French Quarter, especially around hotels, but if you're out somewhere without a lift, call **White Fleet** (948-6605), **Yellow-Checker Cabs** (525-3311), or **United** (524-9606). New Orleans cabs run on meters—base charge $2.50, plus $1 a mile—but if you come during a special event, such as Jazz and Heritage Fest, there may be a base $3 charge in effect. Taxis can also usually be hired for a flat rate if a group of several people want to tour a few attractions; call the dispatcher's office and see what sort of deal you can get. Or if you happen to be picked up by one of the really friendly ones (and New Orleans cabbies can be hilariously well informed), find out if he freelances.

You can also rent a bicycle and combine touring and exercise: **Bicycle Michael's** has a variety of mountain bikes, three-speeders, and even bicycles built for two (622 Frenchmen Street, 945-9505). **French Quarter Bicycles** stocks mostly mountain bikes (522 Dumaine Street, 529-3136; www.fqbikes.com). Rental prices range from $5 an hour to $20 a day.

Walking the Walk

Much of New Orleans can be covered on foot, and that's a good thing, because it means you can settle for pedestrian directions such as "turn right" and "go three blocks on." What you *don't* want to get into is traditional directions—north, south, etc.—because in New Orleans, it just isn't very helpful. Because of the Mississippi River's snaking, the city somewhat resembles an open fan: although various neighborhoods have right angles within themselves, including the Garden District and the French Quarter, just about the only intersection that aligns with the compass is Napoleon Avenue and Tchoupitoulas Street.

So directions in New Orleans are given according to the biggest land-marks around: the Mississippi River and Lake Pontchartrain. Locals speak of going "toward the river" or of something's being "riverside"; an address "toward the lake" might also be "lakeside"—very roughly north. "Uptown" is above—that is, more or less west of—Canal Street, while "downtown" is said to be below, or on the French Quarter side, of Canal. That also helps tell you which is "upriver"—toward uptown—vs. "down-river." Audubon Park is upriver, as are the River Road plantations, but the French Quarter is downriver from the Garden District. Got it?

Other apparently specific directions are merely relative. South Claiborne actually goes mostly northwest, and North Claiborne swings in a curve that runs mostly east and southeast. As for the West Bank . . . it's south and east of the city, somewhere between Algiers and Gretna. The East Bank, naturally, is to the west.

Public Accommodations

The *Unofficial Guides* are starting to get a reputation for worrying about rest rooms, or rather, about your being able to find them. This is a trib-ute to the relatively short staying power of our founder, Bob Sehlinger, and someday we'll stop teasing him about it. But he has a good point: being uncomfortable doesn't help you enjoy a walking tour or a museum. And especially in summer, when New Orleans can be so hot, it's tempt-ing to drink a lot. (When, while in New Orleans, is it *not* tempting to drink a lot?)

The greatest concentration of rest rooms in the French Quarter is down near the water (no pun intended, surely): Riverwalk, Jax Brewery–Millhouse Complex, Canal Place, and World Trade Center all have good, clean bathrooms, as does the French Market (two sets, in the 900 and 1200 blocks). Across from Jackson Square, there are rest rooms in Waldenburg Park. City Park and the Audubon Park tennis courts also have public rest rooms. Museums and department stores are equipped as well. Some places have pay toilets, so it's a good idea to keep some emer-gency change around; and where there is an attendant, it's considered polite to leave a tip, though you need leave only a quarter or so—cheap by big-city standards.

The large-hotel lobbies usually have rest rooms, although you should only take advantage of them in an emergency, and when you are reason-ably well dressed. If you are really in a pinch, go to a bar and at least order a soda before you hit the john.

Part Eight

Sight-Seeing, Tours, and Attractions

The nice thing about sight-seeing is that you can choose your own pace, looking closely at what intrigues you, and pushing right on past what stirs not a flicker of interest. New Orleans is particularly well suited to walking tours, and that's what we recommend. So the latter portion of this chapter is given over to introductory walks around the most important (at least, to visitors) neighborhoods, with a little background flavor and a few landmarks for orientation. We've also suggested ways to customize your visit according to your own interests, by zeroing in on just the military sites, the otherworldly media, etc. The "inside stuff"—the museums, historic houses, and so on—are described in more detail in the next part, on "New Orleans Attractions," which also includes some general walking-tour tips.

But as we said before, we know that not everybody prefers do-it-yourself tours. Some people find it distracting to read directions and anecdotes while walking, and others use packaged tours as a way of getting a mental map of the area. So first we'll run through some of the guided tours available. (These are surely not all of them: Tourism is a boom industry in New Orleans, and you'll see flyers for new tours every month. If you want to take a guided tour, check through the material at the information desks and visitors' centers or even in your hotel lobby; you may find a discount coupon.)

In New Orleans, you can tour by land or sea, mule carriage or coach. You can see historic spots or "haunts," literary sites or cemeteries, battlefields or bayous. And you can pay nothing or, well, something.

The last thing to consider is that New Orleans is not a one-size-fits-all town. Walking is wonderful if you're young and fit, but if your party includes children or seniors, make sure to pace yourself. Build in a timely stop in a park; split the touring day into shifts, so that those with less stamina can head back to the hotel for a rest while the others continue.

Or lay out the schedule on the democratic scheme—that is, plan to visit the attractions everyone wants to see first, the could-be-missed ones later, and the only-for-fanatics excursions last. That way, whoever wants to drop out can.

If each member of the party has his own must-sees, then set a particular hour to split up and a clearly understood place to regroup—General Jackson's statue, for example. If you're worried about a teenager getting wound up in whatever museum or exhibit he's into and losing track of the time, schedule this separate tour session just before lunch; there are few things that can override a kid's stomach alarm. Finally, because the food and beverage lures are everywhere, better carry a supply of snacks in plastic bags.

Guided Sight-Seeing

Walking Tours

Members of the nonprofit **Friends of the Cabildo** lead two-hour walks that focus on the more important historic exteriors and some of the state's museum-system exhibits (see more detail on the Louisiana State Museums below and in the attraction profiles at the end of this chapter). Admission is called a "donation," and the quality of the work done on the museums in recent years gives resonance to the word. Besides, it costs only $10 for adults and $8 for those over 65 or between 13 and 20 (free for children). You can either buy tickets in advance at the Museum Store on St. Ann Street in Jackson Square (523-3939) or just arrive with the funds in hand. Tours begin daily at 10 a.m. and 1:30 p.m., except Mondays (1:30 p.m. only) and holidays.

Rangers from the **Jean Lafitte National Historical Park** (of which the Vieux Carré is part) also lead tours from their new visitors center at 419 Decatur Street (589-2636). There are two each day, one at 10:30 a.m., which lasts about 90 minutes and covers about a mile of the French Quarter; and a 3:30 p.m. walk covering various subjects. These tours are limited to 30 people, so each person must pick up a (free) pass before the walk begins.

One of the most interesting tours is **Le Monde Créole,** which explores the intertwined lives of the white and black, free and slave societies within the two sides (and four generations) of the family that owned the Laura Plantation (see the description in "Plantation Tours and Excursions," below). The family also owned seven townhouses in the Quarter, some of which the Tour can access; tours are also available in French. Walks are offered at 10:30 a.m. and 2:30 p.m. Monday through Saturday, 10 a.m. and 2:30 p.m. Sundays; reservations are required (568-1801).

Bus Tours and Trolleys

There is no shortage of tour companies—you'll find flyers at any visitors center and most hotel lobbies—but you may wish to ask a concierge or one of the volunteers at a state or city information booth as to which are the more reliable tour operators. Also, look for discount coupons for tours and attractions in brochures and tourist maps.

Gray Line Tours (569-1401 or (800) 535-7786), one of the largest operators nationwide, offers a variety of packages, including walking tours of the French Quarter and Garden District, plantation tours, and a combination tour with lunch aboard the steamboat *Natchez*. The bus tour covers the whole city, but you don't get out and really see anything. The main advantages are that a large group can arrange a tour in advance, and the buses make pick-ups from the major hotels.

More recently, Gray Line has partnered with the Audobon Institute, operators of the zoo, aquarium, and IMAX to offer "passports" to all the attractions (or to as many as you choose). For more information, consult **www.audoboninstitute.org.**

New Orleans Tours (592-0560) can arrange walking tours, cruises, nightlife jaunts, swamp tours, and combos.

Carriage Tours

These are becoming common in many cities around the country (and elsewhere—imagine Florence by open buggy), and they're the sort of thing that grabs at your nostalgic heartstrings every once in a while. The French Quarter, especially at night, lends itself to such time travel. A relatively quick two-mile route does help orient you a little, and children will definitely enjoy this.

Most of the carriages just line up along Decatur Street around Jackson Square; the cost ranges from about $10 to $60, depending on the length of the ride. There are a few things to note about such tours, however: Local color definitely doesn't stop at the bridle ribbons. The quality—the factual accuracy, not necessarily the entertainment quotient—varies tremendously, which is one reason there is a movement afoot to license carriage drivers as entertainers rather than as tour guides. And most of the horses are really mules, which doesn't really affect the ride but might affect your view of the ride's authenticity. (Some seem more aromatic than horses, but that may be imagination.) On the other hand, there are drivers usually until midnight, so you can fit this into your schedule at almost any time.

If you want a more elaborate (more expensive) personal tour, contact **Good Old Days Buggies** (523-0804); they will pick you up at your hotel or even at some of the major restaurants. **Royal Carriage** (943-8820) offers tours not only of the French Quarter but also St. Louis Cemetery No. 1 (a relatively safe way to go); the Garden District'

Faubourg Marigny; and—inevitably—a Ghost and Mystery Tour. And since they're open until midnight . . .

Special-Interest Tours

Le'Ob's Tours (288-3478) offers a look at New Orleans that focuses on special connections to African-American culture and its contribution to the city. The **Hermann-Grima/Gallier Historic Houses** (535-5661) offer a special tour on "the African-American Experience in 19th-Century New Orleans" throughout the month of February and year-round to groups of ten or more.

Lawyer/funny guy **David Naccari** offers a "hysterical" history tour; call 899-1431. **Hidden Treasures Tours** (529-4507), which range through both the Upper and Lower Garden District, emphasize women's history, including monuments and authors' homes. They will also take you inside a Garden District home and through one of the fabled New Orleans cemeteries. One nice aspect of these tours is that they'll pick you up from your hotel. Advance reservations are required; the cemetery tours are $17, and the Garden District tours are $25.

The "faculty" of **Bienville Tours** (945-6789) will lead you on tours geared to a variety of special interests, including black history, women's contributions, and gay cultural history. University of New Orleans professor Kenneth Holditch, of **Heritage Tours,** will lead you through a tour of literary-interest sites and homes (by appointment, 949-9805). **Gay Heritage** tours are offered Wednesdays and Saturdays at 1 p.m., leaving from Alternatives at 909 Bourbon Street. For two-and-a-half hours and $20, guides dish the gossip on Tennessee Williams, Truman Capote, Claw Shaw, and even Lillian Hellman; call 945-6789. If you read the French Quarter self-guided walking tour we've laid out below, you'll find quite a few of the literary spots listed.

The **Southern Comfort Cocktail Tour** (587-0861) winds through the French Quarter to track the evolution of such famous New Orleans concoctions as the Sazerac, the Hurricane, and, of course, Southern Comfort. Tours leave from the Gray Line office on Toulouse at 4 p.m. daily.

Finally, music lovers should call **Cradle of Jazz** tours to get the score on New Orleans's earliest masters (283-9136).

Walking on the Dark Side

Haunted tours, voodoo tours, and cemetery tours are all the rage in New Orleans, and you can go at practically any hour (and with guides in full capes and pointy-toothed glory, if you want). They cover essentially the same ground, so to a great extent, you just pick your style.

On the straight side is **Save Our Cemeteries** (525-3377), a nonprofit group whose proceeds go toward the restoration of these "cities of the dead." SOC offers a serious and informative tour of St. Louis No. 1 every

Sunday at 10 a.m., leaving from Royal Blend Coffee and Tea Room at 621 Royal Street, and leads tours of Lafayette Cemetery in the Garden District every Monday, Wednesday, Friday, and Saturday at 10:30 a.m; suggested donation of $6 adults, $5 seniors, and $4 students.

The longest-running haunted tours are probably those offered by the **New Orleans Historic Voodoo Museum** at 724 Rue Dumaine (523-7685). Their cemetery tour, not surprisingly, focuses on Marie Laveau's still-revered tomb and allows you to participate in a wishing ritual, but also explains why the "cities of the dead" are all above ground and shows off various personalities' resting places. The 90-minute tours begin at 10:30 a.m. and 1 p.m. daily (Sundays 10:30 a.m. only) and cost $15 apiece. Also offered is a "Singing Bones" tour (Sundays and Mondays at 4:30 p.m. for $14 per person), which explores voodoo's relationship with traditional New Orleans music. (Subtract 20% from all Voodoo Museum tour prices for groups of 10 or more and 30% for teenagers or AARP members.) Arrive 20 minutes early, and you can tour the museum for free as well.

The voodoo walking tour visits the great voodoo priestess's tomb, and covers haunted houses, Congo Square—emphasizing its history as a voodoo-ritual meeting ground rather than its musical roots—and a Catholic church with a voodoo saint among its statues. This two-and-a-half-hour tour costs $19 per person and begins Monday through Saturday at 1 p.m. and Sunday at 10:30 a.m.

And its "original" voodoo tour, the "Tour of the Undead" route, includes a visit to a voodoo temple, a live witch, and witchcraft and voodoo shops. Each participant gets a gris-gris bag to wear for protection throughout the two-hour tour ($16).

Robert Florence, who has written books on the New Orleans way of death, leads one voodoo and cemetery tour that also includes a temple visit and explores St. Louis No.1; he also leads groups through Lafayette Cemetery and other Garden District sites. The French Quarter tour leaves from the Decatur Café Beignet at 1031 Decatur Street every day at 10:30 a.m. Prices are $12 for adults, $10 for students and seniors; the two-hour tour is free for children younger than 12. Reservations are not required, but come 15 minutes early. For information, call Historic New Orleans Walking Tours at 947-2120 or visit **www.tourneworleans.com.**

The New Orleans Ghost and Vampire Tours were created by Thomas Duran, who used to lead Jack the Ripper and Sherlock Holmes tours (plus Shakespeare and Dickens tours) in London; the staff members, not surprisingly, are very into their subjects . One tour is cemetery oriented, and leaves (appropriately) from the Morgue Pub at 626 St. Philip daily at 8 p.m. ($18); the Literary Garden District tour leaves from the lobby of the Ponchartrain Hotel (streetcar stop 13) on St. Charles Monday through Saturday at 11 a.m. ($15). Both last about two hours; call 524-0708.

Magic Walking Tours (588-9693) offers a similar barrage of mystery-history—a voodoo tour, a haunted-house roundup, a cemetery tour, a vampire tour, and a ghost hunt, in addition to relatively straight neighborhood walks—but they are generally accurate as such things go (they do not mistake one old mansion with a calm history for its sanguine neighbor, as do some self-anointed tour guides). You don't have to make reservations, but the meeting place for each tour differs, so call ahead. Adult tickets range from $9 to $13; kids come along for free.

New Orleans Spirit Tours also runs a Cemetery and Voodoo Tour that leaves the Royal Blend Coffee & Tea House at 621 Royal daily at 10:30 a.m. and 1:15 p.m. (no Sunday afternoon tour); the Ghost and Vampire Tour meets every night at 8 p.m. in the lobby of the Bourbon Orleans at 717 Orleans. Tours last about two hours ($18); call 314-0806.

The **Haunted History Tours** are by far the most theatrical of the bunch—the Lafitte-cum-Lestat hosts of the vampire tours can't be beat—but they do cover a lot of ground, and in grand Gothic style. (And why not? The owners, believers both, threw themselves a vampire wedding.) The Journey into Darkness vampire tour, which focuses both on real-life sites and cinematic backgrounds, leaves every night at 8:30 p.m. from St. Louis Cathedral near the Jackson Square gates (hey, even Lestat went to church there). The Voodoo-Cemetery tour leaves from Rev. Zombie's Voodoo Shop at 723 St. Peter Street daily at 10 a.m. and Monday through Saturday at 1:15 p.m. The Haunted History Tour, which focuses on reported hauntings and paranormal readings, also leaves from Zombie's at 2 p.m. and 8 p.m. daily. And the Garden District tour, which includes both architectural discourse and the obligatory salute to Anne Rice and Lafayette Cemetery, leaves from the Ramada Plaza Hotel at the corner of St. Charles and Jackson. Again, no reservations are necessary (except for large groups), but participants are asked to come 15 minutes early. All Haunted History Tours are $18 ($9 for kids 12 and under) and last about two hours. For more information call 861-2727.

If you religiously tour beautiful churches or seek out stained glass, be sure to visit the partially restored **St. Alphonsus Church** in the Irish Channel—the fictional Mayfair family church, and Anne Rice's family's church as well—which has some of the most astonishing stained-glass panels you will ever see, a contemporary but slightly smaller replica of the Black Madonna, and at least one of the graves of Pere Antoine.

Swamp Tours

The bayous of Louisiana are among the nation's great natural treasures, filled with herons and ospreys, bald eagles, wild hogs, turtles, nutria, mink, deer, bear, and, of course, alligators. Several companies offer guided boat tours. Among the most popular is **Lil' Cajun Swamp Tours** (call 689-3213 or (800) 689-3213), whose guide, Captain Cyrus Blanchard, is as authentic as his Cajun accent and intimately familiar with the twists and turns of his home. If you can take the tour from the boat launch in Crown Point, it's $17 for adults, $15 for seniors, and $13 for children, but it's probably better to arrange with Blanchard for transportation, even though it kicks in another $14 per adult.

Honey Island Swamp Tours of Slidell (641-1769) offers professional naturalists as guides through this rich area; the cost is $20 for adults, $10 for children under age 12; tours begin at 10:30 a.m. and 1 p.m., but like Lil' Cajun, you'll pay extra for transportation from the city. **Blue Dog Seafood Tours** also operates out of Slidell (call 649-1255 or (800) 875-4287). The daylong party includes a jaunt through and even a bit beyond Honey Island Swamp, with a short nature walk thrown in. Tours cost $75 for adults, plus meals and a cooking demonstration, with the usual extra charge for pick-up.

Cajun Pride Swamp Tours combines visits to the Manchac bayou and two plantations, either Destrehan and San Francisco (Sunday, Monday, Wednesday and Friday afternoons) or Laura and Oak Alley (Tuesday, Thursday, and Saturday). Combo tours include lunch and cost $90 for adults and $65 for children. Call 467-0758 or (800) 467-0758. **Louisiana Swamp Tours** (689-3599 or (888) 30-SWAMP) has combo packages for Destrehan, airboat tours, and cruises, with costs ranging up to $80.

Other swamp tours are offered by **Jean Lafitte Swamp Tours** (592-0560) and Gray Line (569-1401 or **www.graylineneworleans.com**). For fishing tours of the bayou, see Part Eleven, Exercise and Recreation.

If you prefer the walking-tour approach to wildlife, the **Barataria Unit of the Jean Lafitte National Park** (589-2330) has trails and boardwalks through three different ecosystem routes: bottomland hardwoods, a cypress swamp, and a freshwater marsh. There are fine exhibits in the visitors center as well; take US 90 south and west of the city to state Highway 45/Barataria Boulevard and continue about seven miles.

Almost directly across Lake Pontchartrain from New Orleans, about 45 miles away on Highway 51, is the **Joyce Wildlife Management Area.** There, a 1,000-foot boardwalk strikes deep into Manchac Swamp and offers great vistas for bird watching, nature photography, and sketching. It's open sunrise to sunset. Stop by the Tangipahoa Parish visitors center (542-7520) at the Exit 28 ramp from I-55 for a free map and birding and animal guide.

A little farther is the **Global Wildlife Center** (624-9453) on Highway 40, about 15 miles east of I-55, one of only three preserves for endangered and threatened species of birds and animals in the country. It covers 900 acres and is devoted to safe breeding and free ranging of zebras, giraffes, camels (one hump and two), wildebeests, llamas, gazelles, impalas, and even kangaroos. Staffers will drive you right up to the animals for a photo op, and since many of the animals have learned to beg for treats, you may get quite a close-up—maybe even a frog. The one-

and-a-half-hour tour costs $10 for adults, $9 for seniors over age 62, and $8 for children ages 2–11; feed bags are $1 apiece.

River Cruises

Several boats cruise the nearby Mississippi River, some with meals, some with music, but to put it bluntly, a port is not the most scenic of sites. Huge tankers, rusting wharves, and old smokestacks are not exactly what Mark Twain saw when he fell in love with "Life on the Mississippi."

The paddle-wheeler steamboat *Creole Queen* (call (800) 445-4109 or 524-0814), for example, offers two-and-a-half-hour cruises leaving at 10:30 a.m. and 2:30 p.m. from in front of the IMAX/Aquarium complex to Chalmette Battlefield, site of the Battle of New Orleans. The boat churns past the old Jackson Barracks (where four commanding generals of the Civil War—P.G.T. Beauregard, Robert E. Lee, U.S. Grant, and George McLellan—all did Army time); the Doullut Houses, twin-glazed, white-brick "Victorian Steamboat Gothic" mansions; the Greek Revival–cum–French Colonial home of Rene Beauregard, planter son of the general; and Pitot House. But the Doullut and Pitot houses are surrounded by smokestacks in a way that is much more obvious from a distance, and you go back past the old naval cruiser *Cabot,* onetime berth of President Bush, and the wharves to Poydras Street. The Beauregard House is now the battlefield visitors center; you can see it up close (and walk the battlefield itself) and visit the homes, too, by yourself if you like (see attraction profiles later in this chapter). The cruise, including lunch and a 45-minute stop at the battlefield, is $23 for adults and $15 for kids ages 6–12 (without lunch, $17 and $9).

Creole Queen also offers a jazz dinner cruise at 7 p.m.; costs are $48 for adults, $25 for kids ages 6–12 ($24 and $15 without dinner). Buy your tickets at the booth by the berth in front of the IMAX.

The *Natchez* (call (800) 233-BOAT or 586-8777), a three-deck stern-wheeler that docks behind the Jax Brewery, also offers daytime and jazz dinner cruises with optional buffet; tickets for adults cost $24.50 for daytime ($15.50 sans lunch) and $49 for jazz dinner ($24.50 sans dinner).

The best cruises, especially for those with children (since a couple of hours can be a long time to have to sit still), are probably the **John James Audubon Aquarium–Zoo** cruise or the free *Canal Street Ferry* across to Algiers (and perhaps Blaine Kern's Mardi Gras World). The *John James Audubon* cruises the seven miles between the Aquarium of the Americas and the Audubon Zoo. It leaves the Aquarium at 10 a.m., noon, 2 p.m., and 4 p.m., and comes back from the zoo at 11 a.m., 1 p.m., 3 p.m., and 5 p.m. Ticket prices vary, but you can expect to pay about $16.50 for an adult fare; there are various combination fares that save you some money. Boat/aquarium passes are $24.50 and $12.25, boat/zoo passes are $22.50 and $11.25, and so on. Tickets to all four attractions—the zoo, aquarium,

IMAX, and a round-trip cruise ticket—are $38.75 adults and $11.25 kids. For more information, call (800) 233-boat or 586-8777.

The *Canal Street Ferry* just putters back and forth every day except Christmas to Algiers, touching the foot of Canal Street every half hour from 6 a.m. to 11:30 p.m., with the last trip returning at midnight. (The ferry spends the night in Algiers, which you don't want to do.) If you want to visit Mardi Gras World, you can pick up a free shuttle bus at the Algiers dock.

There are also various overnight trips on the paddle wheelers **Delta Queen, Mississippi Queen,** and their younger sibling, the **American Queen.** The *Delta Queen* is a true wooden ship, while the two larger ones are steel ribbed, but all have etched glass, bright trim, antebellum-costumed staff, and so on. These are three-day to fortnight-long trips, and take you out of New Orleans to see Natchez and Memphis. Call (800) 543-1949 or 586-0631.

Self-Guided Tours

Exploring New Orleans's Diversity

New Orleans has a pleasant case of multiple-personality syndrome. Even in between the big festivals, you can indulge in self-designed tours spotlighting Mardi Gras, music or literature, Creole society, or history; or you can fill your days (and nights) dabbling in that suddenly pervasive supernatural stuff, hauntings and voodoo and vampire lore. If you're sticking to the family-rated attractions, such as those mentioned in Part Two, Planning Your Visit to New Orleans, you'll be pleased to see how many of them are indoors, so you won't have to worry about the rainy-day blahs, which always hit kids the hardest.

Of course, not all attractions are encased in cemetery stone or museum glass. One easy thing to do is to check through the local papers for announcements of the week's cultural offerings (this is true for music, garden, church, and home tours, as well as special receptions and taste-of-the-town events, many of which may be held in historic sites or houses of special interest).

The *Times-Picayune* newspaper produces a special section on Fridays called "Lagniappe," which lists the best events—concerts, exhibits, tastings, art openings, even flea markets—of the weekend; this is also where you'll find cultural calendars. And remember that bookstores and coffee shops are traditionally neighborhood "bulletin boards" for such events.

But for a few informal do-it-yourself tour ideas, read on. Most of the sites in boldface are described in more detail in the attraction profiles later in this chapter or in Part Ten, Shopping in New Orleans.

Mardi Gras and Music

Hangover-wary veterans of Carnival celebrations, or those who prefer the more sophisticated Mardi Gras parades of earlier decades, can get their fill of the frills by visiting the **Old U.S. Mint** and the free **Germaine Cazenave Wells Mardi Gras Museum** at Arnaud's Restaurant, both in the French Quarter; **Blaine Kern's Mardi Gras World** across the river, where the floats are made; and perhaps the smaller **Mardi Gras Museum** in Rivertown. There are also a few Mardi Gras outfits at the **House of Broel** on St. Charles in the Garden District.

You could also browse through mask and costume shops all over town, notably **MGM Costume Rentals** (1617 St. Charles, 581-3999), which has thousands of outfits from the studio's old storerooms; **Momus Masks** (638 St. Peter, 524-6300); **Masquerade Fantasy** (1233 Decatur, 593-9269); or the **Little Shop of Fantasy** (523 Dumaine, 529-4243).

If you're interested in the history of jazz, surprisingly, there isn't as much as you might expect. Start by calling **Cradle of Jazz** tours to make an appointment with one of their guys on the beat (282-3583). The first museum stop for you is also the **Old U.S. Mint,** which has a rare collection of early instruments; then browse the bins at area record stores (see Part Ten, Shopping in New Orleans). There is no trace of the famed Storyville red-light district, where jazz is generally said to have been born, although there is a re-creation and figures of some famous musicians in the **Musée Conti Wax Museum. Congo Square** in Armstrong Park still hosts some concerts, but it is not a neighborhood to visit without knowledgeable company. At night, however, be sure to check out **Preservation Hall** on St. Peter Street, a sort of living-history music museum.

Cruise Bourbon Street and you can still find a little Dixieland struggling to be heard through the rock-and-roll din. Try the Famous Door at Bourbon and Conti Streets, **Maxwell's Cabaret** on Toulouse between Chartres and Royal, the **Mystick Den** in the Royal Sonesta Hotel, or **Lafitte's Blacksmith Shop. Donna's Bar & Grill** on North Rampart presents only brass bands, but very good ones. Sunday jazz brunches are popular all over town (the **Court of Two Sisters** offers a jazz buffet for lunch every day). If you're more into zydeco or Cajun or gumbo music, make sure to check the schedules at the legendary **Tipitina's** on Tchoupitoulas Street, Tipitina's French Quarter offshoot, or at the **House of Blues** on Decatur. For some foot stomping, go take a free Cajun dance lesson at happy hour at **Alex Patout's** bar on Bourbon Street. For more on jazz and music clubs, see the nightclub profiles in Part Twelve.

Despite the city's history, literary tours are a little harder when self directed, primarily because only a few of the former writers' haunts are identifiable from the street (but we've pointed some out in the walking tours). Your best bet is to see the "Special-Interest Tours" section earlier in this chapter.

History and Culture

American-history buffs have an easy time setting their agendas: the **Cabildo** and **Presbytere** complex on Jackson Square; the **Historic New Orleans Collection;** the **National D-Day Museum,** the **Confederate Museum, Jackson Barracks Military Museum,** and **Chalmette Battlefield.**

As for historic houses, there are a number that are maintained as museums and decorated with original or period furnishings. For a quick-time dance through New Orleans history, compare the 1792 **Merieult House** of the New Orleans Historic Collection (a must-see); the West Indies plantation-style **Pitot House,** circa 1800; the **Hermann-Grima House,** which shows the influence of early 19th-century American society on traditionally Creole architecture; the **Beauregard-Keyes House,** an 1826 "raised cottage" that in its time sheltered both General P.G.T. Beauregard and novelist Frances Parkinson Keyes; and the 1857 **Gallier House Museum,** home of one of the city's premier architects. There is also the **1850 House,** a restored middle-class residence in the Pontalba Apartments on Jackson Square, and **Longue Vue Gardens.** All these sites are profiled in other chapters, along with a few others that are open for viewing only by appointment. And throughout the book, certain buildings of interest are cited as you may come upon them.

As famous as the Garden District is, few buildings there are actually open to the public—but then, the exteriors are what really distinguish them. We have put together a limited walking tour of the area and a bit of streetcar touring later in the chapter.

If you have time, you should take an excursion to the great plantations west of town, but that requires some extra planning, especially if you want to spend the night in the country, or need professional guidance: see "Plantation Tours and Excursions" below. Similarly, if you're captivated by Cajun culture, you'll want to head a few hours west to Lafayette and its environs, but that almost certainly requires two days. See "Cajun Country Festivals" on in Part Three, New Orleans's Major Festivals.

Don't overlook the **New Orleans Museum of Art** in City Park. On the off chance that you happen to be a fan of the Impressionist painter Degas, note that the **Edgar Degas House** at 2306 Esplanade Avenue, where he may have finished as many as 17 works, has recently been restored as a bed-and-breakfast, but visitors are welcome to look around (821-5009 or www. degashouse.com). In fact, there are several houses in town with Degas connections: the building that now houses Brennan's Restaurant was originally built for his great-grandfather, Don Vincenze Rilleaux, and the Pitot House for his great-grandmother, Maria Rilleaux. The Musson House, at 1331 Third Avenue (call (800) 755-6730) in the

Garden District, was built for his uncle, who later built the Degas House; and some sources claim the Waldhorn & Adler building on Royal Street at Conti was built for Don Vincenze Rilleaux, too. The offices pictured in Degas' masterpiece, "A Cotton Office in New Orleans," were at 407 Carondelet in Factor's Row. There's a tour in itself.

If your preference runs to the literary, there are plenty of traces of **Tennessee Williams** about (several are mentioned in the self-guided walking tours of the French Quarter below) and an annual festival dedicated to Williamsesque stories, drinking, and bellowing contests ("Stellaaaaa!"). For festival information, call 581-1144.

Anyone interested in black Southern culture should take the subway out to **Tulane University's Amisted Research Center,** the world's largest collection of arts and letters on race history, both in this country and elsewhere. Contemporary black art is the specialty of **La Belle Galerie** (309 Chartres, 529-3080); **YA/YA** (628 Bayonne, 529-3306); **Barrister's Gallery** (1724 O. Haley Boulevard, 525-2767), and the **Stella Jones Gallery** in the Bank One Center (201 St. Charles, 568-9050).

The Great Hereafter

If you love old churches, make sure to see **St. Louis Cathedral** in Jackson Square, **St. Patrick's** in the Warehouse/Arts District, and the remarkable but only partly restored **St. Adolphus** in the Irish Channel. For quirkier saints, visit **Our Lady of Guadalupe** in the Central Business District and the **Chapel of St. Roch's** east of the French Quarter. If you're particularly interested in stained glass, which is the real treasure at St. Adolphus, be sure to contact the **Preservation Resource Center** (923 Tchoupitoulas, 581-7032) to see when their next "Stained Glass in Sacred Places" tour is scheduled. Also, see the Garden District walking tour for directions to the Tiffany Glass at Tulane University.

If, on the other hand, it's cemeteries you love, you can either experience them straight or gussied up with vampire and voodoo lore. You can visit several of the "cities of the dead," the most famous being **St. Louis Cemetery No. 1** (where the tomb of the city's famous voodoo madam Marie Laveau still gets nightly petitions) and **Lafayette Cemetery** in the Garden District (where Anne Rice's creation, Lasher, is "buried" in a cast-iron tomb), but you should never go after dark, and preferably go in a group even during the day. Your best bet is to drive out to **Lake Lawn Metairie Cemetery,** which has all the extravagant tombs you could want to see. You can tour Gallier House, but the guides there probably won't mention the sometimes residence there of the Vampire Lestat.

If voodoo queens and vampire lovers are your thing, you can, uh, drink your fill. There are now probably as many "haunted," "voodoo," or "magic" tours of New Orleans as general history ones, though not all are particularly serious; see "Walking on the Dark Side" under "Special-Interest Tours" above for more information. Or stop into the **New Orleans Voo-doo Museum,** or the **Voodoo Spiritual Temple** (828 North Rampart, 522-9627).

Neighborhood Walking Tours

Okay, this is the fun part, at least as far as we're concerned—putting the "tour" back in the "tourist," so to speak. We've designed three routes for you, one in the French Quarter, one giving the flavor of the Garden District, and a third to help orient you to the newer pleasures of the Warehouse/Arts District and a bit of the Central Business District (CBD) at the same time.

How long they will take you depends on your pace and whether you stick to the sidewalk; you can, of course, stop at any museum or site that interests you. But none is either exhausting or exhaustive (to be frank, we think most walking tours tell you more than you need or want to know). These are just pleasant, informative, and intriguing strolls—a little history, a bit of legend, some literary notes, architectural details, and anecdotes. The French Quarter walk is the longest, of course, but then there are the greatest number of opportunities to sit, get something to eat or drink (remember, alcohol dehydrates), or duck into a store. The Garden District tour is the shortest, but it opens onto several other options, including Audubon Park, the zoo, the Riverbend neighborhood, etc.

The Vieux Carré/French Quarter (Zone 1)

It's nicer to think of the Quarter as the "old block" because there are so many influences at play on the tour: Spanish, German, American, and African-Caribbean, as well as French. Our route is divided into two double-loop halves, somewhat as though a huge E-3 monogram had been printed over the map with the two middle strokes meeting in front of St. Louis Cathedral. The longer part comes first, so that you can stop midway if you like and have an easier return. (This is also designed to help you get the layout of the Quarter in your head and not worry about going too far astray, because the loops go out and come back within view of the cathedral spire.)

The tour begins in the heart of **Jackson Square,** with a mental salute to the statue of Gen. Andrew Jackson. As pointed out in "A Too-Short History of a Fascinating Place," in Part One, this was originally called Place d'Armes by the French, re-accented to Plaza de Armas by the Spanish, and altered permanently after the glorious victory of 1815. It was also the "inspiration," or in-spite-ation, for Lafayette Square in the American sector. The statue was erected to honor the hero of 1815, of course, but the inscription, which reads, "The Union must and shall be preserved," was added by federal forces during the Civil War occupation. (To be fair, it is an accurate expression of Jackson's political sentiments.)

Straight before you is **St. Louis Cathedral,** the oldest cathedral in the United States (and even at that, this is the third church to occupy that space since 1722). Constructed in 1794, it was partially remodeled in the late 1840s. The flagstone piazza just outside the church doors is officially called Place Jean Paul Deux, to commemorate the 1987 visit of Pope John Paul II.

To the left of the cathedral is the **Cabildo,** so named because during the Spanish administration, the governing council, or Cabildo, met here. It transferred to the French authorities, of course and the Louisiana Purchase was ratified here. To the left of that is the **Arsenal,** built in 1803 on the site of what had been a Spanish prison, and now, like the Cabildo, it is part of the Louisiana State Museum complex.

Walk around the corner of the Arsenal onto St. Peter, and then turn right into the short **Cabildo Alley** and left again into **Pirates Alley.** This is one of several places in which Jackson and Jean Lafitte are frequently said to have plotted strategy for the Battle of New Orleans, but unfortunately, the alley wasn't cut through until 1831. Its real name is Ruelle d'Orleans, Sud—Little Orleans Way, South. However, there are two spots of interest here. **Faulkner House Books,** at 624 Pirates Alley, is not only a fine Southern literature bookstore but also the house where Faulkner lived while working on his first novel. It borders **St. Anthony's Garden,** officially named the Cathedral Garden but long considered a memorial to the Capuchin Father Antonio de Sedella (the beloved "Pere Antoine," as the Creoles re-christened him), who arrived in 1779 and served the colony for nearly a half century. (The good father's garden was also, oddly, the most popular dueling ground for young aristocrats.) The monument in the middle of the garden was erected by the government of Napoleon III to honor 30 French marines who died serving as volunteer nurses during one of the great yellow-fever epidemics.

Pirates Alley ends at Royal Street; turn left onto Royal and begin enjoying the old buildings around you. Walk a block and cross St. Peter Street. In the next block, on your right, at 627 Royal Street, is the **Old Town Praline Shop,** on the site of an apartment that once was home to 19th-century French opera prodigy Adelina Patti and that still sweetly opens its lovely old courtyard to the public. Just beyond that at 613 Royal is the **Court of Two Sisters,** which a century ago was the dry-goods shop of Emma and Bertha Camors and is now a restaurant and jazz bar with its own fine courtyard and informal aviary.

At the next intersection, turn right onto Toulouse Street. On the left at 710 Toulouse, in what is now the Coghlan Gallery, is the house known as the **Court of Two Lions,** named for the two royal beasts that mount the gate pillars. It was bought in 1819 by Vincent Nolte, whose autobiography inspired the huge, and at one point hugely popular, novel-turned-movie *Anthony Adverse.* Next door at 722, which was a boarding house during the Depression, a young Tennessee Williams paid $10 a month for a room (and worked as a waiter in his landlady's restaurant to pay even that). In the 1940s, a little better off, he took an apartment at St. Peter Street, where he wrote *A Streetcar Named Desire.* But in the 1950s and 1960s, with both money and fame to support his writing habit, he moved back to 727 Rue Toulouse, specifically to room 9 at the **Hotel Maison de Ville.**

At the next corner, turn left onto Bourbon Street (you can't miss it!), and after one block turn right again onto St. Louis Street. Halfway up on the left at 820 St. Louis is the **Hermann-Grima Historic House,** one of the finest examples of early American architectural shifts and well worth coming back to tour.

At the corner of Dauphine Street, look catty-corner across to 509 Dauphine and the **Audubon Cottages,** also run by the Hotel Maison de Ville; John James Audubon lived in No. 1 while writing and painting his 1821 masterpiece, *Birds of North America.* In the next block of Dauphine Street (turn left) are some buildings with less illuminated histories: at 415 Dauphine is the Dauphine Orleans, whose lounge, **May Bailey's Place,** used to be a bordello (and they can prove it). And at the corner of Conti Street is the **Déjà Vu** bar, said to be haunted and more reliably said to have housed an 1880s opium den.

At the corner of Conti look right; halfway up the block is the **Musée Conti Wax Museum,** but it's not worth staring at unless you're ready to visit it. If not, keep strolling along Dauphine to Bienville Street and turn left, back toward Bourbon Street. Halfway down on the left is the Arnaud's complex, which includes not only the restored old mansion of a restaurant (potted palms and ceiling fans, leaded glass, and mosaic tile), dining rooms filled with krewe memorabilia, and a fine old-fashioned bar, but the **Germaine Wells Mardi Gras Museum** upstairs, where you can view for free the fine collection of Carnival costumes.

When you get to Bourbon Street, turn left one block back to Conti and right again to Royal Street; turn left. Now, remember that Royal Street was once the financial center of town. On the right, at 334 Royal Street, is the **French Quarter Police Station,** housed in the 1826 Bank of Louisiana building (it has also served as the state capitol, among other things, and has a visitor information center inside). On the left, at 343 Royal Street, is the **Waldhorn Company** antique store, a huge, balconied, and wrought iron–decorated Spanish Colonial edifice built around 1800 as the Bank of the United States. And in the next block, on the opposite corner of Conti Street, is a building designed in 1818 by U.S. Capitol architect Benjamin Latrobe as the Louisiana State Bank (look for the "LB" entwined in the forged ironwork on the balcony).

Across the street at 417 Royal is the celebrated **Brennan's Restaurant,** originally built for Edgar Degas's Spanish grandfather. A few years later it was sold and became yet another bank office, the Banque de la Louisiane, gaining its own wrought-iron monogram in the balcony, a "BL." A few years after that, it was sold again, this time becoming the private residence of the socially prominent Martin Gordon (Andrew Jackson danced here several times when he returned to the city in 1828). But when Gordon went bankrupt, it was sold yet again, at auction, to Judge Alonzo Morphy (perhaps not coincidentally, he was the son-in-law of the auctioneer). Morphy is interesting for two reasons: in the 1850s, his son Paul became the world chess champion at 21, and before buying the house at 417, he lived in what is now the Beauregard-Keyes House (see below).

At **437 Royal,** in what is now the Cohen rare-coins gallery, was the Masonic Lodge where pharmacist Antoine Peychard served his fellow Masons his special after-dinner drink, poured out into little egg cups. The word for the cups was *coquetier,* which some people believe became "cocktail," and Peychard himself became immortalized as a brand of bitters. (His tonic included absinthe and Sazerac-de-Forge cognac, the original Sazerac cocktail.)

The huge white building that takes up the whole **400 block of Royal** on your right was built just after the turn of the 19th century as the civil-courts building. Later it housed the Louisiana Department of Wildlife and Fisheries and its wildlife museum; the U.S. Circuit Court of Appeals for the Fifth Judicial District; most recently (having been wrested back from the feds by the state) it was expensively renovated for the Louisiana Supreme Court. It was also used as a set for Oliver Stone's *JFK.*

Cross St. Louis Street to the TV-station building at **520 Royal** and walk through to the fine four-sided courtyard; take note of the "S" worked into the fan-shaped ironwork at the left corner of the third-floor balcony. In the early 19th century, this was built for wine merchant and furniture maker Francois Seignouret, who always used to carve that same initial into his furniture. The straightforward Spanish building at **536 Royal** was constructed just after the second great fire in 1794; the three-story Maison LeMonnier at 640 Royal, built in 1811, was considered the city's first "skyscraper." (The fourth story was added in 1876.) Note the initials "YLM," for Dr. Yves LeMonnier, in the wrought iron of the balcony.

Across the street, at 533 Royal is the **Historic New Orleans Collection** and the **Merieult House.** The Collection, which faces onto Royal, often has fine historical exhibits (a small but first-class assortment of Mardi Gras costumes, early propaganda posters promising streets of gold to would-be settlers, etc.) and is open and free. It also houses the finest research archives in the city, open to scholars only. Behind it is the late-18th-century Merieult House, one of only two important structures to survive the great fire of 1794, and a 19th-century cottage, which are now open for tours with paid admission. Madame Merieult, née Catherine McNamara, had hair of Irish copper that made her the toast of New

Orleans. And when she and her husband visited Paris, Napoleon offered her her own castle in return for parting with her hair, which he wanted to make into a wig to woo the Sultan of Turkey (who himself wanted to woo a reluctant harem lady) into an alliance. The high-spirited Merieult refused, however.

Go another block along Royal Street and stop at the corner of St. Peter Street. The **Royal Café** building, one of the most popular postcard and photograph subjects in town, is sometimes called the LaBranche House, and its oak-and-acorn-pattern wrought-iron balconies are in very fine condition. Actually, there are 11 LaBranche row houses altogether, built in the 1830s by a sugar planter, that run from the corner of Royal around the block of St. Peter toward Pirates Alley.

Turn right down St. Peter Street. On the right, at the corner of Chartres Street, is **Le Petit Théâtre du Vieux Carré,** home to the country's oldest continuously operating community theater (dating from a 1916 production in the Pontalba Apartments). The whole building is a sort of theatrical set: built in 1922, it's a faithful reproduction of the 18th-century residence of Joseph Xavier de Pontalba, last Spanish governor of New Orleans. The chandeliers and the courtyard fountain are of more recent origin; the wrought-iron balcony rail inside the theater is real, though, made in 1796. Le Petit Théâtre is believed to be haunted by a *Phantom*-like, well, phantom, in the balcony, who has been "photographed"; the now-defunct Society for Paranormal Research claimed to have recorded him several times.

Glance across the corner at the back of the Arsenal, and you will see that we have looped back toward Jackson Square for the first time. Now turn your back again and head out along Chartres Street, which is full of strange and wonderful shops and old facades. After you cross Toulouse, look left; at 514 Toulouse is the **New Orleans Pharmacy Museum,** housed in the 1816 shop (believed to have been designed by architect J.N.B. DePouilly) of apothecary Louis Defilho Jr. A little beyond, at the corner of Chartres and St. Louis Streets is the **Napoleon House,** which may look as though the entire plaster interior were about to collapse but which has probably seen more hard living than even its French Quarter peers and remains a favorite of locals despite the tourists. It owes its name to the loyal sentiments of pirate Jean Lafitte (yes, again), New Orleans mayor Nicholas Girod, and various other Creole leaders who fixed up the 1797 house and offered it to the deposed emperor, who was then languishing on the island of St. Helena. A plot was under way to rescue him when he died in 1821. (The third-floor "Appartement de l'Empereur" has been restored in real style, but can only be rented for private functions.) Make sure you look beyond the aging bar to the ageless courtyard.

If you're a fan of Paul Prudhomme, you can walk one more block and sniff the spicy air outside **K-Paul's Louisiana Kitchen** at 416 Chartres;

then turn left at Conti Street and head toward Decatur Street. Turn left again onto Decatur and the "new New Orleans," the big-name franchise promenade, stretches out before you. As you head back toward Jackson Square, you pass the Hard Rock Café opposite St. Louis Street, the Crescent City Brewhouse, the Millhouse/Jax Brewery complex with its Hooters, and so on. By the time you make it to the square, and see those silly mules in their hats and ribbons, you'll be delighted to look right and mount the steps up to Washington Artillery Park and the Moonwalk overlooking the river.

Now settle yourself in for a cup of reviving coffee at the **Café du Monde,** tour the caricaturists or just relax in Jackson Park. This is the end of Loop 2, and intermission time for the tour.

Here beginneth Loop 3, as they used to say. Walk along St. Ann Street from Decatur toward Chartres, looking up at the **Pontalba Apartments.** Halfway up the block, at 525 St. Ann, is the **1850 House,** a restored three-story apartment showing how a middle-class Creole family lived at the time the Baroness Micaela Almonester Pontalba built her still-sought-after apartments. This is another part of the Louisiana State Museum, and tickets can be bought here for all LSM buildings. Right next to it, at 529 St. Ann, is a **Louisiana visitors center,** with scores of brochures, maps, and coupons. Intriguingly, while the state of Louisiana owns the block of apartments along St. Ann, the city of New Orleans owns the opposite block along St. Peter, including No. 540, where in the mid-1920s, Sherwood Anderson wrote *Dark Laughter.*

At the corner of St. Ann and Chartres is the **Presbytere,** the fourth Louisiana State Museum property right on Jackson Square, and the most conventional of the buildings in that it hosts both permanent and rotating exhibits about New Orleans and Louisiana history, maritime culture, society, portraiture, and decorative arts. Its most famous possession is Napoleon's death mask.

Walk past the door of the Presbytere and turn right up the 1830s flagstone walkway called **Pere Antoine's Alley,** which borders St. Anthony's Garden on the other side. (Like Pirates Alley, its official name is more pedestrian: Ruelle d'Orleans, Nord—Little New Orleans Way, North.) Jog left onto Royal and then right onto Orleans Street to the Bourbon Orleans Hotel on your right. The **Orleans Ballroom,** which has now been restored within the hotel complex, was built by entrepreneur John Davis in 1817 to house theatrical productions and opera. Although some of the official walking tours don't mention it, it was also the site of the famous Quadroon Balls, where Creole aristocrats formally courted mixed-race beauties for their concubines. It apparently served, as did many public buildings, as a hospital during the Civil War, and in 1881 was acquired by an order of black nuns to serve as an orphanage and school. The order sold the building about 30 years ago to the hotel, and there have been rumored ghost sightings around the place, including one of a Confederate soldier and another of a young woman.

Turn right at Bourbon Street and there on the corner is **Marie Laveau's House of Voodoo,** one of the more popular spots for tarot readings, charms, and souvenirs. Keep strolling past St. Ann and Dumaine Streets to St. Philip; on the left, at 941 Bourbon, is **Lafitte's Blacksmith Shop,** yet another probably apocryphal site but much loved. The story is that the Lafitte brothers, Jean and Pierre, used the blacksmith shop as a front for their smuggling network, but although there are deeds of ownership on the property dating to the early 1770s, none indicates a smithy. Still, it's architecturally interesting—one of the last bits of post-and-brick construction, which means that the bricks were set inside a wooden frame because the local clay was so soft—and is still a great candlelight jazz bar that draws locals even more than tourists. (It's such an old reliable that a few years ago, three sheriff's deputies were moonlighting behind the bar when a fugitive came in for a drink; they arrested him on the spot.) It was also the favorite watering hole of Tennessee Williams.

Continue down Bourbon two more blocks to Governor Nicholls Street and turn right. Locate 721 Governor Nicholls Street and the **Thierry House,** built around 1814 to a design proferred by Benjamin Latrobe when he was only 19 years old. Its neoclassical Greek style inspired the whole Greek Revival that characterized Creole architecture.

At the end of the block, turn the corner right again onto Royal. On the left corner, at 1140 Royal, is what is still known as the **LaLaurie House,** and to tour guides as *the* Haunted House. In 1834, it was the home of Delphine LaLaurie, a sort of Creole Elizabeth Bathory, who hosted many brilliant and elaborate soirées there, which despite their popularity fueled gossip about the pitiable appearance of many of her servants. Several of these slaves committed suicide, or so LaLaurie said. One neighbor reported that LaLaurie had savagely beaten a young black girl, who shortly thereafter "fell" from the roof to her death, but a court merely fined her. But on April 10, 1834, when the house caught fire, neighbors, hearing the screams of slaves, broke in to find them chained in a secret garret, starving and bearing the marks of torture. Rumors spread that Madame LaLaurie herself might have set the fire. The house was stormed, and she and her family barely escaped, making their way to Europe. She never returned, although the house was rebuilt, but her body was smuggled back to New Orleans and secretly buried. Some people swear they have heard the shrieking of slaves and the snapping of whips at night, and it is a very popular late-night tourist stop for ghost hosts. Madame LaLaurie is so infamous, in fact, that she is memorialized at the Musée Conti Wax Museum.

The neighboring buildings have a much finer reputation, fortunately. Just alongside at 1132 Royal Street is the **Gallier House Museum,** built in 1857 by James Gallier, Jr., son of the architect of the city hall and a prominent architect himself. He designed the building with many ingenious and then-rare fixtures. The house is administered as a museum by Tulane University.

Continue on Royal, past St. Philip, to 915 Royal, where the wrought-iron fence that gives the **Cornstalk Hotel** its name holds court. It was cast in the 1830s in Philadelphia for Dr. Joseph Biamenti as a present for his homesick Midwesterner wife, and its twin can be seen in the Garden District in front of the house at 1448 Fourth Street.

Across the street at **900, 906,** and **910 Royal** are the three Miltenberger houses, built in 1838 and now housing art galleries. The granddaughter of one Miltenberger was Alice Heine, the Barbara Hutton or Pamela Harriman of her day; she married first the Duc de Richelieu and then moved on to Prince Louis of Monaco.

Turn right onto Dumaine and duck up to the **New Orleans Historic Voodoo Museum** at 724 Dumaine, which is part museum (some pretty grisly), part souvenir shop/fortune-telling temple, and part tour central. Then double back down a block to 632 Dumaine and **Madame John's Legacy,** which is put forth by many historians as the oldest existing building in the lower Mississippi River valley. It was originally built between 1724 and 1726 for Don Manuel Lanzos, the captain of the regiment; but it was either repaired or entirely rebuilt to the same design (hence the debate) after the Good Friday fire of 1788. In either case, it is a fine example of French Colonial architecture of the style called a "raised cottage," with a steeply pitched room and dormers, living quarters high above flood level, half timbering on the back of the rear stairs on the second floor (called columbage), and storage below. The name comes from "Tite Poulette," a short story by the 19th-century writer George Washington Cable, about a beautiful quadroon whose white lover wills her the house on his deathbed. It is now part of the state museum complex.

At the corner of Chartres, glance right—there it is, Jackson Square—and then turn left onto Chartres for the final loop. At Ursuline Street, turn the corner just long enough to peek at the **Hotel Villa Convento,** 616 Ursuline Street. It's a respectable guest house now, but legend points to it as the famous House of the Rising Sun bordello. Now go back down Ursuline to Chartres and turn left. Just around the corner at 1113 Chartres is the **Beauregard-Keyes House,** built by wealthy auctioneer Joseph Le Carpentier and his son-in-law Judge Alonzo Morphy (see Brennan's, above). In its time it was home to Confederate hero General P.G.T. Beauregard and novelist Frances Parkinson Keyes. Keyes wrote two novels about previous occupants while living here (perhaps she was haunted); the better-known novel is about General Beauregard and is entitled *Madame Castell's Lodger,* and the second one, entitled *The Chess Player,* is about Paul Morphy.

Across the street on the corner of Ursuline and Chartres is the **Old Ursuline Convent,** the strongest candidate for oldest building in

Louisiana. Designed in 1745 and completed in 1752, it is the only structure that we know for sure survived the great fires at the end of the 18th
century. (The Sisters of St. Ursula themselves arrived in 1727, and lived
in the meantime in a building at Bienville and Chartres.) It was not only
the first nunnery in the state; it was the first orphanage, the premier
school for Creole children, and the first school for black and Indian children as well. Between 1831 and 1834 it housed the state legislature—the
ultimate proof of charity.

Continue down Ursuline to Decatur and turn right, back toward Jackson Square. The gold-plated warrior astride her fearless steed is, of
course, Joan of Arc, the patron saint of France, and a gift to this still-
French city from the French government. (She has been almost as restless
as her namesake: this is the statue's third location in about five years.)
The **French Market** runs along your left, with the tracks of the Riverfront Streetcar beyond. Shops and restaurants line Decatur on both sides.
At St. Philip Street look left and locate the National Park Service office
peeking through from North Peters; then keep on, back to the Café du
Monde, or stop at any of the little cafes along the way. Even better, stop
by the legendary **Tujague's** on Decatur at Madison; the long stand-up
bar is a New Orleans tradition. The bar itself, which came from Paris
back in 1827, is nearly 300 years old. And it was probably here that O.
Henry, if he did borrow the pseudonym from a bartender, first got the
idea, because he was a regular.

The Garden District (Zone 3)

Although some guidebooks list scores of homes in the Garden District as
historically or architecturally important, they are mainly so to real devotees, especially as virtually all are private residences and can only be
glimpsed from the outside. You may well see all you want to see by staying
on the St. Charles Avenue Streetcar on the way to Audubon Park. So we
have designed a fairly limited walk-through that will give you the flavor of
the district and several of the celebrity highlights. If you go in the later
morning, you may find a lunch stop at the famous Commander's Palace
convenient. If you are enjoying the stroll, you can just keep wandering and
admiring the facades. (If the present owners are working in the yard, you
might stop and ask if they know much about the history of their homes;
most of them are quite knowledgeable.) If you are seriously interested, contact the New Orleans Visitors Bureau about the Spring Fiesta, which starts
the Friday after Easter and includes many garden and house tours.

The Garden District is the second-largest historic district in the United
States, encompassing 10,700 structures—some with as many as 30 rooms.
It is usually said to be bounded by St. Charles Avenue and Magazine
Street (on the north and south sides, more or less) and Jackson and
Louisiana Avenues on the east and west. But neighboring streets continue

to claim relationship, and there is now what is sometimes called a "Lower Garden District"—lower as in Downtown—to the east back toward Lee Circle. Its look is so different from the French Quarter that it almost seems like another country, and in fact it almost was. This was the "American Quarter," the area where the rich, the *nouveau riche,* and the well connected from all over the United States built extravagant mansions to show up their new fellow citizens of the Creole aristocracy.

We suggest you start by taking the St. Charles Streetcar to Jackson Street. At 2220 St. Charles is the **House of Broel,** which is both a dollhouse collection and a full-sized museum, as well as a bridal and haute couture salon. It was originally built as a two-story pied-à-terre for a planter and his family, but in the 1890s, tobacco tycoon Simon Hernsheim had the whole building lifted and added a new Victorian first floor. It is open for tours, if you want to stop or circle back (522-2220).

Across the street at the end of the block, on the corner of Philip Street at **2265 St. Charles,** is a house that was designed by James Gallier Jr., for Lavinia Dabney in the late 1850s, about the time his own home in the Vieux Carré was completed. Gallier designed it as Greek Revival; the Ionic columns and side galleries were added later. Across Philip, at **2336 St. Charles** is, for comparison, a Greek Revival raised cottage designed by his father, James Gallier Sr., at just about the same time.

At the corner of First Street, turn left, walk a block to Prytania, and turn the corner to get a view. At 2343 Prytania is the Second Empire–style **Louise S. McGehee School,** also known as the Bradish Johnson House after the wealthy sugar planter for whom it was built in 1872, for a then-astonishing $100,000, probably by New Orleans–born, Paris-trained architect James Freret. It has been a prestigious girls' school since 1929; the carriage house is the gymnasium, and the stables have been turned into a cafeteria. According to an odd legend, none of the girls, or anyone else, has been born, died, or married within its walls.

Across the street from the school at 2340 Prytania is what sometimes is called **Toby's Corner,** built sometime before 1838 for Philadelphian Thomas Toby, and believed to be the oldest house in the Garden District. Even better, it's still in the family's hands. It is put in the shade in both senses, however, by the huge Spanish moss–draped live oak on the grounds, which is several hundred years old.

Continue down First Street, noting the ornate cast iron in front of the circa 1869 Italianate home at **1331 First Street** and the matching galleries at the remarkably similar house at **1315 First Street.** Both were designed by Irish immigrant Samuel Jamison in 1869.

Just past Chestnut Street, on the corner at **1239 First Street,** is the 1857 mansion once known as the Rose-Brevard House; it was built for merchant Albert Brevard, and its elaborate ironwork has a rose pattern. It's now far more famous as the residence of former novelist Anne Rice and the setting of the best-selling book *The Witching Hour.* The original structure cost only $13,000 (the hexagonal wing was added a few years later); restoring the gates alone would cost that now.

Across the street, at **1236 First Street,** is a gorgeous Greek Revival mansion built as a wedding gift in 1847. Walk another block to Camp Street and look across the corner to the house at **1134 First Street,** built about 1850 for Judge Jacob Payne (who may have designed it himself). It is also the home where one-time U.S. senator and former president of the Confederate States of America Jefferson Davis died in 1889.

Turn right onto Camp Street and walk to Third Street, turning right at the corner. The arched and eaved mansion at **1213 Third Street** was built during the Reconstruction for Irish carpetbagger Archibald Montgomery, president of the Crescent City Railroad. Continue on to the Italianate home at **1331 Third Street,** designed in 1850 by James Gallier Sr., for New Orleans postmaster Michel Musson, who married Edgar Degas's aunt. (The elaborate cast-iron or "iron lace" galleries were added later.)

Across Coliseum at **1415 Third Street** is the Robinson House, one of the Garden District's largest and most attractive homes: its curving front seems especially spacious because both stories are the same height, with identical iron balconies and columns. It was built just before the Civil War by architect Henry Howard for Virginia tobacco trader Walter Robinson, and is thought to have been one of the first homes in New Orleans to have indoor plumbing.

Turn left onto Coliseum Street and walk two blocks to Washington Street. On the corner is **Commander's Palace,** where you can stop for lunch or just cast an admiring glance at the courtyard (or finish the tour and circle back around). This stately old-liner of the Brennan's restaurant fleet has been a restaurant for well over a century, and owes its name not to a naval officer but to owner Emile Commander. It's terribly respectable now—it claims to be the birthplace of oysters Rockefeller, and nobody much has contested it—but back during Prohibition, the second story was a high-stakes, high-society bordello.

Behind the high brick walls of Washington and Coliseum is **Lafayette Cemetery No. 1,** named for the American sector it served, then the City of Lafayette. Laid out in 1833, the cemetery was designed for the well-to-do; its wide aisles were intended to carry extravagant funeral processions to elaborate tombs. However, it was nearly filled within 20 years by victims of repeated epidemics. The cemetery has many fine examples of the above-ground tombs that are New Orleans trademarks, including the cast-iron tomb Anne Rice uses for the elemental spirit Lasher (the cemetery itself served as a setting for scenes from the movie version of *Interview with the Vampire*). The Jefferson Fire Company No. 22 tomb with its bas-relief firetruck is also here, as are other monuments that might look familiar to fans of the seminal film, *Easy Rider*. (Eternal rest or eternal bliss? In 1980, a Neiman Marcus executive and his bride were married here, on Friday, the 13th of June, wearing full black.) Unfortunately, even this cemetery is no longer safe to wander without company, and in any case the gate may be locked. However, if you are waiting at the Washington Street gate at 10:30 a.m. Monday, Wednesday, or Friday, you can hook onto the Save Our Cemeteries tour; or contact one of the commercial tour groups mentioned above in "Walking on the Dark Side."

Walk along the Washington Avenue cemetery wall to Prytania and turn back to the right. (If you're a literary type, turn left and go to **2900 Prytania** at Sixth Street; that boardinghouse was where Jazz Age icon F. Scott Fitzgerald lived in 1919–1920.) Glance down Fourth Street to No. 1448 if you want to see the wrought-iron twin to the fence at the Cornstalk Hotel in the French Quarter. Continue on to **2605 Prytania** at the corner of Third Street: the guest house of this pointy-arched Gothic Revival house, designed by the senior Gallier in 1849, is a perfect miniature of the main house.

Just across Third Street at 2521 Prytania is the former Redemptorist Fathers chapel, **Our Lady of Perpetual Help**—"former" because the Italianate home, built in 1857 for a coffee merchant, had fallen into disrepair before being purchased, like several other dilapidated historic buildings in the District, by Anne Rice. Across from that, at 2520 Prytania, is the **Gilmour-Parker home,** a Palladium-fronted house built in 1853 for an English cotton trader named Gilmour and later sold to John Parker, father of a future governor. The building around the corner at **1417 Third Street** used to be its carriage house, but later was considerably expanded.

Inside the home at **2507 Prytania,** built in the early 1850s for *New Orleans Daily Crescent* publisher Joseph. H. Maddux, is a fireplace of hand-painted tiles depicting a dreamy bayou landscape. The Queen Anne–Greek Revival–style hybrid **Women's Opera Guild House,** on the far end of the block at 2504 Prytania Street, was designed by James Freret in 1858, except for the octagonal turret, which was added toward the end of the century and holds a music room and bedrooms. It was bequeathed to the Opera Guild by its last inhabitant, Nettie Seebold, and its collection of 18th- and 19th-century antiques, along with some Guild mementos, can only be viewed Mondays from 1 to 4 p.m. (a small donation is requested).

Turn left onto Second Street, walk back to St. Charles, and turn left again. At 2524 St. Charles, on the corner of Third Street, is what is known both as the Dameron House and more romantically—and far more widely, thanks to the publication of Anne Rice's *Violin*—as the **Claiborne Cottage.** Rice's story has it that the Greek Revival raised cottage was the home of Bernard Xavier Phillipe de Marigny de Mandeville, son of one of the wealthiest and more influential Creoles of old New Orleans society, and his wife Sophronia Claiborne, daughter of the diplomat who would become the first American governor of Louisiana. Their match marked the first great union of the two societies of New Orleans, but Marigny, who had inherited so much land and money, gambled so obsessively that he is said to have lost a million dollars—not in modern money, but a million dollars *then*—by the time he was 20. In fact, it may have been Marigny who brought back dicing from England: It became known to the Americans as "Johnny Crapaud's game," something like "the Frog's game," and eventually "craps." (Marigny tried to name Burgundy Street "Craps Street," but it didn't take.) Unfortunately, the more people he taught the game to, the more people he lost to. He still managed to live well, but by the time he died at 83, he was a pauper; the neighborhood of Faubourg Marigny is almost the last reminder of his huge holdings. Meanwhile, the house became a convent, a guest house, a rectory, and a school, and was nearly razed several times under various development schemes. However, in the 1950s, when Anne Rice was a teenager, her parents rented the house for several years, and *Violin* was inspired by her memories of the place. She has, needless to say, now purchased the property.

And here you are back at the streetcar.

The Warehouse/Arts and Central Business District (Zone 2)

This is a somewhat mixed tour, primarily pointing out historical buildings, but with a few arts sites thrown in. The neighborhood is undergoing such a dramatic transformation with constant redevelopment and construction that some sites may not be visible or open at all times. If you are a more serious student of contemporary art, you should also plan to take a walk up and down Julia Street, from Commerce to St. Charles, where there are many fine galleries and studios.

With the former World Trade Center on your left, walk along Convention Center Boulevard toward Lafayette Street. Look left down Poydras Street as you pass to flash a victory "V" back to the statue of **Winston Churchill** (the green is called English Place). Turn right at Lafayette and walk three blocks to Commerce Street and the **Piazza d'Italia.** The Piazza d'Italia was designed by Charles Moore, and its fountain (shaped like Italy) and partial arches were supposed to suggest a classical ruin, but the heavy, and in many cases unresolved, construction in the neighborhood has added rather unkindly to the effect. However, plans are afoot to renovate and reopen it.

Continue on Lafayette until it runs into **Lafayette Square,** laid out in 1788 and named for the noble marquis who had joined the American Revolution. On the right is a 1974 sculpture by Clement Meadmore entitled "Out of There," and straight ahead, just inside the park, is the Benjamin

Franklin monument created in 1871 by Hiram Powers. The statue in the center of the park of statesman Henry Clay, dedicated in 1860, originally stood at the intersection of St. Charles and Canal, and the place of honor in this park once belonged to a statue of the king of Spain. Clay was moved here in 1901, after serving as a gathering place for repeated anti-integration riots. And at the far side of the square, facing St. Charles Avenue, is the John McDonogh monument, portraying the philanthropist surrounded by grateful children. McDonogh endowed several public schools in the mid-19th century; until his will was known, he was just considered a cranky old miser with radical ideas about educating slaves.

Turning left onto Camp Street (from Lafayette Street) notice the building on the left between Lafayette and Capedeville. The more or less Italian Renaissance building is now the **U.S. Court of Appeals for the Fifth Circuit,** but was built in 1914 as the post office.

Continue on Camp past Girod Street to **St. Patrick's Church** and its rectory. The high and narrow Gothic Revival building, built in the 1830s and for many years the undisputed high point of the area, was modeled after England's York Minster Cathedral by Irish architects Charles and James Dakin, and meant as a rival and rebuke to the closed-minded French communicants of St. Louis Cathedral. (The shorthand for their attitude was, "God speaks only in French," though how He felt about canonical Latin is unclear.) Their revenge was complete in 1851, when St. Louis Cathedral was being rebuilt, because Bishop Antoine Blanc had to be ordained as archbishop in St. Patrick's. The design was completed by James Gallier Sr. (born James Gallagher in Dublin), who was responsible for the high, vaulted interior—the nave is 85 feet high, the tower 185—and ribbed sanctuary ceiling with floral bosses. The stained glass over the altar and the three large murals, painted in 1840 by Leon Pomarede, are very fine. (The one on the left shows St. Patrick baptizing the princesses of Ireland; take that, St. Louis!) The Italianate rectory to the church's left was built by Garden District and plantation architect Henry Howard in 1874. The pews, incidentally, are cypress.

At the end of the block, catty-corner across Julia Street, you can see what's called **Julia Row** or the **Thirteen Sisters,** a block of 13 red brick rowhouses of a type that was extremely popular among upper-class residents of the American sector from about 1825 (these were built in the early 1830s) to about 1885. Notice the fan-light transom windows, attic cornices, and iron balconies. These are among the most important buildings being restored in the Warehouse District, and in fact the offices of the Preservation Resource Center of New Orleans are at 604 Julia. (You might stick your head in and ask about their walking tour maps or architectural brochures, if you'd like to see more.)

Continue along Camp past St. Joseph Street to 900 Camp Street and the **Contemporary Arts Center.** This renovated, 40,000-square-foot, turn-of-the-19th-century warehouse is both a "living museum," with studios for practicing artists and rotating exhibits, and a theater, with two stages and sometimes concerts. Even the furniture is art—the glass-wave front desk, the lobby information board, the elevator panels, and the lighting sconces are all creations of fine local artists.

At the other end of the block at 929 Camp Street is the **Confederate Museum,** which has the second-largest collection of Confederate memorabilia (after Richmond's Museum of the Confederacy) in the nation. It is also the oldest museum in the state, designed in 1891 with a cypress hallway, 24-foot ceiling, and fireproof cases for its collection of restored battle flags. The body of Jefferson Davis, who died here in 1889 (see the Garden District tour above), lay in state at the museum before being taken to Richmond, and many of his family effects are here, along with uniforms, weapons, insignia, and photographs.

Turn the corner right onto Howard Avenue and you will see the greatest Confederate of them all, Robert E. Lee, on eternal vigilant guard against invasion from the north in the center of **Lee Circle.** (Talk about revered—he's not just on a pedestal, he's on a 60-foot pedestal.) The memorial was dedicated in 1884 (at which time the former Tivoli Circle was renamed), and Jefferson Davis and New Orleans hometown hero P.G.T. Beauregard were still around for the ceremony. The **Isamu Noguchi fountain** at 1055 St. Charles is a sort of echo of the Lee statue; its crescent-shaped stone (entitled *The Mississippi*) is mounted on a sculpted version of the Doric column Lee stands on.

This is becoming an even more important arts district: As you approach Lee Circle you will pass the Howard Memorial Library, an 1888 sandstone extravaganza by Romanesque Revival champion Henry Hobson Richardson that is being renovated as the **Roger Ogden Museum of Southern Art.** And facing the circle to the left of Howard Avenue is the **Lee Circle Center for the Arts.**

On the circle to Lee's back is the **K&B Plaza,** an indoor-outdoor sculpture garden including not only Noguchi's fountain, but also other pieces by an international group of artists including George Rickey, Frank McGuire, Michael Sandle, and Pedro Friedeberg. (The indoor gallery is open weekdays 8:30 a.m. to 4:30 p.m.)

Swing around Lee Circle to Andrew Higgins Drive; two blocks over, at Magazine street, is the **National D-Day Museum,** easily spotted from here. Continue around the circle, watching out for streetcars, and head back downtown along St. Charles. Many of these buildings have great but sad histories—the three-story brick Greek Revival townhouse at **827 St. Charles** is the only survivor of three—but within a few years, many of them will be prime commercial territory again.

At 545 St. Charles, looking out toward Lafayette Square, is **Gallier Hall,** designed in the late 1840s by the senior James Gallier as City Hall for the Second Municipality (i.e., the American Sector) and one of the most beautiful examples of the Greek Revival style in the city—and many believe in the entire country. The figures on the pediment represent Justice, Liberty, and Commerce (the one toting barges and lifting bales).

Stay on St. Charles Avenue for several blocks—past the new **Hotel Monaco,** formerly a Masonic temple and with much of its lavish public space intact—to Common Street; turn left for two blocks and then go right onto Baronne Street. At 132 Baronne is the outlandish Alhambra-Moscovy romantic **Church of the Immaculate Conception,** informally known as the Jesuit Church. The original church, erected in the mid-19th century, had so much wrought and cast iron, some 200 tons of it, that it had nearly collapsed after five years. It was replaced in 1930 by an almost identical structure which still has the old church's cast-iron pews and the bronze-gilt altar, designed by James Freret, which won first prize at the Paris Exposition of 1867. And except for rude intervention of the French Revolution of 1848, the statue of the Virgin Mary would have been installed at the Tuileries.

Go to the corner, turn right onto Canal Street, and head back toward the river. This was for many years "the" shopping area for upper- and middle-class New Orleanians ("I wore white gloves to come here," says one native), and after a dispiriting decline, Canal Street is coming back to life with a raft of brand-name shops and luxury hotels.

Past Decatur, at 423 Canal Street, is the restored Egyptian/Greek Revival **U.S. Customs House,** begun in the 1840s (when the Mississippi was within eyeshot) but not usable until 1889, and not fully completed until 1913. Henry Clay, still in favor, broke the ceremonial ground. The statuary niches along the Decatur Street side are still unfilled. In the meantime, it housed Confederate prisoners of war during the Union occupation. The huge third-floor Marble Hall, with its 55-foot skylight and 14 marble columns, is breathtaking.

Finally, walk one last block of Canal and turn back onto Convention Center Boulevard. On the roof of the old World Trade Center is **Top of the Mart,** a slowly rotating 500-seat bar on the 33rd floor of the World Trade Center building. It takes 90 minutes to make a complete circuit, and the view of New Orleans—from the riverfront around the business districts to the genteel old French Quarter—is especially attractive at night, when the bridges seem hung with Christmas lights and the cathedral spire salutes the sky. Though the building is currently closed, it is being bid out for renovation and will likely become another hotel, at which time the bar will almost certainly reopen.

Plantation Tours and Excursions

It is unlikely that you will have enough time to visit the plantations as part of a business trip, and unless you have figured such an excursion into your family vacation schedule (and are planning to rent a car), you may have to settle for a half-day group tour.

There are some good tour packagers who can bus you to a few of the houses, such as **New Orleans Tours** (call 592-0560 or (800) 543-6332). **Gray Line Tours** (call 587-0709 or (800) 535-7786) offers a seven-hour tour of Nottoway and Oak Alley, but lunch is not included in the $47 fee. There are also steamboat tours, but they offer no more than a glimpse of the houses from the water, and so are not very satisfying for the time they require.

However, if you would like to strike out by yourself, we have laid out a few options, including a half-day's drive, a full day's tour, and an overnight route that would be a romantic highlight.

There are a half dozen houses along what is called River Road, and a seventh a bit to the south (plus many smaller houses, churches, etc.). What makes this statement a little misleading, is that some are on one side of the Mississippi, and the rest on the other. In fact, there is no great single "River Road." There is instead a pair of two-lane River Roads, one on each side of the river—generally Route 44 or 75 on the north bank and Route 18 on the south—called various names as you continue west. Just try to keep a sense of where the river is, and watch for the house signs. It's not as difficult as it may sound—these are, after all, major tourist attractions and are well marked.

Because the tour companies are on tight schedules, they usually take Interstate 10 at least part of the way into plantation territory. However, we suggest you try a slightly more scenic route: Head west out of New Orleans on River Road (also marked as Route 44 or Jefferson Highway) and stay on the north side of the Mississippi River past Destrehan, San Francisco Plantation, Tezcuco Plantation, and Houmas House. Then cross the Sunshine Bridge (Route 70) to the southern bank of the river, taking Route 1 a bit farther west to Nottoway and then heading back east, mostly on Route 18 past Oak Alley and back to the city.

The ideal trip would be overnight, stopping for lunch at Texcuco (or holding out for dinner at Lafitte's Landing) and taking a room at Nottoway Plantation, where you can have dinner or do the big breakfast thing. You can see Destrehan without leaving town; you could drive an hour or so and spend the night at Oak Alley. Or you could probably see Destrehan, San Francisco, Tezcuco, and Houmas and be back in New Orleans for dinner.

All the plantation homes described here have been immaculately restored and are open for tours. However, if you keep your eyes open, you will see many other fine old homes that are still private residences.

The first and closest is **Destrehan Manor** at 13034 River Road/LA 48, just eight miles west of the airport in Kenner (phone (985) 764-9315). Built in 1787 in the French Colonial style by a free man of color, it was given its wings just after the turn of the 19th century and renovated by the next generation into a Greek Revival style. Its Doric columns, double porch, and hipped roof will look very familiar to fans of the film *Interview with the Vampire,* and many of the haunted–New Orleans tours mention sightings and even alleged photos of phantasmic shapes here. Restored in 1970, Destrehan is the oldest plantation still intact in the entire Lower Mississippi Valley. Admission is $5 adults, $3 teens, and $3 ages 6–12; open daily 9 a.m.–5 p.m.; for more information, consult **www.destrehanplantation.org.**

San Francisco Plantation (535-2341) on Highway 44 a little beyond Reserve is an old and elaborately Gothic Creole-style home begun in the mid-1850s by a planter named Edmond Marmillion and finished in the most fantastical manner—double galleries, widow's walk, highly decorative mouldings and painting, carved woodwork—by his sons, one of whom remarked at the end of the construction that he was now *sans fruscin,* or "without a penny." So the house was first called St. Frusquin, eventually corrupted to San Francisco. Its elaborate, almost paddle-wheeling look inspired the setting of Frances Parkinson Keyes' *Steamboat Gothic.* Admission: $10 adults, $5 ages 12–17, $3 ages 6–12, age 6 and under free; open daily, tours every 20 minutes, 9:20 a.m.–4:40 p.m.

About 25 miles farther at 3138 Highway 44 is **Tezcuco Plantation** (call (225) 562-3929), one of the bed-and-breakfast facilities (for $60–$160, you can stay in one of the cottages or in a room in the main house, take a tour, drink some welcoming wine, etc.). It also has a restaurant where you can have breakfast or lunch if you're going on. This was built just before the Civil War, using bricks made on the grounds, local timber, and, of course, slave labor. The owner was a veteran of the Mexican war, and gave the mansion the Aztec word for "resting place." The outbuildings include an African American cultural museum, a life-sized dollhouse, a chapel, and more. Admission: $9 adults, $8 seniors and AAA members, $7 ages 13–17, $4 ages 5–12, age 4 and under free; open 9 a.m.–5 p.m.

A couple of miles farther along 44/River Road at Highway 942 is **Houmas House** (call (225) 473-7841 or (888) 323-8314). It was named for the Indians who originally owned the land and was for decades the largest sugar plantation in Louisiana. The original house was only four rooms; what looks like the main house now, the two-and-a-half-story Greek Revival mansion with columns around three sides, was added on the front in 1840. Built to the fancy of a South Carolinian, it, too, was a film set, in this case for the Southern Gothic *Hush, Hush Sweet Charlotte* with Bette Davis. The hexagonal houses on either side, called "garconnieres," were used by the bachelor sons of the family (the "boys") or by house guests. Admission: $10 adults, $6 ages 13–17, $3 ages 6–12, 5 and under free; open 10 a.m.–5 p.m. (closes at 4 p.m. November through January).

Retrace Highway 44 to near Tezeuco, cross the Sunshine Bridge (so named because a former Louisiana governor, Jimmy Davis, wrote the song "You Are My Sunshine") over the Mississippi River to Donaldsonville, and look right toward Frontage Street. There you'll see a famous restaurant called **Lafitte's Landing** (which burned in late 1998, but has since reopened at 404 Claiborne Avenue; call (225) 473-1232); it has interest, as you may have guessed from the name. It used to be known as the Old Viala Plantation, and was supposed to have been one of the pirate's bases. In any case, his son and entrepreneurial successor, Jean Pierre Lafitte, married the Viala heiress.

From Lafitte's Landing, turn onto Highway 1/Mississippi River Road and head west again for about 15 miles. Near White Castle on Highway 405 is **Nottoway Plantation Inn & Restaurant,** a spectacular and almost unique building which was called "the white castle" and so gave its name to the town. Nottoway, built in 1859 by John Hampden Randolph, is the largest plantation home in the South, a hybrid neoclassical beauty with 64 rooms, 22 enormous columns, and a series of staggered porches and bays. Inside is a spectacular ballroom with hand-carved Corinthian columns, plaster friezes, and crystal chandeliers, and a surprising list of then-rare conveniences such as hot and cold running water and gas lights. As the name suggests, you can have lunch or dinner (and swim in the walled garden that once held roses), or stay overnight with breakfast and a tour tossed into the $105–$250 room rate. Otherwise, the admission is $10, $4 ages 6–12, ages 5 and under free; open 9 a.m.– 5 p.m. with the last tour at 4:30 p.m.; call (225) 545-8632.

(Incidentally, when you get as far as Nottoway Plantation, you are only about another 30 miles from Baton Rouge, around which are other plantations and attractions. If you want to go on, contact the Baton Rouge Convention and Visitors Bureau, P.O. Box 4149, Baton Rouge, LA 70821, or (225) 383-1825, and ask for their tour brochures.)

Here's yet another option: If you have the time, or haven't worn out yet, you could instead go south from Donaldsonville on Highway 308 to **Madewood Plantation** on Bayou Lafourche (call (985) 369-7151), a widely admired 1848 Greek Revival manor whose modern travel-mag style restoration has earned it high ratings from *Travel & Leisure*, etc. (How Creole is this region? See Napoleonville just across the river.) Again, you can stay in the main house or the cottages and have dinner in the original dining room and a continental breakfast before moving on. Otherwise, admission is $8 adults, $4 children; open 10 a.m.–4 p.m.

If you still want to head back toward New Orleans, take Highway 18 from near the Sunshine Bridge about 15 miles to the east and look for the signs to **Oak Alley** (call (800) 44-ALLEY or (225) 265-2151), another Greek Revival beauty whose long drive between rows of 300-year-old live oaks, which gave it its nickname, has become famous through photographs as an example of antebellum architecture. (The real name was Bon Séjour, or "Pleasant Sojourn.") It was built in 1839, and has as many Doric columns, 28, as the oaks themselves. It stood in for the Florida governor's family home in the movie version of *Primary Colors*. It also has several outbuildings that have been turned into overnight rooms ($105–$135) and a restaurant open for breakfast and lunch if you just want to drive over from New Orleans. Admission is $10 adults, $5 students, $3 ages 6–12, (cash only); age 5 and under free; open 9 a.m.–5:30 p.m. (closes at 5 p.m. November through February).

A few miles south of Oak Alley on Highway 18 is the beautifully preserved 1805 West Indies–style plantation, **Laura,** where Louisiana's multi-cultural heritage is even more obvious. Built by Senegalese craftsmen, it was situated on 12,000 acres deeded to a French Catholic family by the King of Spain. Among the tours available are discussions of Creole life, German immigrants, slave history (there are slave cabins among the historic buildings), and the particular role of women landowners. The Laura folks claim that it was here that Joel Chandler Harris heard and recorded the adventures of "Compair(sic) Lapin" and transformed them into the tales of "Br'er Rabbit." However, most scholars believe that Harris's character was an amalgam of three elderly cooks, particularly one known as "Uncle" George Terrell, who Harris knew as a teenage laborer on the Turnwold Plantation in Putnam County, Georgia, during the Civil War. Tours are also given in French daily. Admission is $10 adults, $5 ages 3–17; open daily 9:30 a.m.–4:30 p.m.; call (225) 265-7690.

You can take Highway 18/River Road back to the intersection of Route 90, then take the Huey Long Bridge across the Mississippi back into New Orleans. Or go the other way, southwest, on Highway 18 to Route 641, cross the bridge to I-10 and go back that way.

New Orleans Attractions

As you can tell from the walking tours and our suggestions in Part Two, Planning Your Visit to New Orleans, about designing your own special-interest tour, New Orleans is a lot more, and a lot more interesting, than Bourbon Street. Some of the finest attractions, such as City Park and the New Orleans Museum of Art, the Historic New Orleans Collection, the Jackson Barracks Museum, and Longue Vue House and Gardens, are often overlooked as tourists rush to the more obvious sites. So we've tried to evaluate most of the attractions in a way that may help you choose what you want to see depending on who's in the party, what your interests are, and how in-depth you would like to get.

We begin below with general information about some of the zones not already covered elsewhere, then continue with attraction profiles listed alphabetically by name. However, keep in mind that some cross-zone transportations—the St. Charles Avenue streetcar, the *John James Audubon,* and the Canal Street ferry—are attractions in themselves.

Incidentally, remember that most museums are closed on state as well as federal holidays, and in New Orleans that also means Mardi Gras and frequently All Saint's Day (November 1) as well as the more familiar dates such as Christmas. Many places have group-ticket rates, so if you are traveling with more than just your immediate family, call ahead and ask about discounts. Also remember that ticket prices have a way of inching up without warning, so carry a little extra with you or call in advance.

Zone 2: The Central Business District

We've said several times that you should not venture into **St. Louis Cemetery** without a tour group or at least several friends. One way to get a glimpse of its setting and historic role is to visit **Our Lady of Guadalupe,** which was once used as a virtual assembly line for yellow-fever victims. Unfortunately, the other important site in this area, **Louis Armstrong Park,** can't be recommended as a tourist attraction either, although plans to renovate and secure it in the future may change that. The park is a sort of ghost of Storyville (now vanished under an eyesore of a housing project). It is bordered on one side by Basin Street and includes **Congo Square,** the legendary tribal gathering spot turned jammin' ground; a bandstand (where off and on, free Sunday concerts are scheduled), a community center, and several historic buildings; a jazz and blues radio station (WWOZ 90.7); and even a performing arts center, not to mention the 12-foot statue of Satchmo himself. The neighborhood is gradually reviving, partly thanks to the sentimental "homecoming" of many musicians, but it is not a good idea to walk here. If you do want to hear and see this historic area, contact Cradle of Jazz Tours (283-9136).

Zone 3: Uptown below Napoleon (Garden District)

Unless you have several days, are making a return trip, or have a real shopping "jones," it is unlikely you will spend much time around here. The run of Magazine Street from the Central Business District through Zone 3 to **Audubon Park** in Zone 4 is often touted as the new antiques center, though it is extremely drawn out; you could get off the St. Charles streetcar and walk about three blocks south (that is, turning left as you face uptown from the French Quarter). If you love stained glass, however, jump off at St. Andrew Street and walk four blocks to Constance for **St. Alphonsus.**

Zone 4: Uptown above Napoleon/University

Although they do not qualify as "attractions" in the usual sense, the campuses of both **Loyola University** and **Tulane University** make for nice strolling if you happen to be in the neighborhood. They sit virtually side by side at streetcar stops 36 and 37 on St. Charles Avenue across from **Audubon Park.** (The statue that greets you at the entrance to Loyola, which seems to be running with its arms flung high, has been known on campus for decades as "the touchdown Jesus.") On the Tulane campus is the **Amistad Research Center,** which has the world's largest collection of documents, letters, diaries, photographs, and even art concerning civil rights and black history; the collection is open from 9 a.m.–4:30 p.m., Monday–Saturday, and is housed in the three-story Tilton Hall right at the St. Charles entrance (865-5535). Tulane is also home to the **Newcomb Art Gallery** (835-5328), a collection of Newcomb pottery housed along with rotating exhibits. And there are a few Tiffany studio stained-glass windows at Tulane's **Rogers Chapel,** which is about four blocks off St. Charles on Audubon Place.

If you take the streetcar out to Audubon Park, you may want to notice a few buildings (although there are so many fine fronts that the ride itself qualifies as an attraction). At 3811 St. Charles, between Penniston and General Taylor Streets, is the sweeping double-porch-fronted **Columns Hotel,** (899-9308) designed by architect Thomas Sully in 1883 for a wealthy tobacco merchant and used as the setting for, among other movies, *Pretty Baby.* (If you want to jump off and admire the interior, Esquire magazine once rated its Victorian Lounge the best bar in the city; look for the "private" room.) At 4010 St. Charles, between General Taylor and Constantinople streets, is the Queen Anne home Sully designed for himself. He also designed some three dozen houses along St. Charles, but unfortunately only a few remain. What is now the **New Orleans Public Library** (Latter Branch) at 5120 St. Charles (596-2625), between Soniant and Dufossat, is a fine turn-of-the-19th-century house that was home to, among others, aviator Harry Williams and his film star wife Marguerite Clark; the reading rooms still have their ceiling murals and chandeliers. And just past the edge of the park at Walnut Street is the **Park View Hotel** (861-7564), an ornate Victorian that was originally built to accommodate visitors to the 1884 World Cotton Exposition in Audubon Park.

Finally, you may want to spend a few hours wandering the Riverbend neighborhood for a window-shopping variety as nice as the Quarter's but much less touristy. Take the St. Charles streetcar just past the big right turn onto South Carrollton Avenue (or ask for stop 44), and start strolling up and down Maple Street and then a little farther along Carrollton. There are fine artisan shops here, including boutiques from both

Mignon Faget and Yvonne LaFleur; cafes and coffee shops; bookstores; and bars. Among local favorites: **Brigtsen's** for a Cajun and Creole dinner (chef Frank Brigtsen is a protege of Paul Prudhomme), and the **Camellia Grill** for a locally popular version of steak tartare called the Cannibal Special.

Zone 5: Downtown/St. Bernard

We remind you again that cemeteries, as distinct a New Orleans feature as they are, can be dangerous places for solitary visitors or even small groups. However, if you are seriously intrigued by the offbeat, stop by **St. Roch Cemetery** (945-5961) at Derbigny Street and St. Roch Avenue, modeled on Campo Santo dei Tedeschi near the Vatican in Rome. The story begins with the French-born St. Roch (or Rocco) who, at the beginning of the 14th century, gave away all his possessions and turned to nursing victims of the plague, often curing them by making the sign of the cross. When he himself fell ill, he was kept alive by a dog who brought him food (he's the patron saint of dog-lovers); nevertheless, he was so altered that when he went home he was thrown into prison (he's also the patron of prisoners). Visited in his cell by an angel for five years, he finally died there. In Europe, VSR ("Viva Saint Roch") was often carved over doorways to ward off disease.

When yellow fever broke out in 1868, Father Thevis of nearby **Holy Trinity Church** prayed to St. Roch, promising to build a monument with his own hands if the saint would intercede. The epidemic ended, and Father Thevis built this little chapel, which is now absolutely crammed with prostheses, crutches, glass eyes, and bandages from those who have come here praying for recovery from their injuries. What you see is just what's arrived recently; there are hundreds of such offerings in storage.

If you are with a group and call in advance, you may be able to get inside the **Doullut Steamboat House** on Egania Street near the river (949-1422). It and its neighbor, built just after the turn of the 19th century by Milton Doullut, are two of the most extravagant examples of what is called Victorian Steamboat Gothic architecture, with cypress furbelows, glazed brick, marching columns, great steamboat-style galleries, and glass pilot houses perched on the tops.

Zone 7: Lakeview/West End/Bucktown

If you're headed toward City Park, and you should be, you can visit **Lake Lawn Metairie Cemetery** on Pontchartrain Boulevard at Metairie Road (486-6331), probably the only safe cemetery for tourists to explore (but don't just wander off by yourself, even here). It's younger than the others, built after the Civil War, and not so crowded, but it houses some of the most elaborate sepulchers around: Moorish, Japanese, Greek, Egyptian,

Gothic, you name it. At the foot of the 85-foot obelisk are four statues, because although grieving widower Daniel Moriarty was told there were only three Graces, he insisted there be one at each side, so they've been nicknamed Faith, Hope, Charity and Mrs. Moriarty. You can borrow a general recorded tour at the funeral home, as well as one that locates Civil War veterans and statesmen.

Zone 10: Metairie above Causeway/Kenner/ Jefferson Highway

If you are staying out near the airport, **Destrehan Manor** is very close, about eight miles farther west. However, since most people consider the River Road plantations as out-of-town attractions, we have included it in our self-guided plantation home tour earlier in this chapter.

Type & Name	Zone	Author's Rating
NEW ORLEANS ATTRACTIONS BY TYPE		
Fun & Curiosities		
Blaine Kern's Mardi Gras World	11	★★★
Musée Conti Wax Museum	1	★★½
New Orleans Historic Voodoo Museum	1	★★★
Rivertown	10	★★★★
Six Flags New Orleans	8	t.b.d.
Historic Places		
The Beauregard-Keyes House	1	★★★
Chalmette National Battlefield	5	★★★
The 1850 House	1	★½
Hermann-Grima House	1	★★★
Old Ursuline Convent / Archbishop Antoine Blanc Memorial	1	★★
Pitot House	6	★★★
St. Alphonsus Church	3	★★★★★
Museums & Culture		
Aquarium of the Americas / IMAX Theater	1	★★★★
The Cabildo and Arsenal	1	★★½
Confederate Museum	2	★★★
Gallier House Museum	1	★★★½
Germaine Wells Mardi Gras Museum	1	★★★
Historic New Orleans Collection	1	★★★
Jackson Barracks Museum	5	★★★★

NEW ORLEANS ATTRACTIONS BY TYPE *(continued)*

Type & Name	Zone	Author's Rating
Museums & Culture (continued)		
Longue Vue House and Gardens	7	★★★★★
Louisiana Children's Museum	2	★★★★
National D-Day Museum	2	★★★★★
New Orleans Contemporary Arts Center	2	★★★★
New Orleans Museum of Art	7	★★★★★
New Orleans Pharmacy Museum	1	★★★
The Old U.S. Mint	1	★★★★★
The Presbytere	1	★★★
Parks & Gardens		
Audubon Park	4	★★★★½
Audubon Zoo	4	★★★★
City Park	7	★★★★★
Longue Vue House and Gardens	7	★★★★★
Louisiana Nature Center	8	★★½
New Orleans Botanical Gardens	7	★★★★

NEW ORLEANS ATTRACTIONS BY ZONE

Attraction	Description	Author's Rating
Zone 1: French Quarter		
Aquarium of the Americas /	Marine museum IMAX Theater	★★★★
The Beauregard-Keyes House	Restored home of general and novelist	★★★
The Cabildo and Arsenal	Flagship of Louisiana State Museum complex	★★½
The 1850 House	Mid-19th-century apartment	★½
Gallier House Museum	Period-correct restored home	★★★½
Germaine Wells Mardi Gras Museum	Costume and jewelry collection	★★★
Hermann-Grima House	Restored Federal-style home	★★★
Historic New Orleans Collection	Complex of free exhibits	★★★

NEW ORLEANS ATTRACTIONS BY ZONE (continued)

Zone & Name	Description	Author's Rating
Zone 1: French Quarter (continued)		
Musée Conti Wax Museum	History, horror, and Mardi Gras in wax	★★½
New Orleans Historic Voodoo Museum	Schlock and awe	★★★
New Orleans Pharmacy Museum	Restored apothecary	★★★
The Old U.S. Mint	Part of Louisiana State Museum complex	★★★★★
Old Ursuline Convent / Archbishop Antoine Blanc Memorial	250-year-old religious sites, gardens, archives	★★
The Presbytere	Part of Louisiana State Museum complex	★★★
Zone 2: Central Business District		
Confederate Museum	Civil War museum	★★★
Louisiana Children's Museum	Children's activity center	★★★★
National D-Day Museum	Military museum and veterans' memorial	★★★★★
New Orleans Contemporary Arts Center	Arts and performing arts complex	★★★★
Our Lady of Guadalupe / Shrine of St. Jude	Chapel of "St. Expedite"	★★½
Zone 3: Uptown below Napoleon		
St. Alphonsus Church	Chapel with stained glass	★★★★★
Zone 4: Uptown above Napoleon		
Audubon Park	Public green, pool, playgrounds, etc.	★★★★½
Audubon Zoo	Zoo	★★★★
Zone 5: Downtown/St. Bernard		
Chalmette National Battlefield	Scene of Battle of New Orleans	★★★
Jackson Barracks Museum	Military museum	★★★★
Zone 6: Mid-City/Gentilly		
Pitot House	19th-century home	★★★
Zone 7: Lakeview/West End/Bucktown		
City Park	Municipal park	★★★★★
Longue Vue House & Gardens	Historic home, museum, gardens	★★★★★
New Orleans Botanical Gardens	Gardens and conservatory	★★★★
New Orleans Museum of Art	Fine and decorative arts	★★★★★

NEW ORLEANS ATTRACTIONS BY ZONE *(continued)*		
Zone & Name	**Description**	**Author's Rating**
Zone 8: New Orleans East		
Louisiana Nature Center	Nature preserve and planetarium	★★½
Six Flags New Orleans	Amusement park	t.b.d.
Zone 10: Metairie above Causeway/Kenner/Jefferson Highway		
Rivertown	Family amusement & education complex	★★★★
Zone 11: West Bank		
Blaine Kern's Mardi Gras World	Mardi Gras floats and costumes	★★★

Attraction Profiles

Aquarium of the Americas / IMAX Theater

Type of attraction A state-of-the-art and interactive marine museum with a good mix of science and fun

Location Zone 1 French Quarter; along the Mississippi Riverfront at the foot of Canal Street

Admission Aquarium alone: $14 adults, $10 seniors, $6.50 kids ages 2–12. IMAX alone: $8 adults, $7 seniors, $5 kids age 12 and under. Combination tickets: $18 adults, $15 seniors, $10.50 children. Additional discount tickets available for boat/aquarium/zoo packages or boat/zoo/aquarium/IMAX.

Hours Aquarium: Sunday–Thursday, 9:30 a.m.–6 p.m.; Friday and Saturday, 9:30 a.m.–7 p.m.; IMAX (shows every two hours): Sunday–Thursday, 10 a.m.–6 p.m.; Friday and Saturday, 10 a.m.–8 p.m.

Phone 861-2537; (800) 774-7394

Website www.auduboninstitute.org

When to go Early, if not to see it before it gets crowded, at least to get timed tickets for later in the day, when the air conditioning may be welcome

Special comments One of the 1990s generation of marine installations, very pleasant and user-friendly and a best bet for mixed-age groups

Appeal by Age Group

Pre-school ★★½	Teens ★★★★	Over 30 ★★★★
Grade school ★★★★	Young adults ★★★★	Seniors ★★★

Author's rating Visually and intellectually stimulating, with unusual care taken to make legends both legible and intelligible. ★★★★

How much time to allow At least an hour for the aquarium, even if you have restless children; two hours for IMAX, counting standing in line

Description & comments It's hard to go wrong here unless you are so blasé that you can't get a thrill out of stroking the tough-suede skin of a small sand shark (one of the most popular queues) or of marveling at the beautiful, transparent, and snowflake-complex bodies of lacy jellyfish, one of the more astounding exhibits. The museum houses several large permanent exhibits, including a multilevel, multispecies Amazon rain forest, a penguin house, Caribbean reef and Mississippi River environments, and a 400,000-gallon saltwater mini–Gulf of Mexico with 14-foot-tall glass walls and all the sharks and stingrays any kid could desire. There is a café on the second floor and the usual concessions at the IMAX. The IMAX rotates at least two movies a day, many on historical or environmental themes (even if they are sometimes the Disney version); a few viewers may find the super-realistic wide-angle photography (and sometimes 3-D effects) dizzying.

Touring tips Wear comfortable shoes with no-slip soles; although the ramps in and out of various environments are not slick, you may be distracted by all that's going on around you. This is a nice spot to meet in the afternoon if the party wants to split up during the day, because you can buy timed IMAX tickets in advance. Everything is wheelchair accessible, another fact worth noting in a city as old and often inconvenient as New Orleans.

Audubon Park

Type of attraction Public green and pedestrian retreat with riding stables, conservatory, swimming pool, miniature train, playgrounds, golf course, bandstands, soccer fields, jogging path, etc.

Location Zone 4 Uptown above Napoleon; entrances at 6800–7000 St. Charles Avenue and 6500 Magazine Street

Admission Free

Hours 6 a.m.–10 p.m.

Phone 861-2537

When to go Anytime except after dark, no matter what the signs say

Special comments One of the reasons to choose to stay in the Garden District instead of the French Quarter; not quite as fine a facility as City Park but very close

Appeal by Age Group

Pre-school ★★★	Teens ★★★	Over 30 ★★★★
Grade school ★★★	Young adults ★★★★★	Seniors ★★★

Author's rating If you're staying in town long enough to seek out exercise and recreation, this is prime; even a jog or hour's reading in one of the shady gazebos can be an essential break for a visiting executive. And, of course, it has something for everyone in a family. ★★★★½

How much time to allow Varies by activity

Description & comments This is the classic ideal of a public green, built on what was originally a sugar plantation (in the very beginning, it belonged to the Sieur de Bienville himself) and which still boasts live oaks from before the city's founding, along with magnolias, lagoons, formal plantings, hothouse flowers (the Heymann Memorial Conservatory), benches, and trails. The 365-acre park was laid out in the 1890s by John Olmstead, son of the architect of New York's Central Park, after the Cotton Exposition of 1884 was held there. Cars are prohibited around the St. Charles end, so you can wander without fear. Across the railroad tracks toward the Mississippi is the less-publicized area called River View, popular for picnics or jogging. For more on the sport and exercise facilities, see Part Eleven, Exercise and Recreation.

Touring tips Most of the more organized activities and the zoo are at the Magazine Street end of the park. It's a fairly long walk from St. Charles Avenue if you're only trying to get from here to there, but the zoo operates a shuttle van from St. Charles around to the parking lot.

Audubon Zoo

Type of attraction Popular and professionally acclaimed zoological park with naturalistic environments, hands-on exhibits, a tropical bird house, live-animal feedings, etc.

Location Zone 4 Uptown above Napoleon; 6500 Magazine Street in Audubon Park

Admission $10 adults, $6 seniors, $5 kids ages 2–12

Hours 9:30 a.m.–5 p.m. daily (ticket booths close at 4 p.m.)

Phone 861-2537; (800) 774-7394

Website www.auduboninstitute.org

When to go Anytime

Appeal by Age Group

Pre-school ★★★	Teens ★★★	Over 30 ★★★
Grade school ★★★★	Young adults ★★★½	Seniors ★★★

Author's rating Extremely well designed and stocked, with huge family appeal. ★★★★

How much time to allow 2–3 hours

Description & comments There are nearly 2,000 animals here, many of them rare or endangered species, in carefully re-created environments such as the 6½-acre Louisiana Swamp, crisscrossed with boardwalks so you can spy on the white alligators. It's only a short stroll to other continents, however: the Asian Domain, with its Indian temple, rhinos, elephants, and a white tiger; the African Savannah; the South American pampas, the primate house . . . well, you get the idea. For kids of the *Jurassic Park* generation, there's good info on dinosaurs, a group of "living dinosaurs," namely Komodo dragons, and so on. And all around, the keepers offer chances to stroke or feed the tamer animals.

Touring tips The Cypress Knee Café has great food. Remember to consider the package tickets which combine zoo admission with a cruise from the aquarium, etc. However, the number of steps and escalators in the park may make you wish you hadn't brought the stroller; piggy-backing may save some trouble

The Beauregard-Keyes House

Type of attraction Restored 19th-century "raised cottage" and former residence of Gen. P.G.T. Beauregard and novelist Frances Parkinson Keyes, with personal effects and open gardens

Location Zone 1 French Quarter; 1113 Chartres Street, between Ursulines and Governor Nicholls streets

Admission $5 adults, $4 seniors and students, $2 kids ages 6–12, ages 5 and under free

Hours Monday–Saturday, 10 a.m.–3 p.m.

Phone 523-7257

When to go Anytime

Appeal by Age Group

Pre-school —	Teens ★★★	Over 30 ★★★
Grade school ★★	Young adults ★★★	Seniors ★★★★

Author's rating Low-key, but lovely and a little sad if you know your history. ★★★

How much time to allow No more than an hour, including guided tour and stroll around the gardens

Description & comments This is a lovely old home, even without its many historical connections. It was built in 1826 in raised-cottage style with a lovely twin staircase, Doric columns, and elegant side gallery. The formal gardens probably date back to the 1830s, when it belonged to the Swiss consul. It was a boardinghouse during the Civil War, and when Confederate general and native son Pierre Gustave Toutant Beauregard returned to the area, his own plantation in ruins, he and several members of his family lodged there for about 18 months. It was almost demolished in the 1920s, but a group of ladies lobbied for its restoration, and in 1944 the novelist Frances Parkinson Keyes (rhymes with "eyes") moved in and began meticulous reconstruction, eventually turning the big house over to a charitable foundation and living in the rear cottage, also part of the tour. Many of the furnishings and personal effects belonged to Beauregard. The gift shop has copies of most of Keyes' books, many of them historical novels dealing with Creole society and the house itself.

Touring tips Like many New Orleans homes, this is strictly a guided tour, with costumed docents. But now that PBS has made *The Civil War* so lively again, even students may find Beauregard's old study intriguing. The gardens make for a nice respite, as well.

Blaine Kern's Mardi Gras World

Type of attraction Year-round factory of flamboyant Mardi Gras floats and costumes

Location Zone 11 West Bank; 223 Newton Street, Algiers (across the river from the World Trade Center)

Admission $13.50 adults, $10 seniors, $6.50 children ages 3–11

Hours Daily, 9:30 a.m.–4:30 p.m.

Phone 361-7821

Website www.mardigrasworld.com

When to go Anytime

Special comments One of the four major year-round ways to experience Mardi Gras, and a sure-fire kids' favorite, especially combined with the free ferry ride

Appeal by Age Group

Pre-school ★★★	Teens ★★★★	Over 30 ★★★
Grade school ★★★	Young adults ★★★★	Seniors ★★★

Author's rating Impressive and fantastical, if a little static. ★★★

How much time to allow 1½–2 hours

Description & comments Blaine Kern is known as "Mr. Mardi Gras," and for good reason: He made his first float in 1947, at the age of 19; and since then has become probably the busiest float-makers in the world, responsible for not only more than half of the floats and multistory-sized figures for Mardi Gras, which brings in a reported $20 million a year alone, but also for Macy's Thanksgiving Day parade, the Bastille Day celebrations in Cannes, France, and more than 40 other parades around the world. They even make sculptures and props for Disney. The sculpture company was founded right before the 1984 World's Fair in New Orleans to build the giant characters for that event, and now works for amusement parks all over the world. These huge warehouses, more than 500,000 square feet of them, called "dens," are filled with props, celebrity statues, royal regalia, and the artists creating them; you can even dress in costume and have your picture taken alongside one of the characters.

Touring tips Take the Canal Street Ferry across and look for the shuttle bus. For older visitors, the architecture of the Algiers neighborhood may hold some interest, but it is not a great area to walk around, especially late in the day.

The Cabildo and Arsenal

Type of attraction Flagship building of the Louisiana State Museum complex in the city. Entrance to the Arsenal, which only occasionally has exhibits, is through the Cabildo.

Location Zone 1 French Quarter; on Chartres Street facing Jackson Square

Admission $5 adults; $4 seniors, students, and active military; kids ages 12 and under free

Hours Tuesday–Sunday, 9 a.m.–5 p.m.

Phone 568-6968

Website www.lsm.crt.state.la.us

When to go Anytime

Special comments Be sure to check at the front desk for information on changing exhibits or exhibits in the Arsenal.

Appeal by Age Group

Pre-school —	Teens ★★	Over 30 ★★★
Grade school ★★	Young adults ★★★	Seniors ★★★

Author's rating Not terribly engaging, and sometimes stiffly explained, but if you skim through, picking up the more intriguing exhibits, particularly some of the more subtle folk-art pieces, mildly entertaining. ★★½

How much time to allow 30–60 minutes

Description & comments This is not a very hands-on museum, and compared to the new-generation facilities it can be rather dry; you will probably find yourself skimming through unless you stop to watch videos. But there are a few particular exhibits that may hold even a child's attention, such as the Indian pirogue; weapons and uniforms from the Civil War and the Battle of New Orleans; that apocryphal symbol of slavery, the cotton gin; a lock of Andy Jackson's hair; antique medical tools, including a leech jar; a young child's casket; and Napoleon's death mask, sporting a dark and surprisingly philosophical visage unfamiliar from the typical portraits. African Americans and Native Americans may find the exhibits devoted to their contributions a little stiff but well intentioned. The building itself has historical significance: The official transfer of the Louisiana Territory from France to the United States was signed here, and since it also housed the State Supreme Court from 1868 to 1910, it saw the arguing of several famous legal cases, including *Plessy v. Ferguson.*

Touring tips The Cabildo is wheelchair accessible and even offers wheelchairs for use; visitors with other disabilities should check in at the front counter for assistance.

Chalmette National Battlefield

Type of attraction Scene of the Battle of New Orleans, Jackson's famous victory over the British in 1815

Location Zone 5 Downtown/St. Bernard; 8608 St. Bernard Highway (Rampart/St. Claude extended)

Admission Free

Hours 9 a.m.–5 p.m.

Phone 281-0510

When to go January 7–8 to see battle re-enactment; otherwise anytime

Special comments Although the car gate closes at 5 p.m., there is a pedestrian entry near the cemetery.

Appeal by Age Group

Pre-school —	Teens ★★	Over 30 ★★★
Grade school ★★	Young adults ★★½	Seniors ★★★

Author's rating Admittedly, battlefields (and military cemeteries) don't appeal to everyone, but if you do find wandering such grounds moving, this is an unusually reassuring and well-marked route. It's an unalloyed, Hollywood-cheerful victory, not a haunting experience like revisiting Antietam, for example. And you can't beat the scenery. ★★★

How much time to allow 1–2 hours

Description & comments The bare bones of this battle, so to speak, are familiar to most Americans, by film and pop-music history, if nothing else. Here, on January 8, 1815, British forces under Lt. Gen. Edward Pakenham, brother-in-law of the great Duke of Wellington, were crushed (and Pakenham killed) by the ragtag coalition of Tennessee volunteers, other Southern regiments hustled down for support, free men of color, and Barataria pirates under the able and often ruthless Andrew Jackson. More than 2,000 British were killed on that last day (there had been skirmishes since before Christmas), but only 13 Americans were lost, all but two of them black. The other ironies are almost as well known: The Treaty of Ghent, ending the war, had been signed on Christmas Eve, making the battle moot; Jackson made several errors in judgment that might easily have thrown the victory the other way; and Jackson, who had unsuccessfully tried to persuade President Jefferson to name him governor of Louisiana, wound up far more famous as a result of the battle—the city threw him a triumphal parade modeled on those of the conquering Caesars—which was in effect the first great stroke of his own presidential campaign. It also marked a great turning point in the city's history, uniting Creoles and Americans (and pirates) against a common threat. The annual re-enactment is highly theatrical, beginning the night before with staged spying on Pakenham and Jackson. Oddly, the adjoining Chalmette National Cemetery dates from the Civil War and holds only two veterans of the Battle of New Orleans; most of the other bodies, some 14,000 of them, are Union soldiers.

Touring tips You can just drive past the landmarks, but the visitors center, once the plantation home of Rene Beauregard, son of the general, holds good exhibits that help you understand the battle's waves, a half-hour film, and well-informed rangers. Be sure to walk over to the levee and look onto the Mississippi River.

City Park

Type of attraction Municipal park with a variety of recreational and cultural attractions

Location Zone 7 Lakeview/West End/Bucktown; 1 Palm Drive off I-10 (City Park/Metairie exit)

Admission Park free; museum, botanical gardens, and some recreational centers have fees.

Hours Sunrise to sunset

Phone 482-4888

When to go Anytime

Appeal by Age Group

Pre-school ★★★	Teens ★★★	Over 30 ★★★★★
Grade school ★★★★★	Young adults ★★★★★	Seniors ★★★

Author's rating An unrivaled family venue, with attractions for kids, jocks, picnickers, nature-lovers, and general romantics. ★★★★★

How much time to allow 1–4 hours

Description & comments This is an extraordinary municipal gift, 1,500 acres from the old Allard Plantation. It was presented to the city by John McDonough, whose statue stands in Lafayette Square, and is home to the largest stand of mature live oaks in the world. City Park has an almost unequaled variety of recreational facilities, golf courses, tennis courts, batting cages, riding stables, lagoons, etc., plus a bandstand (the Beatles played here in 1964), the New Orleans Museum of Art, the Botanical Gardens, and the famous Dueling Oaks beneath which hundreds of formal duels were fought during the 19th century. The park also has many simpler attractions, including the Storyland Amusement Park, an old-fashioned but swell children's fairyland where kids can climb over, around, and into the larger-than-life storybook exhibits and hear the out-loud stories straight from the "books'" mouths. *Child* magazine calls this one of the top ten playgrounds in the United States. Next door is Carousel Gardens, known to locals as The Flying Horses, one of the few surviving carved wooden merry-go-rounds in the country. And beyond that are a kid-scaled Ferris wheel, miniature trains, bumper cars, a roller coaster, and so on.

Touring tips From Thanksgiving through New Year's, nearly a million tiny lights are strung among the trees, and the Carousel stays lighted and alive into the evening. Long lines of locals make this an annual holiday event. That's Beauregard at the front gate, of course. Also be sure to notice the WPA symbols, chisels, hammers, and so on, worked into the iron of the bridges around the grounds.

Confederate Museum

Type of attraction Traditional but unusually large and somber Civil War museum

Location Zone 2 Central Business District; 929 Camp Street, at Howard Avenue

Admission $5, $4 students and seniors, $2 kids age 12 and under

Hours Monday–Saturday, 10 a.m.–4 p.m.

Phone 523-4522

When to go Anytime

Appeal by Age Group

Pre-school —	Teens ★★	Over 30 ★★★★
Grade school ★	Young adults ★★★★	Seniors ★★★★★

Author's rating Moving and interesting. ★★★

How much time to allow 1½ hours

Description & comments "Everybody thinks it's a church, but it's not," says the staffer about this medievally somber shrine to the Glorious

Cause, the oldest Civil War museum in the country. Homegrown architect Thomas Sully designed it as a complement to the Romanesque Howard Memorial Library next door (itself becoming a museum, as noted in the walking tour of the Warehouse/Arts District), and it looks every bit the sepulcher—as it surely must have in 1893 when 50,000 mourners came to pay respects to the body of Jefferson Davis. There's no substitute for artifacts in a museum: That ineffable dignity that lingers in objects handled by long-dead humans suffuses the most sophisticated installation, and in such items the museum, also known as Confederate Memorial Hall, is rich indeed. Its collection, the second largest in the country, turns arms and armaments into an eloquent commentary on the social impact of the war on men and women alike. Among the most moving items are the frock coats worn by generals Beauregard and Braxton Bragg, whose physical slightness provides a poignant counterpoint to the magnitude of the conflict; the modest headgear of one Landon Creek, who survived 7 battles and 3 wounds to make it to his 15th birthday; a pair of boots, long interred with its owner and now on eerie, empty display; a child's Zouave-style jacket from Marshall Field's, a high-fashion flirtation with rebellion; and part of Lee's battlefield silver. Among the women honored here are those who resisted the occupation of "Beast" Butler's troops by spitting or recoiling in their presence.

Touring tips Street parking available

The 1850 House

Type of attraction Mid-19th-century middle-class apartment with period furnishings

Location Zone 1 French Quarter; in the Pontalba Apartments at 523 St. Ann Street facing Jackson Square

Admission $3 adults; $2 seniors, students, and active military; kids age 12 and under free

Hours Tuesday–Sunday, 9 a.m.–5 p.m.

Phone 568-6968

Website www.lsm.crt.state.la.us

When to go Anytime, though this might qualify as rainy-day stuff

Special comments One of the most intriguing things about these apartments is that they are still occupied, and there's still a waiting list. Also note the Spring Fiesta Association house at 826 St. Ann; open by appointment only (945-2744, or Fridays 581-1367).

Appeal by Age Group

Pre-school —	Teens ★	Over 30 ★★
Grade school ★	Young adults ★★	Seniors ★★

Author's rating Just a snapshot of social history, but oddly chilly—less palpably lived-in than the Hermann-Grima or Gallier houses. ★½

How much time to allow 15–20 minutes

Description & comments This is a sort of single museum exhibit expanded over several stories, a real-sized dollhouse in a way. If you are not curious about the evolution of American social customs, you may not get much out of it. Some of its antiques, particularly the rococo revival bedroom furniture and the rare complete 75-piece set of Vieux Paris tableware will be very significant to some and merely pretty to others. What is intriguing is the apartment's history: Baroness Micaela Almonester de Pontalba, daughter of the Spanish grandee who rebuilt the Presbytere, Cabildo, and Cathedral after the great fires of the late 18th century, wanted both to transform the square from a military-parade ground into a European-style public plaza and to improve the value of her land in the declining old city. She went through several of New Orleans's best architects, including James Gallier Sr. and Henry Howard, and micromanaged the contractors who survived (if you see the portraits of the baroness in the Presbytere, you won't be surprised); but the row houses were ultimately a great success, 16 on each side and all with storefronts on the sidewalk level, just as they are today. Note the entwined "A" and "P" cartouche—for Almonester de Pontalba—in the balcony railing.

The apartments did eventually become fairly run-down, but were restored by massive WPA projects. The State of Louisiana owns the Lower Pontalbas (the side including the 1850 House), and the city owns the Upper Pontalbas.

Touring tips This museum is not wheelchair accessible, and the rather steep and narrow stairs may be difficult for older or physically limited visitors. The booklet given to visitors for the self-guided tour offers a great deal of information about the original facilities and decoration.

Gallier House Museum

Type of attraction Period-correct restoration of the house designed by prominent architect James Gallier Jr. for his own family

Location Zone 1 French Quarter; 1118–1132 Royal Street, between Ursulines and Governor Nicolls streets

Admission $6 adults, $5 seniors and students, kids under age 8 free; $10 adults and $9 seniors and students for both Gallier and Hermann-Grima houses

Hours Monday–Saturday, 10 a.m.–4 p.m. (last tour begins at 3:30 p.m.)

Phone 525-5661

When to go Anytime, although unlike most historic houses, it's difficult in the rain because you have to go along the upstairs gallery.

Special comments Particularly interesting because Gallier designed so many more elaborate homes in the Garden District for American patrons.

Appeal by Age Group

Pre-school —	Teens ★	Over 30 ★★★
Grade school ★	Young adults ★★	Seniors ★★★

Author's rating House tours are attractions requiring a fair amount of imagination (or desire for imitation), but Gallier's design is both gracious and clever, crammed full of fine architectural and decorative detailing. ★★★½

How much time to allow 30–45 minutes

Description & comments Administered by Tulane University, this is one of the most meticulously correct restorations in town, partly because Gallier's own designs and notes have been preserved. Though not perhaps as wealthy as many of his patrons, Gallier would certainly qualify as comfortably well-off. His house was very up-to-date in many ways—the chandeliers were gas-burning, the bathroom had hot running water, and the whole house had a sort of primitive air-conditioning system with vents and ice-cooled air—but it is also revealing about customs of the times, with its servants' quarters, dish pantry, summer matting vs. winter carpets, children's sickroom, high brick garden walls, etc. The faux painting of the cypress to resemble pine is also very characteristic. The decorative molding and plaster work, gilded capitals, 12-foot ceilings, marble, and paneling are very fine, and the docents here are extremely knowledgeable about the entire inventory. The work on outbuildings continues. Be sure to admire the carriage in the alley between the two buildings.

Touring tips Not truly wheelchair accessible, but not impossible.

Germaine Wells Mardi Gras Museum

Type of attraction Costume and jewelry collection

Location Zone 1 French Quarter; upstairs at Arnaud's Restaurant at 813 Bienville Street, between Bourbon and Dauphine streets

Admission Free

Hours Monday–Friday, 11:30 a.m.–2:30 p.m. and 6–10 p.m.; Saturday, 6–10 p.m.; Sunday 10 a.m.–2 p.m. and 6–10 p.m. (these are the restaurant hours)

Phone 523-0611

When to go Anytime

Appeal by Age Group

Pre-school ★	Teens ★★	Over 30 ★★★
Grade school ★★	Young adults ★★★	Seniors ★★

Author's rating This covers less territory than the Mardi Gras exhibit in the Old U.S. Mint, since it's primarily his-and-her gowns, but they speak volumes about the lost sophistication of old New Orleans. As a fast, free diversion, hard to beat. ★★★

How much time to allow 20 minutes

Description & comments The family of restaurateur Arnaud Cazenave, and particularly his daughter, Germaine Cazenave Wells, were mainstays of the old-society Carnival for decades; Germaine alone reigned as queen of nearly two dozen balls, more than anyone else in history. Her collection of royal outfits and jewelry, many of them astonishingly luxurious and accompanied by pictures of the corresponding ball, has been rescued and placed in glass cases in a pretty but simple wing. When you find the spangled gown she wore as the 1954 Queen of Naiades, tip your hat: she loved the gown so much she was buried in a replica of it. A small case outside displays some of her almost equally exuberant Easter bonnets.

Touring tips The costumes are fragile, so the air conditioning is often up pretty high.

Hermann-Grima House

Type of attraction Beautifully restored home from the early Federal period, with unusually extensive outbuildings

Location Zone 1 French Quarter; 818–820 S. Louis Street between Bourbon and Dauphine streets

Admission $6 adults, $5 seniors and students, kids age 8 and under free; $10 adults, $9 seniors and students for combined ticket to Gallier House

Hours Monday–Saturday, 10 a.m.–4 p.m. (last tour leaves at 3:30 p.m.)

Phone 525-5661

When to go Anytime

Special comments Occasionally there are special cooking demonstrations in the rear kitchen; ask at the ticket counter in the carriage house.

Appeal by Age Group

Pre-school —	Teens ★★	Over 30 ★★★
Grade school ★	Young adults ★★★	Seniors ★★★

Author's rating An unusual house and one that says quite a bit about its owners; more fun when the live demonstrations are scheduled. ★★★

How much time to allow 45 minutes–1 hour

Description & comments This is an unusual home in that it represents the style of the so-called Golden Age of New Orleans, meaning the first great commercial boom under U.S. administration. Though it's usually hard to get younger people interested in old homes, the peculiarities of this one—the shared bathroom, the outdoor kitchens, the young woman's furnishings—make it more accessible than most. The house was built in 1831 for a wealthy merchant named Samuel Hermann. It was constructed in the Federal style, with a central doorway and divided rooms rather than the 18th-century side-hall style; the exterior plaster is scored to look like brick, which was very expensive and showy. (Much of the decorative work was produced by the free men of color then flourishing in New Orleans.) The house was sold in 1844 to Judge Felix Grima, whose family remained there for five generations. The period furniture is very fine. The master bedroom actually faces the street and has a pocket-door opening to the middle hall and second bedroom for ventilation. The long garden, outbuildings for cooking and household work, and even the original carriage house (the one used for tickets and souvenirs was attached to the house next door) are finely restored. There are special black history tours available throughout February or year-round for groups of ten or more.

Touring tips Because you can buy timed tickets in advance, you may want to ask the guides if there are any large groups already scheduled for a particular tour. You can also stop by in the morning and get tickets for the time of your choice, pass them out, and meet at the appointed hour. Because you don't get to go upstairs, this is a good choice for those with physical limitations, although there are a few steps; those unable to mount the front steps might ask at the counter if they can be brought through from the courtyard.

Historic New Orleans Collection

Type of attraction A complex of free exhibits, a late-18th-century residence and a 19th-century residence remodeled for 1940s society

Location Zone 1 French Quarter; 533 Royal Street between Toulouse and St. Louis streets

Admission Williams galleries free; Williams residence and Louisiana History Galleries in the Merieult House, $4

Hours Tuesday–Saturday, 9 a.m.–5 p.m.; tours at 10 and 11 a.m. and 2 and 3 p.m.; free gallery talks are given Wednesdays at 12:30 p.m.

Phone 523-4662

Website www.hnoc.org

When to go Anytime, but calling ahead is recommended

Special comments One of the most satisfying tours in town, historically and culturally

Appeal by Age Group

Pre-school —	Teens ★★	Over 30 ★★★★
Grade school ★	Young adults ★★★★	Seniors ★★★

Author's rating If you have limited time and want to get a flavor of the social, cultural, and historical evolution of New Orleans, this is the tour to take. Even if you have lots of time, it's the one. ★★★

How much time to allow Up to 2 hours including tours

Description & comments This is partly a research center, partly a group of restored architectural gems, and a bit of an art gallery as well. The entrance-level Williams galleries have first-class rotating exhibits on Mardi Gras, renovation, arts and crafts, etc., that are free for the browsing. Behind that is the glorious 1792 Merieult House of romantic legend, whose airy rooms now house rare materials from the landmark collection of the late Kemper and Leila Williams, including maps, documents concerning the Louisiana Purchase, wildly inflated propaganda posters, rare photographs, and so on. (The extraordinary bulk of their collection is now housed in its own lovely library, the Williams Research Center, at 410 Chartres.) The 19th-century brick cottage at the end of the courtyard was the Williams' residence, which they had renovated to suit their own high standards of comfort and hospitality, and to showcase their collections of fine porcelain, antique furniture, and textiles.

Touring tips This is a one-stop whirlwind tour of New Orleans history, and a particularly evocative one, since you literally step off Royal Street into a gracious residence of two centuries' standing. Even the gifts in the shop have some historical appeal. Wheelchair access available; ask at the counter.

Jackson Barracks Museum

Type of attraction Military museum with antique and modern armaments and aircraft from the Revolutionary War through the 1990s

Location Zone 5 Downtown/St. Bernard; 6400 St. Claude Avenue (Rampart Street extended)

Admission Free

Hours Monday–Friday, 8 a.m.–4 p.m.; Saturday, 9 a.m.–3 p.m.

Phone 278-8242

When to go Anytime

Appeal by Age Group

Pre-school ★	Teens ★★★	Over 30 ★★★★
Grade school ★★★★	Young adults ★★★★	Seniors ★★★★

Author's rating Fantastic variety of exhibits in this small space, and almost guaranteed to make kids happy. Since even a Phantom jet and a Russian-made tank abandoned in the Gulf War are here, veterans or students of any war in U.S. history will find something to marvel at. ★★★★

How much time to allow 1½ hours

Description & comments Tanks, artillery, jets, battle flags, decorations, uniforms, maps. . . . This military museum seems to have acquired relics from every skirmish and siege in the nation's history, but without the sometimes-morbid touch of the Confederate Museum. The museum's main building is a powder magazine dating to 1837, but not surprisingly, it had to expand into an annex. The presence of Guardsmen may make this even more realistic for youngsters.

Touring tips This is now headquarters for the National Guard, and subject to "internal business," so it wouldn't hurt to call ahead. As you pass the Jackson Barracks next door, you may feel the ghosts even more strongly: The base was built by order of (President) Andy Jackson, and Civil War generals Robert E. Lee, P.G.T. Beauregard, Ulysses S. Grant, and George McLellan were all stationed here as young West Point graduates.

Longue Vue House and Gardens

Type of attraction Historic home, decorative arts museum, and formal gardens

Location Zone 7 Lakeview/West End/Bucktown; 7 Bamboo Road off I-10 (Metairie Road exit)

Admission $10 adults, $6 seniors, $5 students and children

Hours Monday–Saturday, 10 a.m.–4:30 p.m. (last tour at 4 p.m.); Sunday, 1–5 p.m. (last tour at 4 p.m.)

Phone 488-5488

Website www.longuevue.com

When to go Anytime, but flowering gardens peak in spring

Appeal by Age Group

Pre-school ½	Teens ★★	Over 30 ★★★★★
Grade school ★	Young adults ★★★	Seniors ★★★★★

Author's rating Elegant, interesting, and satisfying. ★★★★★

How much time to allow 2 hours (1 each for house and gardens)

Description & comments The sumptuous Greek Revival home of philanthropist Edgar Bloom Stern and Edith Rosenwald Stern, daughter of Sears tycoon Julius Rosenwald, was constructed with the express idea that it would be left as a museum. It was designed by William and Geoffrey Platt, and the gardens were laid out by Ellen Biddle Shipman, who also oversaw much of the interior decoration, which features important antiques, rice-paper wall coverings, needlework, Oriental carpets, and Wedgwood creamware. The house also offers rotating exhibits in its galleries. Among the gardens are the Spanish Court (modeled after the gardens of the Alhambra), the Portuguese Canal, the Wild Garden, and the Walled Garden.

Touring tips The home is wheelchair accessible and a good choice for older visitors. Tour guide brochures are available in French, German, Italian, Spanish, and Japanese, as well as large print. Educational programs are offered for both children and adults; inquire at the desk.

Louisiana Children's Museum

Type of attraction State-of-the-art children's activity center

Location Zone 2 Central Business District; 420 Julia Street, at Constance Avenue

Admission $6

Hours Tuesday–Saturday, 9:30 a.m.–4:30 p.m.; Sunday, noon–4:30 p.m.; Monday (June–August only), 9:30 a.m.–4:30 p.m.

Phone 523-1357

When to go After lunchtime, when the daytrippers and school groups have left

Appeal by Age Group

Pre-school ★★★★★	Teens ½	Over 30 ½
Grade school ★★★★★	Young adults ½	Seniors ½

Author's rating The way early learning is supposed to be—exciting and fun. ★★★★

How much time to allow 1½–2 hours

Description & comments In a colorful, noisy converted warehouse, this science- and math-oriented facility teaches kids the inner workings of things by letting them simply have a good time. Pulleys, gears, wind machines, bubble rings, and sound-wave amplifiers are offered, along with an innovative and kindly minded exhibit introducing kids to the difficulties of handicapped—but not limited—life: they shoot baskets from a wheelchair, stack blocks wearing thick, clumsy gloves, etc. There are Sesame Street–style areas, such as the café where they can pretend to cook, a grocery store, a Cajun cottage, and an art gallery. There's a special room for toddlers, so siblings don't feel tied down.

Touring tips Being subjected to constant battering means some of the hands-on exhibits need maintenance; just move on to the next thing. Food is limited to vending machines. Street parking available.

Louisiana Nature Center

Type of attraction Nature preserve and planetarium

Location Zone 8 New Orleans East; Joe W. Brown Memorial Park, 11000 Lake Forest Boulevard (off I-10)

Admission $5 adults, $4 seniors, $3 children

Hours Tuesday–Friday, 9 a.m.–5 p.m.; Saturday, 10 a.m.–5 p.m.; Sunday, noon–5 p.m.; public planetarium shows Wednesday–Friday at 3:30 p.m.

Phone 861-2537; planetarium schedule, 246-star

When to go Anytime

Special comments Parts of the nature trails have wheelchair-accessible boardwalks.

Appeal by Age Group

Pre-school ★★	Teens ★★	Over 30 ★★
Grade school ★★★	Young adults ★★★	Seniors ★★★

Author's rating A rare urban reserve. ★★½

How much time to allow 1–2 hours

Description & comments This may be one of those places you don't get to until the second trip, but it would be worth visiting: an 86-acre forest and wetlands reserve with trails, greenhouses, changing science exhibits in the center, and a hands-on Discovery Loft with fossils, skeletons, etc., plus some live specimens. Local wildlife can be observed either from the trails or from window overlooks at the Wildlife Garden.

Touring tips Weekend visitors should inquire about special activities such as canoeing, bird-watching, etc.

Musée Conti Wax Museum

Type of attraction Pretty much what it sounds like, a Madame Toussaud's of New Orleans history with a little requisite scary stuff mixed in and some surprising Mardi Gras outfits as a lagniappe

Location Zone 1 French Quarter; 917 Conti Street, between Dauphine and Burgundy streets

Admission $6.75 adults, $6.25 seniors and students, $5.75 ages 4–17, kids age 3 and under free

Hours 10 a.m.–5:30 p.m. Monday–Saturday, 12–5 p.m. Sunday

Phone 525-2605

Website www.get-waxed.com

When to go Anytime, though this makes a very diverting rainy-day stop and a cool one on the hottest afternoons.

Special comments The special "haunted dungeon" of more or less hor-rific stuff is off to one side, so young or susceptible children don't have to see it.

Appeal by Age Group

Pre-school ★★	Teens ★★★	Over 30 ★★½
Grade school ★★★	Young adults ★★★	Seniors ★★

Author's rating This is not the sort of attraction to visit twice (unless you're a kid), but the first time around it has its fun moments. ★★½

How much time to allow 45 minutes

Description & comments Wax museums may be corny, but they have a certain appeal to even the youngest of kids, who are fascinated by their immovability, and to seniors, for whom they represent the attractions of an earlier, more innocent age. These are pretty good as such things go, with German glass eyes, human hair imported from Italy, and figures straight from Paris. Many of the exhibits are purely historical—Andy Jackson and Jean Lafitte (and the Battle of New Orleans in panorama), and the hilari-ous vision of the Emperor Napoleon, ensconced in his bathtub, impul-sively offering to sell the entire Louisiana Territory—while others are more theatrically gory (Marie Laveau leading a voodoo ritual and lovely Del-phine LaLaurie gloating over her chained slaves). A few are downright cheerful—there are wax models of Louis Armstrong, Pete Fountain, Huey Long, and Mardi Gras Indian Chief Montana. Even the long-lost Storyville has its moment in the artificial sun. Dracula, the Wolf Man, Frankenstein, and two dozen or so of their friends are kept off to one side.

Touring tips Consider before taking small children; a few will find the peculiar, almost-real quality of these mannequins spooky even before they get to the chamber of horrors. International travelers may be sur-prised at the variety of translated tours available for rent.

National D-Day Museum

Type of attraction Military museum and veterans' memorial

Location Zone 2 Central Business District; 945 Magazine Street (entrance on Andrew Higgins Drive)

Admission $10 adults, $6 seniors and students, $5 children ages 5–17; students with I.D., $6; military in uniform, free

Hours Daily 9 a.m.–5 p.m.

Phone 527-6012

Website www.ddaymuseum.org

When to go Anytime

Appeal by Age Group

Pre-school ★		Teens ★★★		Over 30 ★★★★
Grade school ★★★		Young adults ★★★		Seniors ★★★★

Author's rating Even-handed presentations; film more effective than exhibits ★★★★★

How much time to allow 1–2 hours

Description & comments Housed in an old warehouse that has been effectively opened up into exhibit space that almost suggests barracks and aerodromes, this still-unfinished museum—an ambitious, $130 million plan will ultimately give it 230,000 square feet, almost quadrupling its current space—combines the now-familiar "voices" (taped recollections of veterans played as background) with uniforms, weapons, rebuilt barracks bunks, radio and newspaper clips and recruitment and bonds posters into a simple but, especially for those who lived through World War II, moving tribute. So far, the museum is comprised of two "theatres" of war, the Atlantic and Pacific. The Atlantic's introductory half-hour film, narrated by David McCullough (the new Walter Cronkite of documentaries) is laudably free of bias and respectful; children may find a few scenes of battlefield casualties upsetting, but they'll probably be fascinated by the helmet with the bullet hole, etc. Some of the exhibits are a little hard to follow. The Pacific's corresponding film is narrated by the late Stephen Ambrose, one of the museum's premier supporters. The museum gift shop has some rather intriguing items, ranging from the inexpensive soldier paper dolls and reproduction pin-up posters to action figures and vintage recordings to personalized leather jackets for $550. The nicest gift for a veteran, however, would probably be a memorial brick for the Road to Victory; the $100 fee is tax-deductible.

Touring tips Good wheelchair access, though the exhibits twist and turn a little. There's a café/coffeeshop on site.

New Orleans Botanical Gardens

Type of attraction Formal gardens and conservatory

Location Zone 7 Lakeview/West End/Bucktown; Victory Avenue in City Park, across from the tennis center

Admission $5 adults, $2 children ages 5–12, kids age 4 and under free

Hours Tuesday–Sunday, 10 a.m.–4:30 p.m.

Phone 483-9386

When to go Anytime; seasonal exhibits

Special comments A quiet respite, not as elaborate as Longue Vue Gardens, but only a few minutes' stroll from the New Orleans Museum of Art and emotionally well paired with it

Appeal by Age Group

Pre-school ★	Teens ★★	Over 30 ★★★★
Grade school ★★	Young adults ★★★★	Seniors ★★★★★

Author's rating A fine refuge. ★★★★

How much time to allow 15 minutes–1 hour

Description & comments This was the city's first public classical gardens, an Art Deco–style WPA creation marrying art and nature. Today its 10 acres house about 2,000 varieties of plants grouped into theme gardens and settings, among them a tropical conservatory, aquatic gardens, an azalea and camellia garden, a rose garden, cold frames, and horticultural trails.

Touring tips The Garden Study Center offers 90-minute educational and how-to programs for about $15; call 483-9427 for a schedule.

New Orleans Contemporary Arts Center

Type of attraction Multidisciplinary arts and performing arts complex

Location Zone 2 Central Business District; 900 Camp Street, at St. Joseph Street

Admission $5 adults, $3 seniors and students; free on Thursdays. Performance ticket prices vary.

Hours Tuesday– Sunday, 11 a.m.–5 p.m.

Phone 523-3800

Website www.caco.org

When to go After lunchtime on weekdays to avoid school-class groups

Appeal by Age Group

Pre-school ½	Teens ★★★	Over 30 ★★★★
Grade school ★★	Young adults ★★★★	Seniors ★★★★

Author's rating Worth a visit for the high caliber of exhibitions. ★★★★

How much time to allow 1–1½ hours

Description & comments The CAC's gallery spaces total 10,000 square feet and rotate about every six to eight weeks among international as well as national and local artists' exhibits. It also includes spaces for theatrical, musical, and dance performances, as well as some cutting-edge performance art. Call for a schedule of events. That's the up-side. The slight down-side is that this somewhat raw, accessible renovated warehouse can be very loud when groups of school kids come in.

Touring tips Street parking available

New Orleans Historic Voodoo Museum

Type of attraction Part museum, part weird-camp souvenir shop—or to put it simply, part shock, part schlock

Location Zone 1 French Quarter; 724 Rue Dumaine Street, between Royal and Bourbon streets

Admission $6 adults, $5 seniors and students; sign up for a guided tour, and the museum tour is free

Hours 10 a.m.–5 p.m.

Phone 523-7685

When to go Anytime

Special comments One of the hot spots for psychic readings and gris-gris charms as well as "voodoo tours"

Appeal by Age Group

Pre-school ★	Teens ★★★	Over 30 ★★
Grade school ★★	Young adults ★★★	Seniors ★★

Author's rating This absolutely requires that you get into the spirit of things; think of it as an adventure, rather than as a museum per se. ★★★

How much time to allow 30 minutes

Description & comments If something like the Historic New Orleans Collection is the quintessential above-board museum, this is the height of neo–New Orleans exotica—rather grim and sometimes grisly artifacts, strange bones and potions, a voodoo altar, plenty of Marie Laveau lore, stuffed cats and live snakes, low light, and sometimes local low life as well. If you like atmosphere, you'll love this; in fact, if it weren't so dim and dilapidated, they'd have to curse it.

Touring tips Children are generally fascinated by the grotesque, but take your own kids' sensitivities into account. Teens and novice occultists will probably think it very cool, but seniors may find it all a little too grim. The museum staff not only arranges readings and tours, but also occasional "rituals."

New Orleans Museum of Art

Type of attraction Wide-ranging fine arts and decorative arts collection

Location Zone 7 Lakeview/West End/Bucktown; Lelong Avenue and Dueling Oak Drive in City Park

Admission $6 adults, $5 seniors, $3 children ages 3–17; free admission Thursdays 10 a.m.–noon for Louisiana residents only

Hours Tuesday–Sunday, 10 a.m.–5 p.m.

Phone 488-2631

Website www.noma.org

When to go Anytime

Special comments An all-ages introduction-to-art exhibit called "The Starting Point" is as good as it gets.

Appeal by Age Group

Pre-school ★		Teens ★★★		Over 30 ★★★★★
Grade school ★★★		Young adults ★★★★★		Seniors ★★★★★

Author's rating Art lovers should not miss this. ★★★★★

How much time to allow 1–3 hours

Description & comments This neoclassical building, commissioned in 1910 by Jamaican-born New Orleans philanthropist Isaac Delgado to benefit "rich and poor alike," lives up to its mission, housing more than 35,000 works by not only the premier American and European artists— Picasso, Miro, and Degas, whose studio was nearby—but African, Japanese, Chinese, and Native American art as well. Its "Art of the Americas" collection, ranging from pre-Columbian through Spanish Colonial times, is one of the largest, as is its decorative glass works. There are miniatures, furnishings, and regional arts and crafts from the 19th century to today. Sketching of these masterworks is welcome, but in dry media only (pencil, charcoal, etc.) and on a single tablet no larger than legal size. One wing is devoted to rotating exhibits. General tours and special exhibition lectures are offered daily; the courtyard café serves lunch and afternoon beverages.

Touring tips Free parking

New Orleans Pharmacy Museum

Type of attraction Restored apothecary with period exhibits, old potions, and pharmaceutical supplies

Location Zone 1 French Quarter; 514 Chartres Street, between Toulouse and St. Louis streets

Admission $2, $1 seniors and students, kids age 12 and under free

Hours Tuesday–Sunday, 10 a.m.–5 p.m.

Phone 565-8027

When to go Anytime; good rain alternative

Appeal by Age Group

Pre-school ★		Teens ★★		Over 30 ★★
Grade school ★★		Young adults ★★		Seniors ★★★

Author's rating This is another of those "atmospheric" venues that has to draw you. The subject may seem somewhat limited, but it's quite intriguing if you're not squeamish. ★★★

How much time to allow 30 minutes

Description & comments This was the pharmacy of the very first apothecary to be licensed in the United States, Louis Dufilho, who was certified in 1816 and opened this store in 1823. It's an impressive piece of restoration, with German mahogany cases, antique handblown canisters and apothecary jars, a leech pot, and such famous patent medicines of the past as Pinkham's pills, the vitamin concoctions of Miss Lydia Pinkham that were supposed to resolve both ladies' vapors and, though not said openly, sexual indifference; and Spanish fly, the male equivalent still hotly sought after today. The black and rose marble soda fountain, made in Italy in 1855, is a nostalgic highlight.

Touring tips Bring your sense of humor. This will be of some interest to most ages, since the idea of applying leeches and trepanning skulls to relieve pressure (or possession) has a perverse appeal. The courtyard is a nice place to sit for a few minutes, and with the revival of interest in botanicals and alternative medicine, almost trendy. In a funny way, however, this has more appeal to older visitors who recognize more of the names and may even remember tales of defunct medical techniques.

The Old U.S. Mint

Type of attraction Another part of the Louisiana State Museum complex, an imaginatively reconditioned installation housing two of the city's best-kept secret exhibits

Location Zone 1 French Quarter; 400 Esplanade Avenue, at Decatur Street

Admission $5 adults; $4 seniors, students, and active military; kids age 12 and under free

Hours Tuesday–Sunday, 9 a.m.–5 p.m.

Phone 568-6968

Website www.lsm.crt.state.la.us

When to go Anytime

Special comments Because of its music exhibits, the museum sometimes hosts concerts of jazz, big band, spiritual, and early ballroom music; inquire at the desk. Also browse through the music collection in the gift shop.

Appeal by Age Group

Pre-school ★★★	Teens ★★★★	Over 30 ★★★★★
Grade school ★★★★	Young adults ★★★★★	Seniors ★★★★★

Author's rating This is virtually the only exhibit on New Orleans music, and requires perhaps a little personal knowledge for the fullest effect, but even the tone-deaf will be floored by the Mardi Gras rooms. ★★★★★

How much time to allow 1–2 hours

Description & comments The building itself, a huge but not clumsy Greek Revival facade with Ionic details, was designed during Andrew Jackson's administration by William Strickland, the most prominent public architect of the day. Its polished flagstone floors, double staircase, and rear galleries are still pretty impressive (although it has to be admitted that engineer P.G.T. Beauregard had to be called in to perform a little facelift in the 1850s). One side of the second floor holds the jazz collection, which arranges old photographs of Jelly Roll Morton, King Oliver, Sidney Bechet, and Fate Marable's Orchestra alongside early instruments (including Louis Armstrong's first cornet), sheet music, and other memorabilia. Snatches of vintage recordings play overhead, and the often overlooked women of early music are also saluted. (Be sure to notice the copy of the notorious "Blue Book," the social register of Storyville ladies, and the delicate stained-glass panels rescued from a demolished bordello.) The other side of the building houses the Mardi Gras exhibit, an astonishing cornucopia of mocked-up floats and authentic costumes, scepters, crowns, krewe decorations and "honors," hat pins, watches, and Carnival favors. The lavish outfits are made of gold lamé, fake fur, appliquéd satin, beads, feathers, velvets, and silk tassels. Even if your kids can resist the music rooms, they'll be stunned by the chief of the Wild Tchoupitoulas in all his glory, and the picture of Louis Armstrong as King of the Zulu Krewe in 1949. Look also at the paintings depicting the duel between rival club owners (that spelled the beginning of the end of Storyville) and the third-floor hallway mural with many famous faces from the musical past. Down in the basement, where the remnants of the mint equipment can be seen, are a few intriguing exhibits as well, including the carved hearse, built at the turn of the 19th century.

Touring tips This is good wheelchair access territory, with wide aisles and new bathrooms. And if you like old homes, take the time to wander up and down Esplanade Avenue. Although the neighborhood is in mid-revival, it is likely to be the next Garden District. Take particular note of the house at 704 Esplanade, at Royal Street: the Gauche House (so called for owner John Gauche, not as an editorial comment) was built in 1856 supposedly from a drawing by Albrecht Dürer, including cast-iron balconies, cupids, and all. Also note that you are very near the end of the Riverfront Streetcar line, if you're getting tired or want to get across the Quarter easily.

Old Ursuline Convent / Archbishop Antoine Blanc Memorial

Type of attraction A 250-year-old complex incorporating several religious sites, formal gardens and archives

Location Zone 1 French Quarter; 110 Chartres Street, at the corner of Ursuline Street

Admission $5 adults, $4 seniors and students, $2 kids age 9 and up; kids age 8 and under free; groups of 20 or more, $3 adults and $1 children

Hours Tuesday–Friday, 10 a.m.–3 p.m. (tours on the hour, except noon); Saturday and Sunday, tours at 11:15 a.m. and 1 and 2 p.m. only

Phone 529-3040

When to go Anytime

Special comments Not a lively, elaborate, or particularly varied site, but oddly atmospheric; obviously appeals more to Catholic visitors

Appeal by Age Group

Pre-school —	Teens ★	Over 30 ★★
Grade school —	Young adults ★	Seniors ★★

Author's rating Of more historical and religious than visual appeal; an unusually serene tour. ★★

How much time to allow 1 hour

Description & comments This is the only surviving example of pure French Creole construction, begun in 1745, and most people believe it's the oldest surviving building in New Orleans of any sort; it was saved from the fire of 1788 by Pere Antoine and his bucket brigade. The Sisters were the guiding social hand of the city's young people for centuries, educating not only the children of aristocrats (Micaela de Pontalbas, for example) but blacks, Indians, and orphans as well. They served as religious guides, chaperones (it was they who brought over the "casket girls" as brides to the early settlers), nurses, housekeeping instructors, and welfare workers, braving epidemics and massacres alike. Andrew Jackson sent word to the Sisters to ask them to pray for his forces on the eve of the Battle of New Orleans; they responded by spending the entire night in prayer at the chapel here before a statue of the Virgin Mary, and were still there when the messenger brought word of victory. Jackson came in person to thank them, and to this day a celebratory Mass is said on January 8 at the Ursulines' other chapel, the National Shrine of Our Lady of Prompt Succor at State Street and South Claiborne. The lovely old cypress spiral staircase, antique furniture and relics, medicinal garden, and restored chapel, known variously as Our Lady of Victory Church, St. Mary's Italian Church, and the Archbishop's Chapel, are very pretty— but again, of somewhat limited appeal. Incidentally, in the early years of U.S. government, the convent seemed threatened by anti-Catholic educational reforms; the Mother Superior wrote first to President Jefferson and again to President Madison, asking that the school be allowed to continue, and both wrote back assuringly. The Shrine of Our Lady has not only her petitions, but both presidential responses.

Touring tips This is pleasant, but rather a lot of walking for the effect.

Our Lady of Guadalupe / Shrine of St. Jude

Type of attraction Simple but quirky little chapel built to serve St. Louis Cemetery, but with a couple of not-so-strict saints in charge

Location Zone 2 Central Business Dist.; 411 North Rampart St., at Conti Street

Admission Free (donations welcome)

Hours 7 a.m.–6 p.m.

Phone 525-1551

When to go Anytime

Special comments This is the official chapel of the city's fire and police departments, so don't be surprised by any uniforms.

Appeal by Age Group

Pre-school —	Teens ½	Over 30 ★½
Grade school ½	Young adults ★½	Seniors ★★

Author's rating An eccentric but lively side trip. ★★½

How much time to allow 15 minutes; also tours by appointment

Description & comments This little chapel, built in 1826 as the Chapel of the Dead and originally opening directly onto the cemetery (there's a street between now), is intriguing for several reasons. First, because in the days of continual epidemic, it operated at tragic speed: Bodies were brought in, a swift service was said, and they were shipped right into the waiting graves. (The victims were brought here instead of St. Louis Cathedral in a vain effort to limit contagion.) The second intriguing aspect, for those who take saintly intercession with a grain of salt, is that the shrine is now dedicated to St. Jude, he of the lost causes, who might be considered a sort of lost cause himself: Despite his connections—he may have been the brother of either Jesus or James—he has lost a little status, although the petitions and published notices of thanks continue to flow in. Step to the right into his grotto, and see for yourself how active he is. Third, this is also the shrine of the one and only (as far as anyone knows) St. Expedite, whose statue arrived at the chapel without its papers or even an address. Look to the right just as you enter the chapel. He had no identifying attributes, and no other church in New Orleans claimed to be expecting a new saint, so the only thing written on the packing crate—Expedite!—was carved into the base by the confused workers, who didn't speak much English. Gradually petitioners began taking him at his word. The legend goes that if you have a request, you go out toward St. Louis Cemetery and say five rosaries; if your prayer is answered (it will be within 36 hours, or probably not at all), you return to the chapel and leave him a teaspoon of salt and a slice of pound cake.

Pitot House

Type of attraction Historic, early-19th-century home

Location Zone 6 Mid-City/Gentilly; 1440 Moss Street

Admission $6 adults, $4 seniors and children under 12

Hours Wednesday–Saturday, 10 a.m.–3 p.m.

Phone 482-0312

When to go Anytime

Appeal by Age Group

Pre-school —	Teens ★	Over 30 ★★★
Grade school ½	Young adults ★★★	Seniors ★★★

Author's rating Evocative and in fine condition. ★★★

How much time to allow 1–2 hours, depending on your interest

Description & comments When it was built in 1799 for Degas' great grandmother (it's named for James Pitot, first mayor of the city, who bought it soon after), this West Indies–style home—encircled by porches, protected by full shutters—was a block away where the Catholic school now stands. It was used in this century as a convent by Mother Francis Xavier Cabrini, the first canonized saint of the United States. It has been beautifully restored to its original condition and furnished with period antiques.

Touring tips Under the aegis of the State Landmarks Society, who moved it in the 1960s, this house has been made wheelchair accessible.

The Presbytere

Type of attraction Of the Louisiana State Museum properties in the French Quarter, the most traditional one, with both permanent and rotating exhibits

Location Zone 1 French Quarter; 751 Chartres Street, facing Jackson Square

Admission $5 adults; $4 seniors, students, and active military; kids age 12 and under free

Hours Tuesday–Sunday, 9 a.m.–5 p.m.

Phone 568-6968

Website www.lsm.crt.state.la.us

When to go Anytime

Appeal by Age Group

Pre-school —	Teens ★	Over 30 ★★★
Grade school ★	Young adults ★★★	Seniors ★★

Author's rating Like the Cabildo, you have to follow your nose to what interests you, but the rotating exhibits can be very intriguing. ★★★

How much time to allow 45 minutes–1½ hours

Description & comments Architecturally speaking, this is a somewhat mongrelized building. Though not unattractive, it has been renovated and expanded several times, and most recently its really fine plank floors have been reconditioned to fine advantage. Intended to be used as an ecclesiastical residence, it wound up as a courthouse; the mansard roof and hurricane-demolished cupola were supposed to mirror the Cabildo. The exhibits are a bit haphazard but cheerful mishmash: portraits of influential Creoles, such as Don Almonester and his formidable daughter, Baroness Almonester; fine decorative arts, from an 18th-century gold- and silver-embroidered velvet altar cloth and local art glass, to wrought iron from the staircase of the great domed (and doomed) St. Charles Hotel; crosses, cameos, and earrings; hand-tinted Audubon plates; silver table settings; etc. Among the busts are two faces of Beauregard, one young and confident, the other older and wiser.

Touring tips Although the age rating shows low for children, it does depend somewhat on the subject of the rotating exhibits. Among fairly recent examples, the collection of very elaborate to-scale builders' ship models, haute couture (à la the Metropolitan Museum in New York), or antique maps might interest certain youngsters, and the rather weird *Tales from the Crypt* effect of the bust-lined second-floor arcade gallery might tickle others' fancy.

Rivertown

Type of attraction Family amusement/education complex, with small museums and activity centers along three blocks in suburban Kenner

Location Zone 10 Metairie above Causeway/Kenner/Jefferson Highway; welcome center at 405 Williams Boulevard off I-10

Admission All-complex pass $15 adults, $11 seniors, $9 children ages 2–12; single venues vary

Hours Tuesday–Saturday, 9 a.m.–5 p.m. (last admission at 4:30 p.m.); observatory, Thursday–Saturday, 7:30–10:30 p.m.

Phone 468-7231

Website www.rivertownkenner.com

When to go Anytime

Special comments Business travelers bringing the family along may find this a good reason to stay in an airport-area hotel.

Appeal by Age Group

Pre-school ★★	Teens ★★★	Over 30 ★★★★
Grade school ★★★★★	Young adults ★★★★	Seniors ★★★

Author's rating A mixed bag, but at least something for everyone. ★★★★

How much time to allow 2–4 hours

Description & comments Families with children can duck the Bourbon Street barrage for at least a half day by heading toward this Victorian village–style complex a half mile from the airport. The Louisiana Toy Train

Museum is one of the all-ages attractions, with a half dozen large dioramas crisscrossed with tracks for the vintage Lionel, American Flyer, and other small-gauge collections (most dating to the 1950s). The Mardi Gras Museum conveys the trashy, flashy fever of Carnival at safe and PG-rated distance, with costumes, beads, a simulated costume shop, and lots of live-action video. Probably only the most hardcore football fans, or small children, will find more than a few minutes' entertainment at the New Orleans Saints Hall of Fame, which is primarily a giant locker room of helmets, uniforms, game balls, etc. The Daily Living Science Center, a hands-on if lightweight introduction to car engines, weather, dental hygiene, commercial laundries, and other strange and sundry aspects of everyday life leads into a full-sized NASA space station, complete with weightlessness chamber. It also has a planetarium and an observatory, which is open Thursday through Saturday, 7:30–10:30 p.m. (468-9231). On the other hand, the Louisiana Wildlife Museum and Aquarium is well organized and attractive, with over 700 preserved specimens of indigenous mammals and reptiles and a 15,000-gallon tank holding marine life. Literally in the backyard of the Wildlife Museum is the Cannes Brulee Native American Center of the Gulf South, a living history installation that re-creates a Native American village, complete with live hogs, poultry, rabbits, and crayfish, and staffed by serious and well-spoken native craftsmen and "residents." There is also a 300-seat Repertory Theatre, and the Children's Castle offers puppet shows, magic displays, and storytelling.

Touring tips Like many children's museums, this tends to be busier before lunch than after. Walk across to LaSalle's Landing for a good view of the mighty Mississippi.

St. Alphonsus Church

Type of attraction Stunning, partially restored chapel with extraordinary stained glass

Location Zone 3 Uptown below Napoleon; 2029 Constance Street, at St. Andrew

Admission None

Hours Tuesday, Thursday, and Saturday, 10 a.m.–2 p.m.

Phone 524-8116

When to go Anytime

Appeal by Age Group

Pre-school —	Teens ★★	Over 30 ★★★
Grade school ★★	Young adults ★★★	Seniors ★★★

Author's rating Absolutely beautiful. ★★★★★

How much time to allow 30–45 minutes alone

Description & comments It's astonishing to consider by what scrimping and sweating the Irish immigrants of the mid-19th century managed to erect this lovely church. Note the unusual "repertory cast" of faces used in the astonishing stained-glass windows, shamrocks in the floor tiles, and tomb of the popular Redemptorist priest, Father Francis X. Seeles, who is credited with several miracles. This was the home church of Anne Rice and her family, and served as the model for the church the Mayfair sisters attend.

Touring tips Contact the Preservation Resource Center (604 Julia Street; 581-7032) to obtain info on their next "Stained Glass in Sacred Places" tour.

Six Flags New Orleans

Type of attraction Amusement park with cartoon/adventure hero themes, popular music shows, and a sprinkling of Cajun/Creole style

Location Zone 8 New Orleans East; at the intersection of I-10 and I-510 east of downtown (exit 246-A off I-10)

Admission $32.99 adults, $22.99 seniors and children under 48" tall, free ages 2 and under

Hours Weekends mid-April through mid-May and mid-August through October; daily mid-May to mid-August. Call or check website for specific hours.

Phone 278-8100

Website www.sixflags.com

When to go Spring and fall, when storms are less likely (no refunds for rain closures)

Appeal by Age Group

Pre-school ★★	Teens ★★★★	Over 30 ★★★
Grade school ★★★	Young adults ★★★★	Seniors ★★

Author's rating At press time, the park was not quite completed, so some attractions—including the live entertainment productions, street performers, fireworks show, and stunt shows—were not available for evaluation.

How much time to allow 3–5 hours, depending on age

Description and comments Depite the half-dozen music revues, ranging from a country music revue to a Vegas-style spectacular to a recap of 50 years of pop hits; and the Batman-vs.-supervillains stunt show, the park,'s emphasis seems to be on thrill rides, with a smattering of temporary tattoo and hair-wrap booths in between. The two largest roller coaster-style rides are the Batman ride, a pretty complex series of loops, corkscrews, and vertical reverses taken at 50 mph from hanging seats; and the Jester, with a full 360° loop and an 80-foot drop. However, even the Batman ride lasts only one minute, minus the initial climb, and some riders seem underwhelmed. Similarly, the bungee-style ride is only one drop and a half rebound. (There was unexpected enthusiasm for the old-fashioned bumper cars, which may be more of a novelty these days.) The 4,000-foot-long Mega-Zeph is intriguing because it's a wooden roller coaster. The Pirates attraction uses the same NASA-style motion vehicles used to good effect by Disney World, though on a much simpler scale.

Aside from the various rides, there are jugglers, stilt walkers, and the like wandering about. A teen dance club is planned, with guest DJs and local radio personalities serving as rotating MCs. For the younger kids, there's a playground area and opportunities to meet various Looney Tunes characters, such as Bugs Bunny, Tweety Bird, and Daffy Duck. Most of the food is typical concessionaire fare, although Rita's Creole Kitchen near the front entrance has grown-up choices (and one of the handful of beer licenses). The day ends with a laser and fireworks show.

Touring tips Shirts and shoes are mandatory, so don,'t go too far into beachwear whatever the temperature. Guests must pass through security gates, and guards will remove any sharp items such as bottle openers and pocket knives. Also, season passes are $49.99, so if you're planning to go even twice, they may save you a little. Parking is $7; if you take a taxi out to the park, despite its proximity to the airport, be sure to arrange a pickup in advance; otherwise, you may wait a very long time for someone to accept the hail, as the park has no regular cabstand.

Part Nine

Dining in New Orleans

Chowing Down in the Big Easy

Food is THE big deal in New Orleans.

Observe the conversations in any restaurant. In other cities, they'd concern sports, politics, or business. In New Orleans, the talk is all about eating. It's entered into with earnestness and knowledge, and occasionally even seriousness.

Although the whole country is food-mad these days, the passion in New Orleans wells up through six or seven generations. There was a full-blown regional cuisine here over a century ago, long before America got the gourmet bug.

To best enjoy eating in New Orleans, understand that it's intensely local. In just the way that French or Italian towns offer their culinary styles to the near-exclusion of anything else, so too is Southeast Louisiana obsessed with Creole and Cajun cooking.

Which brings up a question that will only get you into trouble. "What's the difference between Creole food and Cajun food?" After noting that Creole is city and Cajun is country, and that Creole cooks like to use tomatoes more than Cajun chefs do, just abandon the matter. Creole and Cajun have influenced each other so much in recent years that you find the same menus and flavors throughout Southeast Louisiana. It's a vaporous issue. Which means, of course, that it gets talked about a lot, usually in restaurants.

Creole and Cajun chefs cook with the same raw materials. Which is a big reason why they're both so good. For starters, this is a land of superb seafood, starting with the Big Four: oysters, shrimp, crabs, and crawfish. Supporting them (or vice versa) is a large cast of finfish from local waters.

There's nothing quite like the freshness of seafood that came to your plate by way of a beat-up old truck that only had to drive a few miles.

There are restaurants in New Orleans where you can eat a fish while watching his relatives swim and jump in the lake right outside the window.

I suppose you're expecting me to define the Creole taste now. Well, I give up. I'm blinkered by having eaten Creole food all my life, which makes me think of it as normal. What I can tell you is what I miss when I travel. I find non-Creole American food lacking in salt, pepper, richness, and general intensity of flavor.

One of the explanations for this is the amount of salt, pepper, cream, butter, and other fats in classic Creole cooking. Indeed, an often-cited characteristic of New Orleans recipes is that they have a way of beginning, "First you make a roux." (Roux, a blend of flour and oil, butter, or other fat, cooked to various shades of brown, is the main active ingredient in dishes from gumbo to oysters Rockefeller.) As a result, much of Creole and Cajun cooking in the old style is high in all those things that the food police tell us to stay away from.

But during the past decade there's been a revolution in Creole cooking, spurred by intense competition among the hundreds (this is no exaggeration) of new restaurants that have opened. Diners have come to expect new dishes, ingredients, and flavors, and the younger, higher-profile chefs have been happy to invent them. Most of the new Creole cuisine is much lighter than its predecessors. Even roux is becoming rarer. Occasionally it's even left out of gumbo (a state of affairs that an old-time Creole cook would consider heresy).

The more innovative local chefs are, at this writing, pulling back from the one-big-world-of-taste fusions they spent the 1990s creating. We're seeing a revival of classic, local ideas. The dishes don't taste or look like they did 20 years ago—the ingredients, for one thing, are a lot better now. But you can see a lot of familiar old friends under the new guises.

During the past ten years, a flood of ethnic restaurants moved onto the scene. Local diners welcome the diversity, and at last some of the exotic cuisines are getting their due in terms of quality foodstuffs, skilled chefs, and pleasant restaurants. I've included a good assortment of them among the restaurants recommended in this book.

If that last fact causes you to cock an eyebrow and wonder whether our gustatory island will lose its distinctiveness, rest easy. No matter how enthusiastically even the most sophisticated New Orleans diner waxes about some new Vietnamese-Mexican fusion bistro, you can be sure that in his most relaxed moments he's still munching poor-boy sandwiches, boiled crawfish, jambalaya, and bread pudding. As will all other aficionados of Creole food from near or far. Because we all know that, like all the world's other great ethnic cuisines, great Creole and Cajun cooking is only found in the land of its birth.

A New Orleans Culinary Calendar

Because the cuisine of New Orleans is so intimately tied to the indigenous ingredients, it's important to pay attention to the seasons. Although many restaurants serve, say, crawfish year-round, there's no question that crawfish are incomparably better in the peak of their natural cycle. Here's the schedule:

Crabs, Soft-Shell and Otherwise April through October. There's a dip in quality in July, then they get good again. Usually the warmer it is, the better the crabmeat.

Crawfish Christmas through the Fourth of July, with the peak of quality in April and May.

Creole Tomatoes These meaty, sweet, gigantic, sensual tomatoes have a short season, in April and May, but they are worth waiting for. Lately we've seen a second crop of Creoles in the fall.

Oysters Good year-round, but a little off during the spawn in July and August. (In other words, forget that months-with-an-R myth.) The best months are November and December, especially if a convincing cold front has passed through.

Pompano July through October.

Shrimp There are several species, so seasons click on and off. The best times are late spring, late summer, and most of the fall. The only poor month for shrimp is March.

Speckled Trout October through January.

Tuna May through September.

The calendar is also reliable in predicting when restaurants will be at their best. Absolutely the worst time to eat in New Orleans is during the Mardi Gras season, which extends three weeks before the movable Ash Wednesday (in February or early March). The city's restaurants are stretched thin at that time of year by tourists, conventions, and Mardi Gras balls. What's more, waiters and other restaurant personnel tend to be heavy participants in Carnival hi-jinks and are, shall we say, not at their peaks.

The best times for a serious eater to come to town are the months of October and April. The weather is beautiful for patio dining, the food supplies are at their best, and the conventions aren't overwhelming. Also good are the summer months, especially July and September. The heat and humidity convince tourists and conventions to stay away (despite the fact that there may be no better air-conditioned city on earth), and the restaurants are eager to please.

Also of note are two superb food festivals. The New Orleans Jazz and Heritage Festival takes place on the last week of April and the first week of May, with an outdoor surfeit of music and indigenous food. Then, in June or July (the date varies from year to year), the New Orleans Wine and Food Experience brings you indoors for an extended weekend of special feasting with the city's best chefs and drinking with the world's best winemakers.

Hype and Glory

In the restaurant profiles that make up most of this book, you may notice that a few well-known or highly visible restaurants are missing. This is not an oversight. The following restaurants may come to your attention, but in my opinion they're not as worthwhile as other comparable options.

Central Grocery 923 Decatur; 523-1620. As this old emporium of imported food allowed its floor space to become more taken over for the vending of muffulettas to tourists, both the store and the muffulettas have declined.

Court of Two Sisters 613 Royal, French Quarter; 522-7273. There's no question that tourists dominate this beautiful restaurant and its lush courtyard tables. Most locals will tell you to stay away. In fact, dinner here is better than decent, with old-style Creole dishes done reasonably well. The daily breakfast-lunch buffet has less appealing food, but does sport a live jazz trio.

Deanie's Seafood 1713 Lake Avenue, Bucktown; 831-4141. Deanie's is immensely popular, but what brings that about is the eye-popping size of its just-okay seafood platters.

House of Blues 225 Decatur, French Quarter; 529-2583. The place has great music almost every night, including name acts. And sometimes the food is good. But not predictably. The Foundation Room is a private club within the club and has a very ambitious kitchen, but first you have to get in—and I have no advice for you there.

Jimmy Buffet's Margaritaville Café 1104 Decatur; 592-2565. A must for parrotheads—but only after eating somewhere else.

Landry's Seafood House 400 N. Peters; 558-0038. A regional chain, Landry's has the look of a great old middle-of-nowhere Louisiana roadhouse, but the food is strictly formula and not very good.

Mulate's 201 Julia; 522-1492. A mammoth place copied from the original Cajun dance restaurant in Breaux Bridge, Mulate's does indeed have good Cajun music, but the food is only occasionally interesting.

Patout's Cajun Cabin 501 Bourbon; 524-4054. They occupy the space where Al Hirt plays when he's in town, supplying gilded versions of Cajun food. Although it can be quite good, the inconsistency is so extreme as to make the place unrecommendable.

New Restaurants

Here are a few restaurants that opened too soon before we went to press for a review to be reliable in the long term. I include them for those who like to hit the new places and who don't mind being part of a work in progress.

Clementine's Belgian Bistrot 366-3995; 2505 Whitney Avenue; Gretna; Zone 11 West Bank. The owners and chef are from Brussels, and they serve every dish from the much-underrated cuisine of Belgium. It has a mostly French tilt, with particular specialties of mussels, fondue, and grilled beef. Very inexpensive.

Muses 219-0770; 200 Hammond Highway, Bucktown; Zone 7 Lakeview/West End/Bucktown. What started as a slightly upscale seafood restaurant evolved into a slightly downscale French-American bistro. This is a response to the change in Bucktown from a scruffy fishing community to a concentration of expensive lakefront condominiums. The food is polished, ranging from a great homemade pâté through simple but elegant essays on a short list of entrées to a spectacular cheese selection.

Unnamed Restaurant #1 (formerly Tavern on the Park) 900 City Park Avenue; Zone 6 Mid-City/Gentilly. The most-anticipated restaurant opening in 2003 is owned by Ralph Brennan (of Bacco and the Red Fish Grill), with chef Gerard Maras in the kitchen. Maras has been a trend-setting chef for over a decade, with a dedicated following for his French-inspired food. The antique premises (this has been a restaurant since before the Civil War) are lovely and tap into the verdant climes of City Park across the street. Richard Shakespeare, long-time manager and cellarmaster at Commander's Palace, will run the dining room.

Unnamed Restaurant #2 In the Renaissance Hotel, Girod at Tchoupitoulas; Zone 2 Central Business District. This restaurant, also planned to open in the summer of 2003, is a partnership between Rene Bajeux (chef-owner of Rene Bistrot) and Bingo Starr (former chef of Cuvee). Both are alumni of the Windsor Court and have track records that bode well for this new place. The new restaurant will focus on seafood—not just local fish, but species from all over the world, especially the Mediterranean.

The Restaurants

Our Favorite New Orleans Restaurants: Explaining the Ratings

We have developed detailed profiles for what we consider the best restaurants in town. Each profile features an easy-to-scan heading that allows you to check out the restaurant's name, cuisine, star rating, cost, quality rating, and value rating very quickly.

Overall Rating   The overall rating encompasses the entire dining experience, including style, service, and ambience in addition to the taste, presentation, and quality of the food. Five stars is the highest rating possible and connotes the best of everything. Four-star restaurants are exceptional, and three-star restaurants are well above average. Two-star restaurants are good. One star is used to connote an average restaurant that demonstrates an unusual capability in some area of specialization—for example, an otherwise unmemorable place that has great barbecued chicken.

Cost   To the right of the star rating is an expense description which provides a comparative sense of how much a complete meal will cost. A complete meal for our purposes consists of an entrée with vegetable or side dish, and choice of soup or salad. Appetizers, desserts, drinks, and tips are excluded.

Inexpensive $14 and less per person   **Moderate** $15–$25 per person

Expensive $26–$40 per person   **Very Expensive** Over $40 per person

Quality Rating   The food quality rating is rated on a scale of one to five stars, with five stars being the best rating attainable. It is based expressly on the taste, freshness of ingredients, preparation, presentation, and creativity of food served. There is no consideration of price. If you are a person who wants the best food available and cost is not an issue, you need look no further than the quality ratings.

Value Rating   If, on the other hand, you are looking for both quality and value, then you should check the value rating. The value ratings, expressed as stars, are defined as follows:

★★★★★	Exceptional value, a real bargain
★★★★	Good value
★★★	Fair value, you get exactly what you pay for
★★	Somewhat overpriced
★	Significantly overpriced

Location   Just below the restaurant address and phone number is a designation for geographic zone. This zone description will give you a general idea of where the restaurant described is located. For ease of use, we divide New Orleans into 12 geographic zones.

Zone 1	French Quarter
Zone 2	Central Business District
Zone 3	Uptown below Napoleon
Zone 4	Uptown above Napoleon
Zone 5	Downtown/St. Bernard
Zone 6	Mid-City/Gentilly
Zone 7	Lakeview/West End/Bucktown
Zone 8	New Orleans East
Zone 9	Metairie below Causeway

Zone 10   Metairie above Causeway/Kenner/Jefferson Highway
Zone 11   West Bank
Zone 12   North Shore

If you are in the French Quarter and intend to walk or take a cab to dinner, you may want to choose a restaurant from among those located in Zone 1. If you have a car, you might include restaurants from contiguous zones in your consideration. (See the detailed zone maps at the end of the Introduction.)

Our Pick of the Best New Orleans Restaurants

Because restaurants are opening and closing all the time in New Orleans, we have tried to confine our list to establishments—or chefs—with proven track records over a fairly long period of time. Those newer or changed establishments that demonstrate staying power and consistency will be profiled in subsequent editions.

The list is highly selective. Non-inclusion of a particular place does not necessarily indicate that the restaurant is not good, but only that it was not ranked among the best or most consistent in its genre. Detailed profiles of each restaurant follow in alphabetical order at the end of this chapter. Also, we've listed the types of payment accepted at each restaurant, using the following codes:

AE	American Express	DC	Diners Club
CB	Carte Blanche	MC	MasterCard
DS	Discover	V	Visa

THE BEST NEW ORLEANS RESTAURANTS

Cuisine & Name	Overall Rating	Cost	Quality Rating	Value Rating	Zone
Cajun					
K-Paul's Louisiana Kitchen	★★★★	Very Exp	★★★½	★★	1
Bon Ton Café	★★★	Mod–Exp	★★★½	★★★	2
Alex Patout's Louisiana Restaurant	★★★	Exp	★★★½	★★★	1
Chinese					
Trey Yuen	★★★	Inexp–Mod	★★★½	★★	12
China Blossom	★★★	Inexp–Mod	★★★	★★★	11
Contemporary Creole					
Dakota	★★★★★	Exp	★★★★★	★★★	12
Emeril's	★★★★★	Very Exp	★★★★★	★★★	2
Delmonico	★★★★★	Very Exp	★★★★★	★★	3

THE BEST NEW ORLEANS RESTAURANTS (continued)

Cuisine & Name	Overall Rating	Cost	Quality Rating	Value Rating	Zone
Contemporary Creole (continued)					
Marigny Brasserie	★★★★	Mod–Exp	★★★½	★★★	5
Wolfe's of New Orleans	★★★★	Mod–Exp	★★★½	★★★	7
Gabrielle	★★★★	Exp	★★★½	★★★	6
Commander's Palace	★★★★	Very Exp	★★★½	★★★	3
Dick & Jenny's	★★★★	Mod–Exp	★★★	★★★	4
Indigo	★★★★	Exp	★★★	★★★	6
Bella Luna	★★★★	Very Exp	★★★	★★★	1
Cuvee	★★★★	Very Exp	★★★	★★	2
Dante's Kitchen	★★★	Mod	★★★½	★★★	4
201 Restaurant and Bar	★★★	Mod–Exp	★★★½	★★★	1
Belle Forche	★★★	Exp	★★★½	★★★	5
Muriel's	★★★	Exp	★★★½	★★★	1
Lee Circle Restaurant	★★★	Mod	★★★	★★★	3
Mat & Naddie's	★★★	Mod–Exp	★★★	★★★	4
Bourbon House	★★	Mod	★★½	★★★	1
Creole					
Galatoire's	★★★★★	Exp	★★★★★	★★★	1
Jacques-Imo's	★★★★	Inexp–Mod	★★★½	★★★	4
Clancy's	★★★★	Mod–Exp	★★★½	★★★	4
Palace Café	★★★★	Mod–Exp	★★★½	★★★	2
Pascal's Manale	★★★★	Mod–Exp	★★★½	★★★	4
Brigtsen's	★★★★	Exp	★★★½	★★★	4
Mr. B's Bistro	★★★★	Exp	★★★½	★★★	1
Broussard's	★★★★	Very Exp	★★★½	★★	1
Upperline	★★★★	Mod–Exp	★★★	★★★	4
Christian's	★★★★	Exp	★★★	★★★	6
Le Parvenu	★★★★	Exp	★★★	★★★	10
Nola	★★★★	Exp	★★★	★★★	1
Arnaud's	★★★★	Very Exp	★★★	★★	1
Brennan's	★★★★	Very Exp	★★★	★★	1
Begue's	★★★	Exp	★★★½	★★★	1
Mandina's	★★★	Inexp–Mod	★★★	★★★★★	6
Gumbo Shop	★★★	Inexp	★★★	★★★	1
Mandich	★★★	Inexp–Mod	★★★	★★★	5
Café Sbisa	★★★	Exp	★★★	★★★	1
Antoine's	★★★	Very Exp	★★★	★★	1
Coffee Pot	★★	Inexp–Mod	★★½	★★★	1

THE BEST NEW ORLEANS RESTAURANTS (continued)

Cuisine & Name	Overall Rating	Cost	Quality Rating	Value Rating	Zone
Eclecitc					
Pelican Club	★★★★★	Very Exp	★★★★★	★★★	1
Peristyle	★★★★★	Very Exp	★★★★★	★★★	1
Bayona	★★★★	Exp	★★★½	★★★	1
Bistro at Maison de Ville	★★★★	Exp	★★★½	★★★	1
Gautreau's	★★★★	Exp	★★★½	★★★	4
Stella!	★★★★	Exp	★★★½	★★	1
August	★★★★	Very Exp	★★★½	★★	2
Victor's	★★★★	Very Exp	★★★½	★★	1
Marisol	★★★★	Mod–Exp	★★★½	★★★	1
Grill Room	★★★★	Very Exp	★★★½	★★	2
French					
French Table	★★★★	Exp	★★★½	★★★	10
La Crêpe Nanou	★★★★	Mod	★★★	★★★★★	4
Herbsaint	★★★	Mod–Exp	★★★½	★★★	2
Lilette	★★★	Exp	★★★½	★★★	4
Rene Bistrot	★★★	Mod	★★★	★★★	2
Greek/Middle Eastern					
Byblos	★★★	Inexp	★★★	★★★★★	3
Indian					
Nirvana	★★★	Inexp–Mod	★★★	★★★	3
Italian					
Irene's Cuisine	★★★★	Mod–Exp	★★★½	★★★	1
Sal & Judy's	★★★★	Mod	★★★	★★★	12
Bacco	★★★★	Mod–Exp	★★★	★★★	1
Café Giovanni	★★★★	Mod–Exp	★★★	★★★	1
Andrea's	★★★★	Exp	★★★	★★★	9
Ristorante Filippo	★★★	Mod	★★★½	★★★	9
Vincent's	★★★	Inexp–Mod	★★★	★★★	4, 10, 12
La Riviera	★★★	Mod–Exp	★★★	★★★	10
Mosca's	★★★	Exp	★★★	★★★	11
Japanese					
Sake Café	★★★★	Mod–Exp	★★★½	★★★	3, 10
Ninja	★★★	Inexp–Mod	★★★	★★★	4
Shogun	★★★	Inexp–Mod	★★★	★★★	9

THE BEST NEW ORLEANS RESTAURANTS (continued)

Cuisine & Name	Overall Rating	Cost	Quality Rating	Value Rating	Zone
Korean					
Genghis Khan	★★★	Inexp–Mod ★★★		★★★	6
Mediterranean					
La Provence	★★★★	Exp	★★★	★★★	12
Vega Tapas Café	★★★	Inexp–Mod ★★★½		★★★	9
Maple Street Café	★★★	Inexp–Mod ★★★		★★★★★	4
Sandwiches					
Mother's	★★	Inexp	★★½	★★	2
Seafood					
Drago's	★★★★	Inexp–Mod ★★★½		★★★	10
RioMar	★★★★	Mod	★★★	★★★	2
Bozo's	★★★	Inexp	★★★½	★★★	9
Red Fish Grill	★★★	Mod–Exp	★★★½	★★★	1
GW Fins	★★★	Exp	★★★½	★★	1
Bruning's	★★★	Inexp	★★★	★★★★★	7
Barrow's Shady Inn	★★★	Inexp	★★★	★★★	4
Galley Seafood	★★★	Inexp	★★★	★★★	9
Fury's	★★★	Inexp–Mod ★★★		★★★	9
Mike Anderson's	★★★	Inexp–Mod ★★★		★★★	1
Uglesich's	★★★	Inexp–Mod ★★★		★★	3
Steak					
Ruth's Chris Steak House	★★★★	Very Exp	★★★½	★★	6, 10
Chateaubriand	★★★★	Exp	★★★	★★★	6
Dickie Brennan's Steakhouse	★★★★	Very Exp	★★★	★★★	1
Steak Knife	★★★	Mod–Exp	★★★	★★★	7
Mr. John's Steak House	★★★	Exp	★★★	★★★	3
Thai					
Basil Leaf	★★★★	Inexp	★★★½	★★★	4
Sabai Thai Cuisine	★★★	Inexp	★★★	★★★★★	11
La Thai Cuisine	★★★	Mod	★★★	★★★	9
Vietnamese					
Kim Son	★★★	Inexp	★★★	★★★★★	11
Pho Tau Bay	★★	Inexp	★★½	★★★★★	10

THE BEST NEW ORLEANS RESTAURANTS BY ZONE

Name	Cuisine	Overall Rating	Cost	Quality Rating	Value Rating
Zone 1: French Quarter					
Galatoire's	Creole	★★★★★	Exp	★★★★★	★★★
Pelican Club	Eclectic	★★★★★	Very Exp	★★★★★	★★★
Peristyle	Eclectic	★★★★★	Very Exp	★★★★★	★★★
Irene's Cuisine	Italian	★★★★	Mod–Exp	★★★½	★★★
Bayona	Eclectic	★★★★	Exp	★★★½	★★★
Bistro at Maison de Ville	Eclectic	★★★★	Exp	★★★½	★★★
Mr. B's Bistro	Creole	★★★★	Exp	★★★½	★★★
Stella!	Eclectic	★★★★	Exp	★★★½	★★
Broussard's	Creole	★★★★	Very Exp	★★★½	★★
K-Paul's Louisiana Kitchen	Cajun	★★★★	Very Exp	★★★½	★★
Victor's	Eclectic	★★★★	Very Exp	★★★½	★★
Bacco	Italian	★★★★	Mod–Exp	★★★	★★★
Café Giovanni	Italian	★★★★	Mod–Exp	★★★	★★★
Marisol	Eclectic	★★★★	Mod–Exp	★★★	★★★
Nola	Creole	★★★★	Exp	★★★	★★★
Bella Luna	Cont. Creole	★★★★	Very Exp	★★★	★★★
Dickie Brennan's Steakhouse	Steak	★★★★	Very Exp	★★★	★★★
Arnaud's	Creole	★★★★	Very Exp	★★★	★★
Brennan's	Creole	★★★★	Very Exp	★★★	★★
Red Fish Grill	Seafood	★★★	Mod–Exp	★★★½	★★★
201 Restaurant and Bar	Cont. Creole	★★★	Mod–Exp	★★★½	★★★
Alex Patout's Louisiana Restaurant	Cajun	★★★	Exp	★★★½	★★★
Begue's	Creole	★★★	Exp	★★★½	★★★
Muriel's	Cont. Creole	★★★	Exp	★★★½	★★★
GW Fins	Seafood	★★★	Exp	★★★½	★★
Gumbo Shop	Creole	★★★	Inexp	★★★	★★★
Mike Anderson's	Seafood	★★★	Inexp–Mod	★★★	★★★
Café Sbisa	Creole	★★★	Exp	★★★	★★★
Antoine's	Creole	★★★	Very Exp	★★★	★★
Coffee Pot	Creole	★★	Inexp–Mod	★★½	★★★
Bourbon House	Cont. Creole	★★	Mod	★★½	★★★

THE BEST NEW ORLEANS RESTAURANTS BY ZONE (continued)

Name	Cuisine	Overall Rating	Cost	Quality Rating	Value Rating
Zone 2: Central Business District					
Emeril's	Cont. Creole	★★★★★	Very Exp	★★★★★	★★★
Palace Café	Creole	★★★★	Mod–Exp	★★★½	★★★
August	Eclectic	★★★★	Very Exp	★★★½	★★
RioMar	Seafood	★★★★	Mod	★★★	★★★
Cuvee	Cont. Creole	★★★★	Very Exp	★★★	★★
Grill Room	Eclecitc	★★★★	Very Exp	★★★	★★
Bon Ton Café	Cajun	★★★	Mod–Exp	★★★½	★★★
Herbsaint	French	★★★	Mod–Exp	★★★½	★★★
Rene Bistrot	French	★★★	Mod	★★★	★★★
Mother's	Sandwiches	★★	Inexp	★★½	★★
Zone 3: Uptown below Napoleon					
Delmonico	Cont. Creole	★★★★★	Very Exp	★★★★★	★★
Sake Café	Japanese	★★★★	Mod–Exp	★★★½	★★★
Commander's Palace	Cont. Creole	★★★★	Very Exp	★★★½	★★★
Byblos	Greek/Middle Eastern	★★★	Inexp	★★★	★★★★★
Nirvana	Indian	★★★	Inexp–Mod	★★★	★★★
Lee Circle Restaurant	Cont. Creole	★★★	Mod	★★★	★★★
Mr. John's Steak House	Steak	★★★	Exp	★★★	★★★
Uglesich's	Seafood	★★★	Inexp–Mod	★★★	★★
Zone 4: Uptown above Napoleon					
Basil Leaf	Thai	★★★★	Inexp	★★★½	★★★
Jacques-Imo's	Creole	★★★★	Inexp–Mod	★★★½	★★★
Clancy's	Creole	★★★★	Mod–Exp	★★★½	★★★
Pascal's Manale	Creole	★★★★	Mod–Exp	★★★½	★★★
Brigtsen's	Creole	★★★★	Exp	★★★½	★★★
Gautreau's	Eclectic	★★★★	Exp	★★★½	★★★
La Crêpe Nanou	French	★★★★	Mod	★★★	★★★★★
Dick & Jenny's	Cont. Creole	★★★★	Mod–Exp	★★★	★★★
Upperline	Creole	★★★★	Mod–Exp	★★★	★★★
Dante's Kitchen	Cont. Creole	★★★	Mod	★★★½	★★★
Lilette	French	★★★	Exp	★★★½	★★★

THE BEST NEW ORLEANS RESTAURANTS BY ZONE *(continued)*

Name	Cuisine	Overall Rating	Cost	Quality Rating	Value Rating
Zone 4: Uptown above Napoleon (continued)					
Maple Street Café	Mediterranean	★★★	Inexp–Mod	★★★	★★★★★
Barrow's Shady Inn	Seafood	★★★	Inexp	★★★	★★★
Ninja	Japanese	★★★	Inexp–Mod	★★★	★★★
Vincent's	Italian	★★★	Inexp–Mod	★★★	★★★
Mat & Naddie's	Cont. Creole	★★★	Mod–Exp	★★★	★★★
Zone 5: Downtwon/St. Bernard					
Marigny Brasserie	Cont. Creole	★★★★	Mod–Exp	★★★½	★★★
Belle Forche	Cont. Creole	★★★	Exp	★★★½	★★★
Mandich	Creole	★★★	Inexp–Mod	★★★	★★★
Zone 6: Mid-City/Gentilly					
Gabrielle	Cont. Creole	★★★★	Exp	★★★½	★★★
Ruth's Chris Steak House	Steak	★★★★	Very Exp	★★★½	★★
Chateaubriand	Steak	★★★★	Exp	★★★	★★★
Christian's	Creole	★★★★	Exp	★★★	★★★
Indigo	Cont. Creole	★★★★	Exp	★★★	★★★
Mandina's	Creole	★★★	Inexp–Mod	★★★	★★★★★
Genghis Khan	Korean	★★★	Inexp–Mod	★★★	★★★
Zone 7: Lakeview/West End/Bucktown					
Wolfe's of New Orleans	Cont. Creole	★★★★	Mod–Exp	★★★½	★★★
Bruning's	Seafood	★★★	Inexp	★★★	★★★★★
Steak Knife	Steak	★★★	Mod–Exp	★★★	★★★
Zone 9: Metairie below Causeway					
Andrea's	Italian	★★★★	Exp	★★★	★★★
Bozo's	Seafood	★★★	Inexp	★★★½	★★★
Vega Tapas Café	Mediterranean	★★★	Inexp–Mod	★★★½	★★★
Ristorante Filippo	Italian	★★★	Mod	★★★½	★★★
Galley Seafood	Seafood	★★★	Inexp	★★★	★★★
Fury's	Seafood	★★★	Inexp–Mod	★★★	★★★
Shogun	Japanese	★★★	Inexp–Mod	★★★	★★★
La Thai Cuisine	Thai	★★★	Mod	★★★	★★★
Zone 10: Metairie above Causeway/Kenner/Jefferson Highway					
Drago's	Seafood	★★★★	Inexp–Mod	★★★½	★★★
Sake Café	Japanese	★★★★	Mod–Exp	★★★½	★★★
French Table	French	★★★★	Exp	★★★½	★★★

THE BEST NEW ORLEANS RESTAURANTS BY ZONE *(continued)*

Name	Cuisine	Overall Rating	Cost	Quality Rating	Value Rating
Zone 10: Metairie above Causeway/Kenner/Jefferson Highway *(continued)*					
Ruth's Chris Steak House	Steak	★★★★	Very Exp	★★★½	★★
Le Parvenu	Creole	★★★★	Exp	★★★	★★★
Vincent's	Italian	★★★	Inexp–Mod	★★★	★★★
La Riviera	Italian	★★★	Mod–Exp	★★★	★★★
Pho Tau Bay	Vietnamese	★★	Inexp	★★½	★★★★★
Zone 11: West Bank					
Kim Son	Vietnamese	★★★	Inexp	★★★	★★★★★
Sabai Thai Cuisine	Thai	★★★	Inexp	★★★	★★★★★
China Blossom	Chinese	★★★	Inexp–Mod	★★★	★★★
Mosca's	Italian	★★★	Exp	★★★	★★★
Zone 12: North Shore					
Dakota	Cont. Creole	★★★★★	Exp	★★★★★	★★★
Sal & Judy's	Italian	★★★★	Mod	★★★	★★★
La Provence	Mediterranean	★★★★	Exp	★★★	★★★
Trey Yuen	Chinese	★★★	Inexp–Mod	★★★½	★★
Vincent's	Italian	★★★	Inexp–Mod	★★★	★★★

More Recommendations

Best Sunday Brunch

Andrea's 3100 19th Street, Metairie   834-8583

Arnaud's 813 Bienville, French Quarter   523-5433

Begue's 300 Bourbon, French Quarter   553-2278

Brennan's 417 Royal, French Quarter   525-9711

Commander's Palace 1403 Washington Avenue, Garden District   899-8221

Delmonico 1300 St. Charles Avenue, Uptown   525-4937

Grill Room 300 Gravier, Central Business District   522-1992

Mr. B's Bistro 201 Royal, French Quarter   523-2078

Palace Café 605 Canal, Central Business District   523-1661

Victor's 921 Canal, French Quarter   524-1331

Best Breakfast

Abita Café 22132 Level, Abita Springs (985) 867-9950

Begue's 300 Bourbon, French Quarter 553-2278

Brennan's 417 Royal, French Quarter 525-9711

Café du Monde 800 Decatur, French Quarter 525-4544

Camellia Grill 626 S. Carrollton Avenue, Riverbend 866-9573

Cobalt 333 St. Charles Avenue, Central Business District 565-5595

Coffee Pot 714 St. Peter, French Quarter 524-3500

Deanie's 1016 Annunciation, Warehouse District 250-4460

Grill Room 300 Gravier, Central Business District 522-1992

Morning Call Coffee Stand 3325 Severn Avenue, Metairie 885-4068

Mother's 401 Poydras, Central Business District 523-9656

Peppermill 3524 Severn Avenue, Metairie 455-2266

Rene Bistrot 817 Common, Riverbend 412-2580

Best Hamburgers

Beachcorner 4905 Canal, Mid-City 488-7357

Bud's Broiler 6325 Elysian Fields Avenue, West End, 282-6696; 500 City Park Avenue, Mid-City, 486-2559; 3151 Calhoun, Riverbend, 861-0906; several other locations

Camellia Grill 626 S. Carrollton Avenue, Riverbend 866-9573

Clover Grill 900 Bourbon, French Quarter 523-0904

Lee's Hamburgers 904 Veterans Boulevard, Metairie 836-6804

Michael's Mid-City Grill 4139 Canal, Mid-City 486-8200

Port of Call 838 Esplanade, French Quarter 523-0120

Snug Harbor 626 Frenchmen, Marigny 949-0696

Sugar Magnolia 1910 Magazine, Garden District 529-1110

Ye Olde College Inn 3016 S. Carrollton Avenue, Uptown 866-3683

Most Striking Architecture

56 Degrees 610 Poydras, Central Business District 212-5656

Antoine's 713 St. Louis, French Quarter 581-4422

Arnaud's 813 Bienville, French Quarter 523-5433

Bella Luna 914 N. Peters, French Market 529-1583

Brennan's 417 Royal, French Quarter 525-9711

Broussard's 819 Conti, French Quarter 581-3866

Christian's 3835 Iberville, Mid-City 482-4924

Commander's Palace 1403 Washington Avenue, Garden District 899-8221

Court of Two Sisters 613 Royal, French Quarter   522-7273
Delmonico 1300 St. Charles Avenue, Uptown   525-4937
Emeril's 800 Tchoupitoulas, Warehouse District   528-9393
Galatoire's 209 Bourbon, French Quarter   525-2021
Sake Café 2830 Magazine, Garden District   894-0033
Trey Yuen 600 Causeway Boulevard, Mandeville   626-4476

Best Cafés for Dessert and Coffee
Angelo Brocato 214 N. Carrollton Avenue, Mid-City   486-1465
Café du Monde 800 Decatur, French Quarter   525-4544
Coffee Cottage 2559 Metairie Road, Old Metairie   833-3513
La Marquise 625 Chartres, French Quarter   524-0420
Morning Call Coffee Stand 3325 Severn Avenue, Metairie   885-4068

Best for Children
Andrea's 3100 19th Street, Metairie   834-8583
Bozo's 3117 21st Street, Metairie   831-8666
Bruning's West End Park, West End   282-9395
Corky's 4243 Veterans Boulevard, Metairie   887-5000
Fury's 724 Martin Behrman Avenue, Metairie   834-5646
Miyako 3837 Veterans Boulevard, Metairie   779-6475
Mr. Ed's 1001 Live Oak, Metairie   838-0022
New Orleans Food & Spirits 210 Metairie-Hammond Highway
  Bucktown, 828-2220
Peppermill 3524 Severn Avenue, Metairie   455-2266
Pizza Man Of Covington 1248 Collins Boulevard (US 190),
  Covington   892-9874.
Red Fish Grill 115 Bourbon, French Quarter   598-1200
Remoulade 309 Bourbon, French Quarter   523-0377
Restaurant des Familles 7163 Barataria Boulevard at Lafitte-Larose
  Highway (LA 45 at LA 3134), Crown Point   689-7834
Zea Rotisserie and Brewpub 4450 Veterans Boulevard (Clearview
  Mall), Metairie   780-9090
Zeke's 1517 Metairie Road, Old Metairie   832-1133

Best Local Color
Antoine's 713 St. Louis, French Quarter   581-4422
Arnaud's 813 Bienville, French Quarter   523-5433
Bella Luna 914 N. Peters, French Market   529-1583

Best Local Color *(continued)*

Brennan's 417 Royal, French Quarter   525-9711

Broussard's 819 Conti, French Quarter   581-3866

Bruning's West End Park, West End   282-9395

Café du Monde 800 Decatur, French Quarter   525-4544

Commander's Palace 1403 Washington Avenue, Garden District
    899-8221

Court of Two Sisters 613 Royal, French Quarter   522-7273

Galatoire's 209 Bourbon, French Quarter   525-2021

Muriel's 801 Chartres, French Quarter   568-1885

Napoleon House 500 Chartres, French Quarter   524-9752

Royal Café 706 Royal, French Quarter   528-9086

Tujague's 823 Decatur, French Quarter   525-8676

Uglesich's 1238 Baronne, Lee Circle Area   523-8571

Best Muffulettas

Central Grocery 923 Decatur, French Quarter   523-1620

Come Back Inn 8016 W. Metairie Avenue, Metairie   467-9316

Johnny's Po-Boys 511 St. Louis, French Quarter   524-8129

Mr. Ed's 1001 Live Oak, Metairie   838-0022

Napoleon House 500 Chartres, French Quarter   524-9752

Nor-Joe Imports 505 Frisco Avenue, Metairie   833-9240

Radosta's 249 Aris Avenue, Old Metairie   831-1537

Remoulade 309 Bourbon, French Quarter   523-0377

Two Tonys 105 Metairie-Hammond Highway, Bucktown   831-0999

Best Outdoor Dining

Bayona 430 Dauphine, French Quarter   525-4455

Broussard's 819 Conti, French Quarter   581-3866

Café Degas 3127 Esplanade, Mid-City   945-5635

Café Volage 720 Dublin, Riverbend   861-4227

Coffee Pot 714 St. Peter, French Quarter   524-3500

Commander's Palace 1403 Washington Avenue, Garden District
    899-8221

Court of Two Sisters 613 Royal, French Quarter   522-7273

Feelings 2600 Chartres Bywater   945-2222

Jacques-Imo's 8324 Oak, Riverbend   861-0886

Louis XVI 730 Bienville Street, French Quarter   581-7000

Marisol 437 Esplanade Avenue, Marigny   943-1912

Martinique 5908 Magazine, Uptown   891-8495

Mat & Naddie's 937 Leonidas, Riverbend   861-9600

Wolfe's of New Orleans 7224 Pontchartrain Boulevard, Lakeview   284-6004

Dante's Kitchen 736 Dante, Riverbend   861-3121

Best Pizza

Bacco 310 Chartres, French Quarter   522-2426

Café Nino 1519 S. Carrollton Avenue, Riverbend   865-9200

Figaro Pizzerie 7900 Maple, Uptown   866-0100

Mark Twain's Pizza Landing 2035 Metairie Road, Metairie   832-8032

New York Pizza 5201 Magazine, Uptown   891-2376

Pizza Man Of Covington 1248 Collins Boulevard (US 190), Covington   892-9874.

Tower of Pizza 2104 Veterans Boulevard, Metairie   833-9373

Venezia 134 N. Carrollton Avenue, Mid-City   488-7991

Best Casual Seafood Houses

Bourbon House 144 Bourbon, French Quarter   522-0111

Bozo's 3117 21st Street, Metairie   831-8666

Bruning's West End Park, West End   282-9395

Casamento's 4330 Magazine, Uptown   895-9761

Charles Sea Foods 8311 Jefferson Highway, Harahan   737-9190

Drago's 3232 N. Arnoult Road, Metairie   888-9254

Felix's 739 Iberville, French Quarter   522-4440

Galley Seafood 2535 Metairie Road, Old Metairie   832-0955

Middendorf's Manchac, Akers   386-6666

Mike Anderson's 215 Bourbon Street, French Quarter   524-3884

New Orleans Food & Spirits 2330 Lapalco Boulevard, Harvey, 362-0800; 210 Metairie-Hammond Highway, Bucktown, 828-2220

Restaurant des Familles 7163 Barataria Boulevard at Lafitte-Larose Highway (LA 45 at LA 3134), Crown Point   689-7834

Uglesich's 1238 Baronne, Lee Circle   523-8571

Zeke's 1517 Metairie Road, Old Metairie   832-1133

Restaurant Profiles

Alex Patout's Louisiana Restaurant   ★★★

CAJUN | EXPENSIVE | QUALITY ★★★½ | VALUE ★★★

720 St. Louis; 525-7788 • French Quarter Zone 1

Reservations Recommended **When to go** Anytime **Entrée range** $14–$25 **Payment** All major credit cards **Service rating** ★★★ **Friendliness rating** ★★★★ **Parking** Pay parking lots nearby **Bar** Full bar **Wine selection** Substantial list, emphasis on California **Dress** Jacket recommended but not required **Disabled access** Limited **Customers** Tourists, some locals

Dinner Sunday–Thursday, 6–10 p.m.; Friday and Saturday, 6–11 p.m.

Setting & atmosphere The restaurant is down the carriageway of an old French Quarter building, past the unassociated Gennifer Flowers' bar (yes, that Gennifer Flowers). It's handsomer than you'll expect.

House specialties Boudin & andouille sausages; baked oysters; gumbo; grilled fish; crabmeat imperial; crawfish étouffée; roast duck with rice dressing; bread pudding; sweet-potato pie.

Summary & comments Alex Patout is one of very few restaurants in New Orleans that cooks the food of the Cajun country—as opposed to the Creole food of New Orleans. Alex comes from a family with a long history in New Iberia, and his style of cooking incorporates the classic ingredients and methods of Cajun country. On the other hand, his cooking has an almost gourmet finish in many dishes, which is an accomplishment—Cajun food doesn't much lend itself to fancy service. Although the chef uses a lot of cream and butter, he also likes things like crab fat and tasso. The restaurant is somewhat inconsistent, but when it's hot, it can serve quite a meal.

Andrea's   ★★★★

ITALIAN | EXPENSIVE | QUALITY ★★★ | VALUE ★★★

3100 19th Street; 834-8583 • Metairie below Causeway Zone 9 • andreasrestaurant.com

Reservations Recommended **When to go** Anytime **Entrée range** $14–$32 **Payment** All major credit cards **Service rating** ★★★★ **Friendliness rating** ★★★ **Parking** Free lot adjacent **Bar** Full bar **Wine selection** Substantial list, mostly Italian and French; a bit overpriced **Dress** Jacket recommended but not required **Disabled access** Full **Customers** Businessmen at lunch; daters.

Lunch & dinner Monday–Thursday, 11 a.m.–10 p.m.; Friday, 11:30 a.m.–11 p.m.; Saturday, 4–11 p.m.; Sunday, 11 a.m.–9 p.m.

Setting & atmosphere The restaurant feels distinctly suburban, but 15 years of bringing in Italian furnishings has given it personality. Lots of private dining rooms.

House specialties Antipasto; angel hair pasta Andrea; mussels marinara; straciatella di Medici (spinach and chicken soup); fish basilico (snapper, trout, drum); veal chop Valdostana; duck with green peppercorns; steak with three-pepper sauce; pannéed veal Tanet; tiramisu; strawberry cake.

Entertainment & amenities Live piano most nights. Strolling accordionist at Sunday brunch.

Summary & comments Capri native Andrea Apuzzo and his restaurant are a formidable presence on the New Orleans Italian dining scene. Andrea's is certainly the city's most ambitious Italian restaurant, with an enormous menu and an offer from the chef to cook anything you want on top of it. The quality of the ingredients (especially seafood and vegetables) is unimpeachable. It started out as a pure Northern Italian restaurant, but as time goes by, Andrea's has acquired a greater and greater New Orleans flavor. What comes out of the kitchen is always beautiful and usually ample in portion, but can range from brilliant to just okay. Seafood is the best bet, followed by poultry. At its best, Andrea's puts out an unforgettable dinner, with the chef constantly in the room flattering his customers and making people laugh. Don't come here on a big holiday; they always overbook.

Antoine's

CREOLE | VERY EXPENSIVE | QUALITY ★★★ | VALUE ★★

713 St. Louis; 581-4422 • French Quarter Zone 1 • antoines.com

Reservations Recommended **When to go** Lunch and early evenings; avoid days before holidays **Entrée range** $16–$40 **Payment** All major credit cards **Service rating** ★★★ **Friendliness rating** ★★ **Parking** Pay garages nearby **Bar** Full bar **Wine selection** Distinguished cellar, with tremendous inventory, and French-dominated. Many older vintages. The wine cellar presents a great visual treat. **Dress** Jacket and tie required at dinner **Disabled access** Limited **Customers** Tourists, some locals

Lunch Monday–Saturday, 11:30 a.m.–2 p.m.

Dinner Monday–Saturday, 5:30–10 p.m.

Setting & atmosphere Antoine's rambling, antique premises are amazing. The many dining rooms recall different eras and flavors of the city's social life. The front dining room is charming, but only at lunch; at dinner, the bustle of arriving diners dominates the atmosphere. Most locals eat in the red-walled (well, we think it's red—most of the surface is covered by framed memorabilia) Annex.

House specialties Oysters Rockefeller; oysters Foch; escargots Bordelaise; shrimp rémoulade; crawfish cardinale; grilled pompano; soft-shell crabs Colbert; chicken Rochambeau; chicken bonne femme; tournedos marchand de vin; lamb chops béarnaise; baked Alaska.

Summary & comments Antoine's is a living museum of New Orleans dining. Founded in 1840, it's the oldest restaurant in America under continuous operation by one family. And it's not for everybody. If you're fascinated by the history of Creole food, you'll be able to put up with the many peccadilloes. If history is not your bag, this may not be the place for you. The best time to figure it all out is lunch, which is rarely busy and offers the same menu as dinner. Antoine's best dishes, once common elsewhere, are now unique to the restaurant. The beef, chicken, and more straightforward seafood dishes provide the best eating here. But the best bet of all may be to make an entire meal of appetizers, of which there is a large array. The best food here is served to regulars, so either be one or go with one. That might not even work these days; there's been more waiter turnover than usual lately.

Arnaud's ★★★★

CREOLE | VERY EXPENSIVE | QUALITY ★★★ | VALUE ★★

813 Bienville; 523-5433 • French Quarter Zone 1 • arnauds.com

Reservations Recommended **When to go** Anytime **Entrée range** $18–$40 **Payment** All major credit cards **Service rating** ★★★★ **Friendliness rating** ★★★ **Parking** Validated (free) at garage corner Dauphine and Iberville **Bar** Full bar **Wine selection** Distinguished cellar, good international balance; a bit pricey. **Dress** Jacket and tie recommended for dinner, but not required **Disabled access** Full **Customers** Tourists, some locals

Brunch Sunday, 10 a.m.–2:30 p.m.

Lunch Monday–Friday, 11:30 a.m.–2:30 p.m.

Dinner Sunday–Thursday, 6–10 p.m.; Friday and Saturday, 6–10:30 p.m.

Setting & atmosphere Nobody ever gave a moribund old restaurant a better rebirth than did Arnaud's owner Archie Casbarian. Its an atmospheric exemplar of the old-style New Orleans Creole restaurant, with tiled floors, tin ceilings, beveled-glass windows, and ancient overhead fans. If you have time, tour the huge restaurant's many private dining rooms and its Mardi Gras museum.

House specialties Shrimp Arnaud (rémoulade); oysters Arnaud (five different); shrimp Bellaire; oysters stewed in cream; trout meunière; pompano David; pompano en croûte; steak tartare (lunch); veal tournedos Chantal; crème brûlée; bananas Foster; bread pudding; café brûlot.

Entertainment & amenities A small jazz band plays through dinner in the Richelieu Room for a small cover charge. Strolling jazz trio at Sunday brunch.

Summary & comments In its first heyday, Arnaud's was the leading restaurant of New Orleans, reinventing the way people dined out. It slipped into obscurity in the 1970s, but was brought back to life in 1979. The modern Arnaud's blends dishes created eons ago by Count Arnaud with spiffy new food—all with an unmistakable New Orleans flavor. The only thing missing is a strong local clientele, but that's a problem all over the French Quarter these days. The wine list's pricing is a bit dear, but the selection is excellent. There are also an exceptional collection of ports, Cognacs, and cigars.

August ★★★★

ECLECTIC | VERY EXPENSIVE | QUALITY ★★★½ | VALUE ★★

301 Tchoupitoulas; 299-9777 • Central Business District Zone 2

Reservations Required **When to go** Dinner **Entrée range** $22–$36 **Payment** All major credit cards **Service rating** ★★★ **Friendliness rating** ★★★★ **Parking** Free valet parking **Bar** Full bar **Wine selection** Excellent wine list, including many selections by the glass **Dress** Jacket recommended but not required **Disabled access** Full **Customers** Business people at lunch, gourmets at dinner

Lunch Monday–Friday, 11:30 a.m.–2 p.m.

Dinner Monday–Saturday, 6–10 p.m.

Setting & atmosphere The ground floor of an early-1800s building, the restaurant has towering ceilings, antique-wood walls and columns, large windows, and a general feeling of antebellum grandeur. The wine room and the bar look a bit more modern but are equally comfortable.

House specialties Most of the menu changes seasonally or more often. Gnocchi with crabmeat and white truffles; lobster ravioli; soft-shell crab BLT; Alain Assaud's fish soup; Duke's oyster stew; roast chicken grandmere's style; dessert assortment.

Summary & comments August was built as a venue for chef John Besh, who's had an impressive career in a succession of first-class restaurants around town. Besh is a local guy, but he spent a lot of time in kitchens in France, which informed his style of cooking in a rustic way. Look for dishes involving homely items like rabbit, chicken, and variety meats. This is strictly a place for those who get a kick out of eating offbeat items prepared in highly original combinations. Everything changes with the seasons, which sometimes bring dishes from far-flung origins.

Bacco ★★★★

ITALIAN | MODERATE–EXPENSIVE | QUALITY ★★★ | VALUE ★★★

310 Chartres; 522-2426 • French Quarter Zone 1 • bacco.com

Reservations Recommended **When to go** Anytime **Entrée range** $12–$24 **Payment** All major credit cards **Service rating** ★★★★ **Friendliness rating** ★★★★★ **Parking** Free valet parking in hotel garage **Bar** Full bar **Wine selection** Substantial list, mostly Italian and California. Many interesting, offbeat bottles. **Dress** Jacket recommended but not required **Disabled access** Full **Customers** Mostly locals, a few tourists

Lunch Daily, 11:30 a.m.–2:30 p.m.

Dinner Sunday–Thursday, 6:30–9:30 p.m.; Friday and Saturday, 6–10:30 p.m.

Setting & atmosphere Striking dining spaces, shaped largely from concrete, create a distinctive environment. Particularly interesting is the vaulted rear dining room.

House specialties White pizza; grilled eggplant; pasta rags, spinach, and chicken; crawfish ravioli; grilled fish; grilled veal T-bone; roasted pork tenderloin; tiramisu; homemade ice creams.

Summary & comments Bacco's menu is mainly that of a Tuscan trattoria, with the best offerings cooked by burning wood: pizza, meat roasts, poultry, and fish. Beyond that, there's a significant New Orleans component to the menu (crawfish ravioli, a specialty, comes to mind). Service is unusually good, and the wine list has one of the best selections of Italian bottles in town. The October-long white-truffle festival is worth scheduling a trip for.

Barrow's Shady Inn ★★★

SEAFOOD | INEXPENSIVE | QUALITY ★★★ | VALUE ★★★

2714 Mistletoe; 482-9427 • Uptown above Napoleon Zone 4

Reservations Not accepted **When to go** Anytime **Entrée range** $10–$12 **Payment** Cash only **Service rating** ★★ **Friendliness rating** ★★★★ **Parking** Free lot adjacent **Bar** Full bar **Wine selection** A few house wines **Dress** Anything goes **Disabled access** Limited **Customers** Neighborhood people

Lunch Thursday–Saturday, 11 a.m.–2 p.m.

Dinner Tuesday–Saturday, 6–10 p.m.

Setting & atmosphere It looks more like a bar than a restaurant, but more people eat than drink.

House specialties Fried catfish with potato salad.

Summary & comments Barrow's, well-hidden Uptown since 1943, fries incomparably light catfish that's so good you eat it like popcorn. And that's all they have. The fish has a little touch of pepper in the flavor that makes it unusual. You also get some fine homemade potato salad.

Basil Leaf ★★★★

THAI | INEXPENSIVE | QUALITY ★★★½ | VALUE ★★★

1438 S. Carrollton Avenue; 862-9001 • Uptown above Napoleon Zone 4

Reservations Accepted **When to go** Anytime **Entrée range** $9–$24 **Payment** AE, DC, MC, V **Service rating** ★★★★ **Friendliness rating** ★★★ **Parking** Curbside parking only **Bar** Full bar **Wine selection** Much better selection of wines than typically found in Asian restaurants **Dress** Casual **Disabled access** Full **Customers** Uptowners, mostly on the young side

Lunch Monday–Friday, 11:30 a.m.–3 p.m.

Dinner Monday–Saturday, 6–10 p.m.

Setting & atmosphere A single room decorated simply but tastefully, with lots of windows.

House specialties Seared scallop salad; spring roll; sautéed calamari; daily soups; pad Thai; grilled chicken or beef noodle salads; green curry with chicken; soft-shell crabs with sesame.

Summary & comments After making a hit in an unpromising space in Metairie, the Basil Leaf moved to more accessible, more comely quarters in Carrollton, near the streetcar barn. Here the ambitions of the chef are fully realized, such that the Basil Leaf now serves the best Thai food in the area. Thai food is usually well presented, but this is notably beautiful. The menu deviates from those of all the previous Thai restaurants hereabouts, at least a little. As in other gourmet bistros, the chef sees no reason why he shouldn't create new ideas. Service is also a cut or two better than what you're used to finding in local Asian restaurants.

Bayona ★★★★

ECLECTIC | EXPENSIVE | QUALITY ★★★½ | VALUE ★★★

430 Dauphine; 525-4455 • French Quarter Zone 1

Reservations Required **When to go** Anytime **Entrée range** $14–$28 **Payment** All major credit cards **Service rating** ★★★★★ **Friendliness rating** ★★★★ **Parking** Validated at garage across the street **Bar** Full bar **Wine selection** Distinguished cellar, with many interesting, offbeat bottles; many by-the-glass selections **Dress** Jacket recommended but not required **Disabled access** Limited **Customers** Mostly locals, a few tourists

Lunch Monday–Friday, 11:30 a.m.–2:30 p.m.

Dinner Monday–Thursday, 6–9:30 p.m.; Friday and Saturday, 6–11 p.m.

Setting & atmosphere All dining rooms other than the main one are small and can get a bit noisy. In decent weather, you may also dine under the banana trees in the courtyard—very pleasant. Avoid the cramped upstairs rooms.

House specialties Grilled shrimp with coriander; sweetbreads any style; roasted garlic soup; shrimp curry; salmon with choucroûte and Gewurztraminer; pork, lamb, or veal chops; quail dish of the day; lemon tart; apple-almond gratin.

Summary & comments The understated personal cuisine of Susan Spicer may underwhelm you during the menu-reading part of the repast. But her brilliant sense of taste and culinary curiosity comes though where it counts—on the plate. This is particularly impressive given the wide range of flavors you encounter here. French, Indian, Mediterranean, New Orleans, Far Eastern . . . she seems to understand the essence of every style she comes in contact with. You'll be presented with two menus of equal length: one of the house specialties, another of the day's offerings. Either card will serve you well. Wine-drinking here is rewarding; the list is full of rare and unusual bottles. Both wine and food are sold at prices a bit below what you'd find in comparable restaurants, and lunch is an excellent bargain.

Begue's ★★★

CREOLE | EXPENSIVE | QUALITY ★★★½ | VALUE ★★★

300 Bourbon; 553-2278 • French Quarter Zone 1

Reservations Recommended **When to go** Anytime; Friday's lunch buffet is particularly inviting **Entrée range** $12–$22 **Payment** All major credit cards **Service rating** ★★★★ **Friendliness rating** ★★★★ **Parking** Validated free in Royal Sonesta garage, downstairs **Bar** Full bar **Wine selection** Decent list, good international balance **Dress** Jacket recommended but not required **Disabled access** Full **Customers** Tourists, some locals; mostly local for Sunday brunch

Breakfast Daily, 7–10 a.m.

Lunch Daily, 11:30 a.m.–2:30 p.m.

Dinner Daily, 6–10 p.m.

Setting & atmosphere The large, very comfy room is surrounded by fanciful paintings of New Orleans scenes on three walls, and large windows view a densely planted courtyard on the fourth.

House specialties Eggs with crabmeat & lobster sauce (breakfast); crab cake; shrimp and crabmeat rémoulade; seafood gumbo; sautéed shrimp with refried grits; grilled double pork chop; roasted lamb chops with spaetzle; steamed lobster with vanilla; sorbets and ice creams; chocolate pecan pie.

Entertainment & amenities Pianist plays throughout dinner and at Sunday brunch.

Summary & comments The flagship restaurant of the Royal Sonesta Hotel is best known for its buffets: lunch Friday, brunch Sunday. Both are among the best of their kind. But the à la carte service at all three meals the rest of the week is also worthy of interest. The kitchen is original and employs first-class local ingredients; what comes out is food with a New Orleans flavor but a continental look. The breakfast menu is one of the best around. Service is a little lackluster, but the restaurant is always a pleasure.

Bella Luna ★★★★

CONTEMPORARY CREOLE | VERY EXPENSIVE | QUALITY ★★★ | VALUE ★★★

914 N. Peters; 529-1583 • French Quarter Zone 1

Reservations Recommended **When to go** Anytime **Entrée range** $18–$32 **Payment** All major credit cards **Service rating** ★★★★ **Friendliness rating** ★★★★ **Parking** Validated free for French Market lot, immediately adjacent **Bar** Full bar **Wine selection** Distinguished cellar, many interesting, offbeat bottles; many by-the-glass selections **Dress** Jacket recommended but not required **Disabled access** Limited **Customers** Mostly locals, a few tourists; couples

Dinner Sunday–Thursday, 6–10 p.m.; Friday and Saturday, 6–11 p.m.

Setting & atmosphere Bella Luna's matchless asset is a view of the Mississippi River—something few New Orleans restaurants have. The long dining room, with its panoramic windows, stretches along the second floor of the French Market.

House specialties Crab cakes rémoulade; fettuccine Reggiano; pasta with truffles; Caesar salad; shrimp quesadillas; grilled or blackened tuna; osso buco; grilled pork tenderloin; veal T-bone with herb olive oil; any game special; dessert assortment.

Summary & comments Take away the great view, and avid diners would still come here for the cooking of chef-proprietor Horst Pfeifer, who unites Italian, Southwestern, and Creole flavors into singular creations. All methods of cooking are explored, but grilling, roasting, and smoking are specialties. The chef ranges wide with his ingredients, too, buying more different species of fish, birds, and chops than most places. A few blocks away, in the garden of the historic Ursuline Convent, he grows fresh herbs. The consistency is not perfect, and the front door greeting could stand a great deal of warming up. But few places can provide the package of gustatory and atmospheric pleasure that Bella Luna does.

Belle Forche ★★★

CONTEMPORARY CREOLE | EXPENSIVE | QUALITY ★★★½ | VALUE ★★★

1407 Decatur; 940-0722 • Downtown/St. Bernard Zone 5

Reservations Accepted **When to go** Late night **Entrée range** $10–$26 **Payment** All major credit cards **Service rating** ★★★ **Friendliness rating** ★★★

Parking Curbside parking only **Bar** Full bar **Wine selection** Decent but unexceptional list **Dress** Dressy casual **Disabled access** Full **Customers** People who like to drift among the many restaurants and clubs along the Marigny strip, and visitors

Dinner Tuesday, Wednesday, and Sunday, 6–11 p.m.; Thursday–Saturday, 6 p.m.–2:30 a.m.

Setting & atmosphere An old shop in an older building has an odd dogleg bend, separating the casual half of the restaurant from the very casual half. An aquarium, a mural, and the scene outside the big windows give the eye something to dwell on between courses.

House specialties Flash-fried oysters "in tuxedo"; duck confit with spaghetti squash; seviche with conch and calamari; grilled fish amandine; Puerto Rican hot pepper chicken; barbecue salmon; duckling with mushrooms and pomegranate; grillades and grits; twice-jerked catfish; pineapple and coconut crème brûlée.

Summary & comments They have two complete menus here. The main menu is ambitious and original, but it works in three styles: old-style Creole, Caribbean, and contemporary American. It all comes together interestingly and incorporates offbeat ingredients, cooking techniques, and presentations. The "café menu" is about half the price of the main card, includes a greater predominance of home-style Creole cooking, and consigns the diner to the bar area. It is also kept in force until the wee hours of the morning on weekends, and is probably the most interesting late-night selection of food in town. All of this is the work of chef-owner Matt Yohalem, a widely-traveled Commander's Palace alumnus.

Bistro at Maison de Ville   ★★★★

ECLECTIC | EXPENSIVE | QUALITY ★★★½ | VALUE ★★★

733 Toulouse; 528-9206 • French Quarter Zone 1

Reservations Recommended **When to go** Anytime **Entrée range** $18–$40 **Payment** All major credit cards **Service rating** ★★★★ **Friendliness rating** ★★★★ **Parking** Several pay lots within two blocks **Bar** Full bar. Many single-malt Scotches, Cognacs, Armagnacs, etc. **Wine selection** Decent list, many interesting, offbeat bottles; many by-the-glass selections **Dress** Jacket recommended but not required **Disabled access** Limited **Customers** Mostly locals, a few tourists

Lunch Daily, 11:30 a.m.–2:30 p.m.

Dinner Daily, 6–10 p.m.

Setting & atmosphere There's a serious shortage of space, both in the quaint dining room as a whole and at your teeny table. More elbow room can be had on the small courtyard, if the weather's tolerable for outdoor dining.

House specialties Crawfish rémoulade; steamed mussels with pommes frites; grilled sea scallops with saffron risotto; sautéed salmon with ravioli of lobster and spinach; grilled double pork chop with apples; pan-seared venison with spaetzle; chocolate cake; crème brûlée.

Summary & comments Claustrophobic but chic, the Bistro (as it's simply called by its regulars) has a history of hiring hot young chefs on their way up.

Nowadays, it's hard to imagine the Bistro without chef Greg Picolo, who's been on the job longer than all his predecessors combined. It's a Bistro tradition for the menu to be unpredictable, but there's a certain hard-to-nail-down style that's consistent. Ingredients and techniques tend to the unusual, and a certain Mediterranean aspect seems always to be present. The dining room is orchestrated by the always-accommodating Patrick Hoorebeek, whose stamp is even more pervasive than chef's. Make him your instant friend by mentioning his homeland, Belgium. Patrick's wine collection is as gratifying as his service style.

Bon Ton Café   ★★★

CAJUN | MODERATE–EXPENSIVE | QUALITY ★★★½ | VALUE ★★★

401 Magazine; 524-3386 • Central Business District Zone 2

Reservations Recommended **When to go** Anytime **Entrée range** $15–$24 **Payment** AE, DC, MC, V **Service rating** ★★★ **Friendliness rating** ★★★★ **Parking** Pay lot and curbside (metered) **Bar** Full bar **Wine selection** A few house wines **Dress** Jacket recommended but not required **Disabled access** Limited **Customers** Mostly locals at lunch, mostly tourists at dinner

Lunch Monday–Friday, 11 a.m.–2 p.m.

Dinner Monday–Friday, 5–9:30 p.m.

Setting & atmosphere One big brick-walled room, its tables covered with checked tablecloths, full of people who look like regulars.

House specialties Turtle soup; fried catfish fingers; shrimp rémoulade; Cajun Caesar salad; crawfish dinner (crawfish four ways: étouffée, bisque, fried, and omelette); crabmeat au gratin; redfish Bon Ton; oysters or soft-shell crab Alvin; pan-broiled oysters; bayou étouffée; bread pudding.

Summary & comments The Bon Ton has specialized in crawfish longer than anyone else in New Orleans and can claim to be the town's oldest Cajun (as opposed to Creole) restaurant. Cajun cooking is itself regional; the Bon Ton's style comes from the Bayou Lafourche area. It's mild in its pepper levels and a bit old-fashioned. You'll see touches you haven't been treated to since the early 1960s. (The service style is definitely from that era.) It's a charming, unaffected place delivering good food and value. But go with the specialties, and don't make it jump through hoops.

Bourbon House   ★★

CONTEMPORARY CREOLE | MODERATE | QUALITY ★★½ | VALUE ★★★

144 Bourbon; 522-0111 • French Quarter Zone 1

Reservations Recommended **When to go** Anytime **Entrée range** $14–$25 **Payment** All major credit cards **Service rating** ★★★ **Friendliness rating** ★★★★ **Parking** Pay parking lots nearby **Bar** Full bar **Wine selection** Good wine list, including many selections by the glass **Dress** Jacket recommended but not required **Disabled access** Full **Customers** Mostly local at lunch, a mix of locals and visitors at dinner

Breakfast Daily, 6–10 a.m.

Lunch Monday–Friday, 11:30 a.m.–2:30 p.m.

Dinner Daily, 5–10 p.m.

Setting & atmosphere An expansive, tall space with large windows, the Bourbon House stands at what's considered the gateway to Bourbon Street. Just inside the door is a lavish display of the current seafoods, with an inviting, polished raw bar.

House specialties Oysters on the half shell; chilled seafood platter; oyster stew with cream; oysters Bienville; stuffed crab meunière; soups 1-1-1; redfish "on the half shell"; fish Grieg with crabmeat; fish with pecans; shrimp Chippewa; barbecue shrimp; pannéed veal with crabmeat; Mississippi mud pie.

Summary & comments Dickie Brennan attempts to do with seafood here what he did with steak at his restaurant a half-block away. Which is to say simple service of top-class foodstuffs in a pleasant but informal environment. But the greatest success of the Bourbon House is in returning to an active menu the best food served at Commander's Palace (that's family) about 20 years ago, when Paul Prudhomme and Emeril Lagasse ruled that kitchen. It's the same pleasure as listening to oldies music—no less good, but old hat. Not all the kinks are worked out at this writing, but that's normal for new Brennan restaurants.

Bozo's

SEAFOOD | INEXPENSIVE | QUALITY ★★★½ | VALUE ★★★

3117 21st Street; 831-8666 • Metairie below Causeway Zone 9

Reservations Not accepted **When to go** Anytime except the very busy Fridays **Entrée range** $8–$16 **Payment** MC, V **Service rating** ★★★ **Friendliness rating** ★★★ **Parking** Free lot adjacent **Bar** Full bar **Wine selection** A few house wines **Dress** Casual **Disabled access** Full **Customers** Mostly locals, a few tourists

Lunch Tuesday–Saturday, 11 a.m.–3 p.m.

Dinner Tuesday–Thursday, 6–10 p.m.; Friday and Saturday, 6–11 p.m.

Setting & atmosphere Two modern, high-ceilinged, but casual rooms connected by the oyster bar and an open kitchen.

House specialties Oysters on the half shell; boiled crawfish or shrimp in season; chicken andouille gumbo; fried oysters; fried catfish; broiled shrimp; stuffed shrimp; stuffed crab; hot sausage poor boy; bread pudding.

Summary & comments Bozo's demonstrates how great simple fried seafood can be when it's meticulously selected and prepared. The catfish, for example, are small, wild Des Allemandes cats (as opposed to the inferior farm-raised fish). They're fried to order and served while still crackly hot. Each seafood is fried separately, which keeps everything from tasting the same. They also have great boiled seafood here, especially crawfish in season. The portions are not piled as high as elsewhere, but the quality is consistently satisfying. The gumbo, raw oysters, and broiled shrimp are the major specialties on a menu full of good food.

Brennan's ★★★★

CREOLE | VERY EXPENSIVE | QUALITY ★★★ | VALUE ★★

417 Royal; 525-9711 • French Quarter Zone 1

Reservations Required **When to go** Late mornings or lunchtime **Entrée range** $20–$40 **Payment** All major credit cards **Service rating** ★★★★ **Friendliness rating** ★★★★ **Parking** Validated free for Omni Royal Orleans Garage, Chartres at St. Louis **Bar** Full bar **Wine selection** Easily the finest restaurant wine cellar in New Orleans. Tremendous inventory, variety and depth. Lots of unusual, rare, and older wines, very well stored. Prices are alarming on the low side. **Dress** Dressy casual **Disabled access** Full **Customers** Mostly tourists; a few local regulars and wine buffs

Lunch Monday–Friday, 11:30 a.m.–2 p.m.

Dinner Daily, 6–10 p.m.

Setting & atmosphere You can't get much more French Quarter atmosphere than this. The historic building has dining rooms surrounding (and looking onto) a big, lushly planted, slate-paved courtyard. The best rooms are the first one past the bar and the long gallery along the courtyard. The upstairs dining rooms are also beautiful, but they tend to be reserved for tourists.

House specialties Breakfast: oyster soup; eggs Sardou; eggs Hussarde; eggs St. Charles; grillades and grits. Dinner: oysters Rockefeller; oysters casino; buster crabs with pecans; seafood crêpes Barbara; turtle soup; Jackson salad; filet mignon Stanley; filet mignon Diane; veal Kottwitz; fish Jaime; bananas Foster.

Summary & comments Breakfast at Brennan's is one of the most original and enjoyable meals you'll ever have—if you can break out of the crowd of tourists who come for it. (Tell them at every contact that you're local and that you don't want to sit upstairs.) You also must get past the idea that $40 and up is ridiculous for breakfast. It is, of course, but forget it. At dinner, Brennan's menu is made up almost entirely of the dishes we ate in New Orleans in the 1950s. However, nobody gets tired of it—diners or chefs. The latter use first-class raw materials, served generously. But the best part of dinner here is exploring the wine list. It's the best in New Orleans, full of superb and unusual bottles, sold at prices well below what oenophiles are used to seeing.

Brigtsen's ★★★★

CREOLE | EXPENSIVE | QUALITY ★★★½ | VALUE ★★★

723 Dante; 861-7610 • Uptown above Napoleon Zone 4

Reservations Required **When to go** Early evenings **Entrée range** $16–$32 **Payment** All major credit cards **Service rating** ★★★★ **Friendliness rating** ★★★★ **Parking** Curbside **Bar** Full bar **Wine selection** Modest list, but wines well chosen for the food **Dress** Jacket recommended but not required **Disabled access** Limited **Customers** Mostly locals, a few tourists

Dinner Tuesday–Saturday, 5:30–10 p.m.

Setting & atmosphere It's a 100-year-old cottage, lightly remodeled to provide three small dining rooms. The best tables are in the windows up front. The conviviality among customers keeps the walls from closing in.

House specialties Grilled rabbit tenderloin; sesame-encrusted foie gras; shrimp rémoulade; soup or gumbo of the day; pannéed rabbit; veal specials; fish specials; tournedos of beef; chicken with hot and sweet peppers; banana bread pudding; ice creams; double chocolate cake.

Summary & comments Unless you have a problem with small dining rooms, you'll find Brigtsen's hospitable and easy to love. Marna Brigtsen acts more like the hostess of a guest house than that of a restaurant. The familiarity and informality are perfect for husband/chef Frank's original but very Creole cooking style. Because the menu changes every day and because the chef loves to experiment, you'll find fish and vegetables here you never heard of before, as well as more familiar eats. The problem will be that too much of it will sound irresistible, and ordering may be traumatic. The wine list is short but right for the food and attractively priced.

Broussard's ★★★★

CREOLE | VERY EXPENSIVE | QUALITY ★★★½ | VALUE ★★

819 Conti; 581-3866 • French Quarter Zone 1 • broussards.com

Reservations Recommended **When to go** Anytime **Entrée range** $17–$30 **Payment** All major credit cards **Service rating** ★★★ **Friendliness rating** ★★★★ **Parking** Pay parking lots nearby **Bar** Full bar **Wine selection** Decent list, good international balance; a bit overpriced **Dress** Jacket recommended but not required **Disabled access** Full **Customers** Tourists, plus a few adventuresome locals

Dinner Daily, 5:30–10 p.m.

Setting & atmosphere Three plush, old-style, romantic dining rooms surround one of the French Quarter's largest and handsomest courtyards. You can dine out there if you like.

House specialties Delice ravigote; shrimp and crab cheesecake; baked oyster trio; sweet potato, corn, and shrimp bisque; poussin Rochambeau; pecan-stuffed salmon; pompano Napoleon; veal filet on braised leeks; wild game grill; chocolate pava; crêpes Broussard; bananas Foster.

Summary & comments Broussard's opened in 1920 and is a grande dame among Creole restaurants. It went through more changes than Galatoire's, Arnaud's, and other members of its generation, but it's at its all-time best right now. Chef Gunter Preuss—an old hand in continental restaurants locally—is the current owner, and with his wife and son run Broussard's as a dynastic restaurant. While the menu is dominated by the Creole classics you expect to find in restaurants like this, the chef keeps the flavor palette up to date and sprinkles the menu with many of his polished originals. The best news about Broussard's is, after years of dwindling interest among local diners, the Preusses have managed to woo many of them back in, especially for special occasions.

Bruning's ★★★

SEAFOOD | INEXPENSIVE | QUALITY ★★★ | VALUE ★★★★★

West End Park; 282-9395 • Lakeview/West End/Bucktown Zone 7

Reservations Not accepted **When to go** Anytime, but Fridays are very crowded **Entrée range** $8–$16 **Payment** All major credit cards **Service rating** ★★★

Friendliness rating ★★★★ **Parking** Free lot adjacent **Bar** Full bar **Wine selection** A few house wines **Dress** Anything goes **Disabled access** Limited **Customers** Locals, families

Lunch & dinner Daily, 11:30 a.m.–10 p.m.

Setting & atmosphere   The original restaurant was decimated by a 1998 hurricane, and it still has not been rebuilt. In the meantime, a smaller but equally scenic building nearby is open. There's a nice view of the lake from the upstairs dining room.

House specialties   Oysters on the half shell; seafood gumbo; boiled crabs, crawfish, or shrimp; whole broiled flounder; whole fried trout; fried seafood platter; broiled redfish; stuffed shrimp; fried chicken; bread pudding.

Summary & comments   Possibly the oldest continuously operated fried-seafood house in the world, Bruning's opened in 1859 at West End. Now owned by the sixth generation of the founder's family, its old original building has been out of action since Hurricane Georges in 1999. In the interim quarters, the food didn't change. They cook the archetypal platters of fried seafood and mounds of boiled seafood. The distinctive specialty is a whole flounder—the size that fishermen call "doormats"—fried or broiled. A very casual place for eating, drinking, and reveling in the New Orleans life.

Byblos   ★★★

GREEK/MIDDLE EASTERN | INEXPENSIVE | QUALITY ★★★ | VALUE ★★★★★

3218 Magazine; 894-1233 • Uptown below Napoleon Zone 3
1501 Metairie Road; 834-9773 • Metairie below Causeway Zone 9

Reservations Accepted **When to go** Anytime **Entrée range** $10–$18 **Payment** All major credit cards **Service rating** ★★★ **Friendliness rating** ★★★★ **Parking** Ample parking lot adjacent **Bar** Full bar **Wine selection** A few house wines **Dress** Casual **Disabled access** Full **Customers** Locals

Lunch & dinner Monday–Saturday, 11:30 a.m.–10 p.m.

Setting & atmosphere   Both locations are large, agreeable restaurants. The Metairie original has lofty ceilings and a Mediterranean décor. The Magazine Street restaurant is in an 1830s building, but has a generally contemporary design and an open kitchen inside.

House specialties   Hummos; baba ghanooj; stuffed kibbeh; falafel; stuffed cabbage rolls; cheese pie; tabbouleh salad; beef shawarma; beef kabob; chicken kabob; kafta kabob; fried kibbeh; kibbeh nayyi; ashta (flaky dessert pastry).

Summary & comments   Byblos (named for an ancient city in Lebanon) is the best Middle Eastern restaurant this area has ever had. The ingredients are first-class (i.e., filet mignon is used for the beef kabob), and the cooking is careful and light. Much care is given to plate presentation, but everything comes out hot anyway. The appetizer meza brings forth an assortment of some 15 appetizers for 4 to 6 people—a great way to eat. Byblos is usually populated by Lebanese, Syrians, Israelis, Turks, and others who know what this food is supposed to taste like.

Café Giovanni ★★★★

ITALIAN | MODERATE–EXPENSIVE | QUALITY ★★★ | VALUE ★★★

117 Decatur; 529-2154 • French Quarter Zone 1

Reservations Recommended **When to go** Anytime **Entrée range** $18–$30 **Payment** All major credit cards **Service rating** ★★★★ **Friendliness rating** ★★★ **Parking** Valet parking, $5 **Bar** Full bar **Wine selection** Substantial list, mostly Italian; many by-the-glass selections **Dress** Jacket recommended but not required **Disabled access** Full **Customers** Mostly locals, a few tourists

Dinner Daily, 5:30–6 p.m.

Setting & atmosphere Café Giovanni is one of the gems on the revived Lower Decatur strip. Its dining spaces straddle two old townhouses and the courtyard between them. The busy, rather noisy main rooms has a striking and uniquely New Orleans look.

House specialties Antipasto; oysters Giovanni; grilled scallops and shrimp with sake soy sauce; eggplant LoCicero (shrimp and crabmeat); Sicilian wedding soup; crabmeat Siciliana salad; pasta Gambino; cioppino; seared pork loin with crawfish and tasso; filet mignon Tuscany; tiramisu.

Entertainment & amenities Several nights a week, waiters who sing opera (or, more appropriately, singers who wait tables) put on a substantial show. They also do a bit of singing on the off-nights.

Summary & comments Chef-owner Duke LoCicero emphasizes both Sicilian and Creole culinary traditions, but doesn't hesitate to employ tastes from anywhere else in the world. All this is rendered with polish, interesting local ingredients, and fresh, original touches. The best strategy is to let the chef feed you an assortment of small portions of the day's specials for about $50. Regardless of which way you order, you will almost certainly get too much to eat here. Plates are really overloaded.

Café Sbisa ★★★

CREOLE | EXPENSIVE | QUALITY ★★★ | VALUE ★★★

1011 Decatur; 522-5565 • French Quarter Zone 1 • cafesbisa.com

Reservations Recommended **When to go** Anytime **Entrée range** Prix fixe, $35–$47 **Payment** All major credit cards **Service rating** ★★★ **Friendliness rating** ★★★★ **Parking** Validated (free) at French Market lot, one block **Bar** Full bar **Wine selection** Decent list, French-dominated **Dress** Jacket recommended but not required **Disabled access** Limited **Customers** Mostly locals, a few tourists

Brunch Sunday, 10:30 a.m.–3 p.m.

Dinner Sunday–Thursday, 5:30–10:30 p.m.; Friday and Saturday, 5:30–11 p.m.

Setting & atmosphere In its third incarnation and second century, this charming two-level parlor of antique wood panels and mirrors recalls a different era, when the French Market across the street was a bustling place of commerce.

House specialties Shrimp rémoulade; crab cakes with horseradish cream sauce;

turtle soup; trout amandine; trout Eugene; barbecue shrimp; duck with green peppercorns; eggs Sardou (brunch); grillades and grits (brunch); pecan pie; chocolate sin cake.

Entertainment & amenities Various jazzy, bluesy live music at Sunday brunch.

Summary & comments Café Sbisa concentrates on the traditional classics of Creole cooking, but has no hesitation about dressing them up with new ingredients and styles. The food never quite achieves brilliance or originality, but the total package always winds up creating an enjoyable evening. On Sundays, there's a lively brunch.

Chateaubriand ★★★★

STEAK | EXPENSIVE | QUALITY ★★★ | VALUE ★★★

310 N. Carrollton Avenue; 207-0016 • Mid-City/Gentilly Zone 6

Reservations Recommended **When to go** Anytime **Entrée range** $18–$30 **Payment** All major credit cards **Service rating** ★★★ **Friendliness rating** ★★★ **Parking** Ample parking lot adjacent **Bar** Full bar **Wine selection** Good wine list, including many selections by the glass **Dress** Jacket recommended but not required **Disabled access** Full **Customers** Locals, Francophiles, Uptowners, and (at lunch) a business crowd

Lunch Monday–Friday, 11:30 a.m.–2:30 p.m.

Dinner Daily, 6–10 p.m.

Setting & atmosphere The all-time best adaptation of a former Shoney's, the restaurant is in the ground floor of a fine old Mid-City warehouse. The walls are decorated with trompe l'oeil paintings. Large windows and high ceilings give an opulent feeling of spaciousness.

House specialties Duck pâté; escargots; grilled duck breast "Apicius"; Chateaubriand for two; sirloin strip au poivre; filet mignon Perigeux; double-cut pork chop with apples; rack of lamb; Dover sole meunière; fish specials; lemon cakes; cheese selection.

Summary & comments Chef-owner Gerard Crozier ran the best French bistro in town for 25 years, sold it, and retired young. A year later, he was persuaded that his reputation and the prime-steakhouse trend could unite in a successful restaurant—and they did. The beef here is all prime grade, but rendered distinctive by being cooked, sauced, and presented in a decidedly French style. The namesake dish, a 20-ounce tube of tenderloin, is grilled to order and sent out with béarnaise, peppercorn, or Perigeux sauces as perfectly made as you'll find anywhere outside of France. The menu goes on to include not only all the big chops, but also a full selection of seafood, poultry, and seasonal French specialties. But it's hard to pass up the beef, which was always Crozier's specialty at his old place.

China Blossom ★★★

CHINESE | INEXPENSIVE–MODERATE | QUALITY ★★★ | VALUE ★★★

1801 Stumpf Boulevard; 361-4598 • West Bank Zone 11

Reservations Accepted **When to go** Anytime **Entrée range** $9–$18 **Payment** All major credit cards **Service rating** ★★★ **Friendliness rating** ★★★★

Parking Free lot adjacent **Bar** Full bar **Wine selection** Limited list of ordinary wines **Dress** Casual **Disabled access** Full **Customers** Locals

Lunch Tuesday–Friday, 11 a.m.–2 p.m.; Sunday, noon–3 p.m.

Dinner Tuesday–Thursday, 5–9 p.m.; Friday and Saturday, 5–10 p.m.; Sunday, 3–9 p.m.

Setting & atmosphere It's a storefront in a strip mall and rather spare, but pleasant enough.

House specialties Spring roll; pot stickers; hot-and-sour soup; crab claws with black bean sauce; tong-cho shrimp, trout, or oysters; soft-shell crab with crawfish sauce; Maine lobster with ginger; spicy flaming chicken; wor shu op (crisp half duck); ming steak; beef with oyster sauce; lotus banana.

Summary & comments The China Blossom is the best Chinese restaurant near the center of town (it's across the river, but just). Its menu started out almost identical to that of Trey Yuen, from which most of the staff came. But over the years they've evolved their own style, with a strong specialty in seafood. They buy great fresh fish and shellfish and cook it with excitement and great sauces. Many of the dishes involve interesting tableside preparations. The dining rooms are understated and comfortable, and you will be better served here than in the average Chinese place.

Christian's ★★★★

CREOLE | EXPENSIVE | QUALITY ★★★ | VALUE ★★★

3835 Iberville; 482-4924 • Mid-City/Gentilly Zone 6

Reservations Recommended **When to go** Dinner **Entrée range** $16–$26 **Payment** AE, DC, MC, V **Service rating** ★★★★ **Friendliness rating** ★★★★ **Parking** Ample parking lot adjacent **Bar** Full bar **Wine selection** Substantial list, about equally French and Californian; very attractive prices **Dress** Jacket recommended but not required **Disabled access** Limited **Customers** Mostly locals, a few tourists; couples; gourmets

Lunch Tuesday–Friday, 11:30 a.m.–2:30 p.m.

Dinner Tuesday–Saturday, 6–10 p.m.

Setting & atmosphere The restaurant is housed in a former church, although it was called Christian's (after one of the founders) before it moved there. Cathedral ceilings and tall windows create a delightful effect. Still, some diners may find the deuces along the perimeter a little too close to their neighbors.

House specialties Oysters Roland; oysters en brochette; shrimp rémoulade; saffron shrimp; crawfish Carolyn; smoked salmon; smoked soft-shell crab; stuffed eggplant; trout meunière amandine; filet mignon stuffed with oysters; strip sirloin au poivre; crème caramel; homemade ice creams.

Summary & comments No gimmicks here. Christian's is a serious, consistent, original restaurant, grounded in the classics of New Orleans restaurant cuisine, more or less in the style of Galatoire's (there's a family connection). But it has always included dishes influenced by country French cooking and some entirely new ideas. The service staff has an easy, good style. The menu is not the bargain it once was, particularly at lunch.

Clancy's ★★★★

CREOLE | MODERATE–EXPENSIVE | QUALITY ★★★½ | VALUE ★★★

6100 Annunciation; 895-1111 • Uptown above Napoleon Zone 4

Reservations Recommended **When to go** Anytime **Entrée range** $15–$30 **Payment** All major credit cards **Service rating** ★★★★ **Friendliness rating** ★★★★ **Parking** Curbside parking only **Bar** Full bar **Wine selection** Substantial list, full of oddities. The owner is an oenophile and buys many short-lot wines he's interested in. Many by-the-glass selections. **Dress** Dressy casual **Disabled access** Limited **Customers** Locals, gourmets

Lunch Tuesday–Friday, 11:30 a.m.–2:30 p.m.

Dinner Monday–Saturday, 6–10 p.m.

Setting & atmosphere It used to be a neighborhood bar, and still has a neighborhood feeling. The long downstairs dining room is convivial and bright. Upstairs tables are in a sort of maze. Many people dine at the bar.

House specialties Oysters with Brie and spinach; crabmeat ravigote; shrimp rémoulade; house salad; smoked soft-shell crab and crabmeat; smoked shrimp with ginger; seafood pasta specials; veal liver Lyonnaise; veal and lamb chops; smoked duck; filet mignon with port and Stilton; crème caramel.

Summary & comments Clancy's was one of the original crop of bistros that redefined Creole cooking in the early 1980s. It's matured into an Uptown answer to Galatoire's, with a passionate local following. Its kitchen leans largely on traditional Creole restaurant dishes that most hip places are afraid to serve. It blends these with adventuresome specials and a few unique signature dishes. It was the first local restaurant with an in-house capability of smoking food, and those dishes are a good part of the menu. The service staff jokes around and take certain unusual informalities with the mostly-regular clientele. Clancy's has a great bar, and is one of the few you can trust to make a fine cocktail. The collection of Cognacs, Armagnacs, single-malt Scotches, and small-batch Bourbons is tremendous. The wine selection is so large that they bought a house next door to store it.

Coffee Pot ★★

CREOLE | INEXPENSIVE–MODERATE | QUALITY ★★½ | VALUE ★★★

714 St. Peter; 524-3500 • French Quarter Zone 1

Reservations Not accepted **When to go** Anytime **Entrée range** $7–$15 **Payment** AE, MC, V **Service rating** ★★★ **Friendliness rating** ★★★ **Parking** Pay garages nearby **Bar** Full bar **Wine selection** A few house wines **Dress** Casual **Disabled access** None **Customers** Tourists, a few Quarterites

Open Daily 7 a.m.–midnight

Setting & atmosphere The dining room is the parlor of an old Quarter residence. Alfresco tables are in the carriageway.

House specialties Salad Jayne; Seafood gumbo; red beans and rice; fried chicken; fried seafood platter; daily blackboard specials; omelettes; bread pudding; fruit cobblers; breakfasts; calas.

Summary & comments Although the Coffee Pot is largely given over to the tourist trade these days, it's a historic restaurant. For over fifty years, the place has served the home-style Creole classics with pizzazz. This is, for example, the last stand for calas, the nearly-extinct but delicious Creole breakfast rice cake. A few Quarterites still use it as their neighborhood restaurant, coming mainly for the good breakfasts, served all day long. Oddly, the coffee is consistently forgettable.

Commander's Palace   ★★★★

CONTEMPORARY CREOLE | VERY EXPENSIVE | QUALITY ★★★½ | VALUE ★★★

1403 Washington Avenue; 899-8221 • Uptown below Napoleon Zone 3

Reservations Required **When to go** Lunch and weekday dinners **Entrée range** $24–$39 **Payment** All major credit cards **Service rating** ★★★★ **Friendliness rating** ★★★★ **Parking** Valet (free) **Bar** Full bar **Wine selection** Distinguished cellar, good international balance. Many rare wines (although not many older ones) from France and California. **Dress** Jacket required at dinner **Disabled access** Limited **Customers** Half tourists, half socializing locals; couples

Brunch Saturday, 11:30 a.m.–1 p.m.; Sunday, 10:30 a.m.–1:30 p.m.

Lunch Monday–Friday, 11:30 a.m.–2 p.m.

Dinner Daily, 6–10 p.m.

Setting & atmosphere The Victorian mansion and adjacent courtyard were built in the mid-1800s and are part of the fabric of the surrounding Garden District. The upstairs Garden Room is most popular with locals, but every part of the restaurant has its own distinctive, antique charm.

House specialties Shrimp rémoulade; tasso shrimp Henican; rabbit and foie gras pie; oysters and caviar Trufant; turtle soup; Lyonnaise fish; sautéed fish with pecans; veal chop Tchoupitoulas; roasted strip sirloin steak; rack of lamb; bananas Foster; bread pudding soufflé.

Entertainment & amenities Strolling jazz trio at Sunday brunch.

Summary & comments Commander's Palace is the flagship of the Brennan family's restaurant empire. For decades, it was New Orleans's most popular first-class restaurant. Its kitchen has many illustrious alumni (Paul Prudhomme and Emeril Lagasse, to name two). The menu combines both old and new styles of Creole cooking, using first-class, interesting foodstuffs. The barrage of Brennan service gambits reaches a peak here. One of those is value: a four-course dinner can be had for $40, lunch for $18. Another is service, so well planned that it may be a bit too mechanical. Be sure to tell the waiter you're in no hurry. Commander's slipped a bit when the Brennans decided to distribute ownership of its restaurants among the various branches of the family, instead of managing everything centrally. The Brennans who stayed at Commander's Palace next opened a gourmet-to-go, then a Las Vegas restaurant. At about the same time, they suffered the tragic death of Chef Jamie Shannon. The impact was that Commander's lost much consistency and inspiration. Still, dining here is a lot of fun, and the environment and clientele are essential New Orleans.

Cuvee ★★★★

CONTEMPORARY CREOLE | VERY EXPENSIVE | QUALITY ★★★ | VALUE ★★

322 Magazine; 587-9001 • Central Business District Zone 2

Reservations Recommended **When to go** Dinner **Entrée range** $18–$32 **Payment** AE, DC, MC, V **Service rating** ★★★ **Friendliness rating** ★★★★ **Parking** Free valet parking **Bar** Full bar **Wine selection** Distinguished wine cellar, with wide variety from all around the world **Dress** Jacket recommended but not required **Disabled access** Full **Customers** Gourmets and wine buffs

Lunch Monday–Friday, 11:30 a.m.–2:30 p.m.

Dinner Monday–Thursday, 6–10 p.m.; Friday and Saturday, 6–11 p.m.

Setting & atmosphere Wine dominates the décor. Chandeliers, for example, are made out of large-format Champagne bottles. The brick-walled dining room is artfully hard-edged, but there are soft corners here and there.

House specialties Mirliton and shrimp Napoleon; smoked chèvre and lamb tortilla; roast poussin on tasso-smothered greens; chive-battered salmon with crawfish-vegetable slaw; sugar cane–smoked duck breast, crisp confit leg, and foie gras; peach tarte Tatin; Good Humor ice-cream plate.

Summary & comments It's currently hip for major restaurants to start with a wine cellar and build a menu around it. This is such a place, as the name implies. (*cuvee* is a French wine word that refers to the art of blending, particularly in Champagne.) The potential pretentiousness of this theme has been kept under control at Cuvee. If you're interested in sampling a very unusual bottle, you will be apprised of its availability and told all you need to know about it. If you just want a good glass of wine to go with dinner, the waiters are sensitive to that need, too, and back off the heavy oeno-speak. The original chef here came out of the Windsor Court a few years ago, and installed menu that manages to blend ambitiousness with more than a little playfulness. Many of the dishes will make you smile twice: first, when you read about and imagine them, and again when you taste them. A contemporary version of the local flavor predominates, with admixtures from other traditions here and there. The six-course degustation with matching wines is one of the best and most affordable such schemes in New Orleans. The waiters stop by a little too often, even in a romantic situation.

Dakota ★★★★★

CONTEMPORARY CREOLE | EXPENSIVE | QUALITY ★★★★★ | VALUE ★★★

629 N. US 190; (985) 892-3712 • North Shore Zone 12

Reservations Recommended **When to go** Weeknights **Entrée range** $17–$32 **Payment** AE, DC, MC, V **Service rating** ★★★★★ **Friendliness rating** ★★★★★ **Parking** Ample parking lot adjacent **Bar** Full bar **Wine selection** Distinguished cellar, emphasis on California. Many excellent boutique wines; the owner is a wine buff who travels around looking for discoveries. **Dress** Jacket recommended but not required **Disabled access** Full **Customers** Locals, couples, gourmets

Lunch Monday–Friday, 11:30 a.m.–2:30 p.m.

Dinner Monday–Thursday, 6–10 p.m.; Friday and Saturday, 6–11 p.m.

Setting & atmosphere The two large dining rooms are spacious almost to the point of echoing. They're furnished in a distinctive modern style, with particularly interesting floral arrangements.

House specialties Seared beef tenderloin or seared tuna salad; seafood beignets with lobster sauce; grilled rabbit tenderloin; smoked chicken gumbo; roasted salmon with fried spinach; stuffed soft-shell crab; cane-smoked pork tenderloin; mixed grill; rack of lamb; bread pudding; dessert pastries.

Summary & comments Dakota raised the standard of dining on the North Shore when it opened in 1990. It's still the best restaurant across the lake, and among the best in the metro area at large. Chef and co-owner Kim Kringlie (he's the Dakota connection) cooks contemporary Creole food in its most intensely flavorful forms, and shows no shyness about using salt, pepper, cream, butter, smoke, or anything else that might make flavors detonate. More exotic styles work their ways into a few dishes. Good daily specials round out a fascinating array of food. Dakota is rare among North Shore restaurants in having a well-trained service staff and a distinguished wine cellar.

Dante's Kitchen ★★★

CONTEMPORARY CREOLE | MODERATE | QUALITY ★★★½ | VALUE ★★★

736 Dante; 861-3121 • Uptown above Napoleon Zone 4

Reservations Recommended **When to go** Anytime **Entrée range** $17–$23 **Payment** All major credit cards **Service rating** ★★★ **Friendliness rating** ★★★★ **Parking** Curbside parking only **Bar** Full bar **Wine selection** Modest list matched to food **Dress** Dressy casual **Disabled access** Limited **Customers** Neighborhood people and curious gourmets from the rest of the city

Lunch Tuesday–Saturday, 11:30 a.m.–2:30 p.m.

Dinner Tuesday–Saturday, 5:30–10 p.m.

Setting & atmosphere An old cottage with haphazard add-ons gives a motley assortment of dining areas, including a small alfresco dining area.

House specialties Crabmeat and Brie French toast; escargots with pancetta; iceberg wedge with Roquefort; falafel-crusted fish; redfish "on the half-shell"; lemon and rosemary chicken; oyster chowder with bacon; filet mignon trio with three sauces; hazelnut crème brûlée.

Summary & comments Chef and co-owner Emanual Loubier was one of the stalwarts in the kitchen at Commander's Palace during that restaurant's glory years before he opened this bistro. His cooking is imaginative, yet tends to the less-expensive side of the gourmet Creole spectrum. Always a surprise or two on the menu here, even for regulars. Service can be a little quirky. The other partner is a wine buff, and he keeps the list supplied with interesting bottles.

Delmonico ★★★★★

CONTEMPORARY CREOLE | VERY EXPENSIVE | QUALITY ★★★★★ | VALUE ★★

1300 St. Charles Avenue; 525-4937 • Uptown below Napoleon Zone 3

Reservations Recommended **When to go** Anytime **Entrée range** $21–$40

Payment All major credit cards **Service rating** ★★★★ **Friendliness rating** ★★★★★ **Parking** Free valet parking **Bar** Full bar **Wine selection** Distinguished wine cellar, managed by a well-informed sommelier **Dress** Jacket recommended but not required **Disabled access** Full **Customers** A lot of overflow from Emeril's winds up here (read: tourists). Locals dominate at lunchtime.

Brunch Sunday, 10:30 a.m.–2:30 p.m.

Lunch Monday–Friday, 11:30 a.m.–2 p.m.

Dinner Sunday–Thursday, 6–10 p.m.; Friday and Saturday, 6–11 p.m.

Setting & atmosphere Delmonico was a 100-year-old Creole standby when Chef Emeril bought it in 1998. After he treated it to an expensive, well-wrought renovation, the place looks fresh and contemporary, while retaining enough suggestions of antiquity to make it very different from Emeril's other, trendier local establishments.

House specialties Turtle soup; shrimp rémoulade; barbecue shrimp; redfish meunière; hickory-roasted duck; veal Marcelle; sirloin strip steak; double-cut pork chop; chèvre cheesecake; bananas Foster; coconut cream pie.

Entertainment & amenities Live piano nightly.

Summary & comments When Delmonico opened, it promised classic dishes and service from the past. That didn't really fly as a theme, though, and as time goes on the style grows more contemporary. Still, it's far back from the cutting edge Emeril's chefs wield at his other places. And some of the best food here remains dishes you may not have had for a decade or two. (Although don't come here expecting anything from the old Delmonico.) The most recent menu addition was a complete collection of prime-grade steaks. These are dry-aged on the premises and cooked with bravado. The steaks' crusty-exterior-juicy-inside bids fair to make these the best steaks in New Orleans.

Dick & Jenny's   ★★★★

CONTEMPORARY CREOLE | MODERATE–EXPENSIVE | QUALITY ★★★ | VALUE ★★★

4501 Tchoupitoulas; 894-9880 • Uptown above Napoleon Zone 4

Reservations Not accepted **When to go** Early dinner **Entrée range** $14–$26 **Payment** AE, MC, V **Service rating** ★★ **Friendliness rating** ★★★★ **Parking** Curbside parking only **Bar** Full bar **Wine selection** Modest list of wines matched to food **Dress** Casual **Disabled access** Limited **Customers** Clientele tends to the younger side and others who have time to wait in line.

Dinner Tuesday–Saturday, 5:30–10 p.m.

Setting & atmosphere An old corner café on the Uptown riverfront, with enough New Orleans raffishness to make it appealing. You'd want to check it out even if there weren't food inside.

House specialties Crab cakes; duck and Brie pain perdu; filet mignon with foie gras; pecan catfish; seafood hot pot.

Summary & comments Dick is Richard Benz, formerly the chef of the Upperline and a few other good places. Jenny is his wife, a former floral designer. Both of them had their eyes on this grubby-but-cool old joint for a long time. When the previous tenants folded they moved in and fixed the place up—but not too much. The whole idea caught on with the younger end of the Uptown gourmet spectrum, and suddenly everybody was hanging around inside and outside waiting for a table (no reservations). It's a little uncomfortable, but the prices are lower than average for a place like this.

Dickie Brennan's Steakhouse   ★★★★

STEAK | VERY EXPENSIVE | QUALITY ★★★ | VALUE ★★★

716 Iberville; 522-2467 • French Quarter Zone 1 • dbrennanssteakhouse.com

Reservations Recommended **When to go** Anytime **Entrée range** $20–$35 **Payment** All major credit cards **Service rating** ★★★ **Friendliness rating** ★★★★ **Parking** Validated parking next door **Bar** Full bar **Wine selection** Excellent wine list, including many selections by the glass **Dress** Jacket recommended but not required **Disabled access** Full **Customers** Professionals at lunch, couples at dinner; some tourists and conventioneers

Lunch Monday–Friday, 11:30 a.m.–2:30 p.m.

Dinner Daily, 5:30–10 p.m.

Setting & atmosphere The only sub-street-level restaurant in New Orleans, this is a handsome place. Tile floors, banquette seating, and unusual displays of antique weapons in the private dining rooms make for a distinctly local and masculine environment.

House specialties Baked oyster combination; tomato and onion salad with blue cheese and rémoulade; turtle soup; strip steak; porterhouse steak; house filet mignon (with oysters); grilled fish; pontalba potatoes; bananas Foster bread pudding.

Summary & comments Dick Brennan, Sr. had the idea for this back in the 1960s: a steakhouse with a simple menu of first-class beef and chops, in a comfortable restaurant with great service and a real wine list. But it didn't happen until his son opened this place in the late 1990s. In the meantime, of course, a few national chains ran with the same idea. But that doesn't make this any less good. The beef is USDA prime without exception. Each cut is cooked differently: The filet is broiled, the strip is cooked in a hot black iron skillet, and the ribeye is roasted. The menu is significantly more original than what we're used to finding in steakhouses. And the Brennan style honed at Commander's Palace is very much in evidence.

Drago's   ★★★★

SEAFOOD | INEXPENSIVE–MODERATE | QUALITY ★★★½ | VALUE ★★★

3232 N. Arnoult Road; 888-9254 • Metairie above Causeway/Kenner/Jefferson Zone 10

Reservations Not accepted **When to go** Anytime **Entrée range** $14–$37 **Payment** All major credit cards **Service rating** ★★ **Friendliness rating** ★★★ **Parking** Small parking lot adjacent **Bar** Full bar **Wine selection** A few house wines, including a few from Croatia **Dress** Casual **Disabled access** Full **Customers** Locals, families

Lunch Monday–Friday, 11:30 a.m.–2:30 p.m.

Dinner Monday–Saturday, 5–10 p.m.

Setting & atmosphere This old seafood house has exploded into an insanely popular restaurant in recent years. Getting a table will take some time, particularly on Fridays. The dining rooms came out of the last renovation a bit too high-tech and noisy. Best place to eat: the bar.

House specialties Raw oysters; char-broiled oysters; grilled, stuffed drumfish Tommy; oyster brochette; boiled lobster; Shuckee Duckee (grilled duck breast with oysters and pasta); shrimp Herradura; La-Mex (black beans with fried chicken or fried catfish); seafood gumbo; Cajun surf-and-turf (steak with shrimp and oysters).

Summary & comments Ambitious as casual seafood restaurants go, Drago's is our premier oyster specialist, both at the raw bar and in the kitchen. The great cooked dish is char-broiled oysters (grilled in the shell, basted with garlic-herb butter). Almost everything else in the way of local seafood is here, often in highly original concoctions. They also sell more Maine lobster than any place else in town, at attractive prices.

Emeril's ★★★★★

CONTEMPORARY CREOLE | VERY EXPENSIVE | QUALITY ★★★★★ | VALUE ★★★

800 Tchoupitoulas; 528-9393 • Central Business District Zone 2

Reservations Required **When to go** Lunch and early evenings **Entrée range** $18–$40 **Payment** All major credit cards **Service rating** ★★★★ **Friendliness rating** ★★★★ **Parking** Valet (free) **Bar** Full bar **Wine selection** One of the city's most distinguished cellars, with extremely wide range and many rarely-seen bottles, many by-the-glass **Dress** Dressy casual **Disabled access** Full **Customers** Mix of tourists and locals; hip, gourmet crowd

Lunch Monday–Friday, 11:30 a.m.–2:30 p.m.

Dinner Monday–Sunday, 6–10p.m.

Setting & atmosphere Emeril's first and flagship restaurant is in a warehouse. A renovation a few years ago softened the industrial aspect and the acoustics (although it remains a loud restaurant), and moved the furnishings far into the realm of artful design. Particularly interesting is the arch over the food bar, where those most interested in cooking can watch the action while eating atop barstools.

House specialties Specials are always the best bets. Others include barbecue shrimp; smoked trout dumplings; gumbo of the day; andouille crusted redfish; pannéed quail; filet of beef with blue cheese; double-cut pork chop with green mole; banana-cream pie; chocolate pecan pie; chocolate Grand Marnier soufflé; cheeses.

Summary & comments Emeril Lagasse is America's best-known chef, thanks to his winning personality, his television shows, and his constant flow of cookbooks. His media activities and growing empire of seven restaurants (at latest count; the other two in New Orleans are Nola and Delmonico) mean that your chances of seeing him here are slim. The staff makes up for that by talking about him, a line of conversation encouraged by most customers. But this is where it all started, and he's kept Emeril's a first-class restaurant. The menu is based on Louisiana flavors. It's also highly ingredient-driven. Emeril's ruling principle is that the menu should obey the vagaries of the fresh food market. The rarer the food, the better. The result is big taste and high adventure. A great way to sample it is to get the tasting menu, which gives maximum attention to the specials—usually the best food here.

French Table   ★★★★

FRENCH | EXPENSIVE | QUALITY ★★★½ | VALUE ★★★

3216 W. Esplanade; 833-8108 • Metairie above Causeway/Kenner/Jefferson
   Zone 10

Reservations Recommended **When to go** Weeknights, lunch **Entrée range** $16–$32 **Payment** AE, DC, MC, V **Service rating** ★★★★ **Friendliness rating** ★★★★ **Parking** Ample parking lot adjacent; valet parking at lunch **Bar** Full bar **Wine selection** Decent list, French-dominated **Dress** Dressy casual **Disabled access** Full **Customers** Locals, couples

Lunch Monday–Friday, 11:30 a.m.–2 p.m.

Dinner Tuesday–Thursday, 5–10 p.m.; Friday and Saturday, 5–11 p.m.

Setting & atmosphere The restaurant is in an anonymous strip mall. That makes its small, pretty dining rooms a charming surprise.

House specialties Pâté maison; magret of duck; escargots bourguignonne; onion soup gratinée; salade maison; poached fish hollandaise; coq au vin; sweetbreads Grenobloise; veal Crozier; steak au poivre; filet mignon Perigourdine; gratin dauphinoise; floating island; gâteau de pain au whiskey.

Summary & comments For 26 years, this was Crozier's, a very personal bistro run by Lyon-born chef Gerard Crozier. He sold it and moved on, but the new owners were former customers who didn't want to see the place vanish. Although the menu, premises, and hours were amplified, eating here does still have most of its old magic and romance. Service and presentations are understated, and there's nothing stuffy.

Fury's   ★★★

SEAFOOD | INEXPENSIVE–MODERATE | QUALITY ★★★ | VALUE ★★★

724 Martin Behrman Avenue; 834-5646 • Metairie below Causeway Zone 9

Reservations Not accepted **When to go** Anytime **Entrée range** $8–$15 **Payment** All major credit cards **Service rating** ★★ **Friendliness rating** ★★★ **Parking** Small parking lot adjacent **Bar** Full bar **Wine selection** A few house wines **Dress** Casual **Disabled access** Full **Customers** Neighborhood people

Lunch & dinner Sunday–Thursday, 11:30 a.m.–10 p.m.; Friday and Saturday, 11:30 a.m.–10:30 p.m.

Setting & atmosphere A tight L-shaped room, with a small bar in the back.

House specialties Onion rings; seafood gumbo; crabmeat au gratin; barbecue shrimp; crawfish étouffée; seafood platters; trout amandine; fried or broiled chicken; chicken or veal Parmesan; bread pudding.

Summary & comments A neighborhood seafood café in the old style, with all that implies both in the way of honest, cooked-to-order food as well as outmoded (but also honest) atrocities. The shortcomings are easily ignoreable in view of the low prices and goodness of the basic specialties. Seafood dominates, with every imaginable combination platter, fried or broiled. But the specials are pure back-street New Orleans cuisine, served to a clientele as regular as ever patronized a corner café.

Gabrielle ★★★★

CONTEMPORARY CREOLE | EXPENSIVE | QUALITY ★★★½ | VALUE ★★★

3201 Esplanade Avenue; 948-6233 • Mid-City/Gentilly Zone 6

Reservations Required **When to go** Early evenings, weeknights **Entrée range** $20–$30 **Payment** All major credit cards **Service rating** ★★★ **Friendliness rating** ★★★ **Parking** Curbside **Bar** Full bar **Wine selection** Modest list, mostly California. Wines well-chosen for the food. Many by-the-glass selections. Attractive prices. **Dress** Dressy casual **Disabled access** Limited **Customers** Locals, couples, gourmets

Lunch Friday, 11:30 a.m.–2:30 p.m.

Dinner Tuesday– Saturday, 5:30–10 p.m.

Setting & atmosphere The restaurant is tiny, crowded, and noisy, and even with a recent addition there is never enough room for all the people who want to dine here. The effect is more convivial than claustrophobic.

House specialties Oysters Gabie; sausage mixed grill; grilled rabbit tenderloin; blackened steak; blackened tuna; pork chop any style; roasted duck; fish specials; apple upside-down bread pudding; dessert specials.

Summary & comments Gabrielle is the personal restaurant of Greg and Mary Sonnier, husband and wife, both chefs. After Mary prepares the evening's desserts, she spends her time running the dining room. From the micro-kitchen proceeds a menu of imaginative but distinctly Louisiana-style dishes. The repertoire supplies a slightly different menu every day. Sonnier opened this place after stints at K-Paul's and Brigtsen's, and like those restaurants it prizes robustness of flavor above niceties of atmosphere and service. The Friday lunch is easygoing and a good introduction. It's also popular among the regulars, so don't figure on just sauntering in.

Galatoire's ★★★★★

CREOLE | EXPENSIVE | QUALITY ★★★★★ | VALUE ★★★

209 Bourbon; 525-2021 • French Quarter Zone 1 • galatoires.com

Reservations Accepted only for upstairs rooms **When to go** Late lunch or early dinner. Locals completely take over on Fridays and Sundays. **Entrée range** $14–$27 **Payment** All major credit cards **Service rating** ★★★ **Friendliness rating** ★★★ **Parking** Pay garages nearby **Bar** Full bar. Drinks are very generously poured and modestly priced. **Wine selection** Peculiar list of French and California wines with the absolute minimum of identification of maker and vintage. Very attractive prices. **Dress** Jacket and tie required at dinner and all day Sunday **Disabled access** Full **Customers** Both tourists and locals. The latter tend to be regulars who know all the other regulars.

Lunch & dinner Tuesday–Sunday, 11:30 a.m.–10 p.m.

Setting & atmosphere A cornerstone of fine Creole dining throughout the 1900s, Galatoire's ended the century with a major renovation—the first in the restaurant's 100-year history. The main dining room downstairs kept its tiled floors, mirrors, motionless ceiling fans, and bright, naked light bulbs. The second-floor dining room, open for the first time since the 1940s, is a touch less distinctive. A new bar and waiting area all but eliminated the troublesome queue on the sidewalk.

House specialties Shrimp rémoulade; crabmeat maison; canapé Lorenzo; oysters Rockefeller; oysters en brochette; green salad with garlic; trout meunière or amandine; grilled pompano; poached salmon or drum hollandaise; shrimp Marguery; crabmeat Yvonne; chicken Clemenceau; filet or strip steak béarnaise; lamb, veal, or pork chop; crème caramel; crêpes maison.

Summary & comments Fears that a management change and renovation at Galatoire's would ruin this essential, traditional Creole restaurant proved unfounded. The definitive French-Creole menu remained inviolate, as did the loose, generous operating style of the cooks and waiters. Know that Galatoire's has the style of a bistro, and its best food is made from great, fresh ingredients cooked in a generally simple, sometimes even homely style. Seafood is the main draw, but they cook everything deftly. Regular diners can recommend their own favorite mystery dishes from the catalog-like menu. The service staff works in an old-fashioned, unceremonious way.

Galley Seafood

SEAFOOD | INEXPENSIVE | QUALITY ★★★ | VALUE ★★★

2535 Metairie Road; 832-0955 • Metairie below Causeway Zone 9

Reservations Not accepted **When to go** Anytime **Entrée range** $6–$15 **Payment** AE, DC, MC, V **Service rating** ★★ **Friendliness rating** ★★★★ **Parking** Free lot adjacent **Bar** Beer and wine **Wine selection** A few house wines **Dress** Casual **Disabled access** Full **Customers** Neighborhood people

Lunch & dinner Tuesday–Saturday, 11:30 a.m.–9:30 p.m.

Setting & atmosphere A converted convenience store with a few tables in a covered area outside makes for a pleasant neighborhood café.

House specialties Seafood gumbo; any other soup; boiled shrimp, crabs, or crawfish; spicy meat pies; spicy crawfish pies; fried seafood platters or sandwiches; pecan catfish.

Summary & comments The proprietors are famous for the soft-shell crab poor boy at the Jazz Festival. This little place serves that offbeat savory year-round, as well as a menu of small and large seafood platters, usually fried lightly to order. The blackboard shows off a passel of home cooking every day; the soups here are always especially good. They also boil the usual crustaceans for eating in or removing to home. Good news: The boiled seafood is served hot, instead of refrigerated.

Gautreau's ★★★★

ECLECTIC | EXPENSIVE | QUALITY ★★★½ | VALUE ★★★

1728 Soniat; 899-7397 • Uptown above Napoleon Zone 4

Reservations Recommended **When to go** Anytime **Entrée range** $19–$34 **Payment** All major credit cards **Service rating** ★★★★ **Friendliness rating** ★★★★ **Parking** Valet (free) **Bar** Full bar **Wine selection** Modest list, but wines well chosen for the food **Dress** Jacket recommended but not required **Disabled access** Limited **Customers** Locals, couples, gourmets

Dinner Monday–Saturday, 6–10 p.m.

Setting & atmosphere The small dining room was once an antique pharmacy, from which some relics remain. There's more room upstairs, but they don't use it every night. The place can be noisy.

House specialties Crisp duck confit with mustard and sage; seared sea scallops; cold poached lobster with smoked corn; salmon tartare with sesame seaweed salad; cream of corn soup with crabmeat; roasted grouper and fennel; roast chicken with wild mushrooms; beef tournedos and artichoke ragout; roasted lamb chops and truffle risotto; crêpes with cherry fig sauce; crème brûlée.

Summary & comments Deep in an Uptown residential neighborhood, Gautreau's many regulars (they're the only ones who can find the place) have come to expect a certain hard-to-define but polished style of contemporary cooking. The abbreviated menu has one of just about everything, whipped up with light touches of both innovation and Creole flavor. The best dishes tend to be the least exotic—the filet mignon and roast chicken, to name two such. Service has a rather chummy style about it; the servers give frank opinions about everything. It's difficult to get a table here on short notice, and there's no comfortable place to wait.

Genghis Khan ★★★

KOREAN | INEXPENSIVE–MODERATE | QUALITY ★★★ | VALUE ★★★

201 Baronne; 299-9009 • Mid-City/Gentilly Zone 6

Reservations Accepted **When to go** Anytime **Entrée range** $12–$25 **Payment** AE, MC, V **Service rating** ★★★★ **Friendliness rating** ★★★ **Parking** Curbside **Bar** Full bar **Wine selection** A surprisingly large collection of wines, most of them displayed on retail-style racks at one end of the dining room. **Dress** Casual **Disabled access** Limited **Customers** Locals

Lunch Monday–Friday, 11:30 a.m.–2 p.m.

Dinner Sunday–Thursday, 6–10 p.m.; Friday and Saturday, 6–11 p.m.

Setting & atmosphere A long dining room on the ground floor of a downtown hotel is dominated by a grand piano at its center.

House specialties Fried mandu (dumpling); calamari tempura; kim (seaweed wafers) and rice; spinach namul; kimchee; bulgoki; whole marinated tempura fried fish; shrimp Genghis Khan; chongol hot pot (beef and shrimp in broth); tempura banana split.

Entertainment & amenities Talented artist-waiters perform vocally and instrumentally at every meal. The owner is himself a violin virtuoso, and plays every time he gets a break.

Summary & comments For over 25 years, classical violinist Henry Lee has operated a terrific restaurant featuring the food of his homeland. Korean food offers the same appeal that Chinese and Japanese eats do, but in its own distinctive way. If you've had Korean food before, be aware that this menu is much adapted to Western tastes, but what comes out is undeniably delicious. Charcoal-grilled, marinated beef is an essential part of the menu; so are very full-flavored, cold concoctions of leafy green vegetables. Some of the food is quite spicy. But the most popular dish here among the regulars is the whole fried fish, ample and greaseless. Genghis Khan is a couple of blocks from both the Orpheum (where the symphony performs) and the Saenger (the main house for big theatrical events here).

Grill Room ★★★★

ECLECTIC | VERY EXPENSIVE | QUALITY ★★★ | VALUE ★★

300 Gravier; 522-1992 • Central Business District Zone 2

Reservations Required **When to go** Wednesday through Friday nights **Entrée range** $24–$40; tasting menu, $75 **Payment** All major credit cards **Service rating** ★★★★★ **Friendliness rating** ★★★★★ **Parking** Valet (free) **Bar** Full bar **Wine selection** One of the town's best wine cellars, with a thick book of unusual bottles from all over the world. The large stock of older French wines was assembled by buying private collections at auction. **Dress** Jacket required for dinner **Disabled access** Full **Customers** A mix of locals, hotel guests, and tourists; gourmets

Breakfast Daily, 7–10:30 a.m.

Lunch Monday–Saturday, 10:30 a.m.–2 p.m.

Dinner Daily, 6–10:30 p.m.

Setting & atmosphere The best and most expensive napery, china, silverware, flowers, foodstuffs, and wines are placed at your disposal by an extremely cooperative service staff. The dining room is modern but furnished with an impressive collection of art and antiques, most with a British cachet.

House specialties Complete menu changes frequently; Windsor Court salad; crab cakes; chef's tasting menu.

Entertainment & amenities Live chamber music in lounge.

Summary & comments The Grill Room is the restaurant of the Windsor Court Hotel, which has been called by various authorities one of the best hotels in the world. The clientele that reputation attracts calls for unusual tastes, ingredients, and presentations at the highest levels of service and price. The best way to experience the Grill Room is through the degustation—some eight courses of the night's best specials. With accompanying wines it tops $100, but it will provide an evening you will not soon forget. There may be a dish or two in there that may appeal more to the brain than to the palate, but what the stylish want is what the stylish get. The wine list was built from private collections and boasts rare vintages from all over. A frequent turnover of chefs in recent years has prevented the Grill Room from maintaining the eminence it had in past years. It's rarely less than a pleasure, however.

Gumbo Shop ★★★

CREOLE | INEXPENSIVE | QUALITY ★★★ | VALUE ★★★

630 St. Peter; 525-1486 • French Quarter Zone 1

Reservations Not accepted **When to go** Middle of the afternoon or evening **Entrée range** $8–$20 **Payment** All major credit cards **Service rating** ★★★ **Friendliness rating** ★★★★ **Parking** French Market pay lot, one block **Bar** Full bar **Wine selection** A few house wines **Dress** Casual **Disabled access** Limited **Customers** Tourists, some locals

Lunch & dinner Sunday–Thursday, 11 a.m.–10 p.m.; Friday and Saturday, 11 a.m.–11 p.m.

Setting & atmosphere The restaurant isn't as old as its yellowed murals or antique dining room make it look. But it feels good anyway. They also have a few tables in the carriageway.

House specialties Shrimp rémoulade; seafood gumbo; jambalaya; red beans and rice; crawfish pie; crawfish étouffée; redfish Florentine; blackened redfish; pecan pie; bread pudding.

Summary & comments This best-named of all New Orleans restaurants is a great resource. If it's traditional everyday New Orleans eats you want, here they are. Gumbo and the other homestyle Creole specials are very credibly done every day, and the menu can even turn out something fancy with élan. Prices are a lot lower than they could be, given the popularity and great location (less than a block from Jackson Square). Unfortunately, that attracts a large following, and waiting for a table here is unavoidable save in the dead of summer.

GW Fins ★★★

SEAFOOD | EXPENSIVE | QUALITY ★★★½ | VALUE ★★

808 Bienville; 581-3467 • French Quarter Zone 1

Reservations Recommended **When to go** Anytime **Entrée range** $18–$30 **Payment** All major credit cards **Service rating** ★★★ **Friendliness rating** ★★★★ **Parking** Pay parking lots nearby **Bar** Full bar **Wine selection** Excellent wine list, with plenty of offbeat bottles and dozens of wines by the glass **Dress** Jacket recommended but not required **Disabled access** Full **Customers** A mix of locals and visitors, tending toward the younger side

Lunch Friday, 11:30 a.m.–3 p.m.

Dinner Daily, 6–10 p.m.

Setting & atmosphere A big, modern room with the best tables arrayed in an arc around the main seating area. The wall of windows in front allows a great view of Arnaud's, across the street.

House specialties Most of the menu changes daily. A few of the good regular items include: sizzled, smoked oysters; bouillabaisse; seared tuna wrapped in nori;

sautéed red snapper with crawfish étouffée; apple pie for two.

Summary & comments GW Fins does with seafood what the prime steak-houses do with beef. They fly in top-quality finfish and shellfish from all over the world, and blend it with the seasonal local seafood into a menu of interesting but uncomplicated dishes. The menu changes daily along with the market availability of everything. The intrinsic merits of the fish get all the spotlight, while the chef's tricks generally recede into the background. This works better for some species than for others. An around-the-world crab platter, for example, was fascinating. Appetizers and side dishes are okay; service varies widely.

Herbsaint ★★★

FRENCH | MODERATE–EXPENSIVE | QUALITY ★★★½ | VALUE ★★★

701 St. Charles Avenue; 524-4114 • Central Business District Zone 2

Reservations Recommended **When to go** Anytime **Entrée range** $10–$25 **Payment** All major credit cards **Service rating** ★★★ **Friendliness rating** ★★★★ **Parking** Free valet parking **Bar** Full bar **Wine selection** Good wine list with an emphasis on French bottles **Dress** Dressy casual **Disabled access** Full **Customers** Couples by night, long-lunch-hour types by day

Lunch Monday–Friday, 11:30 a.m.–2:30 p.m.

Dinner Monday–Saturday, 6–10 p.m.

Setting & atmosphere The L-shaped dining room, with its big windows onto the increasingly green urban streetscape, is sharply furnished and comfortable.

House specialties Tomato and shrimp bisque; arugula with rabbit croquettes; charcuterie plate; fried frogs' legs with fines herbes; seared scallops with risotto; braised pork belly with beluga lentils; warm chocolate beignets; lavender crème brûlée.

Summary & comments Herbsaint is named for a New Orleans–made anise-flavored liqueur, famous for its use in oysters Rockefeller. The chef here uses it in other dishes as well, but stops short of turning it into a leitmotif. The real theme here is a contemporary American interpretation of French country cooking, leavened a bit with some local dishes and local ingredients. Both the prices and ambitions of the kitchen are kept in the moderate range, but the food's goodness excels. Susan Spicer of Bayona is an owner, but her style is not much in evidence here.

Indigo ★★★★

CONTEMPORARY CREOLE | EXPENSIVE | QUALITY ★★★ | VALUE ★★★

2285 Bayou Road; 947-0123 • Mid-City/Gentilly Zone 6

Reservations Recommended **When to go** Dinner **Entrée range** $20–$30 **Payment** All major credit cards **Service rating** ★★★ **Friendliness rating** ★★★ **Parking** Curbside parking only **Bar** Full bar **Wine selection** The cellar is over-populated with expensive bottles, but you'll be able to find something moderate and good with the food. **Dress** Jacket recommended but not required **Disabled access** Full **Customers** A blend of local gourmets on the younger side; hip visitors

Lunch Friday, 11:30 a.m.–2:30 p.m.

Dinner Tuesday–Saturday, 6–10 p.m.

Setting & atmosphere On the grounds of the House on Bayou Road, an historic 1798-vintage guest house, the restaurant is in an imaginatively-renovated old nightclub. Tall ceilings, etched concrete floors, and an outdoor dining area verging on the house's gardens add up to a singular antique dining environment.

House specialties Mussels with fennel and chorizo; oyster gratin with artichokes; confit duck crêpes; sautéed redfish with fried oysters; grilled fish with corn; tournedos with crabmeat and mushrooms; double-cut pork chop with demi-glace; crème brûlée; passionfruit torte.

Summary & comments After opening with a pretentious, unappetizing, avant-garde menu, Indigo started over again in 2002 with Chef Kevin Vizard, one of the best of the Baby Boom chefs who transformed New Orleans dining in the 1980s. His talents are as sharp as ever. His menu performs the appealing miracle of remaining well within the flavor and ingredient palette of New Orleans cooking, while at the same time coming across as exciting and original. However, the chef has a record of remaining only so long at any particular restaurant, although he usually leaves inspiration in his wake. Just hope he's still there when you arrive.

Irene's Cuisine ★★★★

ITALIAN | MODERATE–EXPENSIVE | QUALITY ★★★½ | VALUE ★★★

539 St. Philip; 529-8811 • French Quarter Zone 1

Reservations Not accepted **When to go** Early evenings **Entrée range** $12–$22
Payment AE, DC, MC, V **Service rating** ★★★ **Friendliness rating** ★★★
Parking Curbside **Bar** Full bar **Wine selection** Decent list, mostly Italian
Dress Casual **Disabled access** Full **Customers** Mostly locals, a few tourists; many Quarterites

Dinner Sunday and Monday, 5:30–10 p.m.; Tuesday–Saturday, 5:30–11 p.m.

Setting & atmosphere The main dining room is in an old paper warehouse, and is pleasantly rough. A big part of the experience of dining here involves who you'll socialize with during the almost-inevitable wait for a table.

House specialties Mussels marinara; Oysters Irene (pancetta and Romano); oysters Vittorio (Italian style, plus artichokes); grilled shrimp and pannéed oysters; roasted chicken with rosemary and garlic; veal Sorrentino; roast duck with spinach and mustard; sautéed soft-shell crab and pasta; lamb rack à la Provence; tiramisu; Italian ice creams.

Summary & comments Irene DiPietro cooks up lusty, robust, generally simple food with a country Italian flavor—meaning lots of fresh herbs, garlic, and olive oil. It's a style you don't run into much around here (Mosca's is about the only other place), which may explain the crowds that usually make it at least a little difficult to get a table. Service operations are overseen by former Sazerac maître d' Tommy Andrade (a co-owner), but the trattoria-authentic bustle can reach chaos at times. A recent addition has loosened things up a bit, fortunately. This is one of the few restaurants deep in the French Quarter that has a substantial local clientele.

Jacques-Imo's   ★★★★

CREOLE | INEXPENSIVE—MODERATE | QUALITY ★★★½ | VALUE ★★★

8324 Oak; 861-0886 • Uptown above Napoleon Zone 4

Reservations Accepted for parties of five or more **When to go** Avoid Fridays and Saturdays **Entrée range** $12–$18 **Payment** All major credit cards **Service rating** ★★ **Friendliness rating** ★★★ **Parking** Curbside parking only **Bar** Full bar **Wine selection** Modest list of wines matched to food **Dress** Anything goes **Disabled access** Limited **Customers** Younger crowd, plus hip visitors with a taste for New Orleans funk

Dinner Monday–Saturday, 5:30–10:30 p.m.

Setting & atmosphere A little front dining room and the rear courtyard are both available. Both have a slight hint of Creole voodoo in their décor. Extraordinarily popular in a near-cult way, and not easy to penetrate without at least a short wait.

House specialties Eggplant with oyster dressing; fried oysters with spicy garlic sauce; fried green tomatoes with shrimp rémoulade; fried chicken; smothered chicken; broiled escolar with shrimp; stuffed pork chop; Cajun bouillabaisse; blackened tuna; pannéed rabbit with oyster-tasso pasta; sautéed veal Bienville; banana cream pie; white chocolate bread pudding.

Summary & comments Jack "Jacques" Leonardi, a former K-Paul's chef, teamed up with legendary soul-food chef Austin Leslie to create a convincing neighborhood Creole café. The food here is unapologetically lusty, fresh, and local. Most of the cooking can be found in other restaurants, but few places add the funky spin that this place does. Always interesting, sometimes amazingly good.

K-Paul's Louisiana Kitchen   ★★★★

CAJUN | VERY EXPENSIVE | QUALITY ★★★½ | VALUE ★★

416 Chartres; 524-7394 • French Quarter Zone 1

Reservations Not accepted downstairs, required upstairs **When to go** Lunch, and during slack tourist and convention periods **Entrée range** $26 and up **Payment** AE, MC, V **Service rating** ★★★ **Friendliness rating** ★★★ **Parking** Jackson Brewery pay lot, one block **Bar** Full bar **Wine selection** Good wine list, including many selections by the glass **Dress** Casual **Disabled access** Full **Customers** Mostly tourists at dinner, a good contingent of locals at lunch; gourmets

Dinner Monday–Thursday, 5:30–10 p.m.; Friday and Saturday, 5:30 p.m. until late

Setting & atmosphere Chef Paul Prudhomme's original headquarters has changed a lot since the early days, both physically and spiritually. In the casual downstairs dining room, small parties still share tables with others, and amenities are still minimal. The new upstairs dining room offers greater amenities: tablecloths, private tables, and even reservations. You are not likely to see Chef Paul himself.

House specialties Chicken-andouille gumbo; Cajun popcorn with sherry sauce; shrimp or crawfish étouffée; stuffed soft-shell crab choron; blackened tuna; fried mirliton and oysters with tasso hollandaise; roast duck with pecan gravy; pan-fried veal with roasted stuffed peppers; blackened beef tenders in debris sauce; sweet potato pecan pie; bread pudding with lemon sauce; chocolate mocha cake.

Summary & comments Chef Paul Prudhomme's fame as the archetypal Cajun chef allowed his restaurant to be high-handed for years. But K-Paul's is now much friendlier—even to the point that locals are returning. Whether you sit upstairs or downstairs, you get the unique recipes of Chef Paul, with his consistently impressive ability to make the first-class ingredients they buy here explode with flavor— not always along Cajun lines. Also still in place: unexpectedly lofty prices.

Kim Son   ★★★

VIETNAMESE | INEXPENSIVE | QUALITY ★★★ | VALUE ★★★★★

349 Whitney Avenue; 366-2489 • West Bank Zone 11

Reservations Accepted **When to go** Anytime **Entrée range** $7–$14 **Payment** AE, MC, V **Service rating** ★★ **Friendliness rating** ★★★★ **Parking** Free lot adjacent **Bar** None **Wine selection** Limited list of ordinary wines **Dress** Casual **Disabled access** Limited **Customers** Locals, gourmets

Lunch Monday–Saturday, 11:30 a.m.–2:30 p.m.

Dinner Daily, 6–10 p.m.

Setting & atmosphere A large room with the usual Asian kitsch. An alarmingly big fish levitates in a tank. Men should check out an amazing apparatus in the restroom.

House specialties Imperial roll; spring roll; Vietnamese hot-and-sour fish soup; charcoal-broiled beef and cold noodles; salt-baked crab; salt-baked scallops; fish cooked in clay pot; steamed whole fish; clay-pot chicken curry with coconut; leaf–bound beef; beef fondued in boiled vinegar; eggplant and bean cake in clay pot.

Summary & comments Kim Son was the city's first successful Vietnamese restaurant. Although it, like all other ethnic places, has assimilated its food somewhat over the years, it's still loaded with great dishes. The cooking usually involves the heavy use of fresh herbs and grilled meats—both hallmarks of Vietnamese cooking. It's best to bring a large group, the better to sample the wide range of the menu. Some of the best dishes involve charcoal-grilling, clay pot–braising, and salt-baking. They also have some unexpectedly wonderful noodle and vegetarian dishes. The staff is very helpful about the more exotic fare. Make sure you stay away from the Chinese food, which is not bad but not as good as the Vietnamese dishes.

La Crêpe Nanou   ★★★★

FRENCH | MODERATE | QUALITY ★★★ | VALUE ★★★★★

1410 Robert ; 899-2670 • Uptown above Napoleon Zone 4

Reservations Not accepted **When to go** Early evenings **Entrée range** $12–$24 **Payment** AE, MC, V **Service rating** ★★★ **Friendliness rating** ★★★

Parking Curbside. Robert Street side of parking lot **Bar** Full bar **Wine selection** Substantial list, French-dominated. Many by-the-glass selections. Attractive prices. **Dress** Casual **Disabled access** Limited **Customers** Uptowners, Francophiles; a baby-boomer favorite

Dinner Sunday–Thursday, 6–10 p.m.; Friday and Saturday, 6–11 p.m.

Setting & atmosphere It looks as if it had been transported here from a Parisian back street. The premises are a collage of mismatched decors and furnishings. Always busy, with a happy crowd of locals waiting for tables.

House specialties Pâté maison; mussels marinière; escargots de bourguignonne; onion soup au gratin; crêpes, especially crab, crawfish, Florentine, and Provençal; grilled salmon béarnaise; roast chicken; grilled quails with mushrooms; filet mignon with green peppercorn sauce; lamb chops with Cognac sauce; dessert crêpes, especially Antillaise, Belle Helene, and Calvados.

Summary & comments Evolved far beyond its origins as a crêpe shop, Nanou is a fix for Francophiles. Understandably popular, meals here usually include at least a short wait for a table. The social scene during the delay is a subspecies of the Uptown cocktail party. The food is classic bistro fare: fresh, French, inexpensive, and more delicious than you anticipate. Crêpes—both entrée and dessert varieties—remain a specialty that no other local restaurant can match.

La Provence   ★★★★

MEDITERRANEAN | EXPENSIVE | QUALITY ★★★ | VALUE ★★★

25020 US 190; (985) 626-7662 • North Shore Zone 12

Reservations Required **When to go** Sunday afternoon **Entrée range** $15–$32 **Payment** AE, MC, V **Service rating** ★★★ **Friendliness rating** ★★★ **Parking** Free lot adjacent **Bar** Full bar **Wine selection** Distinguished cellar, French-dominated. The policy on corkage is draconian. **Dress** Jacket recommended but not required **Disabled access** Full **Customers** Gourmets from all over the area; couples

Brunch Sunday, noon–9 p.m.

Dinner Wednesday–Thursday, 4–10 p.m.; Friday and Saturday, 4–11 p.m.

Setting & atmosphere Dining at La Provence is like dining in the countryside of Europe. Still surrounded by forest on the old Mandeville-Slidell highway, it feels rural and sophisticated at the same time.

House specialties Merguez (lamb sausage); shrimp with peppercorn cocktail sauce; quail gumbo; baked oysters three ways; duck à l'orange; tournedos Bordelaise; sweetbreads braised in port wine; rack of lamb; roast chicken with herbs; Greek salad.

Entertainment & amenities Pianist in lounge nightly.

Summary & comments Chef-owner Chris Kerageorgiou has been a delightful character on the dining scene for three decades. He assumes that he knows everybody in the dining room, so even if you're a stranger you'll get a visit and maybe even a hug or an invitation to take a tour of the kitchen. Chris blends the flavors of his French and Greek heritage with Creole touches for some endlessly delicious, original food. While the food is not as consistent as it once was, an amazing thing has happened: the prices have dropped, with a particularly attractive, three-course, $15 early-evening special. The somewhat casual service style (again, much like what one finds in the French countryside) is off-putting to some diners, but you can easily get over it.

La Riviera ★★★

ITALIAN | MODERATE–EXPENSIVE | QUALITY ★★★ | VALUE ★★★

4506 Shores Drive; 888-6238 • Metairie above Causeway/Kenner/Jefferson
  Zone 10

Reservations Recommended **When to go** Anytime **Entrée range** $11–$26 **Payment** All major credit cards **Service rating** ★★★★ **Friendliness rating** ★★★ **Parking** Ample parking lot adjacent **Bar** Full bar **Wine selection** Substantial list, mostly Italian **Dress** Jacket recommended but not required **Disabled access** Full **Customers** Locals, couples

Lunch Monday–Friday, 11:30 a.m.–2:30 p.m.

Dinner Monday–Thursday, 6–10 p.m.; Friday and Saturday, 6–11 p.m.

Setting & atmosphere The slightly gaudy dining room feels a bit formal—at least until it fills up, when it gets more than a little noisy.

House specialties Crabmeat ravioli; fried calamari; fettuccine La Riviera; baked oysters Italian style; stuffed mushrooms; broiled trout; seafood-stuffed eggplant; soft-shell crab with crabmeat; spaghetti and meatballs; osso buco; veal pizzaiola; veal piccata; filet mignon with Madeira sauce; spumoni; Amaretto kiss.

Summary & comments The first successful effort at serving classical (as opposed to Creole) Italian food to the New Orleans dining public has run for over 30 years, and founder-chef Goffredo Fraccaro is still at it. The menu is easy to get into. For example, completely out of place, here is the best plate of meatballs and spaghetti around. But more ambitious dishes abound, particularly in the veal and seafood departments. Nobody does better broiled fish, osso buco, or fried calamari. And Goffredo's signature creation—crabmeat-stuffed ravioli—is such a hit that every Italian restaurant in town now serves it. Outgoing service and well-selected Italian and other wines complete an agreeable lunch or dinner.

La Thai Cuisine ★★★

THAI | MODERATE | QUALITY ★★★ | VALUE ★★★

933 Metairie Road; 828-3080 • Metairie below Causeway Zone 9

Reservations Recommended **When to go** Wednesday dinner, when featured wines are included in the price **Entrée range** $9–$16 **Payment** AE, DS, MC, V **Service rating** ★★ **Friendliness rating** ★★★ **Parking** Ample parking lot adjacent **Bar** Full bar **Wine selection** Good wine list **Dress** Casual **Disabled access** Full **Customers** Old Metairie crowd dominates

Lunch Monday–Friday, 11:30 a.m.–2 p.m.

Dinner Daily, 5–10 p.m.

Setting & atmosphere A renovated gas station has big windows, high ceilings, and a generally spacious, clean look.

House specialties Thai shrimp soup; pecan-crusted oysters with wasabi artichoke; crawfish spring rolls; tamarind duck; Thai pork chop; sea scallops with spinach and pepper flakes.

Summary & comments New Orleans's first reverse-fusion restaurant, La Thai is owned by the family that opened the first Thai restaurant here in the 1980s. By blending Thai flavors and ingredients with those of the local cuisine, the kitchen arrives at a fascinating, unique style of cookery. Some dishes are straight Asian, some are pure Creole, but most are a combination of the two. Surprisingly, they almost never trip up on this adventure, and the eating is terrific and light.

Le Parvenu ★★★★

CREOLE | EXPENSIVE | QUALITY ★★★ | VALUE ★★★

509 Williams Boulevard; 471-0534 • Metairie above Causeway/Kenner/Jefferson Zone 10

Reservations Recommended **When to go** Anytime **Entrée range** $13–$24 **Payment** All major credit cards **Service rating** ★★★ **Friendliness rating** ★★★ **Parking** Small parking lot adjacent; lots of curbside parking nearby **Bar** Full bar **Wine selection** Modest list of wines matched to food **Dress** Jacket recommended but not required **Disabled access** Limited **Customers** People from the nearby towns along the river

Lunch Tuesday–Saturday, 11:30 a.m.–2 p.m.

Dinner Tuesday–Saturday, 6–10 p.m.

Setting & atmosphere Le Parvenu is by far the best restaurant in the vicinity of the airport, and worth going to even when you're not going anywhere. It's a porch-surrounded cottage in the historic Rivertown part of Kenner. Le Parvenu's dining spaces are small but kept from being claustrophobic by its many windows.

House specialties Crabmeat Patricia; lemon-smoked snapper; mirliton, shrimp, and crab bisque; artichoke and garlic cheese soup; lobster Le Parvenu; lamb chops with rosemary and mint sauce; filet mignon with shrimp and peppercorns; roast duck with smoked orange sauce; lemon crêpes; crème brûlée.

Summary & comments The name means "the newcomer," but chef-owner Dennis Hutley could not be called that, really. He cooked in glitzy restaurants for years before opening this fine little bistro. While he made an immediate shift from continental to Creole food, a touch of Europe remains in the polish he applies to every presentation. A good strategy for dining here is "And Den Sum" (try to ignore the name), a four-course, twelve-dish sampler. Service is more casual than the dramatically overdressed maître d' (a familiar and welcoming face) might suggest.

Lee Circle Restaurant ★★★

CONTEMPORARY CREOLE | MODERATE | QUALITY ★★★ | VALUE ★★★

936 St. Charles Avenue; 962-0915 • Uptown below Napoleon Zone 3

Reservations Recommended **When to go** Anytime **Entrée range** $16–$27 **Payment** All major credit cards **Service rating** ★★★★ **Friendliness**

rating ★★★★ **Parking** Free valet parking **Bar** Full bar **Wine selection** Excellent wine list, including many selections by the glass **Dress** Jacket recommended but not required **Disabled access** Full **Customers** People working downtown at lunch, convivial crowd from the entire city at dinner

Lunch Monday–Friday, 11:30 a.m.–3 p.m.

Dinner Daily, 6–10 p.m.

Setting & atmosphere The single dining room and its expansive glass facade curve around the contour of Lee Circle, with a full view of the Confederate general's statue. An abundance of hard surfaces and an overdone modernity make the place feel a little cool and sound loud.

House specialties Shrimp rémoulade; baked shrimp with artichokes and basil; fried oysters with Brie and spinach; veal sweetbreads Creole; crabmeat salad maison; crabmeat and mirliton bisque; red snapper and crabmeat Kell Marie; duck with smoked orange sauce; filet mignon with oyster demi-glace; crème brûlée.

Summary & comments The restaurant of Le Cirque Hotel is independently operated by the principals of two first-class restaurants: Clancy's and Le Parvenu. The menu includes the better specialties from both, but most of it is original, primarily along contemporary Creole lines, often with a suggestion of French polish. When it opened, Lee Circle was much less avant-garde than the other members of its class, but that conservatism was actually welcome. Service is attentive. At Mardi Gras time, when parades pass right in front, the restaurant reverts to a much more primitive menu.

Lilette   ★★★

FRENCH | EXPENSIVE | QUALITY ★★★½ | VALUE ★★★

3637 Magazine; 895-1636 • Uptown above Napoleon Zone 4

Reservations Accepted **When to go** Dinner **Entrée range** $9–$20 **Payment** AE, DS, MC, V **Service rating** ★★★ **Friendliness rating** ★★★ **Parking** Curbside parking only **Bar** Full bar **Wine selection** Modest, somewhat eccentric list matched to the food **Dress** Dressy casual **Disabled access** Full **Customers** Youthful crowd of Uptown gourmets

Lunch Tuesday–Saturday, 11:30 a.m.–2:30 p.m.

Dinner Tuesday–Sunday, 6–10 p.m.

Setting & atmosphere This is a small restaurant, but it feels spacious because the dining room's ceilings are so tall. Tables are placed in a haphazard way, such that not even the ones along the windows are what you could call a good table.

House specialties Eggplant crisps with skordalia; escargots with mushrooms; warm crabmeat with snap pea vinaigrette; boudin noir; sizzling shrimp with oregano; braised veal cheeks salad; roasted chicken or duck breast; hanger steak with marrow; seared tuna with brown butter; grilled veal paillard.

Summary & comments Lilette serves the personal cuisine of chef-owner John Harris, a local fellow with a long-standing taste for the country flavors of France. Most of his menu reflects that, to a delightful extreme. Harris doesn't hesitate to offer the likes of veal cheeks, boudin noir, and whatever other rarity strikes his fancy. All this is cooked with a bit more herbalness and garlic than the average

French bistro uses, to great effect. The specials are absolutely the best food here. Service is a bit New Age in its demeanor, but just look them right in the eye and tell them what you're after.

Mandich   ★★★

CREOLE | INEXPENSIVE–MODERATE | QUALITY ★★★ | VALUE ★★★

3200 St. Claude Avenue; 947-9553 • Downtown/St. Bernard Zone 5

Reservations Accepted **When to go** Anytime **Entrée range** $12–$18 **Payment** MC, V **Service rating** ★★★ **Friendliness rating** ★★★★ **Parking** Free lot adjacent **Bar** Full bar **Wine selection** A few house wines, arrayed on the bar with supermarket-style price tags **Dress** Casual **Disabled access** Limited **Customers** Neighborhood people

Lunch Tuesday–Friday, 11:30 a.m.–2:30 p.m.

Dinner Friday and Saturday, 5–10 p.m.

Setting & atmosphere The dining room looks like something out of the early 1960s.

House specialties Oysters Bordelaise; seafood gumbo; red-bean soup; trout Mandich (broiled with a crisp breading, with lemon butter); crab cakes; oyster platter four ways; stuffed shrimp; garlic chicken; sweet potato duck; pannéed veal; filet mignon; cheesecake; bread pudding.

Summary & comments Mandich is predominantly a lunch place; its original clientele worked in the port, which starts and ends early. That legacy lives on in the food, which is a cut or two better than that of the typical neighborhood restaurant. All of it is the kind of food Orleanians feasted on before we became self-conscious gourmets. Most of the customers are regulars, but they always welcome unfamiliar faces. Few enough restaurants of this ilk survive these days that a meal here becomes special.

Mandina's   ★★★

CREOLE | INEXPENSIVE–MODERATE | QUALITY ★★★ | VALUE ★★★★★

3800 Canal; 482-9179 • Mid-City/Gentilly Zone 6

Reservations Not accepted **When to go** Off-peak lunch and dinner hours to avoid waiting **Entrée range** $9–$17 **Payment** Cash only **Service rating** ★★ **Friendliness rating** ★★ **Parking** Ample parking lot adjacent **Bar** Full bar **Wine selection** A few house wines **Dress** Casual **Disabled access** Limited **Customers** Locals, families; professionals at lunch

Lunch & dinner Monday–Thursday, 11 a.m.–10:30 p.m.; Friday and Saturday, 11 a.m.–11 p.m.; Sunday, noon–9 p.m.

Setting & atmosphere A recent expansion made it only a little easier to get a table, while doing nothing to change the worn-out, always-bustling original dining rooms. The front room's tables vie for space with customers waiting at the bar. The whole place is furnished with neon, old painted signs, beer clocks, and other relics.

House specialties Shrimp rémoulade; crab fingers in wine sauce; oyster and artichoke soup; fried soft-shell crab; trout amandine; spaghetti and Italian sausage; daily specials, especially: red beans with Italian sausage (Monday); beef stew (Tuesday); braciolone (Thursday); trout amandine (Friday); shrimp Creole (Sunday); bread pudding.

Summary & comments Mandina's comes to most Orleanians' minds when they try to conjure up the cherished image of the old-time neighborhood café. The best food on any given day will be the homestyle specials. These are almost uniformly good across the board, and when you factor in the prices, the appeal of the place becomes obvious. All portions are titanic, but somehow avoid grossness. You might hesitate to order it, but they have one of the best roast-beef poor boys around here. The service staff have been here a long time, and they have seen it all, likely more than once. A recent, big improvement: a parking lot.

Maple Street Café ★★★

MEDITERRANEAN | INEXPENSIVE–MODERATE | QUALITY ★★★ | VALUE ★★★★★

7623 Maple; 314-9003 • Uptown above Napoleon Zone 4

Reservations Accepted **When to go** Anytime **Entrée range** $9–$22 **Payment** All major credit cards **Service rating** ★★★ **Friendliness rating** ★★★★ **Parking** Small parking lot at corner **Bar** Full bar **Wine selection** Good wine list, including many selections by the glass **Dress** Casual **Disabled access** Limited **Customers** Uptowners; many people from nearby shops come in at lunch

Lunch Monday–Saturday, 11:30 a.m.–2:30 p.m.

Dinner Sunday–Thursday, 6–10 p.m.; Friday and Saturday, 6–11 p.m.

Setting & atmosphere This part of Maple Street is a quaint shopping district. Even the restaurants are storefronts designed for pedestrians. This one is split-level, bright, and convivial.

House specialties Eggplant cake with crabmeat cream sauce; stuffed shrimp in phyllo; Greek salad in a bread bowl; rigatoni sui-sui (garlic-tomato sauce); angel hair pasta with three wild mushrooms; filet mignon with grilled portobello; fresh fish Florentine or baked in pastry; caramel custard.

Summary & comments The Maple Street Café is where the Maple Street shop-keepers go for lunch, but it's good all the time. The menu is a mix of Italian, Creole, and continental cooking, with a few fillips of Middle Eastern taste thrown in here and there. (The chef/owner is Jordanian, but he learned how to cook locally.) The cooking here is more ambitious than one expects given the prices or the pretensions; there's even a degree of polish. The young service staff is well-spoken and eager to please.

Marigny Brasserie ★★★★

CONTEMPORARY CREOLE. | MODERATE–EXPENSIVE | QUALITY ★★★½ | VALUE ★★★

640 Frenchmen; 945-4472 • Downtown/St. Bernard Zone 5

Reservations Recommended **When to go** Anytime **Entrée range** $10–$20 **Payment** AE, MC, V **Service rating** ★★★ **Friendliness rating** ★★★ **Parking** Curb-side parking only **Bar** Full bar **Wine selection** Good wine list **Dress** Casual **Disabled access** Limited **Customers** Marigny residents; couples and singles

Brunch Saturday and Sunday, 8 a.m.–2:30 p.m.

Lunch Daily, 11:30 a.m.–2:30 p.m.

Dinner Sunday–Thursday, 5–11 p.m.; Friday and Saturday, 5 p.m.–2 a.m. or later

Setting & atmosphere A corner restaurant at the midpoint of Restaurant Row in the Faubourg Marigny, this place takes full advantage of the passing parade with big windows onto the busy sidewalks. The main dining room is an airy, open space with two rows of banquettes.

House specialties Duck-andouille spring rolls; seafood wontons; grilled vegetable Napoleon; grilled tuna with artichoke hearts and tomatoes; grilled smoked veal chop; arroz con pollo; pannéed veal with fettuccine Alfredo.

Summary & comments It started down the block as a coffeehouse, graduated into serving food, and has continued to get better and more ambitious as years go on. The last two chefs have left Cajun and Spanish touches on a menu of contemporary Creole cooking. Familiar dishes get ratcheted up with a special ingredient or fine detail. The consistency is less than perfect, but it's always fun to come here, particularly late in the evening.

Marisol ★★★★

ECLECTIC | MODERATE–EXPENSIVE | QUALITY ★★★ | VALUE ★★★

437 Esplanade Avenue; 943-1912 • French Quarter Zone 1 •
  marisolrestaurant.com

Reservations Recommended **When to go** Dinner **Entrée range** $18–$32 **Payment** AE, DC, MC, V **Service rating** ★★★ **Friendliness rating** ★★★ **Parking** Curbside parking only **Bar** Full bar **Wine selection** Good if abbreviated wine list **Dress** Dressy casual **Disabled access** Full **Customers** Local gourmets and visitors

Lunch Tuesday–Friday, 11:30 a.m.–2:30 p.m.

Dinner Sunday and Tuesday–Thursday, 6–10 p.m.; Friday and Saturday, 6–11 p.m.

Setting & atmosphere A charming, rustic room spills out through the often-open doors into a small courtyard. The alfresco tables are nice in spring and fall, but a touch warm and loud (from the air conditioning compressors) in the summer.

House specialties Tapas (early evening); steamed mussels; ravioli with lobster sauce; foie gras "en bocal"; duck confit with spiced honey; Thai crabmeat and coconut soup; whole crispy fish with ginger sauce; pan-roasted Guinea hen; rack of venison; grilled hanger steak; Key lime pie; cheese selections.

Summary & comments Chef-owner Peter Vazquez works up a highly personal cuisine at Marisol. It begins with a French bistro inspiration, adds a Mediterranean freshness, then departs for every other part of the world. The menu changes daily, but you can count on finding some predictable aspects. Mussels, foie gras, unusual fish (much of it bought through the same channels that sushi bars use), and cuts of meat involving bones and slow cooking have been there on my every visit. All of it is cooked with inspiration, sometimes rising into the upper levels of brilliance. One of the best reasons to eat here is the presence of the town's best cheese assortment. You're guaranteed to have a cheese you've never tasted (or perhaps heard of) before, in pristine condition. Desserts seem to revolve around the availability of fresh fruit. The wine list is quirky, but that's a perfect match to the widely varied style of the cooking. At lunchtime, Marisol offers an appealing buffet of antipasto.

Mat & Naddie's ★★★

CONTEMPORARY CREOLE | MODERATE–EXPENSIVE | QUALITY ★★★ | VALUE ★★★

937 Leonidas; 861-9600 • Uptown above Napoleon Zone 4

Reservations Recommended **When to go** Dinner **Entrée range** $12–$24 **Payment** All major credit cards **Service rating** ★★★ **Friendliness rating** ★★★★ **Parking** Curbside parking only **Bar** Full bar **Wine selection** Modest list of wines matched to the food **Dress** Casual **Disabled access** Limited **Customers** Uptowners

Lunch Tuesday–Friday, 11:30 a.m.–2:30 p.m.

Dinner Tuesday–Saturday, 6–10 p.m.

Setting & atmosphere Operations are in an old house on the Uptown riverfront, where the freight trains that pass in the night somehow become romantic. The feeling that you've discovered a hidden gem charms you.

House specialties Oysters Rockefeller pizza; charbroiled oysters; barbecue shrimp; pan-sautéed salmon; roasted rack of lamb; filet mignon with peppered chèvre; crème brûlée.

Summary & comments The name is a kidspeak version of the founder's kids' names. The restaurant is now in the hands of the former sous chef, who—if anything—has made the food even better. The cooking starts from a platform of contemporary Creole dishes that stop short of avant-garde, but incorporate a few fusion elements here and there. It's done with enough skill and distinction to make this an enjoyable, if offbeat, place to eat.

Mike Anderson's ★★★

SEAFOOD | INEXPENSIVE–MODERATE | QUALITY ★★★ | VALUE ★★★

215 Bourbon Street; 524-3884 • French Quarter Zone 1

Reservations Not accepted **When to go** Anytime **Entrée range** $10–$22 **Payment** All major credit cards **Service rating** ★★ **Friendliness rating** ★★★ **Parking** Pay garages nearby **Bar** Full bar **Wine selection** A few house wines **Dress** Casual **Disabled access** Limited **Customers** Tourists, some locals; professionals at lunch

Lunch & dinner Sunday–Thursday, 11 a.m.–10 p.m.; Friday and Saturday, 11 a.m.–11 p.m. or later

Setting & atmosphere The original New Orleans–area branch of the LSU football hero's seafood restaurant chain is one of the busiest restaurants in the French Quarter. One long, dark room is filled with funky swamp décor.

House specialties Oysters on the half shell; three-way alligator; baked oysters four ways; turtle soup; fried seafood platter; broiled seafood platter; crawfish, shrimp, or crab dinner; fish stuffed with crab and shrimp; jolie rouge (broiled fish topped with crabmeat).

Summary & comments Portions greatly exceed appetites here, which explains some of the popularity. However, the eating is good. They cook fresh across the board, sending out very good grilled, broiled, stuffed, and sauced seafoods as well as fried. There's more of a Cajun touch here than in most other New Orleans restaurants. A major specialty is the seven-way dinner, made with your choice of crawfish, crab, or shrimp. Not all of the seven will be great, but if you eat only the top four you'll still have too much to eat.

Mr. B's Bistro ★★★★

CREOLE | EXPENSIVE | QUALITY ★★★½ | VALUE ★★★

201 Royal; 523-2078 • French Quarter Zone 1

Reservations Accepted **When to go** Early evenings **Entrée range** $14–$26 **Payment** All major credit cards **Service rating** ★★★★★ **Friendliness rating** ★★★★★ **Parking** Validated (free) at Dixie Parking, behind restaurant on Iberville Street **Bar** Full bar **Wine selection** Substantial list, almost entirely West Coast **Dress** Dressy casual **Disabled access** Limited **Customers** Mostly locals, some tourists; gourmets, couples

Brunch Sunday, 10:30 a.m.–3 p.m.

Lunch Monday–Saturday, 11:30 a.m.–3 p.m.

Dinner Daily, 5:30–10:30 p.m.

Setting & atmosphere One big, somewhat dark, moderately noisy room with a semi-open kitchen. The engaging bar is usually full at dinner with people waiting for tables, a product of a reservation system that favors locals and walk-ins.

House specialties Shrimp and pork spring rolls; skillet shrimp with garlic; crabtini (crabmeat rémoulade in a martini glass); gumbo ya-ya; hickory-grilled fish; pasta jambalaya; barbecue shrimp; hickory-roasted chicken with garlic glaze; seafood-and-pasta specials; bread pudding; Mr. B's chocolate cake; profiteroles and chocolate sauce.

Entertainment & amenities Pianist at dinner nightly and at Sunday brunch.

Summary & comments In 1979 the Brennans transformed the New Orleans dining scene by opening this, the archetype of the casual, contemporary Creole bistro. It was so widely imitated that restaurants like Mr. B's now dominate the scene. Its kitchen creates innovative and excellent Creole dishes from top-rung fresh ingredients, but serves them in an easy, informal way. Hickory-grilled fish, now common, was pioneered here; so was using pasta as the basis for new Creole concoctions. The chicken-andouille gumbo and barbecue shrimp are definitive. The service staff and the wine list are both better than they need to be.

Mr. John's Steak House ★★★

STEAK | EXPENSIVE | QUALITY ★★★ | VALUE ★★★

2111 St. Charles Avenue; 566-1212 • Uptown below Napoleon Zone 3

Reservations Recommended **When to go** Dinner **Entrée range** $14–$34 **Payment** All major credit cards **Service rating** ★★★ **Friendliness rating** ★★★★ **Parking** Free valet parking **Bar** Full bar **Wine selection** Good wine list **Dress** Casual **Disabled access** Full **Customers** Hotel guests for breakfast and lunch; uptowners and steak lovers at dinner

Breakfast Daily, 7–10 a.m.

Lunch Daily, 11:30 a.m.–2:30 p.m.

Dinner Daily, 6–10 p.m.

Setting & atmosphere The tiled dining room and the tables on the sidewalk offer a pleasant view of the passing streetcars. The style of the place is loose and easy.

House specialties Onion rings; crawfish cakes with smoked tomato butter; barbecue shrimp; filet mignon; strip sirloin; chicken with mushrooms and artichokes; spinach or broccoli au gratin; bread pudding; pineapple fluff.

Summary & comments Mr. John Santopadre is an operator of first-class small hotels and restaurants. He always wanted to open a New Orleans–style steakhouse, so here it is—in the ground floor of his Avenue Plaza Hotel. The beef is USDA prime all the way, available in all the classic cuts, broiled in a superheated broiler until crusty, and then sent out with the New Orleans–style sizzling butter. The rest of the menu is a touch more ambitious than is found in other steakhouses, and includes a substantial selection of seafood platters, both fried and grilled. Side dishes and salads are simple, well made, and huge.

Mosca's   ★★★

ITALIAN | EXPENSIVE | QUALITY ★★★ | VALUE ★★★

4137 US 90; 436-9942 • West Bank Zone 11

Reservations Accepted but rarely honored **When to go** Weeknights; closed August **Entrée range** $16–$24 **Payment** Cash only **Service rating** ★★ **Friendliness rating** ★★ **Parking** Ample parking lot adjacent **Bar** Full bar **Wine selection** Decent list, almost entirely Italian; several Amarones **Dress** Casual **Disabled access** None **Customers** Mostly locals (many of them regular customers), a few tourists; families of adults

Dinner Tuesday–Saturday, 5–10 p.m.

Setting & atmosphere A two-room shack, stark and noisy. The location is daunting: way out on the highway out of town, surrounded by marshland. It does not look inviting from the outside, but ignore that. Civilization is approaching, but it's still the last thing for miles.

House specialties Crab salad; chef's bean soup; oysters Italian style; shrimp Italian style; chicken grandee; roast chicken; roast quail or squab; Italian sausage; filet mignon; pineapple fluff.

Summary & comments Mosca's has hardly changed, except in price, since it opened in the 1940s. Finally, here is all the olive oil, garlic, and rosemary you always wanted, scattered around roasted chickens, sausage, shrimp, and oysters. All this is delivered with a startling lack of ceremony—big platters of food accompanied by stacks of plates and utensils for you to distribute among yourselves. Come with at least four people to best enjoy; six is even better. The dining rooms are still almost always full, and the staff still turns a deaf ear to your complaints about the wait for a table or anything else.

Mother's ★★

SANDWICHES | INEXPENSIVE | QUALITY ★★½ | VALUE ★★

401 Poydras; 523-9656 • Central Business District Zone 2

Reservations Not accepted **When to go** Anytime except around noon and during large conventions **Entrée range** $7–$18 **Payment** Cash only **Service rating** ★★ **Friendliness rating** ★★★ **Parking** Curbside; pay lot nearby **Bar** Beer **Wine selection** A few house wines **Dress** Anything goes **Disabled access** None **Customers** Tourists, some locals; professionals at lunch

Open Monday–Saturday, 5 a.m.–10 p.m.; Sunday, 7 a.m.–10 p.m.

Setting & atmosphere A cramped, concrete-floored dining room with a line of customers snaking through it.

House specialties Breakfast special; Mae's omelette; pancakes; ham poor boy; ferdi (ham and roast-beef debris); turkey poor boy; fried-seafood poor boys; red beans and rice; gumbo of the day; jambalaya; corned beef and cabbage; bread pudding; brownies; muffins.

Summary & comments The world's most famous vendor of poor-boy sandwiches, Mother's is also among the city's busiest restaurants on a volume-per-square-foot basis. There's almost always a line. While standing in it, you may have cooks break through with their buckets of hot gravy or beans or whatever from the kitchen. Everything is cooked on site—exceptional for a poor-boy shop. Portions on the plate specials are absurdly large, and the food tends to the heavy side. Lunch and supper are the main meals, but breakfast is terrific, too. Don't come here when there's a large convention in town, or when you have less than $15 cash in your pocket.

Muriel's ★★★

CONTEMPORARY CREOLE | EXPENSIVE | QUALITY ★★★½ | VALUE ★★★

801 Chartres; 568-1885 • French Quarter Zone 1

Reservations Recommended **When to go** Anytime **Entrée range** $18–$27 **Payment** All major credit cards **Service rating** ★★★ **Friendliness rating** ★★★★ **Parking** Validated parking at Place d'Armes Hotel next door **Bar** Full bar **Wine selection** Good wine list, including many selections by the glass **Dress** Dressy casual **Disabled access** Limited **Customers** A mix of visitors and locals

Lunch Monday–Saturday, 11:30 a.m.–3 p.m.

Dinner Daily, 6–11 p.m.

Setting & atmosphere If your idea of New Orleans atmosphere includes an ancient, slightly crumbling old building with quirky, rumpled furnishings and aspects of voodoo and the bordello, this is the place for you. Actually, even Orleanians find this place interesting, particularly the upstairs rooms, which are illuminated almost entirely by candles in chandeliers. All this is on Jackson Square, the spiritual center of New Orleans since its earliest years.

House specialties Appetizer sampler; shrimp rémoulade with fried green tomatoes; crawfish étouffée in puff pastry; grilled barbecue shrimp; stuffed flounder; duck and lamb cassoulet; tournedos of beef.

Summary & comments The food at Muriel's blends with the old Creole environment. While you won't find the same menu served at the places that really are as old as Muriel's looks, it has a decidedly old Creole flavor. The concoctions are dominated by local seafood, which make for the best eating here. They cook everything else here, too, and even when you press them on some of the more ambitious dishes, the kitchen shows great skill. The dining room staff is not as experienced nor as hospitable as it could be—the only potential catch in dining here. Even then, the place is fun and utterly unique.

Ninja ★★★

JAPANESE | INEXPENSIVE–MODERATE | QUALITY ★★★ | VALUE ★★★

8433 Oak; 866-1119 • Uptown above Napoleon Zone 4

Reservations Accepted **When to go** Anytime **Entrée range** $7–$16
Payment AE, DC, MC, V **Service rating** ★★ **Friendliness rating** ★★★★
Parking Curbside **Bar** Full bar **Wine selection** A few house wines **Dress** Casual
Disabled access None **Customers** Neighborhood people; college types

Lunch Tuesday–Sunday, 11:30 a.m.–2:30 p.m.

Dinner Tuesday–Sunday, 6–10 p.m.

Setting & atmosphere Downstairs is a darkish, low-ceilinged bar where you might have to wait for a table. It gives no suggestion of the brighter, sleeker dining room upstairs. All this is a welcome change from the cramped cottage Ninja used to occupy.

House specialties Gyoza; sushi specials; ninja dinner; mixed seafood platter; chirashizushi; beef tataki; barbecued eel; teriyaki beef; tempura shrimp.

Summary & comments Ninja is one of the best and most consistently creative sushi bars around. The menu includes the usual array of fried and grilled dishes, but sashimi, sushi, and the like are clearly the specialties. The regular clientele is particularly vociferous in its opinion that there's no better place than this. However, newbies are treated to the same fine food and service as the regulars.

Nirvana ★★★

INDIAN | INEXPENSIVE–MODERATE | QUALITY ★★★ | VALUE ★★★

4308 Magazine; 894-9797 • Uptown below Napoleon Zone 3

Reservations Accepted **When to go** Dinner **Entrée range** $9–$14 **Payment** All major credit cards **Service rating** ★★★ **Friendliness rating** ★★★ **Parking** Curbside parking only **Bar** Full bar **Wine selection** A few house wines **Dress** Casual
Disabled access Full **Customers** Uptowners, bohemians, Indians

Lunch Tuesday–Sunday, 11:30 a.m.–2:30 p.m.

Dinner Sunday and Tuesday–Thursday, 6–10 p.m.; Friday and Saturday, 6–11 p.m.

Setting & atmosphere A big space in an old Magazine Street storefront offers room for the aromas to spread. Nice pressed-tin ceiling.

House specialties Seenkh kebab; saag paneer (creamed spinach with home-made cheese); tandoori chicken; malai kebab (chicken marinated in yogurt and cream cheese); macchi tikka (marinated, roasted fish); lamb Goa (spicy coconut-milk curry); mint-encrusted lamb; chicken, lamb, or vegetarian biryani.

Summary & comments Nirvana is the fifth and most ambitious restaurant from the Keswani family, who introduced Indian food to New Orleans. The kitchen dispatches tandoori dishes, many isotopes of curry, dishes with other sauces ranging from mild and buttery to flamethrowing, a vast array of vegetarian offerings, and even some of the Southern Indian dosa—crêpe-like dishes remarkable for their many condiments. Like every other Indian restaurant in the world (it seems), they serve from a buffet here, but that won't show you what this place is capable of.

Nola ★★★★

CREOLE | EXPENSIVE | QUALITY ★★★ | VALUE ★★★

534 St. Louis; 522-6652 • French Quarter Zone 1

Reservations Recommended **When to go** Anytime **Entrée range** $18–$32 **Payment** All major credit cards **Service rating** ★★★★ **Friendliness rating** ★★★★ **Parking** Validated at Omni Royal Orleans Hotel **Bar** Full **Wine selection** Substantial list, emphasis on California; many by-the-glass selections **Dress** Dressy casual **Disabled access** Full **Customers** A mix of tourists and locals, with a hip, young tilt

Lunch Monday–Saturday, 11:30 a.m.–2:30 p.m.

Dinner Sunday–Thursday, 6–10 p.m.; Friday and Saturday, 6 p.m.–midnight

Setting & atmosphere The building is old, but they did it up in a swell, high-tech way. The whole place is a sort of modern sculpture.

House specialties Pizzas; crab cake with chili aïoli; shrimp pasta with warm rémoulade; Vietnamese-style seafood salad; cedar plank–roasted fish; double-cut pork chop; New York strip steak; slow-roasted duck; coconut bread pudding; lemon chess pie; chicory coffee crème brûlée.

Summary & comments The second restaurant of local chef superstar Emeril Lagasse, Nola duplicates Emeril's in using extremely well-selected fresh ingredients in innovative ways, while holding to a distinctly Louisiana flavor. Emeril's superstar status draws large crowds of tourists looking for a glimpse of him. They probably won't get one, but the wait staff is happy to tell the visitors all about him. The open kitchen sports a wood-burning oven and grill. Full advantage is taken of that resource. The chefs like to use planks of wood to roast and serve various fish and meats upon; this is a major specialty. The other menu entries are either interesting twists on local standards, or totally innovative concoctions—all about equally good. The first-class pastry department makes an exceptionally good assortment of desserts. Locals love this place because it's not as expensive or as hard to negotiate as Emeril's other two New Orleans establishments.

Palace Café ★★★★

CREOLE | MODERATE–EXPENSIVE | QUALITY ★★★½ | VALUE ★★★

605 Canal; 523-1661 • Central Business District Zone 2

Reservations Recommended **When to go** Anytime **Entrée range** $15–$26 **Payment** All major credit cards **Service rating** ★★★★ **Friendliness rating** 5 **Parking** Validated (free) at Holiday Inn and Marriott garages **Bar** Full bar **Wine selection** Substantial list, almost entirely from the West Coast **Dress** Dressy casual **Disabled access** Full **Customers** A mix of locals and tourists; professionals at lunch; families

Lunch Monday–Friday, 10:30 a.m.–2:30 p.m.

Dinner Daily, 5:30–10 p.m.

Setting & atmosphere The Palace Café occupies the historic old Werlein's Music Building, with big windows opening onto Canal Street and its new streetcar tracks. There is no better restaurant for watching Mardi Gras parades. When full, the tile floors and large windows conspire to create high sound levels.

House specialties Crabmeat cheesecake with pecan crust; corn-fried oysters with artichokes; oyster pan roast with rosemary cream; shrimp rémoulade; turtle soup; andouille-crusted fish; catfish pecan; roast dry-aged duck; veal chop with rock-shrimp risotto; Palace potato pie; white chocolate bread pudding; bananas Foster.

Entertainment & amenities Unusually good player piano rolls all the time. Live blues supports the Sunday brunch.

Summary & comments The PC is the flagship of Dickie Brennan's group of restaurants. The food is polished Creole, and in some ways it reminds me of what its big sister Commander's Palace was doing ten years ago. That was a great style, and it's perfect for the location. In just a few years they've created a few widely copied dishes here—most notably white chocolate bread pudding. Service appears to be casual, but suddenly they roll up a gueridon and start flaming or carving something.

Pascal's Manale ★★★★

CREOLE | MODERATE–EXPENSIVE | QUALITY ★★★½ | VALUE ★★★

1838 Napoleon Avenue; 895-4877 • Uptown above Napoleon Zone 4

Reservations Recommended **When to go** Anytime **Entrée range** $12–$30 **Payment** All major credit cards **Service rating** ★★★ **Friendliness rating** ★★★ **Parking** Ample parking lot adjacent **Bar** Full bar **Wine selection** Not what it should be; mostly ordinary Italian wines **Dress** Casual **Disabled access** Limited **Customers** A mix of Uptown locals and tourists

Lunch & dinner Monday–Friday, 11:30 a.m.–10 p.m.

Dinner Daily, 6–10 p.m.

Setting & atmosphere Manale's feels like neighborhood café, with a certain scruffiness that's surprising considering its fame as a venerable local eatery.

House specialties Raw oysters; oysters Bienville; oysters Rockefeller; stuffed mushrooms; crab and oyster pan roast; shrimp and crabmeat rémoulade; turtle soup; New Orleans barbecue shrimp; broiled fish with crabmeat and hollandaise; veal Puccini; filet mignon; double pork chop with peppercorns; spaghetti Collins; bread pudding; chocolate mousse.

Summary & comments New Orleans's oldest Italian restaurant serves the epitome of Creole-Italian cuisine—a hybrid so well blended now that no Italian would recognize it as being from his homeland. The famous dish is widely copied around town. Barbecue shrimp, completely misnamed, aren't grilled or smoked, nor is there a barbecue sauce. Other restaurants now do the dish better, but these are still lusty: gigantic heads-on shrimp cooked in a distinctive pepper-butter sauce. They do terrific things with oysters, veal, and beef. Avoid red-sauce dishes and you'll eat well. Service is a little too casual.

Pelican Club ★★★★★

ECLECTIC | VERY EXPENSIVE | QUALITY ★★★★★ | VALUE ★★★

615 Bienville; 523-1504 • French Quarter Zone 1

Reservations Recommended **When to go** Anytime **Entrée range** $15–$30 **Payment** All major credit cards **Service rating** ★★★★ **Friendliness rating** ★★★ **Parking** Validated (free) at Monteleone Hotel garage **Bar** Full bar **Wine selection** Substantial list, good international balance; many by-the-glass selections **Dress** Jacket recommended but not required **Disabled access** Limited **Customers** A mix of locals and tourists; couples; gourmets

Dinner Sunday–Thursday, 5–10 p.m.; Friday and Saturday, 5–11 p.m.

Setting & atmosphere The three dining rooms line up into a long hall, with enough hard surfaces to make the acoustics uncomfortably lively when the place is full.

House specialties Scallop stuffed artichoke; beef and shrimp pot stickers; escargots with crawfish and mushrooms; Creole Caesar salad; Thai seafood salad; smoked duck and shrimp gumbo; Louisiana bouillabaisse; grilled fish with ginger lime glaze; filet mignon with Cabernet mushroom sauce; jambalaya; dessert specials.

Summary & comments Keeping a low profile on mysterious Exchange Alley, the Pelican Club can wine and dine you with the best of them. Chef-owners Richard Hughes and Chin Ling combine Creole, Italian, Chinese, Southwestern, and various other flavors into dishes using ingredients of impressive pedigree. The result is immensely appealing, perhaps because the food has the taste of familiarity for all its innovation. Although one is served well, and although many locals have made this restaurant one of their regular places to eat grandly, I've never felt a sense of warm accommodation from the dining-room staff. But that's not something that will ruin the evening, especially on nights when the kitchen is really on.

Peristyle ★★★★★

ECLECTIC | VERY EXPENSIVE | QUALITY ★★★★★ | VALUE ★★★

1041 Dumaine; 593-9535 • French Quarter Zone 1

Reservations Required **When to go** Early evenings **Entrée range** $18–$28 **Payment** All major credit cards **Service rating** ★★★ **Friendliness rating** ★★★

Parking Free valet parking **Bar** Full bar **Wine selection** An impressive list—not for its size, but for the wide variety of styles it represents. Very interesting to oenophiles. **Dress** Jacket recommended but not required **Disabled access** Limited **Customers** Gourmets, couples; mostly locals

Lunch Friday, 11:30 a.m.–2 p.m.

Dinner Tuesday–Saturday, 6–10 p.m.

Setting & atmosphere This space has been a restaurant for nearly a hundred years. A renovation following a fire in 1999 freshened up the dining room, but retained the antique fixtures and two old murals—one of which depicts the namesake structure in City Park.

House specialties Most of the menu changes frequently, but these standards are usually on: crabmeat ravigote with beets; grilled sea scallops; seared foie gras; roasted squab.

Summary & comments Chef-owner Anne Kearney was rising to national prominence when her restaurant closed for nine months due to a bad fire. When Peristyle reopened, it did so with even more popularity than before, and tables are more than a little difficult to obtain. (Try getting in here for the Friday lunch.) The chef's ruling principle is polish: perfect leaves of greens, vivid and simple sauces, beautiful seafood, and stunning but straightforward presentations. The style is clearly French-inspired, but also very American and a little bit New Orleans. The wait staff has a little snootiness, but they know what they're doing, and can converse intelligently about both the food and wine offerings.

Pho Tau Bay ★★

VIETNAMESE | INEXPENSIVE | QUALITY ★★½ | VALUE ★★★★★

3116 N. Arnoult; 780-1063 • Metairie above Causeway/Kenner/Jefferson Zone 10

Reservations Accepted **When to go** Anytime **Entrée range** $5–$9 **Payment** AE, MC, V **Service rating** ★★ **Friendliness rating** ★★ **Parking** Small parking lot adjacent **Bar** Full bar **Wine selection** A few house wines **Dress** Anything goes **Disabled access** Limited **Customers** Mostly young; many Asians

Lunch & dinner Monday–Saturday, 11 a.m.–10 p.m.

Setting & atmosphere The small, minimally furnished dining room is clean and comfortable enough.

House specialties Spring rolls; Vietnamese shrimp and pork omelette; chicken, beef, or vegetables with rice noodles in broth (pho); char-broiled pork or beef with vermicelli or rice; fish in clay pot; beef in vinegar hot pot.

Summary & comments The best of the many restaurants around New Orleans serving the Vietnamese whole-meal soup called pho, Pho Tau Bay ("airplane soup"—ask about the name) has a menu that's more to the point than in most Vietnamese places. They have the pho in several configurations, all involving a light broth brought to the table with beef or chicken or shrimp (you order), noodles, and a plate of leafy vegetables. Don't worry about whether you're doing it right—just eat it. Great both on the hottest summer days and the coldest winter days, somehow. They also make an assortment of good grilled dishes on pillows of room-temperature noodles.

Red Fish Grill ★★★

SEAFOOD | MODERATE–EXPENSIVE | QUALITY ★★★½ | VALUE ★★★

115 Bourbon; 598-1200 • French Quarter Zone 1

Reservations Accepted **When to go** Anytime **Entrée range** $14–$30 **Payment** AE, DC, MC, V **Service rating** ★★★★ **Friendliness rating** ★★★★ **Parking** Pay parking lots nearby **Bar** Full bar **Wine selection** Good wine list, mostly Californian **Dress** Dressy casual **Disabled access** Full **Customers** A mix of locals and visitors, with a sizable local lunch crowd

Lunch Daily, 11 a.m.–3 p.m.

Dinner Daily, 5–11 p.m.

Setting & atmosphere What once was the menswear section of a department store looks like it was hit by a bomb, then painted over. Walls, floors, and tabletops are fancifully decorated by artist Luis Colmenares in a way that almost suggests a slick chain restaurant, but this is the one and only.

House specialties Coconut shrimp; shrimp rémoulade with fried green tomatoes; oysters three ways; red bean soup; crabmeat-stuffed shrimp; hickory-grilled redfish; oyster-crusted redfish; sweet potato catfish; chocolate bread pudding.

Summary & comments The decoration as well as the name tell you the specialty is seafood. But this casual place has ambitions well above those of the standard fried-fish place. The owner is Ralph Brennan, who started Mr. B's and Bacco before dreaming the Red Fish up. The namesake dish—grilled redfish—is seared over an all-wood fire, which cooks up a lot of other tasty dishes here, too. Appetizers are not to be missed, particularly the unique preparations of oysters and shrimp. The menu is decidedly New Orleans in taste, and, the cute descriptions notwithstanding, represents a talented kitchen.

Rene Bistrot ★★★

FRENCH | MODERATE | QUALITY ★★★ | VALUE ★★★

817 Common; 412-2580 • Central Business District Zone 2

Reservations Recommended **When to go** Anytime **Entrée range** $12–$23 **Payment** All major credit cards **Service rating** ★★★ **Friendliness rating** ★★★ **Parking** Free valet parking in Renaissance Hotel **Bar** Full bar **Wine selection** Good wine list **Dress** Dressy casual **Disabled access** Full **Customers** Professionals at lunch; locals and a few hotel guests at dinner; pre-theatre crowd

Breakfast Daily, 7–10 a.m.

Lunch Daily, 11:30 a.m.–3 p.m.

Dinner Daily, 6–10 p.m.

Setting & atmosphere The tiles and rectangularity suggest the modernism of the 1950s. The room reminds me of a minimized version of the Four Seasons restaurant in Manhattan. The theatres for music and big performances are very nearby, and this makes a good place to stop and eat beforehand.

House specialties Roasted oysters with leeks; mussels Basquaise; foie gras with white truffle flan; salade Niçoise; sweetbreads with morels; braised veal cheeks with garlic potatoes; sautéed skate with artichoke; tuna Rossini; rotisserie chicken or duck; daily table d'hôte lunches; chèvre cheesecake with poached pears.

Summary & comments French Chef Rene Bajeux departed the Windsor Court Hotel to open his entry in the currently popular French bistro trend. Ducks, chickens, roasts, and even fish rotate on rotisseries; these produce some of the best food in the house. The plats du jour are the next-best bets, along with any kind of offbeat fish or meat that the service staff might seem enthusiastic about. At its best, this place serves terrific food, but this is not a consistent thing.

RioMar ★★★★

SEAFOOD | MODERATE | QUALITY ★★★ | VALUE ★★★

800 S. Peters; 525-3474 • Central Business District Zone 2

Reservations Recommended **When to go** Anytime **Entrée range** $13–$22 **Payment** All major credit cards **Service rating** ★★★ **Friendliness rating** ★★★ **Parking** Pay parking lots nearby **Bar** Full bar **Wine selection** Good wine list, with Spanish wines a specialty, many by the glass **Dress** Dressy casual **Disabled access** Full **Customers** A mix of locals and people attending events at nearby Morial Convention Center

Lunch Monday–Friday, 11:30 a.m.–2 p.m.

Dinner Monday–Saturday, 6–10 p.m.

Setting & atmosphere The dining rooms are spare but attractive, with most surfaces made of concrete or stucco.

House specialties Seviche; mussels with chorizo; grilled giant squid; xarzuela; seafood romesco; "unilateral" salmon; steak with chimichurri sauce; hanger steak; arroz con anything; tres leches.

Summary & comments Chef-owner Adolfo Garcia is an Orleanian, but his family is from Panama, and his career has been marked by an interest in the entire range of Hispanic cuisines. RioMar's main theme is seafood, but it differs dramatically from other seafood specialists around town in a) offering nothing fried and b) focusing on the flavors of Central America and Spain. RioMar always has at least four distinct preparations of seviche, for example. The chef also likes to find and experiment with little-seen species; razor clams are a big deal here when he can get them. There's a little beef and sausage and chicken, but you should come here with an appetite for fish.

Ristorante Filippo ★★★

ITALIAN | MODERATE | QUALITY ★★★½ | VALUE ★★★

1917 Ridgelake; 835-4008 • Metairie below Causeway Zone 9

Reservations Recommended **When to go** Anytime **Entrée range** $12–$20 **Payment** AE, DC, MC, V **Service rating** ★★★ **Friendliness rating** ★★★★ **Parking** Small parking lot adjacent **Bar** Full bar **Wine selection** Good wine list **Dress** Dressy casual **Disabled access** Limited **Customers** Metairie professionals at lunch; small coterie of regulars sharing secrets at dinner

Lunch Monday–Friday, 11:30 a.m.–2 p.m.

Lunch & dinner Tuesday–Saturday, 6–10 p.m.

Setting & atmosphere Nothing about the utilitarian exterior suggests the intimate, casually elegant dining rooms inside. The owner was an interior designer before he became a chef.

House specialties Oysters al oreganate; mussels marinara; house soup; pasta aglio olio; pork chop; chicken speidini; veal Sorrentino; fish specials. tiramisu.

Summary & comments In a funny location that's easy to see but hard to get to, Phil Gagliano cooks a wide-ranging menu of smart, well-buffed Italian dishes. Although he's a native, his food relies more on herbs, olive oil, and careful roasting than red sauces and melted cheese. This comes as a surprise to first-timers, who size the place up as a neighborhood meatball-and-spaghetti house from the exterior. The well-spoken Gagliano runs not only the kitchen but the dining room, and he visits all his customers and caters to their desires.

Ruth's Chris Steak House   ★★★★

STEAK | VERY EXPENSIVE | QUALITY ★★★½ | VALUE ★★

711 N. Broad; 486-0810 • Mid-City/Gentilly Zone 6
3633 Veterans Boulevard; 888-3600 • Metairie above Causeway/Kenner/
  Jefferson Zone 10

Reservations Accepted **When to go** Anytime **Entrée range** $16–$32 **Payment** All major credit cards **Service rating** ★★★★ **Friendliness rating** ★★★★ **Parking** Valet (free) **Bar** Full bar **Wine selection** Substantial list, heavily tilted toward the red end of the spectrum, from all over the world. Nothing extraordinary, though, which is just as well because they don't handle wine well here. **Dress** Dressy casual **Disabled access** Full **Customers** Politicians, media figures, professionals, couples at dinner

Lunch & dinner Sunday–Friday, 11:30 a.m.–11 p.m.; Saturday, 4–11 p.m.

Setting & atmosphere The Ruth's Chris chain started in New Orleans, but the two local outlets have been largely homogenized into the standard chain look. The dining room has a masculine, clubby feel, with well-padded tables either out in the middle of things or secluded, as customers' needs be.

House specialties Shrimp rémoulade; stuffed mushrooms; salad with Creole French dressing; filet mignon; New York strip; porterhouse for two; lamb chops; veal chops; pork chop (lunch only); boiled lobster; Lyonnaise potatoes; French fries; baked potato; bread pudding; cheesecakes.

Summary & comments During the current resurgence of interest in top-notch beef, Ruth's Chris rides higher than ever. Long the dominant steakhouse in New Orleans, it's also now a major player nationally. What you get is a top-grade, fresh, dry-aged steak from rigorously selective sources, brought to something like the temperature you ordered in a superheated broiler. It is rendered sinful and irresistibly aromatic by the addition of bubbling butter, the traditional New Orleans abetment to steak. Also here are big lobsters, great lamb and veal chops, and thick flanks of salmon. Side dishes are prosaic but prepared well. Service is effective but unceremonious. Regulars favor one location or the other, but both locations are equally good.

Sabai Thai Cuisine ★★★

THAI | INEXPENSIVE | QUALITY ★★★ | VALUE ★★★★★

550 Gretna Boulevard #16; 367-2810 • West Bank Zone 11

Reservations Accepted **When to go** Anytime **Entrée range** $6–$12
Payment All major credit cards **Service rating** ★★★ **Friendliness rating** ★★★
Parking Ample parking lot adjacent **Bar** Full bar **Wine selection** A few house
wines **Dress** Casual **Disabled access** Full **Customers** West Bank people and
fans of Asian food

Lunch & dinner Daily, 11:30 a.m.–10 p.m.

Setting & atmosphere The single room was adapted from an old taco shop,
painted white, and decorated with a restrained amount of Thai art. Pleasant and
clean.

House specialties Thai spring rolls; stuffed chicken wings; shrimp toast; clay
pot shrimp; beef musaman curry; panang curry; green curry with chicken and
eggplant; whole steamed fish; pad Thai.

Summary & comments A "sabai" is the name of a sash worn by Thai women;
it's what the statue is wearing. The family that operates Sabai takes a less West-
ernized approach to its cooking, even when it seems to go against their customers'
habits. Many dishes here are served with a far greater liquid component than is
seen in other Thai restaurants, such that many Americans might interpret them
as soups. Get past that, and you'll find great flavors and expert cooking. They
have a greater than average range in the Thai curry department. At lunch, ask for
the dinner menu, which is already a bargain.

Sake Café ★★★★

JAPANESE | MODERATE–EXPENSIVE | QUALITY ★★★½ | VALUE ★★★

2830 Magazine; 894-0033 • Uptown below Napoleon Zone 3
817 West Esplanade Avenue; 468-8829 • Metairie above Causeway/Kenner/
   Jefferson Zone 10
4201 Veterans Boulevard ; 779-7253 • Metairie above Causeway/Kenner/
   Jefferson Zone 10

Reservations Accepted **When to go** Anytime **Entrée range** $8–$17
Payment All major credit cards **Service rating** ★★★ **Friendliness rating** ★★★
Parking Ample parking lot adjacent **Bar** Full bar **Wine selection** Good wine list
Dress Casual **Disabled access** Full **Customers** Suburban Gen-X-ers and other
sushi buffs

Lunch & dinner Daily, 11:30 a.m.–10 p.m.

Setting & atmosphere The Sake Café is hidden in a corner of a strip mall otherwise populated by the likes of Houston's and Chili's. So its good looks come as
a surprise. It is the handsomest Japanese restaurant we've seen in our town so far,
with a cool sophistication.

House specialties Seaweed salad; salmon skin salad; shu-mai; oshitashi
(steamed spinach with bonito flakes); sushi and sashimi; negimaki (grilled beef
rolls); bento box dinners.

Summary & comments The environment signals the most ambitious kind of dining, and the kitchen is up to the task. The uncommonly large menu moves in arenas of Japanese cooking few other places trouble with. The intrinsic merit of the sushi fish is clearly good, and this extends throughout the menu. The staff works more along the lines of Western service, and is forthcoming and knowledgeable. And, as you might imagine, the sake selection is pretty good. The wine collection, too.

Sal & Judy's ★★★★

ITALIAN | MODERATE | QUALITY ★★★ | VALUE ★★★

27491 U.S. 190; (985) 882-9443 • North Shore Zone 12

Reservations Not accepted **When to go** Weeknights **Entrée range** $10–$19 **Payment** AE, DS, MC, V **Service rating** ★★ **Friendliness rating** ★★★ **Parking** Ample parking lot adjacent **Bar** Full bar **Wine selection** Limited list of Italian wines **Dress** Casual **Disabled access** Limited **Customers** North Shore people, families

Lunch & dinner Sunday, noon–10 p.m.

Dinner Wednesday–Saturday, 5:30–10 p.m.

Setting & atmosphere After decades as a dump way out on the highway, Sal and Judy's is now a conventionally nice-looking Italian restaurant—but still way out on the highway. Always a wait for a table, but everybody knows everybody else.

House specialties Fettuccine Alfredo; stuffed artichoke (with bread crumbs and garlic); fried calamari; baked oysters Cinisi (mushrooms and Italian sausage); trout Jimmy (with artichokes and lemon); soft-shell crabs; spaghetti aglio olio with Italian sausage and roasted peppers; spaghetti with oysters; cheesecake; gelato.

Summary & comments Sal & Judy's is one of the best and most popular restaurants on the North Shore. Sal Impastato's menu incorporates many New Orleans tastes as well as basic Italian ideas, and the result is a palette of food so appealing that it's easy to understand why it's tough to get a table here. The large portions on the absurdly small plates and the low prices also have something to do with this. The printed menu is unimpressive, but the specials provide very good eating, mostly of the veal and seafood.

Shogun ★★★

JAPANESE | INEXPENSIVE–MODERATE | QUALITY ★★★ | VALUE ★★★

2325 Veterans Boulevard; 833-7477 • Metairie below Causeway Zone 9

Reservations Not accepted **When to go** Anytime **Entrée range** $8–$20 **Payment** All major credit cards **Service rating** ★★★ **Friendliness rating** ★★★ **Parking** Ample parking lot adjacent **Bar** Full bar **Wine selection** A few house wines **Dress** Casual **Disabled access** Full **Customers** Locals, singles; families at the teppan-yaki tables

Lunch Sunday–Thursday, 11:30 a.m.–2:30 p.m.

Lunch & dinner Friday and Saturday, 11:30 a.m.–10 p.m.

Dinner Sunday–Thursday, 6–10 p.m.

Setting & atmosphere Three restaurants in one: a large sushi bar, an area of Benihana-style hibachi tables, and conventional tables.

House specialties Baked seafood appetizer; gyoza; red miso soup; sushi and sashimi; teishoku (box) dinners; shabu shabu (thinly sliced beef quickly boiled at the table); seafood nabe.

Summary & comments Shogun was the first successful sushi bar in the area, and remains very busy. The oversized sushi bar has a wider assortment than most others around. At the teppan-yaki tables, Shogun's showy chefs grill steak and shrimp and all that; it's a good show the first time, ordinary thereafter. At the standard tables you can get the entire range of Japanese cookery. The most interesting are the teishoku lunches and the boiled meat or seafood dinners prepared at the table. You can also get a kaiseki, the elaborate many-course formal dinner, with advance notice.

Steak Knife ★★★

STEAK | MODERATE–EXPENSIVE | QUALITY ★★★ | VALUE ★★★

888 Harrison Avenue; 488-8981 • Lakeview/West End/Bucktown Zone 7

Reservations Recommended **When to go** Weeknights; early-evening period is a good deal but very busy **Entrée range** $13–$27 **Payment** AE, MC, V **Service rating** ★★★ **Friendliness rating** ★★★★ **Parking** Valet (free) **Bar** Full bar **Wine selection** Decent list, good international balance; many by-the-glass selections **Dress** Dressy casual **Disabled access** Full **Customers** Neighborhood people, couples, families

Dinner Sunday–Thursday, 6–10 p.m.; Friday and Saturday, 6–11 p.m.

Setting & atmosphere Most of the tables are in the paneled environment of a former bank. The manager's office is a good private room.

House specialties Crabmeat au gratin; shrimp rémoulade; coconut beer-battered shrimp; cream of crabmeat soup; seraphine salad (avocado, asparagus, hearts of palm, artichokes, and greens); filet mignon; strip sirloin; lamb chops with mint demi-glace; roasted chicken with rosemary and mushrooms; chocolate mousse; bread pudding.

Summary & comments The Steak Knife has been an upscale Lakeview neighborhood hangout for decades. When it moved across the street into much grander digs, it became a more ambitious, livelier place. It's still the beef specialist that its name implies, but the menu now encompasses a broad range of foodstuffs. Nothing here is either especially original or the best of its kind, but everything is prepared consistently well using fine raw materials. Some of the side dishes are inspired. Good service except during the early-evening mob scene.

Stella! ★★★★

ECLECTIC | EXPENSIVE | QUALITY ★★★½ | VALUE ★★

1032 Chartres; 587-0091 • French Quarter Zone 1

Reservations Recommended **When to go** Dinner **Entrée range** $22–$32 **Payment** All major credit cards **Service rating** ★★ **Friendliness rating** ★★ **Parking** Free valet parking **Bar** Full bar **Wine selection** Good wine list, including many selections by the glass **Dress** Jacket recommended but not required **Disabled access** Full **Customers** A blend of local gourmets and visitors who happen to stumble onto the place

Dinner Wednesday–Monday, 6–10 p.m.

Setting & atmosphere Enclosed by but not part of the Provincial Hotel, Stella! has two dining rooms flanking the carriageway of a very old French Quarter mansion. The dining room nearer the street is smaller and isolated, but overlooks the street and a row of townhouses. Missing: a guy yelling "Stella!"

House specialties Lobster gnocchi; risotto; Oriental appetizer assortment; duck breast with foie gras wontons; scallops and shrimp with caviar butter; lobster-scented fish; rack of lamb with sweetbreads and prosciutto; morel-crusted breast and confit leg of pheasant; bananas Foster French toast.

Summary & comments Chef-owner Scott Boswell is one of a brilliant group of chefs who worked together at the Windsor Court a decade ago, then went on to run their own personal kitchens in other restaurants. Boswell's style blends local ingredients, flavors, and techniques with those of nearly all the rest of the world, with particular attention to Italy, France, and Japan. What results is original, artfully turned out food whose only flaw is an occasional recurrence of the undercooking habits of the late 1990s. The chef vacillates on his offer to do a tasting menu, but if it's on, that's a great way to eat here.

Trey Yuen ★★★

CHINESE | INEXPENSIVE–MODERATE | QUALITY ★★★½ | VALUE ★★

600 Causeway Boulevard; 985-626-4476 • North Shore Zone 12

Reservations Not accepted **When to go** Weeknights **Entrée range** $11–$24 **Payment** All major credit cards **Service rating** ★★★ **Friendliness rating** ★★★★ **Parking** Ample parking lot adjacent **Bar** Full bar **Wine selection** Decent list, emphasis on California **Dress** Casual **Disabled access** Full **Customers** North Shore people, families

Lunch Wednesday–Friday, 11:30 a.m.–2 p.m.

Lunch & dinner Sunday, 11:30 a.m.–10 p.m.

Dinner Tuesday–Thursday, 6–10 p.m.; Friday and Saturday, 6–11 p.m.

Setting & atmosphere A large, airy rotunda suggests a temple from the outside, an effect compounded by the well-kept gardens that surround the restaurant. Busy and a little noisy inside.

House specialties Spring rolls; pot stickers; hot and sour soup; seafood with tong cho sauce; wor shu op; satay squid; shrimp in a cloud; lobster with black bean sauce; scallops Imperial; Presidential chicken; spicy lemon chicken; steak kew; lotus banana; ice cream.

Summary & comments This striking Chinese palace turned the Asian restaurant scene around when it opened in 1981. The surroundings, service, and food were way above what most of us were used to. That resulted in a degree of popularity that makes dining here occasionally inconvenient. Seafood is a particular strength, but they cook everything well. The wines and desserts are far above Chinese-restaurant standards. One wishes that the Wong brothers would up the ante again, but they seem to be comfortable with the way things are. Service is unceremonious and sometimes can bog down when the place is busy—which it often is.

201 Restaurant and Bar ★★★

CONTEMPORARY CREOLE | MODERATE–EXPENSIVE | QUALITY ★★★½ | VALUE ★★★

201 Decatur; 561-0007 • French Quarter Zone 1

Reservations Accepted **When to go** Dinner **Entrée range** $16–$26 **Payment** All major credit cards **Service rating** ★★★ **Friendliness rating** ★★★ **Parking** Pay parking lots nearby **Bar** Full bar **Wine selection** Good wine list, including many by the glass **Dress** Casual **Disabled access** Limited **Customers** A mix of visitors and locals early; later, waiters and bartenders come in from other Quarter restaurants

Dinner Sunday–Thursday, 6–11 p.m.; Friday and Saturday, 6 p.m.–midnight.

Setting & atmosphere The one spacious room could be cast in a movie as the lobby of a bordello. Big double-hung windows open onto both Iberville and Decatur streets and their constant pedestrian traffic. Very casual, with a busy bar.

House specialties Barbecue shrimp; steamed mussels with saffron tomato broth; grilled quail with pears; baked oysters of the day; crab and oyster-stuffed shrimp; pasta with wild mushrooms, asparagus and truffle oil; grilled pork tenderloin with blackberry sauce; crème brûlée with berries.

Summary & comments The premises feel more like a hangout than a serious restaurant, and when the bar fills up it's noisy. But that only makes what the kitchen does into a pleasant surprise. The chef is enormously creative without leaving the precincts of familiar Creole bistro food, and his presentations and ingredients leave nothing wanting. The service staff is very friendly and well-informed, even about the ample assortment of wines by the glass. 201 stays open later than most full-service places—till midnight on Friday and Saturday.

Uglesich's ★★★

SEAFOOD | INEXPENSIVE–MODERATE | QUALITY ★★★ | VALUE ★★

1238 Baronne; 523-8571 • Uptown below Napoleon Zone 3

Reservations Not accepted **When to go** Avoid noon hour **Entrée range** $8–$16 **Payment** Cash only **Service rating** ★★ **Friendliness rating** ★★★★ **Parking** Small parking lot adjacent **Bar** Beer and wine **Wine selection** A few house wines **Dress** Anything goes **Disabled access** Limited **Customers** A mix of locals and tourists, most on the young side; lots of restaurant people

Lunch Monday–Friday, 11:30 a.m.–2:30 p.m.

Setting & atmosphere Uglesich's is a concentrated dose of New Orleans funk—a bit much for some who, after eyeballing the place and its neighborhood, drive on by. There's never an open table when you walk in, but there will be by the time the food comes out.

House specialties Oysters on the half shell; barbecued oysters; shrimp rémoulade on fried green tomatoes; crawfish bisque; grilled fish plate; fried oyster poor boy; roast beef poor boy; French fries; blackboard specials.

Summary & comments Those who seek out Uglesich's are rewarded with food that some gourmet restaurants would do well to imitate. The oyster poor boy, for example, is made from oysters that are not only fried but shucked to order. Anthony and Gail Uglesich have expanded their range far beyond sandwiches in recent years; you can now get an astounding assortment (considering the rudimentary kitchen) of grilled, sautéed, and fried platters, many highly original. Beware: If they tell you something is spicy, believe them. Those raw oysters at the bar are good, too.

Upperline ★★★★

CREOLE | MODERATE–EXPENSIVE | QUALITY ★★★ | VALUE ★★★

1413 Upperline; 891-9822 • Uptown above Napoleon Zone 4

Reservations Recommended **When to go** Anytime; the garlic festival in summer is always interesting **Entrée range** $17–$25 **Payment** All major credit cards **Service rating** ★★★★ **Friendliness rating** ★★★★ **Parking** Small parking lot adjacent **Bar** Full bar **Wine selection** Excellent wine list, with many delightful surprises **Dress** Casual **Disabled access** None **Customers** A mix of locals and tourists; lots of arts crowd, gourmets, and oenophiles

Dinner Wednesday–Sunday, 5:30–10 p.m.

Setting & atmosphere The original dining room—inherited from an old neighborhood café—flows into an adjacent cottage to make a string of small dining rooms. All are filled with artworks, with primitive and folk artists dominating the theme.

House specialties Fried green tomatoes with shrimp rémoulade; duck gumbo; watercress, Stilton, and pecan salad; onion-crusted fish with tapenade and mustard and fennel sauce; shrimp curry with jasmine rice; rack of lamb with mint and Madeira; filet mignon with garlic port sauce; roast duck with ginger peach sauce; garlic-stuffed pork tenderloin; pecan pie; double chocolate Amaretto mousse.

Summary & comments One of the original gourmet Creole bistros that changed the dining scene in the 1980s, the Upperline's greatest asset is the fertile mind of owner JoAnn Clevenger. Eating here is to open oneself to a barrage of her creative statements about art, drama, literature . . . and, yes, food, too. Her most famous culinary idea is the summer-long garlic menu, but there's almost always a festival of something or other here. Not everything is offbeat: The Upperline's menu is full of classic Creole dishes, including a tasting menu of traditional local dishes. Prices are lower than you'd expect, and the wine list much more impressive. Never a dull moment here.

Vega Tapas Café ★★★

MEDITERRANEAN | INEXPENSIVE–MODERATE | QUALITY ★★★½ | VALUE ★★★

2051 Metairie Road; 836-2007 • Metairie below Causeway Zone 9

Reservations Accepted **When to go** Anytime **Entrée range** $7–$15 **Payment** All major credit cards **Service rating** ★★★ **Friendliness rating** ★★★★ **Parking** Small parking lot adjacent **Bar** Full bar **Wine selection** Modest list of wines matched to food **Dress** Casual **Disabled access** Full **Customers** Younger, more adventuresome gourmets

Dinner Monday–Thursday, 5–10 p.m.; Friday and Saturday, 5–11 p.m.

Setting & atmosphere One long room is broken up by wait stations into semi-discrete areas. The lights are dim, and the environment seems perfect for a first date.

House specialties Carp roe dip; roasted beet and goat cheese salad; smoked salmon and avocado salad; sweetbreads with crimini mushrooms; wild mushroom risotto with white truffle oil; seared scallops with polenta; Moorish pork; paella; smoked duck breast with couscous; marinated shrimp, calamari, and baby octopus.

Summary & comments Allison Vega cheffed in a number of with-it cafés around town before opening her own place. Although it's billed as a tapas restaurant, Vega's offerings are more substantial than the traditional Spanish one-or-two-bite dishes. Almost everything is the size of a large appetizer or small entrée. The variety of flavors, textures, and ingredients makes for fascinating ordering and eating, especially with a group of friends. While some of the food has a Spanish taste, inspirations come from all over the place. The menu changes frequently enough to make this a fun place to explore with some frequency. All the food is fresh, imaginative, and well turned out.

Victor's ★★★★

ECLECTIC | VERY EXPENSIVE | QUALITY ★★★½ | VALUE ★★

921 Canal; 524-1331 • French Quarter Zone 1

Reservations Recommended **When to go** Anytime **Entrée range** Table d'hôte, $65–$115 **Payment** All major credit cards **Service rating** ★★★★★ **Friendliness rating** ★★★★★ **Parking** Free valet parking **Bar** Full bar **Wine selection** Excellent wine list, including many selections by the glass **Dress** Jacket recommended but not required **Disabled access** Full **Customers** Hotel guests and local gourmets at the most ambitious level

Breakfast Daily, 7–10 a.m.

Lunch Monday–Friday, 11:30 a.m.–2 p.m.

Dinner Every night, 6–10 p.m.

Setting & atmosphere Two walls of windows to the lobby give the room a wide-open quality. A pair of very private dining cloisters (you can close the curtains if you like) grant the ultimate in exclusivity. All furnishings are the best of their kind: flowers, napery, silverware, china.

House specialties Menu changes unpredictably every day.

Entertainment & amenities A light jazz trio with a vocalist plays in the lounge just outside the dining room..

Summary & comments Victor's is the culinary buzz generator for the new Ritz-Carlton Hotel. Although it's named for a historic New Orleans restaurant from the late 1800s, there's nothing either traditional or New Orleans about it. You choose from an assortment of table d'hôte repasts, ranging from six to ten courses. The courses, however, are about the size of tapas, inspiring many diners to focus on the tininess of the portions. By dinner's end you will have had enough to eat, and the many different places the chef took you will fill your soul, too. The menu changes daily, with the only predictable aspect being that the ingredients will be unusual and almost never from the local area. You can arrange to have any dinner accompanied by wines on a course-by-course basis, and the master wine book shows a well-stocked cellar of full bottles. All of this largesse is supplied by a staff that, on principle, will satisfy your any need. Of course, you will pay for all this. But all the elements are here for a special celebration or an advance in your state of gourmandise.

Vincent's ★★★

ITALIAN | INEXPENSIVE–MODERATE | QUALITY ★★★ | VALUE ★★★

7839 St. Charles Avenue; 866-9313 • Uptown above Napoleon Zone 4
4411 Chastant Street; 885-2984 • Metairie above Causeway/Kenner/Jefferson Zone 10
4250 Louisiana 22, Suite B; (985) 624-2300 • North Shore Zone 12

Reservations Not accepted **When to go** Anytime **Entrée range** $10–$21 **Payment** All major credit cards **Service rating** ★★ **Friendliness rating** ★★★★ **Parking** Curbside parking only **Bar** Full bar **Wine selection** A few house wines **Dress** Casual **Disabled access** Limited **Customers** Neighborhood people, college students

Lunch Tuesday–Friday, 11:30 a.m.–2:30 p.m.
Dinner Tuesday–Sunday, 6–10 p.m.

Setting & atmosphere All three locations of Vincent's are casual neighborhood cafés. The uptown and Metairie locations are the most utilitarian; in Mandeville, they accidentally made the place look a little nice.

House specialties Eggplant sandwich; artichoke Vincent (with crawfish and shrimp); veal meatballs on garlic toast; corn and crab bisque en croûte; veal cannelloni in a crêpe; soft-shell crab with tomato garlic sauce; pannéed fish with crab cream sauce; garlic chicken; braciolone; veal Florentine; osso buco; tiramisu; chocolate mousse cake; torroncino ice cream.

Summary & comments Vincent Catalanotto, a former waiter, discovered he could cook as well as any of the chefs who shouted at him. So he opened this unpretentious side-street café and started cooking some of the most impressive food ever sold at prices this low. The style is Creole-Italian, with enough polish that it could be sold in a much more expensive restaurant. Seafood is especially fine, served with terrific and original sauces. Salad, vegetable, and dessert courses are less impressive, but hardly grounds for complaining. The service staff is chummy. Problem: getting a table, particularly on weekends, is a tough deal. If you're in the mood for a raunchy but funny joke, ask for Vincent.

Wolfe's of New Orleans ★★★★

CONTEMPORARY CREOLE | MODERATE–EXPENSIVE | QUALITY ★★★½ | VALUE ★★★

7224 Pontchartrain Boulevard; 284-6004 • Lakeview/West End/Bucktown Zone 7

Reservations Required for dinner **When to go** Dinner **Entrée range** $16–$28 **Payment** AE, MC, V **Service rating** ★★★ **Friendliness rating** ★★★★ **Parking** Free lot adjacent **Bar** Full bar **Wine selection** Decent list, emphasis on California; many by-the-glass selections **Dress** Casual **Disabled access** None **Customers** Couples and foursomes of gourmets

Lunch Monday–Friday, 11:30 a.m.–2 p.m.

Dinner Monday–Saturday, 5:30–10 p.m.

Setting & atmosphere The restaurant is an appealing cottage near the West End Marina. The dining room was made by opening up two parlors around a fireplace, and furnishing it with handsome contemporary tables and chairs: very comfortable. In pleasant weather, you can dine on the porch in front.

House specialties Gumbo of the day; shrimp and celery root rémoulade; grilled scallops; crab cakes; baked oysters three ways; filet mignon with three-potato gratin; cane syrup roast duck; panco crusted redfish; lamb or pork chops; white chocolate butter bars.

Summary & comments Chef Tom Wolfe became well known at Emeril's, where he cooked many a meal for that restaurant's patrons at the food bar. In 2000 he took over this little spot in West End and started cooking. His style shows the Emeril influence, with big Louisiana flavors in an original way. Some of the dishes are avant-garde, particularly in their use of too-hip ingredients. Others (the better ones) are modern reworkings of some funky old stuff. All very deftly prepared, generously served, and priced attractively. Service is also more careful than one ordinarily finds in Creole bistros.

Part Ten

Shopping in New Orleans

Probably the only reason visitors to New Orleans spend any less time shopping than they do eating and drinking is that the stores tend to close earlier—and even at that, you'll find a surprising number of merchants open until 8 or even 10 p.m. After all, trade and conspicuous consumption are at the heart of New Orleans history. In the mid-18th century, it was the third-busiest port in the United States and had the highest per capita income of any city in the country, according to some figures.

So you can easily shop until you drop. Stores and galleries are abundant in the Vieux Carré, making for spectacular window shopping, and that can be the danger as well. Just as there is a tendency to keep eating because you can smell all that food around you, there's a tendency to keep falling in love with jewelry and posters and rings and masks. (And remember, alcohol loosens your inhibitions, including the financial ones.) If you have a budget, or if you are looking for something particular, it's best to know in advance where you want to go, or you might get sidetracked.

Also, if you think of shopping by "type"—high-end antiques or specialty stores, upscale supermalls or souvenir troves—you can head to the neighborhood with the most options. If you have a couple of days to spare, then you can range a little farther, but even then, if you don't have a background in antiques, a knowledgeable companion, or a friend who lives in town, you're probably not going to stumble onto a hidden treasure.

Among the neighborhoods with good browsing are the most famous shopping strip in New Orleans, Royal Street; the entire riverfront strip from the Farmers Market to the Convention Center; and Magazine Street, uptown from Canal over to Audubon Park. You might also enjoy the somewhat more relaxed **Riverbend District** in Carrollton, which you can stroll as part of the St. Charles streetcar tour (see Part Eight, Sight-Seeing, Tours, and Attractions).

Incidentally, sales tax in New Orleans is 9%, so if what you're buying is large, you might consider having it shipped to you; the handling charge may well be less than the tax. If you are visiting from another country, you can take advantage of Louisiana's Tax-Free Shopping, although this will mean carrying your passport (or at least a good photocopy) with you instead of putting it in the hotel vault; Canadian visitors may bring a driver's license or birth certificate. Here's how it works: If the store posts an LTFS sticker (or ask at the counter), show the passport and ask for the special refund voucher. You'll still pay the tax, but when you get to the airport, stop by the LTFS counter—in the main lobby across from the American Airlines counter—and show them your receipts *and* refund vouchers. Up to $100 will be refunded in cash, up to $500 by check; anything over $500 will be mailed to your home. You will have to pay a handling fee of $18 for refunds up to $1,000, or $30 for refunds up to $2,000, to a maximum fee of $75. For more information, call 467-0723.

The French Quarter

As Bourbon Street is to nightlife, so **Royal Street** is to antiques—and if it's not there, it's probably on Chartres. That's an exaggeration, of course, but the Royal antiques row goes back several generations, on both the selling and buying sides. Royal Street makes for the most riveting window-shopping in the city: cases of earrings, necklaces, cufflinks, and enamels; chandeliers and candelabra; gold leaf, crystal, and silver; china dolls; silver-headed walking sticks; and sterling cigarette cases, all glittering with the mystique of Creole culture. Some of these stores advertise all over the country (which is a consideration that cuts both ways—somebody has to pay for all that publicity); still others capitalize on Royal Street's reputation to embellish both the value and the actual cost of their goods.

Many hotels and visitors centers carry a brochure produced by the Royal Street Guild that lists members (or call the guild at 524-1260), but the choices are almost overwhelming, so visitors should start with these reputable dealers: One of the oldest names in the antiques game here is **Keil's** (325 Royal Street, 522-4552), founded before the turn of the 19th century and still among the best choices for French and English art and furnishings, chandeliers, and decorative arts. It remains a family concern, and other stores in the clan's hands are **Royal Antiques** (307–309 Royal Street, 524-7033), its annex around the corner (715 Bienville Street), and **Moss Antiques** (411 Royal Street, 522-3981). Another good spot is the **French Antique Shop** (225 Royal Street, 524-9861). Its collection of bronzes, chandeliers, and Baccarat crystal loom out of the dark to draw you in. Peter Patout specializes in French and American antiques and decorative arts (920 Royal Street, 522-0582).

For Asian art and antiquities, contact **Diane Genre,** a member of the International Association of Appraisers and a specialist in Japanese woodblock prints, temple carvings, lacquer work, and extraordinary Japanese and Chinese textiles, including such gold- and silver-embroidered dragons as would bring your fantasies to life. She has closed her retail store but is working out of an apartment showroom overlooking Royal; call for an appointment (595-8945).

If you're interested in fine estate jewelry, **Ida Manheim Antiques** (409 Royal Street, 620-4114) specializes in 17th-, 18th-, and 19th-century mantels, chandeliers, and bronze and marble statuary. Or consult Nancy Kittay, who runs her jewelry business, specializing in Victorian and Early American pieces, from inside **Waldhorn & Adler** (343 Royal Street, 581-6379).

This used to be the financial heart of the Vieux Carré, and several of the old financial institutions are into their second lives as antiques stores. The Waldhorn building, for example, served as the Bank of the United States in 1800, and the former Manheim Galleries building at Royal and Conti Streets was designed in 1818 by Benjamin Latrobe as the Louisiana State Bank.

For the hostess with the mostest, nothing could be more fun than a lesson in preparing an absinthe cocktail—the sharp-tipped, perforated absinthe spoons range from $65–$125—from Patrick Dunne, proprietor of **Lucullus** (610 Chartres, 528-9620). Lucius Licinius Lucullus was a famous Roman epicure, and Dunne's shop stocks cookware, silver, and culinary objets d'art dating to the 17th century.

The old **M.S. Rau** store has taken to offering one-day "specials," à la the Manhattan merchants, on such items as walking sticks (many of them hiding rapiers), music boxes, and decanters; pick the right day, and you might pick a prize (630 Royal Street, 523-5660).

Really serious collectors should be aware of the seasonal and special sales at the **New Orleans Auction Galleries** located upstairs at 801 Magazine Street (call 566-1849), although it's a few blocks outside the French Quarter.

Kurt E. Schon, Ltd. (510 St. Louis, 524-5462) has what he advertises as the largest inventory of 19th-century European paintings in this country, particularly featuring works by Impressionist, Post-Impressionist, French Salon, and Royal Academy artists, and the price tags are as breathtaking as the collection. (If your budget only goes up to $100,000 or so, don't even attempt the six floors of private showrooms, open by appointment only.) If you love the styles, but can't quite afford the Schon prices, try the Vincent Mann Gallery (713 Bienville Street, 523-2342), which specializes in the second rank, but high second rank, of predominantly French Post-Impressionists.

Books, Records, and Prints

Not surprisingly, a literary town like New Orleans is rich in bookstores, particularly those specializing in out-of-print titles, first editions, and rare publications. **Faulkner House Books** is in the building overlooking St. Anthony's garden, where William Faulkner lived while writing *Soldier's Pay* and various short stories set in New Orleans. It naturally features first editions of his works and other titles important to Southern literature (624 Pirate's Alley, 524-2940). The house where Tennessee Williams wrote *A Streetcar Named Desire,* coincidentally, is right through Exchange Alley, in the next block, at 632 St. Peter Street.

Other good bookshops in the Quarter, especially for those who love to linger among the shelves, include **Beckham's** (228 Decatur Street, 522-9875) and its sibling **Librarie** (823 Chartres Street, 525-4837); the scholarly **Crescent City Books** (204 Chartres Street, 524-4997); **Arcadian Books and Art Prints** (714 Orleans Street, 523-4138); and **Dauphine Street Books** (410 Dauphine Street, 529-2333).

At the north end of the Quarter is **Kitchen Witch** (1214 North Rampart Street, 569-8450), a collection of used and vintage cookbooks. Hours vary, so it's best to call ahead.

Faubourg Marigny Bookstore, on Frenchman Street at Chartres (943-9875), specializes in gay, lesbian, and feminist literature. Most of these stores belong to an association of antiquarian and second-hand booksellers, and any one of them can give you a list and a simple map of the others. In the same way, a musical town like this is a great place to dig up old recordings. For jazz (mostly re-recorded and available on cassette or CD), stop by the shop at the **Old U.S. Mint** on Esplanade.

New converts to the regional sounds of jazz, zydeco, Cajun, blues, swamp pop, and gospel sounds may also want to flip through the 25,000 albums at **Louisiana Music Factory** (210 Decatur Street, 586-1094). For those just as interested in music memorabilia as the recordings themselves, check out the autographed albums—Sinatra to Stevie Ray Vaughan—at **Vintage 429** (429 Royal Street, 529-2288).

If you're interested in photographs, either vintage or contemporary, **A Gallery of Fine Photography** (322 Royal Street, 568-1313) carries works by such artists as Berenice Abbott, Eadweard Muybridge, Edward Weston, Yousuf Karsh, Edward Steichen, Henri Cartier-Bresson, Diane Arbus, Ansel Adams, and Helmut Newton. For fine mezzotints and other vintage prints, try the **Stone and Press Galleries** (238 Chartres Street, 561-8555). For animation art and limited-edition prints from Jerry Garcia or Ron Wood, visit **America's Gallery** (522 Royal Street, 586-0801).

Stamp collector extraordinaire **Raymond H. Weill** sold his entire collection to a London firm ten years ago for a staggering $14 million, and has been restocking ever since (407 Royal Street, 581-7373).

For maps, fine-art prints, architectural drawings, star charts, medical diagrams, and official documents—layers and layers of them—try the **Centuries Antique Prints and Maps** (517A St. Louis Street, 568-9491).

Other French Quarter Collectibles

Once you get into New Orleans music, you'll want to join the parade. So for a really unusual souvenir, consider a "second-line" umbrella—the ones you see waving behind the band in those parades—or a fine plantation-worthy parasol. **Anne B. Lane** is the Umbrella Lady (1107 Decatur Street, 523-7791), whose fashionable wares can often be seen on the balcony overlooking the street, if she herself is not waving them in an impromptu kick-line. For a hat you can wear to the Ritz or on a Royal Streeet balcony, consult Tracy Thompson of **Kabuki** (1036 Royal Sreet, 523-8004) or **Fleur de Paris** (712 Royal Street, 525-1899). Men can look to the venerable **Meyer the Hatter** (120 St. Charles Avenue, 525-1048) for classic Stetson Panamas.

Weapons and ammunitions—flintlocks, pistols, muzzle loaders, swords, bayonets, sabers, shot, and even cannonballs—are the signature stock at the fourth-generation **James H. Cohen & Sons** (437 Royal Street, 522-3305). The entrance is guarded—perhaps a little cruelly—by a wooden Indian.

For those who prefer their warfare a little less realistic, **Le Petit Soldier Shop** (528 Royal Street—or as they continue to put it, 528 Rue Royale, 523-7741) carries not only vintage lead and more modern toy soldiers of the familiar Civil War and Napoleonic eras, but figures of Sherlock Holmes and Watson, "Kagemusha"-style samurai, Roman emperors, Winston Churchill, and even Hitler, along with service decorations and pilots' wings. For dolls, check out **Boyers Antiques & Doll** shop (241 Chartres Street, 522-4513). For dollhouse furniture and miniatures, stop by Boyers Miniature Shop (330 Chartres Street, 522-4513), the **Black Butterfly** (727 Royal Street, 524-6464), or the Ginja Jar Too (611 Royal Street, 523-7614).

The most fanciful and zoological furniture—alligator fainting couches, zebra side tables, heron-necked CD towers—can be found at **The Private Collection** (1116 Decatur Street, 593-9526) and **Tropical Reflections** (51 French Market, (800) 264-6117). Vintage paintings and ceramics of beloved pets and champions are the attraction at **Animal Art Antiques** (617 Chartres Street, 529-4407).

Great-looking pens can be had for $4 or $5 apiece at the **MMC Enterprises** stand inside the French Market, or call Charles Chen at 433-2838.

George Rodrigue's **Blue Dog paintings,** which refer in part to the old *loup-garou* or werewolf legends of the artist's childhood, have become cult items. His gallery is at 721 Royal Street (581-4244).

What would a trip to the voodoo capital of the country be without a little mysticism? For charms, potions, mojo dolls, and the most atmospheric palm or tarot readings, head to the **New Orleans Historic Voodoo Museum** (724 Dumaine Street, 523-7685), which is more theater than museum; or visit **Marie Laveau's House of Voodoo** (739 Bourbon Street,

581-3751). If you prefer to walk on the sunnier side, the **Bottom of the Cup Tearooms** stock crystals, wrought-iron stands and heavy crystal balls, and scores of tarot decks reproduced from various countries and centuries (732 Royal Street, 523-1204 and 616 Conti Street, 524-1997).

Another New Orleans must is pralines, those brown sugar–pecan sweets. While there are several fine and old confectionaries, the **Old Town Praline Shop** (627 Royal Street, 525-1413) has even more than its candy to recommend it—hometown ladies behind the counter and a lovely courtyard in the back, one of the few still open to visitors and a welcome respite from the shopping grind. French Opera diva Adelina Patti, who set Creole hearts aflame during the 1860 season, used the house as her residence, and photos of her triumphal tour dot the walls.

To check your e-mail over your morning coffee, start at **Royal Blend Tea & Coffee** (621 Royal Street) and then head upstairs to **Royal Access Internet Café** (525-0401). Or try the **Bastille Internate Café** (605 Toulouse, 581-1150); a mere $2.75 gets you 15 minutes of online time.

For neo-Creos who can't live without their morning stogie, there's **Café Havana** (842 Royal Street, 569-9006 or (800) 860-2988); **Crescent City Cigar Shop** (730 Orleans, 522-4427); or **The Epitome** (631 Royal Street, (800) 444-3741 or 523-2844). The cigars aren't truly Cuban, of course, but they are sufficiently showy.

If those frozen-drink bars on Bourbon Street that resemble laundromats aren't your style, or you're invited to someone's house, the selection at **Vieux Carré Wine and Spirits** (422 Chartres, near K-Paul's; 568-9463) is quite good. And they're even open on Sunday. Hey, this is New Orleans, after all.

Although it's now in the Pontalba complex next to the 1850 House, **Bourbon French Perfume** (525 St. Anne Street, 522-4480) used to be on the street it's named for—back in 1843, when it opened. You can either get French scents like those preferred by Creole society (see the super economy-sized bottles in the Hermann-Grima House, for fun) or have one blended for you.

There are masks and Mardi Gras paraphernalia all over, but unless you just want a mass-produced version, head for the **Little Shop of Fantasy** (523 Dumaine Street, 529-4243), which stocks all handmade masks and costumes by about two dozen local artists. This is also where you can get those Victorian stovepipes and ubiquitous *Cat in the Hat* toppers, if you must. Not far away are the elaborate and fantastic leather disguises of Masquerade Fantasy (1233 Decatur Street, 593-9269).

If your boss is the sort of guy who has everything, here are a few leather items that might save you the annual Christmas-list blues: hanging suit bags for $335; golf bags, tooled or smooth, for $495; roll-on suitcases for $265, even cellular phone carriers of various sizes. The smartest idea yet is a leather duffel weekender that folds flat into itself so you can pack it inside another suitcase for souvenirs. All, as well as belts, shoes, totes, and purses, are at **Leather Creations** (837 Decatur Street, 527-0033).

Finally, for those interested in restoring old homes, it's worth heading over to **Architectural Antiques** (4531 North Rampart Street, 942-7000) to look over the mantelpieces, corbels, and columns. **Sigle's Antiques and Metalcraft** is stocked with balcony iron and ornamental hangings and brackets (935 Royal Street, 522-7647). **Bevolo Gas and Electric Lights** has been turning out handmade and hand-riveted lamps, including the gas-look fixtures around Jackson Square, for half a century (521 Conti Street, 522-9485).

(For more architectural and salvage spots, see the description of the Warehouse/Arts District below.)

Magazine Street

In recent years, with rising rents and stiffer competition, many antiques dealers have either moved off the main drag or out of the French Quarter altogether. A number of stores and galleries have opened on **Magazine Street** in the Uptown/University area, and the Magazine Street merchants have been promoting their association with brochures and maps—which brings up a sticky point: there are a great number of interesting stores along Magazine Street, to be sure, but whether it actually makes sense for visitors to the city, especially those staying only a few days, to venture over there is another issue.

For one thing, despite the promotional brochures raving about "six miles of antique shops, art galleries, restaurants, and specialty shops in Historic Uptown New Orleans," the road is still primarily residential; there is a block or two with a lot of stores, and then it may be several blocks before another cluster. If you don't have a car, it's difficult to see more than a few stores at a time. The confusion is increased by the fact that Magazine Street begins in the new Warehouse/Arts District near the Convention Center, so that some visitors believe they can walk to the antiques strip, whereas it's quite a hike to the real clusters.

Second, alongside many of the nicer stores are still lower-scale salvage shops, more like flea market or "granny's-attic" affairs. So if you don't already know something about antiques, and if you aren't willing to spend a couple of hours sorting through showrooms and comparing prices, you may be disappointed.

One possibility is to hire a professional antiquing companion, such as Macon Riddle of **Let's Go Antiquing,** who's made a career of designing half- or full-day shopping tours geared to your interests. For $100 an hour, minimum three hours, you get her expert advice too; call 899-3027 or visit **www.neworleansantiquing.com.** Another possibility is to drive about 45 minutes to Ponchatoula, on the other side of Lake Pontchartrain, which has more than 30 antiques shops at non-Royal prices.

If you do want to go to Magazine, here are a few clusters of specialty shops of particular interest, so you can make at least some sort of park-and-walk visit or walk over from the streetcar without exhausting yourself. Or consult with the Regional Transit Authority about bus routes and VisiTour passes, as described in "Getting Around New Orleans."

Start off near St. Mary Street at **Jim Russell Rare Records** (1837 Magazine Street, 522-2602) for eight-tracks and semi-precious vinyl. Next stop is **Bush Antiques,** which has an amazing assortment of ecclesiastical remnants, so to speak: gilded high altars; heavy bishops' chairs; old chapel statuary, including the Virgin Mary and various saints; iron crucifixes from cemeteries; stained glass; and even vestments (2109–2111 Magazine Street, 581-3518). If you're attracted to the vividly painted bayou folk art of the sort that adorns the House of Blues, be sure to step through to the courtyard for a look at the "studio" there.

Across the street are **Hands** (2042 Magazine Street, 522-2590), where owner Rachel Dalessandro specializes in pre-Columbian art and artifacts as old as 3,000 years (some astonishingly affordable); and **Gerry White Glass** (2036 Magazine Street, 522-3544), the showroom/studio of a man whose custom architectural glass, etched and carved, ranges from tables to standing screens. (The panels in the window, etched to look like venetian blinds, won him his wife.)

The sleazy-chic name of the **House of Lounge** just about says it all, from lingerie to furniture (2044 Magazine Street, 671-8300). A few blocks farther is **George Herget Books,** which is one of the most important rare and secondhand bookstores outside the French Quarter, housing an estimated 20,000 volumes (3109 Magazine Street, 891-5595). Missing that sterling silver fork? **As You Like It** (3038 Magazine Street, 897-6915) has rounded up an array of silver julep cups, antique flatware, candelabras, and the like. **Magazine Arcade Antiques** (3017 Magazine Street, 895-5451) stocks thousands of music boxes, home furnishings, high-end bric-a-brac, porcelain, and cloisonné; and a mix of American, European, and Asian antiques. And if you've got the money, honey, they've got the time: **Kohlmaier and Kohlmaier** (1018 Harmony Street, just off the 3200 block of Magazine Street, 895-6394) specializes in standing and cabinet clocks, mantel clocks, and personal timepieces.

Another few blocks out is a cluster for decorators with an eye for decorative accessories and ethnic and folk arts. Jewelry designers **Katy Bell** (3701 Magazine Street, 896-9600), **Mignon Faget** (3801 Magazine Street, 891-6789), and **Anne Pratt** (3937 Magazine Street, 891-6532) are local artists developing national reputations. And **Neal Auction Co.** at 4038 Magazine Street (899-5329) specializes in estate jewelry as well as art. Pottery fans will be drawn to the studio showroom of **Pots Alot** at Shadyside Pottery

(3823 Magazine Street, 897-1710). Bohn served his apprenticeship in Japan but also loves classical Greco-Roman styles. And, if you dare, see the beautifully finished pieces by furniture designer **Mario Villa** (3908 Magazine Street, 895-8731); it was Villa who made the sconces for the Contemporary Arts Center, which gives you an idea how highly his peers regard his work. **Cole Pratt Gallery** (3800 Magazine Street, 891-6789) handles several local artists' works.

For collectors of African art, the **Davis Gallery** (904 Louisiana Avenue, 895-5206) is a must-see: household items, baskets, personal items, cookware, and masks from Central and West Africa—all actually used, not mass manufactured—are displayed in a museum-quality setting. The nearby **Private Connection** does a similar good turn for Indonesian artifacts—shadow puppets, "flying" temple figurines, batik fabrics, and jewelry—along with colonial-era antiques (3927 Magazine Street, 899-4944).

This Old House has nothing on **Architectural Salvage and Collectibles** (3983 Tchoupitoulas, 891-6080). **Crescent City Architecturals** is another treasure trove for home renovators (3101 Tchoupitoulas Street, 891-0500). And farther uptown in the Garden District, **Armadillo South** reclaims iron gates, mantlepieces, transoms, doors, and other architectural elements from private homes and—judging from some of the more elaborate bar fixtures and lamps—a few "public houses" (4801 Washington Avenue, 486-1150).

Lucullus, the culinary antique store, has a branch at 3922 Magazine Street (894-0500). **Jacqueline Vance Rugs** (3944 Magazine Street, 891-3304) specializes in both antique and contemporary Kilims and dhurries. And if you've become one of the retro tea–party crowd, visit **Jon Antiques** (4605 Magazine Street, 899-4482), which specializes in smaller, more portable, but elegant items such as 18th- and 19th-century porcelains, tea caddies, and fireplace screens.

Finally, hop to **Beaucoup Books** for a full range of Southern fiction (5414 Magazine Street, 895-2663); then move over to **Scriptura** for handmade papers (5423 Magazine Street, 897-1555); and wrap it up at **Pied Nu** for gourmet edibles (5521 Magazine Street, 899-4118).

The Warehouse District

Another neighborhood emerging as a shopping center is the old Warehouse/Arts District, a loosely defined area roughly squared off by the convention center, Lafayette Street to Lafayette Square, St. Charles Avenue between Lafayette and Lee Circle, and Howard Avenue from Lee Circle back to the convention center. A number of former mills, machinery suppliers, and storehouses have been gutted and refurbished as art spaces and condominiums, although there are still pockets of industry all over. Taking most of its impetus from the 1984 World's Fair (which was a *succès d'estime* if not an economic one), this neighborhood is an intriguing combination of retail and residential. It is home to Emeril's Restaurant, the Contemporary Arts Center, the D-Day Museum, the Ogden Museum of Southern Art (still under construction), and the new Louisiana Children's Museum, as well as such historic landmarks as St. Patrick's Cathedral. (See the walking tour of the Warehouse District and the museum profiles in Part Eight, Sight-Seeing, Tours, and Attractions.)

The main strip, nicknamed **Gallery Row,** is along Julia Street between St. Charles and the convention center. Since art is definitely a matter of taste, you'll just have to wander around the galleries and check them out. You can get to the Warehouse District from the French Quarter by riding the Riverfront Streetcar to the Julia Street stop; and if you're not tired afterwards, you can wind up at St. Charles and take that streetcar for a spin out to the Garden District.

Some of the best-known galleries in this district include **Marguerite Oestreicher** (720 Julia Street, 581-9253), who has the sculpture from the estate of Milton Avery, among others; **Simonne Stern** (518 Julia Street, 529-1118), who was one of the first, and remains one of the premier, dealers in contemporary regional art; **LeMieux Galleries** (332 Julia Street, 522-5988); **Stella Jones** (201 St. Charles, 568-9050), who stocks vivid and evocative African-American sculptures and textiles; **Heriard-Cimino** (440 Julia Street, 525-7300); **d.o.c.s.** (709 Camp Street, 524-3936); **Arthur Roger** (432 Julia Street, 522-1999); and the **New Orleans Auction Galleries** (801 Magazine Street at Julia, 566-1849), which innovatively employs only women auctioneers.

This is also a great neighborhood in which to find one-of-a-kind handmade furniture. **Ariodante** (535 Julia Street, 524-3233) displays contemporary art glass, ceramics, jewelry, decorative accessories, and furniture by regional and national artisans. **Christopher Maier** makes King Tut-inspired thrones; gilded and enameled bureaus; rope-seated, lion's paw-footed chairs; even an armoir with the sun's rays stretching to the floor (329 Julia Street, 586-9079). And **YaYa—Young Artists, Young Aspirations**—is a nonprofit showcase for inner-city youths with artistic talent (601 Baronne Street, 529-3306).

The cult favorite art bikes of the **Confederate Motorcycle Company** (845 Carondelet, 561-9122) are on view at their new state-of-the-art plant and showroom. These hogs and choppers are the preferred steeds of Bruce Springsteen and Nicolas Cage, among others.

Mart Viola Walker (834 Julia Street, 523-0562), who began by designing witty home accessories, has turned to striking but affordable jewelry collections. One, the "cocktail collection," includes pieces combining freshwater pearls, jade "olives" and garnet "pimentos," and evening bags made of semiprecious stones and silver wire.

Aside from the art galleries and studios, there are a couple of particularly noteworthy addresses along Magazine Street. The New Orleans School of **GlassWorks & Gallery** (727 Magazine Street just off Julia, 529-7277) is the largest contemporary glass-arts studio in the South, and it offers glass-blowing classes to the public—not only six-week courses, but two-day, intensive introductions to the art and even private tutoring. Exhibitions go on constantly, and the studio shares space with fine book-makers and print- and paper-makers, who also offer exhibitions and workshops. This is a first-class family attraction as well as an art gallery.

And although it may be a little fine for beginners, good amateur and even professional musicians should make a special trip to **International Vintage Guitars** (1011 Magazine Street, 524-4557), which has used and vintage Martin, Rickenbacher, Fender, and Gibson instruments, along with accessories, amplifiers, etc.

Malls of the Americas

New Orleans has developed an almost continuous line of those prepackaged, upscale-label shopping malls stretching along the waterfront from Jackson Square to the convention center, or commercially speaking, from the French Market to the Riverwalk Marketplace. This baby-boomer boomtown also houses that most notorious of souvenir franchises, the Hard Rock Café (and was home to the now-defunct Planet Hollywood); across Decatur Street is the Crescent City Brewpub. The whole area is bookended by two other theme-sales centers: the Jimmy Buffett shop, filled with Parrothead paraphernalia, at the corner of Decatur and Ursuline, and the House of Blues souvenir store on Decatur past Bienville.

This Great Wall o' Malls winds in and out among the various riverside promenades, cruise-ship landings, and the Aquarium of the Americas, and in good weather the kite flyers and Rollerbladers wind in and out of tourists hefting huge shopping bags and wielding baby strollers. This can be somewhat wearing, whether or not you're actually purchasing anything, so it's best to stop periodically and admire the river, or get a 15-minute neck massage or a hair wrap.

Starting at the east end of the French Quarter and stretching along North Peters Street to the Café du Monde at Jackson Square is the **French Market,** which legend says was a trading post for Native Americans long before the Europeans arrived. Nowadays the complex comprises a half-dozen nicely restored pink stucco buildings housing everything from high-priced souvenirs to jazz bars to orange-juice stands. The building closest to Barracks Street is the **Old Farmers Market**—or, rather, what is now called the Old Farmers Market. The crates of live poultry, rabbits, turtle, and squid that locals used to buy right off the dock have pretty much been replaced by stands of pepper sauce and braided ropes of garlic being sold at inflated prices to credulous tourists as "Cajun hot garlic."

The next stretch of the market, which spills out into the street on weekends, is the **Community Flea Market,** a grab bag of tie-dyed dresses, carved masks, old chairs, and mass-produced "stained glass" that for most people provides all the cheap souvenirs their officemates can stand. Inside these buildings are scores of vendors offering voodoo dolls, T-shirts, earrings, cheap ties (including Jimi Hendrix patterns and copies of Nicole Miller designs for $5), rock posters, sunglasses, blackface pecan-shell magnets, reproduction grocery labels, fabric pins, mobcaps, novelty ballpoint pens (including some that resemble syringes), rubber-band guns, and sports caps. Hot-sauce and Cajun-spice fans can find stalls like the **N'awlins Cajun & Creole Spices** (1101 North Peters Street, 566-2325 or (800) 237-2325) selling hundreds of gumbo mixes and seasonings bearing both old names (Zatarain's, McIlhenny) and new celebrity imprints (Paul Prudhomme's and Emeril's). You can even have your name inscribed on a grain of rice for $8.

As you work your way toward Jackson Square, you'll find some clothing boutiques, indoor-outdoor bars (there are usually at least two jazz trios playing at any given time), and gift shops with pralines and pepper sauce and cutesy statuettes of Louis Armstrong. (Note that the similarly styled building a little behind the French Market at about St. Philip Street is the Jean Lafitte National Park Visitors Center; see Part Eight, Sight-Seeing, Tours, and Attractions.) Beyond the legendary **Café du Monde,** where you can buy chicory coffee and beignet mix right from the source, the commercial strip briefly gives way to Washington Artillery Park and the wooden Moonwalk promenade along the river. Of course, down along the Square, the sidewalks will be full of mule carriages, caricaturists, and clowns; and Artillery Park will probably have some street theater or music going on, but that's just for fun.

Then the shopping picks up again at the old **Jackson Brewery,** one-time house of Jax beer (as it's familiarly known), now with a river-view branch of Pat O'Brien's (called **POB's**) at the top, along with a host of very expensive condos; and the **Marketplace,** home of the **Hard Rock Café.** The Marketplace is big-time retail media: it also boasts **Tower Records & Video and Bookstar.**

There is another pretty stretch—Waldenburg Park—which meanders over to the Aquarium of the Americas; just west of the Aquarium, the Spanish Plaza segues into the huge **Riverwalk Marketplace** complex, an upscale Rouse development of 200 boutiques and eateries (one with seven-pound live lobsters and another with pizza slices almost as big) that connects to the Hilton Hotel and the Convention Center. Most of these stores seem to come as a package deal now, and even in duplicate:

Warner Bros., the Gap, Banana Republic, Ann Taylor, Speedo, and Circo's, Sharper Image and **Brookstone, Eddie Bauer** and **Abercrombie & Fitch, Victoria's Secret** and . . . well, you get the idea. On the other hand, there are also a half-dozen shoe stores, including several specializing in comfortable walking shoes that might come in handy if you're facing the agony of da feet.

For something a little less predictable, look into the shop of **Yvonne LaFleur,** who not only carries upscale fashions but custom-designed hats, cocktail dresses, evening gowns, and even wedding dresses. From the river, you can see where the facade of Riverwalk was torn away by the runaway barge—it looks a little like an intentional architectural model, actually—but you'd never know from strolling through the glossy mall inside that anything had ever happened. And there's a cute little magic shop, where the free demonstrations keep the kids cool.

At the foot of Canal Street, across the streetcar tracks from the Aquarium, is **Canal Place,** a lushly appointed and label-conscious mall that blazons the logos of its Gucci, Saks, and Brooks Brothers tenants. Be sure to browse through **RHINO,** which is an acronym for "Right Here in New Orleans," describing where the store's crafts were made. It's a non-profit shop, and the clothing and art are extremely attractive. Canal Place is also the home of jewelry designer **Mignon Faget,** whose creations in silver, 14-karat gold, and bronze d'or for both men and women are highly prized.

There is another upscale mall called the **New Orleans Centre** (1400 Poydras Street, by the Superdome) that houses both **Lord & Taylor** and **Macy's,** but it covers a lot of the same brand-label territory as Riverplace.

Part Eleven

Exercise and Recreation

Working Out and Playing Hard

A few years ago, it would have seemed silly to put a chapter on exercise in a vacation guide—particularly a guide to a city as famed for self-indulgence as New Orleans. But most of us at the *Unofficial Guides* are into some form of exercise, if only as a matter of self-preservation: it reduces stress, helps offset those expense-account and diet–holiday meals (no, it's not true that food eaten on vacation has no calories), and even ameliorates some of the effects of jet lag. Even more remarkably, we have discovered that jogging, biking, and just plain walking are among the nicest ways to experience a city on its own turf, so to speak, and we're happy to see that more and more travelers feel as we do.

However, remember what we said in the beginning about the climate of New Orleans—hot and humid, cool and damp. In the summer months, it's really a good idea to schedule exercise early in the day or in the first cool of the evening; those late-afternoon showers can make a nice difference. (On the other hand, insects prefer the cooler hours, too, so pack some bug spray. Better yet, double up and get sunscreen with repellent built in.) It's rarely too cold for a run even in January, but again it may be damp, so pack a weather-resistant layer as well as a first-aid kit: we go nowhere without sports-style adhesive strips, ibuprofen or some other analgesic, petroleum jelly, and a small tube of antiseptic. Blisters can ruin the most perfect vacation. We know.

Walking

Considering how strongly we've urged you to walk at least the French Quarter, you may have already guessed that we find not agony but ecstasy in the feet. And in addition to the neighborhood walks, New Orleans has several picturesque options, starting with the roughly two miles of **Riverwalk** from Esplanade Avenue to the Spanish Plaza, which takes you past Jackson Square, the various cruise ships, and a wonderful assortment of vendors and relaxing natives. (Keep an ear out; this is also popular among rollerbladers.) If you take the St. Charles Avenue Streetcar to where St. Charles ends, you'll discover the tracks take a sharp right turn onto Carrollton Avenue; that's because the Mississippi River takes a hard right as well, and you can get off and walk the levee there, too, before exploring the shops and cafes of the **Riverbend** neighborhood.

City Park covers 1,500 acres, twice the size of New York's sweeping Central Park, and you can wander pretty much as long as you like. If you like those walking trails with built-in exercise stations equipped with chin-up bars and stretching posts and the like, go to Audubon Park; part of the macadam bike trail over by the duck pond has 18 mild challenges.

Running and Jogging

Again, the riverfront area is a common draw for runners who deal in limited distance, and the long, lovely stretch of **St. Charles Avenue** down through the Garden District is a great possibility. You could run as far as you like and then ride the streetcar back—the annual Crescent City 10K starts in Jackson Square and ends at the zoo—or even go half-marathon distance by running to Audubon Park, circling the two-mile path around the golf course, and returning. If you'd like to participate in the Crescent City Classic and its sports and fitness expo, call 861-8686. The race is usually run in mid-April, which is a great time to be in the city.

Along with its pleasure paths, City Park has two 400-meter polyurethane tracks built for the 1992 Olympic trials and 1993 NCAA championships, one inside **Tad Gormley Stadium** (call City Park at 482-4888). At the **Chalmette Battlefield** there is a dirt track that is ideal for runners of the contemplative sort; although the car gate is locked at dusk, there is a smaller pedestrian gate next to the national cemetery that will give you access. And if you're used to running with a club, contact the **New Orleans Track Club** (482-6682) or **Southern Runner Productions** (899-3333) for event schedules.

Biking

We already mentioned that it's easy to rent a bike or even a two-seater in the French Quarter. **Laid Back Tours** provides recumbent bikes for $35 a day for two people and will arrange a "Ride 'Em & Blues" tour with guides; call (800) 786-1274 or go to **www.laidbacktours.com** for information. **Bicycle Michael's** on Frenchman Street (945-9505) has a 25-mile map for serious bikers that goes out Esplanade Avenue to City Park, around the lake, through mid-city to Audubon Park and the university area, and back along St. Charles. A new riverfront path now extends all the way from Jefferson Parish through Orleans Parish and St. Charles as well. And that two-mile track in Audubon Park is very popular with rollerbladers and bikers, particularly on weekends. You can also contact the **Crescent City Cyclists** (276-2601) for group-ride information.

Tennis

There are public courts in both **City Park** (482-4888)—which has 31 lighted synthetic–surface courts (making it the largest public facility in the South), USPTA instructors, and even racquet rentals—and in **Audubon Park** at the Magazine Street end (895-1042), which has 10 clay courts and is nice but not lighted. Both charge fees and accept reservations, but they are not required.

There are eight indoor tennis courts, four racquetball courts, and three squash courts at the **Rivercenter Racquet and Health Club,** which is in the Hilton Riverside at 2 Poydras Street (556-3742); it's open to guests at other city hotels, too. It also offers lessons, a stringing service, and a match-a-partner service, so if you can make arrangements in advance, it's a good place to go.

Golf

Like much of the South, this is popular golf territory, and as usual, you can start at the City Park, where **Bayou Oaks** club (483-9396) is (again) the largest municipal facility in the South. It offers four 18-hole courses, PGA teaching pros, and a huge, 100-tee, double-decker driving range open until 10 p.m. Greens fees are $8–$20; $19 with a cart with a $10 deposit. **Audubon Park** (212-5290) has recently completed an ambitious renovation of its 18-hole, par-62 course under the direction of Dennis Griffiths. Greens fees are $27 weekdays and $35 weekends, with an additional $11 per person for the cart. There is also **Joe Bartholomew Course** (288-0928), located in Ponchartrain Park, in the northeast part of the city. It charges a greens fee of $8 on weekdays and $12 on weekends, and a $20 cart fee. There are also two public courses just across the river on the West Bank: **Brechtel Park** course (362-4761), which charges $7.75–$10 for greens fees and $18 for carts; and **Bayou Barriere** (394-0662), which combines fees for carts and greens. On weekdays, it's $21 for residents and $35 for nonresidents; on weekends, it's $30 for residents and $35 for nonresidents. The PGA-sanctioned Compact Classic is played in early April at **English Turn** (pro shop, 391-8018), which is on a curve of the Mississippi River, a pretty drive down St. Bernard Highway.

Gyms and Health Clubs

The **Y** in the Superdome (412-9622) has an assortment of Nautilus machines, treadmills, bikes, free weights, a sauna, and aerobics. The cost is $10.

The **Downtown Fitness Center** in the Canal Place complex has aerobics, treadmills, bikes, stair machines, free weights and leveraged machines, saunas, and even personal trainers. You can get a daily pass for $12 and a three-day pass for $30 (525-2956).

The **Ritz-Carlton** charges non-guests $35 a day for use of its fitness center, but its spa is the most luxurious in town, and a $35 service there makes the workout free.

In addition, the **Rivercenter Club** at the Hilton has massage therapists, a whole list of name-brand machines, salon treatments, and even a tanning bed.

Other Recreational Activities

If you want to swim and are not staying in a hotel with a pool (which only a few in the French Quarter or Garden District have), check with the Y or the health and fitness clubs. There is a public swimming pool at **Audubon Park** as well.

If you like a little outdoor entertainment, but don't go for regimented exercise, you have a couple of other choices. You can ride at a few stables including, of course, **City Park** (482-4888), which has only a ring, but offers 1-hour group lessons and 30-minute individual lessons in English-style riding. Audubon Park's **Cascade Stables** (891-2246), allows riders to go out into the park a bit.

City Park also offers **canoes and paddleboats;** docks for a little light **catfish and bass fishing** (you have to get a license at the boat dock behind the park casino, which is the only so-called casino in town without a deck of cards to its name; **soccer** fields; **baseball** diamonds; and a **batting cage** at the four-field softball center.

And if you're interested in serious fishing and hunting a little farther outside the city, perhaps for your second New Orleans visit, there are dozens of guides and charters. There are two famous names, or at least faces, in the fishing biz. One is former TV weatherman Nash Roberts, of **Fishhunter Guide Service,** which will not only supply you with everything you need but come and get you at the hotel (call 837-0703 or (800) 887-1385). The other is TV sportfishing-series character Phil Robichaux of **Captain Phil's Saltwater Guide Services** (689-2006), whose charters leave from the Lafitte Marina near the Barataria unit of the Jean Lafitte National Historic Park and Preserve, about an hour's drive from the French Quarter. You can probably get several other names and numbers out of promotional brochures or by calling marinas and fishing stores, but we suggest you contact the New Orleans Visitors Bureau for a list of reliable guides. Remember, you *do* need a permit from the **Department of Wildlife and Fisheries** (568-5636). Permits are available from most sporting goods stores, marinas, and guide companies. You can get a one-day license for $20, a four-day

license for $60, and a full-season license for $90. You will need to bring
your driver's license.

Spectator Sports

New Orleans is not a great football town—which may mean that it's a
great football town for tourists. Although in most cities with NFL franchises, tickets are sold out well in advance and have to be scalped at the
scene, the **New Orleans Saints** (731-1700) do not sell out and there are
regularly seats available. The Saints play in the legendary (and newly
spiffed-up) Superdome, so you can also call TicketMaster at 522-5555
for information. **Tulane University** also plays its Saturday home games
at the Superdome, and every other year, there's a rousing, old-fashioned,
rah-rah LSU–Tulane grudge match there; call the Dome offices at 587-
3810 or 587-3822 for schedules and ticket information. You can also
inquire about ticket availability for the **Sugar Bowl** collegiate duel, but
you'll need to do so well in advance of the match.

There are times when New Orleans is a super football town, and that
is during the years when the **Super Bowl** is played there. It's a long shot,
but you can try to get in on the ticket lottery not by besieging the Superdome itself but by sending a certified letter to the National Football
League offices at 410 Park Avenue, New York, NY 10022.

The **New Orleans** (née Charlotte) **Hornets** basketball team have
moved into the 18,500-seat Sports Arena behind the Superdome. Call
301-4000 for information, or consult **www.hornets.com.**

New Orleans does better in baseball with the **New Orleans Zephyrs**
(the Houston Astros AAA affiliate). Zephyr Stadium in Metairie, which
opened for the 1997 season, cost $23 million and seats 12,000 in the
height of retro-stadium style. For game schedules and ticket information, call the Zephyrs's office at 734-5155.

Zephyr Stadium is also home to the **New Orleans Storm** (734-5155),
a minor-league soccer team, which plays from April through September.

New Orleans also does well by the blue-blooded sport of horse racing
(as you might expect from such a royalist colony). The **Fair Grounds**
(944-5515) near City Park hosts thoroughbred racing from Thanksgiving to mid-April, when it gives way to the Jazz and Heritage Festival.

Entertainment
and Nightlife

Performing Arts

Let's be up-front about this: Few people head for New Orleans intending
to spend a night at the theater. But that's not to say you shouldn't look
around for something beyond the strip joints and jazz bars. There is no
multistate performing-arts center here like New York's Lincoln Center or
Washington's Kennedy Center, but there are several venues, most in the
Central Business District, that book touring companies of Broadway
shows, concerts, etc. Most shows will be listed in the *Times-Picayune*.

The main theatrical venue to check into is the **Saenger Performing
Arts Center** (524-2490) at Rampart and Canal, a gorgeously restored
Renaissance-style cinema worth visiting just for its "living sky" ceiling of
drifting clouds and constellations; it books national touring companies
of Broadway productions and the occasional big-name pop star. The
State Palace Theater (522-4435) at Rampart and Basin is another old
venue whose boxes and chandeliers go rather strangely with some of its
non-middle-of-the-road music acts. The grand-old-style **Mahalia Jackson Theatre of the Performing Arts** (565-7470 or 565-8081), although
in the somewhat questionable Louis Armstrong Park at the edge of the
French Quarter, is home to the New Orleans Opera Association and the
primarily imported productions of the New Orleans Ballet Association.

The **Louisiana Philharmonic Orchestra** (523-6530) performs, in a
season that roughly matches the school year, at the ornately restored
Beaux Arts **Orpheum Theatre**—part of the original Orpheum vaudeville circuit—on University Place just off Canal; Maxim Shostakovich,
conductor of the LPO's predecessor, the bankrupt New Orleans Symphony, occasionally picks up the baton. The only Equity company in
New Orleans, the **Southern Repertory Theater** (861-8163), has a small
150-seat house on the third floor of Canal Place. It's not the most professional of companies yet, but the fact that so many of its productions have

local connections—plays by Tennessee Williams, Lillian Hellman, and others—makes it interesting. **Le Petit Théâtre du Vieux Carré** (522-2081) has plenty of atmosphere and a reputed phantom to boot, though its seasons aren't as ambitious as they once were.

The **Contemporary Arts Center** (523-3800) in the Warehouse/Arts District books more cutting-edge productions, which sometimes are merely artsy-for-art's-sake and more apt to draw local residents than tourists. (On the other hand, Edward Albee directed his own "Fragments" at CAC, using local actors.) The Center has two stages, so sometimes dance and theatrical performances are booked at the same time. **Le Chat Noire** (581-5812) offers an entertaining array of cabaret, spoken word, and alternative theater productions in one of the city's more stylish stage settings.

Uptown, both **Loyola** and **Tulane** universities frequently offer classical or dramatic works; contact the Loyola ticket office (865-3492) or Tulane box office (865-5360).

Big-name rock and pop concerts are usually scheduled either for the **Louisiana Superdome** (call 587-3663 or TicketMaster), the more intimate **New Orleans Arena** next door (phone number same as for Superdome), or the University of New Orleans's **Kiefer Lakefront Arena,** a 10,000-seat venue near Lake Pontchartrain at UNO's east campus (280-7222).

New Orleans Nightlife

The Quarter

New Orleans is indeed a nightlife town. For all the city fathers' efforts to portray the Big Easy as a family-oriented destination, there's little doubt that legions of folks come here to do what they can't or won't do back home—holler in the streets, drink all night, and show their, er . . . wits. They've come to the right place, with its relaxed laws, lusty hideaways, and rich, sultry nights. There are hundreds of bars here to cater to every conceivable appetite and mood. And it all starts in one special place—the French Quarter.

When most folks think of the French Quarter, they think Bourbon Street—with its tawdry parlors, beer-soaked juke joints, strip clubs, and drunken college kids stumbling about with go cups full of super-potent hurricanes. The street has a reputation for being the epicenter of improvisational jazz and blues, but the fact is, it isn't and never really was.

Bourbon Street is and always has been a mishmash of nightlife styles—elegant, rowdy, punky, sleazy, gay (in all senses of the term). But a majority of the city's great hangouts and, in particular, the great venues for live music, are not on Bourbon Street. The street's live music scene is largely relegated to a series of average cover bands, karaoke clubs, and cheap trios playing to recorded drum machine accompaniment. There are, of course, exceptions, and plenty of visitors find on Bourbon Street just what they're looking for.

Howl at the Moon (125 Bourbon, 410-9000), **Big Bad Wolf** (433 Bourbon, 561-8200), and **Razoo** (511 Bourbon, 522-5100) would probably qualify as your prototypical Bourbon Street hangouts: too loud, too young, lots of booze, lots of hooking up and making out. The pretty waitresses selling test tubes full of multi-colored vodka and Everclear shots complete this boisterous tableau.

At the **Chris Owens Club** (500 Bourbon, 523-6400) the club's name-sake matriarch cranks out two high-energy dance shows a night, despite her rapidly advancing septuagenarianism. Whoopi Goldberg, a devout Owens fan, has been known to jump onstage during her frequent visits to New Orleans. The clientele is mostly retirees and snowbirds, but it's a lark worth checking out just for its camp factor. It's the closest thing New Orleans has to Branson, Missouri.

Patout's Cajun Cabin (501 Bourbon, 529-4256) offers spirited and visitor-friendly Cajun music, long on familiar favorites but often wanting a true roadhouse feel.

Oddly, the most popular and crowded spot on Bourbon is often the **Cat's Meow** (701 Bourbon, 523-2788), the city's flagship karaoke bar. The most romantic spot on Bourbon is undoubtedly **Lafitte's Black-smith Shop** (941 Bourbon, 523-0066), which is dimly lit, heated by fire in the winter, and an ideal spot to disappear into a dark corner (by the piano bar in the back). Three of the city's major gay dance clubs are clus-tered on Bourbon: the **Bourbon Pub and Parade** (801 Bourbon, 529-2107), **Café Lafitte in Exile** (901 Bourbon, 522-8397), and the upstart **Oz** (800 Bourbon, 592-8200), a straight-friendly, anything-goes, dance-all-night kind of place.

There are a bunch of strip clubs on Bourbon Street, both elegant and sleazy. Larry Flynt's **Hustler Club** (225 Bourbon, 524-0010) and **Rick's Cabaret** (315 Bourbon, 524-4222) are two of the city's premier upscale gentlemen's clubs. Flynt's joint is pretty interesting during the Tuesday night "Hustler Honey" amatuer stripper contests, when tourist passersby indulge their stage fantasies in front of their fellow conventioneers.

During Mardi Gras, *Playboy's* bunnies-for-hire take over the balcony at **Temptations** (327 Bourbon, 525-4470), lending it an air of credibility. **Big Daddy's** (522 Bourbon, 581-7167) is famous for the mannequin legs that swing in and out of its front window, but it's kind of a dive. **Papa Joe's** next door is a female impersonator lounge ; the sign above the joint says "Seeing is Believing" but we'll leave that determination up to you. (Note about strip clubs: You probably already know this, but they're a hustle. Expect to be relieved of a minimum of several twenties when you walk into these joints.)

There are literally dozens of other hangouts where beer and Jell-O shots outpace scintillating conversation. Not everyone cruising down Bourbon Street is on the make for the second coming of Buddy Bolden; in fact,many just want a good, clean place to let it hang out a bit. The **Famous Door** (339 Bourbon, 522-7626), the **Funky Pirate** (727 Bourbon,523-1960), and **Krazy Korner** (640 Bourbon, 524-3157) book jazz, R&B, and the occasional Cajun cover bands to amuse the masses who stream in.

The **Tropical Isle** (721 Bourbon, 529-4109) is an island-theme hangout with lots of Jimmy Buffett sing-alongs, both from the jukebox and the bands that sit in. At Tropical Isle's original location around the corner (738 Toulouse, 525-1689) various Buffett cover bands have been pulling in a hardcore local following for more than 15 years. It's loud and late. And fun.

Johnny White's **Sports Bar** (718 Bourbon, 588-1239) is a corner dive featuring round-the-clock Mardi Gras videos for voyeurs who have come in the off season and need their fix of flesh. **735 Club** (735 Bourbon, 581-6740) offers cutting-edge dance music and various Goth and glam-themed evenings

Then there's the dozen or so daiquiri specialty shops on Bourbon. And the windows that dispense with any pretense and just serve to pedestrians on the sidewalk. Add to all this the scores of taverns with courtyard hideaways for intimacy or second-story balconies offering a visual feast of the sea of stumbling, bead-mongering party animals from across the globe below, and you realize what the truth is: just about every 20 feet down the street there's another bar beckoning you inside. We are confident that you can find a giggle or two on this most lively and entertaining stretch of American roadway.

The rest of the French Quarter is also a mesh of varying styles and atmospheres, from the impressive and ornately decorated **House of Blues** (225 Decatur, 529-blue), where the biggest names in the music business congregate; to the affected elegance of the **Bombay Club** (830 Conti, 586-0972), where $9 martinis rule the roost; to the ultimate in barroom bizarro, the **Dungeon** (738 Toulouse, 523-5530), which opens at midnight and offers an experience not unlike the LSD sequence by Peter Fonda in *Easy Rider,* complete with black lights, Gothic décor, and heavy-metal dance tapes. To get an idea of just how late this place goes, the happy hour 3-for-1 starts at 4 a.m.

The well-known **Pat O'Brien's** (718 St. Peter, 525-4823) is said to boast the largest alcohol sales of any bar in America, but New Orleans is full of stories like that. Check out the dueling-pianos bar and the flaming water fountain in the courtyard.

Over on Rampart Street are **Donna's Bar and Grill** (800 N. Rampart, 596-6914) and the **Funky Butt at Congo Square** (714 N. Rampart, 558-0872), two venues featuring hot young brass bands from around the city, often till the wee hours.

The **Shim Sham Club** (615 Toulouse, 299-0666) is a mixed bag of jazz, country, punk, and retro music; of special note are the Sunday-night revues by the Shim Shammettes, a retro burlesque troupe that stunningly recreates the mood and look of Bourbon Street in the 1940s. It's a treat.

El Matador (504 Esplanade, 569-8361) is a hip and retro club featuring weekly flamenco shows, brass-band blowouts, and mellow jazz and swing nights. **O'Flaherty's** (514 Toulouse, 529-1317) and **Kerry Irish Pub** (331 Decatur, 527-5954), the area's only Irish music clubs, feature live music and Guinness on tap. (**Kerry** and **Margaritaville**—mentioned just below—are great places to hear quality local musicians in the late afternoons and early evenings, long before most places crank to full volume.) **Ryan's Irish Pub** (241 Decatur, 523-3500) offers no live musical fare, but is a lively, well-lit tavern and pool hall, often filling up after House of Blues concerts have ended just up the block.

You'll rarely run into the owner at **Jimmy Buffett's Margaritaville Café** (1104 Decatur, 592-2565), but the open-air windows along the sidewalk and the good-time music—pop, blues, piano bangers, and such—make for an atmosphere that would please the boss.

Another local and international favorite is the **Napoleon House** (500 Chartres, 524-9752), a watering hole for the Quarter's literary folk, a dark and dusty corner tavern where the classical music on the stereo mixed with the clop-clop of the mule-drawn buggies outside and the many languages of the clientele make for a European nostalgia.

There are loads of neighborhood hangouts (yes, people live in the Quarter) for straight folks (notably, the 1100 block of Decatur Street) and gay (perhaps best known is the low-key **Good Friends** at 740 Dauphine, 566-7191).

A place not to be missed for cutlure vultures and aficianados of camp and questionable Americana is **Gennifer Flowers Kelsto Club** (720 St. Louis, 524-1111). That's right, the former tabloid queen, perky peroxide princess, and Bill Clinton's longtime paramour shed her scandalous ways, moved to New Orleans, and opened a very tasteful and visually appealing piano bar across the street from the famed Antoine's restaurant. She sings, she greets, she smiles that famous smile. Definitely worth a visit because, well . . . why not?

And, of course, New Orleans boasts one of the notorious **Coyote Ugly** franchises (225 N. Peters, 561-0003). You know the drill: Country music on the jukebox, hot bartenders dancing on the bar top, free-flowing shots. Think Hooters meats Urban Cowboy.

At press time, the newest kid in the Quarter is **Lounge Lizards** (200 Decatur, 598-1500), a small music club of great promise located across the street from the hulking House of Blues. This place offers a French Quarter rarity—nightly sets from various roots- and jazz-oriented local musicians who rarely venture away from the comfort and safety of their low-paying Uptown gigs into the oft-less appreciative tourist district. Jazz, R&B, and general eclectica fill the bill. The New Orleans Klezmer Allstars are a special treat—here or wherever else you find them listed.

The Quarter has more, so much more. Literally dozens more juke joints, pool halls, daiquiri bars, meat markets (both gay and straight), strip clubs of all varieties, video-poker hangouts, and sports bars. All of this is just a start. There are so many establishments of so many colors that, at times, it seems there are as many bars in the French Quarter as there are T-shirt shops. But this is only an illusion.

The Jazz Scene

Yes, jazz is everywhere. In many forms, variations, and presentations, from the cobblestones of Jackson Square to the overdressed cigar bars around town, someone somewhere is carrying on the traditions of the great masters of American improvisational music.

In the French Quarter alone, the strains of horn solos pour forth, it seems, from every street corner. The music ranges from the sublime to the downright cheesy, but it's what people come to hear, and the city aims to please. For the most part, the term "jazz" in New Orleans refers to traditional Dixieland, the stuff of old Satchmo and Al Hirt records. On Bourbon Street, the **Maison Bourbon Jazz Club** (641 Bourbon, 522-8818) is probably the best spot to catch a feel of the Bourbon Street swing set, circa 1954. It's an old, wide-open room with crumbling brick décor, and the rotating teams of old men in tuxedos file in shortly after lunchtime and start banging out classics until around midnight.

The **Famous Door Jazz Café** (339 Bourbon, 522-7626) offers Dixieland among its many afternoon and evening music shows. The **Jazz Bistro** at Arnaud's restaurant (corner of Bienville and Bourbon streets, 523-2847) and **The Court of Two Sisters** (613 Royal, with an entrance on Bourbon, 522-7261) offer jazz while you eat. The lobby bar of the **Royal Sonesta Hotel** (300 Bourbon, 586-0300) generally offers low-key combos in the evenings.

Across the French Quarter spectrum, there's **Preservation Hall** (726 St. Peter, 522-2841), where tourists congregate in thick lines to hear some of the great old traditional jazzmen of the city play in a dusty and dim old-time listening hall. (The thirsty beware: there are no refreshments served.)

The **Palm Court Jazz Café** (1204 Decatur, 525-0200) is a prime venue for traditional New Orleans jazz, and the **Crescent City Brewhouse** (527 Decatur, 522-0571) is the Quarter's only brewpub and a playground for some of the area's fresh-faced young jazz players.

The many cafés and public kiosks of the French Market host jazz bands nightly on the sidewalks, free for the listening from nearby benches. A great moment to remember in the city is the night you danced arm-in-arm on the curbside while a mule buggy clopped by and a saxman serenaded you in the rain. It happens all the time.

Outside the Quarter, several hotels offer jazz samplings in their lobby bars. Among these are the **Fairmont** (123 Baronne, 529-7111), the **Hotel Inter-Continental** (444 St. Charles, 525-5566), and the **Marriott New Orleans** (555 Canal, 581-1000). Down in the city's Ninth Ward, one of the area's favorite jazz traditions unfolds Thursday nights, when Kermit Ruffins, the second coming of Louis Armstrong, cooks turkey-neck stew or red beans and rice on the back of his pickup truck, then plays trumpet at **Vaughan's Lounge** (4229 Dauphine, 947-5562). This scene attracts all manner of celebs, from Mick Jaggar to Peter Jennings. (Who knew he was so hip?)

A little farther off the path are the **Steak Knife** restaurant (888 Harrison, 488-8981) in the Lakeview neighborhood, offering late-night weekend shows, and the **Sandbar** pub, located in the Cove student-union building at the University of New Orleans. Here, university students, studying in the music program founded by jazz grandaddy Ellis Marsalis, perform for intimate and undersized crowds. Check local or university listings for the times of these rare and thrilling performances—you just might catch the next Harry Connick, Jr.

Sweet Lorriane's (1931 St. Claude, 945-9654) is a mellow jazz joint of a mature thread, the closest thing to a Cotton Club left in New Orleans. Nearby, in the hip and happening Faubourg Marigny entertainment district, **d.b.a** (618 Frenchmen, 942-3731) and **The Spotted Cat** (623 Frenchmen, 943-3887) are top-quality intimate nightclubs offering contemporary and retro jazz foremost among their many musical samplings. If the Hot Club of New Orleans is listed at either joint, make a point to see this tight—and very nicely dressed—gypsy jazz band. A high-quality jazz destination in the Uptown direction is the luxurious **Dos Jefes Uptown Cigar Bar** (5535 Tchoupitoulas, 891-8500), which offers live jazz seven nights a week in a comfortable neighborhood setting with, yes, plenty of cigar accompaniment.

And, finally, for those who really want to get away from the maddening crowd, the famed Dukes of Dixieland play weekend dinner shows on the **Steamboat Natchez** (at the Toulouse Street Wharf behind the Jax Brewery, 586-8777).

What Else Is There?

Indigenous Louisiana music forms other than jazz—primarily Cajun and zydeco—are among the state's great exports. In New Orleans, they are plentiful. **Mid City Lanes, Mulate's,** and **Tipitina's** are all profiled in the following section, but fiddles and accordions abound in lesser-known areas as well. **Patout's Cajun Cabin** (501 Bourbon, 529-4256) pulls crowds off the street for dancing and fun, lured by the crazy syncopated washboard rhythms. **Michaul's** (840 St. Charles, 522-5517) offers Cajun cuisine and two-stepping six nights a week in a roadhouse atmosphere.

The blues is the stepchild of New Orleans musical tradition: every bit as vital and necessary to the development of the city's heritage, but often overlooked as a cultural staple.

The name notwithstanding, the **House of Blues** is not actually a blues club, per se, as much as a blues museum. Its actual live musical fare covers all spectrums, from Latin to punk to funk to fusion. **Tipitina's, The Maple Leaf,** and **The Showcase** are all profiled in the following section, but there are plenty of other spots around town where you can drown your sorrows in wailing guitar riffs.

The **Canal Bus Stop** (2828 Canal, 822-2011) recalls the many soulful neighborhood clubs around town from the 1950s through the 1970s, before the street corners got scary and the bar scene started re-segregating itself. The amazing New Orleans ambassador of love, Walter "Wolfman" Washington holds court on weekends and consistently churns out some of the hottest and most genuine American soul and R&B not only in New Orleans, but anywhere.

Ernie K-Doe's **Mother-in-Law Lounge** (1500 N. Claiborne, 947-1078) is an out-of-the-way musical museum dedicated to the curious career of the famed R&B warrior, who scored a hit with "Mother-in-Law" in the late 1950s and milked a career out of the song for the next 40 years. This is a one-of-a-kind place. K-Doe is dead now, but a life-size statue greets you at the door; his wife Antoinette serves up complimentary beans and rice most Sunday nights. Some nights it's empty, other nights it positively rocks. Never can tell. They don't have a bar like this in your hometown. (Note: Very edgy neighborhood; take a cab.)

The Circle Bar (1032 St. Charles, 588-2616) is a late-night hangout for singers and songwriters of various stripes, from Latin to lounge. It's loud and uber-hip, but a fun place to melt into the wee hours.

The blues mix with rock and pop at a legion of other clubs around town. **Jimmy's** (8200 Willow, 861-8200) and the neighboring **Carrollton Station** (8140 Willow, 865-9190) both offer local and regional acts in intimate Uptown surroundings. **Checkpoint Charlie** (501 Esplanade, 947-0979) on the outer fringe of the French Quarter, dabbles in all forms of contemporary music, from jazz to funk to folk. Curiously, it also houses a laundromat and a paperback book exchange as well.

Le Bon Temps Roule (4801 Magazine, 895-8117) is a boozy neighborhood pool palace with live bands in the back room several nights a week. More often than not, one of the city's totally hot young brass bands has the place jumping until 2 a.m.

Out on River Road, past the Uptown section of the city, the **Rivershack Tavern** (3449 River Road, 834-4938) boasts the largest tacky-ashtray collection in the world and also a roster of offbeat and always lively weekend music shows that spill out into the gravel parking lot where, on the good nights, the fog off the river touches your soul and maybe even scares you a little.

The **Acadian Brewing Company** (201 N. Carrollton, 483-3097) is one of two New Orleans brewpubs, featuring homemade suds and occasional folk- and rock-music sets. (The other brewpub, Crescent City, is featured in the following section.)

For the nonalcoholic set, the **Neutral Ground Coffee House** (5110 Daneel, 891-3381), tucked away in a residential Uptown neighborhood, is the city's foremost folk and singer/songwriter showcase, with no cover charge.

For those seeking more mainstream singles nightlife—and by that we mean generic big-city fare—**Ampersand** (1100 Tulane, 587-3737) and **Club 360** (2 Canal, 595-8900) are big, bold and loud contemporary downtown dance clubs. Throbbing lights, tight shirts, hair gel . . . those kinds of places. Club 360, in particular, offers a smashing view of the Mississippi River from 32 floors up. Bonus value: 360 is the favored watering hole for Saints and Hornets players and—best of all (we think)—it's hometown diva Britney Spears' favorite New Orleans club.

Contrary to popular belief, not every bar in New Orleans is a jazz club, or even a music or dance club, for that matter. Conversation and the art of flirting are alive and well on the bayou, and places abound to indulge. A favorite of artists and celebrities is the deliciously offbeat and out-of-the-way **Saturn Bar** (3067 St. Claude, 949-7532), where Alec Baldwin, Sam Shepard, Robbie Robertson, and Nicolas Cage are among the many notables who have dropped in to drop out of the local scene for a night. It's dark, quiet, and full of bad art and poets who smoke too much.

The **Balcony Bar** (3201 Magazine, 895-1600) and the **Bulldog** (3236 Magazine, 891-1516) are anchors of the expanding yuppie nightlife scene in the arts and antiques district Uptown, both offering big beer selections and great people-watching venues.

In the Warehouse District, the **Ernst Café** (600 S. Peters, 525-8544) is a popular happy-hour hangout for upwardly mobiles, and is one of local hero John Goodman's many favorite spots.

And finally, a rising star on the singles/couples scene is **Monkey Hill Bar** (6100 Magazine, 899-4800). This tasteful Uptown tavern gathers on its couches and barstools an eclectic mix of young lawyers, politicians, Saints players, and posh nightclubbers. The drink selections are choice. The free pool table is a nice touch. Stay away on Friday and Saturday nights, though; it's much too crowded.

A Note on Safety

New Orleans is a city with predictable danger zones and drug-peddling neighborhoods. Most visitors are aware of the city's high murder and robbery rates, and you should always bear these unflattering statistics in mind. Fringe areas of the French Quarter are particularly vulnerable spots for robbery. Always be aware when walking the streets, and don't hesitate to cross a street or turn around to avoid coming face to face with what appears to be an unsavory character. The risk of offending said stranger is far outweighed by ensuring your personal safety. In short, the deal is this: In the highly commercial areas of the French Quarter, feel free and safe to walk about. In all other areas, we recommend you take a cab. They're cheap and efficient.

Also, there is a common scam on Bourbon Street that goes like this: A stranger approaches you and says, "I bet I know where you got them shoes. I know the street and the city and the state where you got them shoes." Don't take the bet. He knows: You got them shoes on your feet on Bourbon Street, in New Orleans, Louisiana.

Get it? No matter. If you take the bet, be prepared to pay up or face a bad scene on the street. Never play games on other people's playing fields. That's it for the lecture. Now go ahead, have fun.

NEW ORLEANS NIGHTCLUBS BY ZONE

Zone & Name	Description	Cover
Zone 1: French Quarter		
Arnaud's Bar	Beau monde hideaway	None
Bombay Club	Delightfully pretentious gin joint	Varies
Cat's Meow	Bourbon Street karaoke	None–$5
Crescent City Brewhouse	Brewpub and jazz joint	None
Donna's	Live brass-band jazz	$5
El Matador	Hipster hangout	$5–$10
French Quarter Bar	See and be scene	None
Funky Butt at Congo Square	Jazz, blues, and jazzy blues	None–$20
Gennifer Flowers's Kelsto Club	Former tabloid queen follows lounge dream	None
House of Blues	National-, regional-, local-circuit music club	Varies
Lafitte's Blacksmith Shop	Romantic hideaway and piano lounge	None
Margaritaville Café	Beachy music club	Varies
Molly's on the Market	French Quarter media hangout	None
Napoleon House	French Quarter institution	None
O'Flaherty's	Live Irish music club and entertainment complex	Varies
Palm Court Jazz Café	Jazz bar and restaurant	None–$5
Pat O'Brien's	International tourist mecca	None
Preservation Hall	Old-time jazz hall	$5

NEW ORLEANS NIGHTCLUBS BY ZONE (continued)

Zone & Name	Description	Cover
Zone 2: Central Business District		
The Howlin' Wolf	Regional, alternative, progressive country, and folk music	Varies
Loa	Swinging singles meet hip hop nation	None
Lucy's Retired Surfer's Bar	Singles sidewalk hangout	None
The Mermaid Lounge	Live performance art, lounge music, and unsavory misfits	$2–$10
Mulate's	Cajun dance and dinner hall	None
Whiskey Blue	What Fashion Café was probably meant to be	None
Zone 3: Uptown below Napoleon		
The Columns	Sophisticated singles and debutante ball	None
Zone 4: Uptown above Napoleon		
Dos Jefes Uptown Cigar Bar	Cigar bar and jazz joint with speakeasy feel	None
F&M Patio Bar	Late-night party bar	None
The Maple Leaf	Live regional music	None
Mid City Lanes	Rock 'n bowl	$5–$15
Tipitina's	New Orleans's quintessential music club	Varies
Zone 5: Downtown/St. Bernard		
Café Brasil	International watering hole	$0–$10
d.b.a.	Energetic and intellectual watering hole	None
Saturn Bar	Offbeat lounge	None
Snug Harbor	Jazz club	$10–$25

Nightclub Profiles

Arnaud's Bar

BEAU MONDE HIDEAWAY

Who goes there Lawyers, old-line locals, tourists, former Queens of Mardi Gras, 30+

813 Bienville Street, 523-5433 • French Quarter Zone 1

Cover None **Minimum** None; jazz club $4 **Mixed drinks** $3.75 and up **Wine** $5.75 and up **Beer** $3.50 and up **Dress** Suits, party dresses, casual elegance, and the occasional black tie **Food available** Creole, with a sophisticated twist **Disabled access** Yes

Hours French 75 open 6–10:30 p.m.; restaurant open 11:30 a.m.–2:15 p.m. for lunch, and 6 –9:45 p.m. weekdays; open till 10:15 p.m. Friday and Saturday

What goes on Arnaud's is primarily known as one of the great high-end, old-line Creole restaurants of the French Quarter, often mentioned in the same breath as Antoine's, Broussard's, and Brennan's. Off to the far side of the 17-room restaurant is the old lounge, a bar filled with diners who are waiting for their tables, and those who have already polished off their pompano plates and are enjoying the rewards of classic New Orleans post-supper culture. In the midst of these restaurant patrons are locals who have just come for a drink and to revel in this beautiful cocktail chamber, where local wags and kingmakers decide who will back the next mayor of New Orleans and who will be named the next Queen of Mardi Gras—equally important decisions in these curious times.

Setting & atmosphere "Count" Arnaud Cazenave (he had no bona fide claim to the title) opened the restaurant in an antebellum mansion in 1918, and it has been a local high-society staple ever since. With its player piano and green, upholstered men's-club motif, a small but well-stocked humidor, and the requisite white tile and period gas lamps, Arnaud's interior reminds one of a Victorian parlor. This is a great place to knock back a few martinis and argue with the ghost of Huey Long.

If you go Seek out proprietor Archie Casbarian, who serves two valuable functions. A cigar aficionado from the days before super models posed with stogies on trendy magazine covers, Casbarian is the man to consult for an after-dinner smoke. He also presides over the restaurant's famous Mardi Gras museum, a series of tiny rooms that offer life-size renditions of the gowns and finery and feathers of Mardi Gras past. It's all such a long story—the New Orleans Mardi Gras and attendant mysteries, controversies, and layers of social complexity. The small but endearing exhibit poses more questions than it answers, but then that's the charm. Don't miss it.

Bombay Club

DELIGHTFULLY PRETENTIOUS GIN JOINT AND ARMCHAIR LOUNGE

Who goes there 30–75, movers, shakers, pols, yuppies, buppies, second sceners, the courthouse crowd

830 Conti Street, 586-0972; www.thebomabyclub.com • French Quarter Zone 1

Cover Festivals and major shows only **Minimum** None **Mixed drinks** $4.25–$15 **Wine** $5–$7 **Beer** $3–$4.50; drinks at least $6 for festivals and major shows **Dress** The sign says "Proper attire required." Let that be your guide. Jackets for men. **Specials** When it's offered, "New Orleans

Networking Night" is a promotion enhanced by free drinks for women all night. **Food available** Small but appealing bistro menu as well as appetizers along the lines of pâté, salmon plates, and cheese boards **Disabled access** Yes

Hours Tuesday–Saturday, 4 p.m.–2 a.m.; late night menu Wednesday–Saturday

What goes on Networking, schmoozing, flirting, and general bedazzling, both physical and verbal. The Bombay is where monied but demure locals gather to chatter and booze to the soft piano strains of local and generally very talented ivory ticklers. The Bombay was the first of the city's upscale cigar and martini bars—by ten years—and still stands above the others.

Setting & atmosphere Downright Churchillian, the Bombay has the trappings of a British men's club, which is what it was supposed to be when it opened. But there are not many Brits here, and it turns out women like it too. It is darkly paneled with rich reds amid the décor, and a variety of bar stools, booths, and sofas, in comfy living-room settings. The subtle hints at old-line decadence, the hushed conversation emanating from the booths, and the background sound of tinkling glasses make for a convivial step back in time to an era when a slew of martinis after work was considered classy, not reprehensible.

If you go Demure, please. Remember, everyone is putting on a show, but no one wants to look like it. Play the game. Overtip. Don't sing along to the piano. Don't ogle the enhanced cleavage, although there is plenty. Overdress—go ahead, get your stones out of the hotel safe for this one. Recommended refreshments: clear liquors are the toast of the Bombay—all the great, triple-distilled, and overpriced gins and vodkas. Try one. Try two and take a cab. Please.

Café Brasil

INTERNATIONAL WATERING HOLE AND LIVE-MUSIC CLUB

Who goes there Latins, Africans, rastas, punks, rockers, Liv Tyler, and New Yorkers who miss the Village

2100 Chartres Street, 949-0851 • Downtown/St. Bernard Zone 5

Cover None–$10 **Minimum** None **Mixed drinks** $3 and up **Wine** $3 and up **Beer** $3 and up **Dress** Turtlenecks, sandals, dreads, tie-dyes, leather, kenta cloth, Sex Pistols T-shirts **Food available** None **Disabled access** Yes

Hours Varies. Generally, daily, 6 p.m.–3 a.m., but much is left to the whims of club management

What goes on Situated just a block outside the French Quarter, in the trendy Faubourg Marigny section of town, Café Brasil led the revival of this funky and decidedly hip neighborhood, now full of bistros and music clubs. Brasil is an international town hall, with many complexions, dialects, and orientations at play. The music is mellow early, a place for young lions of jazz to show their chops, then more dance oriented in the later evening, generally along the lines of funk, Latin, or reggae.

Setting & atmosphere Wide open and neon, it looks more like New York—or perhaps Brazil—than New Orleans. The clientele spills onto the street and sidewalk nightly, creating a vibrant and colorful neighborhood atmosphere. Plenty of Harleys, tattoos, lounging dogs, and clove cigarettes to make for a funky, underground feel.

If you go Relax and enjoy. No one here is in a hurry. Drink coffee or imported beer and soak up the international flair. Close to the French Market side of the Quarter, it's a safe walk. Also, check out the handful of other music clubs in the area—The Dragon's Den, Dream Palace, Checkpoint Charlie's, Café Negril, Blue Nile, and Snug Harbor—Frenchmen Street has become the city's bohemian and musical epicenter. These clubs and the smattering of bistros on Frenchmen Street have made the Marigny an unofficial extension of the Vieux Carré, with a considerably more local and multicultural accent.

Cat's Meow

BOURBON STREET KARAOKE

Who goes there 20–45, suburban singles, folks who wouldn't be caught dead in a place like this back home

701 Bourbon Street, 523-2788 • French Quarter Zone 1

Cover Friday and Saturday $5 for those under 21 only **Minimum** None **Mixed drinks** $4.50–$5.75 **Wine** $4 **Beer** $3.75 **Dress** Anything goes **Specials** Happy hour 4–8 p.m. weekdays, with three-for-one drinks **Food available** None **Disabled access** Yes

Hours Monday–Friday, 4 p.m.–4 a.m.; Saturday and Sunday, 2 p.m.– sunrise

What goes on For reasons no one seems able to explain, this is on many nights the most crowded and raucous club on a very crowded and raucous street. It is certainly the city's premier karaoke club and has the best sound, the most selections, and a staff of professional hosts/singers to keep the night running with controlled chaos and provide at least the occasional bearable performance. If you want to participate, be prepared to wait—as you'll see, a lot of people think they belong onstage in this world, and most of them wind up here.

Setting & atmosphere We're talking dead-center, ground-zero Bourbon Street here. People are stacked shoulder to shoulder, so you never really see the décor, other than the bright stage lights and the pink-and-green neon backdrop. If the street level proves too crowded for your taste, walk up to the balcony; Mardi Gras plays out 365 days a year on the street below. Hooting, hollering, bartering for plastic beads, and flashing are part of the nightly ritual.

If you go Be prepared to wear some beer on your clothes. It's hot and crowded, and jostling for space and movement is inevitable. Along with tourists, the place draws younger suburban folks looking for a good drink and a few laughs. This is no place for the uptight or the overdressed. Also, Cat's Meow is the location of the infamous Bourbo-Cam, a streaming video camera set up on the sidewalk outside where drunk revelers can stand, call their friends back in Boston, and tell them to go online and witness their, well . . . revelry. Lots of flashing here. (The website is **nola.com**.)

The Columns

PART SOPHISTICATED-SINGLES CLUB, PART DEBUTANTE BALL

Who goes there Debs, old frats, old money, Uptowners, porch potatoes

3811 St. Charles Avenue, 899-9308; • Uptown below Napoleon Zone 3

Cover None **Minimum** None **Mixed drinks** $3–$6.50 **Wine** $2–$6.50 **Beer** $2.50–$3.50 **Dress** Rumpled seersucker, Dockers, $75 shorts **Specials** Weekdays, happy hour 5–7 p.m., $2 house wines **Food available** Hot-plate munchies during happy hour only **Disabled access** Yes

Hours Monday–Thursday, 3 p.m.–midnight; Friday, 2 p.m.–2 a.m.; Saturday, 11 a.m.–2 a.m.; Sunday 11 a.m.–midnight

What goes on From the expansive Victorian front porch, watch the streetcars run up and down the oak-lined, placidly genteel avenue—New Orleans's most famous and beautiful. Inside the rich and lusty barroom, tell your best investment stories. On some Tuesday or Wednesday nights your might find some jazz trio noodling around in the side parlor. Mostly, it's just a relax-and-be-smug-that-you're-in-New-Orleans kind of place.

Setting & atmosphere This old hotel was the setting for *Pretty Baby,* Brooke Shields' breakout film, but don't hold that against the place. It's musty and a little lopsided, but full of the charm and mystery of old-line Uptown New Orleans—eccentric, monied, and talkative. It is cozy, romantic, sultry, and on hot nights, sweaty—but in the best sense. Take the time to soak in the architectural details of the parlors off the main bar, a trove of pilasters, cornices, chandeliers, gilded frames, and Victorian mirrors and furniture.

If you go Make no plans after The Columns: you could get stuck here for hours, imprisoned by the absolute passivity and laissez-faire of the locals who congregate to tell the stories of their gloried pasts. If this all sounds pretentious, it's not. In fact, consider the place to be one of the city's communal living rooms, where family and friends gather in sloe-gin comfort.

Crescent City Brewhouse

FRENCH QUARTER BREWPUB AND JAZZ JOINT

Who goes there 25–75, tourists, home brewers

527 Decatur Street, 522-0571; www.crescentcitybrewhouse.com • French Quarter
Zone 1

Cover None **Minimum** None **Mixed drinks** $4.75+ **Wine** $4.75+ **Beer**
$3.95–$5.95 **Dress** Business casual, suits to sandals **Specials** Weekday
happy hour 5–7 p.m., two-for-one beer and free hors d'oeuvres **Food
available** Full menu of pastas, seafood, steaks, gumbo, and an oyster bar
Disabled access Yes

Hours Sunday–Thursday, 11 a.m.–10 p.m.; Friday and Saturday, 11
a.m.–midnight; bar sometimes open later than restaurant

What goes on This is a spacious and lively brewpub pushed right up on
one of the busiest sidewalks in the Quarter. Music is usually provided by
trios of wannabe young lions, cutting jazz chops. Sometimes it's a Latin
combo. Either way, the band is usually background to chatter and conversation, though Wynton Marsalis did show up one night when his little brother was playing, and that pretty much shut everybody up.

Setting & atmosphere Before your very eyes are the huge copper vats in
which Red Stallion and Black Forest ales are brewed, as well as Crescent
City Pilsner and a variable beer of the month—maybe a nice bock or a
Christmas ale. Fine brews, all. Lots of exposed and shiny wood, very
clean, very beer-gardeny, if that's a word. Lots of room. Plenty of light.
Always a friendly and energetic crowd.

If you go Check a stool at the bar; it gives you a look at the brewing
process, the band, and the sidewalk, where an endless parade of buggies,
buses, skateboarders, gutter punks, waiters, and Kansans loll by. If the
band doesn't impress you and you long for grander vistas, go upstairs on
the balcony overlooking Decatur, where the view affords Mississippi
River traffic, with its tankers, steamers, barges, and paddle wheelers.

d.b.a.

ENERGETIC AND INTELLECTUAL-FRIENDLY WATERING HOLE

Who goes there Writers, musicians, public radio DJs, occasional suits, discrimi-
nating imbibers

618 Frenchmen Street, 942-3731 • Downtown/St. Bernard Zone 5

Cover None **Minimum** None **Mixed drinks** $4 and up **Wine** $4 and
up **Beer** $3.50–$6 **Dress** Casual to suits **Specials** Happy hour intil
7p.m., $1 off drinks **Food available** None **Disabled access** Yes

Hours Daily, 4 p.m.–4 a.m.

What goes on Despite its somewhat pretentious lowercase nomenclature, d.b.a. has been a most welcome addition to the "smart bar" scene since opening at the dawn of the new century. The music is smart—nightly sets by extremely game and talented local jazz, fusion, R&B, and lounge acts. The clientele is smart—you're more likely to hear conversations about international affairs and Lars von Trier's latest film than the latest reality TV show. (This is not to say that mindless chatter about the Saints or J-Lo's latest dress are unwelcome; it's just that the TV in the corner is as likely to be turned to CNN as to ESPN.) And the booze is very smart. Indeed, d.b.a.'s trademark—both here and at its New York City sister bar—is the creative selections of wine, Scotch, port, and beer. Great stuff; perhaps the most alluring selections in town for fans of the juice.

Setting & atmosphere It's laid back; no worries or pretentions about dress code, social status, or smoking (or even kids and dogs on very relaxed and not-too-crowded evenings). The staff is (generally) very helpful with your selections and service. It's dark and spare inside—unadorned cypress paneling and dark tables and stools, candlelight, plenty of space overhead for conversation and smoke to dissipate. In general, a very good vibe. Also, there's a pool table and a private back room with revolving art exhibitions, perfect for small parties, the occasional celeb visitor (Nicolas Cage is a regular here), and private poker games and such. Best to call ahead to secure this room.

If you go Relax and enjoy the place. Just one thing: d.b.a. is clearly divided into two halves—two long rooms linked by openings at both ends. One side is the "tavern," where conversation is the bill of fare. The other side is the music room, and as the music here is always of high integrity (and generally not overpoweringly loud), you'd be advised to respect the audiophiles' wishes by keeping to the tavern side if your party is chatty.

Donna's

LIVE BRASS-BAND JAZZ

Who goes there Euro jazzhounds, second liners, old hats, thrill seekers, the mayor

800 N. Rampart Street, 596-6914; www.donnasbarandgrill.com • French Quarter Zone I

Cover $5 **Minimum** One drink per set **Mixed drinks** $3–$5.50 **Wine** $3 **Beer** $3 **Dress** Very casual, umbrellas optional **Specials** Free barbecue chicken and red beans and rice at first break and between sets on Mondays **Food available** Southern barbecue, ribs, pulled pork sandwiches, étouffée, and burgers **Disabled access** Adequate

Hours Thursday–Monday, 6:30 until; closed Tuesday and Wednesday

What goes on Donna Sims has built the headquarters for the city's hottest musical renaissance—brass-band jazz, the swirling and frenetic interplay of horns and percussion. This is the place for nationally touring acts like Kermit Ruffins, the Rebirth Brass Band, the Tremé Brass Band, and lesser-known yet more adventurous gangs like the Soul Rebels and Newbirth Brass bands, who mix urban shades of hip-hop with the traditional brass. Also, this has become the after-hours hangout for the friends and appointees of Ray Nagin, the city's extremely popular, telegenic, and nightclubbing mayor.

Setting & atmosphere The bar stools, beer lights, and industrial carpet don't make much for aesthetics, but that's not why people come here. Be ready to dance and sashay or grab a space out of the way and against the wall. Locals will pull out hankies and umbrellas and act like their old Uncle Joe just died and this is his jazz funeral. Out of respect for old Uncle Joe, get off your duff and live a little. Do the funky chicken. Grab a stranger and dance. You may already have gotten this impression, but Donna's is loose on structure and form. What else can you say about a place where you have to part soloing trombonists to get to the rest rooms? If the joint is cooking, a night at Donna's will be something you remember forever.

If you go Beware: Rampart Street is the dark side of the Quarter, literally and figuratively. It is seedier and more dangerous than the spry and lively Bourbon and Decatur streets. This doesn't mean don't go there. It means take a cab to the door. If you're already nearby in the Quarter and are with a group of three or more, feel safe to hoof it, but be on maximum alert in the street.

Dos Jefes Uptown Cigar Bar

CIGAR BAR AND JAZZ JOINT WITH A SPEAKEASY FEEL

Who goes there Locals, music students, jam-session junkies, dates, off-duty Uptown waiters

5535 Tchoupitoulas Street, 891-8500 • Uptown above Napoleon Zone 4

Cover None **Minimum** None **Mixed drinks** $4 and up **Wine** $3.75 and up **Beer** $2.25 and up **Dress** Suits to shorts; casual but clean **Specials** Happy hour 5–8 p.m. **Food available** Limited menu of bar food **Disabled access** None, but doorman will help with steps

Hours Every day, 5 p.m. until

What goes on Yeah, yeah, the big American cigar craze has run its course, but realize this—the trend didn't get to New Orleans until it was playing out on the East and West coasts, so let us have our fun. Cigars aren't really the buzz here anyway; the 50 brands or so in the wall humidor are just lagniappe, a New Orleans term for something special to go with the regular fare of the place. It's a sit-and-chat jazz joint, with high-quality music seven nights a week, ranging from local piano professors and guitar pickers to improvisational Latin and bebop combos. Some of the younger Marsalis brothers sit in here from time to time.

Setting & atmosphere It's got a nice speakeasy feel to it: tables pushed close together and a couch or two to sink into while the music flows over the place. There's a cozy outdoor beer garden, brightly painted and surrounded by lush flora, rendering a Caribbean feel to the place. It's a loose locale with no general rules; sometimes the crowd drowns the music, sometimes, when the personalities and compositions intertwine on one of those magic nights, the horn sessions get to some smoking levels that even Satchmo might admire, and that reminds the oft-jaded locals in the house why they live in New Orleans.

If you go First of all, don't complain about the smoke. It's part of the program, but it shouldn't be too much of a problem since the air-filter system works pretty well. The musicians here are paid peanuts, so a fiver in the jar might be nice. This is a polite, genteel, and comfortable place to close out an evening spent at any one of the top-shelf Uptown fine-dining restaurants, like the Upperline, Clancy's, Gautreau's, Martinique, or Brigtsen's.

El Matador

HIPSTER HANGOUT

Who goes there Bohemians, Hollywood bad boys, adventurers

504 Esplanade Avenue, 569-8361 • French Quarter Zone 1

Cover $5–$10 **Minimum** None **Mixed drinks** $2.50–$7 **Wine** $3.50–$4.50 **Beer** $2–$4 **Dress** Punk, boho, casual or retro **Specials** None **Food available** None **Disabled access** Yes

Hours Monday–Wednesday, 9 p.m.–until; Thursday–Sunday, 5 p.m.–until

What goes on One allure—among many—is the musical fare offered here: top-notch local jazz, lounge, roots, and soul. (Watch the listings for Ingrid Lucia, the Soul Rebels, and Jeremy Lyons—all inventive young acts with seekly gigs here.) That said, the place can be a little intimidating to the Dockers set. The content of tragically hip customers (tattoos, piercings, porkpie hats, and sideburns of intriguing design and variation) can be overwhelming at times, but it's impossible to keep this off any serious list of go-to clubs in the city. The Matador is a central link between lower Decatur Street and nearby Frenchmen Street—the two frontiers where locals outnumber tourists downtown. The place is owned by Rio Hackford, the son of director Taylor Hackford and actress Helen Mirren. Hackford's star power (he's an L.A. native and sometime actor) draws young Hollywood types in from time to time, most notably cinematic bad boy Vince Vaughn, who is so at home here that he's more likely to take a turn at the bar serving drinks than hang around in the public areas surrounded by adoring women. And the women, they love that Vince.

Setting & atmosphere The Matador has a red velvet and retro look to it. Very loungey with deep-set booths and little direct lighting. The stage looks like 1956. It's no coincidence that Hackford (and Vaughn, of course) was in Swingers, the cult hit film about the L.A. lounge scene. This place has the feel of those old Hollywood and Vine lounges that have become extremely popular among young nightclubbers out on the coast these days.

If you go Enjoy the music. The players love this joint and generally deliver spirited late-night sets. Safe to say anything goes here. The best advice we can offer is: Don't get caught leering at the tattoos that crawl out of the cleavages of the female clientele. But you knew that, didn't you? And look, if Vince has that "don't bother me—I am very drunk" look on his face, it's best to comply. We know this from experience.

F&M Patio Bar

LATE-NIGHT PARTY BAR

Who goes there Uptowners, debs, post-debs, lawyers, post-grads, cops, insomniacs, John Goodman

4841 Tchoupitoulas Street, 895-6784 • Uptown above Napoleon Zone 4

Cover None **Minimum** None **Mixed drinks** $3 and up **Wine** $3 and up **Beer** $2.50 and up **Dress** Parrothead chic, Saints jerseys, loose ties, torn jeans, food stains from dinner **Food available** New Orleans bar food: cheese fries, quesadillas, burgers, and po'boys **Disabled access** Adequate, but men's rest room is inaccessible.

Hours Everyday, 5 p.m.–4 a.m. or later

What goes on This is the party after the party, the place where folks go after the Quarter, after the music, after the Carnival ball, and after their other favorite bars have closed. Nowhere do well-heeled Orleanians display more consistently and more forcefully the city's all-night colors than here, shouting lyrics to Beatles tunes on the jukebox, dancing on pool tables, and cramming four at a time into the bar's trademark photo booth. The scene plays out on many levels, from last-chance pick-up joint to a place to wind down the wee hours.

Setting & atmosphere Truthfully, there is nothing particularly New Orleanian about the place. It's a basic fraternity house basement décor: bare cement floors, neon beer signs, pinball tables, etc. The jukebox is rich with pop classics, from Haley to Hootie. Sometimes the smell of beer is a little pungent.

If you go It can be rowdy sometimes, and a little too collegiate for some tastes, but it's mostly a harmless place to catch up on the goings-on of

Uptown locals, many of whom have cell phones, children, and 401k plans and know better than to be here at this hour. It is a party until the last gasps of dawn have surrendered to the sun, so bring your sunglasses—it can be awfully harsh walking out into the sunny glare of the industrial Tchoupitoulas Street corridor.

French Quarter Bar

SEE AND BE SCENE

Who goes there Social climbers, out-on-the-towners, famous people

921 Canal Street (lobby of the Ritz Carlton hotel), 524-1331 • French Quarter Zone 1

Cover None **Minimum** None **Mixed drinks** $5–$10 **Wine** $8–$18
Beer $4–$5 **Dress** Sharp **Specials** No **Food available** Full-service Cajun/Creole/traditional bistro **Disabled access** Yes

Hours Daily, 11 a.m.–2 a.m.

What goes on FQB, as locals—and the hotel's promotional staff—call the joint, has became a favorite of locals and visitors alike in the last year or two. Now that New Orleanians have finally (begrudgingly) come to terms with the era of the $10 mangotini, they have embraced the French Quarter Bar as a quintessential see-and-be-seen scene. The music is great fun; young house bandleader and trumpeter Jeremy Davenport is a classic crooner and entertainer in an Old School sense—lots of stage banter and set lists of listener-friendly jazz standards. One allure of the place is its celebrity content, perhaps for no other reason than the bar is located in the hotel where all A-list visitors to New Orleans check in. No less stellar lights than Paul McCartney, Sting, and hometown boy (and former Davenport mentor) Harry Connick, Jr., have sat in with the band on occasion. Davenport's star is rising in such a manner that there is even a featured drink called the "Davenportini." We've never tried it. Let us know if it's any good.

Setting & atmosphere Truth is, with its smartly arranged tables and fine linen tablecloths, FQB looks more like a restaurant than a bar (and the vittles are first rate, by the way), but there's no mistaking the tenor of the joint once night takes hold in the city. It's a long and wide-open setting by day, but the place shrinks in a hurry when the crowds start pressing in, particularly on weekends. Whether celebs are present or not, FQB always has a house-party, forget-your-cares atmosphere. Also a plus: a learned staff that knows how to put sublime touches on some New Orleans classics, like Sazeracs, mint juleps, Pimm's Cups, and a not-as-deadly-as Bourbon Street Hurricane.

If you go Dress sharp. It is the Ritz, after all. If you want to focus on the music—and it is worth the effort to listen here—you need to get a perch close to the stage. The back of the house can get pretty noisy sometimes with loose-lipped locals or tourists who've spent the day getting socially lubricated. Of note: If it gets too crowded or beery in the FQB, you can retreat to the dark, secluded Library Lounge on the far side of the hotel's sprawling lobby. It's a dark, intimate club better suited to get-to-know-you kinds of evenings or low-key conversation.

Funky Butt at Congo Square

JAZZ, BLUES, AND JAZZY BLUES IN A DECO SETTING

Who goes there Lounge lizards, nighthawks, poets, bohos, jazzheads

714 N. Rampart Street, 558-0872; www.funkybutt.com • French Quarter Zone 1

Cover None–$20 **Minimum** One drink per set **Mixed drinks** $3–$5 **Wine** $3.50–$7 **Beer** $2–$6 **Dress** Anything goes; Gothic to black tie **Specials** Funky Buttjuice, a $6 concoction of secret ingredients, for the daring only **Food available** Gumbo, jambalaya, étouffée **Disabled access** Adequate; wheelchair access through kitchen; upper level is inaccessible. **Hours** Daily, 7 p.m.–3 a.m.

What goes on When proprietor Richard Rochester isn't giving guided tours of French Quarter haunted properties (that's another story), he is here hosting one of the hippest music clubs in town. Carved out of the classic and formerly exclusive Art Deco restaurant called Jonathan, the Funky Butt is a lively mélange of conversation and dance, seven nights a week, with the likes of piano professors Henry Butler or Jon "King" Cleary and other world-class keyboard and horn players holding court. The Funky Butt, by the way, was the name of a dance that accompanied the music of the pioneering Buddy Bolden, the city's first King of Jazz and a cornet player with chops so loud that legend tells of listeners enjoying his solos from half a mile away. We cannot, however, document this.

Setting & atmosphere Downstairs, the lounge retains many of the Deco treasures and details from the Jonathan era—black-lacquered woods, cut-glass fixtures, and Erte prints. The jukebox is one of the great archives of New Orleans music history. Upstairs, the live-music club is dark, with a few hidden corners for discreet couples. One reviewer called the décor "a cross between a 1930s jazz crib and a brothel," and we think the description fitting.

If you go Like its neighbor Donna's (see profile), the Funky Butt hovers on the sketchy side of the Quarter. We suggest alertness when coming and going, and a cab to do both.

Gennifer Flowers's Kelsto Club

FORMER TABLOID QUEEN FOLLOWS HER LOUNGE DREAM

Who goes there Quarterites, high society, the curious and the easily amused

720 St. Louis Street, 524-1111 • French Quarter Zone 1

Cover None **Minimum** 1 drink **Mixed drinks** $4–$30 **Wine** $5–$9 **Beer** $3–$9 **Dress** Scandalous, of course. Bluck cocktail dresses? (Oops, sorry . . . wrong scandal.) **Specials** No **Food available** Alex Patout's full-service Cajun restaurant is upstairs. **Disabled access** Yes **Hours** Daily, 5 p.m. until

What goes on Well, well, well. They certainly don't have this in your home town. Gennifer Flowers, the tabloid queen of the 1990s, the peppery peroxide paramour of Bill Clinton, relocated to New Orleans a few years ago to follow her first love: music. That's right, she's a torch singer. She opened a piano bar, and she meets and greets and sings Patsy Cline a couple nights a week, whenever the mood strikes. Naturally, the middle American masses are checking in to check it out.

Setting & atmosphere Great history at this location: In the early 1900s, the original Kelsto Club was a brothel. In the 1970s, famed trumpeter Al Hirt opened a Frank Sinatra tribute bar here. In the 1980s, a woman named Verita Thompson—who was Humphrey Bogart's mistress for more than a decade—opened a joint called Bogey & Me. After that closed, the property became Lucky Cheng's, a Creole restaurant staffed entirely by Asian drag queens. And now . . . Gennifer Flowers. Even by New Orleans standards, that's a colorful history. Lordy, if these walls could talk. It's a gloriously beautiful room, full of fancy furniture, precious fixtures, and fine crown molding and, of course, the requisite framed clippings of Flowers's 15 minutes of fame.

If you go Don't hesitate to introduce youself to the proprietor; she's a wide-open personality, full of mischief and much smarter than she was portrayed during the Clinton scandal era. Also, seek out her husband, the improbably named Finis Shellnut, who is a singular character all his own. All in all, the place is a great lark. Caveat emptor: Bring a ton of money. As much as we are amused by this place, $9 for draft beer strikes us as, well . . . downright scandalous!

House of Blues

NATIONAL-, REGIONAL-, AND LOCAL-CIRCUIT MUSIC CLUB

Who goes there Dan Aykroyd and friends, out-of-towners, locals because it's the only place left to see the Neville Brothers

225 Decatur Street, 529-blue; www.hob.com • French Quarter Zone I

Cover Varies from $5 for good local acts to $50+ for heavy hitters like Sheryl Crow or Bob Dylan. The back bar—where you can watch the show on live TV—is free. **Minimum** None **Mixed drinks** $3.75–$7 **Wine** $4.50–$9 **Beer** $3.75–$4.50 **Dress** To fit the show. For Trisha Yearwood, boots and buckles would suit; for the Nevilles, perhaps something in unity colors. For the Gospel Brunch, dare to be different: dress nice.

Food available Full menu of Louisiana, Cajun, and American café dishes
Disabled access Yes

Hours Restaurant: Monday–Wednesday 11:30 a.m.–11:30 p.m. and Thursday–Saturday 11:30 a.m.–midnight. Music Hall: Daily 8 p.m. until

What goes on When the House of Blues opened in 1994, its New Age–friendly motto, "Help Ever, Hurt Never," was tarnished by the club's cutthroat pursuit of every major player in the local rock, blues, and jazz circles, outbidding and nearly snuffing out several local and long-established music clubs. In the ensuing years, an easy equilibrium has settled over the local industry; it's a given now that the House gets the biggest names in the business, from Eric Clapton to Mystikal to Norah Jones. And the biggest crowds. Also, the addition of The Parish—a nightclub within a nightclub—has allowed the House to book smaller and more daring acts—jazz trios, lonesome songwriters and such—many of them well suited to the smaller and more intimate stage setting of this cozy second-story ballroom.

Setting & atmosphere This is a New York club in a small town; the goon-sized bouncers with headsets and ear phones, quite frankly, scare the hell out of some locals, who prefer to hang out at a place where they can park within three or four blocks of the front door. On the positive side, HOB has amassed an awesome collection of Southern folk art, which hangs everywhere, including the rest rooms. Take the time to look at these colorful treasures from Louisiana, Mississippi, and Alabama.

If you go First and foremost, never mess with the bouncers. There are stories. Second, be ready to pay the price—both monetarily and in comfort. There is not enough seating available, and what there is seems always reserved for visiting celebrities who hinted to management that they were coming, but never showed up. This leaves the great seats empty on the most crowded nights and adds to the generally antagonistic relationship between the club and longtime local music fans who have lived by a first come, first served basis for decades. But these ill-wishing locals realize that the House of Blues will succeed, even thrive, on one-time customers or those who will put up with the club's icy treatment because it's the only place to catch the great national tours. And the Nevilles.

The Howlin' Wolf

LIVE REGIONAL, ALTERNATIVE, PROGRESSIVE COUNTRY, AND FOLK MUSIC

Who goes there Rockers, cow punks, guitar gods, slackers

828 S. Peters Street, 522-9653; www.howlin-wolf.com • Central Business District Zone 2

Cover Varies with act, roughly $10–$30 **Minimum** None **Mixed drinks** $3.50–$6 **Wine** $4 **Beer** $2.50–$5 **Dress** Rock-club casual **Food available** None (only during JazzFest and Mardi Gras) **Disabled access** Yes

Hours 9 p.m. until the show ends (anywhere from midnight to 8 a.m.)

What goes on The Wolf is the musicians' music club; half the house on any night may be the city's rock fraternity checking out the latest acts on the local alternative, rockabilly, or singer/songwriter circuit. The Wolf also draws an array of lesser-known but established national acts—anybody from country-crooning Iris Dement to jazz poet John Sinclair to surf-guitar guru Dick Dale. This is where up-and-coming bands play before the House of Blues gets wind of who they are and books them on the next tour.

Setting & atmosphere A roomy two-level music hall decorated with old movie-set signs, the Wolf is dimly lit but very clean. The clientele is respectful of the music, so don't be surprised to find the pool-table light extinguished before the performance; many acoustic acts will request your attention. It's a mix of listening and dancing crowds; feel free to do either. If you need to be off your feet for the evening, get there early, as available bar stools at the raised tables are rare.

If you go The Wolf operates on a time-honored rock tradition—the music begins when the music begins, and ends when it ends. The news-paper will no doubt list a performance at 10 p.m., and this raises a strategic riddle: Do you go on time and end up cooling your heels for an hour while band members drift in, or do you arrive late and risk missing the rare prompt performer? Our advice: Go on time, get a table, and if the show is late, chill out to the great sound system and a cold Abita draft.

Lafitte's Blacksmith Shop

ROMANTIC HIDEAWAY AND PIANO LOUNGE

Who goes there Couples, romantics, Quarter rats, pirates, and ghosts

941 Bourbon Street, 523-0066; www.lafittes.com • French Quarter Zone 1

Cover None **Minimum** One drink (not strictly enforced) **Mixed drinks** $3.75 and up **Wine** $3.50 **Beer** $3.50 and up **Dress** Casual **Food available** None **Disabled access** Yes, but access to the rest rooms is hindered by a step; staff members are glad to help.

Hours Daily, 24 hours

What goes on Located in one of the oldest buildings in the city, Lafitte's is said to be America's oldest bar, but that's another one of those oft-repeated stories. . . What we do know is that the building actually belonged to the famed privateer Jean Lafitte—or one of his colleagues—and was used for the storage of loot pilfered from ships in Barataria Bay and the Gulf of Mexico. Somewhere along the line, many years after Lafitte disappeared into the Confederate mist, the building became one of the city's most beloved bars.

Setting & atmosphere Other than a single bulb behind the bar, the only light in here is provided by candles and, during cool seasons, the fireplace.

It is dark, damp, and lusty inside, made of old brick, stone, crumbling mortar, and exposed beams. In the back cove, local piano-bar aficionados gather around the keys and sing along to time-honored classics every night except Wednesday. There's an overgrown and musty courtyard on the side for those who truly want to disappear.

If you go This is an ideal spot to get to know that special someone you met at the planning seminar earlier in the day at the Marriott conference center. Lafitte's is a port of calm on Bourbon Street's sea of bedlam, so if the racket is getting to you but you still want to be a part of the night scene, pull in here for a couple of hours. The close quarters and slow, easy pace of the staff and clientele beg for intimacy. This is a great bar.

Loa

SWINGING SINGLES MEET THE HIP-HOP NATION

Who goes there 21–75, suburban voyeurs, downtown lawyers, rap stars, buppies and the ghost of Marie Laveau

221 Camp Street, 553-9550 • Central Business District Zone 2

Cover None **Minimum** None **Mixed drinks** $4.50 and up **Wine** $5.50 **Beer** $4 and up **Dress** Suits, loose ties, and the occasional casual elegance **Specials** None **Food available** No **Disabled access** Yes

Hours Monday–Saturday, 11–2 a.m.; Sunday, closed

What goes on Loa is a trendy hotel bar in a trendy hotel, a watering hole for the suit-and-seersucker set after the factory whistle blows, and a busy singles hangout by nightfall. Thrown into this mix is the fact that the hotel in question, the International House, has emerged as ground zero for high-end African American travelers, therefore the joint attracts more than its share of bold-face names—particularly rap and R&B stars, former pro athletes and the occasional TV star or supermodel.

Setting & atmosphere The place is small but the turnover is steady; most folks seem to stop by Loa on their way to or from someplace else. (Though it doesn't matter if the crowd surges; the hotel lobby can easily accommodate.) The décor is muted pales and off whites, lit almost entirely by votive candles at night. High windows along two walls lend Loa its big-city, downtown feel. It could be Manhattan, really, but it has a warm feel to it.

If you go Dress sharp and be prepared to wait for drinks if the crowd numbers in the dozens. And one more thing: Loa is a word from the voodoo dictionary that means the pantheon of the gods. Don't be surprised if you walk in on an impromptu voodoo ceremony; they're held now and then to keep the spirits clean. Just so you know.

Lucy's Retired Surfer's Bar

SINGLES SIDEWALK HANGOUT

Who goes there 25–45, suits, debs, hot shots, climbers, condo-dwellers

701 Tchoupitoulas Street, 523-8995 • Central Business District Zone 2

Cover None **Minimum** None **Mixed drinks** $3.50 and up **Wine** $3.50 **Beer** $3.25 and up **Dress** Loose ties, Hawaii Five-O, Banana Republic **Specials** Monday happy hour 4–7 p.m., drinks $1.50–$2.50 **Food available** A full California/MexAmerican menu **Disabled access** Yes

Hours Monday, happy hour, 4 p.m.–7 p.m.; Tuesday–Saturday, 11 a.m.–2 a.m.; Sunday, closed

What goes on Big on happy hour and weekend nights, Lucy's fills to capacity with young banker and lawyer types from the neighboring Central Business District and with the rising number of yuppie Warehouse District inhabitants escaping from the confines of their nearby cubicle condos. Though everyone seems to know everyone else here, a well-timed compliment on a tie or nail color may open doors for strangers in the crowd. (At press time, Lucy's was preparing to open a second location on Magazine Street near Audubon Park, where the young, monied, Uptown crowd will no doubt provide a steady clientele.)

Setting & atmosphere Sidewalk chic; even in the heat of summer, the crowd at Lucy's flows into the street, making for a super-casual block-party environment. The interior is exposed brick with hints of South Pacific blues and greens. Generally patrons stand three or four deep at the bar, but there are booths and a back room for stretching out.

If you go The scene at Lucy's is somewhat interchangeable with a smaller, funkier, less hustling, and more intimate tavern across the street, Vic's Kangaroo Café, a Down Under joint serving up imported drafts and Aussie meat pies. This is a late-night watering hole for the black-and-white-clad waiters and waitresses of the many chic bistros of the Warehouse District. Vic's also has the last and only Asteroids video game that we have found in the city, if that matters.

The Maple Leaf

LIVE REGIONAL MUSIC

Who goes there Dancers, poets, chessmen, Uptowners, celebrities escaping the fuss

8316 Oak Street, 866-9359 • Uptown above Napoleon Zone 4

Cover Varies with act, generally $5–$10; higher for jazz festival **Minimum** None **Mixed drinks** $3.50 and up **Wine** $3 and up **Beer** $3.25 and up **Dress** Bowling shirts, sundresses, jeans, bandannas **Food available** None **Disabled access** Yes

Hours Sunday–Thursday, 3 p.m.–2 a.m.; Friday and Saturday, 3 p.m.–3 a.m.

What goes on Dancing and drinking nightly, with a broad range of local and regional musical offerings: poetry on Sunday afternoons, Cajun and zydeco on Thursdays, and blends of the blues, Latin, and funk the rest of the week. Shows get rolling around 10:30 p.m. The Tuesday-night brass-band jam, hosted by the Rebirth Brass Band, is a weekly microcosmic Mardi Gras. Packed with locals and visitors alike, the frenetic three-hour sessions literally pulse with energy and serious second-line spirit. At 2 a.m. you'll look around and wonder just what kinds of jobs all these dancing people have, but until then just enjoy being a guest at the city's most rollicking weekly house party. Go see this.

Setting & atmosphere One of the great old survivors of the local music scene, The Maple Leaf long ago ditched its courtyard laundromat—a local favorite—but retains all the other aspects of its funky Uptown charm: the pressed tin ceiling; the skinny yet inviting dance floor; the overgrown and candle-lit patio; the reliable musical palette; and the loveable, unemployable intellectuals who plop on bar stools every afternoon and bet on TV's "Jeopardy"—and always score better than anyone on the show.

If you go Be ready for one of New Orleans's favorite contact sports, two-stepping. The Leaf's dance floor is famously narrow, and when the likes of Rockin' Jake or Jumpin' Johnny's Blues Party open the throttle, it gets a little bouncy. If you get bumped, get out of the way or bump back. No whining. Also, the Leaf is two short blocks off the streetcar line Uptown. Take the St. Charles line there, then take a cab home.

Margaritaville Café

FRENCH QUARTER BEACHY MUSIC CLUB

Who goes there Tourists, Parrotheads, afternoon souvenir shoppers on rum break

1104 Decatur Street, 592-2565; www.margaritaville.com • French Quarter Zone 1

Cover Only for main stage and during festivals **Minimum** None **Mixed drinks** Margaritas start at $5.50 **Wine** $3.25 and up **Beer** $3 and up **Dress** Bermudas, sandals, and Hawaiian shirts **Specials** Happy hour Monday–Friday 2 for 1 from 5–7 p.m. **Food available** Gulf Coast cookin' with a late-night menu til 10:30 p.m. **Disabled access** Yes

Hours 11 a.m.–midnight or so, every day

What goes on As the name might imply, Margaritaville is part of pop-music icon and Gulf Coast favorite son Jimmy Buffett's considerable business empire. He's not quite a mogul of his cousin Warren's caliber, but the Margarita Man's publishing, music, real-estate, and retail accomplishments are impressive. The proprietor comes around occasionally, as New Orleans is among his preferred ports of call. His appearances on stage are always unannounced, yet jammed with loyal fans—the Parrotheads—who communicate on these matters via the Internet. Mostly, though, the musical fare is top-of-the-line New Orleans folk and R&B, from lunchtime 'til the wee hours, with several sets of music throughout the day performed by varying solo artists, duos, and full bands. Hoodoo guitar slinger Coco Robicheaux is a favorite here, playing late-afternoon sets of down-and-dirty Delta blues with a touch of local gris-gris thrown in for kicks, and 9th Ward country crooner Mike West is creating a whole new genre of hillbilly Cajun music here. You really should hear it.

Setting & atmosphere It has Buffett's personality: laid back, tropical, lazily seductive. It's a carefully contrived Key West/Caribbean setting that doesn't offend. Set along the busy lower Decatur Street sidewalk, home to edgy boutiques and vintage-clothing stores, there's lots of roomy seating in both the back and front bars, and plenty of exposure to the busy and eclectic street traffic. The décor is a biography of Buffett's career.

If you go No rules, really. It's a prime spot to waste away again in Margaritaville, slurping the plenitude of fancy tequila- and rum-based specialties of many hues and flavors, served in those towering, frou-frou cocktail glasses for which these kinds of places are known. Since you're here, you might as well stock up on the multitude of colorful Buffett-inspired and island-related gifts, T-shirts, and various paraphernalia. You can pass many hours here and wonder where the day went.

The Mermaid Lounge

LIVE PERFORMANCE ART, LOUNGE MUSIC, AND THE GENERAL RANTS AND RAVES OF MUSIC-MINDED IF SOMETIMES UNSAVORY MISFITS

Who goes there 25–45, Goths, rockers, the Paisley Parade, human tattoos, poseurs, the Lounge Nation

1100 Constance Avenue, 524-4747 • Central Business District: Zone 2

Cover $2–$10 **Minimum** None **Mixed drinks** $3–$4 **Wine** $3 **Beer** $3.50–$4 **Dress** Glitter, gloss, Elton John as Pinball Wizard, black tie, whatever. Go ahead, try to be noticed. **Specials** $1.50 Schaefer beers **Food available** The consortium of 30- and 40-something partners likes to host impromptu cookouts, buffets, and barbecues, but when it happens is up to whimsy. **Disabled access** Poor

Hours 9:30 p.m. until

What goes on When the Mermaid opened in 1994, it gave a nightclub presence to a varied and overlooked array of Louisiana artists: Glyn Styler, the local angst-ridden crooner and champion of lounge lizards; the Hackberry Ramblers, an octogenarian Cajun swing band; C.C. Adcock, a guitar-blazing swamp-pop incarnation; and Quintron, a local curiosity who locks himself in a room offstage and raises racket out of old electric organs. The club also books the more daring and unknown acts out of towns like Austin, Atlanta, and New York City. The Mermaid has become the epicenter of the alternative nightclub scene, wonderfully bizarre and calculatingly offbeat.

Setting & atmosphere The bar hosts rotating art shows and could be hanging anything from neon art to ersatz porn on any given weekend. There is no describing how casual this place can be, so full of slacker attitude and European cigarettes. The crowd generally spills out onto the sidewalk for impromptu street scenes among the Harleys and 1972 Impalas. Its reclusive location and costumed clientele often give it the feeling of being on the set of a Mad Max movie.

If you go Take a cab, not because it's so dangerous, but because the Mermaid is the hardest club in the city to find, tucked away under an interstate ramp at the end of a one-way street. Just hope the cab driver can find it.

Mid City Lanes

ROCK 'N BOWL

Who goes there Bowlers, rockers, two-steppers, Zydecajuns, Hollywood, the Rolling Stones (just to watch, not play)

4133 S. Carrollton Avenue, 482-3133 • Uptown above Napoleon Zone 4

Cover $5–$15 **Minimum** None **Mixed drinks** $3.50–$5 **Wine** $3 **Beer** $1.50–$4.50 **Dress** Zydeco Festival T-shirts, shorts, bandannas, bowling shoes **Food available** New Orleans bar food: cheese fries, shrimp po'boys, buffalo wings **Disabled access** No

Hours For bowling, seven days a week, open at noon; music: Tuesday–Saturday, noon–10 p.m. or later

What goes on Bizarre story. Johnny Blancher, a down-on-his-luck crawfish broker, makes a pilgrimage in the late 1980s to Medjogore, the Yugoslavian village where the Virgin Mary is said to appear to the Catholic faithful. He asks for a sign, something to dig his family out of debt. Back home, he is approached about the sale of an old bowling alley. The sellers—the Knights of Columbus! He figures that's the sign he was waiting for. He buys this charming but crooked alley above a strip shopping center, starts booking bands, and in short time, is running the happiest and most interesting bar in the city. It's a hotbed of zydeco music Wednesday and Thursday nights. On weekends, the playlist is pumped-up R&B, soul, and more zydeco. It's a celebrity magnet; Ashley Judd, Tom Cruise, Liv Tyler, and Sharon Osbourne are just a few of the famed visitors. It's loud, lively, fun, and frenetic. Mid City Lanes is, quite frankly, the best bar in America. Do not miss it. If you don't go anywhere else in New Orleans, go here.

Setting & atmosphere It's a place lost in time, a bowling alley where you still keep score in pencil. There's plenty of dancing room, and plenty of places to get off your feet. Tom Cruise's rental shoes hang alongside portraits of Elvis and the Virgin Mary. Let's just say there's nothing like this where you come from. On Saturday nights and during peak seasons, Blancher opens up a dance hall underneath the alley, called Bowl Me Under (get it?) and books more zydeco. On big nights, he'll book four bands from around southwest Louisiana, and the place absolutely throbs.

If you go Look for Blancher—he's the guy in the pink bowling shirt doing the funky chicken. He'll get you a lane or teach you how to two-step, whatever you want. Don't be intimidated by the local dancers; they're real good and they know it. Fake it, stumble over your feet, give it a whirl—no one will laugh at you. We recommend going early and locking in a lane for the night. The ten bucks an hour is worth it. Once you have zydeco-stomped to Nathan and the Zydeco Cha-Chas in bowling shoes, you will never be the same. Also, when Jon "King" Cleary is on the bill, don't be surprised if Bonnie Raitt shows up to play with him. They're pals.

Molly's on the Market

FRENCH QUARTER WATERING HOLE, MEDIA HANGOUT

Who goes there The press, their sources, pols, tattoos, locals, former professional athletes, video-poker junkies, gutter punks

1107 Decatur Street, 525-5169 • French Quarter Zone 1

Cover None **Minimum** None **Mixed drinks** $2.75–$5 **Wine** $2.50 **Beer** $2.50–$3.75 **Dress** Suits to grunge **Specials** Frozen Irish coffee, bloody mary, $3 **Food available** A full Chinese menu from restaurant behind bar **Disabled access** Yes

Hours Daily, 10 a.m.–6 a.m.

What goes on Local and visiting media 30 years ago established Molly's as a news bureau of sorts, where rookies and old pros trade stories and shooters. On Thursday nights there's usually a celebrity bartender from the worlds of journalism, sports, or politics, and a complimentary cocktail for members of the working press. The rest of the week offers a general mix of French Quarter regulars: tourists, a few local drunks, a skinhead or two, and often a pretty good political argument at one of the raised tables.

Setting & atmosphere Nothing fancy. A pub atmosphere with a long bar down one side and a few tables with bar stools up the other. The walls are crammed with press clippings about the place, from *Esquire* to *Le Monde* to the local *Times-Picayune*. The jukebox plays mostly rock, oldies, and New Orleans music. The open-air window on the sidewalk makes for quality people-watching on this busy nightlife stretch of the Quarter.

If you go Keep an open mind about the eclecticism of the Quarter and its many thirsty denizens. Don't fear the skinhead bartenders; they won't bite. Remember, they're somebody's kids, too.

Mulate's

CAJUN DANCE AND DINNER HALL

Who goes there Bus tours, Kansans, local two-steppers, folks too short on time to drive to Lafayette

201 Julia Street, 522–1492 • Central Business District Zone 2

Cover None **Minimum** One drink **Mixed drinks** $4.25–$6 **Wine** $3.75 and up **Beer** $3.25 and up **Dress** Last year's Festivals Acadiens T-shirt, Bermudas, cotton **Food available** Full-service Cajun restaurant—blackened catfish, gumbo, couscous, crawfish salad **Disabled access** Yes

Hours Daily, 11 a.m.–11 p.m. (music Monday–Thursday, 7–10:30 p.m.; Friday–Sunday, 7–11 p.m.)

What goes on The first Mulate's opened nearly 30 years ago in the little town of Breaux Bridge, Louisiana, and along with New Orleans chef Paul Prudhomme and the famed bayou band Beausoleil, it helped put Cajun culture on the forefront of the American pop-culture landscape. The recipe was simple: good, hot Cajun food and nightly dancing. The Breaux Bridge location's remarkable success in sales and patronage has been duplicated in Baton Rouge and at this New Orleans location. Mulate's takes great care to book the best available Cajun musicians, importing them nightly from southwest Louisiana.

Setting & atmosphere There's no way anyone can reproduce the old-time Cajun dance halls of Acadiana here in the city, but Mulate's nearly pulls it off. It's huge, and they've tried their best to give it a country feel, with attention to faux-rustic detail and artwork by some of Cajun Country's notable painters like George Rodrigue—he of Blue Dog fame—and Francis Pavy, "the zydeco painter."

If you go Lose your fear and dance. There are enough locals on hand to show you how to two-step, Cajun style. It is more fun than it looks, and it looks very fun. Caveat: Cajun dancing is a contact sport—be tolerant of the occasional butt-bounce from the couple next to you. And never, ever be afraid to ask a stranger to dance in a place like this. That's why strangers come here.

Napoleon House

FRENCH QUARTER INSTITUTION

Who goes there Writers, intellectuals, tourists, yuppies, bar flies, and storytellers

500 Chartres Street, 524-9752 • French Quarter Zone 1

Cover None **Minimum** None **Mixed drinks** $3.50 and up **Wine** $3.50 and up **Beer** $3 and up **Dress** Whatever you're wearing **Food available** Salads, jambalaya, po'-boys, and the best muffulettas in town **Disabled access** Yes

Hours Monday–Thursday, 11 a.m.–midnight; Friday and Saturday, 11 a.m.–1 a.m.; Sunday, 11 a.m.–7 p.m.

What goes on Nothing, and that's the joy. It's a place to sit and think, or sometimes just sit. The building was secured in the 19th century to be the great Emperor Bonaparte's residence in exile after his defeat at Waterloo, but he died before ever making it to the States. Now it's just a French Quarter corner bar, albeit a classic, where locals and visitors alike gather to cool their heels.

Setting & atmosphere Sublime. The building is hundreds of years old, dark, with fading paint, chipped plaster, and a variety of Napoleon renderings on the walls. The stereo—a turntable!—spins classical and opera recordings. It is sultry, romantic, and intimate. The staff is indifferent at best, surly at worst.

If you go There is no better way to beat the city heat than to duck into any of the dark tavern or patio corners and sip a Pimm's Cup, a New Orleans standard made of ginger-spiced gin, lemonade, and 7-Up, with a slice of cucumber. Totally refreshing. If you're on a fast track, stay away—conversation is the currency of the club and few here are in a hurry, including the waiters.

O'Flaherty's

LIVE IRISH MUSIC CLUB AND ENTERTAINMENT COMPLEX

Who goes there 30–75, beer drinkers, dart players, tourists, neo-folkies, and sing-along lovers

514 Toulouse Street, 529–1317 • French Quarter Zone 1

Cover Thursday–Sunday only, $5+ **Minimum** One drink per set in music club **Mixed drinks** $2.25 and up **Wine** $2–$6 **Beer** $1.50–$5 **Dress** Casual **Food available** Shepherd's pie, Irish stew, and such **Disabled access** Yes

Hours Daily, noon–3 a.m.; music starts at 7:30 p.m.

What goes on Plenty. One room holds the lively music club, which features local, national, and international Celtic performers seven nights a week. Another room is a traditional Irish pub with darts on the wall, slow-rolling Guinness on tap, and traditional dancing on Saturday nights. There's also a sultry courtyard in the back for lounging about, and a gift shop selling not only souvenirs but Irish groceries as well. O'Flaherty's is also a gathering point for European soccer fans; there's almost always a match on the tube.

Setting & atmosphere A grand old 18th-century building and courtyard, with traditional exposed-brick French Quarter comfort and a hint of Old World decadence. Added attractions are the four ghosts said to inhabit the premises, from spurned lovers to old generals. They live upstairs. For more on that, ask proprietor Danny O'Flaherty to fill you in.

If you go The folks are friendly here, but won't hesitate to remind you to be respectful of the music. If you want to sing the chorus, fine. If you want to chatter, head for the pub so as not to disturb.

Palm Court Jazz Café

JAZZ BAR AND RESTAURANT

Who goes there 35–75, jazz pilgrims, hipsters, Europeans

1204 Decatur Street, 525-0200 • French Quarter Zone 1

Cover $5 for table seat; free to lean on the bar **Minimum** None **Mixed drinks** $4–$6 **Wine** $3.50–$6 **Beer** $3.50 **Dress** Casual to casually elegant **Food available** Traditional Creole and international cuisine **Disabled access** Yes

Hours Wednesday–Saturday, 7–11 p.m.

What goes on George Buck gave his wife, Nina, a birthday present back in the 1980s, something she always wanted—a jazz club. Now Nina Buck runs the classiest traditional jazz joint in town, while upstairs, George presides over the industry's largest independent jazz record distributorship. This club is where Danny Barker, Pud Brown, and Louis Nelson finished their careers, and where their legacy plays on five nights a week from the likes of rising tradjazz masters Lucien Barbarin, Gregg Stafford, and the 90-something and charmingly cranky Lionel Ferbos.

Setting & atmosphere With its expansive tile-floored layout, mahogany bar, Steinway piano, and overhead lamps, the Palm Court suggests Roaring 1920s décor. It's a wide-open place with plenty of seats and a comfortable bar to lean on. Nina Buck sets the tone for the night; if she breaks out her umbrella and handkerchief for a second line, fall in behind. Between sets, there's plenty of history in the paintings, photographs, and record albums displayed throughout the hall. The records—that's right, vinyl!—are for sale.

If you go Make a night of it. The food is good, and the shows are top-class performances by the old generals and young lions of New Orleans Dixxieland jazz. Every night at Palm Court is a celebration of the city's vibrant musical history.

Pat O'Brien's

INTERNATIONAL TOURIST MECCA

Who goes there Tourists—all of them, visiting football fans, suburban 20-somethings seeking French Quarter thrills

718 St. Peter Street, 525-4823 • French Quarter Zone 1

Cover None **Minimum** None **Mixed drinks** $3.50 and up; Hurricanes start at $5.50 **Wine** $3.50 and up **Beer** $3 and up **Dress** Anything goes

Specials None **Food available** In adjacent Courtyard restaurant until 2 a.m. **Disabled access** Yes

Hours 10 a.m.–4 a.m. and until 5 a.m. Friday and Saturday

What goes on Purported to rack up the highest alcohol sales of any bar in America, Pat O's is a big rollicking adult fun house where folks from around the world come to drink the trademark Hurricanes—four ounces of rum mixed with red fruit juice and served in a souvenir glass that most people get too buzzed to remember to take home with them.

Setting & atmosphere Pat O's is a three-in-one venue. Down the carriageway and to the left is a standard saloon with a loud jukebox and a handful of locals hanging out among the tourists. To the right is the dueling piano bar, a tribute to the kind of New Orleans portrayed in Elvis Presley's *King Creole*. Through the afternoon and evening, two big-haired, painted, and leggy dames (or the occasional dudes) with attitude crank out tons of barrelhouse fun, from holiday tunes to famous American standards to contemporary pop hits. It's loud in here, and the huge collection of steins hanging from the ceiling give it a beer-garden sort of atmosphere. The place draws big visiting crowds during football weekends in the fall, and the fans who've followed their teams to town for games against Tulane, LSU, or the Saints get absolutely wild with joy that the piano players know their beloved alma mater's fight song—and they always know. The third venue is the lush and gigantic courtyard in the back, a big draw for bachelor parties and roving gangs of conventioneers who slurp Hurricanes and talk too loud. A beautiful water fountain with a natural-gas flame burning inside the water spray is a treat to behold. Night-blooming vines lend a sweet Southern smell to the place in summer and fall.

If you go Don't wear your nice shoes; it's pretty sticky. It's also really touristy, but necessarily so. It's fun and you should experience it, if only once. However, watch the Hurricane intake if you've got appointments in the morning. More than a few folks who consider themselves tavern veterans back home go down for the count after an exuberant evening of John Denver sing-alongs here.

Preservation Hall

OLD-TIME JAZZ HALL

Who goes there Tourists—all of them

726 St. Peter Street, 522-2841; www.preservationhall.com • French Quarter Zone I

Cover $5 **Minimum** None **Mixed drinks** Drinks are prohibited **Wine** None **Beer** None **Dress** Casual **Food available** None **Disabled access** Yes

Hours Daily, 8 p.m.–midnight, music at 8:30 p.m.

What goes on Although the building—and the musicians—appears to have been standing here since the dawn of jazz, the place actually opened in 1961. Since that time, it has become synonymous with the great tradition of New Orleans Dixieland jazz, and deservedly so, for the musicians are top notch. The club hosts changing bands and musicians nightly, and also puts together national and world tours of musicians under the name Preservation Hall Jazz Band. Everyone who was anyone during the past 30 years has been associated with this place, including Danny and Blue Lu Barker, Kid Thomas, Tuba Fats, and the Olympia Brass Band.

Setting & atmosphere Comfort is not a premium here. It's a small room with very limited seating—just a few benches. Overflow sits on the floor and stands around the walls on the side and in back. The band's enthroned on chairs in the front, looking every bit like a 50-year-old postcard.

If you go Be prepared to invest time in this one; lines can be long. The hall does not serve refreshments of any kind, and there is no smoking. We suggest a cocktail sipped from one of the city's famed go-cups while you wait in line. This is one of those must-see deals in guidebooks and travel stories, and apparently readers take the recommendation seriously. The show is only about 40 minutes long; then you're quickly ushered out to make room for next crowd in. But we've never heard people complain about the brevity—perhaps because they were getting thirsty toward the end.

Saturn Bar

OFFBEAT LOUNGE AND CULTURE-VULTURE HIDEOUT

Who goes there Mad poets, off-duty cabbies and Lucky Dog salesmen, famous actors, guys who actually were at Woodstock

3067 St. Claude Avenue, 949-7532 • Downtown/St. Bernard Zone 5

Cover None **Minimum** None **Mixed drinks** $3 and up **Wine** $3 and up **Beer** $2.25 and up **Dress** Anything goes **Specials** None **Food available** Prepackaged snacks **Disabled access** None

Hours Every day, 4 p.m.–12 or 1 a.m.

What goes on Okay, it's kind of down-and-out at times, smoky and booze soaked, a little bit of a *Barfly* thing going on here, but the Saturn is a true New Orleans classic, a tavern that casts no judgment on its patrons, no matter their stripe. It's a hard-drinking hangout for folks who don't want to be bothered with anything loud or trendy, and that includes a number of Hollywood A-list bad boys who hang out in dark corners when they're in town—Sean Penn, Nicholas Cage, Sam Shepard, Dennis Quaid, and John Goodman among them.

Setting & atmosphere It's a generally dark place lit in small sections by interesting neon sculptures salvaged from an old French Quarter saloon. The main décor comes from the delightfully twisted artistic vision of a local painter named Mike Frolich, who has painted his version of the history of the universe on the walls and ceilings. We are in no position to interpret these bizarre murals; we'll let them speak their own message to you.

If you go Beware the occasional angry alcoholic intellectual, the sort who can polish off the *New York Times* Sunday crossword puzzle in 18 minutes but hasn't managed to hold down a steady job since graduating cum laude in economics from Tulane back when LBJ was President. They like to argue about anything, and unless you've got a strong command of LSU football rosters, circa 1955 through 1972, as well as a more-than-passing knowledge of Louisiana's Byzantine political structure and personalities (the difference between Huey and Earl Long, for instance), then steer clear of these types. Also, the Saturn is a bit on the edge, geographically. St. Claude Avenue is a wide and well-lit roadway, but it's fairly run-down and borders the proverbial wrong side of the tracks. Plus, the side streets are a little sketchy. Be aware. (By the way, Earl was the one who dated stripper Blaze Starr; Huey was assassinated in the state capital in 1934.)

Snug Harbor

JAZZ CLUB

Who goes there Hipsters, buppies, mellow fellows, and anyone named Marsalis

626 Frenchmen Street, 949-0696 • Downtown/St. Bernard Zone 5

Cover Varies, usually $10–$25 **Minimum** None **Mixed drinks** $4.25 and up **Wine** $5 **Beer** $2.75 and up **Dress** Classy but comfortable **Food available** A separate dining room full of meat and seafood entrees, salads and soups, and such. Killer burgers. **Disabled access** Yes, limited

Hours Daily, 5 p.m.–about 2 a.m. Shows at 9 p.m. and 11 p.m.

What goes on Marsalis, Connick, Batiste, Neville, Payton—this is where the great families of modern New Orleans jazz gather and grow. Snug is the link between the city's past and present musical forms, the serious contemporary jazz club in town, low-down and cool. It's a sit-down joint, not much for hootin' and hollerin', but more prone to an evening of Scotch-sipping, finger-snapping solos, and such. It's where the next toast of New York is playing tonight in New Orleans. You can say you saw them when.

Setting & atmosphere Very cozy, befitting the name. The outer bar is dark, cool, and romantic—an ideal spot for a starter drink. Inside the small, two-tiered music hall, it is warmly lit and mirrored. Tables are small and tightly packed, and the upstairs has some view-obstructed seats and tables, hence the big mirror on the stage-left wall.

If you go Parking's tight. It's only two blocks out of the safe side of the Quarter, so walking is fine. There are usually two shows a night, so call and check it out. Arrive early if a big name is on the bill; prime seating can make all the difference. Ellis Marsalis—that's Wynton and Branford's daddy—is one of the city's sublime performers, a Snug regular, and one heck of a lot more fun to watch than his uptight kids.

Tipitina's

NEW ORLEANS'S QUINTESSENTIAL MUSIC CLUB

Who goes there Frat boys and debs, mods and rockers, aging hippies, and people who actually saw Professor Longhair play

501 Napoleon Avenue, 895-8477 • Uptown above Napoleon Zone 4

Cover Varies from occasional free weeknight shows to about $15 for big names **Minimum** None **Mixed drinks** $3.50 and up **Wine** $3 and up **Beer** $2.75 and up **Dress** Khakis, old Jazz Fest T-shirts, tie-dyes, and suits **Specials** Free beans and rice on Sunday 5–9 p.m. with Cajun music **Food available** Burgers, red beans and rice, cheese fries **Disabled access** Yes **Hours** Sunday, 5–10 p.m.; Monday–Thursday, 5 p.m.–2 a.m.; Friday and Saturday, 5 p.m.–3 a.m.; bar opens at 9 p.m.

What goes on Tip's is the heart and soul and somewhat faded glory of the city's musical renaissance of the 1970s, when Fess, James Booker, Dr. John, and the Neville Brothers got everybody hip to the city's non–Dixieland musical heritage. Although the House of Blues has definitely altered Tip's ability to book big-name talent, Tip's is still the place to go for New Orleans R&B, rock, and the occasional big name from the college circuit. The Sunday-afternoon fais-do-do (Cajun dance) with Bruce Daigrepont is a New Orleans institution—good, sweaty family fun.

Setting & atmosphere Wide-open spaces and the checkerboard floor give it an old dance-hall feel. There are stools down the two side bars, and that's about it for seating. Pressure from the House of Blues finally forced Tip's to put up a new coat of paint, fix up the rest rooms, get new refrigeration, and increase the cool-air circulation, so the place is darn near comfortable these days. For big shows, the balcony upstairs offers a respite from the crowd.

If you go Rub the statue of Professor Longhair inside the front door; it's a tradition and will remove any gris-gris suspended in your aura. Move slowly and take in the amazing history of the club's past performers via posters plastered all over the walls. And, if you go to the Sunday fais-do-do (which we highly recommend you do), you may want to bring a second, dry shirt to wear home. It can be a barn burner.

Whiskey Blue

WHAT THE FASHION CAFÉ WAS PROBABLY MEANT TO BE

Who goes there 25–50, Armani fashion victims, players, paralegals and guys with really expensive watches

333 Poydras Street, 525-9444 • Central Business District Zone 2

Cover None **Minimum** None **Mixed drinks** $5 and up **Wine** $6 and up **Beer** $4 and up **Dress** No shorts, hats, or logo shirts **Food available** None **Specials** None **Disabled access** Yes

Hours Saturday–Tuesday, 4 p.m.–2 a.m.; Wednesday–Sunday, 4 p.m.–4 a.m.

What goes on The most glaring example of the bi-coastalization of New Orleans nightlife is Whiskey Blue—the city's slow cultural homogenization. In other words, there is absolutely nothing local about the joint, except the staff. Whiskey Blue is one of the links in the chain of nightclubs owned by entrepreneur Rande Gerber, better known as Mr. Cindy Crawford. His bars are generally exclusive, expensive, and sexy. This is all three. It's somewhat of a celebrity hangout, due primarily to its location in the lobby of the very tony W Hotel. That said, don't expect the owner's wife; she's never been seen in the joint.

Setting & atmosphere The décor is predominantly black, broken up by patches of a very appealing electric ice blue. It's L.A. chic: Too small to dance, too loud to talk. Perfect, in others words, for a singles hangout. Outside the door is the lobby of the hotel, and the W chain's trademark funky padded-chaise lounges and carpeted backgammon tables are more suitable environs in which to catch up with old friends or pursue conversation with a new one.

If you go Be beautiful. When Whiskey Blue opened, talent scouts were sent to the city's modeling agencies and most fashionable nightspots to recruit bartenders and cocktail waitresses. The women wear revealing black dresses, the guys wear tight black turtlenecks, and they are all uniformly supermodelish—and after a couple of beers, they can make you feel pretty miserable about yourself.

Index

Acadians, arrival of, 28
Accents on Arrangements, children's tours at, 60
Admission. *See* Tickets; *specific attractions*
African-Americans
  Amisted Research Center collection on, 169, 191
  artifacts of, shopping for, 315
  festivals for, 53
  history of, 31–33
  Mardi Gras clubs for, 69, 73
Airports, 138–40
Allergy season, 62
Amisted Research Center, 169, 191
Amtrak service, 141
Amusement parks, 226–27
Antiques, shopping for, 308–9, 313–15
Aquarium of the Americas, 196–97
Archbishop Antoine Blanc Memorial, 220–21
Armed and Dangerous, 75
Arrival and orientation, 138–53
  by airport, 138–40
  by bus, 141
  by car, 140–41
  dress recommendations, 56–57, 146
  geography, 141–43, 156–57
  highways, 140–41
  local customs and protocols, 144–45
  name pronunciations, 145–46
  radio stations, 148
  safety guidelines, 144–45, 148–53
  strip establishments, 147–48
  tipping, 147–48
  by train, 141
  visitor guides, 141
Arsenal, 171, 201–2
Art
  festivals for, 56
  museums for, 168, 184, 191, 217–18
  shopping for, 309, 316–17
  studios for, 183–84
Arts center, 183–84, 216, 326

Attractions, 189–227. *See also specific attractions*
  Central Business District, 190, 195
  for children. *See under* Children
  Downtown/St. Bernard, 192
  French Quarter, 194–95
  Lakeview/West End/Bucktown, 195–96
  types of, 193–96
  Uptown
    above Napoleon, 191–92
    below Napoleon, 190
Audubon Cottages, 172
Audubon Park, 190, 191, 197–98
  recreation in, 322–23
  safety of, 150
Audubon Zoo, 54, 60, 198–99
  Halloween events at, 56
Automated teller machines, at airport, 138

Ballet, 325
Balls
  Halloween, 75–76
  Mardi Gras, 63, 67
Banking services, 61, 138
Barataria Preserve, 60
Bars and nightclubs
  Cajun music in, 332
  French Quarter, 326–30
  jazz in, 330–31
  profiles of, 335–63
  safety in, 333–34
  zydeco music in, 332
Bartenders, tipping of, 147
Baseball, 52, 323, 324
Battle of New Orleans, anniversary celebration of, 52
Battlefield sites, 202–3, 321
Bayou Food Festival, 78
Bayou tours, 163–64
Beauregard-Keyes House, 177, 199–200
Bicycles, rental of, 156

Bienville Tours, 161
Biking, 321–22
Blacksmith Shop, Lafitte's, 176
Blaine Kern's Mardi Gras World, 167, 200–201
Blue Dog Seafood Tours, 164
Blues, 332
Boating, 165–66, 323
Boo at the Zoo, 56
Book shops, 171, 309–10
Botanical Gardens, 215–16
Bourbon Street, 36
   geography of, 143–44
   nightlife on, 326–33
   safety on, 333–34
Breakfast, restaurants for, 242
Brennan's Restaurant, 172–73
Breweries, 318
Brewpubs, 333
Broel, House of, 167, 279
Brunch, restaurants for, 241
Bucktown (Lakeview/West End/Bucktown)
   attractions, 195–96
   map of, 20
   restaurants, 240
Burgundy Street, 144
Buses, 156
   to/from airport, 139–40
   arrival by, 141
   tours on, 160
Business District, Central. *See* Central
   Business District
Business travelers, 132–37
   convention center for, 132–37
   food for, 137
   lodging for, 133–34

Cabildo, 171, 201–2
Cabot (ship), 165
Cabs. *See* Taxis
Cajun(s)
   arrival of, 28
   cooking of, 228–29, 234, 318
   festivals of, 78
   music of, 331–32
   region of, swamp tours in, 163–64
Cajun Mardi Gras, 78
Cajun Pride Swamp Tours, 164
Cajun Queen cruises, 165–66
Calendar
   of food seasons, 230–31
   of special events, 52–57
Canal Place mall, 319
Canal Street, 28, 142, 143, 156
   walking tours of, 185
Canal Street Ferry, 60, 165–66
Captain Phil's Saltwater Guide Services,
   323
Carjackings, 153
Carnival. *See* Mardi Gras
Carriage tours, 160–61

Cars
   arrival by, 140–41
   crime prevention in, 153
   impoundment of, 154
   parking, 150, 154
   plantation tours in, 186–89
   rental of, 50, 86, 138
Cascade Stables, 323
CBD. *See* Central Business District
Celebration in the Oaks, 57
Cemeteries, 202–3
   Lafayette, 169, 180–81
   Lake Lawn Metairie, 192–93
   safety of, 147
   St. Roch, 192
   tours of, 161–63, 169–70
Central Business District
   attractions, 190, 195
   description of, 37–38
   French Quarter, 239
   maps of, 14–15
   nightlife in, 335
Chalmette National Battlefield, 202–3, 321
Chapel of St. Roch's, 169
Chartres Street, 143
Children
   attractions for, 59–60, 165–66
      carriage tours, 160–61
      Creole Christmas, 76–77
      Mardi Gras, 73–74
      museums, 59–60, 212
      Rivertown, 60, 224–25
   bookstores for, 309–10
   restaurants for, 243
Christmas events, 44, 57, 76–77
Churches
   Church of the Immaculate Conception, 185
   Holy Trinity Church, 192
   Our Lady of Perpetual Help, 181
   St. Alphonsus, 163, 169, 190,
      225–26
   St. Louis Cathedral, 169, 171
   St. Patrick's, 169, 183
   tours of, 163, 169–70
Churchill, Winston, statue of, 182
City Park, 40, 60, 203–4
   Celebration in the Oaks, 57
   Creole Christmas, 76–77
   recreation in, 321–23
   safety of, 150
Civil War, 33–34
   museums of, 60, 184, 204–5
Claiborne Auto Pound, 154
Claiborne Cottage, 181–82
Clothing
   costumes, 167, 207–8
   recommendations for, 56–57, 146
Clubs
   health, 322–23
   Mardi Gras, 65–70, 73

Clubs *(continued)*
    travel, 82–83
Coffee, in restaurants, 243
Coffee houses, 333
Columns Hotel, 191
Commander's Palace, 180
Commercial area. *See* Central Business
    District
Commuting, to Morial Convention
    Center, 132–33
Compaq Classic, 54
Confederate Museum, 60, 184, 204–5
Conference Child Care Service, 60
Congo Square, 167, 190
Consolidators, for lodging, 84–85
Contemporary Arts Center, 183–84,
    216, 326
Convention and Visitors Bureau, 46
Convention Center. *See* Morial
    Convention Center
Convents, Ursuline, 177–78, 220–21
Cornstalk Hotel, 177
Corporate rates, for lodging, 82
Costumes
    museums for, 207–8
    rental of, 167
Court of Two Lions, 171
Court of Two Sisters, 171
Craft festivals, 78
Crawfish season, 230
Credit cards, 61
Creole(s)
    cooking of, 228–29, 234–35
    history of, 31–33
Creole Carnival, 67
Creole Christmas, 44, 76–77
Creole Queen cruises, 165
Crescent City, 142
Crescent City Classic race, 54
Crime, 144–45, 148–53
    carjackings, 153
    at Mardi Gras, 63
    in nightlife, 333–34
    personal attitude toward, 152
    precautions against, 150–53
    scams, 333–34
    self-defense against, 152–53
Crowds, seasonal, 44, 45
Cruises, river, 165–66
Cultural museums, 193–94
Culture, walking tours related to, 168–69
Currency exchange, 61–62
Customs, local, 144–45
Customs office, 61

D-Day Museum, 184
Dauphine Street, 144
Decatur Street, 143
Degas, Edgar, 168–69
Delta Queen cruises, 166
Desserts, in restaurants, 243

Destrehan Manor, 187
Disabled visitors, services for, 62, 138
Discounts, for lodging, 82–87
Districts. *See* Zones
Dollhouse museums, 279
Dolls, shopping for, 311
Doullut Steamboat House, 192
Downtown Fitness Center, 323
Downtown/St. Bernard
    attractions, 192
    description of, 39–40
    maps of, 18
    nightlife in, 335
    restaurants, 240
Drama, 325–26
Dress recommendations, 56–57, 146
Driving. *See* Cars
Drugs, international travel and, 61
Duty-free allowances, 62

East New Orleans
    description of, 40
    map of, 21
Eating. *See* Restaurants
Edgar Degas House, 168–69
1850 House, 205–6
Entertainment
    bars. *See* Bars and nightclubs
    French Quarter, 326–31
    jazz scene, 330–31
    music. *See* Music
    performing arts, 325–26
    safety in, 333–34
    strip establishments, 147–48
Ernest N. Morial Convention Center. *See*
    Morial Convention Center
Esplanade Street, 143
Essence Music Festival, 55
Exercise. *See* Recreation

Fairgrounds
    horse racing at, 324
    Jazz and Heritage Festival at, 74–75
Faubourg Marigny neighborhood, 39
Faulkner, William, 310
Faulkner House Books, 171
Ferries, 60, 165–66
Festivals. *See also* Mardi Gras (Carnival)
    calendar for, 52–57
Festivals Acadiens, 78
Fiction books. *See* Literature
Film festivals, 55
Films, IMAX Theater, 196–97
First Street, walking tour of, 179–80
Fishing, 323–24
Fishunter Guide Service, 323
Fitness clubs, 322–23
Flea markets, 318
Food, restaurants for. *See* Restaurants
Food festivals, 54–55, 78, 230–31
Football, 52, 57, 324

Foreign visitors, 61–62
French influence, 27–28
French Market, 59, 143, 178, 317
French Quarter
  attractions, 194–95
  crime in, 149–50
  description of, 36–37
  entertainment in, 326–31
  geography of, 143–44
  jazz scene, 330–31
  maps of, 12–13
  music in, 330–31
  nightlife in, 326–31, 334
  rest rooms in, 157
  restaurants, 238
  shopping in, 308–13
  walking tours of, 170–78
French Quarter Festival, 53–54
Fresh Art Festival, 56
Friends of the Cabildo, walking tours, 159

Galleries, 309, 316–17
Gallier House Museum, 176–77, 185
Garden(s), 194
  botanical, 215–16
  Long Vue, 211–12
  St. Anthony's, 171, 220–21
Garden District
  description of, 38
  walking tours of, 178–82
Gay Heritage tours, 161
Gays and lesbians, information sources
    for, 141
Gentilly. See Midcity/Gentilly
Geography, 141–43, 156–57. See also Maps
Germaine Wells Mardi Gras Museum,
    167, 172, 207–8
German festivals, 55
Gilmour-Parker House, 181
Glass works, shopping for, 317
Global Wildlife Center, 60, 164
Go Fourth on the River celebration, 55
Golf, 322
Gray Line Tours, 160, 186
Great French Market Tomato Festival, 54–55
Greater New Orleans Black Multicultural
    Network, 46
Greater New Orleans Multicultural
    Tourism Network, 141
Greek Festival, 54
Greyhound Bus Lines, 141
Gyms, 322–23

Half-price programs, for lodging, 82–83
Halloween events, 44, 56, 75–76
Hamburger restaurants, 242
Handicapped visitors, services for, 62, 138
Haunted History Tours, 163
Haunted tours, 161–63
Health clubs, 322–23
Heritage Tours, 161

Hermann-Grima House, 172, 208–9
Hidden Treasures Tours, 161
Highways, 140–41
Historic New Orleans Collection, 173,
    209–10
History, 26–35
  museums for, 193, 209–10
  walking tours related to, 168–69
Hockey, 324
Holy Trinity Church, 192
Honey Island Swamp Tours, 164
Horse racing, 56–57, 324
Horseback riding, 324
Hotel Villa Convento, 177
Hotels. See Lodging
Houmas House, 187–88
House of Broel, 167, 279
House of Voodoo, Marie Laveau's, 176
Houses, historic, walking tours of, 168–69
Hurricanes, 34, 46

IMAX Theater, 196–97
Immaculate Conception, Church of the, 185
Information sources, 46–51, 56
  at airport, 138
  Mardi Gras, 68
  tourist, 141
  walking tours, 137, 166
International travelers, 61–62
Internet, planning information on, 47–51

Jackson Barracks Museum, 60, 210–11
Jackson Brewery, 318
Jackson Square, 59, 170
Jazz
  in nightspots, 330–31
  records of, shopping for, 310
  tours related to, 161
Jazz and Heritage Festival, 44, 54, 74–75
Jazz Awareness Month, 55
Jean Lafitte National Historical Park, 159,
    163–64
Jean Lafitte Swamp Tours, 164
Jeff Fest, 56
Jesuit Church (Church of the Immaculate
    Conception), 185
Jewish Community Center, 46–47
John James Audubon cruises, 165
Joyce Wildlife Management Area, tours
    in, 164
Julia Row, 183
July Fourth celebration, 55

Keyes, Frances Parkinson, 177, 199–200
Kiefer Lakefront Arena, music at, 326
King Rex, 64–65, 67, 69–70
Krewes, in Mardi Gras, 65–70

Lafayette, Cajun Mardi Gras at, 78
Lafayette Cemetery, 169, 180–81
Lafayette Square, 182–83

368 Index

Lafitte's Blacksmith Shop, 176
Lafitte's Landing, 188
Lake Lawn Metairie Cemetery, 192–93
Lake Pontchartrain, 142
Lakefront Airport, for private planes, 140
Lakeview/West End/Bucktown
    attractions, 195–96
    maps of, 20
    restaurants, 240
LaLaurie House, 176
Language assistance, 62
Laura plantation, 189
Laveau, Marie, 176
Le Chat Noire, 326
Le Monde Crèole Tour, 159
Le Petit Théâtre du Vieux Carré, 60, 174, 326
Lee Circle, 184
Lent, celebration before. *See* Mardi Gras
    (Carnival)
Le'Ob's Tours, 161
Library, 191
Lil' Cajun Swamp Tours, 163–64
Limousines, to/from airport, 139
Literature
    festivals for, 53
    with New Orleans settings, 42–43, 53
    shopping for, 309–10
Lodging, 79–131
    for business travelers, 133–34
    from consolidators, 84–85
    near convention center, 133–34
    corporate rates for, 82
    costs of, 82. *See also specific hotels in
        alphabetical list*
        for business travelers, 133–34
        comparison of, 91–101
        discounts for, 82–87
        half-price, 82–83
        jazz in, 331
        preferred rates for, 83–84
        profiles of, 104–31
        public rest rooms in, 157
        rating/ranking of, 91–101
            best deals (top 30), 101–3
            room characteristics in, 88–91
        reservations for, 48–50
            for busy seasons, 44–45
            for conventions, 133–34
            services for, 84–85
            travel agent help with, 86–87
        selection of, 79–81
        tipping for, 147
        travel agent help with, 86–87
        with travel package, 85–86
        travel packages sponsored by, 86
        value season for, 82
        weekday rates for, 82
        from wholesalers, 84–85
Long Vue House and Gardens, 211–12
Louis Armstrong Park, 190
Louisiana Black Heritage Festival, 53
Louisiana Children's Museum, 60, 212

Louisiana Nature Center, 60, 213
Louisiana Philharmonic Orchestra, 325
Louisiana Purchase, 30
Louisiana Superdome, 52, 324, 326
Louisiana Swamp Tours, 164
Louisiana Visitors Center, 175
Lower Quarter, 143
Loyola University, 191, 326
Lundi Gras, 53, 67–68, 73

McGehee, Louise S., School of, 179
Madame John's Legacy, 177
Madewood Plantation, 188
Magazine Street, shopping in, 313–15
Magic Walking Tours, 163
Mahalia Jackson Theatre of the Performing
    Arts, 325
Malls of the Americas, 317–19
Maps, 12–25
    Central Business District, 14–15
    Downtown/St. Bernard, 18
    East New Orleans, 21
    French Quarter, 12–13
    Lakeview/West End/Bucktown, 20
    Metairie
        above causeway, 23
        below causeway, 22
    Midcity/Gentilly, 19
    Morial Convention Center, 135, 136
    North Shore, 25
    Uptown
        above Napoleon, 17
        below Napoleon, 16
    West Bank, 24
Mardi Gras (Carnival), 44–45, 52–53,
    63–75
    lodging during, 80
    museums for, 167–68, 172, 207–8, 219–20
    walking tours related to, 167–68
Mardi Gras World, 200–201
Marie Laveau's House of Voodoo, 176
Marine museums, 196–97
Masks
    rental of, 167
    shopping for, 312
Merieult House, 173
Metairie
    above causeway
        description of, 41
        maps of, 23
        restaurants, 240–41
    below causeway
        description of, 41
        maps of, 22
        restaurants, 240
Midcity/Gentilly
    description of, 40
    maps of, 19
    restaurants, 240
Military museums, 60, 184, 204–5, 210–11,
    214–15
Mint, United States, 60, 167, 219–20

Mississippi River
  cruises on, 165–66
  orientation of, 142
Moisant International Airport, 138–40
Money
  at airport, 138
  for international travelers, 61–62
  stealing of, 150–51
Morial Convention Center
  commuting to, 132–33
  description of, 133, 137
  eating at/near, 137
  lodging near, 133–34
  map of, 135, 136
  walking distance to, 134
Motels. See Lodging
Muffulettas, restaurants for, 244
Musée Conti Wax Museum, 60, 167,
    213–14
Museum(s)
  art, 168, 184, 191, 217–18
  for children, 59–60, 212
  Civil War and Confederate, 60, 184,
    204–5
  costume, 207–8
  cultural, 193–94
  dollhouse, 279
  for families, 59–60
  Gallier House, 176–77, 185
  history, 193
  Mardi Gras, 167–68, 172, 207–8,
    219–20
  marine, 196–97
  military, 60, 184, 204–5, 210–11,
    214–15
  music, in Old Mint, 60, 167, 219–20
  pharmacy, 60, 174, 218–19
  voodoo, 162, 177, 216–17
  wax, 213–14
Music. See also Jazz
  blues, 332
  Cajun, 78, 331–32
  festivals for, 54–55, 78
  French Quarter, 326–31
  Jazz and Heritage Festival, 44, 54,
    74–75
  in lodging, 331
  museums for, 60, 167, 219–20
  radio stations for, 148
  records of, shopping for, 310
  in restaurants, 331
  rock, 326, 332
  symphonic, 325
  tours related to, 167–68

Napoleon House, 174
Natchez cruises, 165
National D-Day Museum, 184
National Shrine of Our Lady of Prompt
    Succor, 220–21
Natural disasters, 34
Nature centers, 60, 213

Nature tours, 163–64
Neighborhoods. See Zones
New Orleans Botanical Gardens, 215–16
New Orleans Centre mall, 319
New Orleans Film & Video Festival, 55
New Orleans Food & Wine Experience, 54
New Orleans Gay and Lesbian
    Community Center, 46
New Orleans Historic Voodoo Museum,
    162, 177, 216–17
New Orleans Jazz and Heritage Festival,
    44, 54, 74–75
New Orleans Lakefront Airport, for private
    planes, 140
New Orleans Metropolitan Convention
    and Visitors Bureau, 46, 141
New Orleans Moisant International
    Airport, 138–40
New Orleans Museum of Art, 168, 217–18
New Orleans Pharmacy Museum, 60,
    174, 218–19
New Orleans Public Library, 191
New Orleans Spirit Tours, 163
New Orleans Tours, 186
New Year's Eve celebrations, 57, 77
Newcomb Art Gallery, 191
Newspapers, special event information in,
    141
Nightclubs. See Bars and nightclubs
Nightlife, 325–63. See also Entertainment
  jazz scene, 330–31
  safety in, 333–34
North Shore
  description of, 42
  maps of, 25
  restaurants, 241
Nottoway Plantation Inn & Restaurant, 189

Oak Alley, 189
Octoberfest, 55
Offbeat magazine, 141
Oil and gas industry, 35
Old Farmers Market, 317–18
Old Town Praline Shop, 171, 312
Old United States Mint, 60, 167, 219–20
Old Ursuline Convent, 177–78, 220–21
Opera house, historic, 181
Opera performances, 325
Orleans Ballroom, 175–76
Orpheum Theatre, 325
Our Lady of Guadalupe, 190, 221–22
Our Lady of Perpetual Help, 181
Outdoor recreation, 320–24
Oysters, season for, 230

Parades, Mardi Gras, 65–74
Parishes, of New Orleans, 35–36
Park(s), 194. See also City Park
  Audubon Park, 150, 190, 191, 197–98,
    322–23
  Louis Armstrong Park, 190
  safety of, 150

Park(s) *(continued)*
   Waldenburg Park, 318
Park View Hotel, 191
Parking, 150, 154
Parties
   Cajun Mardi Gras, 78
   facilities for, 58–59
   Halloween, 75–76
Passport requirements, 61
Pere Antoine's Alley, 175
Performing arts, 325–26
Perfume, shopping for, 312
Pharmacy Museum, 60, 174, 218–19
Photographs, shopping for, 310
Piazza d'Italia, 182
Pirates Alley, 170
Pitot House, 222–23
Pizza restaurants, 245
Plantation tours, 186–89
Police department
   corruption in, 149
   old French Quarter station of, 172
Pralines, shopping for, 171, 312
Preferred rates, for lodging, 83–84
Presbytere, The, 175, 233–34
Prescriptions, of international travelers, 61
Preservation Hall, 167
Preservation Resource Center, 169
Protocols, local, 144–45
Prytania Street, walking tours of, 181
Public transportation, 154–56
Pubs, 333

Racing, horse, 56–57, 324
Radio stations, 148
Railroad, arrival by, 141
Rainfall, seasonal, 45–46
Rampart Street, 144
Reconstruction era, after Civil War, 33–34
Record shops, 310
Recreation, 320–24
   biking, 321–22
   boating, 323
   fishing, 323–24
   golf, 322
   gyms, 322–23
   health clubs, 322–23
   horseback riding, 323
   jogging, 321
   in parks, 323
   running, 321
   spectator sports, 324
   swimming, 323
   tennis, 322
   walking, 156–57, 321–22
Reggae Riddums Festival, 55
Regional Transit Authority, 139, 156
Rental
   bicycles, 156
   cars, 50, 86, 138
   costumes, 167

   masks, 167
Reservations
   Internet resources for, 48–50
   lodging. *See* Lodging, reservations for
   restaurants, 146–47
   travel, 48–50
Rest rooms
   in airport, 139
   in lodging, 157
   at Mardi Gras, 70–71
Restaurants, 228–306
   with architecture, 242–43
   breakfast, 242
   brunch, 241
   Cajun, 234
   for children, 243
   Chinese, 234
   coffee, 243
   at/near Convention Center, 137
   Creole and variations, 234–35
   desserts in, 243
   dress recommendations for, 146
   eclectic, 236
   French, 236
   Greek, 236
   hamburger, 242
   Indian, 236
   Italian, 236
   Japanese, 236
   Korean, 237
   with local color, 243–44
   Mediterranean, 237
   muffulettas in, 244
   music in, 331
   new, 232
   outdoor dining in, 244–45
   pizza, 245
   private party facilities at, 58–59
   profiles of, 246–306
   rating of, 232–34
   reservations in, 146–47
   on riverboats, 165–66
   sandwiches, 237
   seafood, 230, 237, 245
   seasonal differences and specialties in,
      230–31
   steak, 237
   Thai, 237
   tipping in, 147
   Vietnamese, 237
   by zone, 238–41
Rex, King of Carnival, 64–65, 67, 69–70
Riding, horseback, 323
River cruises, 165–66
Riverbend, 39
Rivercenter Racquet and Health Club, 322
Riverfront Streetcar, 154–56
Rivertown, 60, 224–25
Riverwalk, for walking, 321–22
Riverwalk Marketplace, 318–19
Robbery, 150–51

Roger Ogden Museum of Southern Art, 184
Rogers Chapel, 191
Royal Cafe, 174
Royal Street, 142, 143
   shopping on, 308
   walking tour of, 172–74
Running, 54, 321

Saenger Performing Arts Center, 325
Safety, 144–45, 148–53, 333–34
St. Alphonsus Church, 163, 169, 190, 225–26
St. Ann Street, 144, 175
St. Anthony's Garden, 171
St. Bernard. *See* Downtown/St. Bernard
St. Charles Avenue, 142
   for running, 321
   streetcar on, 155
   walking tours of, 179, 185
St. Joseph's Day celebration, 53
St. Jude, Shrine of, 221–22
St. Louis Cathedral, 169, 171
St. Patrick's Churches, 169, 183
St. Patrick's Day celebration, 53
St. Peter Street, 144
St. Roch Cemetery, 192
Sales taxes, 308
San Francisco Plantation, 187
Sandwiches, restaurants for, 237
Save Our Cemeteries tours, 161–62
Scams, 333–34
Science centers, 60, 213
Seafood
   restaurants for, 237, 245
   seasonal specialties in, 230–31
Seasons for visiting, 45–46
   allergies and, 62
   lodging values, 82
   seafood specialties in, 230–31
   special events calendar, 52–57
Self-defense, 152–53
Services
   at airport, 61, 138
   for disabled visitors, 62
   for international travelers, 61–62
Shopping, 307–19. *See also specific items*
   French Quarter, 308–13
   Magazine Street, 313–15
   Malls of the Americas, 317–19
   tax-free, 308
   Warehouse District, 315–17
Shrimp, season for, 230
Shrine of St. Jude, 221–22
Shuttles, to/from airport, 139
Sightseeing. *See also* Tours
   guided, 159–66
   self-guided, 166–85
Six Flags New Orleans, 226–27
Slave population, history of, 31–33
Soccer, 323, 324
Southern Comfort Cocktail Hour, 161
Southern Repertory Theater, 325–26

Spanish influence, 28–29
Special events calendar, 52–57
Sports
   recreational. *See* Recreation
   spectator, 324
   in Superdome, 52, 324, 326
Spring Fiesta, 53
Stables, 323
Stamps, collectible, shopping for, 310
State Palace Theater, 325
Steak, restaurants for, 237
Steamboat cruises, 165–66
Streetcars, 154–56, 160
Strip establishments, tipping in, 147–48
Sugar Bowl, 44, 52, 324
Super Bowl, 44, 52, 324
Superdome, 52, 324, 326
Swamp Festival, 55
Swamp tours, 163–64
Swimming, 323
Symphonic music, 325

Tad Gormley Stadium, 321
Taxes, sales, 308
Taxis, 156
   to/from airport, 139
   crime in, 152
   queues for, 152
   tipping for, 147
Telephones, at airport, 138
Temperatures, seasonal, 45–46
Tennessee Williams New Orleans Literary
      Festival, 53
Tennis, 322
Tezcuco Plantation, 187
Theater, 325–26
   for children, 60
Thierry House, 176
Third Street, walking tour of, 180, 181
Thirteen Sisters, 183
Tickets. *See also specific attractions*
   bus, 156
   festivals, 52
   Mardi Gras seats, 68
   New Orleans Jazz and Heritage Festival, 75
   parking, 150
   spectator sports, 324
   train, 141
Tipping, 147–48
Toby's Corner, 179
Tomato festival, 54–55
Top of the Mart, 185
Tours
   antique shopping, 313–14
   bus, 160
   carriage, 160–61
   cemetery, 161–63, 169–70
   for children, 60
   church, 163, 169–70
   cultural, 168–69
   French Quarter, 170–78

Tours (continued)
  Garden District, 178–82
  guided, 159–66
  haunted places, 161–63
  historical, 168–69
  Mardi Gras-related, 167–68
  music-related, 167–68
  nature, 163–64
  plantation, 186–89
  river cruises, 165–66
  self-guided, 166–85
  special interest, guided, 161–63
  swamp, 163–64
  taxi, 156
  trolley, 160
  walking. See Walking tours
  Warehouse/Arts District, 182–85
Train, arrival by, 141
Transportation
  to/from airport, 139–40
  crime in, 152
  public, 154–56
  to/from Morial Convention Center, 132–33
Travel, reservations for, 48–50
Travel agent, reservations through, 86–87
Travel clubs, discounts from, 82–83
Travel packages, 85–86
Traveler's Aid Society, at airport, 138, 141
Travelers checks, 61, 138
Treme neighborhood, 37
Trolleys, 154–56, 160
Tujague's, 178
Tulane University, 191
  Amisted Research Center, 169, 191
  Gallier House, 176–77, 185
  performing arts at, 326
  sports teams of, 324
Twelfth Night, 52

Umbrellas, shopping for, 311
Union Terminal, 141
United States Customs, for international
    travelers, 61
United States Mint, 60, 167, 219–20
University neighborhood, 39
Upper Quarter, 143
Uptown
  above Napoleon
    attractions, 191–92
    description of, 38–39
    maps of, 17
    nightlife in, 335
    restaurants, 239–40
  below Napoleon
    attractions, 190
    description of, 38
    maps of, 16
    restaurants, 239
Ursuline Convent, 177–78, 220–21

Vieux Carré. See French Quarter
Voodoo
  artifacts of, shopping for, 176, 311–12
  museums for, 162, 216–17
  tours related to, 161–63, 169–70

Waldenburg Park, 318
Waldhorn Company, 172
Walking, 156–57, 321–22
Walking tours, 156–57
  cemetery, 169–70
  church, 169–70
  cultural, 168–69
  French Quarter, 170–78
  Garden District, 178–82
  guided, 159
  haunted places, 161–63
  historical, 168–69
  information on, 137
  Mardi Gras-related, 167–68
  music-related, 167–68
  Warehouse/Arts District, 182–85
  wildlife, 163–64
Warehouse/Arts District
  description of, 37–38
  shopping in, 315–17
  walking tours of, 182–85
Washington Street, tours of, 181–82
Wax museums, 167, 213–14
Weapons, shopping for, 311
Weather, 45–46
Weddings, facilities for, 59
Weekday rates, at lodging, 82
West Bank
  description of, 42
  maps of, 24
  restaurants, 241
West End (Lakeview/West End/Bucktown)
  attractions, 195–96
  map of, 20
  restaurants, 240
Wheelchairs, accessibility to, 62, 138
White Linen Night, 55
Wholesale room brokers, 84–85
Wildlife centers, 60
Wildlife tours, 163–64
Williams, Tennessee, 53, 310
Witches' Run parties, 76
Women's Opera Guild House, 181

Zephyr Stadium, 324
Zones, of New Orleans, 8–9. See also specific
    zones
  description of, 36–43
  map of, 10–11
Zoo, 54, 60, 198–99
  Halloween events at, 56
Zulu Social Aid and Pleasure Club parade,
    69, 73